THE ENCYCLOPEDIA OF FEMALE PIONEERS IN ONLINE LEARNING

The Encyclopedia of Female Pioneers of Online Learning is the first volume to explore the lives and scholarship of women who have prominently advanced online learning. From its humble origins as distance education courses conducted via postal correspondence to today's advances in the design and delivery of dynamic, technology-enhanced instruction, the ever-evolving field of online learning continues to be informed by the seminal research and institutional leadership of women. This landmark book details 30 preeminent female academics, including some of the first to create online courses, design learning management systems, research innovative topics such as discourse analysis and open resources, and speak explicitly about gender parity in the field. Offering comprehensive career profiles, original interviews, and research analyses, these chapters are illuminating on their own right while amounting to an essential combination of reference material and primary source.

Susan Bainbridge is Sessional Instructor of Distance Education in the Faculty of Humanities and Social Sciences at Athabasca University, Canada and with the Centre for Lifelong Learning at Carl von Ossietzky University of Oldenburg, Germany.

Norine Wark is a freelance researcher, writer, and consultant in the field of distance education.

"Historically, the online and distance learning (ODL) field has been dominated by men, *but where are the women?* This much-needed book answers that question and provides a unique historical perspective into the groundbreaking contributions that women have made to ODL research and practice: from instructional design and pedagogy development to exploring new technologies and influencing public and political policy. Bainbridge and Wark's book is an essential legacy to the pioneering work of these women in ODL."

—**Lisa Marie Blaschke**, *Ph.D., Program Director of the Master in Management of Technology Enhanced Learning at the Center for Lifelong Learning at University of Oldenburg, Germany*

"Women are disproportionately attracted to open and distance learning (ODL) as students. Moreover, the slow adoption of fair selection procedures in conventional higher education led many brilliant women to opt for careers in ODL. This book is a splendid attempt to tell the stories of some of these stars, many of whom I have worked with during my career. I hope this book will inspire other scholars to explore this field more widely."

—**Sir John Daniel**, *O.C., Chancellor of the Acsenda School of Management – Vancouver, Canada, and former Chair of the International Board of the United World Colleges and Vice-Chancellor at the Open University, UK*

THE ENCYCLOPEDIA OF FEMALE PIONEERS IN ONLINE LEARNING

Susan Bainbridge and Norine Wark

NEW YORK AND LONDON

Cover image: Shutterstock

First published 2023
by Routledge
605 Third Avenue, New York, NY 10158

and by Routledge
4 Park Square, Milton Park, Abingdon, Oxon, OX14 4RN

Routledge is an imprint of the Taylor & Francis Group, an informa business

© 2023 Susan Bainbridge and Norine Wark

The right of Susan Bainbridge and Norine Wark to be identified as authors of this work has been asserted in accordance with sections 77 and 78 of the Copyright, Designs and Patents Act 1988.

All rights reserved. No part of this book may be reprinted or reproduced or utilised in any form or by any electronic, mechanical, or other means, now known or hereafter invented, including photocopying and recording, or in any information storage or retrieval system, without permission in writing from the publishers.

Trademark notice: Product or corporate names may be trademarks or registered trademarks, and are used only for identification and explanation without intent to infringe.

Library of Congress Cataloging-in-Publication Data
A catalog record for this book has been requested

ISBN: 978-1-032-23035-1 (hbk)
ISBN: 978-1-032-22343-8 (pbk)
ISBN: 978-1-003-27532-9 (ebk)

DOI: 10.4324/9781003275329

Typeset in Bembo
by Apex CoVantage, LLC

This book is dedicated to the participants who were not able to see the finished product. They were so pleased to be part of this research, and we feel deeply privileged to have captured their voices.

Chere Campbell Gibson 1945–2020

Chandra Gunawardena 1940–2021

CONTENTS

Author Biographies   *xvi*
List of Tables and Figures   *xvii*
Foreword   *xix*

PART ONE

1   Initial Thoughts   3
    Introduction 3
    Background 3
    Aim 4
    Scope 5
    Content and Structure 6
    References 7

2   Belawati, Tian   8
    Interview 9
        Transcript Analysis Summary 9
        Transcript of Interview 11
    Interview Questions 11
    Publications 15
        Books 15
        Book Chapters 16

3   Beukes-Amiss, Catherine Margaret (Maggy)   18
    Interview 19
        Transcript Analysis Summary 19
        Transcript of Interview 20
    Interview Questions 21

      Publications 27
         Journal Articles 27
         Conference Presentations and Interviews 28

4   Brindley, Jane Elizabeth   29
      Interview 30
         Transcript Analysis Summary 30
         Transcript of Interview 31
      Interview Questions 32
      Publications 38
         Books 38
         Book Chapters 38
         Journal Articles 39
         Conference Presentations 39

5   Burge, Elizabeth June (Liz)   40
      Interview 41
         Transcript Analysis Summary 41
         Transcript of Interview 43
      Interview Questions 43
      Publications 51
         Books 51
         Book Chapters 51
         Journal Articles 52
      References 53

6   Chen, Li   54
      Interview 55
         Transcript Analysis Summary 55
         Transcript of Interview 56
      Interview Questions 57
      Publications 59
         Books 59
         Journal Articles 59
         Conference Presentations 62

7   Fainholc, Beatriz   63
      Interview 64
         Transcript Analysis Summary 64
         Transcript of Interview 65
      Interview Questions 66
      Publications in English 68
         Books 68
         Book Chapters 68
         Journal Articles 69
      Publications in Spanish 69

8   Farley, Helen Sara   70
    Interview 71
        Transcript Analysis Summary 71
        Transcript of Interview 73
    Interview Questions 73
    Publications 83
        Books 83
        Book Chapters 83
        Journal Articles 84

9   Gibson, Chere Campbell   87
    Interview 88
        Transcript Analysis Summary 88
        Transcript of Interview 89
    Interview Questions 90
    Publications 96
        Books 96
        Book Chapters 96
        Journal Articles 97
        Conference Presentations 98

10 Glennie, Jennifer (Jenny)   99
    Interview 100
        Transcript Analysis Summary 100
        Transcript of Interview 101
    Interview Questions 102
    Publications 109
        Books 109
        Book Chapters 109
        Journal Articles 110
        Conference Presentations 110

11 Gregory, Sue   111
    Interview 112
        Transcript Analysis Summary 112
        Transcript of Interview 113
    Interview Questions 114
    Publications 120
        Books 120
        Book Chapters 120
        Journal Articles 122

12 Gunawardena, Chandra   124
    Interview 125
        Transcript Analysis Summary 125
        Transcript of Interview 126

    Interview Questions 127
    Publications 133
        Books 133
        Book Chapters 134
        Journal Articles 135

13 Gunawardena, Charlotte Nirmalani (Lani)   137
    Interview 138
        Transcript Analysis Summary 138
        Transcript of Interview 140
    Interview Questions 140
    Publications 151
        Books 151
        Book Chapters 151
        Journal Articles 153
        Conference Presentations 154

14 Henri, France   156
    Interview 157
        Transcript Analysis Summary 157
        Transcript of Interview 159
    Interview Questions 159
    Publications 167
        Books 167
        Book Chapters (Chapitres de Livre) 167
        Journal Articles and Blog Postings (Articles de Revues et Billets de Blog) 168

15 Herring, Susan   170
    Interview 171
        Transcript Analysis Summary 171
        Transcript of Interview 173
    Interview Questions 173
    Publications 186
        Books 186
        Book Chapters 186
        Journal Articles and Blog Postings 189
        Conference Presentations 191

16 Hiltz, Starr Roxanne   194
    Interview 195
        Transcript Analysis Summary 195
        Transcript of Interview 196
    Interview Questions 196
    Publications 203

    Books 203
    Book Chapters 204
    Journal Articles 205

17 Jung, Insung   209
  Interview 210
    Transcript Analysis Summary 210
    Transcript of Interview 211
  Interview Questions 211
  Publications 219
    Books 219
    Book Chapters 219
    Journal Articles 220
    Conference Presentations 224

18 Kanwar, Asha   225
  Interview 226
    Transcript Analysis Summary 226
    Transcript of Interview 228
  Interview Questions 228
  Publications 231
    Books 231
    Book Chapters 232
    Journal Articles 232
    Conference Presentations 233

19 Keough, Erin M.   234
  Interview 235
    Transcript Analysis Summary 235
    Transcript of Interview 237
  Interview Questions 237
  Publications 250
    Books 250
    Book Chapters 250
    Journal Articles 250
    Conference Presentations 251

20 Koroivulaono, Theresa   252
  Interview 253
    Transcript Analysis Summary 253
    Transcript of Interview 254
  Interview Questions 254
  Publications 261
    Book Chapters 261

      Journal Articles 262
      Conference Presentations 262

21 Kurtz, Gila   263
    Interview 264
      Transcript Analysis Summary 264
      Transcript of Interview 265
    Interview Questions 265
    Publications 269
      Books 269
      Book Chapters 269
      Journal Articles 270
      Conference Presentations 270

22 Lamy, Thérèse   273
    Interview 274
      Transcript Analysis Summary 274
      Transcript of Interview 275
    Interview Questions 276
    Publications 280
      Books and Courseware 280
      Book Chapters 280
      Journal Articles 280
      Conference Presentations 280

23 Meeks Gardner, Julia (Julie)   282
    Interview 283
      Transcript Analysis Summary 283
      Transcript of Interview 284
    Interview Questions 284
    Publications 290
      Books 290
      Book Chapters 290
      Journal Articles 291
      Conference Presentations 293

24 Moran, Louise   294
    Interview 295
      Transcript Analysis Summary 295
      Transcript of Interview 296
    Interview Questions 297
    Publications 304
      Books 304

  Book Chapters 304
  Journal Articles 305
  Commissioned Reports 305

25 Murray, Denise 307
 Interview 308
  Transcript Analysis Summary 308
  Transcript of Interview 310
 Interview Questions 310
 Publications 317
  Books 317
  Book Chapters 318
  Journal Articles 319

26 Roberts, Judy 321
 Interview 322
  Transcript Analysis Summary 322
  Transcript of Interview 324
 Interview Questions 324
 Publications 330
  Books and Courseware 330
  Book Chapters 330
  Journal Articles 330
  Conference Presentations 331

27 Seelig, Caroline 332
 Interview 333
  Transcript Analysis Summary 333
  Transcript of Interview 334
 Interview Questions 335
 Publications 340
  Book Chapters 340
  Journal Articles 341
  Conference Presentations 341

28 Simmons-McDonald, Hazel 342
 Interview 343
  Transcript Analysis Summary 343
  Transcript of Interview 344
 Interview Questions 344
 Publications 356
  Book Chapters 356
  Conference Presentations 356
 References 358

29 Spronk, Barbara 359
 Interview 360
  Transcript Analysis Summary 360
  Transcript of Interview 361
 Interview Questions 361
 Publications 369
  Books 369
  Book Chapters 369
  Journal Articles 369

30 von Prümmer, Christine 370
 Interview 371
  Transcript Analysis Summary 371
  Transcript of Interview 372
 Interview Questions 372
 Publications 380
  Books 380
  Book Chapters 380
  Journal Articles 381
  Conference Presentations 382

31 Young, Arlene M. C. 383
 Interview 384
  Transcript Analysis Summary 384
  Transcript of Interview 385
 Interview Questions 385
 Publications 389
  Books and Reports 389
  Book Chapters 389
  Journal Articles 390

PART TWO

32 Analysis of Interviews 393
 Introduction 393
 Discussion and Definition of Terms 393
  Distance Education, CMC, ODL, and Online Learning 393
  Pioneers: Founders, Leaders, Researchers/Writers 394
 Research Methodology 395
  Research Questions 395
  Selection of Respondents 396
  Data Analysis Process 397
 Results 398
  Coding Themes 398

    Background 399
    Learning Environment 404
    Challenges 405
    Accomplishments 407
    Changes over Time 409
    Research Interests 409
    Goals 410
    Interesting Memories 411
    Early Founders 412
    Others for the Book 413
    Final Comments 413
    Emergent Codes 414
  Discussion 416
    Background 417
    Learning Environment 420
    Challenges 422
    Accomplishments 427
    Changes over Time 428
    Research Interests 429
    Goals 429
    Interesting Memories 430
    Early Founders 431
    Others for the Book 433
    Final Comments 433
    Emergent Codes 433
  Conclusion 435
    Research Limitations 438
  References 439

33 Final Thoughts   441
  Introduction 441
  Key Findings 441
  Conclusion 442
    Key Implications for Stakeholders 442
    Future Research 448
  References 448

Appendix A: Interview Version A   451
Appendix B: Interview Version B   452
References   453
Index   457

AUTHOR BIOGRAPHIES

Susan Bainbridge

Dr. Susan Bainbridge has worked globally for the past 30 years. She has lived in the Canadian Arctic, Japan, South Korea, United Arab Emirates, and Honduras. She is currently an instructor and co-supervisor with the Faculty of Humanities and Social Sciences for the Distance Education graduate/post-graduate programmes at Athabasca University in Canada. She also works with Oldenburg University in Germany in the Online Teaching and Learning Programme, and consults for the United Nations Development Programme (UNDP). Susan holds a Doctor of Education in Distance Education, obtained at Athabasca University in 2013. Her doctoral research was centred in Nepal with the development of a pedagogical model for online learning. She earned her MA in applied linguistics at the University of Southern Queensland in Australia and her BA in religious studies/history at Laurentian University in Canada. Her research interests include online learning in underdeveloped countries, leadership, and online pedagogy and design, as well as gender issues in education.

Norine Wark

Dr. Norine Wark is an educational consultant, researcher, and writer in the field of distance education. She holds a teaching certificate and five-year Bachelor of Education from Simon Fraser University, Canada, as well as online Master of Education in Distance Education and Doctor of Distance Education degrees from Athabasca University, Canada. Upon graduating from the doctoral programme, she was awarded the Governor General of Canada's Gold Medal for scholarly achievements and contributions to the academic community. Norine has taught K–12, special education, adult advocacy, higher education, and other educators in face-to-face, online, and blended learning environments since the late 1980s. She has also developed multimedia instructional resources for these learners and other stakeholders. Her primary research interests include historic and emerging theory and practice in distance learning, self-determined learning, learner empowerment, and the technologies that enable such learning. She has contributed numerous peer-reviewed international publications and conference presentations to the field of distance education, some of which have received awards from the academic community. Norine's academic volunteer activities include board membership and other contributions to international educational associations, mentorship for graduate and post-graduate students, online K–12 teaching in Honduras, and peer-review services for international conferences and journals.

TABLES AND FIGURES

1.1	Female Pioneers Included in This Volume, by Country	6
2.1	All Respondents' Versus Tian Belawati's Parent Codes	10
3.1	All Respondents' Versus Margaret (Maggy) Beukes-Amiss's Parent Codes	20
4.1	All Respondents' Versus Jane Brindley's Parent Codes	31
5.1	All Respondents' Versus Elizabeth (Liz) Burge's Parent Codes	42
6.1	All Respondents' Versus Li Chen's Parent Codes	56
7.1	All Respondents' Versus Beatriz Fainholc's Parent Codes	65
8.1	All Respondents' Versus Helen Farley's Parent Codes	72
9.1	All Respondents' Versus Chere Campbell Gibson's Parent Codes	89
10.1	All Respondents' Versus Jennifer (Jenny) Glennie's Parent Codes	101
11.1	All Respondents' Versus Sue Gregory's Parent Codes	113
12.1	All Respondents' Versus Chandra Gunawardena's Parent Codes	126
13.1	All Respondents' Versus Charlotte (Lani) Gunawardena's Parent Codes	138
14.1	All Respondents' Versus France Henri's Parent Codes	158
15.1	All Respondents' Versus Susan Herring's Parent Codes	172
16.1	All Respondents' Versus Starr Roxanne Hiltz's Parent Codes	195
17.1	All Respondents' Versus Insung Jung's Parent Codes	210
18.1	All Respondents' Versus Asha Kanwar's Parent Codes	227
19.1	All Respondents' Versus Erin Keough's Parent Codes	236
20.1	All Respondents' Versus Theresa Koroivulaono's Parent Codes	253
21.1	All Respondents' Versus Gila Kurtz's Parent Codes	264
22.1	All Respondents' Versus Thérèse Lamy's Parent Codes	275
23.1	All Respondents' Versus Julia (Julie) Meeks Gardner's Parent Codes	284
24.1	All Respondents' Versus Louise Moran's Parent Codes	296
25.1	All Respondents' Versus Denise Murray's Parent Codes	309
26.1	All Respondents' Versus Judy Roberts' Parent Codes	323
27.1	All Respondents' Versus Caroline Seelig's Parent Codes	334
28.1	All Respondents' Versus Hazel Simmons-McDonald's Parent Codes	344
29.1	All Respondents' Versus Barbara Spronk's Parent Codes	360
30.1	All Respondents' Versus Christine von Prümmer's Parent Codes	371
31.1	All Respondents' Versus Arlene Young's Parent Codes	384
32.1	Inter- and Intra-Coder Reliability Statistics	397

32.2	All Respondents' Interview Parent Codes	399
32.3	Locations Where Female Pioneers Worked	400
32.4	Pioneers' Educational Background by Field	401
32.5	Pioneers' Experiential Background by Career Field	401
32.6	When Respondents Became Interested in the Field	402
32.7	Initiating Circumstances: Respondents vs Coded Units	402
32.8	Who Influenced Pioneers to Join the Field	403
32.9	Challenges Identified by Respondents	406
32.10	Respondents' Accomplishments	407
32.11	Respondents' Research Interests	410
32.12	Respondents' Goals	411
32.13	Respondents' Interesting Memories	412
32.14	Respondents' Final Comments	413
32.15	Respondent-Identified Benefits of DE	414
32.16	Technology Sub-Themes: Respondent vs Coded Unit	416
32.17	Respondents' Gender-Related Comments	416

FOREWORD

It is my pleasure to offer the foreword to this outstanding review of historical thought leaders in the field of education. This book release will occur on the heels of UNESCO's 2021 Report *Reimagining Our Futures Together: A New Social Contract for Education*. This report makes explicit the need for, and benefit of, diverse voices in shaping the future of global education. The question "Can you hear us now?" included in the cover image of this book is a reminder of the exclusions of the past. Presenting the stories of this sample of women pioneers in distance and online education brings their voices out of the subtext and into the foreground, where their contributions can be understood and acknowledged.

Authors Bainbridge and Wark, two women researchers of current online education innovation, "introduce researchers, historians, writers, and students of distance education and online learning to the pioneering female researchers and leaders in online learning." The adjective *pioneering* is most aptly used in this case. The women represented here, visible through their stories and the lists of their published contributions, are easily described as pioneers: they are some of the first to apply and use new ideas, concepts, and applications of what was, and still is, an evolving education enterprise.

Identified as those embracing education change, the labels *founder*, *trailblazer*, *leader*, *researcher*, and *writer* are used to identify the roles these women played. Insights into both the individual and shared realities of these significant contributors provide context in which to interpret the struggle and impact these change agents offered to teachers and students in the field of distance education and online learning.

A detailed interview process with a sample of women engaged in the evolution of education prior to 1980, anywhere in the world, is the substance of this book. Data are presented through a thematic structure, and the results beautifully interpreted. As you read, take note of the social justice imperative that provides a red thread to follow. Like our recent call to action in UNESCO's report on education futures, equity, inclusion, and fairness were driving forces for change in the histories of the women highlighted here.

The report of this history could not be better timed. Edging toward a post–COVID-19 social reality, the use of alternative forms of education delivery must be informed not by the emergency remote teaching employed for protection during the global pandemic, but instead by the lessons of distance education and online learning research of the past. The female pioneers of online learning are a significant part of this past.

Foreword

I believe many education researchers, developers, teachers, and students will find this book an invaluable resource. It is an exciting piece of work that will be of interest to anyone wanting to claim broad expertise in the field of distance education and online learning. It fills an obvious void in the historical research that many have not noticed. I applaud and congratulate Drs. Bainbridge and Wark for embracing this challenge and seeing it through to completion.

Dr. Martha Cleveland-Innes
Professor and Programme Director
Master of Education Programme
Athabasca University
Visiting Professor of Pedagogy
Mid Sweden University
Editor-In-Chief
Canadian Journal of Learning and Technology

PART ONE

This encyclopedia is divided into two parts. Part One contains an introductory chapter, Initial Thoughts, which describes the background, aim, scope, content, and structure of this volume about female pioneers in online learning. Chapter 1 is followed by a series of chapters, each of which is devoted to contributions of one pioneer. These chapters are arranged alphabetically by the pioneers' surnames.

1
INITIAL THOUGHTS

Introduction

The main goal of this book is to capture and share the voices and contributions of female pioneers in online learning. Most of the content comes directly from the pioneers. As a result, this book serves as a timeless, living record of these women's stories, experiences, and achievements during a period when most of the world transitioned from traditional, print-based correspondence to a dizzying array of technology-enhanced immersive learning experiences. These direct contributions, merged with a qualitative research study on the pioneers' interview data, are intended to help readers understand the challenges and accomplishments of these female pioneers; their experiences, perceptions, and motivations; and their research/leadership interests. The concluding chapter, Final Thoughts, summarizes the key implications that the content of this book may hold for policymakers, administrators, educators, historians, researchers, writers, and students who are interested in distance education (DE), online learning, educational technology, and gender issues topics.

Background

The impetus for this book began as a rather offhand observation that the first author, Dr. Susan Bainbridge, shared with the second author, Dr. Norine Wark. Having learned and worked in the field for quite some time, Bainbridge had begun to notice an absence of references to female pioneers among colleagues and students in the field of DE. During the conversation, she further speculated that acknowledgement of female pioneers in the literature might be sparse as well. This prompted Wark, who had obtained most of her education by various DE means and who was also working in the field, to reflect in earnest upon her own encounters with female pioneers in the field. While both authors were able to come up with a number of possible female pioneer candidates, neither could recall a single literary reference that acknowledged these pioneers' contributions. The authors could, however, cite a number of such references extolling the contributions of male pioneers. Bainbridge mused that perhaps a book in honour of our female pioneers was in order. The conversation ended with the authors agreeing to do a little more independent research to confirm the validity of their speculations.

A few months of further research yielded countless books, journal articles, blogs, newscast interviews, and podcasts on male pioneers in the field (see, for example, Bates, 2016; EDEN Secretariat, 2016; Kentnor, 2015), but negligible results showcasing female pioneers. One periodical, the *Journal* of *Learning for Development (JL4D)*, included a paragraph or two on a handful of women in a series of articles in Volume 4, Issues 1–3 (2017) and Volume 5, Issue 1 (2018) on leaders in DE from across the globe. A second periodical, the *International Women Online Journal of Distance Education (intWOJDE*; www.wojde.org/; Demiray, 2012), initiated in 2012, also invited (and continues to invite) submissions on the history of DE. A single podcast featuring one pioneer was uncovered. The remaining collection of pioneering women's contributions seemed to be found on educational institution faculty web pages, which typically offered a short biography, research interests, and some publications, and was usually written by the pioneer. It seemed that Bainbridge's speculations held credence. Although the authors viewed themselves as pure feminists in that they believed in gender equality, neither came from the feminist tradition with regard to research or active feminist ideology. Nonetheless, both felt that it was a grave injustice to history and a profound loss of insight into our field to ignore the contributions that these outstanding female pioneers had made, and continue to make, to our field. It was determined that the most comprehensive, timeless offering that the authors could produce would be a reference book. To be most valuable, this book had to reflect, if not amplify, the living voices and comprehensive works of female pioneers in online learning from around the world.

Originally, the authors thought about including female pioneers within the broad context of DE. This would mean, however, that first-person pioneering accounts would be unlikely, if not impossible, since original print-based, snail mail correspondence traced back to the 1700s (Anderson & Simpson, 2012). Educational radio broadcasts began in the 1930s (Foss, n.d.), and educational television broadcasts dated back to at least 1958 (Zaitz, 1960). The authors faced a conundrum if they relied on second- or third-hand resources to piece together the stories and contributions of pioneers. How could the authors determine what resources were truly authoritative? If they could speak for themselves, would the pioneers agree with these sources? In other words, how could the authors assure stakeholders that the information gathered authentically represented the pioneers' voices and contributions? Second- or third-hand sources were simply not acceptable.

As the first interviews began to unfold, it became apparent that the authors needed to focus on female pioneers of online learning. This was the era in distance learning where the greatest number of female pioneers were still alive and able to tell their stories in their own words.

Although initially driven by passion and dedication to this worthy undertaking, the authors had little idea that they were about to embark on such an epic journey. Wild tales about hitching with gun-toting guerrillas in far-off jungle islands and heart-wrenching stories about unimaginable life-or-death suffering at the hands of those who systematically denied others the right to education were peppered amongst amusing tales about the novelty of red hair, being covered from head to toe in correcting fluid and ink, and Coca-Cola truck deliveries of DE materials. Through the recruitment, interview, data analysis, and writing process, these pioneers secured a special place in the hearts and minds of the authors. By sharing so much of themselves so openly, and often with such great humour, the astounding pioneers in this book have invited all of us to experience the world of DE and online learning through their eyes.

Aim

The primary aim of this book is to introduce female pioneers in online learning to researchers, historians, writers, students, and other stakeholders of DE and online learning. In doing so, this book aims to honour and accurately portray these intrepid pioneers by sharing their stories, experiences, and achievements in their own words, rather than from an outside perspective. It is hoped that this living record will become a timeless historical testament of who these women are, what they believe, and what they offer to our field.

A related aim is to provide stakeholders with a handbook that affords easy access to a comprehensive, chronologically organized list of each woman's publications in the field. This list is found at the end of each pioneer's chapter in this book.

A third aim is to assist stakeholders in acquiring new insight into the perspectives, experiences, and contributions made by female pioneers in online learning. To achieve this, data from the pioneers' individual and collective interviews are analyzed and assessed in this book to determine patterns of commonality between pioneers, unique characteristics of individual pioneers, and what remains to be uncovered by future research.

Scope

This book includes information on 30 female pioneers of online learning. Potential candidates for the book were identified using a two-step recruitment approach (described in greater detail in the Research Methodology section of Chapter 32). In brief, the first step involved the authors generating a list of potential candidates. This list was compared to a set of author-determined guiding terms and related definitions that they perceived to constitute the profile of a pioneer. These terms were: *founder/trailblazer*, *leader*, and *researcher/writer* (defined in the Methodology section of Chapter 32). A second author-determined criterion was founding date. That is, in order to be considered for the book, a potential candidate had to have initiated their founding activities somewhere between 1970 and 2000. If a woman began her pioneering activity after 2000, it had to be because online learning had just been introduced in her country, or the activity was novel in some respect (e.g., initiating the use of new technologies and pedagogies).

After purging the authors' list of potential candidates whose profiles did not meet the established criteria, the authors used a snowballing strategy to garner the names of more pioneers. This strategy (explained in greater detail in the Research Methodology section of Chapter 32) involved asking the female pioneers participating in the study to volunteer the names of other females who might be candidates for the book. This two-stage approach to identifying candidates resulted in the inclusion of 30 pioneers in this volume. Each of these women's profiles matched one or more of the guiding terms and the date criterion established by the authors.

The authors believe that the 30 women included in this book fairly represent female pioneers from across the globe, especially those who are able to communicate in the English language (Table 1.1). The inception and expansion of the Internet and the expansion of the World Wide Web occurred in American institutions, spreading across North America and into other English-speaking countries, before expanding into the rest of the world (Berners-Lee, 2021; Press, 2015). The advent of these emerging technologies precipitated the development of online learning. The number and distribution of female pioneers included in this book reflect this historic pattern of development in online learning.

Outside of literary citations intended as luminary references for understanding specific phenomena or patterns in research findings, the scope of this book is limited to direct contributions by the participating pioneers and the authors' interpretations of these contributions. Direct contributions published in this volume are located within each pioneer's chapter. These contributions include a recording of their interview (accessible through embedded YouTube links and QR codes in the chapters), a transcript of the interview that has been edited and verified by the pioneer, and a list of publications and related references provided by the pioneer.

The authors offer no attempt to clarify existing definitions used in our field for such terms as *distance education*, *online learning*, and *educational technologies*. Our field possesses a plethora of "authoritative" multimedia resources that establish a myriad of often confusing and contradictory definitions for such terms (see, for example, Bates, 2008). Our purpose herein is not to join the debate or even

Table 1.1 Female Pioneers Included in This Volume, by Country

Female pioneers by country

Argentina	**China**	**New Zealand**
Fainholc, Beatriz	Chen, Li	Seelig, Caroline
Australia	**Germany**	**South Africa**
Burge, Liz	von Prümmer, Christine	Glennie, Jenny
Gregory, Sue		
Moran, Louise	**Indonesia**	**Sri Lanka**
Murray, Denise	Belawati, Tian	Gunawardena, Chandra
Australia/ New Zealand	**India/Canada**	**Sri Lanka/USA**
Farley, Helen	Kanwar, Asha	Gunawardena, Lani
Canada	**Israel**	**USA**
Brindley, Jane	Kurtz, Gila	Gibson, Chere
Henri, France		Herring, Susan
Keough, Erin	**Korea/Japan**	Hiltz, Starr Roxanne
Lamy, Thérèse	Jung, Insung	
Roberts, Judy		**West Indies**
Spronk, Barbara	**Marshall Islands**	Meeks Gardner, Julie
Young, Arlene	Koroivulaono, Theresa	Simmons-McDonald, Hazel
	Namibia	
	Beukes-Amiss, Maggy	

to negotiate agreed-upon definitions of terms used by the pioneers in this book. Instead, the authors have accepted each pioneer's perspective on what these terms mean in the attempt to reduce filters between the pioneers' voices and those who read this book. Furthermore, the authors' use of the terms *online learning* and *emerging technology* are meant to reflect all related terms used by the pioneers and other literary references in this book.

Content and Structure

This volume is divided into two parts. In Part One, this chapter, Initial Thoughts, is followed by one chapter devoted to each female pioneer in online learning. The chapters are alphabetically organized according to the pioneers' surnames. Each chapter begins with a photo and succinct biography of each pioneer. The biography presents a snapshot of the pioneer's education, career history, major achievements, current role, and research interests. This is followed by a brief qualitative thematic analysis of the pioneer's interview data as it relates to the average interview profile generated from the research data. Fourteen thematic areas arising from the collective interview data analyses are considered in this review. Listed in alphabetical order, these areas are: accomplishments, background, benefits of DE, career history, challenges, changes over time, early founders, final thoughts, general gender-related comments, goals, interesting memories, learning environment, names of others for the book, and research interests. A comparative chart of these results is included in the discussion of this analysis. Located after the thematic analysis is an embedded YouTube link and a QR code that provide access to the recorded interview. This recording is followed by a transcription of the interview, which has been edited and verified by the pioneer. The chapter concludes with a chronologically ordered presentation of the published works that the pioneer has chosen to share with readers.

The second part of the book begins with the presentation of the qualitative research study that was conducted on the pioneers' collective interviews. The first chapter in this part introduces the research methodology employed and then goes on to present the findings from the data analysis process. The subsequent discussion on the findings and resultant conclusions are merged with external references, where appropriate, in order to provide further insights and to assist in placing research findings within the context of known literature. The chapter ends with a review of the limitations of the research study.

The last chapter in this book, Final Thoughts, summarizes the key findings derived from the compilation of this book and the related research project. The conclusion of this chapter begins by pointing out key implications that this book holds for policymakers, administrators, educators, historians, researchers, writers, students, and any other stakeholders who are interested in DE and online learning. The final part of this chapter delineates possible avenues for future research.

References

Anderson, B., & Simpson, M. (2012). History and heritage in distance education. *Journal of Open, Flexible, and Distance Learning, 16*(2). https://files.eric.ed.gov/fulltext/EJ1080085.pdf

Bates, A. W. (2008, July 7). What do you mean by...? [Web log post]. *Tony Bates*. www.tonybates.ca/2008/07/07/what-is-distance-education/

Bates, A. W. (2016, September 18). Who are the founding fathers of distance education? [Web log post]. *Tony Bates*. www.tonybates.ca/2016/09/17/who-are-the-founding-fathers-of-distance-education/

Berners-Lee, T. (2021). The history of the World Wide Web [Web log post]. *World Wide Web Foundation*. https://webfoundation.org/about/vision/history-of-the-web/

Demiray, E. (Ed.). (2012). *International women online journal of distance education (intWOJDE)*. www.wojde.org/

EDEN Secretariat. (2016, September 16). Learn from three founding fathers of distance education interviewed by Steve Wheeler [YouTube video]. *#EDEN16*. www.youtube.com/watch?v=OEZU89Drkj4

Foss, K. A. (n.d.). Remote learning isn't new: Radio instruction in the 1937 polio epidemic [Web log post]. *The Conversation*. http://theconversation.com/remote-learning-isnt-new-radio-instruction-in-the-1937-polio-epidemic-143797

Kentnor, H. (2015). Distance education and the evolution of online learning in the United States. *Curriculum and Teaching Dialogue, 17*(1–2). https://digitalcommons.du.edu/cgi/viewcontent.cgi?article=1026&context=law_facpub

Panda, S. (Ed.). (2017–2018). *Journal of Learning for Development (JL4D)*. https://jl4d.org/index.php/ejl4d

Press, G. (2015, January 2). A very short history of the Internet and the Web [Web log post]. *Forbes*. www.forbes.com/sites/gilpress/2015/01/02/a-very-short-history-of-the-internet-and-the-web-2/?sh=88a49d07a4e2

Zaitz, A. W. (1960). The history of educational television – 1932–1958 (PhD Thesis). Wisconsin University: Madison. https://eric.ed.gov/?id=ED016919

2
BELAWATI, TIAN

Photo of Tian Belawati contributed by Tian Belawati

> *Lately it is becoming my little obsession for Indonesian people to embrace modern higher education methods such as online learning, mobile learning, and those sorts of things.*

Dr. Tian Belawati received her undergraduate degree in agricultural economics from the Bogor Agricultural Institute in Indonesia. Then she went on to study at Simon Fraser University in Canada where she obtained a Master of Education in Management of Distance Education. Her PhD focused on adult education at the University of British Columbia in Canada.

Dr. Belawati held the position of Rector, Universitas Terbuka (Indonesia Open University) until 2017, when she went back to focus on her teaching and research. She has a long history of affiliation with international organizations, such as:

- 2018 to date

  Majelis Pendidikan, Dewan Pendidikan Tinggi, Kemenristekdikti

- 2017 to date

  Board of Directors, Open Education Consortium (OEC)

- 2015 to date

  Board of Trustees, International Council for Open and Distance Education (ICDE)

- 2012–2015

  President, International Council for Open and Distance Education (ICDE)

- 2009–2011

  Member of the Executive Committee, International Council for Open and Distance Education (ICDE)

- 2009–2010

  President, Asian Association of Open Universities (AAOU)

- 2007–2009

  Secretary General, Asian Association of Open Universities (AAOU)
  Member of the Election Committee, International Council for Open and Distance Education (ICDE)

Dr. Belawati has received many awards throughout her career. The most recent awards honoured her long career and contributions to open and distance learning. These awards included the Asian Association of Open Universities (AAOU) Meritorious Service Award in 2012 and the Distinguished Individual Promoter of ODL from the African Council for Distance Education (ACDE) in June 2014.

Her research interests include online learning pedagogy, online learning quality assurance, MOOCs, and open education resources (OER), as well as new technologies and their use in open and online learning. References included at the end of this chapter reflect these research interests.

Interview

Transcript Analysis Summary

Analysis of all interviews included in this volume led to the identification of 3,545 units of data. The mean of these collective units was 118 per pioneer, the median was 118.5, and the mode was 132.

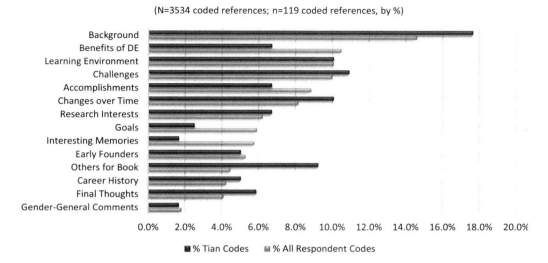

Figure 2.1 All Respondents' Versus Tian Belawati's Parent Codes

Individual interview units ranged from 59 to 217 units, yielding a spread of 158 units between all interviews. Tian Belawati's interview generated 119 units, which placed her interview just over the mean and median of all interviews in terms of unit generation.

A comparision of Tian Belawati's interview to the interviews of all pioneers indicated that half her interview was comparable to the average interview in terms of units produced per thematic area (Figure 2.1). Seven of the 14 thematic codes in her interview yielded a similar numbers of units to the average interview. These included learning environment, challenges, research interests, early founders, career history, final thoughts, and general gender-related comments. Her interview produced more units than the average interview did in three areas: background, changes over time, and others for the book. In responding to interview questions related to her background, Belawati indicated that her educational and experiential history was of an international nature. She also talked about a number of women whom she came to know during these years. These factors led to the higher-than-average number of units in this area. This international history also offered insight into the increased number of units in the changes over time and others for the book categories.

Belawati's interview yielded fewer units than the average interview did in the areas of benefits of DE, accomplishments, goals, and interesting memories. The lower number of units for the benefits of DE would be explained by the fact that none of the interview questions asked about this topic. Perhaps one reason for the lower-than-average number of units in the accomplishment section was that she stated in the interview that she could not remember all the awards that she had received over the years. Lastly, it was not known why she did not elaborate more about her goals or interesting memories during the interview.

Link to recorded interview: tinyurl.com/Belawati-T

Transcript of Interview

Full name: Tian Belawati

Institutional Affiliation: Professor, Indonesian Open University, also known as Universitas Terbuka (UT); International Council for Open and Distance Education (ICDE); Open Education Consortium

Key:

Regular font = Interviewee comments
Italicized font = Interviewer comments

Interview Questions

1. *What was your educational and experiential background before you became involved in online distance learning [ODL]?*

   My first degree was in agricultural economics, but after I graduated, I started to work at the Indonesian Open University. It was just established five months before I joined it. My practical professional life is in open and distance learning at the university level. So, although I have a background in agricultural economics, my work has always been in open and distance learning as it was practiced by the Open University of Indonesia.

   My second and third degrees are in education.

2. *In what year did you begin to look specifically into ODL?*

   I guess as soon as I joined the Open University of Indonesia. That would be in 1985.

3. *What were the circumstances in your world that initiated this interest in ODL?*

At that time in Indonesia, we had a lot of high school graduates who could not be absorbed by the higher education system. So the education policymakers at that time were looking for a model of higher education that could open up access to more people so that the high school graduates could complete a higher education level. We looked at the Open University in the UK and started to think about opening an open university here. But eventually, the actual establishment and organization of the Open University was helped by CIDA, the Canadian International Development Agency. It was with the help of CIDA, the money, the consultants, and everything that Indonesia established its first Open University in September 1984. That was the initial motivation for the Indonesian government to get involved in open and distance learning. But as time went on, it seemed that the learning system attracted more interests of the older adults. After the Open University was first established, we had more adult students than fresh high school graduates.

4. *Which female researchers or female colleagues may have piqued your interest in ODL?*

That is a very difficult question. I cannot recall any particular name at this time. It seems that in my earlier years working in this field, it was mostly men in the literature. So, I read a lot of literature, writings, or research results from, for example, Tony Bates, [Börje] Holmberg, and Otto Peters. That was in the early years. As time went by, I got to know and to work together with many women colleagues in the field of open and distance learning [ODL]. I got to know, for example, a more senior one who was Susan D'Antoni. Susan D'Antoni was in UNESCO [United Nations Educational, Scientific and Cultural Organization] at that time, and she was one of the proponents who worked on projects like OER [open educational resources] in UNESCO. Then there was this lady, Ingeborg Bø, from Norway who was already working very actively through ICDE. And there is Asha Kanwar of the Commonwealth of Learning. She has a long journey in the field of ODL, starting with when she was working with the Indira Gandhi National Open University. Then there is Brenda Gourley, who was the vice chancellor of the Open University of the UK, and many more now. I think that there are many more female enthusiasts now; proponents and also practitioners of ODL, but in the early days, it is a little harder to recall.

5. *Who would you identify as the early female leaders/founders in the field of ODL?*

I don't really know, but in the literature, we find names of those like I just mentioned. In Asia, for example, we have Professor Uma [Coomaraswamy], previous vice chancellor of the Sri Lanka Open University. There is, for example, Insung Jung, who is now working in Japan. There are many colleagues in Asia who are female. These are in later years when I was already involved in the field, but the more senior ones in the early years, I don't have any names. I'm sorry.

6. *What are some of the goals that you strove to achieve in the field of ODL?*

Of course, for my country, where access is still a big issue, one of my personal goals is to really give opportunities to every citizen in my country to enjoy higher education for whatever personal objectives they might have.

Lately, it is becoming my little obsession for Indonesian people to embrace modern higher education methods such as online learning, mobile learning, and those sorts of things. So I am still a little obsessed with those kinds of issues.

7. *What are some of your accomplishments in the field of ODL that you would like to share?*

This question has been asked of me many times. Usually, my answer is that I am very happy with the fact that being the President of our university for two terms until July, 2017. I am very happy and proud to see now that distance education or online education has been socially and officially accepted by the Indonesian people and also by the government and the law. It is not easy to put the words *open and distance education* in the Indonesian National Law, but we did it, and now it is official. It is there. And in fact, starting two years ago, for example, the government was very eager to motivate or even push the other institutes to also go into this field, to start expanding their programmes through the open and mobile learning methods. We have been campaigning on this for a very long time. I have been and still am personally involved in doing the campaign throughout the country. So if people ask me about my personal accomplishments, I think that as an accomplishment through my university, we have made ODL accepted. People are now starting to trust this method of learning as a way of learning. Even though it is not solely my personal effort, I would record it as one of my personal prides. Aside from being acknowledged by people with several prizes, certifications, or being elected as president of the Asian Association of Open Universities [AAOU] and also as past president of ICDE, I guess this is an accomplishment.

I: You mention some of your awards. Would you like to elaborate on any of them?

I can't mention all awards that I have received because I don't remember them all. But I think, professionally, I have received an award from the AAOU that is named the "Meritorious Service Award," that goes to someone who has been dedicating him- or herself to the field of distance education in Asia and is acknowledged as contributing to the field of ODL.

There is also an award from the African Council of Distance Education. The award is called "The Distinguished Individual Promotor of ODL Award." I guess the name says it for itself as to what was awarded.

I was also awarded an honorary professorship from the Tianjin Open University in China, for example, for my contribution to the awareness of open and distance education in China.

I have been awarded the Honoris Causa [Doctor of Letters] from the Wawasan Open University in Malaysia, as they said for my contribution, also to motivate women to be more active, especially in open and distance education.

I guess those were the latest.

8. *What are some of the challenges that you faced in the field of ODL over the years?*

In the past, it has been the trust and acceptance of people over the method. Now I guess we have gotten over that one. We have been able to convince people that this is as effective as any other method of learning. But within the Indonesian context, I guess that we are still struggling with the IT [information technology] infrastructure, which would facilitate quality distance education using the latest technologies that we could use. I feel personally that I am still struggling in campaigning and convincing people to share more of their materials, to make them open, and to also utilize and capitalize on the ample educational resources that are available there. People are still hesitating. People are still having a lot of obstacles to absolve because of the language barriers as well. But I think even though it is slow, we are making progress. Technically, I think that people have a lack of skills in utilizing the materials and resources and everything that can be and should be easily used by people in Indonesia on the technical side.

Gender-wise, as a female in the Indonesia, in the region not in the big cities, sometimes people take it [me as a woman] for granted like, for example, if I visit a regional office in the region and they would be looking for the university president, they would just walk past me because they are looking for a guy for a president. You know, things like that I've gotten used to. Then, when people start to recognize your face, it is a little easier, but there are those things.

9. *What was the "state of DE" when you first entered the field as opposed to ODL in 2019?*

Back in the mid-80s, at that time we didn't have the Internet. I think at that time the most sophisticated Open University was the Open University in the UK, which utilized a lot of different broadcasts and video conferences. In Indonesia, we started with some correspondence with print-based materials supplemented with face-to-face tutorials.

Now we are in a more connected world where we use a lot of Internet-based technology that makes it easier for us to connect to the students, even though in my part of the country, the active use of the Internet is not as high as it probably is in Canada, the United States, or Western Europe, but we are getting there. So I think the difference is really significant and influenced by the advancement of technology or ICT [information communication technologies].

10. *What interesting memories would you like to share about the beginning of ODL?*

When I started, we prepared printed learning materials. My first duty as a contract employee at the university was to do the editing of many materials before they went to the printer. So I had to read and correct it for grammar, and I had to check if the substance was accurate and compare it to the original transcription that was handwritten by the course authors that were outsourced from other universities. If I found any mistakes, I had to erase them with Tipp-Ex, the liquid eraser [correction fluid] and then use [correction tape] that would stick to the paper. So instead of retyping, we would do that for correcting. At the end of the day, all of my clothes would be black with all of this [excess] correcting [tape]. I can laugh about it now, but I used to hate my clothes at the end of the day when doing this work because it was so messy. I went through that probably for about a year, and then I was sent to Simon Fraser University [Burnaby, BC, Canada] to do a master's degree. I was so relieved that I didn't have to deal with that any more.

Now it is so easy with everything. I used to tell the academics at my university, "You are so lucky to start in this era because you don't have the mess at the end of the day, you know."

11. *What were your specific ODL research interests, and have they changed/evolved over the years?*

Yes and no. In the past, I used to be very much interested in factors related to persistence, factors related to withdrawal, those kinds of things: learning habits. Now I'm more into how we can use ICT to make it easier for us and also for the students or how students are learning with, for example, our digital learning materials, how they interact.... So it is still related to the students and to the learning process, but with a different angle, I guess.

12. *Could you please describe the learning environment that you currently work in or have most recently worked in (e.g., geographic and institutional setting, student demographics)?*

The university operates nationwide, but the head office is in the location where I am right now [Jakarta]. We have regional offices throughout the country. I work in the graduate programmes in the Faculty of Education. Because the operation is spread throughout the country, we have what we call "regional offices" throughout the country. We have about 40 offices. I travel to those offices to meet up with the students to see how they are doing. For example, we still organize face-to-face tutorials based on demands, and we organize simultaneous examinations throughout the country. So I usually go to the regions to see how the exams are going, for example, to meet some students. So, yes, I am quite mobile within the country.

We are a totally, entirely a distance education institution, but we do provide face-to-face tutorials for certain courses in response to student demands. The default tutorial system is online.

The student demographics include adult students, but the characteristics of our student demographics are changing over time. Our median age used to be around 55 some 15 years ago. Now

I think the median age is around 35. In the past, about 80% of our students were above 40 [years of age]. Now 40% of our students are below 30, but they are still above college age. I think about 25% of our students are between 19 and 25, so it is getting younger and more similar to campus-based students, but still we have a lot of older students.

13. *Is there anything else you [would] like to address?*

I think, as it has been said in much literature and by many experts as well, because of the character and nature of the distance education learning system, it cannot be separated from technology. So distance education will evolve in line with the evolution of technology. So we don't know what it's going to look like in the future because things change so fast, but I think we have a better way of providing education to the people, and even better in the future.

I was just watching a video in a WhatsApp group this morning about how Japanese are already conceptualizing how society will be in the Industrial Age 5.0. It seems to be better than 4.0 because it is going to be centred in the human being, but helped very much by the technology. So I hope that there will be no dichotomy between distance education and face-to-face education. I think the future will be just education and learning, using the latest technology that can still make the human as the centre of the whole process. That made me happy after seeing the video because now, it is a little scary for me.

I'm optimistic of people. Any challenges or obstacles that we have, we will always find solutions. Knowing the advancement of technology, I think that learning and getting smarter will be as fast as blinking your eyes.

14. *Can you suggest names of other female pioneers in distance education or ODL that you think we should include in the book?*

Maybe they are already in your list. The people that I mentioned: Asha Kanwar, Insung Jung, Ingeborg Bø [she has already passed], Susan D'Antoni. Susan D'Antoni is in Ottawa [Ontario, Canada]. She has retired already. You would like to interview her. She used to be in UNESCO, but she's retired now. Ema Tubella, she is in Spain. I think if you google her, you will find her name. And Brenda Gourley and Belinda Tynan. In United States, I would say, for example, Meg Benke. Who else can I think of? Oh, Sophie . . . in France, but her last name is difficult.

There is Zuraini Wati Abas in Malaysia. There is Grace Alfonso in the Philippines.

Do you have names from Africa? There is Laura from South Africa. Her last name is Czerniewicz and is hard to pronounce.

Publications

Books

Baggaley, J., & Belawati, T. (2010). *Distance education technologies in Asia* (2nd ed.). Sage.
Belawati, T. (2019). *Pembelajaran online (online learning)*. Universitas Terbuka.
Belawati, T. (2000). *Prinsip-prinsip pengelolaan pendidikan terbuka dan jarak jauh [Principles of distance education management]*. PAU-PPAI Universitas Terbuka.
Belawati, T., & Baggaley, J. (2010). *Policy and practice in Asian distance education*. Sage.
Belawati, T., Damayanti, N. S., Puspitasari, K. A. (Eds.). (2015). *Universitas Terbuka di era informasi*. Universitas Terbuka.
Belawati, T., Zuhairi, A., Hardhono, A. P., Zainul, A., Atwi Suparman, M., Sutjiatmo, B., . . . Winataputra, U. S. (Eds.). (1999). *Pendidikan terbuka dan jarak jauh [open learning and distance education]*. Universitas Terbuka.
Jung, I., Wong, T. M., & Belawati, T. (2013). *Quality assurance in distance education and e-learning. Challenges and solutions from Asia*. Sage.

Suciati, S., Belawati, T., Padmo, D. A., & Handayani, S. (Eds.). (2015). *Difusi inovasi pendidikan*. Universitas Terbuka.

Book Chapters

Belawati, T. (1999a). Pendidikan terbuka: Menunggu reformasi pola pikir [Open learning: Waiting for mind setting reform]. In D. P. Pannen (Ed.), *Cakrawala pendidikan* (pp. 200–209). Universitas Terbuka.

Belawati, T. (1999b). Sejarah pemikiran pendidikan terbuka dan jarak jauh [Development of theoretical framework of open and distance learning]. In T. Belawati (Ed.), *Pendidikan terbuka dan jarak jauh* (pp. 30–44). Universitas Terbuka.

Belawati, T. (2001). Open and distance education in the Asia Pacific region: Indonesia. In O. Jegede & G. Shive (Eds.), *Open and distance education in the Asia Pacific region* (pp. 171–188). Open University of Hong Kong Press.

Belawati, T. (2003a). Meta-survey on the use of technologies in education: Indonesia. In G. Farrell & C. Wachholz (Eds.), *Meta-survey on the use of technologies in education in Asia and the Pacific* (pp. 89–94). UNESCO Asia and Pacific Regional Bureau for Education.

Belawati, T. (2003b). Meta-survey on the use of technologies in education: Malaysia. In G. Farrell & C. Wachholz (Eds.), *Meta-survey on the use of technologies in education in Asia and the Pacific* (pp. 107–110). UNESCO Asia and Pacific Regional Bureau for Education.

Belawati, T. (2003c). Meta-survey on the use of technologies in education: Philippines. In G. Farrell & C. Wachholz (Eds.), *Meta-survey on the use of technologies in education in Asia and the Pacific* (pp. 121–128). UNESCO Asia and Pacific Regional Bureau for Education.

Belawati, T. (2003d). Meta-survey on the use of technologies in education: Thailand. In G. Farrell & C. Wachholz (Eds.), *Meta-survey on the use of technologies in education in Asia and the Pacific* (pp. 137–142). UNESCO Asia and Pacific Regional Bureau for Education.

Belawati, T. (2003e). Meta-survey on the use of technologies in education: Vietnam. In G. Farrell & C. Wachholz (Eds.), *Meta-survey on the use of technologies in education in Asia and the Pacific* (pp. 143–146). UNESCO Asia and Pacific Regional Bureau for Education.

Belawati, T. (2019). Massive open online courses: The state of practice in Indonesia. In K. Zhang, C. Bonk, T. Reeves, & T. Reynolds (Eds.), *MOOCs and open education across emerging economies: Challenges, successes, and opportunities*. Routledge.

Belawati, T., & Bandalaria, M. D. P. (2019). Distance education in Asia: Indonesia and Philippines. In M. G. Moore & W. C. Diehl (Eds.), *Handbook of distance education* (4th ed., pp. 557–579). Routledge.

Belawati, T., Kusmawan, U., & Isman, S., I. G. A. K. (2012). Open and distance learning in Asia: A case study. In R. Hogan (Ed.), *Transnational distance learning and building new markets for universities* (pp. 40–50). University of the South Pacific.

Belawati, T., Padmo, D., & Zuhairi, A. (2006). Open and distance education: Development and experience from Universitas Terbuka. In W. Zhang (Ed.), *Global perspectives: Philosophy and practice in distance education* (pp. 293–309). CCRTVU Press.

Belawati, T., & Wardani, I. G. A. K. (2010). Quality assurance in distance teacher education: The experience of Universitas Terbuka. In P. Alan & A. Umar (Eds.), *Teacher education through open and distance learning* (pp. 159–174). Commonwhealth of Learning.

Belawati, T., Zuhairi, A., & Wardani, I. G. A. K. (2012). Quality assurance in a mega university: Universitas Terbuka. In I. Jung & C. Latchem (Eds.), *Quality assurance and accreditation in distance education and e-learning models, Policies and Research*. Routledge.

Darojat, O., & Belawati, T. (2017). Quality assurance in open and distance education: A case of universitas terbuka, Indonesia. In C. Li (Ed.), *Open and distance education international quality assurance case* (pp. 19–28). Beijing Normal University Press.

Daryono, & Belawati, T. (2013). Prospects and challenges for introducing open educational resources in Indonesia. In G. Dhanarajan & D. Porter (Eds.), *Open educational resources: An Asian perspective* (pp. 75–86). Commonwealth of Learning and OER Asia.

Padmo, D., & Belawati, T. (2017). Implementing sustainable ICT-supported innovation policies. Case of Universitas Terbuka – Indonesia. In I. A. Lubin (Ed.), *ICT-supported innovations in small countries and developing regions: Perspectives and recommendations for international education*. AECT/Springer.

Padmo, D., Belawati, T., Idrus, O., & Ardiasih, L. S. (2017). The state of practice of mobile learning in Indonesia. In A. Murphy, H. Farley, L. Dyson, & H. Jones (Eds.), *Mobile learning in higher education in the Asia Pacific: Harnessing trends and challenging orthodoxies* (pp. 173–190). Springer.

Prasetyo, D., & Belawati, T. (2013). Country case study Indonesia: Reaching younger distance learners through social media. In *United Nations Asian and Pacific Training Centre for Information and Communication Technology for Development. Open and Distance Learning in Asia and the Pacific* (pp. 30–39). United Nations Asian and Pacific Training Centre for ICT for Development.

Semiawan, C., & Belawati, T. (2000). Pendidikan tinggi untuk milenium ketiga [Higher education in third millennium]. In D. P. Pannen (Ed.), *Cakrawala pendidikan* (pp. 60–73). Universitas Terbuka.

Journal Articles and Blogs

Anggoro, M. T., Hardhono, A. P., Belawati, T., & Darmayanti, T. (2001). Tutorial elektronik melalui internet dan fax-internet [electronic tutorials through internet and fax-internet]. *Jurnal Pendidikan Terbuka dan Jarak Jauh, 2*(1), 60–77.

Belawati, T. (1998). Increasing student persistence in Indonesian post-secondary distance education. *Distance Education, 19*(1), 81–108.

Belawati, T. (2000). Enhancing learning in distance education through the world wide web. *Jurnal Pendidikan Terbuka dan Jarak Jauh, 1*(1), 1–17.

Belawati, T. (2005). The impact of online tutorials on course completion rates and student achievement. *Learning Media and Technology, 30*(1), 15–25.

Belawati, T. (2006). Financial management system in open and distance learning: An example at Universitas Terbuka. *Educom Asia, 12*(1). www.cemca.org/newsletter/sept2006/sept2006.pdf

Belawati, T. (2014). Open education, open educational resources and massive open online courses. *Journal of Continuing Education and Lifelong Learning (IJCELL), 7*(1). https://w5.hkuspace.hku.hk/journal/index.php/ijcell

Belawati, T., Anggoro, M. T., Hardhono, A. P., & Darmayanti, T. (2002). Electronic tutorials: Indonesian experience. *International Review of Research in Open and Distance Learning, 2*(5), 1–11.

Belawati, T., & Zuhairi, A. (2007). The practice of quality assurance system in open and distance learning: A case study at Universitas Terbuka. *International Review of Research in Open and Distance Learning, 8*(1). www.irrodl.org/index.php/irrodl/article/view/340/782

Darojat, O., & Belawati, T. (2014, May 5). Managing quality assurance in a mega university. *CLICK's Insider*.

Hewindati, Y. T., & Belawati, T. (2017). Massive open online courses as a community programme. *ASEAN Journal of Open and Distance Learning (AJODL), 9*(1), 1–11.

Padmo, D., Huda, N., & Belawati, T. (2000). Pemanfaatan program TV melalui satelit siaran langsung (TV-SSL) di Indonesia: Persepsi dan kesediaan perguruan tinggi negeri/swasta [Direct satellite television for education: Perception and willingness of higher education Institutions]. *Jurnal Pendidikan Terbuka dan Jarak Jauh, 1*(1), 58–67.

3
BEUKES-AMISS, CATHERINE MARGARET (MAGGY)

Photo of Catherine Margaret (Maggy) Beukes-Amiss contributed by Maggy Beukes-Amiss

Most important of the goals that I am trying to achieve is that I would really like to have a total mindset change among our academics regarding use of technology, and to move away from some of the technophobic fears experienced, which I can see will happen through various change management strategies in this area.

Dr. Maggy Beukes-Amiss began her studies with a Higher Education Diploma Secondary from the University of Namibia. She also holds an International Computer Driving Licence (ICDL) from the Computer Society South Africa and an Expert of New Learning Technology from University of Applied Sciences in Furtwangen, Germany. She went on to obtain a Bachelor of Arts degree in Library and Records Management, also from the University of Applied Sciences. Following in the same vein, she obtained a Master of Science in Electronic Information Management from Robert Gordon University in Aberdeen, Scotland. Her tertiary studies were completed at the University of Pretoria in South Africa, where she completed a PhD in Computer-integrated Education.

She is currently Director, Centre for eLearning and Interactive Multimedia, and Director, Centre for Open, Distance and eLearning (CODeL) in Windhoek, at the University of Namibia.

Beukes-Amiss has over 20 years of teaching experience in higher education, focusing on the areas of information communication technology (ICT), web development, systems analysis, design and evaluation information sources, and Internet search engines, as well as information storage and retrieval software (WINISIS).

Beukes-Amiss is very active in her region at various international e-learning conferences, where she has taken on the responsibilities of workshop facilitator, paper presenter, and moderator/chair: for example, Online Educa Conference Berlin (2005, 2006, 2010, 2011, 2012, 2013, and 2014); e-Learning Africa Conferences, Addis Ababa (2006), Nairobi (2007), Accra (2008), Dakar (2009), Lusaka (2010), Dar es Salaam (2011), Cotonou (2012), Windhoek (2013), Kampala (2014), Addis Ababa (2015); and eMerge Online (2006–2012).

Dr. Beukes-Amiss has varied research interests, which are reflected in the reference section at the end of this chapter. Her personal context leads her work with information and communications technology (ICT) implementation and usage, open access, and the role of libraries in e-learning.

Interview

Transcript Analysis Summary

Analysis of all interviews included in this volume led to the identification of 3,545 units of data. The mean of these collective units was 118 per pioneer, the median was 118.5, and the mode was 132. Individual interview units ranged from 59 to 217 units, yielding a spread of 158 units between all interviews. Maggy Beukes-Amiss' interview generated 123 units, which placed her interview near the top of the middle third of interviews in terms of unit generation.

A comparision of Maggy's interview to the interviews of all pioneers indicated that over half of her interview was akin to the average interview in terms of units produced per thematic area (Figure 3.1). Eight of the 14 thematic codes in her interview yielded a similar numbers of unit to the average interview. These included background, benefits of DE, learning environment, accomplishments, early founders, career history, final thoughts, and general gender-related comments. Maggy's interview generated significantly more units than the average interview in the areas of challenges, research interests, and goals. The number of units in the challenges category was most likely due to the trials that she faced, especially in trying to change the mindsets of people in her country about the value and role of online and distance learning, which had been recently introduced. The recent advent of online and distance learning helped explain the many goals and research interests that she talked about during the interview as well. It might be the reason for her less-than-average number of units in the areas of changes over time. Finally, the lack of units in the others for the book section was because Beukes-Amiss asked to provide some names after the interview was over.

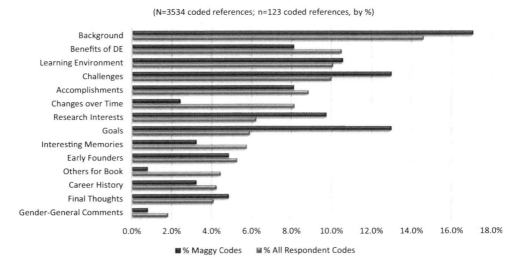

Figure 3.1 All Respondents' Versus Margaret (Maggy) Beukes-Amiss's Parent Codes

Link to recorded interview: tinyurl.com/Beukes-Amiss-CM

Transcript of Interview

Full name: Dr. Catherine Margaret (Maggy) Beukes-Amiss
Institutional Affiliation: The Centre for Open, Distance and eLearning (CODeL), University of Namibia Main Campus, Windhoek, Namibia
Key:

Regular font = Interviewee comments
Italicized font = Interviewer comments

Interview Questions

1. *What was your educational and experiential background before you became involved in distance education [DE] and e-learning?*

   My educational and experiential background is actually quite diverse. I started off studying, from an educational qualification point of view, with a Diploma in Higher Education – Secondary Education [HED Sec], which was a four-year diploma. I then moved on to a Bachelor of Arts, specifically in Library and Records Management because during my first diploma, I majored in Library and Records Management, so it was natural to move to a Bachelor's degree in this area. The Bachelor's was also a four-year programme. Both of these I obtained through the University of Namibia [UNAM]. After that, I moved to Robert Gordon University [RGU] in Scotland, where I studied for a Master's in Science in Electronic Information Management [MSc EIM]. I had curiosities about electronic information and tools and how to use them in accessing information. Eventually after that, I moved into a PhD in Computer-integrated Education [CIE] at the University of Pretoria in South Africa.

   From the technical side, I ensured that I acquired an International Computer Driving Licence (ICDL) from the Computer Society of South Africa. Soon after that, I also engaged in a programme called Expert of New Learning Technology, which was a seven- to eight-month online computer planning course that I was certified for through the University of Applied Sciences in Furtwangen, Germany.

   This is a more or less a formal view of my educational and technical background.

2. *In what year did you begin to look specifically into DE and e-learning?*

   More specifically regarding e-learning, I started when I took that Expert of New Learning Technology certificate, which was actually a blended learning programme because we had face-to-face as well as online interactions. We had a face-to-face session in the beginning, then seven or eight months online, and then another face-to-face session in the end, where we wrote an exam to get the certification. That started way back in 2004. I completed that in 2005.

   For distance education [DE] specifically, I got more interested and involved in a formal capacity from 2016. Why I would say in a formal capacity only from 2016 was because I was the Director for the Centre for eLearning and Interactive Multimedia [CeLIM] in 2015, but then the university went through a restructuring process and basically considered a merger between the then–Centre for External Studies [CES], which was our open and distance learning [ODL] wing in the university, to merge with the Centre for eLearning and Interactive Multimedia, which we called "CeLIM" at the time. After the merger in 2016, we became the Centre for Open, Distance, and eLearning (CODeL). So that is why I am saying formally only from 2016 because we then established a centre, which now carries a dual mandate for distance education as well as e-learning.

   I also got involved in discussions with public stakeholders and consultations regarding the ODL policy of the country. So I had a bit of not-so-official involvement before 2016, and then my formal involvement in ODL, which I guess you refer to as DE, started in 2016.

3. *What were the circumstances in your world that initiated this interest in DE and e-learning?*

   Well a lot, but to be a little bit specific, once I participated in this seven- to eight-month blended learning course, which I started in 2004, I realized that there were a lot of opportunities that we could start to tap into as a country by kicking off with capacity-building opportunities, even though we are faced with lots of challenges like access, bandwidth, lack of digital literacy skills, and also the digital divide due to our country's geographical size. But the interest for me was when I completed that course and decided that it would be good to start building capacity and let people become familiar with this world, so that once these other things [challenges we faced] would fall in place, we could just move ahead. So these are some of the circumstances in my world that initiated my interest in e-learning.

Then, of course, I always had the deep feeling that ODL is definitely a part, and should be a part, and it should be able to benefit from the opportunities that technology can avail to it. So, while it was daunting to know that we had to merge, it was a blessing at the same time that we could start to try and make a difference in terms of the opportunities that the technologies can avail to the distance side.

4. *Which female researchers or female colleagues may have piqued your interest in DE and e-learning?*

I looked at this question, and I said to myself, "I don't want to sound arrogant in answering when I am asked about this," but I just briefly reflected and thought that I would like to believe that it could be quite a number of females that would have piqued on this interest of mine in distance and e-learning as I became so passionate in terms of training in this field, specifically e-learning at that stage, within my country and across several countries through various opportunities that were availed to me. I assisted my country through a trust that we belong to as ODL Institutions, which is called Namibian Open Learning Network Trust [NOLNet]. We got funding in Germany through Gesellschaft für Internationale Zusammenarbeit [GIZ], which helped us to be sponsored and train people in the area, and for that reason, it isn't easy for me to give an exact number, but as I said, I would like to believe that it could be quite a number of females that could have piqued on my interest in distance and e-learning over the years.

5. *Who would you identify as the early female leaders/founders in the field of DE and e-learning?*

It depends whether this question is testing my know-how of female leaders/founders in the world or rather within my own context. In my own context, specifically related to e-learning, I think I, myself, could be one of those early adopters of technology that made the way through with know-how in this area and shared it with others. A couple of female colleagues and I were among the first to explore the area/field of e-learning specifically. Maybe some did not take it to another level, just left it at an interest level, but for me, I then went ahead in terms of studying e-learning as a field, as I explained, in my PhD area. I had a couple of other female colleagues who started with me, but it does depend upon the ones who remained in the area and decided to take it further. For others, as their beliefs turned, they may have moved into other areas as well. In DE in general, there are other females, like at our sister university, Namibian University of Science and Technology [NUST], but there are not a lot of females in both the fields of distance education and e-learning in Namibia. That is one of the aspects that I picked up in 2017 when I started to attend more ODL conferences. Setting e-learning aside and just looking at DE, to my mind, there is only one lady at our National University of Science and Technology.

6. *What are some of the goals that you strove to achieve in the field of DE and e-learning?*

This is an interesting question in terms of goals that I strove to achieve in the integrated field. Now I intend to refer to it as ODeL, with distance and e-learning combined. I am passionate about quality delivery through both the traditional distance mode that I am still supporting within my university, but strengthened through the use of technology as well as online mode, with specific emphasis on ensuring more and more academics and students will become comfortable studying through these modes that we are making available to them and have the opportunity to focus on deeper aspects of learning and not just the superficial aspects. The problem for me currently is that in teaching in the traditional face-to-face environment, we are limited by time. We stick to a timetable in terms of topical areas that we should address. Through my new centre in the university, we get to avail more opportunities in terms of various technologies that we now couple with the traditional distance mode. It allows us to practice things like the flipped classroom and so on, so that we really can focus more on deeper learning instead of just superficial opportunities in terms of how our students learn.

Also, to allow our academics and students to test and try various technologies that can aid in their personal and professional development. So, in this sense, we researched quite a lot of tools and technologies that we integrated into our learning management systems [LMSs] as third-party services that can enhance the learning experience of our students.

Most important of the goals that I am trying to achieve is that I would really like to have a total mindset change among our academics regarding use of technology and to move away from some of the technophobic fears experienced, which I can see will happen through various change management strategies in this area. Eventually, I would like to see the centre that I am the Director for at the moment, which is the Centre of Open, Distance and eLearning, become a hub or a centre of excellence in DE and e-learning.

These are just a few that I am mentioning to you. There could be more, but I decided to focus on these ones only.

7. *What are some of your accomplishments in the field of DE and e-learning that you would like to share?*

Let me start with the most recent one, which had to do with a merit sabbatical, which focused upon leadership within the centre in the university. I received this award for outstanding leadership in the area. It is something that I achieved, and I would like to think because of my hard work and passion for what I live, breathe, and think every day.

I also received an award in the form of a certificate from GIZ, Germany "Ambassador for Quality in Digital Learning" in 2016, after I had successfully participated in and completed a MOOC [massive open online course] that GIZ hosted in quality digital learning. That was another achievement because I didn't realize that it would come with any form of certification because it was a MOOC, it was online, and I obtained quite a number of badges online while I participated, but in the end, I actually received a certificate in that area, and it was very humbling.

I feel very content in my heart about the opportunities that I had to train quite a number of participants in Namibia, and several other countries in Africa and abroad. I was hired as a consultant to facilitate and coach in e-learning, instructional design, e-learning management, online facilitators/tutors, and things like that. So, I think that is another accomplishment in my opinion because in one way or another, I became visible to several people, not just confined to my own country but kind of started an international identity for myself in this way as well.

I have also been very recently classified in the elite category of the top 100 movers and shakers in e-learning in Africa after I was consulted to fill out a short form with my name and details and affiliated institution, and they then carried out independent research in terms of achievements and where I made a difference in my area. So I then was classified in the elite area among the top ten of over a hundred of African movers and shakers that they researched and studied. I think that this is another accomplishment that I feel very pleased about because somehow it cements my passion that I think I'm sharing in this field.

Within the field of ODL, I coordinated, as the current Director of CODeL, huge improvements of what I found as a more print-based distance mode through the effective use of technologies. I tried to couple the benefits of technological tools to what was heavily print-based in terms of DE: things that I think really made a different to the Institution when it comes to the services that we deliver to the students, either through distance mode or online mode.

The other accomplishment that I think that I could also mention is that I got the opportunity to be invited to deliver keynotes at my own Namibia ODL conference and also various e-learning conferences. There's one in particular that we call "eLearning Africa" [eLA]. I started to join that one as of 2006. I try not to miss this event that takes place once a year in different African countries. I also had the opportunity to host it in Namibia with support from the Ministry of Information and Communication Technology and the Ministry of Education. It is rotational from country to country, and I managed to be in charge as overall coordinator and chairperson of the implementing steering committee the year that it came to Namibia. Then I also attend others like Online Educa Berlin so that I can keep in touch with and stay abreast with the international flair of where things are moving within the fields of DE and e-learning. I also participate in interviews like this one and online webinars where I talk about my experiences in this area, or I share some particular tricks in an area, like online facilitation or e-learning management when I am requested to do so.

I will stop there with those. There are definitely more, but I would like to just stick to the couple that I have just mentioned.

8. *What are some of the challenges that you faced in the field of DE and e-learning over the years?*

I think that the field of e-learning, as I explained to you, was a new thing, a new way of doing things, so definitely mindset, mindset of people in terms of that change that I was after to start to embrace what the whole area is about, considering that even now we are in the industrial revolution. For me in particular, I think the biggest obstacle, besides things like bandwidth related to connectivity, access, or digital divide, as I mentioned already, I think a more particular one for me was the issue regarding mindset. To get people to change their perspective of how we could. . . . You know, I used to always get responses like "No, we are not yet there. What are you on about? It's maybe not going to work yet," but I always had the feeling that we need to start somewhere with this. So those are just some of the challenges.

In DE, personally I would say that when I entered this area of the field as I now see as one field combined, which I refer to as ODeL, I had the impression that it was definitely more male dominated. The reason why I'm saying it is because I had the opportunity to represent my vice chancellor last year in Malaysia at a vice chancellors' platform for ODeL institutions worldwide organized by the Commonwealth of Learning [COL]. I think that there were maybe four ladies out of 25 participants. That's when I realized that it is still heavily dominated by the male counterparts and that we would have to work very hard in terms of getting more females visible in the area.

This is something that is more contextual to my country because I do not have evidence that it is happening elsewhere, is this whole secondary treatment of the DE field, almost as if it is not receiving the right attention and priority in terms of budgeting, in terms of understanding. I must confess, however, in Namibia, when I attended a conference in 2016 in Swakopmund where I delivered a keynote, our ministers were in full support of the fact that we need to change the perception that DE is at a lower level in terms of quality and output than the more traditional educational modes. I can't deny that they were in support, but the feeling and the perception in general has been very daunting so far when it comes to the specific area of DE. So that is something that we are working on to address, to try to make a huge impact and difference in.

9. *What was the "state of DE" when you first entered the field as opposed to e-learning in 2019?*

The state of DE when I first entered, unofficially prior to 2016, but now officially from 2016 heading such a centre in my university, I found it to be very heavily print-based. So that was the state. What I have been trying to change from then up to now and will continue to do so is to try and optimize the benefits of technology in shaping manual and print-based processes. If I can just give you one example: When I entered the field of DE, in particular e-learning, the university had 12 campuses across the country, and I was confronted with huge stacks of assignments that students submitted from across all corners of the country, and they got lost in terms of snail mail [postal mail] processes. Sometimes students entered exams without even knowing if they made the continuous assessment requirement or not. Immediately when we started in 2016 as a merged entity, I tried my level best to turn around some of the very manual, text-based processes. To date, I have moved all of our assignment submission processes for our distance and online mode students completely online insofar as having the marking of the assessments online as well.

10. *What interesting memories would you like to share about the beginning of e-learning?*

As I referred to in a previous question, it definitely was tough; even though you are asking me for interesting memories that I would like to share about the beginning of e-learning, it started off very tough because of those challenges that I have already mentioned. But at the same time, I tend to want to see a challenge in terms of a positive perspective in that I want to see it changed into something more positive and more exciting. So that's why I am saying that it was tough in the very beginning because of those challenges that I already mentioned, but at the same time also very exciting for me because I had the opportunity to empower and share my knowledge with so many that never even heard the term *e-learning* before. It was such a rewarding feeling at a conference in my country or another country when I could learn, and I could see another way that I could be assisted through the use of technologies. I never wanted them to believe that technology was a quick fix to any of their problems. I always tried to make sure that I availed and brought across the opportunities that we got through the use of technologies. I still remain very passionate about the area even though I faced a lot of challenges as well.

11. *What were your specific e-learning research interests, and have they changed/evolved over the years?*

My particular problem at the present time is that because my educational background is so diverse, I had the opportunity of building my research profile almost more related to those fields that I worked in because I was the Head of my Department of Information and Communication Studies in the Faculty of Humanities and Social Sciences at two different intervals in my entire span within the faculty of almost 20 years. Therefore, my research at that stage was more geared to the areas in which I worked. I have now started to turn things around and would like to work more on research outputs that would speak more specifically to my passion and interest in terms of e-learning and ODeL. So that's now where I am paving the way in terms of where I should go.

One of the areas of interest that I have right now is that I would like to share with the world the quality drive that I would want to bring across within my centre, but also of benefit to other centres of ODL. So my research interests are now going into that. I would like to finish a paper soon that I would like to deliver later this year at a conference about that quality drive and how I started, planned, and worked for it, in terms of improving quality of distance education.

And then, through my PhD, I have the opportunity of honing in, in terms of the activities of champions in e-learning. Even there, I am working on a couple of publications where I would like to share what I managed, establish what were the feelings and the qualities of those early adopters in the field of e-learning.

And then, of course, another area where I have had a lot of interest in research and where I had the opportunity to also convey through podcasts or interviews internationally was online facilitation.

I don't think that in my area of work that it will ever remain static, so I do think they [my research interests] will change, and they will change quite often. Within my centre, we have started what we call a "research catalogue." Within that research catalogue, I do have quite a number of ideas that I brainstormed with my team that we would like to use as a target to get our research more specifically focused.

12. *Could you please describe the learning environment that you currently work in or have most recently worked in (e.g., geographic and institutional setting, student demographics)?*

Recently in my current workplace, I am stationed at the Centre for Open, Distance and eLearning at the University of Namibia, Windhoek, Namibia. We have at the moment more or less 6,000 distance-mode students, but inclusive of those distance-mode students, since last year we are now starting to work on more fully-fledged online distance learners as well. So those students are incorporated in the 6,000 distance students that I'm referring to. In general, my university has a complement, inclusive of the distance and online-mode students, of around 27,000 altogether.

The full-time students would be typically the same age range as in traditional campuses, coming straight from high school to university. However, the distance-mode student and the online-mode student would be more an adult type of learner who already has more or less a first degree and would like to further their studies while working full time; they have families, etc. So the distance- and online-mode student would definitely be much older, trying to stay in touch with the latest developments in their field. So, therefore, they opt to study further through distance or online mode, where we manage to avail our programmes through various faculties in ODeL modes.

We have quite a range of courses. I would rather go by faculty name, because in each faculty, we have a range of programmes. We support them in terms of online and distance modes. In terms of faculty support through the modes, we've got the Faculty of Education that we support through distance mode but also through online mode specifically in various programmes. We have also got the Faculty of Economic and Management Sciences. There again, we've got quite a range of programmes in distance mode only, but also two certificates through online mode specifically. We've got the Faculty of Humanities and Social Sciences where we also support them in terms of various programmes, like media studies, information and library science, records management, in distance and online mode. We've also got our Faculty of Health Sciences, but specifically our School of Nursing, where we support them with a post-graduate diploma in nursing education. Recently we managed to get our Faculty of Law on board. They started with distance mode with their LLB [Legum Baccalaureus] programme last year, and this past year we moved it online through a staggered approach. Now they are in their second-year distance, so they will move second year online next year. So these are a few faculties through which we run various programmes over these modes that I've explained.

13. *Is there anything else you would like to address?*

That's a tough one because it's interesting that you are posing the question about what are some of the things that I would like to share with someone 50 years from now, but I remain confident that whatever challenges and perceptions in terms of negative perceptions that we face at the moment would be bygones by then, if somebody picks this up 50 years from now. I could almost imagine that by then we would be in a world where this would be commonplace and part of common understanding, that people would want to embrace the opportunities that either technologies or fields of learning like e-learning or DE can avail to them. It's not a warning, but I would just like to, sort of an almost light bulb moment, to say is that I have learned that it is never easy in the beginning, but hard work and passion and believing in the value of what you do will eventually overcome whatever might clutter your mind at the moment. If you are passionate about what you are doing, if you believe in the value of what you are doing in terms of its total contribution to society or a nation, then whatever challenge you face now would not be a challenge then, because of the effort that you put in and all of the sacrifices to make this work and to make it commonplace and part of common understanding. Because I always reflect a little bit and think what I would really love to see in a couple of years from now is that we should reach that tipping point where this would almost become naturally as part of what the future would hold for us, whether it is through artificial intelligence or virtual reality, that we reach that tipping point soon, so that those to come can then also fit in and not see it as daunting as when it started off, but more fitting in the middle, if you want to look at the continuum of where we start with early adopters to where we have the laggards join in. This is just off the cuff. I would have loved for this particular question to reflect a little bit more, because I want it to be powerful. I want it to make a difference. I want it to remain in people's minds. On a lighter note, I'm not sure that I am making that impact, but for now I will leave it at that. If I have another opportunity, I could get back to this again.

I absolutely loved the opportunity granted to me to participate in such an interview where I can share, I hope humbly so, my experiences and, most importantly, my passion for the two combined areas. It's absolutely wonderful. I don't think we often get the opportunity to share on a wider scale with other colleagues in the world what we are experiencing, and that we could almost get the opportunity to identify and come up with synergy in terms of some of the things. We often work so much in isolation in one way or another, so I really appreciated the opportunity that I got today to share my world a little bit with you. And I hope that it is going to make a difference one way or another. Thank you very much for the opportunity.

In terms of the official interview, this is my story. If I could think of anything else that might make a difference in this regard, I guess that we could do this at another stage. But for now, I feel content that I managed to share whatever I had in mind at the moment.

14. *Can you suggest names of other female pioneers in DE, e-learning, or open and distance learning [ODL] that you think we should include in the book?*

I could think of a couple. For this request, I would ask for a little more time so that I could perhaps through email put you in touch with some. As I said, I could only think of one more lady at our sister university within this area, more specifically, ODeL. Then, of course, I could put you in touch with people that we look up to and support us in the area, some of the ladies from the Commonwealth of Learning who also tried some of the initiatives in ODeL. So if I have a bit more time, we could take this particular question offline and engage a bit more so that I can direct and help you in that regard.

Publications

Journal Articles

Banda, F., Beukes-Amiss, C. M., Bosch, T., Mano, W., McLean, P., & Steenveld. L. (2007). Contextualising journalism education and training in Southern Africa. *Ecquid Novi: AJS, 28*, 156–173.

Beukes-Amiss, C. M., & Chiware, E. R. T. (2006). The impact of the diffusion of ICTs into educational practices: A review of the Namibian situation. *Namibia Educational Research Association Journal, 2005/2006*, 33–45.

Mchombu, K. J., & Beukes-Amiss, C. M. (2015). The role of libraries in contemporary African society. *Library Trends, 64*(1), 112–124.

Nengomasha, C. T., Mubuyaeta, M. M., & Beukes-Amiss, C. M. (2017). Organisational knowledge management: A case study of the ministry of Gender Equality and Child Welfare (MGECW) in Namibia. *Journal for Studies in Humanities and Social Sciences. 6*(1), 18–40.

Nyanga, E., Nengomasha, C. T., & Beukes-Amiss, C. M. (2018). Disaster preparedness and management at the national archives and the national library of Namibia. *African Journal of Library, Archives and Information Science (AJLAIS), 28*(1), 77–91.

Yule, W., & Beukes-Amiss, C. M. (2017). Scholarly communication: The value of repositories and e-portfolios at the University of Namibia (UNAM). *International Journal of Library and Information Science, 9*(7), 58–65.

Conference Presentations and Interviews

Beukes-Amiss, C. M. (2006a). *Establishment of a multi-stakeholder eLearning Centre* [Paper presentation]. eLearning Africa Conference, Addis Ababa, Ethiopia.

Beukes-Amiss, C. M. (2006b). *Impact of electronic resources on teaching and learning in selected secondary schools in Scotland and Namibia* [Paper presentation]. WWW Applications Conference, Bloemfontein, South Africa.

Beukes-Amiss, C. M. (2011). *Towards scalable and sustainable implementation of e-Learning processes in higher education* [Paper presentation]. Knowledge 2011 Conference, Knowledge production and higher education in the 21st Century, Cape Town, South Africa.

Beukes-Amiss, C. M. (2015, November 9). Interview by SISTEM®. *Africa Tomorrow*.

Beukes-Amiss, C. M., & Kazondovi, C. (2006). *Research on ICT in education: African and Namibian perspectives* [Paper presentation]. SANGONet ICT Thetha Forum, July 2006. Windhoek, Namibia.

Beukes-Amiss, C. M., & Mchombu, K. (2013). *KM & ICT4D in Education performance improvement through use of KM & ICT4 Education* [Paper presentation]. Faculty of Humanities and Social Sciences, University of Namibia, Windhoek, Namibia.

Beukes-Amiss, C. M., & Mufeti, T. K. (2005). *Benefits of using open source software: A review of Unam's learning management system (LMS)* [Paper presentation]. NOLNet Open and Distance Learning Conference, Windhoek, Namibia.

4
BRINDLEY, JANE ELIZABETH

Photo of Jane Elizabeth Brindley contributed by Jane Elizabeth Brindley

We were all pioneers in a new field trying our best to figure out the best methods for communicating, teaching and supporting students, and researching and evaluating our work.

Jane Elizabeth Brindley comes from a background in psychology with a Master of Arts in Counselling Psychology, University of British Columbia, and a PhD in Clinical Psychology, University of Ottawa. Her academic interests have always been tied to distance education, with her master's thesis, entitled *A Study of Completion and Attrition in Distance Education*, and her PhD thesis being *The Effect of a Social Support Intervention on Distance Learner Behaviour*.

She began her career in 1978 when she joined Athabasca University as Counsellor, Student Services. She remained with Athabasca University for 13 years, leaving the role as Director of the Northern Regional Office in 1991. Her interest in student support in distance education was enhanced during her time with Athabasca University.

Brindley moved on to Sudbury, Ontario, where she worked with Cambrian College and then had internships with the Centre for Psychological Services, University of Ottawa, Ottawa, and Psychosocial Services Department, Northeastern Ontario Regional Cancer Centre. Next, she moved on to serving as a special consultant, Centre for Innovation in Learning with Contact North in 1997.

She worked as Intake Coordinator and then Director of the Psychological Services Centre at the University of Windsor from 2000 to 2008. Simultaneously, she worked as an adjunct faculty member with Oldenburg University, Germany, and University of Maryland University College.

As of the publication date of this book, Brindley is an Adjunct Professor, Department of Educational and Counselling Psychology and Special Education, Faculty of Education, University of British Columbia, Canada.

Brindley's main research interest delves into learner support services in online learning, as well as the tools currently available to enhance student support. Her papers and book chapters listed at the end of this chapter demonstrate her concern for innovative approaches to learner support systems and the need to focus on student success in distance education.

In addition to her research activities, Brindley was involved with the Canadian Association for Distance Education (CADE) and the International Council for Open and Distance Education (ICDE). She was present at the Vancouver meeting of ICDE in 1982, along with many of the women profiled in this book, where women began talking about starting their own group. These women began meeting together at ICDE conferences and other conferences and eventually gained funding to begin the Women's International Network (WIN). Brindley was one of these women who left their mark as leading researchers in the field of distance education despite its being a small group at the time.

Interview

Transcript Analysis Summary

Analysis of all interviews included in this volume led to the identification of 3,545 units of data. The mean of these collective units was 118 per pioneer, the median was 118.5, and the mode was 132. Individual interview units ranged from 59 to 217 units, yielding a spread of 158 units between all interviews. Jane Brindley's interview generated 148 units, placing her interview in the upper fifth of all interviews in terms of unit numbers.

A comparision of Brindley's interview to the interviews of all pioneers indicated that half her interview profile was, generally speaking, akin to that of the average interview profile (Figure 4.1). Her interview produced a similar number of units to the average interview in the following areas: learning environment, challenges, research interests, goals, career history, final thoughts, and general gender-related comments. Her interview yielded a fair number more units than the average interview in the areas of background, early founders, and others for the book. The larger number of background units might be understood within her unique context as a pioneer in developing and delivering DE counselling and support services, as well as DE psychology programmes and courses. The number of units in the topic areas of early founders and others for the book could explained by her early entry into the field and international involvement with other female pioneers of her day.

Brindley's interview had a much lower-than-average number of units in the areas of benefits of DE and accomplishments. There may be two primary reasons for the sparsity of benefits of DE units. First, there was no interview question that asked about the benefits of DE. It was a topic that

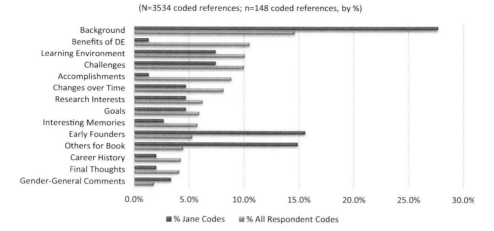

Figure 4.1 All Respondents' Versus Jane Brindley's Parent Codes

naturally arose in responses to other interview questions. Second, it might be possible that Brindley focused on what supports students needed to be successful DE learners, rather than on the benefits learners received from such support resources. One possible explanation for Brindley's low number of accomplishment units is related to social mores that discourage women from talking about their accomplishments. Further evidence to support this theory is found in her response that discussed team accomplishments, rather than her own. This possible explanation is expanded upon in Part 2 of this encyclopedia.

Link to recorded interview: tinyurl.com/Brindley-J

Transcript of Interview

Full name: Jane E. Brindley
Institutional Affiliation: University of British Columbia, British Columbia, Canada

Key:

Regular font = Interviewee comments
Italicized font = Interviewer comments

Interview Questions

1. *What was your educational and experiential background before you became involved in distance education [DE]?*

   I was always taking courses and learning after I started at Athabasca University [AU, Canada], but when I joined the institution, I had a Bachelor's degree in psychology and French, and my main work experience was in the area of career development

2. *In what year did you begin to look specifically into DE? Open and distance learning [ODL]?*

   It was when I started work with AU in 1977.

3. *What were the circumstances in your world that initiated this interest in DE and ODL?*

   I had worked in various aspects of career development doing research, developing self-help materials, and writing about career development, particularly for adults. I was also involved in developing workshops for adults who were making work and career transitions that might involve a return to school. It was in the era when people were thinking a lot about adult education and social justice. Malcolm Knowles and Paolo Freire are examples of the educators and writers who were inspiring our thinking. I saw a job advertised at AU for a career development specialist for counselling. I didn't know very much about AU, but I researched it, and it seemed to be aimed specifically at adults who might not otherwise have the opportunity to take advantage of post-secondary education, so it seemed like a very good fit for me. I applied for it and was successful. Very fortunately for me, I found myself in a context of a very new institution that was still trying to figure out how best to fulfill its mandate, and I had a rare opportunity, particularly for a relatively young person, to influence direction and practice. Open and distance learning [ODL] was very, very new in Canada as envisioned at AU. Of course, there was a long history of DE in Canada, particularly in fields like home economics and agriculture. These types of courses had been offered through correspondence for a long time through continuing education departments. But what AU was trying to do was open up accredited university courses and programmes to any Canadian adult 18 or over. This was not an easy proposition in a country where universities have longstanding and strong traditions about how teaching and learning can take place in order to be credible and accredited. There were competing ideas within AU about how we could make post-secondary education more accessible while still meeting academic standards. During the time I was with AU, the institution was reimagined a number of times with the goal of finding the best way to balance openness and accessibility with academic integrity. I was really fortunate to join the institution at that time because there was constantly rigorous and thoughtful debate about our vision, goals, model of teaching and learning, and everyday practice. When I joined AU, all the faculty and staff could pretty well fit in one large room. There were definitely fewer than 100 – maybe closer to 50 of us, not including the tutors. Being part of this small but passionate group strengthened my commitment to the values inherent in ODL.

4. *Which female researchers or female colleagues may have piqued your interest in DE and ODL?*

I have to say that at the time I joined AU, there were not that many women working in the field, but I was lucky to meet many of them who were really making a difference. At Athabasca, there was [1] Arlene Young, who was my colleague in student services, and she and I worked on a number of projects together in the early days. Arlene became a real pioneer in the area of helping students develop study skills needed for independent learning. Of course, at AU there was [2] Barbara Spronk, who I believe began as a tutor but fairly quickly moved into senior administration and became an international leader in the field. Another woman that I met fairly early on is [3] Margaret Haughey at the University of Alberta, who later (after I had left) came to work at Athabasca.

In the 1970s and 80s, when each country might have only one or two institutions that defined themselves through open and distance learning, practitioners looked beyond their borders to find colleagues working on similar challenges. There was a small international community of distance learning academics and practitioners, and we were always hungry to learn from one another. For example, AU had close ties to the Open University (OU UK) in Britain. I followed [4] Mary Thorpe's writing at the OU UK because she was working in the challenging and very new area of evaluation of quality. Also doing great work at the OU UK were [5] Helen Lentell, who did pioneering work in tutor training; [6] Judith Fage, whose work on supporting students was inspirational and who became director of the London Regional Office; and [7] Gilly Salmon, whose writing on teaching with technology was groundbreaking. Also in the UK was [8] Ros Morpeth, who ran the National Extension College in Cambridge and whose work had a huge international impact. In Germany, [9] Christina von Prummer and [10] Gisela Pravda were DE leaders who always spoke up on behalf of women. When I first met Gisela, she was working in Colombia, organizing training projects with very disadvantaged women. Meanwhile, in Canada, I was lucky to meet [11] Liz Burge, [12] Judy Roberts, [13] Jennifer O'Rourke, and [14] Erin Keough, all of whom made significant contributions to the field and from whose work I learned. These are just some of the women I remember from the early days of national and international meetings where we shared ideas and practices. As time went on, I met others – like Robin Mason (OU UK) working in the area of technology; Yoni Ryan from Australia, one of the few people who wrote about the need for student services; and Chere Gibson from the US, who really inspired me because she was writing about issues that I felt passionate about and which often got overlooked – that is, the need to provide distance learners with the support that would give them the best opportunity to succeed in their studies.

I cannot remember all of the names of the women from whom I have learned and with whom I had great conversations. What I know is that contact with them was essential in developing my own research, theories, and practice. For example, I remember a wonderful woman from Scotland who did training workshops at some of the conferences that I went to in Britain, helping people to communicate better by audio. She would have us do things like sit on chairs back to back in pairs with one person explaining to the other how to build something with Lego while the other person (with a pile of Lego) would actually try to follow the instructions.

So those are some of my early memories. There was a pretty small but strong international group of women involved in distance learning, and we were drawn to each other. We were all pioneers in a new field, trying our best to figure out the best methods for communicating, teaching and supporting students, and researching and evaluating our work.

5. *Who would you identify as the early female leaders/founders in the field of DE and ODL?*

I have already named women who influenced me, and they were all leaders and founders. In Canada, certainly Barbara Spronk, Liz Burge, Jennifer O'Rourke, Judy Roberts, and Margaret Haughey stand out. Beyond Canada, women DE leaders would include Ros Morpeth, Mary Thorpe, Judith Fage, Anne Gaskell, and Helen Lentell in the UK; Chere Gibson in the US; Anne Forster and Louise Moran in Australia; and in New Zealand, Shona Butterfield. In Europe, I would say Gisela Pravda and Christine von Prümmer really stand out. Those would be women that I would say are key pioneers. My list is sadly missing women outside of Canada, the US, Europe, New Zealand, and Australia. I know that there were highly influential women in Asia and Africa, such as Jenny Glennie, with whom I had little to no contact because of who was funded to come to meetings and conferences. In the 1970s and 1980s, I would have met most of my contacts through the Canadian Association for Distance Education [CADE] and the International Council for Open and Distance Education [ICDE]. At the Vancouver meeting of ICDE in 1982, women started talking about starting their own group. We did meet at subsequent ICDE conferences and elsewhere [the Cambridge conferences]. Karlene Faith's book about women in distance education grew from that. We took strength from one another, but it was actually quite a hard path. We struggled to get funding from ICDE to form a sustainable group, but we did make a mark and I think left an indelible impression as women as leaders in the field. Interestingly, I could probably name more men in the field as I look back because they had higher profiles in research, and more were in senior administration, giving them greater access to funding to travel and make presentations. There are many more women leaders in ODL now. When I was teaching online in a master's in distance education program that started in 2000, I met so many brilliant women – faculty and students. But in the early days, the women I have named bucked the odds to be pioneers as well as inspirational leaders.

6. *What are some of the goals that you strove to achieve in the field of DE and ODL?*

I worked in the area of student support, which was an area that I have to say was both undervalued and underfunded. There just weren't that many people working in DE who were trying to figure out how to provide services, such as assessment of readiness for academic study, student advising, student counselling, study skills assessment, special needs assistance, financial aid, library and research skills development – all the kinds of services in which campus-based universities and distance institutions are now investing very heavily to promote student success. At the time I was working in student support, these services were offered "on the side" at campus-based institutions, and they were the first to be cut in times of tight budgets. Most DE institutions didn't have these kinds of student support services (and many still do not offer comprehensive student support). AU was exceptional in that we were trying to figure out how to provide support services for students that would help them develop skills that give each student not a guaranteed, but the best opportunity for success. We had many students, particularly in the early days, who were returning to school after a long time. Some were early school leavers because, for a variety of reasons, they had not been successful. We recognized that, if we were going to have an open door, we needed to figure out how to help our students develop lifelong learning skills such as how to manage their time, plan an academically sound programme, find and use library resources, read effectively, study for exams, write papers, do basic math, plan their careers, and carry out a job search.

If I could wrap it up it a sentence, what we were trying to do at AU in the student services department was to provide a comprehensive set of support services that would give students the best opportunity for success in their studies from the time they made their first inquiry through graduation and beyond. One of the things we did was to set up an inquiry service like a triage.

If a prospective student made an inquiry but AU was not the right place to meet their needs, rather than turning them away, we made sure that our inquiry people had enough information and training so that they could refer them to the right educational institution or the right service. We were dedicated to adult education and believed everyone who approached us deserved assistance in meeting their goals.

When I joined AU, we had a very small department of student services. It grew over the years to include different kinds of specialists based on what we found out about learner needs. In the beginning, we looked at what services were available to students at campus-based institutions and tried to emulate that by offering the same services at a distance. However, as we developed, we recognized the unique demands that distance learning makes on students to be independent and self-directed, the diversity of learners in an open institution, the technologies available for communication, and the implications that these factors have on support needs. By the time I left AU, we offered a comprehensive set of services that students could access throughout their studies. We also had opened regional offices in Fort McMurray, Edmonton, and Calgary. My main goal in choosing to work in student services was to see more students achieve success in their studies.

7. *What are some of your accomplishments in the field of DE and ODL that you would like to share?*

Well, first I would say that I think we made a positive difference for many students at AU through providing good support. As I said, we worked hard to develop a pretty sophisticated and comprehensive model of student support at AU, with many different services and forms of engagement. Beyond that, though, I also felt strongly that I had to be out in the field and champion the need in other places in Canada and the world to have those kinds of services available to distance learners.

I feel very strongly that if, as an institution, you are going to be involved in open and distance learning [ODL], you should not just invite students to the table through being accessible. You have to offer students the kinds of support that will help them develop the skills to be successful. You have a responsibility to do that. I tried to spread that message and help institutions and practitioners develop support services for their students.

8. *What are some of the challenges that you faced in the field of DE and ODL over the years?*

I think the first challenge was just not having any models to follow. At the time, campus-based models of student support were less of a proactive approach to promoting student success and more a suite of services from which students could pick and choose. We had to figure out what kinds of support made the most positive difference and the best way to engage students to use the support we offered. As well, in DE institutions, so much resource was being invested in course development to get programmes up and running, and subsequent to that, there was a lot of focus placed on use of new technologies. Student support development and delivery got a lot less attention. So it was always an uphill climb to get recognition for just how challenging it was for students to study in this way and the kind of support that they required to be successful. Students were very isolated in the early days of DE. However, even now with the kinds of technology that we have that facilitates student-to-student interaction, learners still need support to develop skills (including the skill of learning collaboratively). That is one of the greatest challenges – to continue to remind institutions about the support needs of students studying at a distance. Students on campus have access to a vast array of services, but it still is not a given that distance students do. For example, library support is one of the most important student services – not just providing access to the library – but also offering the support services that really teach students the skills they need to find information, evaluate it, distill it, apply it and how to use a library effectively.

9. *What was the "state of DE" when you first entered the field as opposed to ODL in 2019?*

Well, I told you already that when I joined, it was correspondence education supported by telephone tutoring. That was the case in most places, although in some very large DE institutions in developing countries, all communication was through correspondence. Compared to what we have now, our systems were pretty rudimentary, and our knowledge about learners and how to promote learning was pretty slim.

I would say the main change for me, because subsequent to my being at AU, I taught for about ten years in an international online master's of DE programme, was the communications technology that provided the opportunity for students to engage in collaborative learning and to have much better and timelier communication between learners and the instructor. Course design and teaching methods are based on research and provide much better support for students.

10. *What interesting memories would you like to share about the beginning of ODL?*

My best memories in ODL are to do with colleagues, international exchange, and a sense of shared purpose in contributing to a field of education that in the beginning was all about social justice. I think that there was such a great camaraderie among colleagues that went beyond single institutions and beyond geographical borders. The number of institutions involved in this type of teaching worldwide was relatively small, so there was a great deal of international collaboration that was very productive. That was just so positive in terms of creating community and moving the field forward. Whether it was the small workshops held in Cambridge starting in about 1983 or the big ICDE conferences, staff and faculty exchanges between institutions, or research and writing collaborations, there were people that I continually met who were leaders in the field and helped me to become a better thinker and practitioner. I have very fond memories of a staff exchange, which allowed me to work in the Cambridge and London offices of the OU UK; a fellowship stint at the Open Polytechnic in Wellington, New Zealand, leading workshops and making educational visits to ODL institutions in many different countries; and, of course, the many great pub conversations with colleagues who became lifelong friends.

I feel very fortunate to have worked in a field that I was proud of that made a positive difference in peoples' lives and which brought me into contact with so many committed educators. I guess would be a good way to sum it up.

11. *What were your specific DE and ODL research interests, and have they changed/evolved over the years?*

My background is in psychology, and my initial interest in providing support services for students had to do with my own strong interest in motivation and what learners need beyond instruction in order to set goals and work toward them. I've always been interested in student success, how to define it, and how to promote it. For many years, that manifested in developing support services for ODL and evaluating their effectiveness and culminated in teaching others how to do this. More recently, when I was teaching in the master's of distance education for the University of Oldenburg [Germany], I began looking at how we use online tools such as learning journals, e-portfolios, and social media to promote the kinds of skills, such as self-reflection, self-directed inquiry, and collaborative learning, which help students to become better learners. We embedded specific types of social media in courses and tried to measure the impact on learning goals, including skill development. At UBC [University of British Columbia, Canada], I used a similar approach to design and write an online master's-level research methods course.

I was interested to see if students would be able to identify skills they learned in the course that they would continue to use in academic study and their clinical practice.

12. *Can you please describe the learning environment that you currently work in or have most recently worked in (e.g., geographic and institutional setting, student demographics)?*

    I am a counselling and clinical psychologist, and I teach graduate students at the master's and doctoral level who are in counselling psychology at UBC. Some are coming straight through from a baccalaureate degree, but many are adult students who have been working since graduating from their last degree and are re-entering university at the master's or doctoral level. They are often switching careers to go into a psychotherapy role or become a psychologist.

    I teach and provide clinical supervision in the two free psychological services clinics that UBC has: one on the main campus in Point Grey and one in New Westminster. These clinics are open to the public, and UBC graduate students provide the therapy services. I am very aware that my approach to teaching and supervision is significantly influenced by my years of thinking about what learners need to be successful, how to help them develop skills, how to engage them, and how to help them learn collaboratively.

    I have also written and taught a research methods course online for students in the same programme who live in Central BC [British Columbia, Canada], and this year I will be a visiting expert in the student support course in the Oldenburg MTEL programme, so I haven't completely gone away from ODL, but I would say that my main work now is in a clinical setting.

13. *Is there anything else you [would] like to address?*

    Yes, I'd like to make the observation that in my most recent experience of writing and teaching an online course for UBC, I encountered these very bright, motivated students who were struggling unnecessarily because they lacked appropriate support. For example, most of the students were already part way through a master's programme, but either didn't have library access or didn't have basic library research skills. The students in the course were geographically spread, but we came together as a group a couple of times, and I brought a librarian in to talk to them and do a presentation. The relief and joy they displayed was palpable, and they made great leaps forward in their individual research projects afterwards. A number of the students asked me, "Why didn't someone do this in our first course?" I thought, "Yeah, why didn't someone?"

    To me, it was a glaring example of the tendency to overlook the comprehensive needs of online students, just as was the case with early distance learners. There is still too much focus on, "Let's get the course up." But the course is not everything that students need. They need a holistic educational experience, and that includes all of the supports that will help them develop the skills to be successful learners in formal studies and in life.

14. *Can you suggest names of other female pioneers in DE, e-learning, or ODL that you think we should include in the book?*

    I'm sure there are, but I can't think of any beyond those I have already named. I do have a name that I would pass on to you because she is a new leader and role model for other women in ODL. I first met Lisa Blaschke in 2000 when she was a student in the course that I taught in the MDE for Oldenburg. Subsequently, she taught in the programme and then became the director. I've done some collaborative research and course writing with her and learned from her innovative thinking and mastery of technology as a teaching tool. Lisa has illuminated the concept of heutagogy [learner-determined learning], and is applying it to teaching and learning in a very exciting way, showing how social media and other tools can be used in the online classroom to help learners develop critical skills. Lisa recently completed the final requirements for her PhD, but she has been doing research and generously sharing her work since she entered the master's programme. She is the new female pioneer in the current wave of ODL, collaborating internationally, confidently publishing and presenting, and encouraging other women to do the same. I am inspired by her energy and her achievements.

One last thing that I would say when talking about the international ODL community is that I had a lot of encouragement from many people over the years, including some notable men. Although this book is about women pioneers, I would be remiss if I didn't mention at least a couple of men who made a point of mentoring and promoting women. One is Roger Mills, who for years was director of the Cambridge Regional Office of the OU UK. He's now sadly gone, and I miss him very much, but it is worth noting that he really encouraged and mentored many women, including me, and believed in the difference that women could make in ODL. Another is Tony Bates, who showed an interest in my early attempts to evaluate the impact of learner support and encouraged me in my practice by including me in some interesting and challenging projects. Tony has had an amazing impact on so many researchers and practitioners. He is generous with his knowledge and encouragement. Finally, there is Otto Peters, who inspired so much good thinking and who generously was a visiting expert in dozens of online classes in the Oldenburg MDE programme. Many years ago, Otto came to my first international research presentation (making me somewhat nervous), stayed afterwards, and showed genuine interest by asking challenging and thoughtful questions. He always encouraged me to think deeply about my work and, by being a role model, challenged those of us in the MDE to give our students the best experience.

Thank you for the opportunity to reflect on my experience in ODL. As I look back, I find that despite some of the challenges faced, I learned an astonishing amount, had the opportunity to make a small positive difference, and accumulated a rich and plentiful bank of happy memories.

Publications

Books

Brindley, J. E. (2004). *Researching tutoring and learner support handbook*. Practitioner Research and Evaluation Skills Training in Open and Distance Learning Series. Commonwealth of Learning.

Brindley, J. E., Walti, C., & Zawacki-Richter, O. (Eds.). (2004). *Learner support in open, distance and online learning environments*. Bibliotheks- und Informtionssystem der Universität Oldenburg.

Book Chapters

Blaschke, L., & Brindley, J. E. (2015). Using social media in the online classroom. In M. Ally & B. Khan (Eds.), *The international handbook of e-learning* (Vol. 1). Routledge.

Brindley, J. E. (2014). Learner support in online distance education. In O. Zawacki-Richter & T. Anderson (Eds.), *Online distance education – towards a research agenda*. Athabasca University Press.

Brindley, J. E., Zawacki-Richter, O., & Roberts, J. (2003). Support services for online faculty: The provider and user perspectives. In U. Bernath & E. Rubin (Eds.), *Reflections on teaching and learning in an online program* (pp. 137–165). Biblioteks-und Informtionssystem der Universität Oldenburg.

Paul, R. H., & Brindley, J. E. (2000). Status report on distance education in Canada for CREAD. In P. A. Nelson (Ed.), *Ten years of international collaboration in distance education*. Penn State University.

Paul, R. H., & Brindley, J. E. (2008). New technology, new learners, and new challenges: Leading our universities in times of change. In T. Evans, M. Haughey, & D. Murphy (Eds.), *The world handbook of distance education*. Marrickville, Elsevier Australia.

Roberts, J., Brindley, J. E., Mugridge, I., & Howard, J. (2002). *Faculty and staff development in higher education: The key to using ICT appropriately?* [Report]. Commissioned report for The Observatory, Association of Commonwealth Universities.

Journal Articles

Blaschke, L., & Brindley, J. E. (2011). Establishing a foundational framework for development of reflective thinking: A case study of learning journal use. *European Journal of Open, Distance and E-Learning*, Special Issue: Best of EDEN 2010.

Brindley, J. E., Blaschke, L., & Walti, C. (2009). Creating effective collaborative learning groups in an online environment. *International Review of Research in Open and Distance Learning, 10*(2). www.irrodl.org/index.php/irrodl/article/view/675

Conference Presentations

Brindley, J. E. (2000). *Staying in touch with the learner experience: Evaluating programme effectiveness* [Paper presentation]. 16th Annual Conference of the Canadian Association for Distance Education, Quebec City, Canada.

Brindley, J. E. (2002, February). *Student support in an online environment* [Paper presentation]. Open Learning and Information Network (of Newfoundland and Labrador), St. John's, Canada.

Brindley, J. E. (2003, March). *Learner support: The key to quality learning environments* [Invited presentation]. Manitoba Association for Distributed Learning and Training Conference, Winnipeg, Canada.

Brindley, J. E. (2006, May). *Dancing to the rhythm of change: Dancing at a distance* [Keynote presentation]. Maryland Community College Association for Community Education and Training. Ocean City, MD.

Brindley, J. E. (2006, October). *Using qualitative methods in e-research* [Workshop presentation]. 4th EDEN Research Workshop, Barcelona-Castelldefels, Spain.

Brindley, J. E., & Blaschke, L. (2010, October). *Establishing a foundational framework for development of reflective thinking: Learning journals in the MDE* [Paper presentation]. 6th EDEN Research Workshop, Budapest, Hungary. Winner of the best research paper award.

Brindley, J. E., Blaschke, L., & Walti, C. (2008, October). *Creating effective collaborative learning groups in an online environment* [Paper presentation]. 5th EDEN Research Workshop, Paris, France. **Finalist for best research paper award.

Brindley, J. E., Crawley, A., & Peteres, B. (2017, October). *Student Services for Online Learning: Re-imagined and Re-invigorated* [Workshop presentation]. World Conference on Online Learning, Toronto, Canada.

Brindley, J. E., & Paul, R. H. (2004, March). *The role of learner support in institutional transformation – A case in the making*. 3rd EDEN Research Workshop, Oldenburg, Germany.

5
BURGE, ELIZABETH JUNE (LIZ)

Photo of Elizabeth (Liz) Burge contributed by Elizabeth (Liz) Burge

Roughly only 25% of [International Council for Distance Education conference] attendees were women, but the men didn't know that we were feisty and not going to accept any nonsense.

Dr. Elizabeth (Liz) Burge was born in Australia and began her post-secondary education there. She moved to Canada in 1980 where she completed her post-graduate education. She holds Australian and Canadian citizenships.

DOI: 10.4324/9781003275329-6

She began her studies by receiving professional accreditation from the Library Association of Australia in 1968. She then completed an undergraduate degree in English literature and history from the University of Adelaide in Australia. In 1978, she completed a graduate diploma in educational technology at the University of South Australia. Burge moved to Canada in 1980 when she received a one-year scholarship and was placed in the adult education department of the Ontario Institute for Studies in Education (OISE) at the University of Toronto. It was at the University of Toronto that she completed her MEd in 1981 and her EdD in 1993, both specializing in adult education.

Dr. Burge held various administrative positions with OISE (based at the University of Toronto) until 1993, when she accepted a teaching position with the University of New Brunswick (UNB) in Eastern Canada. Throughout her years at UNB, she also took sabbaticals to work at the University of Helsinki, Finland, and later with Mid Sweden University (Mittuniversitetet) in Sundsvall, Sweden.

As exemplified by the list of her publications at the end of this chapter, Liz Burge is a prolific researcher with works that span four decades. Her interests include gender issues, teaching effectiveness, and new technologies and their value and use, as well as andragogy and how this all fits into online learning.

Burge was very involved with the International Council for Distance Education (ICDE) and stood as a Vice President from 1985 to 1988 and again from 1988 to 1991. She was a Founding Chair of Women's International Network in Distance Education (WIN) from 1982 to 1988. She co-organized the WIN meetings at Penn State University in 1997.

In her interview, she refers several times to her concern with the implementation of new technologies without careful consideration of their value. New technology for the sake of new technology is a topic she speaks of with thoughtfulness and clarity. She advises future students and researchers to look carefully at what a new technology offers and what it replaces, carefully ensuring the replacement "factor" is worth the implementation.

Interview

Transcript Analysis Summary

Analysis of all interviews included in this volume led to the identification of 3,545 units of data. The mean of these collective units was 118 per pioneer, the median was 118.5, and the mode was 132. Individual interview units ranged from 59 to 217 units, yielding a spread of 158 units between all interviews. Liz Burge's interview generated 84 units, placing her interview in the bottom fifth of all interviews in terms of number of units produced.

A comparision of Liz Burge's interview to the interviews of all pioneers indicated that her interview profile held little in common with the average interview profile (Figure 5.1). Her interview yielded relatively similar numbers of units in 4 of the 14 topic areas: changes over time, goals, career history, and final thoughts. Burge's interview produced a significantly greater number of units than the average interview in the topic areas of accomplishments and interesting memories. Part of the reason for this may be that Burge was a prolific writer and made numerous international contributions to our field during her career. Having been retired for some years by the time of the interview, it was possible that Burge had spent time reflecting on the interesting memories that her expansive career offered over the years.

Burge's interview produced a fewer-than-average number of units in a number of topic areas. These areas included benefits of DE, learning environment, research interests, early founders, and others for the book. The interview did not include a question about the benefits of DE, so this

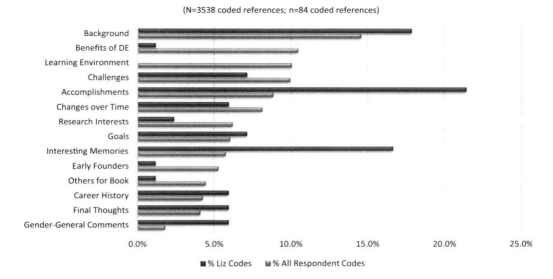

Figure 5.1 All Respondents' Versus Elizabeth (Liz) Burge's Parent Codes

would explain her low number of units for this topic area. Since Burge was retired at the time of the interview, it would be anticipated that her interview would not yield many units in the learning environment or research interest areas, either. Burge explained the lack of units for early founders by saying, "I just can't answer that question; we all have our own opinions, I think." Finally, Burge did not provide any other names for the book at the time of the interview because she needed more time to think about that question.

Link to recorded interview Part A: tinyurl.com/Burge-Liz-A

Link to recorded interview Part B: tinyurl.com/Burge-Liz-B

Transcript of Interview

Full name: Elizabeth June Burge
Institutional Affiliation: University of Toronto; University of New Brunswick
Key:

Regular font = Interviewee comments
Italicized font = Interviewer comments

Interview Questions

1. *What was your educational and experiential background before you became involved in distance education [DE]?*

I have a bachelor of arts degree [University of Adelaide, Australia] and a national librarianship certification that enabled me to be an Associate of the Library Association of Australia. For approximately 16 years, I worked in the state library, various government libraries, and two municipal libraries. Then I got a scholarship from a government department that trains people to work in technical colleges as teachers and as people who can teach others. This one-year scholarship spanned from 1980 to 1981, and I was placed in the adult education department of the Ontario Institute for Studies in Education [OISE] at the University of Toronto where there were world-renowned experts in the field. I thought this was great. After getting my master's degree, people started saying, "Come on. Do a doctorate now. You've got to get some steady work." I ended up after about six years with a doctorate in adult education. My doctorate was the first in Canada and elsewhere that explored adult students' experiences from two master's degree classes using "computer conferencing," which was very innovative at the time!

2. *In what year did you begin to look specifically into DE?*

The very last department that I worked with, in the TAFE world, was where I had to run the DE library. I was dealing with people who were posting out lots of papers to various people and having telephone discussions and whatever. I was managing the library there, and I thought, "There has to be a better way of doing all of this." So I applied for this grant for one year at University of Toronto to look at ways in which we could give the students much better access to an easy way to get information and therefore get better teaching. So, in 1978, I was just coming into the trades educators and their information needs. Then two years later, I am in Toronto to begin a new life in Canada.

3. *What were the circumstances in your world that initiated this interest in DE?*

Well, the Open College in Adelaide where they had the distance education students and me thinking that I have got to change things and make things better, especially for students.

4. *Which female researchers or female colleagues may have piqued your interest in DE and online distance learning [ODL]?*

When I was established as a graduate student at the University of Toronto, I found out about an international conference of the International Council for Distance Education [ICDE] on DE developments at the University of British Columbia [UBC] in Western Canada. Roughly only 25% of attendees were women, but the men didn't know that we were feisty and not going to accept any nonsense. I was sitting there fuming, listening to these men talking about their work and the items and kits that they were sending out to students, both male and female. We had to sit there and listen to *all* the references to "male" for teachers and students. I was sitting in the middle of the hall; so was Gisela Prazda and other women leaders, too. We were all just bubbling and burning! Gisela stood up and asked why women had disappeared. She just blew them away – the men, I mean. And the women were not laughing. We were sitting near her, and we were loudly clapping. I jumped up and said something. A few other women got up and protested. That was a shocker for the men, clearly. For the rest of the three-day conference, they were quieter. But any time that Gisela heard the use of male-oriented language, she would pounce on people, which was very good! The women came away thinking that they must band together and be able to talk easily to each other, so at the next big international conference, they could make a big "splash." That conference was in 1985 in Melbourne [Australia]. That's when the women really got together because we had gathered three years of new talking with each other. I had made a little newsletter, but that wasn't adequate. And we were still seeing learning materials without the words *women* or *girls* in them. So the Melbourne conference helped the tide to turn. Some of the men admitted, "We must do what these colleagues are telling us to do." So that was a big deal for all of us women.

After everyone had left Melbourne, a few of us women started to say, "We have to start recording what's going on here. These women teachers, researchers, administrators, you name it, what is their experience like in their DE activities?" We were all saying, "What is going on out there? How can we help women educators using DE modes? And how can we help male teachers, etc., to consider female perspectives?" With the help of Routledge UK publishers, a new book was distributed around the world. *Toward New Horizons: International Perspectives on Women in Distance Education*, was published in 1988 and edited superbly by Dr. Karlene Faith. It included 20 chapters, a superb introduction, names of pioneers, and case studies. The Carl chapter linked this book to recorded DE practices before 1988. That was a real turning point in terms of equality for women and girls. We began to talk much more boldly, as never before done. We felt legitimized by such needed chapters. My little forward said, "Light a candle, don't curse the dark," because sometimes we got tired of hearing people complaining, rather than changing. Gisela and I were very good at saying to people, "Avoid negative ideas all the time. We have to do something." So that's how things began in earnest: nothing like a set of great chapters!

I concluded the forward by saying:

> Enjoy this book. Be impressed. It is unique as a first event and in its feminist style. It illuminates experience. It celebrates achievement and it reveals inequities. It also seeks companions against the dark.
>
> (p. xii)

Even now when I read that, I am . . . Wow! That's how we had to do it. And so in Melbourne, we just got going. So that was good. The book, *Toward New Horizons*, I think opened a lot of eyes, even some women's eyes. Dr. Karlene Faith died recently. She was fantastic doing it; that was a big job. It certainly got a lot of good comments and all that sort of thing. She was hugely respected and a great guide for me.

In 1988, the conference at Oslo was a small event with Nordic women, which bolstered Karlene's book. Then in 1990 we had the Women's [International] Network [WIN]. There was a meeting in Venezuela where the big ICDE conference was going on. Gisela and I were there; actually, quite a number of women there. Gisela and I ran a workshop for some of the women teachers. My goodness, we thought we had problems! After that, I think I couldn't go to some of these WIN things, but I did stay in touch. After the Karlene book we were getting some good responses from some intelligent and caring men saying, "Yes, we've got to change our documents and things so that it's not all male."

In 1993, the Women's Studies Centre of Umeå University in Sweden hosted a small working conference on feminist pedagogy and women-friendly perspectives.

5. *Who would you identify as the early female leaders/founders in the field of DE and ODL?*

   I just can't answer that question; we all have our own opinions, I think. The Carl chapter in the Dr. Karlene Faith book is a good reference.

6. *What are some of the goals that you strove to achieve in the field of DE and ODL?*

   I am still hoping that people think and apply what Neil Postman said about not getting carried away with the latest technology. [Read the four McLuhan points, cited later in this interview.] I sometimes think that people need to think of simpler ways of helping adults learn. I don't think that I can think of anything else at this stage, except to recall that my teaching will always be lively discussions with students to help them critique.

   Goals. . . . I didn't think in that way. I just saw opportunities, like where someone was talking at a conference about ethics. Then I'd go home and think about it: "There is no book on this in distance education, so I'd better get going, etc." I think it's more like I do things when I hear issues and opportunities popping up, or I see something that I think is not helpful for the students or for the teacher or for the researcher or whatever. All said, having my own learning critiqued would suit me well.

7. *What are some of your accomplishments in the field of DE and ODL learning that you would like to share?*

   I designed and enjoyed (as did others) a kind of poem about a cat and learning technology. I wrote this for a book that was being made. I started a paragraph by saying:

Being an incorrigibly metaphorical thinker, I planned and used a cat analogy to figure out the features of an elegantly applied learning technology. Here they are:

- Flexible software *(ears move to catch passing sounds: fur as both heating and cooling device)*
- Engaging interface *(cute face and silky fur)*
- Proportional & linked parts *(long legs and body curl into a ball)*
- Minimum effort for maximum return *(no unnecessary paw movements)*
- Capacity for self-correction *(lands on feet after a jump or fall)*
- Some toleration for errors *(human care-giver is "forgiven" after return from holidays)*
- Fast feedback on action taken *(hissing or purring in response to others' actions)*
- Evidence for best operational capacity *(claws for climbing but not designed for flying)*
- Ease of interaction *(a little squeak leads to food appearing)*
- Hidden operational software *(millions of invisible smell detectors)*
- Variety of experience possible *(humans are enchanted, then act as domestic slave)*
- Adaptations to various contexts *(lives in summer house as happily as in city house)*

[Excerpt from Burge, E. J. (1999). Using learning technologies: Ideas for keeping one's balance. *Educational Technology, 39*(6), 45–49]

Anyway, it was a big hit to the point where somebody took it to another place with my name on it, and this male professor took my name off and posed it as his own in a big meeting. Well, I was mad when I heard that, but still. . . .

While I was beginning to end my intensive work in DE as such, I was at the University of Toronto and got my doctoral degree, and there came a new position at the University of New Brunswick in Eastern Canada. So I went from Toronto to the east. They asked me to apply to be a professor in the adult education department. So I left Toronto in mid-1983, and I retired in 2012. The work in New Brunswick was shifting. I still had to teach in adult education and keep up with adult education, particularly because I had made some friends in Toronto, and if I need to ask something, I could always call up. But now I was moving away from things like a library book or the well-known refereed journal called *Library Trends*. I planned a whole issue called *Adult Learners: Learning and Public Libraries*. I had some really good people writing for it, so my brain was suitably stretched!

Before I left for Atlantic Canada, the Canadian folks had decided that it was about time that we had the first national workshop of the Canadian Association of Distance Education [CADE]. It was planned for April 25th and 26th, 1984, and it was really a grand one because it involved connecting people with new audio technology across Canada. After it all got launched, participants enjoyed easy access to distant colleagues and students. Almost immediately, I had to help teachers and students in education at OISE. We then started getting the professors to learn about it; for example, how could they learn with some new technologies? The first major one was audio conferencing. Judy Roberts was one of the innovators, and we sure treasured her! We all felt pleased using a technology that linked everyone and rejected lecturing. We thought, "Wow, we are stepping at the beginning of something really good here. We don't know where it's going. We just got to keep our eyes on what the learners need, what they can cope with, what the teachers need, and how they are going to react." OISE had students all over the very wide province of Ontario and elsewhere, so we had to get the professor's help in using audio conferencing. We had a very good professor who had a great sense of humour. We all adored him, but we had to keep reining him in; otherwise, he would go crazy, you see. He came to me one day and said, "Liz, I've got students 2,000 kilometers up north, and I've got many more in the West. That's a long way from where we are, and so I thought to make things happy, could you help me get some sound into my opening and my closing of the three-hour session that we have once a week?"

So, I said, "Well, what's the sound that you want put in, Richard?"

And he said, "I want the sound to come in like a big steam engine that's been going for 2,000 kilometers and is finally arriving at where the students are. That would be so cool" (or words to that effect).

So I said, "What are you going to do when you come back to Toronto at night?"

He said, "Well, I'll do the opposite with the train noise." Well, you can understand the chuckling and laughter and amazement from the students, but it was a very effective technique that Professor Richard used. He began to like it all. We couldn't get any other professor to do something like that. It is lovely sometimes being a pioneer.

I will tell you several other things, too, that were very important to me once I got to New Brunswick and its small, but well-known university. The first was a comment. We had Neil Postman on video from the USA during a teaching gig. He was always saying very intelligent things about the link-up between technologies and people's brains and people's needs. I used his following famous quote as the very first quote from my doctoral dissertation, and here it is:

"Every culture must negotiate with technology, whether it does so intelligently or not. A bargain is struck in which technology giveth and technology taketh away. The wise know this well and are rarely impressed by dramatic technological changes, and are never overjoyed" [Postman, 1992, p. 5].

Wow! So true, yet often ignored or explained.

Two other things quickly. . . . McLuhan and McLuhan, Marshall McLuhan and his son, launched this book in 1988, *The New Science*, [published by] the University of Toronto Press. They are challenging the new technologies as well with four famous questions:

1. What does the technology enhance or intensify?
2. What does it retrieve that it was previously made obsolete?
3. What does the possible change because of the technology render obsolete or displace?
4. What does it produce or become when pushed to an extreme?

(That's the end of the quote. It was on page seven of the McLuhan and McLuhan book. Not bad, eh? Try it in your own life!)

Last thing is a quote from a German writer, Rainer Rilke [1875–1926]. I don't know where this comes from, but it is so good that I've had it on my fridge for many years. "The point of raising powerful questions is not necessarily to find an answer, but to learn to dwell in the questions until you live yourself into the answers." So there is Lizzy with her Rilke, McLuhan and McLuhan, and Postman. (Yes, where are the women?)

I went east in Canada to New Brunswick in mid-1993. I think it was late 1993 in the University of New Brunswick when Neil Postman talked with a number of students in the video session. After all of the students had dealt with all of their work and their questions, I put my hand up and talked to Postman in the video. I dealt my question; I cannot recall it now, but it was about technology issues and cognition. He looked at me. It was all dead silence. And then he said, "Would you marry me?"

So I made some cheeky answer about, "Well, it depends. It just depends." He laughed his head off, and so did I. Students were still sitting quietly in the room, eyes popping out of their heads as Neil and I talked on seriously, using critical minds.

The reason I am telling this to anyone who might be interested is that I have to keep stepping back and thinking, "Why have this now? Do we need this now? Is it okay to have something that is older and cheaper, and is still as good, etc.? Do we design something new?" These ideas and those quotations helped me think of all of my publications – for example, the *Journal of Distance Education's* "Beyond andragogy: Explorations for distance learning design." These were early things before I went to eastern Canada: "Audio conferencing in graduate studies" and those sorts of things. I think that other people and I were trying to sort out "Where should our brains and students be working?"

Then I did some writing: *Journal for Information Science* – "Lessons about learning and technology." I was doing these bits and pieces everywhere I went. I was asking people, "How do you embrace technology without thinking that "technology taketh away?" [Postman, 1992].

Chere Campbell Gibson created a useful book, *Distance Learners in Higher Education: Institutional Responses for Quality Outcomes* [1988]. So now educators were getting a little bit tough. They are not just saying, "Oh, isn't that lovely? We must try that." It was, "These things are coming to stay. We have to start facilitating their use without letting them go wild." So we've got Chere's book, and, of course, Judy Roberts made the classic *Classrooms with a Difference: Facilitating Learning on the Information Highway* [2nd ed., 1998]. Well, isn't this fantastic! We had to do a second edition because it was going everywhere. But we wanted adult learning principles and ideas, plus using technologies to get people thinking and not just be completely taken over by the latest technology. Otherwise, critical thinkers like me go crazy.

Here's another one in 2001: *Using Technologies: A Synthesis of Challenges and Guidelines*. I must have done that because someone must have asked me, "Come on, we've got clarify some key ideas. But don't keep writing too much because people get sick of it." Here's another one: *Libraries and Lifelong Learning*, a publication for librarians, of course. They asked me to do an article with Judy Snow, who was a very top librarian at OISE in Toronto. She and I did a lot of effective work together. She was pioneering when I was when we were both at OISE. Anyway, the title of the book chapter we wrote [in 2000] was called "Candles, corks, and contracts: Essential relationships between learners and librarians." We had great fun and hoped that it would be read. Judy was fantastic with that.

Then in the same year [2000], *New Directions for Adult and Continuing Education: The Strategic Use of Learning Technologies* was published. I find myself being asked to edit a journal volume on technology, so I looked for the best possible authors.

Later, Margaret Haughey and I edited a new book, *Using Learning Technologies: International Perspectives in Practice*. Luckily, we were able to do this fairly quickly. It was published in 2001.

Regarding ethics, two publications arose. One journal published by Routledge, *Open Learning: The Journal of Open and Distance Learning*, produced a special issue. This developed to be a special issue, *Ethical Issues in Open and Distance Learning* [22(2), June, 2007], guest editor, Liz. Then in 2009 I was the editor for a Jossey-Bass periodical, *Negotiating Ethical Practice in Adult Education*.

There's a Routledge journal called *Distance Education* [29(1), May 2008]. I think it is the first item in this prestigious journal, *Future: Pioneer Lessons and Concerns for Today*, by *moi*, Liz, Faculty of Education, University of New Brunswick. I secured a grant from the Social Sciences and Humanities Research Council [SSHRC; Canada], and it enabled me to meet the international interviewees at their place. I think I had 41 (or was it 44?) internationals finally in the group.

They were either retired or were about to shortly. I was thinking, "This is terrible. We're not capturing the brilliant learnings, attitudes, ethics, etc. of these senior distance education folks."

The last book, *Flexible Pedagogy, Flexible Practice: Notes from the Trenches of Distance Education*, was a joy to do. It really was. Chere, her husband, and I had to be very engaging for our readers and our writers. It's getting people to talk honestly, critically, hopefully, happily, and get themselves in a book for other people. They all did a fantastic job. This is a book that you can buy as a paperback or you can download it free on your computer. Worth reading! Truly.

So I think that's about all I've done here in terms of the distance education. And then I had to scurry because my deadline for leaving the university was coming up, but I wanted to do one last thing. I wanted to get a group of older women. They had to be . . . I think it was over 65, from each of the four provinces. I would talk with them with a questionnaire about their lives and particularly about their social activism. What does it mean to be a person like that? What's good, what's bad, etc.? I wanted it not to be in a book priced at $40 or $60 [Canadian dollars]; otherwise, the pricing would reduce sales. So the library of the University of New Brunswick had a special unit, which would make my pieces of paper and layout into a website on the Internet, where they can read through the report, and if they want to print off somebody's profile and comments, they can do that [https://womenactivists.lib.unb.ca]. If you just looked up "women activists' library UNB," you would find it. When I had finished that, I had finished my paid work in New Brunswick, Canada. My unpaid work was a six-and-a-half-year stint as president of the Heritage Association in this small city.

Somehow Finland drops in here. I had done quite a bit of work with Finns and helping them to rethink ideas about learning and teaching and researching, linking to DE in all of its ways.

The only other thing that rises in my brain is that I came home (when I was living in New Brunswick), and I had a fax machine. I came in one day as usual to the University of New Brunswick to find a sheet in the machine. I said, "Who's faxing me? This is weird." So I went over and started reading. It was from my chief colleague in the Nordic countries saying that, "The president of Finland will be in investing you with the White Rose of Finland Knight First Class sometime next year. We hope that you will be available."

I'm standing there in the kitchen, thinking, "I've got to read this again. I must have read it wrong." So I put my things down, papers and whatever, and I read it again. I thought, "What is going on here?" So, I called a friend in Finland a bit later.

She said, "No, Liz, you know the Finns are never silly about things. It is right."

Anyway, I thought that I hadn't earned anything. I didn't ask for money. So it ended up that I now have this beautiful piece wrapped up carefully because I have been instructed that when I die, the insignia must be sent back to the Office of the President of Finland.

It is funny. It's those kinds of things that just come from left side that make you think, "Oh, I should be working better. I must work better here. I must make myself good enough for what the president has just given me." I can't think of anything else, really. I've just enjoyed talking and learning from great colleagues, being supported by them, thinking and planning with them. I couldn't get a better life.

8. *What are some of the challenges that you faced in the field of DE and ODL over the years?*

Men who don't think that women are as clever as they are, if not sometimes more. I can't think of anything much. I quickly learned that if I needed something, it always paid off to talk to the boss, who has to say yes or no, and tell them how they will be positioned in the activity. I'm always careful about that so they know that they've had a good slice of the pie, even though I did all of the work. I always knew that, if I didn't want a whole lot of hassles and problems, I had to make sure that everybody who needs to be involved can get something out of it in the end. And I make it very important if I'm standing out launching something or I'm telling people something new that's going on, I'm always very careful to make sure that the people sitting in the front row and the people in the very back are saying, "Yes, we did this!"

9. *What was the "state of DE" when you first entered the field as opposed to ODL in 2019?*

I'm assuming that "computer conferencing," as we called it when we first started, is very strongly established. I would be sad if that is the only technology that could be used. I always like to see a combination of different ways of how to get information, how to judge it, how to discuss it with colleagues, how to use it with a professor, etc. All of that activity gets fairly complicated.

10. *What interesting memories would you like to share about the beginning of ODL?*

It was interesting because I had done my doctoral thesis on what I think was the first serious look by a professor in OISE at the University of Toronto to run a master's level course using only online (I think it was only; I don't think he brought them together after the first day). . . . I was also getting his ideas as well as my own ideas, so it worked really well. Of course, when the article I had to write about on how the students reacted to online or computer teaching, I found it easy to pull together the results of how the students reacted and what giveth and what taketh away, because previously people were saying, "Oh, this new technology, it's absolutely wonderful! It's perfect! No problem! Let's get on with it." I was at the real cutting edge here.

Then about four days before I was due to defend my doctoral thesis on these two courses that had been done only by computer conferencing, my supervisor came in and said, "Liz, you're not going to believe this, but an American comrade of yours is about to defend his thesis, which is almost exactly the same as yours."

I said, "What do we do? I can't get this person's whole thesis and weave it into mine because where am I going into my own?" Anyway, it all worked out.

The interesting thing was that Postman's adage of "technology giveth, but it also taketh away; the wise know this " [1992, p. 5] fit well into our dissertations.

11. *What were your specific DE and ODL research interests, and have they changed/evolved over the years?*

I haven't been on this since I left New Brunswick in 2012. I don't really think about it. Now I'm on the Council of the National Trust of South Australia, so I'm doing very easy adult education work there. And I'm doing various bits of volunteering as well. I've left academe behind. As I get old and more tired, I'm no good to anybody. For example, I'm not keeping up with the literature. So it's better that I focus on where I can help people repair a sailing ship or help volunteers change the setups of "21st century heritage centres," not old museums filled with unchanging old displays and unmoving "technologies." And that keeps me happy.

I: You started off researching how people were using technologies for learning, correct?

The work linked up with my paid work at a university. That was always on how do the users of any technology for learning and teaching think about how they use them, why do they use them the way that they do, and what are the good things, and what are the bad things, etc.? When I walked out of the university, I remember even asking the top person managing the email system if he would please take me off because I was now retired. He looked at me with his eyes popping out. He said, "No other professors have ever asked this."

I said, "Well, I am not going out of here to keep on doing what I am doing. It's time for a change and new learning. Does that make sense?" The email manager was shocked and then carefully popped the switch, and I slid away. Several years later I am back in "harness" with different tasks and challenges.

12. *Is there anything else you [would] like to address?*

I think a major role in helping people of all ages learn is helping them to learn critically and not just saying, "Oh, that looks good. I think I'll get that."

Two final points: First, your question makes me go back to this quote, and I think it works with all people at all levels: "All cultures must negotiate with technology. A bargain is struck," the quote I read earlier from Neil Postman: "Technology giveth and technology taketh away." I always get hung on this because our lives are getting more and more technological, and if we can't understand that there are various issues involved in looking at machinery, particularly new technology, and say, "How is that fitting with me now?" And giving it three or four years: "Is it changing anything I do?" Then there's McLuhan and McLuhan's [1988] prescient quote, "What does the new technology render obsolete or displace? Where does it help?" [p. 7]. I think those things that were talked about in 1998 and 1992 might be more useful than they were 20 years ago because we have so much more changing technology around us. I have to learn to manage it and manage myself.

Second, I have always experienced from colleagues the skills, courtesies, challenges, and determination to work by thoughtful goals. Thank you so much.

13. *Can you suggest names of other female pioneers in DE, e-learning, or open and distance learning [ODL] that you think we should include in the book?*

Let me think. They have to be people who have been in DE primarily. I will think about that.

Publications

Books

Burge, E. J. (2001). The strategic use of learning technologies. In *New directions in adult and continuing education.* Jossey-Bass/Wiley.

Burge, E. J., & Roberts, J. M. (1998). *Classrooms with a difference: Facilitating learning on the information highway* (2nd ed.). Cheneliere/McGraw-Hill.

Book Chapters

Burge, E. J. (1988). Light a candle, don't curse the dark. In K. Faith (Ed.), *Toward new horizons: International perspectives on women in distance education* (pp. vii–xiv). Routledge.

Burge, E. J. (1991). Making sense of practice: Some inside-out theorising. In M. S. Parer (Ed.), *Development design and distance education* (2nd ed., pp. 233–246). Gippsland Institute of Advanced Education.

Burge, E. J. (1992). *Computer mediated communication and education: A selected bibliography.* Ontario Institute for Studies in Education, Distance Learning Office.

Burge, E. J. (1993). Adult distance learning: Challenges for practice. In T. Barer-Stein & J. A. Draper (Eds.), *The craft of teaching adults* (Enlarged ed., pp. 215–230). Culture Concepts, Inc.

Burge, E. J. (1994). The Tao of writing a thesis. In A. L. Cole & D. E. Hunt (Eds.), *The doctoral thesis journey* (pp 25–33). OISE Press.

Burge, E. J. (1995). Electronic highway or weaving loom? Thinking about conferencing technologies for learning. In F. Lockwood (Ed.), *Open and distance learning today* (pp. 151–163). Routledge.

Burge, E. J. (1998). Gender in distance education. In C. C. Gibson (Ed.), *Distance learners in higher education Institutional responses for quality outcomes* (pp. 25–45). Atwood Publishing.

Burge, E. J. (2001a). Distance and online education. In T. Eater-Stein & M. Kornpf (Eds.), *The craft of teaching adults* (3rd ed., pp. 137–150). Irwin Publishing/Culture Concepts.

Burge, E. J. (2001b). Synthesis: Learning and learners are the issues. In E. J. Burge (Ed.), *The strategic use of learning technologies*. (New Directions in Adult and Continuing Education, # 88). Jossey-Bass.

Burge, E. J., & Frewin, C. C. (1985). Self-directed learning in distance learning. In *International encyclopedia of education: Research and studies* (pp. 4515–4517). Pergamon.

Burge, E. J., & Frewin, C. C. (1989). Self-directed learning in distance learning. In C. J. Titmus (Ed.), *Lifelong education for adults: An international handbook* (pp. 260–262). Pergamon Press (Original work published in 1986).

Burge, E. J., & O'Rourke, J. (1998). The dynamics of distance teaching: Voices from the field. In C. Latchem & F. Lockwood (Eds.), *Staff development in open and distance learning* (pp 193–202). Routledge.

Burge, E. J., & Roberts, J. M. (1993). *Classrooms with a difference: A practical guide to the use of conferencing technologies*. Ontario Institute for Studies in Education.

Burge, L., & Haughey, M. (1993). Transformative learning in reflective practice. In T. Evans & D. Nation (Eds.), *Reforming open and distance education* (pp. 88–112). Kogan Page.

Burge, L., Norquay, M., & Roberts, J. (1987). *Listening to learn: Using the voice in distance education*. Instructional Resources Development Unit, OISE/CJRT FM-Open College (Print and audio cassette manual).

Journal Articles

Burge, E. J. (1977). Change agents or change victims? An exploration of the relevance of an innovation diffusion model for library management. *Australian Library Journal*, *18*(4), 311–315.

Burge, E. J. (1983). Changing perspectives. *Library Trends*, *36*(2), 513–523.

Burge, E. J. (1985). Better connections: Some issues in the use of audio-teleconferencing in higher education. *Hersda News – Higher Education Research and Development Society of Australia*, *7*(2), 3–4.

Burge, E. J. (1986a). Andragogy in distance education. *Education for Librarianship: Australia*, *3*(1), 26–37.

Burge, E. J. (1986b). Audio classrooms: Experience from Ontario. *Media in Education and Development*, *19*(1), 26–29.

Burge, E. J. (1987). Reaching out through distance education. *Insight*, *1*, 94–102.

Burge, E. J. (1988a). Beyond andragogy: Some explorations for distance learning design. *Journal of Distance Education*, *3*(1), 5–23.

Burge, E. J. (1988b). Learner-centredness: Some additional points. *Journal of Distance Education*, *4*(1), 47–50.

Burge, E. J. (1990). Women as learners: Issues for visual and virtual classrooms. *The Canadian Journal for the Study of Adult Education/laRevue canadienne pour l'étude de l'éducation des adultes*, *4*(2), 1–24.

Burge, E. J. (1994). Learning in computer conferenced contexts: The learner's perspective. *Journal of Distance Education*, *9*(1), 19–43.

Burge, E. J. (1996). Inside-out thinking about distance teaching. Making sense of reflective practice. *Journal of the American Society for Information Science*, *47*(11), 843–848.

Burge, E. J. (1998). Thinking about technology; Or, how to be a realist without being a "techno." *Teaching Voices*, *26*, 2–4.

Burge, E. J. (2007). Guest editorial. *Open Learning*, *22*(2), 107–115.

Burge, E. J. (2008). "Crafting the future"- pioneer lessons and concerns for today. *Distance Education*, *29*(1), 5–17.

Burge, E. J., & Davison, P. (2010). Between dissonance and grace: The experience of post-secondary leaders. *International Journal of Lifelong Education*, *29*(l), 111–131.

Burge, E. J., & Fales, A. W. (1984). Self-direction by design: The application of self- directed learning in distance course design. *Canadian Journal of University Continuing Education*, *10*(1), 68–78.

Burge, E. J., & Howard, J. L. (1990a). Audio-conferencing in graduate education: A case study. *The American Journal of Distance Education*, *4*(2), 3–13.

Burge, E. J., & Howard, J. L. (1990b). Graduate level distance learning: The students speak. *Canadian Journal of University Continuing Education*, *16*(1), 49–65.

Burge, E. J., Howard, J. L., & Snow, J. E. (1989). Distance education: Concept and practice. *Canadian Library Journal*, *46*(5), 329–335.

Burge, E. J., Laroque, D., & Boak, C. (2000). Baring professional souls: Reflections on Web life. *Journal of Distance Education*, *15*(1), 81–98.

Burge, E. J., & Lenskyj, H. (1990). Women studying in distance education: Issues and principles. *Journal of Distance Education*, *5*(1), 20–37.

Burge, E. J., & Roberts, J. (1984). Audio-teleconferencing in continuing education: A case study with implications. *Canadian Journal of University Continuing Education, 10*(2), 20–30.

Burge, E. J., & Roberts, J. (1993). Dialogue on dialogue. *Journal of Distance Education, 7*(2), 89–94.

Burge, E. J., & Snow, J. E. (1990). Interactive audio classrooms: Key principles for effective practice. *Education for Information, 8*, 299–312.

Burge, E. J., Smythe, C. L., Roberts, J. M., & Keough, E. M. (1993). The audio-conference: Delivering continuing education for addiction workers in Canada. *Journal of Alcohol and Drug Education, 39*(1), 78–91.

Burge, E. J., & Snow, J. E. (2000). Candles, corks and contracts: Essential relationships between learners and librarians. *The New Review of Libraries and Lifelong Learning, 1*(l), 19–34.

References

Gibson, C. (Ed.). (1998). *Distance learners in higher education: Institutional responses for quality outcomes*. Atwood Publishers.

McLuhan, M., & McLuhan, H. (1988). *Laws of media: The new science*. University of Toronto Press.

Postman, N. (1992). *Technopoly: The surrender of culture to technology*. Knopf.

6
CHEN, LI

Photo of Li Chen contributed by Li Chen

> *I am the first person to deliver online teacher training in China for the local teachers on how to integrate ICT in the face-to-face classroom.*

Dr. Li Chen began her academic studies with a Bachelor of Science degree in Electronics. As she began to pursue graduate studies, her focus shifted to an interest in educational technology. She obtained a Master of Science in Educational Technology in 1992 and then completed a Doctor of Science in Educational Technology in 2003. All her studies were through Beijing Normal University.

Currently, Dr. Chen is an Associate Professor and also Vice President of HR and ICT at Beijing Normal University. She has taught for over 30 years with Beijing Normal University. Li Chen has contributed to Chinese education and has held positions such as President, Society of International Chinese in Educational Technology (2015–2016); Director, Technology Committee, National Lab for Smart Online Learning (2017 to date); Executive Dean, Beijing Institute for Learning Society, Beijing Normal University (2010 to date); and Executive Member of the Council, Chinese Society of Educational Development Strategy (2017 to date).

Her initial interest in distance education was related to satellite technology and how it held the potential to improve education in rural areas.

Li Chen has written 17 books and over 200 papers. Her publications list at the end of this chapter includes her most current publications. She is a prolific researcher; the main focus of her work is concerned with distance education pedagogy and current trends, such as massive open online courses (MOOCs). Much of her work is also focused on learner critical thinking and interactions in online learning environments. Currently, she is exploring the emerging ideas of connectivism and is dedicated to developing a new systematic theory for online learning based on connectivism.

One of her most important achievements was to initiate the first (and, to date, the only) master of distance education programme and doctor of distance education programme in China. At the time of her interview, Beijing Normal University was the only institution in China to offer such programmes, thanks to the foresight and interests of Dr. Chen.

Li Chen has also worked internationally, most recently with helping to co-initiate the annual international symposium between Beijing Normal University and Athabasca University, as well as being Co-chair of the Asian Student Seminar and Round Table between Korea, Japan, and China for over six years.

Interview

Transcript Analysis Summary

Analysis of all interviews included in this volume led to the identification of 3,545 units of data. The mean of these collective units was 118 per pioneer, the median was 118.5, and the mode was 132. Individual interview units ranged from 59 to 217 units, yielding a spread of 158 units between all interviews. Li Chen's interview generated 69 units, placing her interview near the bottom of all interviews in terms of number of units produced. This low number of units may partially be explained by the fact that Li participated in English, which was not her native language.

A comparison of Li Chen's interview to the interviews of all pioneers indicated that her interview profile shared a fair number of commonalities with the average interview profile (Figure 6.1). Her interview yielded a similar number of units in 8 of the 14 topic areas: benefits of DE, challenges, accomplishments, research interests, goals, interesting memories, final thoughts, and general gender-related comments. Relatively speaking, Li Chen generated more units when discussing her educational and experiential background and changes over time than the average interviewee did. This may be because she came into the field from an engineering background at a time when China did not offer DE. As a result, Chen played a pivotal role in the acceptance and rapid expansion of DE initiatives during her career.

Li Chen's interview produced a fewer-than-average number of units in the areas of learning environment, early founders, others for the book, and career history. It is not known why she chose not to provide much information on her learning environment. Career history was a topic that arose during some interviewees' conversations, so it was not unusual for Chen's interview to contain so

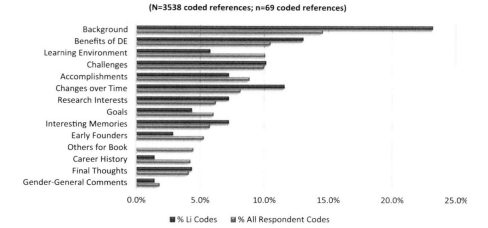

Figure 6.1 All Respondents' Versus Li Chen's Parent Codes

few units in this area. Given that Chen came from an engineering and educational technology background and began her career when DE was not offered in her country, it was not surprising to note the low number of units in these topic areas, either.

Link to recorded interview: tinyurl.com/Chen-L-2018

Transcript of Interview

Full name: Li Chen
Institutional Affiliation: Professor, Research Centre of Distance Education, Beijing Normal University, Beijing, China
Key:

Regular font = Interviewee comments
Italicized font = Interviewer comments

Interview Questions

1. *What is your name and title?*

   My family name is Chen. My given name is Li. Right now, I am a professor in Beijing Normal University. I am a researcher and professor in the Research Centre of Distance Education in Beijing Normal University.

2. *In what year did you begin to look specifically into distance education [DE]?*

   In 1991. My bachelor-level background is in electronics. During a part of my master's degree programme, I made a decision to change my research field from satellite technology into educational technology. My research field is in distance education.

3. *What were the circumstances in your world that initiated this interest in DE?*

   When I was very young in school, I got a lot of support from my teachers. So at that time, I was very interested in becoming a good teacher and was very interested in education. When I was in the university as an undergraduate student, I majored in electronics. At that time, I learned out of the courses from the school of education. So when I was very young, I was very interested in education. I learned out of courses in education. So when I was a master's degree student, suddenly I found that distance education is a very good way to share educational resources, particularly for the people in rural areas. So I found that a new technology, particularly satellite technology, can make it more effective and the field broader. So I made the decision to change my major and to enter into this area.

4. *Which female researchers or female colleagues may have piqued your interest in DE?*

   It was not my peers who supported me. When I talked to my master degree supervisor, she was a scientist working in satellite technology. I talked with her. I was very interested in distance education with satellite technology. She was very supportive. She told me that we need more people to contribute in this area. If I would like to transfer my major, she would like to support me. It was not her that pushed me into that area, but she was the very important supporter for me to make my decision.

5. *Who would you identify as the early female leaders/founders in the DE field?*

   When I entered into this area at the beginning, I never met very many females, but I met a female leader who was leading the China Radio and TV Open University in China at that time. Her name was Xiuyun Yu. I think that she was the first female leader in distance education in China. She made a lot of contributions.

6. *What are some of the goals that you strove to achieve in the DE field?*

   At the beginning when I entered this area, I just wanted to know more about the principles of distance education and to integrate more advanced technology into distance education at that time. Now I am dedicated to developing new systematic theory for online learning based on connectivism.

7. *What are some of your accomplishments in the field of DE that you would like to share?*

   I am very proud of one achievement for my career. I initiated so far the only master's degree and doctoral degree in distance education in China. So Beijing Normal University is the only university to deliver a master's degree and a PhD degree in distance education. We have a lot of degrees *by* distance education, but these are the only degrees *for* distance education.

8. *What was the "state of DE" when you first entered the field as opposed to DE in 2018?*

   In the last century, distance education was the only way to share or deliver non-degree programmes for adults located in all of China. Now, distance education is not only for the people who are out of the school. Even in the school, distance education is kind of the innovative teaching and learning model. So that's the difference.

   At the time that I entered distance education, distance education was not the pedagogical way for China. But now the pedagogy in the school is normal for all schools. It is not only for the Open University or the Radio and TV University. It is not only for the adults but also for the students in the university.

9. *So, is there a lot of blended learning going on now?*

   Yes. Yes, blended learning. We have a different term in Chinese principles, but it is similar. Blended learning in the flipped classroom is very popular, and lots of the teachers in the school university are trying to integrate online learning as the most important part of the dialogue of teaching and learning.

10. *What interesting memories would you like to share about the beginning of online DE?*

    For me or for China? The Internet is developing very fast in China. We have a very ambitious national plan in China to make the Internet a priority everywhere. So far, we can use the Internet everywhere. We have lots of very exciting, very effective applications. Distance education is an area for the Internet application. Now we are already starting to rebuild education through the Internet. We have lots of initial plans for China.

    For me, I am the first person to deliver online teacher training in China for the local teachers on how to integrate ICT in the face-to-face classroom. I am not sure which year, but it was quite early. It was a very important project because I used distance education and the Internet in my project.

    Another thing, our Open University, or Radio and TV Open University, is trying to use online education to build a lifelong learning support system. So we have lots of these kinds of activities in China.

11. *What were your specific DE research interests, and have they changed/evolved over the years?*

    At this stage, there are two kinds of topics that I am working on. One, I am organizing a research team to try to dig out new online learning principles. We have found, particularly with the SNS [social network software], online learning principles are different from face-to-face. Online learning is a collective activity. It is an individual online learning process that is integrated into a collective sharing process, so there are lots of new things. So one of my plans is to dig out the new principles to support online education better.

    Another way is to try to push and try to enhance the central government and different levels of government to rebuild the education system. So we have lots of very initiative activities that we have started in distance education or online education. But the education management system is more suitable for the school education, not distance education. So far, there is lots of the system that we don't have. For example, the qualification certification system we don't have. Today, Professor Zhang organized the symposium. And that's the second part – how to push or enhance the government to make this kind of system? So those are two of my research fields that I am working on.

12. Is there anything else you [would] like to address?

I'm very proud as a professor in distance education. I think that distance education means the future. It means the creative. There are a lot of creative opportunities for me, so I learn a lot. From my experience in distance education, I think that in facing the future, we should broaden our eyes about distance education. So distance education is not only for the Open University. Maybe it is kind of a [power], or maybe it is kind of the new pedagogy; maybe it is kind of a creative idea, a philosophy to rebuild whole education. There are lots of implications for distance education. So we have more opportunities and more challenges.

Publications

Books

Chen, L. (2002). *Teaching guide on integrating ICT into traditional classroom.* China Central Radio &TV University Press.
Chen, L. (2004a). *Foundation of distance education.* High Education Press.
Chen, L. (2004b). *Modern educational technology: Technology innovation and social development.* Beijing Normal University Press.
Chen, L. (2005). *Guide for distance learner: How to be successful learner.* Beijing Normal University Press.
Chen, L. (2007a). *Education innovation: Effective strategy for integrating ICT into teaching & learning.* High Education Press.
Chen, L. (2007b). *E-learning: An inevitable choice for university in information era.* Beijing Normal University Press.
Chen, L. (2011a). *Distance education.* High Education Press.
Chen, L. (2011b). *Transforming teaching and learning by ICT – Innovation by learner-center philosophy.* Central Radio & TV University Press.
Chen, L., & Chen, Q. (2002). *Guide for school net project: Technology & policy making.* China Peace Press.
Chen, L., & Feng, X. (2008). *Policy and management for distance education organization.* Central Radio & TV University Press.
Chen, L., & Sidwell, D. (2014). *Guide for writing distance learning material.* Central Radio & TV University Press.
Chen, L., Wang, Z., & Anderson, T. (2016). *Instructional interaction for distance learning.* Central Radio & TV University Press.
Chen, L., Xie, X., & Wang, X. (2017). *The case study of internal quality assurance for open universities.* Beijing Normal University Press.
Li, S., & Chen, L. (2011). *Principle and guide for learner-center.* Central Radio & TV University Press.
Shen, X., Chen, L., & Zheng, Q. (2017). *Quality assurance standard for Chinese Open University.* Beijing Normal University Press.
Zheng, Q., Chen, L., & Burgos, D. (2018). *The development of MOOCs in China.* Springer.
Zheng, Q., Chen, L., & Lin, S. (2016). *Internet + education: MOOCs in China.* Electronic Industry Press.

Journal Articles

Baggaley, J., Chen, L., & Nian, Z. (2014). Re-thinking MOOCs. *Open Education Research, 1,* 9–15.
Chen, L. (2014a). International review on instructional interaction in distance learning. *Distance Education in China, 11,* 14–19.
Chen, L. (2014b). The new relation between opportunity, quality and cost in the era of internet+. *Journal of Beijing Radio & TV University, 6,* 10–13.
Chen, L. (2016a). The innovative nature and transformative trend of Internet + Education. *Journal of Distance Education, 4,* 3–8.
Chen, L. (2016b). Open University pilot needs new policy and management system. *Journal of Open Education, 2,* 6–9.
Chen, L., & Feng, X. (2015). Learning theory and pedagogy innovation for online course design. *Journal of Beijing Radio & TV University, 1,* 1–8.
Chen, L., Guo, Y., Wang, H., & Zheng, Q. (2018). The framework of education research topic on ICT in education in the new era. *Modern Distance Education Research, 1,* 42–48.

Chen, L., & Ji, H. (2017). Open and connection: The power to transforming radio & TV university to open university. *Lifelong Education Research, 3*, 12–15.

Chen, L., Li, B., Guo, Y., & Peng, D. (2017). New direction and new trend of ICT for K12 in the era of Internet +. *E-Education Research, 5*, 5–12.

Chen, L., & Li, Q. (2015). A study on marketing for Guang Dong Open University on continued education. *Journal of Guang Dong Open University, 4*, 1–8.

Chen, L., & Lin, S. (2014). The rational thinking on MOOCs. *Modern Distance Education, 3*, 3–7.

Chen, L., Lin, S., & Zheng, Q. (2016). The opportunity & challenge for distance education in the era of Internet+. *Modern Distance Education Research, 1*, 3–10.

Chen, L., Shen, X., Wan, F., & Zheng, Q. (2018). Concept of quality assurance for distance education in Internet era. *China Educational Technology*, 15–21.

Chen, L., Wang, F., Li, J., Liu, H., & Li, D. (2015). The new organization structure for Guang Dong Open University based on international experience. *Journal of Guang Dong Open University, 1*, 12–21.

Chen, L., Wang, H., Sun, H., & Liu, C. (2017). The return and Innovation on service of MOOCs in China. *E-Education Research, 8*, 1–6.

Chen, L., & Wang, Z. (2016). The theory of instructional interaction on three generations of distance learning. *Distance Education in China, 10*, 14–21.

Chen, L., Wang, Z., & Zheng, Q. (2017). The reflection on program educational technology in the era of Internet. *E-Education Research, 9*, 5–11.

Chen, L., Zheng, Q., & Lin, S. (2017). The opportunity and challenge for open university in the era of Internet +. *Open Education Research, 1*, 12–20.

Chen, L., Zheng, Q., & Wang, Z. (2014). Review on MOOCs and analysis on three kinds of MOOCs. *China Educational Technology, 7*, 25–33.

Chen, L., Zheng, Q., Xie, H., & Shen, X. (2013). A study on qualification framework for China on the international perspective. *Modern Distance Education Research, 4*, 917.

Chen, L., Zheng, Q., & Yin, B. (2013). The responsibility on improving quality reputation of distance education for China Open University. *China Educational Technology, 10*, 42–46.

Chen, Y., Zheng, Q., Sun, H., & Chen, L. (2016). Online teacher evaluation model based on learning analysis. *E-Education Research, 10*, 35–41.

Feng, X., & Chen, L. (2013). Inter-school collaboration environment: A design-based research. *Journal of Educational Technology Development and Exchange, 6*(2), 5–39.

Guo, W., Chen, L., & Chen, G. (2013). MOOCs: Old & new gene of Internet. *Peking University Education Review, 4*, 173–184.

He, F., Zheng, Q., & Chen, L. (2015). Course development for practical course based on connectivism. *Modern Distance Education, 5*, 24–33.

Jinag, N., Chen, L., & Zheng, Q. (2013). Comparative study on lifelong learning law. *Modern Distance Education, 5*, 3–9.

Li, S., Chen, L., & Zheng, Q. (2016). A study on course design for MOOCs in China. *Journal of Open Education, 2*, 46–52.

Lin, S., Chen, L., & Peng, Y. (2016). External quality assurance for university level distance education. *Distance Education in China, 5*, 43–48.

Nian, Z., Chen, L., & Xie, H. (2014). International review on learning cities. *Comparative Education Review, 11*, 36–41.

Sun, D., Cheng, G., Xu, P., Zheng, Q., & Chen, L. (2019). Using HMM to compare interaction activity patterns of student groups with different achievements in MPOCs. *Interactive Learning Environments, 27*(5–6), 766–781. https://doi.org/10.1080/10494820.2019.1610780

Sun, H., & Chen, L. (2014). A framework for analysing the social affordance of Web 2.0 tools. *International Journal of Social Media and Interactive Learning Environments, 2*(1), 37–59. www.inderscience.com/info/inarticletoc.php?jcode=ijsmile&year=2014&vol=2&issue=1

Sun, H., Chen, L., Wang, Z. (2017). A study on interactivity for distance learning tools. *Distance Education in China, 4*, 33–41.

Sun, H., Zheng, Q., & Chen, L. (2016). A study on instructional interaction on MOOCs in China. *Journal of Open Education, 1*, 72–79.

Sun, H., Zheng, Q., Chen, Y., & Chen, L. (2016). Online course evaluation model based on learning analysis. *E-Education Research, 11*, 33–40.

Wang, Z., Anderson, T., Chen, L., & Barbera, E. (2016). Interaction pattern analysis in cMOOCs based on the connectivist interaction and engagement framework. *British Journal of Educational Technology, 18*. http://onlinelibrary.wiley.com/doi/10.1111/bjet.12433/abstract

Wang, Z., Anderson, T., Chen, L., & Barbera, E. (2017). Interaction pattern analysis in cMOOCs based on the connectivist interaction and engagement framework. *British Journal of Educational Technology*, *48*(2), 683–699. http://onlinelibrary.wiley.com/doi/10.1111/bjet.12433/abstract

Wang, Z., Anderson, T., Chen, L., & Wang, S. (2018). Research methodology and methods on instructional interaction for distance learning. *China Educational Technology*, *1*, 50–59.

Wang, Z., Anderson, T., Wang, S., & Chen, L. (2018). How learners participate in connectivist learning: An analysis of the interaction traces from a cMOOC. *The International Review of Research in Open and Distance Learning*, *19*(1), 44–67.

Wang, Z., & Chen, L. (2014a). How to design good MOOCs based on instructional interaction theory & the taxonomy of learning objectives. *Modern Distance Education Research*, *6*, 59–68.

Wang, Z., & Chen, L. (2014b). Review on connectivism and new development. *Open Education Research*, *5*, 11–29.

Wang, Z., & Chen, L. (2015a). The instructional interaction theory model for connectivism. *Journal of Open Education*, *5*, 25–34.

Wang, Z., & Chen, L. (2015b). The international review on the theory of instructional interaction for distance learning. *Open Education Research*, *2*, 30–39.

Wang, Z., & Chen, L. (2015c). The value and key topics for study on instructional interaction for connectivism. *Modern Distance Education Research*, *5*, 47–54.

Wang, Z., & Chen, L. (2016). Instructional interaction model and way in cMOOCs. *China Educational Technology*, *2*, 49–57.

Wang, Z., & Chen, L. (2017a). Concept interaction and learning evaluation on distance learning. *Distance Education in China*, *12*, 12–20.

Wang, Z., & Chen, L. (2017b). Learning activity design based on theory of instructional interaction hierarchy about distance learning. *Distance Education in China*, *6*, 39–47.

Wang, Z., Chen, L., & Anderson, T. (2014). A framework for interaction and cognitive engagement in connectivist learning contexts. *The International Review of Research in Open and Distance Learning*, *15*(2), 121–141.

Wang, Z., Chen, L., Chen, M., & Li, T. (2017). The study on interactivity for distance learning resource. *Distance Education in China*, *2*, 45–52.

Wang, Z., Chen, L., Chen, M., & Han, S. (2016). The philosophy foundation for instructional interaction of distance learning. *Distance Education in China*, *9*, 7–13.

Wang, Z., Chen, L., & Han, S. (2016). Interactivity analysis framework for distance learning environment. *Distance Education in China*, *12*, 37–42.

Wu, Y., & Chen, L. (2015). A study on critical thinking structure for university students. *Journal of Beijing Radio & TV University*, *2*, 35–41.

Wu, Y., Chen, L., & Zhao, H. (2014). The study on pedagogy for critical thinking development. *E-Education Research*, *11*, 71–77.

Wu, Y., Zhao, H., & Chen, L. (2015). A pilot study on developing critical thinking by Internet. *Model Distance Education Research*, *2*, 76–86.

Xie, H., & Chen, L. (2013). The study on how to make learning city develop sustainably. *Modern Distance Education Research*, *2*, 1–3.

Xie, X., Chen, L., & Wu, Y. (2016). The international experience on building quality reputation for distance organization. *Journal of Open Learning*, *4*, 10–16.

Yin, B., & Chen, L. (2018). The principle of self-organization for online learning. *E-education Research*, *3*, 56–61.

Yin, B., Zheng, Q., & Chen, L. (2016). A study on certificate and accreditation for MOOCs in China. *Journal of Open Education*, *2*, 30–37.

Zhang, J., Li, S., & Chen, L. (2015). The role of the third generation of distance teachers in China on the international perspective. *Journal of Beijing Radio & TV University*, *3*, 26–32.

Zhang, J., Perris, K., Zheng, Q., & Chen, L. (2015). Public response to "the MOOC movement" in China: Examining the time series of microblogging. *International Review of Research in Open and Distance Learning*, *16*(5), 144–160.

Zhao, H., Chen, L., & Panda, S. (2014). Self-regulated learning ability of Chinese distance learners. *British Journal of Educational Technology*, *45*(5), 941–958.

Zhao, H., Chen, L., & Zhao, Y. (2015a). The software design and development on guide for learning strategy based on personal learning style. *China Educational Technology*, *5*, 67–72.

Zhao, H., Chen, L., & Zhao, Y. (2015b). A study on learning strategy for distance learners in Open University. *Journal of Beijing Radio & TV University*, *2*, 26–32.

Zhao, H., Sun, H., Zheng, Q., Zhang, X., & Chen, L. (2017). Study on learning support for MOOCs in China. *Modern Distance Education*, *3*, 10–18.

Zhao, H., Yeonwook, I., & Chen, L. (2016). A study of the effects of learner characteristics on the self-regulated learning ability: A comparison of Korea and China. *Educational Technology International, 17*(1), 59–85.

Zhao, H., Zhang, H., Zheng, Q., & Chen, L. (2017). The study on learning evaluation of MOOCs in China. *China Educational Technology, 9,* 53–61.

Zhao, H., Zheng, Q., & Chen, L. (2017). MOOCs in China: Situation and reflection. *Distance Education in China, 11,* 55–62.

Zheng, Q., Chen, L., & Xu, L. (2015). The cost-effectiveness for distance education in the network era. *Journal of Beijing Normal University, 2,* 107–116.

Zheng, Q., Chen, Y., & Chen, L. (2016). A survey on learner's learning literacy for MOOCs in China. *Journal of Open Education, 2,* 38–45.

Zheng, Q., Chen, Y., Sun, H., & Chen, L. (2016). Online learning evaluation model based on learning analysis. *E-Education Research, 9,* 35–40.

Zheng, Q., Li, Q., & Chen, L. (2015). A study on teaching model for MOOCs in China. *Journal of Open Education, 6,* 71–79.

Zheng, Q., Ma, D., & Chen, L. (2013). Theory model and evaluation framework for adult lifelong learning literacy. *Modern Distance Education Research, 2*.

Zheng, Q., Yu, C., & Chen, L. (2016). A study on instructional interaction on MOOCs based on student perspective. *China Educational Technology, 6,* 77–85.

Zheng, Q., Zhang, X., & Chen, L. (2016). Review on MOOCs in China and study on supporting system. *China Educational Technology, 8,* 44–50.

Zong, Y., Chen, L, Zheng, Q., & Hu, H. (2017). An analysis on academic emotion by online learning data on Moodle. *Journal of Open Learning, 12,* 11–20.

Conference Presentations

Shen, X., Chen, L., & Li, Y. (2013). The construction of quality assurance system for distance education based on ecological view. *Proceedings of EITT2013, International Conference of Educational Innovation through Technology, 2013*(11), 309–316.

Zhao, H., & Chen, L. (2014). Learning styles of distance students attending a pilot e-college in China: survey results. *Proceedings of EITT 2014, 184–191. Re-thinking MOOCs: Open Education Research, 1,* 9–15.

7
FAINHOLC, BEATRIZ

Photo of Beatriz Fainholc contributed by Beatriz Fainholc

> *The goals at any educational programme, basically, have to show understanding and the practices of the values of freedom and democratization.*

Dr. Beatriz Fainholc completed her Bachelor of Education Sciences at Buenos Aires University, Argentina in 1966. She went on to the University of Sao Paulo, Brazil to obtain a Master of Social Sciences in 1970. Her Doctorate in Education Sciences was obtained through the National

University La Plata, Argentina in 1996. She also holds a Post Doctorate in Virtual Pedagogy within the Framework of Cultural Studies completed in 2014 at the University of Chicago in Champaign, Illinois, the United States.

Fainholc's areas of research interest include virtual pedagogy and cultural studies, educational technology, digital humanities in social sciences and education, the development of deep thinking, virtual communities, and the study of reading skills on the Internet, as well as processing big data.

Fainholc currently is a Faculty Professor (face-to-face and virtual) and researcher at the National University La Plata, Argentina; UTN National Technological University, Argentina; and several foreign universities. She is also a consultant in virtual higher education in Uruguay; the doctorate programme at Guadalajara, México; UTEM in Chile; and Polytechnic in Madrid.

Today, Dr. Fainholc is also the General Director of CEDIPROE, a non-government organization (NGO) dedicated to design, production, evaluation, and research at its multimedia material centre in Buenos Aires, Argentina.

Fainholc has been recognized internationally for her work in distance education. She is also a member of numerous associations, such as:

- Founding Member of the Argentine Association of Distance Education, 1979,
- Founding Member of the Association of Graduates in Educational Sciences, 1964, and
- Adherent member of the ICDE International Council of Distance Education, Norway, from 1990 to present.

Fainholc is a prolific researcher in her areas of interest. A list of her books, chapters, and journal articles are found at the end of this chapter, beginning with works written in English. Most of her publications are in Spanish. These Spanish publications are listed as they appear on her website, along with a link to her site.

Interview

Transcript Analysis Summary

Analysis of all interviews included in this volume led to the identification of 3,545 units of data. The mean of these collective units was 118 per pioneer, the median was 118.5, and the mode was 132. Individual interview units ranged from 59 to 217 units, yielding a spread of 158 units between all interviews. Beatriz Fainholc's interview generated 59 units, making her interview the one to produce the least number of units among all interviews. This low number of units may be due in part to the fact that the interview was conducted in English, which was a foreign language to her.

A comparision of Fainholc's interview to the interviews of all pioneers indicates that her conversations yielded a similar number of units in the areas of challenges, accomplishments, changes over time, and final thoughts (Figure 7.1). Since DE was not established when Beatriz began her career, she provided a fairly detailed review of the background that led to her involvement in the field. Much of Fainholc's career was built on meeting the need for educational opportunities for rural and marginalized people in her country. A significant challenge that she faced during her career was a cultural more that dehumanized and demoralized the female poplulation, which had systematically denied them an adequate education. Fainholc has viewed DE as a primary solution to addressing educational challenges in her country; this explains why Fainholc's interview extoled the benefits of

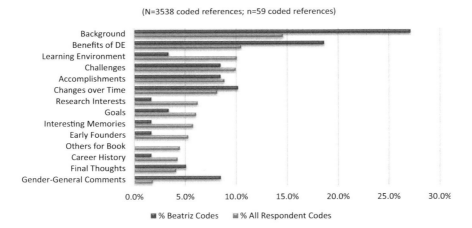

Figure 7.1 All Respondents' Versus Beatriz Fainholc's Parent Codes

DE to such an extent. It also provides insight into why her interview produced more general comments about gender issues than the average interiew did.

Link to recorded interview: tinyurl.com/Fainholc-B

Transcript of Interview

Full name: Dr. Beatriz Fainholc
Institutional Affiliation: Argentine and international higher education institutions
Key:

Regular font = Interviewee comments
Italicized font = Interviewer comments

Interview Questions

1. *In what year did you begin to look into distance education [DE]?*

   In 1983, I wrote the first book of distance education [DE] in Argentina, published by Libreria El Colegio, Buenos Aires. My interest was growing and growing after the two awards that the Canadian government gave me, based on my pioneering study and work in DE programmes. (I was selected from among many people whom I thought knew more about the area.) During my visits in Canada, I saw different groups working in DE, such as the Open Learning Agency in Vancouver, British Columbia (I don't know if this agency exists anymore because the director was Tony Bates, a pioneer in these things. He came from DE on TV. He had worked a lot in DE when I met him, and now he is a great, great friend of mine), the beginning of Athabasca University and the distance education department and so on, and the beginning of the thinking and use of DE for short courses for women to help the communities develop in their hands in Ontario, for example, and other places.

2. *What education and experience did you have before you became involved in DE?*

   Sociology of education in rural education because I have perceived that, in general, the remote areas and their inhabitants were marginalized in society and the modern movements and that the women were marginalized the worst.

3. *What events in your life made you interested in DE?*

   I thought that the first to receive information, training, etc., had to be the remote, poor, and marginalized populations: basically, women who were not integrated into society. In those times, only press material and telephone (if it did exist because of the lack of electricity) had to be the choice for the educational media (if not, nothing). I began to work in the Agricultural Ministry in 1983 when the dictatorship ended in my country and proposed to design the first DE courses (in order to improve the quality of their teaching), which were basically for agricultural technicians in rural areas so that the economic production increased. The women were absent, and the rural secondary schools did not have restrooms for them! Incredible, hmm? Coming back from the travels of these areas, I begged and explained the need to build these courses, but nobody could understand why I thought these courses were needed. In a couple years more, they built restrooms, but the courses abruptly disappeared when the ministries were restructured. . . . Incredible, but it was so. Then I decided to write a book (the first one in Argentina) dedicated to defining and promoting DE and what its possibilities were.

4. *Were there any women who may have helped you become interested in DE?*

   In general, no. The interest in DE and women studies did not exist at the faculty and in other social organizations. The traditional society did not perceive these issues: the traditional role of women had been naturalized, fixed as the ancestral interaction with men, the view of the everyday communication, the silence, and subjacent violence, and so on. The socialization in the cultural framework presented a strict psycho-political dissociation and a deep social differentiation between men and women, with women having minor and prohibited participation in many areas, existing according to stereotypical expectations, first education of the children exclusively in their hands, etc. Also, it was reflected, obviously, in the educational sphere (in formal schooling and informal everyday life), including the teachers training in biased roles, and kept for many centuries until today. The habits, or the mentality, as it is known nowadays, fixes and consolidates the inferiority of women in any social groups and situations.

5. *Who would you say are the early female leaders/founders in the DE field?*

There were not a lot of female leaders specifically in the DE field. But, in general, many sociologists and anthropologists were more interested in studies, for instance, of the Trobriand or Samoa islands [from 1958–1960] and had very, very little interest in rural areas where the women's lives were quite different. Not many psychologists and even less medical doctors, lawyers and so on (till today) could perceive the need to review the epistemological pillars of the "knowledge" that the women produced and how it circulates in the circuits named before. The essence of my point is to be aware of the ancestral roots of women's disparages. The DE movement also had a lot of difficulties to be recognized as an educational modality by the official authorities, and many of its direct possible users (ill people, women that are at home with small children, training workers in specific jobs, and so on).

6. *What are some of the goals that you worked to achieve in the DE field?*

I agree with the feminist view of the women's studies as a cross variable in any kind of subject. So the goals at any educational programme, basically, have to show understanding and the practices of the values of freedom and democratization, to revalue the position and roles of women in society, their invisible domestic work, and their artisan or industrial elaborations. Such as to remark that these issues, at any level, means to produce social productive knowledge that the women are doing, including the economic issues and, moreover, the political issues.

DE is a rich opportunity to break this mentality and in educational terms today, to integrate ICT and the networks (with a didactic processing of information, which is really the main difficulty) for designing and developing many educational proposals to overcome the sexist world. Because, as I understand here, DE delivery that includes this perspective is important, since, in the schools, there is not yet a law to include views of women's situations, and this should be distributed across all educational offerings. So in DE, it is worse. Again, this context helps the commitment of developing many competencies and capacities of different social groups, ethnicities, and so on, where the women are invisible, forced to be excluded, and seen in many violent situations.

7. *What are some of your accomplishments in the field of DE that you would like to share?*

I would like to share the experience of proposals put into practice in different contexts, the plan of concrete educational activities that I have designed and included. For instance, for a couple of years in Mexico, the educational secretary bought three editions of my book, *Towards a Non-Sexist Didactic*, to train teachers. Another book of mine complements and extends this first one. This second book is called *Education and Gender: A Cultural, Social and Technological Perspective* (in Spanish, but it is possible to be translated).

In those proposals, which intend to provoke awareness in the population – and not only among women – I remark to integrate ICT into the design of educational activities, to be used, to put into practice, in a conscious manner, not only for face-to-face educational programmes, but mainly for DE ones.

8. *What were some of the challenges that you found in the field of DE?*

To make visible and to reckon the need to listen and to understand the social, economic, and political presence of women, in an equalitarian position and role with men. It is not a challenge, but mainly a great social responsibility (by public policies), which means to take into account the political oppressive matter of the inferiority of the women, and their little possibilities without recognizing the inclusion of their existence. This is beyond knowing that the social situations change a lot in a historic line if, for example, we compare the life of our grandmother, my mother, and me.

9. *What was DE like when you first entered the field as compared to DE in 2018?*

   It is an incredible difference, but there are a lot of things to do yet: to review many points of view, to include (in my country) sexual education not only in the schools but in any kind of programme, including the design and production of didactic material (nowadays software, websites, gamification), to renovate the framework of the curricula to include activities to integrate families, media, social organizations, governments; taking into account many discussions to participate and to be more aware of the inequality world, referred in this case to the women of my country.

10. *What were your DE research interests, and have they changed over the years?*

    For me, the key is to train professors, tutors, and faculty members at the university through designing, implementing, and evaluating programmes and the epistemological framework with the participants to collaborate via the distance learning experience, in a hurry here!!!!!!!!!

    Nowadays, this includes ICT and their different formats: not being a great specialized expert, but to be aware of the main point to understanding of what democracy is because it is the engine of the social and cultural change in mentality. And of course, the improvement of the quality of the teaching and learning processes, which, at every meeting, a lot of politicians say, and in general, nobody takes into account or does.

    Could you please describe the learning environment in which you currently work?

    I teach and conduct research at our national university and foreign universities and give seminars for designing DE courses (and today, MOOCs) with the cross variables of women studies and cultural studies, which I have dedicated my efforts to since many years ago. I have now completed a post doc two years ago, published by a Spanish university [UOC, Open University of Catalunya (Catalonia), Barcelona, Spain].

11. *Is there anything else you [would] like to address?*

    I would like to apologize for my English, because I have a lot of problems with it yet. [Laughs.]

    I would like to see the work that has been done be widely diffused; thank you a lot!!

Publications in English

Books

Fainholc, B. (2011). *Distance and flexible education applying ICT for an innovative and open learning.* Nova Sciences Publishers.

Book Chapters

Fainholc, B. (2019a). Cultural studies and education. In J. R. Naumov (Ed.), *Selected topics in cultural studies.* Nova Sciences.

Fainholc, B. (2019b). *Distance education in Latin America.* In M. G. Moore & W. C. Diehl (Eds.), *Handbook of distance education.* Routledge.

Journal Articles

Fainholc, B. (2010). The appropriation of wikis in higher blended learning course: A case study. In D. Gearhart (Ed.), *Cases on distance delivery and learning outcomes: Emerging trends and programs*. Troy University Press. DOI: 10.4018/978-1-60566-870-3

Publications in Spanish

(*Also listed on Dr. Fainholc's website: https://bfainhol.wixsite.com/cvbeatrizfainholc*)

Fainholc, B. (1979). *Introducción a la sociología de la educación*. Humanitas, Buenos Aires.

Fainholc, B. (1980a). *Educación a distancia Lib*. El Colegio, Buenos Aires. 1er libro escrito sobre el tema en el país.

Fainholc, B. (1980b). *Educación rural Argentina*. Lib. El Colegio, Buenos Aires.

Fainholc, B. (1984). *La TV y los niños en la Argentina*. Lib. El Colegio, Buenos Aires.

Fainholc, B. (1990). *La Tecnología Educativa y Apropiada*. Editorial Humanitas, Buenos Aires.

Fainholc, B. (1992). *Educación rural: Temas claves*. Editorial Aique, Buenos Aires.

Fainholc, B. (1993). *La Mujer y los medios de comunicación social*. Editorial Humanitas, Buenos Aires.

Fainholc, B. (1994a). *Hacia una escuela no sexista*. Editorial Aique, Buenos Aires.

Fainholc, B. (1994b). *La educación a distancia en Canadá, una vista sugerente para los países de América Latina*. Biblioteca Norte Sur, Entre Ríos. Argentina.

Fainholc, B. (1994c). *La Mujer en la educación y la cultura*. Editorial Sudamericana, Buenos Aires.

Fainholc, B. (1999). *La interactividad en la educación a distancia*. Editorial Paidós. Buenos Aires.

Fainholc, B. (2000). *Formación del profesorado para el nuevo milenio: Aportes de tecnología educativa Apropiada*. Editorial Lumen-Magisterio. Buenos Aires. ISBN 987-00-0003-7

Fainholc, B. (2004). *La lectura crítica en Internet: análisis y utilización de los recursos tecnológicos en educación*. Editorial Homo Sapiens, Rosario. Argentina.

Fainholc, B. (2008). *Programas, profesores y estudiantes virtuales. Una sociología de la educación a distancia*. Editorial Santillana, Buenos Aires. ISBN 978-950-46-1853-9

Fainholc, B. (2009). *Diccionario practico de tecnología educativa*. Editorial Alfagrama, Buenos Aires.

Fainholc, B. (2011). *Educación y género. Una perspectiva social, cultural y tecnológica*. Editorial Lugar, Buenos Aires. ISBN: 978-950-892-392-9

Fainholc, B. (2012a). *Aprendizaje electrónico mixto. El blended learning como propuesta educativa de síntesis creativa para la educación superior*. Editorial Académica Española.

Fainholc, B. (Ed.). (2012b). *Una tecnología educativa apropiada y crítica. Nuevos conceptos. Lumen-Hvmanitas. Buenos Aires*. Tambien Editorial Académica Española.

Fainholc, B. (2017a). *Lectura crítica y escritura estratégica en Internet. Formar lectores críticos y escritores estratégicos para la virtualidad Aprendizaje electrónico mixto*. Editorial Académica Española- EAE.

Fainholc, B. (2017b). *Una pedagogía virtual en el marco de los estudios culturales*. Editorial UOC, Barcelona.

8
FARLEY, HELEN SARA

Photo of Helen Farley contributed by Helen Farley

> [T]here is definitely a tendency to not listen to female academics as much as male academics. There is definitely discrimination there. I can say something, but my voice won't be as loud as a male academic working in the field. That can be very frustrating. Although I can see it with my own work, I probably see it more with other female academics who have struggled to have their voices heard. That's a particular challenge for females working in open and distance learning.

Dr. Helen Farley comes from an eclectic academic background, holding a Bachelor's degree in Veterinary Science, a Master of Arts in Religious Studies, and a PhD in Religious Studies, all of which were obtained at University of Queensland. She also possesses a Master of Education degree with a focus on information and communications technology (ICT) from Macquarie University.

DOI: 10.4324/9781003275329-9

Dr. Farley's early research concentrated on learning in virtual worlds and mLearning. She helped with groundbreaking work on the Second Life platform to create virtual environments for her students to enter and to enhance their online learning experiences. Farley also investigated early mLearning tools to help Australian and Southeast Asian students enhance their learning experiences.

Dr. Farley's unique contribution to modern learning is her pioneering work with incarcerated learners and working to develop offline programmes to allow this particular group of learners to study under the constraints of prison rules. She also combines her experience working with Indigenous peoples to enhance her current work, as a large percentage of incarcerated individuals come from this group. Her publication list at the end of this chapter demonstrates her dedication to these areas of research.

Farley has been instrumental in creating and establishing a learning management system (LMS) that models the online platform used by the University of Southern Queensland (USQ) but works offline to meet the prison regulations in Australia and New Zealand. The platform is operated by USQ and is called "OffLine StudyDesk." According to Farley:

> The USQ OffLine StudyDesk provides access to five programs modified to work without the Internet. The programs are: 1) the Tertiary Preparation Program, 2) the Indigenous Higher Education Pathways Program, 3) the Diploma of Arts (Community Welfare and Development, 4) the Diploma of Science (Environment and Sustainability), and 5) the Associate Degree of Business and Commerce. To date, this project is in Queensland (all but one correctional centre), Western Australia (six correctional centres), Tasmania and the Northern Territory (two correctional centres and one work camp). To date, there have been 1000 enrolments across 2000 courses in the project with a retention rate of 78%.
> (as compared to 65% for USQ across the same programmes;
> H. Farley, personal communication, December 6, 2018)

Interview

Transcript Analysis Summary

Analysis of all interviews included in this volume led to the identification of 3,545 units of data. The mean of these collective units was 118 per pioneer, the median was 118.5, and the mode was 132. Individual interview units ranged from 59 to 217 units, yielding a spread of 158 units between all interviews. Helen Farley's interview generated 146 units, placing her interview in the middle of the upper third of all interviews in terms of unit numbers.

A comparision of Farley's interview to the interviews of all pioneers indicated that her interview profile was, generally speaking, unique to that of the average interview profile (Figure 8.1). Her interview produced a similar number of units to the average interview in the areas of background, accomplishments, and goals. An exceptional number of units in the areas of learning environment, interesting memories, and final thoughts might be contributed to the fact that Farley was (and still is) pioneering the education of prisoners and, in doing so, has been developing a unique DE system.

While it is understandable that Farley would identify a number of challenges in her interview, it is not known why she did not discuss the benefits of DE more. This may be because no research question overtly asked about the benefits of DE. Nonetheless, Farley's results do not match the typical interview, which tended to have slightly more benefit than challenge units. Lesser unit numbers than average in the areas of early founders and others for the book were attributed to two factors: first, Farley was forging new ground in her area of interest, and second, she was aware that the authors had already contacted a number of potential book candidates at the time of her interview. An interview question about career history was not asked. Since this topic arose organically from some interviews, it is not surprising that Farley's interview did not contain many units in this area.

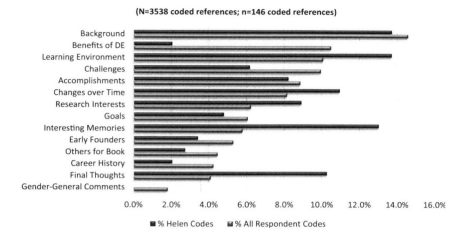

Figure 8.1 All Respondents' Versus Helen Farley's Parent Codes

Link to recorded interview Part A: tinyurl.com/Farley-H-A

Link to recorded interview Part B: tinyurl.com/Farley-H-B

Transcript of Interview

Full Name: Dr. Helen Farley

Institutional Affiliation: Associate Professor, Digital Life Lab, University of Southern Queensland and Practice Manager, Education and Training for the Southern Region, Department of Corrections, New Zealand

Key:

Regular font = Interviewee comments
Italicized font = Interviewer comments

Interview Questions

1. *What was your educational and experiential background before you became involved in online and distance learning [ODL]?*

    I have an undergraduate degree in vet science. I came back to university because I was working as a music journalist. I came back to university to study journalism and also studies in religion. I ended up doing post-grad work on studies in religion, looking at esotericism and divination. While I was doing my PhD, I did a graduate certificate in higher education.

    After I got my PhD, I taught in studies of religion at the University of Queensland, and I completed a Masters of Education in ICT [Information Communication Technology] from Macquarie University.

2. *In what year did you begin to look specifically into ODL?*

    I began my PhD when I was 34, and I was teaching from the very beginning, so that must have been about 2002. We were using the Blackboard learning management system [LMS] at that time, so I was using it straightaway.

    I was working at a face-to-face university. The University of Queensland, where I was working, is a face-to-face university, but I was already aware that a lot of my students had to work. A lot of them couldn't get to class, so I would make my Blackboard site such that they wouldn't have to come to class. I would give the students sufficient links, recordings, and other resources so that they didn't have to come to class; a lot still did, but some didn't. So, even though it was a face-to-face university, I was already designing for distance learning.

3. *What were the circumstances in your world that initiated this interest in ODL?*

    I always had really close relationships with my students. I was talking to them a lot. We would have group lunches once a week or something like that. I realized that so many were working, or they had caring responsibilities; they were parents or had family members that they were looking after. It was really hard for some of them to get to class. That's what made me think about distance learning, even though my university wasn't, and still isn't a distance learning university. The University of Queensland is not a distance learning university.

    So it was that recognition; that my students' lives were challenging and diverse was what made me think about distance learning.

4. *Which female researchers or female colleagues may have piqued your interest in ODL?*

    There was Dr. Caroline Steele. She also worked in the Teaching and Educational Development Institute [TEDI] at the University of Queensland. She was very involved in not so much distance learning but e-learning, with a view, I guess, to distance learning.

Also, Professor Belinda Tynan, that was at the University of New England.

There is Dr. Sue Gregory, who is also at the University of New England. She is still there. She would be a good person for you to talk to. She got me thinking about virtual worlds and using those sorts of immersive environments for distance learning.

And Dr. Julie Willems, who was also at the University of New England. The University of New England was, and still is, a distance learning university. So that was the hotbed of that kind of activity and that kind of research there.

5. *Who would you identify as the early female leaders/founders in the field of DE and/or ODL?*

Probably those people that I just mentioned, particularly Professor Belinda Tynan, who is now at RMIT [Royal Melbourne Institute of Technology] in Melbourne. She was certainly very early into the field.

I am mostly aware of Australian researchers because I wasn't an education academic at that time. I was an academic for studies in religion at that time, so I wasn't looking too far afield to see what people were doing. I'm sure that there were other female leaders in our field internationally. I just wasn't aware of them at that time.

6. *What are some of the goals that you strove to achieve in the field of ODL?*

I really wanted that distance learning experience to make the students feel at home. I didn't want them to feel alone. So I put a lot of effort into creating community in my online courses. I would really try to have active discussion boards. I would do that by asking silly questions (and some good questions, of course), but silly questions like, "What's the greatest rock and roll album of all time? What's your favourite book?" After they did that, they were more likely to contribute to our discussion boards. We always got full engagement.

I always liked to have a forum called "Ask a Dumb Question," where people could ask questions anonymously so that they wouldn't feel silly when they're asking questions. I would plant questions in there as well to things that I thought the students might need answers to.

It was really about making my students feel at home. I also tried to be very cognizant of the fact that the Internet was not very good in Australia at that time. You might say that it is still not very good in some places. So I would always to have a couple alternatives for students if they had bad Internet connections. I would make some things a smaller file size, record the audio, or offer alternative resources or stuff like that. So in case people didn't have good Internet access, they could still download the resources. I tried not to have streaming resources also for that reason. And I flagged what were core resources so that if people had difficulty downloading something or looking at something, they could decide whether to bother or not by determining whether or not it was a core resource. I guess that I was just trying to make it as easy as possible.

I also tried to use all of the file types. So, when Microsoft ended up with .docx formats, I still used .doc formats so that people could still read them. I just tried to cover as wide of range of potentials of what was out there.

I wanted it to be a very engaging experience. I was cognizant of the fact that these students were paying a lot of money to do these courses and programmes. So I wanted to ensure that they had as good and as rich of an experience as possible. I wrote a short piece that went with every week's lesson, talking about what we were doing, when we were doing it, how they should go about it. I didn't just pop the resources up there and hope for the best.

I would have synchronous sessions with students as well, again, so that they wouldn't feel that they were alone and that they were part of a cohort.

So I guess those were the main things that I was thinking of when I was doing that stuff.

7. *What are some of your accomplishments in the field of ODL that you would like to share?*

There are a couple of things that I am probably particularly proud of. One was the use of virtual worlds in my teaching and learning. In particular, early on, I was an early adopter of Second Life. Even though my undergraduate cohort was geographically quite close to me, my post-graduate cohort wasn't, so they were doing PhDs and masters' at a distance. I would have post-grad meetings in Second Life. I created a space in Second Life for my post-grads where we could meet. That was great. I could get my students into our Second Life Island to hook up with my students in Tasmania, and so on.

For my undergraduate cohort, I tried to do a lot of experiential learning. Because I was teaching studies in religion at that time, I created an island called UQ Religion Bazaar, which had a representation of buildings of many faiths. So there was a Christian church, an Orthodox synagogue, a Freemasons' temple, and a Hindu temple to Ganesha; I had a stack of buildings. My students would investigate the religions and perhaps recreate an activity or piece of history from within particular spaces, learn about the religions, and report back to the class on that. So we had some really great activities within that.

I can remember one thing that I used to get my classes to do was to dress their avatars. I'm not so sure that I would do this now, because I'm not sure that it would be considered a very respectful thing to do. But at the time, I would get them to make their avatars female, irrespective of whether they were male or female students and dress their avatars in hijabs and then go to a public space in Second Life and try to experience life as a Muslim woman in the world and to hear what people said. The discussions that occurred because people were very unkind and unfriendly and fairly horrible to my students dressed in this way really turned some of them right around. Some of them who had not be sympathetic at the beginning of the activities became really sympathetic at the end of them, having experienced what an ordinary Muslim woman dressed in a hijab would be experiencing.

So I am proud of my work in Second Life, but without a doubt, I am most proud of the work that I have done with prisons. Getting computers into prisons for distance learning has been really hard, but really rewarding. The computers that I take into prisons don't have Internet access. We've developed a system whereby we have an online kiosk that prison educators can access, and they download materials. They load the materials onto specially adapted computers going to the prisons that don't have Internet access.

We've created software for these computers that scans for illegal activities. The Internet, Bluetooth, recorders, and cameras are disabled. This special software will scan the computers all of the time in case the learners try to re-enable the software or otherwise do anything naughty.

We've developed our version of a learning management system. We use Moodle that will work offline. I believe it is the first time that it has been done successfully in the world, but we individually install Moodle onto a laptop computer that can be opened and closed repeatedly, and Moodle stays stable. It's an instance of Moodle that is not hosted. I understand that has not been done before.

The learners in prison get the whole experience of being a distance learner. They see the videos; they access their resources. Obviously, the courses have been modified so that they can run in the offline environment, so there are no links out to YouTube. We have to find other resources that work with Moodle and load them. They are not able to interact with YouTube, they can't participate in discussion boards – that would be collusion in a prison, and they are not allowed to do that, and obviously we cannot do that offline. So there are modifications that need to be done. We have developed a whole methodology around doing that.

To date, we have had 1,700 prisoners using that particular technology for Australian jurisdictions. So, I'm probably most proud of my prison work.

8. *What are some of the challenges that you faced in the field of ODL over the years?*

[One challenge is] that there is not Internet everywhere. Even in my work at the University of Southern Queensland – that's a regional university – for those students, the Internet is not always available, or for some students, they are not able to access it. So that's definitely been challenging to try and figure out that and how to get digital distance learning to those students.

Prejudice, I guess, is an issue, especially in my work at the prisons. There are a lot of people who don't think very favourably of prisoners. And it's not that I don't understand that when we incarcerate people, we deprive them of their liberty. That is supposed to be their punishment, not everything else that we inflict on top of that. They should still have access to education, and when we don't provide that, I feel that it is a violation of their human rights. Trying to get people to work with me to get education into prisons has definitely been challenging.

I think also there is definitely – and this probably getting worse, I think – but there is definitely a tendency to not listen to female academics as much as male academics. There is definitely discrimination there. I can say something, but my voice won't be as loud as a male academic working in the field. That can be very frustrating. Although I can see it with my own work, I probably see it more with other female academics who have struggled to have their voices heard. That's a particular challenge for females working in open and distance learning.

Another challenge is to get people to do something new. They just want to do something that they have always done. That's particularly true, I guess, when moving from paper-based distance learning to digital distance learning. A lot of people still believe in this day and age that distance learning needs to be a whole stack of .pdfs put up in the learning management system with nothing else, and no other adaptation of their approach or pedagogy or anything. So that's definitely a challenge.

I could probably go on, but these are probably the main challenges.

9. *What was the "state of DE" when you first entered the field as opposed to ODL in 2019?*

I guess when I first started, the tools were not as sophisticated. Certainly, the marketplace wasn't as crowded. So the university that I worked for was probably the first in Australia in this particular strand in this space, the first online programme. I think that might have been around 1999, so a bit before my time. But even then, when I came into it later, there weren't that many online universities or even face-to-face universities weren't using a learning management system. Now they are all using learning management systems. Many traditional face-to-face universities are now putting their courses or programmes online. So it is a very crowded marketplace.

I'd say that there's a lot more flexibility in distance learning now. When I first started everyone pretty much adhered to the same timelines. Students would enrol in the beginning of Semester One or Semester Two, or if your university had a Semester Three, maybe there. But now there a lot of universities offering multiple intakes, seven or eight intakes through the year, or starting whenever students want. So there is more flexibility and more tools.

I think that there has been a shift away from just providing resources. Back in the day, distance learning was still correspondence and was pretty unidirectional. It was from the educator to the student. Now I think that there is a lot more group activity and collaboration. The teacher is far less prominent in distance learning than they used to be, in good distance learning anyway. Unfortunately, in 2019, I think that we can still find courses and programmes that are no more sophisticated than those first programmes offered in 1999. So as much as things have changed, some are still the same as well.

10. *What interesting memories would you like to share about the beginning of your work in ODL?*

I can remember my first encounter with a learning management system, and that was quite significant. I was doing a post-grad course, the one that I referred to earlier, the post-grad certificate that I was doing when I was doing my PhD. Most of it was face-to-face, but one lecture unit was through WebCT. I was so angry. I was so furious because I thought that the lecturer was shirking his responsibility. I remember looking at it. It took forever to download stuff. He wasn't aware of how long it took for some things to download. A seven-and-a-half-megabit file would take an hour and half to download on my dial-up Internet. I was so furious at him. Every opportunity that I had, I riled and riled against it. I complained bitterly to all of my colleagues and friends about how terrible it was that he introduced this thing called "WebCT" into my life.

I was sitting at the university cafeteria one day, having a cup of coffee under the trees, and I thought, "Wow! In five years' time, will there be more or less computers than now?" And it kind of just really dawned on me that of course there were going to be more computers, and computers were going to be a bigger part of our lives, so I had better get onboard with this. From that moment on, I stopped bleating about how awful WebCT was (although it was pretty awful at that time) and started thinking about "How can I use this in my own work? What might I be able to do?"

So I talked to the lecturer instead of being furious at him. I told him, "You know that seven-and-a-half-megabit file takes an hour and a half to download, and that if you did this, this, and this, that would actually be a smaller file?" It was kind of a realization to me that this could be a really powerful, wonderful opportunity before us and not the terrible devastation that I thought it was.

I had a similar kind of revelation when Second Life came into my life. I was talking to a friend, and he said, "I heard on the radio about this thing that is like a world, and you log into it. Your virtual self goes around and stuff. You can meet people and—"

I said, "Why would I do that? What a stupid thing to do! I have trouble leading my first life, let alone my second life!" And then, again, that realization: "Wow. I've been worried about my students being lonely. Maybe this is somewhere where we could meet."

So I made an avatar and went into Second Life. It scared the bejesus out of me. As soon as my avatar landed, people started talking to me. It was like . . . I just quickly shut down my computer because I didn't know what to say to them. I didn't know who they were.

I eventually went back, and this time, when someone came and talked to me, I actually talked back to them. I found out where they were. They were from somewhere in the USA. And it really occurred to me what a great tool this could be. So as soon as I could, I started bringing my students in there just to meet and explore and do stuff. Even before I had my own island, I would bring them in to explore different areas. That would have been around 2007, so probably not early in terms of distance learning, but pretty early in terms of my distance learning.

So you will be pleased to know that when there is a new tool released now, I am actually a bit more optimistic about it and how I might use it.

And I guess probably it was the realization that I was actually beginning to know my distance learning students. Even though I was talking to them through the learning management system over the Internet, I actually knew them better than my face-to-face students. I can't remember a specific memory about that, but I can remember being just blown away about that particular realization. I knew more about those people who I never met than I knew about those people sitting in front of me every week in class.

I guess also in terms of interesting memories is the way that some of us are so enthusiastic about using technology for distance learning that, to some extent, we have forgotten about those people who might have trouble accessing it; this is particularly true with Second Life. Now most computers will run Second Life, although Second Life might be shutting down soon. But now any computer can run Second Life, whereas in those days, it was only pretty high-end, snazzy computers that could run something like a virtual world where the graphics would work and stuff like that. So a lot of my early memories of using distance learning technology was about struggling with the technology and spending a lot of time trying to make that technology work.

Now I am the queen of the backup plan So, if I have a technology that I am using, I also have a backup for those people who can't use it, or are struggling or are having difficulties of some kind.

So, I guess, yeah, those are my most significant memories.

11. *What were your specific ODL research interests, and have they changed/evolved over the years?*

Oh boy, they have changed. I'm one of these terrible people who are interested in everything. Anything I see, I can be distracted by. In the beginning, for me, distance learning was about alternative access to my students, my face-to-face students. When I discovered the wonderful world of open educational resources, I found all of these fascinating things created by people much smarter and more talented than me that I could use in my teaching; that was absolutely fabulous. So I was interested in open educational resources. It's not that I'm not interested in them now – I am, but unfortunately, the rest of the world had not caught up with me. More of the world has caught up with me now.

From there, I went to immersive virtual world environments. So I was really interested in Second Life virtual worlds and what we could do there. I was teaching studies in religion. It was just so fantastic to be able to take my students to that environment and have them explore all of the religious sites that existed in Second Life at that time. Also, to create my own as well, and have them wander around there and do stuff.

Before that, a piece of assessment for my religious students was for them to go to a place of worship in the real world and attend some kind of celebration or service or prayer or something, and observe and write notes and stuff. Now, my university was in Brisbane, which was a big city on the Eastern Seaboard, where most of the people are very boring, middle aged, and white. So mostly it meant that for that piece of assessment, they went to a church. I didn't think that gave them a very broad view of what religion was. And also, I was troubled about them going and observing people like they were zoo animals. I was a bit worried about that. I was also worried about the logistics of it because Brisbane is a big, sprawled-out city with very poor public transport, particularly then. So I felt bad about sending them off on these quests. I was also concerned legally about what the university's responsibility would be should – heaven forbid – one of the students got hit by a car or something while out doing work for the university. So Second Life allowed me to get rid of a lot of those constraints and also for students to question, experiment, and ask without risking upsetting and offending anyone, which I thought was a pretty high danger of in the real world. So that was the virtual environments that I was really interested in.

Then I got really interested in haptic feedback and the other things that you could do virtually, like we could get students who were studying at a distance to have an experience with (this is a bad example) surgery or something that required some movement, feeling, and stuff like that. So I was also interested in MulSeMedia [multiple sensorial media] media, specifically tactile stuff and also olfactory stuff I got into for a while.

One project that I was involved in at the University of South Queensland was to look at if we could make an Aboriginal garden in the real world with lots of plants used by Aboriginal Australians for either food or medicine or whatever. These plants would have stories around them and about them. What I wanted to do was replicate that in Second Life, but also be able to replicate the smells of the plants into Second Life. So I looked into that for a while; it was going to be possible. Not that we've got funding for it. But to send something little that you could hook to your computer that would allow students at a distance to have access to those smells and sights associated with special plants. And also to capture the stories about those plants from the Aboriginal Elders, too, because those Elders are now dying, and that knowledge will be lost. So I was kind of interested in that: all the sounds, smells, sights, and experiences and trying to replicate those in immersive virtual environments.

Then I kind of went completely the other way, only accidently. Instead of thinking about high-tech stuff, I started thinking about low-tech stuff for prisoners and how we could overcome the barriers of how to get technologies into prisons to provide access to education. That was something that I hadn't thought about. The reason why I did think about it was that our university was undergoing restructuring. I don't know about your university, but our university was always undergoing constant restructures, and we lost a staff member. She rang me up after she had left to say that she had started a project looking at how to get technologies into prisons so that our prisoners could have access to the same sort of digital resources that our other students had. I thought, "Oh, I suppose, just as a favour, I'll go and have a meeting with this academic and just see where it goes from there." And that's where that interest began.

That was the exact opposite of what I had been looking at. I had been looking at cutting-edge technologies using gaming consoles and all of those kind of things, and now I was looking at bare bones: getting something from the university to provide access to digital education. Because the University of Southern Queensland was a distance learning university, it had television studios and great facilities for making multimedia materials, all sorts of great things, and yet our prison students weren't getting any of those things. They were getting a block of printed text. And in prison, probably between 30% and 50% of those students are dyslexic or have other learning disabilities. A lot of them have significant levels of hearing loss, all sorts of acquired brain injuries; every kind of compounding factor you can think of happens in a prison. So giving those people big blocks of printed text is firstly, really intimidating for them, and secondly, they just don't deal with it.

Thinking about how we might get some of those resources into a prison, computers into a prison, was really a change for me. Anyway, obviously I stuck with it. I'm still doing it. Now I'm doing it in New Zealand as well.

12. *Could you please describe the learning environment that you currently work in (e.g., geographic and institutional setting, student demographics)?*

Now I am working in New Zealand. I'm still with the University of Southern Queensland, but now my substantive role is within the Department of Corrections in New Zealand. We have about 10,000 prisoners: 92% of them would be male, about 8% female. The real challenge here – well, there are a lot of challenges – but the real challenge here is that Māori are vastly over-represented. They are about 15% of the non-incarcerated population and 51% of the incarcerated population. So the Indigenous over-representation is huge in New Zealand. So there are all sorts of cultural considerations to take into account with that.

In Australia, I was able to slowly introduce technologies. In moving to New Zealand and working with the Department of Corrections here, I am kind of back at the beginning in terms of getting them to experiment with computers and technologies and so on and so forth. So that is a really challenging environment.

Here, too, they have a different view of education. In Australia, I was working in introducing higher education into prisons. In New Zealand, there is very little higher education in prisons. I could probably count the number of students studying at the undergraduate level in New Zealand on two hands, I suspect. So not only is it technologically different; it's also the levels of education that are different, and the cohorts are quite different.

There is an advantage in having 51% Māori. I can now make the argument that because they are our biggest cohort. . . . We have about 51% Māori, 38% white New Zealanders, and the remaining 14 or whatever percent from the Pacific Islands around here. So Māori are our biggest cohort by a long way. I can make the argument that Māori ways of learning are preferable because they are our biggest cohort. And guess what? Everything about Māori education is everything that we love about education, everything that good educators know is important about education, things like putting the student at the centre of learning, basically social-constructivist learning. It's a good argument to use to get away from didactic teaching and learning, which is the predominate style in prisons here. So I'm using Māori education as a good excuse to get better education for everyone. If I can pull this off, every single one of our incarcerated students will be better off.

Geographically, it's interesting. New Zealand has a North and a South Island. I'm on the South Island, which is far less populated. We have fewer prisons. We are a long way off from everywhere else. That's kind of good. That's actually one of the reasons why I moved here, to get away from everyone else. It's bad because people here lose perspective because they are in such a small country a long way away from everyone. They forget that the rest of the world exists. So they feel quite isolated and can work in a silo. Even Australia seems a long way off from New Zealand. The good thing is that they are not encumbered by those other beliefs, either. So it's their strength and their weakness.

Because it is a small country dealing with a relatively small population, I believe that we can be agile in our learning. Learning in prisons is often distance learning necessarily because there's a limit as to how many instructors can go in. Obviously, we can't take the learner to where the learning is. So it is necessarily distance education.

The age range is probably spread, and that is probably noteworthy. We have prisoners here – I don't know; the upper age limit would be their 80s. There are people in their 80s in our prisons. They are eligible for training and education when they are in there. I know for a fact that we have students in their 60s and their 70s here. We do have that here. The lower age level would be 18. They need to be 18 to be in prison, or at least 17. And we do have specialist youth units with a younger demographic, and the way that we approach those is slightly different. But it is pretty well a wide spread.

The only other thing probably to be said in addition to that is that prisoners tend to be a little bit older when they become interested in education. When they are young and they are first in prison, they think it is all very exciting. I would be terrified, but they think it is exciting. They are not sick of it yet. By the time someone's done their second, third, fourth, or fifth stint in prison, they are sick of it. They don't want to come back, and they are looking for something to do. So sometimes it is harder for us to engage those younger people in education, who arguably need it more. And so the demographic is probably a little bit older than those people who are attempting the same qualifications or entering the same programmes on the outside.

13. *Is there anything else you [would] like to address?*

I think that readers 50 years from now should have a good, hard look at distance education to see if it has really changed. I think that is the danger; we keep reinventing the wheel. As I said, I think back to my early distance learning work; I think that it probably looks the same as people's distance learning work in 2019. So, I think, check to make sure that it is really changing.

I think also that we need to be cognizant of the fact that when we use a new technology, we lose some people and to look at those people and how we can bring them along. When we introduced the Internet and put everything on the Internet, we lost all those people who can't access the Internet. And access is not just theoretical access; I think that we have to remember that as well. We know there are people who can't afford Internet access even if it is available.

I think we also need to be aware of our particular cohorts. We need to ensure that our distance learning is safe and good for everyone. That relates to gender, ethnicity, and it relates even to introverts and extroverts. I'm an introvert. Some things just don't suit me, and I won't participate in them. I would appreciate an alternative. I've always tried to create those alternatives for my students – alternative assessments and stuff like that.

I remember asking a class how many essays they had to write in a particular semester we were in because they were in, on average, four courses. On average, they had two papers to write for each course, so many of them were writing eight essays a semester. How good does a student need to be at writing an essay? So I would design alternative assessments for my students. I think that's important. And I think designing alternative assessments for who can't access our tools is important.

In knowing anything about me, I'd say that I'm just an enthusiastic amateur. I don't think that it's hard. You just need to think about what your student may need. I think that you have to meet your student wherever they are. Don't expect them to always come to you – and I don't mean geographically; I mean going to their level and going to where they are comfortable and bringing them with you. I've tried to do that.

It's not rocket science. That's the other thing; it's just not rocket science. I just think good learning takes good planning. I think you should do stuff, even if you are scared. What I am thinking about here is to let people look at what you are doing and examine your practice. I know that is still a big one for people. A lot of educators won't let anyone else into their learning management systems to see what they have done. I think the consequences are pretty horrific. When I've finally gotten into some other people's courses, they have been pretty horrendous. I think that could have been spared if we had the courage to let other people into our courses sooner to see what we're doing and to reinforce the good things, too.

I think it is a really exciting field. It behooves us to think about the "open" in open and distance learning as well, and to get our stuff far and wide because learning is transformative, and it can change people's lives. I have seen that no more evident than in prison. I've seen people's lives completely turned around.

A lot of the prisoners that I deal with have had very difficult relationships and experiences with formal education. You can imagine being in a classroom, being dyslexic, not knowing what is going on, falling farther and farther behind, the teacher yelling at you, always getting bad assessment marks, and so on and so forth, being excluded from activities and that kind of thing. They were often really traumatized by that. So I think that by the time they are in prison and thinking about learning spaces, and we recreate those learning spaces – the desks, the teacher standing at the front – I think it is a very special kind of cruelty. It's a terrible thing for us to do with our learners. So that's why distance learning can be so good. If we can get student-centred distance learning, where they are not in that situation and not having those kinds of experiences, they can productively learn and move forward. Because of their traumatic experiences with formal education, they often think they're stupid.

The other thing is that education is often at completely the wrong time for boys. When they should be in formal education, they are busy showing their bravado, thinking about girls, doing all of those sorts of things, doing outside stuff, and particularly if they can't do it, they're not engaged. And when they fail, they think they're stupid. They think that they have no brains and that they're destined for bad things.

When I actually get to see them and talk to them, I say to them, "Wow! Education was at a completely wrong time for you. It happened at a time when you weren't ready for it. That's bad of us, not bad of you. You're not stupid. You can study. You can learn something." When I see them, it is like a weight dropping off of their shoulders. For the first time, they contemplate thinking about what it means to not be stupid. They can start thinking of themselves as having something to offer the world: that they're not dumb, that they might even be smart. I'm hooked on seeing that look on their faces.

Would I be out of place just to tell a short story about how education has turned someone around?

I: *I think that it would be wonderful.*

OK. In Australia, we had what was called the "Stolen Generations," where the government would take Aboriginal children away from their families. This happened over a long time, maybe 70 or 80 years. A lot of Aboriginal children were taken from their families and put either with foster parents, or they were put into orphanages. Very frequently (and it happens all over the world), these children were sexually abused and beaten and used as slave labour. They had a very difficult time. It was obviously very traumatic for the children, it was traumatic for their families, and it was traumatic for the communities from where they came. The result was that these children would lose their culture and be unaware of where they came from or their heritage. Most often, good parenting was not modelled for them. In turn, they didn't become good parents. They became bad parents very often.

So there was a man in a prison that I would visit. He was one of the Stolen Generations children. He was taken away from his family at six. His mother was Aboriginal, and his father was white. As a child, he was quite pale, so he was taken away from his family. From about the age of fourteen, he was in trouble with the authorities, so he went into the juvenile justice system at the age of fourteen. He didn't behave. He was violent. He was hurting. He was traumatized. After murdering somebody, he made a ready transition into the adult justice system. He was very violent. He was a drug user. They say that there are no drugs in prisons, but most prisons are awash with drugs, unfortunately. And so he was also a drug addict while he was inside. He was known as a tough man of the prison.

Aboriginal Elders very frequently go into prisons to visit with Indigenous prisoners. One of the Elders encouraged this man to start thinking about reading and writing, because he was illiterate, and to think about doing some education. So he engaged with some very basic numeracy and literacy training in the prison. But, basically, he taught himself to read and write while he was held in solitary confinement. He taught himself to read and write using the Bible, using Archie comics, and using those funny, thin little Western novels. (I don't know if you remember those.) He taught himself to read and write that way. He did a bit more education; he did some basic schooling. Then there was a man at University of Southern Queensland called Tas Bedford; he was very interested in prison education. He talked to this man and encouraged him to enrol in pre-tertiary studies at the University of Southern Queensland using the technologies I've been talking about.

And so this man enrolled in the tertiary preparation programme with us. With a laptop computer, he very slowly struggled through, but he got there. And when he finished the tertiary preparation programme, he then went into undergraduate studies with us.

Now to hear him speak, he is a changed man. Where once he used to wake up in the morning, and he used to think about whom he could hurt and whom he could damage, now he was waking up thinking about study, and he was excited to be learning. He would get up at two o'clock in the morning because that is when prison is quiet. Prisons are really noisy places, but prison was quiet at two. He would get up, and he would study and work. And now his life is completely turned around.

It's a long time until he gets out of prison still. He has been very naughty. Now he is no longer a drug user. He very proudly tells me that he has completed 37 clean urines. He is now a role model and mentor to other young Aboriginal men who come into prison. He is encouraging them to study. He speaks very eloquently against violence and about domestic violence. He is helping those young Aboriginal men get in contact with their culture, reconnect with their culture, and also guides them into study. He says that for the first time, he knows that when he gets out of prison this time, he is going to stay out of prison. He'd be my age or a little older, and since 14, he's been out of prison for four months. So I'm thinking for him to say that he knows that he won't go back in is huge. He is unrecognizable as the person that he used to be. I am so proud of him.

And I have so many stories like that. So it is just really worth taking the time and finding ways to overcome those challenges because the differences that it makes to those lives is just unbelievable, and particularly so when talking about prisoners. Distance learning helps them imagine a new life for themselves and for their families, so it's totally worth putting the work into.

I have a million of them [that is, stories]. It is just amazing!

14. *Can you suggest names of other female pioneers in DE or ODL that you think we should include in the book?*

I think Sue Gregory, whom I talked about; I think she did a lot of work and still does a lot of work in Second Life and online, just generally. She's really great. [She's at] the University of New England.

Probably also Belinda Tynan at RMIT, I think. I've got her email address; I can send it to you.

Julie Willems also; again, [she's] a pioneer in using technology in distance learning. She's done some really great research around social media and disaster, which is probably not related but still very interesting.

If I think of any others, I will let you know.

Publications

Books

Murphy, A., Farley, H., Dyson, L., & Jones, H. (Eds.). (2017). *Mobile learning in higher education in the Asia Pacific: Harnessing trends and challenging orthodoxies.* Springer.

Book Chapters

Farley, H. (2010). Interoperability, learning designs and virtual worlds: Issues and strategies. In F. Lazarinis, S. Green, & E. Pearson (Eds.), *Handbook of research on e-Learning standards and interoperability: Frameworks and issues.* Information Science Reference.

Farley, H. (2011). Using multi-user virtual environments in tertiary teaching: Lessons learned through the UQ Religion Bazaar Project. In C. Wankel (Ed.), *Teaching arts and science with the new social media* (pp. 211–237). Emerald Group Publishing.

Farley, H. (2013). Facilitating immersion in virtual worlds: An examination of the physical, virtual, social and pedagogical factors leading to engagement and flow. In B. Tynan, J. Willems, & R. James (Eds.), *Outlooks and opportunities in blended and distance learning* (pp. 189–203). IGI Global.

Farley, H. (2014). Virtual Worlds in higher education: The challenges, expectations and delivery. In M. Gosper & D. Ifenthaler (Eds.), *Curriculum models for the 21st century* (pp. 325–349). Springer.

Farley, H. (2016). The reality of authentic learning in virtual worlds. In S. Gregory, M. J. W. Lee, B. Dalgarno, & B. Tynan (Eds.), *Learning in virtual worlds: Research and applications* (pp. 129–149). Athabasca University Press.

Farley, H., & Murphy, A. (2013). Developing a framework for evaluating the impact and sustainability of mobile learning initiatives in higher education. In R. Sims & M. Kigotho (Eds.), *Education across time and Space: Meeting the diverse needs of the distance learner* (pp. 27–34). http://au.blurb.com/books/4061067-education-across-space-and-time

Farley, H., & Murphy, A. (2015). Evaluation of mobile teaching and learning projects, introduction. In Y. A. Zhang (Ed.), *Handbook of mobile teaching and learning: Design, development, adoption, partnership, evaluation and expectation* (1st ed., pp. 685–689). Springer-Verlag.

Farley, H., Murphy, A., Todd, N. A., Lane, M., Midgley, W., & Johnson, C. (2015). Moving towards the effective evaluation of mobile learning initiatives in higher education institutions. In Y. A. Zhang (Ed.), *Handbook of mobile teaching and learning: Design, development, adoption, partnership, evaluation and expectation* (1st ed., pp. 721–740). Springer-Verlag.

Farley, H., & Pike, A. (2018) Research on the inside: Overcoming obstacles to completing a postgraduate degree in prison. In F. Padró, R. Erwee, M. Harmes, & P. Danaher (Eds.), *Postgraduate education in higher education: University development and administration*. Springer. https://doi.org/10.1007/978-981-10-0468-1_39-1

Farley, H., & Song, H. (2015). Mobile learning in Southeast Asia: Opportunities and challenges. In J. A. Zhang (Ed.), *Handbook of mobile teaching and learning: Design, development, adoption, partnership, evaluation and expectation* (1st ed., pp. 403–419). Springer-Verlag.

Farley, H., & Steel, C. (2011). Multiple sensorial media and presence in 3D environments. In G. Ghinea, F. Andres, & S. Gulliver (Eds.), *Multiple sensorial media advances and applications: New developments in MulSeMedia*. IGI Global.

Jones, J. K., Farley, H., & Murphy, A. (2017). Virtual Worlds as restorative Environments. In S. Gregory & D. Wood (Eds.), *Authentic virtual world education: Facilitating cultural engagement and creativity* (pp. 45–59). Springer.

Lee, C., Farley, H., Cox, J., & Seymour, S. (2017). Tackling Indigenous incarceration through promoting engagement with higher education. In J. Frawley (Ed.), *Indigenous pathways and transitions into higher education: From policy to practice*. Springer.

Moloney, C., & Farley, H. (2015). Digital skills in healthcare practice. In J. Lawrence, C. Perrin, & E. Kiernan (Eds.), *Building professional nursing communication* (pp. 155–181). Cambridge University Press.

Murphy, A., & Farley, H. (2017). Supporting the sustainable implementation of mobile learning for higher education in the Asia-Pacific region. In A. Murphy, H. Farley, L. Dyson, & H. Jones (Eds.), *Mobile learning in higher education in the Asia Pacific: Harnessing trends and challenging orthodoxies*. Springer.

Rees, S., Moloney, C., & Farley, H. (2015). Mobile learning initiatives in nursing education. In Y. A. Zhang (Ed.), *Handbook of mobile teaching and learning: Design, development, adoption, partnership, evaluation and expectation* (1st ed., pp. 275–289). Springer-Verlag.

Rees, S., Moloney, C., & Farley, H. (in press). Mobile learning evolution: Trends in nursing education. In Y. A. Zhang (Eds.), *Handbook of mobile teaching and learning: Design, development, adoption, partnership, evaluation and expectation* (2nd ed.). Springer-Verlag.

Willems, J., Farley, H., Ellis, A., McCormick, D., & Daniel, W. (2013). Supervising higher degree research (HDR) candidates at a distance: What do emerging virtual world technologies have to offer? In B. Tynan, J. Willems, & R. James (Eds.), *Outlooks and opportunities in blended and distance learning* (pp. 369–382). IGI Global.

Journal Articles

Al Lily, A. E., Foland, J., Stoloff, D., Gogus, A., Erguvan, I. D., Awshwar, M. T., . . . Schrader, P. G. (2016). Academic domains as political battlegrounds: A global enquiry by 99 academics in the fields of education and technology. *Information Development Journal, 33*(3). https://doi.org/10.1177/0266666916646415

Cochrane, T., Kearney, M., & Farley, H. (Eds.). (2017). Augmenting learner-generated contexts via mobile augmented reality and mobile virtual reality [Special issue]. *Australasian Journal of Educational Technology*, *33*(6). https://doi.org/10.14742/ajet.4132

Farley, H. (2015). Virtual worlds in distance education: Opportunities and challenges (J. Xiao, Trans.). *Distance Education in China*, *11*, 34–44. https://doi.org/10.13541/j.cnki.chinade.2015.11.008

Farley, H. (2016). Digital technologies for learning in prison: What one Australian university is doing. *Custodial Review* (77), 18–21.

Farley, H. (2018). Using 3D worlds in prison: Driving, learning and escape. *Journal of Virtual Worlds Research*, *1*(1), 1–11. https://doi.org/10.4101/jvwr.v11i1.7304

Farley, H., & Doyle, J. (2014). Using digital technologies to implement distance education for incarcerated students: a case study from an Australian regional university. *Open Praxis*, *6*(4), 357–363.

Farley, H., & Hopkins, S. (2016). The prison is another country: Incarcerated students and (im)mobility in Australian prisons. *Critical Studies in Education*, 1–18. https://doi.org/10.1080/17508487.2016.1255240

Farley, H., & Murphy, A. (2013). Mobile learning in higher education: Moving towards a framework for efficacy and sustainability. *Distance Education in China*, *17*(9).

Farley, H., & Pike, A. (2016). Engaging prisoners in education: Reducing risk and recidivism. *Advancing Corrections*, *1*(1), 65–73. http://icpa.ca/library_category/advancing-corrections-journal/

Farley, H., Cliffe, N., Reardon-Smith, K., Mushtaq, S., Loch, A., & Lindesay, J. (2013). Sweetening climate information for sugar cane farmers with Second Life machinima. *Journal of Virtual Studies*, *4*(1), 34.

Farley, H., Ellis, A., Hassett, A., & Jacobson, N. (2013). Encke virtual university collaboration: Bringing educators together in Second Life. *Journal of Virtual Studies*, *4*(1).

Farley, H., Gregory, S., Grant, S., Butler, D., Jacka, L., Oriwn, L., & Jones, J. K. (2013). The Australian and New Zealand virtual worlds working group: A collaborative community of practice. *Journal of Virtual Studies*, *4*(1), 34.

Farley, H., Harmes, K., & Pike, A. (2019). Identity, bias and diversity behind bars: Overcoming barriers to education for incarcerated students. *International Journal of Bias, Identity and Diversities in Education*, *4*(1).

Farley, H., Jacobsen, N., Hassett, A., Cliffe, N., Reardon-Smith, K., Mushtaq, S., Lindesay, J., & Loch, A. (2013). Machinima as a discussion support system for sugar cane farmers. *Journal of Virtual Studies*, *4*(1).

Farley, H., Murphy, A., & Bedford, T. (2014). Providing simulated online and mobile learning experiences in a prison education setting: Lessons learned from the PLEIADES pilot project. *International Journal of Mobile and Blended Learning*, *6*(1), 17–32.

Farley, H., Murphy, A., Johnson, C., Carter, B., Lane, M., Midgley, W., & Koronios, A. (2015). How do students use their mobile devices to support learning? A case study from an Australian regional university. *Journal of Interactive Media in Education*, *2015*(1), 1–13. https://doi.org/http://doi.org/10.5334/jime.ar

Farley, H., Murphy, A., Jones, J. K., & Moodie, D. (2013). RejuveNation Island: Attentional restoration for pre-service teachers in Second Life. *Journal of Virtual Studies*, *4*(1).

Farley, H., Pike, A., Demiray, U., & Tanglang, N. (2016). Delivering digital higher education into prisons: The cases of four universities in Australia, UK, Turkey and Nigeria. *GLOKALde*, *2*(2), 147–166.

Farley, H., Pike, A., Demiray, U., & Tanglang, N. (2016). Delivering digital higher education into prisons: The cases of four universities in Australia, UK, Turkey and Nigeria (J. Xiao, Trans). *Distance Education in China*, *7*(26), 35–43. https://doi.org/10.13541/j.cnki.chinade.20160726.008

Gregory, S., Scutter, S., Jacka, L., McDonald, M., Farley, H., & Newman, C. (2015). Barriers and enablers to the use of virtual worlds in higher education: An exploration of educator perceptions, attitudes and experiences. *Journal of Educational Technology & Society*, *18*(1), 3–12.

Harmes, M., Farley, H., & Hopkins, S. (2019). Beyond incarcerated identities: Identity, bias and barriers to higher education in Australian prisons. *International Journal of Bias, Identity and Diversities in Education*, *4*(1).

Harmes, M., Farley, H., & Pike, A. (Eds.). (2018). Educating the incarcerated – Bias and identity [Special issue]. *International Journal of Bias, Identity and Diversity in Education*, *4*(1).

Hopkins, S., & Farley, H. (2014). A prisoners' island: Teaching disconnected incarcerated tertiary students in the digital age. *Journal of Prison Education and Re-entry*, *1*(1), 42–51.

Hopkins, S., & Farley, H. (2015). e-Learning incarcerated: Prison education and digital inclusion. *The International Journal of Humanities Education*, *13*(2), 37–45.

Lee, M. J. W., Dalgarno, B., & Farley, H. (Eds.). (2012). Virtual worlds in the Australasian context [Special issue]. *Australasian Journal of Educational Technology*, *28*(3).

Murphy, A., Farley, H., Lane, M., Hafeez-Baig, A., & Carter, B. (2014). Mobile learning anytime, anywhere: What are our students doing? *Australasian Journal of Information Systems*, *18*(3), 331–345.

Mushtaq, S., Reardon-Smith, K., Cliffe, N., Ostini, J., Farley, H., Doyle, J., & Kealley, M. (2017). Can digital discussion support tools provide cost-effective options for agricultural extension services? *Information Technologies & International Development*, *13*, 52–68.

Pooley, A., Midgley, W., & Farley, H. (2019). Informal language learning through mobile instant messaging among university students in Korea. *International Journal of Mobile and Blended Learning*, *3*(2).

Reardon-Smith, K., Farley, H., Cliffe, N., Mushtaq, S., Stone, R., Doyle, J., . . . Lindesay, J. (2014). The development of virtual world tools to enhance learning and real world decision making in the Australian sugar farming industry. *International Journal of Advanced Corporate Learning*, *7*(3), 17–23.

Reardon-Smith, K., Mushtaq, S., Farley, H., Cliffe, N., Stone, R., Ostini, J., & Lindesay, J. (2015). Virtual discussions to support climate risk decision making on farms. *Journal of Economic and Social Policy*, *17*(2), 1–21.

Reushle, S, Farley, H., & Keppell, M. (Eds.). (2015). Proceedings of the 2014 digital rural futures conference [Special issue]. *Journal of Economic and Social Policy*, *17*(1).

9
GIBSON, CHERE CAMPBELL

Photo of Chere Campbell Gibson contributed by Chere Campbell Gibson

Access does not equal success!

Dr. Chere Gibson studied at Macdonald College of McGill University in Montreal, Canada, where she obtained her Bachelor of Science in Nutrition in 1966. She then moved to Madison,

Wisconsin, and completed a Master of Science in Agricultural and Extension Education in 1973 at the University of Wisconsin-Madison. She continued on to complete a PhD in Continuing and Vocational Education with minors in nutrition and sociology at the University of Wisconsin-Madison in 1976.

Gibson remained in Madison and held various administrative roles and teaching roles, with most work within the Department of Continuing and Vocational Education at the University of Wisconsin-Madison.

Dr. Gibson has received many awards over the course of her career, with the most recent being:

- 2011 – Inducted into the International Adult and Continuing Education Hall of Fame, and
- 2003 – Inducted into the United States Distance Learning Association's Hall of Fame.

Her research interests are varied, but a number of papers are concerned with quality assurance in distance learning, learner preferences, and course design, as well as new technologies and their use in computer mediated learning. Her very early work, pre-1990, was published under the name, Chere Campbell Coggins. A list of her many publications can be found at the end of this chapter.

Dr. Gibson began her career working and assisting with traditional distance education programmes, which were correspondence-based, and then moved into computer-mediated education as the University of Wisconsin-Madison transitioned to online learning. Her rich experience is demonstrated through her research, as she holds a firm foundation in adult education before technology and the Internet changed distance education dramatically.

Interview

Transcript Analysis Summary

Analysis of all interviews included in this volume led to the identification of 3,545 units of data. The mean of these collective units was 118 per pioneer, the median was 118.5, and the mode was 132. Individual interview units ranged from 59 to 217 units, yielding a spread of 158 units among all interviews. Chere Campbell Gibson's interview generated 68 units, making her interview the one to produce the third least number of units among all interviews.

A comparision of Campbell Gibson's interview to the interviews of all pioneers indicates that, generally speaking, Campbell Gibson's conversations generated a unique interview profile (Figure 9.1). She provided more details about changes over time, final thoughts, accomplishments, and research interests than most others did. She also furnished more names for book candidates than the average interviewee did. While Campbell Gibson did not mention as many benefits of DE, she also did not recount as many challenges as the average interviewee did. Interestingly, her profile did match the average one in these latter two areas in one respect; both profiles indicated that the number of units generated by the benefits of DE somewhat outnumbered the challenges.

Perhaps one of the most noteworthy difference in the number of units from Chere Campbell Gibson's interview versus the average interview related to the learning environment category. This was because she was retired at the time of the interview. Units collected in this category related to a research study that she was engaged in with her husband during this period. Lastly, Campbell Gibson's interview did not generate any units in the area of career history. This was because no specific interview question dwelt on this topic, although most pioneers did bring this subject up at some point during their interviews.

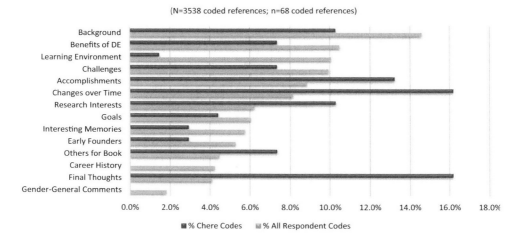

Figure 9.1 All Respondents' Versus Chere Campbell Gibson's Parent Codes

Link to recorded interview: tinyurl.com/Gibson-C-2019

Transcript of Interview

Full name: Chere Campbell Gibson; early publications are under the name Chere Campbell Coggins

Institutional Affiliation: University of Wisconsin-Madison

Key:

Regular font = Interviewee comments
Italicized font = Interviewer comments

Interview Questions

1. *What was your educational and experiential background before you became involved in distance education [DE]?*

    Essentially nutritional sciences at the undergraduate level and adult education at the master's and PhD level. I was aware of distance education [DE], as I worked with Charles Wedemeyer on one of his courses, Michael Moore and I were grad students together as he worked on his theory of transactional distance, and there were a number of others working on distance education–related topics.

2. *In what year did you begin to look specifically into DE?*

    My first experience was as a learner. It was in 1965 as an undergrad at McGill [University] taking a statistics course via a blue programmed learning machine and a red stats book by Steele and Torre. There were 110 in the class with 50 passing the final exam. Five of us passed the retake exam. I learned the importance of learner support the hard way!

    The second more current bumping into DE was in 1981: the University of Wisconsin system administration. This was the administration over the 27 institutions at Wisconsin that launched four extended degrees. These degrees were intended for those who began an undergraduate degree and for whatever reason – health, family responsibilities, etc. – did not complete their degree. I joined the team in 1980.

3. *What were the circumstances in your world that initiated this interest in DE?*

    I was working with a number of individuals who were exploring distance education as a means to solve a problem – that problem being 750,000 persons in Wisconsin with baccalaureate degrees begun but not completed. Building on the British Open University model, the team designed four degree-completion programmes. Initially, it was print-based, as you would guess, and the technology array expanded as we went forward. With my adult education background and the extended degrees being logically aimed at adults, I was seen as a resource and added to the team. It is all about being in the right place at the right time.

4. *Which female researchers or female colleagues may have piqued your interest in DE?*

    I didn't know any at the time.

5. *Who would you identify as the early female leaders/founders in the field of DE?*

    That is a question I have left unanswered because I just didn't know how to answer it. Because I am so old, I'm trying to think about what 80-year-old distance educators were there. I just don't know. I didn't have any early female founders or leaders in mind; they just weren't part of my reality.

6. *What are some of the goals that you strove to achieve in the field of DE?*

    The goals that I strove to achieve in DE . . . To highlight the need for support – learner support, faculty support, and technology support. The former, learner support, grew out of the 1962 experience. In terms of faculty support, it grew out of an understanding that without knowledgeable faculty who understand how to design learning experiences and teach at a distance, the learner is once again the loser, and the technology is key. If it fails or the learner does not know how to use it, there will be no learning. As I have said over the years, sadly many more times than people would like to hear, "Access does not equal success!"

7. *What are some of your accomplishments in the field of DE that you would like to share?*

That is not an easy question – many of my accomplishments were as part of a team – usually as the instructional designer working with subject-matter specialists who were trying to provide access to information to those at a distance, working on anything from a set of learning materials on how to teach nutrition in small groups to a five-university undergraduate credit course on meat evaluation delivered at a distance, to a master's degree in engineering professional practice, etc. So a lot of my accomplishments I owe to the rest of the team, where I was simply a designer.

One of my accomplishments was the launch of a Certificate of Professional Development in Distance Education in 1992. I think that it was building on my belief that faculty support and knowledgeable faculty were so critical. Initially, the certificate was print-based, with audio and/or video tapes and a faculty resource for each course to answer questions and grade papers as students worked through this self-paced programme. We had four core modules: one that focused on the adult learner, another on instructional design, a third on distance delivery technologies, and the fourth being evaluation with additional elective modules on learner support, administration and management, a self-chosen focus, etc.

Many people associate me with the Annual Conference on Teaching and Learning at a Distance that is offered annually by the University of Wisconsin-Madison. I chaired that conference for many years, but my husband, Terry Gibson, originated the conference in 1985, and I took over as chair in 1988. The 34th annual is this year, so it continues. During my years as chair, we were able to grow the conference to 1,000 participants, with a continued focus not on the technology, but on learners and learning.

As I go on, always practice and practitioner focused, my research focused on the learner and trying to understand how to support that learner at a distance from understanding how they see themselves as learners at a distance, the challenges they face in the context they exist in, to the support they need to succeed. Later in my career, I had an opportunity to evaluate some existing programmes to again better understand what helps the learner succeed.

Thanks to Canadian colleagues working with the Canadian International Development Agency, I had an opportunity to spend three years in St. Lucia working with a team to design and deliver upper-level high school courses to those teaching in St. Lucia, so these teachers who had not completed high school could get A or O levels certificates to enter teachers' college. It truly was an experience I'll never forget and eye opening to boot! Who knew the Coca-Cola truck would end up being our delivery mechanism to bring educational materials to remote villages when the roads were bad? But that's what happened.

All in all, I feel I had a fairly well-rounded career and leave behind some absolutely great graduate students who are teaching at a distance, researching the field, writing books, embracing new technologies, and training. The next generation needs to remember that teaching and learning are important, and having access, but no success, is a tragedy.

You can leave in my Wedemeyer Award because it has Jeanette MacDonald's name on it. She was certainly one of my dear graduate students. The Charles Wedemeyer Award is given in his name. He was such a pioneer. He had ideas before his time. He was much beloved around the world, but somehow seen as just a little out of step at his own institution because he was just so far ahead of time. At some point in time, he and his wife decided that they would like to give an award in his name to a researcher or researchers each year. The research was to be published in the *American Journal of Distance Education*. A small team would pick a number of articles and then would have the review team discern which one they thought was the best of the year. So every year at the annual conference of Teaching and Learning at a Distance, the Charles Wedemeyer Award would be presented to a researcher in the field. I was fortunate to be the second name on the plaque, with the first one being Jeanette MacDonald. She was in my first online class, and her research interest was group dynamics and looking at the dynamics of online groups. Interesting enough, they parallel the dynamics of face-to-face groups. The pacing is a little different. She was just so struck by the cohesion that occurs in an online class, or can emerge in an online class, that she just felt inspired to take a look at the group dynamics.

8. *What are some of the challenges that you faced in the field of DE over the years?*

As I thought through this question, there were about three that jumped out. I taught the very first "online" course at the University of Wisconsin-Madison, and there were no end of doubters and a few curious to see how this might work. It was pre-Internet, so the course was taught on a listserv. Its name was "– e-Rita"; that was its password, based on the movie *Educating Rita*, that marvelous old British Open University–related movie. To make it more exciting, we decided to link a number of online courses together. So the course that I taught at the University of Wisconsin-Madison was linked to a somewhat parallel course at the University of Oklahoma, a little more technology-oriented course at San Diego State, a similar course at the University of Wyoming, University of New Mexico, and a university in Australia. It was absolutely great fun, just great fun. One of my students travelled to California and met a few of his online colleagues as he went. We learned a lot! We had great fun. It was an exciting way to start.

The second challenge I think was the limitations of the technology – especially in the beginning when there was more that I wanted to do, but the software wasn't there yet, or the connectivity wasn't there, etc. I worked in Indian country, what you would call "First Nations people." That really helped me understand the digital divide better than I ever had.

I think my last challenge over time was the lack of support for learners, faculty, and the technology. All of my research and evaluation over time have made the need for support abundantly obvious, but the attention to support and dollars are still often missing.

9. *What was the "state of DE" when you first entered the field as opposed to online learning in 2019?*

I come from an institution that launched the first educational radio station in the United States in 1922 and the seventh educational television station in 1954, as well as one of the earliest educational telephone networks in the late 1960s. Slow-scan TV [television] came shortly afterwards. We had the technology, and there were people using it for mainly non-credit teaching. Continuing professional education for physicians was what got our educational telephone network started. They were teaching piano lessons for children over this system. While the radio station was available broadly, the educational television network did not broadcast to the far northwest corner of the state that happened to be where we launched one of our extended degree programmes. (We ended up solving that problem by asking Minnesota's educational television station to broadcast our programmes in the early 1980s as Minnesota reached the missing corner of our state, as an aside.) The educational telephone network required people to come to one of approximately 200 sites, and travelling in the winter can be challenging here in Wisconsin. We also had a spin-off from ARPANET, called "THEORYNET," that in 1977 linked over 100 computer science departments together, one of which was ours at the University of Wisconsin-Madison. Again, we had the technology and were doing considerable linking with other institutions on how to use the technology, but the technology had scant use in the university credit arena. Both Charles Wedemeyer and Burton Kreitlow broke the mold of the face-to-face university teaching by each teaching a course at a distance via the educational telephone network. Interesting enough, two of the people in Wedemeyer's class over this educational telephone network swore that they would devote their entire careers to the educational telephone network, and they did! One is an instructional designer, and one is a top-notch faculty support information technology person.

So when I entered as a student, we didn't have much beyond print in use. When I entered the field as a professional, we had a few more tools, such as audio and video cassettes and our radio, television, and telephone networks, although [they were] not without their challenges in terms of programming and reach. We did not have access to the computer linkages that we now just take for granted. That would come later – early 1990s, as I recall, but initially only open to the university personnel. So that's the technology context when I first started. We had a technology-rich university system, just not used in ways that I wanted to use it.

10. *What interesting memories would you like to share about the beginning of online learning?*

Teaching online without the Internet meant teaching on a listserv with all the messages, regardless of topic, arriving in the same location – none of those wonderful bits of technology where you can have your social discussions in the café in one little spot and have your theoretical discussions in another. So for me, that meant printing out messages and categorizing them if you wanted a record of the class. And so you had piles and piles of papers – social, theory, questions, etc. That was kind of messy and certainly not evidence of an all-digital and paperless society.

The other memory that I have, and I don't have it, but others shared it, was the joy of seeing my online students meet other students for the very first time face-to-face after spending a whole semester together virtually. As I said, I seldom had that joy, but many of my faculty colleagues did see these "reunions," and they certainly shared those memories with me.

11. *What were your specific DE research interests, and have they changed/evolved over the years?*

My interest throughout has been on support in general and learner support more specifically, with an eye to ensuring that the learner can indeed succeed. That said, much of my practice and the outreach focus of my work has been on faculty development: for example, the certificate programme, the DE conference, and instructional design for international development and, at home, instructional design work for the online master of science in engineering.

My research interests continued to focus on the learner. Boy, there is some bad research out there that I have done, and there is some reasonable research. But the focus has always been on the learner: how they feel about themselves as learners, how they use the context in ways that will help them succeed, getting a better understanding of what they need to succeed, emotional support, educational support, logistical support, economic support. And so really, as a result and through that 1962 absolutely dreadful learning experience with the blue programming learning machine and the red stats book, learner support has been my focus throughout. Graduate students take you off in one direction or another, but my focus has remained on the learner.

12. *Can you please describe the learning environment that you most recently worked in (e.g., geographic and institutional setting, student demographics)?*

Most recently, I worked on a grant with my husband after we both retired. It was a grant written for the University of Wisconsin-Oshkosh. It is a four-year institution in Wisconsin in the centre of the state, veering off towards the east side. It is a comprehensive institution that has a wide array of undergraduate degrees, and it offers master's degrees through a variety of faculties but no PhDs. In the Wisconsin system where I have spent most of my life, we only have two institutions that offer PhDs. I had worked with the University of Wisconsin-Oshkosh on a faculty development technology grant, so they asked me if I would work on another grant. The grant was funded by the Robert Wood Johnson Foundation, which is very focused on health issues in the United States. They are part of the Johnson & Johnson enterprise: you know – everything from baby powder to whatever. So the grant was funded by the Robert Wood Johnson Foundation, as I said, a dominant health care foundation in the US. It really enabled my husband and I to use our adult education and distance education as well as evaluation backgrounds. The focus of this particular grant was on comparing educational outcomes of those with a baccalaureate degree who had returned to the university as adults to pursue additional coursework to qualify them for a bachelor of nursing science degree. In the United States, it is often called a "BS to BSN programme." So it was a bachelor of science, regardless of focus, to a bachelor of science in nursing. We studied programmes where students met face-to-face or at a distance to pursue their coursework, and experienced their practical/hands-on training via a traditional method of rotating through various health care situations or a newer preceptor training method that still goes through the traditional training rotation but has a single point of contact throughout the student's practica. Practical training occurred in the student's local community whenever possible. We used surveys with students, interviews with students, practica leaders, faculty and support staff, as well as final grades on the National League of Nursing exams [to] provide the data. So we had a fair amount of data and lots of transcribing that didn't seem to fit into the funding. So that's why I certainly empathize with what you are up against. The institution was comprehensive, across the board with undergraduate degrees and master's degrees. These students were all adult students. I can think of one example. If you look at your right hand with your palm towards you, Oshkosh is sitting up at the base of your finger next to your thumb. There was a student who was living up at the very top of your longest finger. He had a bachelor's degree. I can't remember what he was doing for employment, but he was also an emergency medical technician [EMT]. As he continued on those emergency runs as an EMT, he recognized that whatever he was trained to do with his bachelor of science degree was not what he wanted to do for the rest of his life. Way up in northern Wisconsin, there was only one institution close to him. It did not offer nursing at all. To accomplish his goals, he enrolled in the University of Wisconsin-Oshkosh distance programme so he could pursue his coursework to help him move from a BS to a BSN. With a lot of wangling, he was able to do his practicum up north. The Oshkosh programme had students from all over the country. It is a very small cohort programme. You promise two years of your life to the programme. It's about an 18-month programme overall, but you have some preparatory work to do in advance. But students are from all over the country. And as I recall, the cohort was either 20 or 25, so it's a small cohort, which is absolutely ideal.

The study itself was nationwide. The institutions we had were Oshkosh, one of our key groups was in California, and so there was an array of institutions around the country. The outcomes surprised many, because the students at a distance with a one-on-one practicum relationship far outperformed those at a distance with the traditional practica and students learning face-to-face with either practicum method. So a BS to a BSN could be accomplished was the bottom line. You had a neutral arbiter in the National League of Nursing, test exams, and data scores across a variety of practice areas in nursing. Typical of adult students, if you made it possible for them to accomplish a dream, they are just ecstatic. We just had so many students learning at a distance, pursuing their dreams, accomplishing their dreams. They had information technology support that you would die for. Support was really, really strong, and they accomplished their dreams. And they were very thankful.

13. *Is there anything else you [would like] to address?*

Yes, the joy of being a distance educator was the first thing that came to mind. The joy of being an educator, especially one with instructional design expertise, meant many opportunities to design, implement, and evaluate distance education non-credit programmes, credit-bearing courses, and graduate degrees with colleagues from other faculties at the university. I sat back in response to this question and thought I was privileged to work with faculty and staff in agriculture, engineering, medicine, nursing, human ecology, veterinary medicine, and many areas in extension. A distance educator can bring a lot to a team. Working in a team is absolutely invaluable. Your assumptions are questioned; things you never thought about doing emerge in these conversations. I still so strongly believe in the importance of team design, working with others to strongly evaluate what you are doing, and learning by doing is the only way to go.

I think to neglect your learners, you do so at your own expense. Learners have much to offer in terms of how to structure a strong programme in which they indeed have access and success. For example, with our baccalaureate degree programme, these were people who started and didn't finish sometimes because they had to work on the farm or stay home to work with health-care providers to help Mom live out her last few years, or whatever. But there were others who just failed, simple as that. They were embarrassed that they failed for all the reasons that a 19-year-old can fail at course at school. Now they are trying a second time. You don't want them to fail a second time. You want to have that success. By implementing programmes with the learner in mind, that constant refinement through evaluation and learner feedback, faculty feedback, and technical support feedback, it's absolutely invaluable. You just kind of need that continuous quality improvement. That was drilled through my head when working with engineers.

The international engineering programme that I worked on has won so many national awards. We have much to be proud of because our learners, our faculty, and our support staff provided us with lots of insight so we could simply refine, refine, and refine.

So I would say that it is a joy to be a distance educator. Involve the team as much as possible. Instructional design, [and] evaluate, evaluate, evaluate, keep in touch with those learners and those faculty members.

Faculty development . . . I think that one of the more fun opportunities (we are talking the late 1970s and early 1980s) was doing faculty development. The faculty by then had been teaching for maybe a year or two at a distance, mainly print-based. We got them together to do some faculty development, with opportunities to share in small groups, to problem solve, to share lessons learned, and that was an invaluable experience. You and I can say all the things about what we know, but if some faculty or colleague at some other institution says, "Oh my gosh! I've been there, done that. This is now I resolved it." That peer-to-peer problem solving, lesson sharing, and lessons learned is so much to watch and I think a real growth experience for everybody; a real learning experience to boot.

Thinking back to Athabasca (University) and one of your former colleagues, Dr. Dan Coldeway, who used to say, "An 'N of one' is not really that helpful." As distance educators, we are so busy practicing and so busy designing; we are busy implementing and busy evaluating. We have got to research our practice, [and] continue, continue, continue to research our practice; the larger the N, the better our practice. If we can team up with other faculty colleagues at other institutions or other faculties at our own institutions that are doing distance education, we need more research. It is all well and good to share your research, your "N of one," as Dan Coldeway would say, but we need to go beyond the "N of one." We have got to research our practice to a greater extent than we are doing now.

If you can, as a distance educator, get out there to those conferences. I loved to come to CADE [Canadian Association of Distance Education] conferences and certainly went over to ICDE [International Council of Distance Education] conferences. I can say "over" because I can remember some of them being in Birmingham, England, and Bangkok, Thailand. You meet all sorts of wonderful distance educators – not many females early on, at least in the 1980s and 90s. I think it is much vaster now. But it gives you a sense of what kind of DE is happening around the world, and what other people are doing and how you can start to collaborate internationally. There are great things going on in Australia, as you know, and New Zealand, and Sukhothai Thammathirat Open University has been around forever, and the OU [British Open University]. You just got to get out and over there. Read broadly, but go to these conferences and meet broadly as well.

14. *Can you suggest names of other female pioneers in DE that you think we should include in the book?*

Well, you probably have already thought about Liz Burge. We worked on a book together for Athabasca University Press. She is near and dear to my heart.

Then you've got Diane Conrad not to be forgotten. You know, sometimes you forget the professors who are in your own institution, your own people.

You have mentioned Judy Roberts and Louise Moran. A person you may not know, though, is a person by the name of Chris Olgren, Dr. Chris Olgren. She may not fit your criteria. She did an absolutely marvelous dissertation on learning strategies in DE. She is a great researcher. She directed the Certificate Programme of Professional Development in Distance Education for years and grew it from the old print, audio cassette, and video cassette to online. She's directed the distance conference for years. She was a good researcher who finished her PhD in her 40s. I think ageism got her in terms of getting a faculty position. So she stayed back and did just marvelous work on the certificate programme, the distance education conference, and a whole host of other things that she would know about. Just a solid female distance educator, more of a practitioner than a researcher; you wouldn't find her at all of the ICDE conferences. She was somebody who stayed at home and did a lot of work.

Publications

(Note: Chere's pre-1990 work was published under the name Chere Campbell Coggins.)

Books

American Council on Education. (1996). *Guiding principles for distance learning in a learning society*. American Council on Education (Authored by taskforce).

Burge, E., Gibson, C., & Gibson, T. (2011). *Flexible pedagogy, flexible practice: Notes from the trenches of distance education*. Athabasca University Press.

Gibson, C. (Ed.). (1996). *Distance education symposium 3: Learners and learning* (Research Monograph Number 13). American Center for the Study of Distance Education.

Gibson, C. (Ed.). (1998). *Distance learners in higher education: Institutional responses for quality outcomes*. Atwood Publishers.

Mariasingam, M., Smith, T., & Gibson, C. C. (2019). *Quality assurance in open and distance learning: Global approaches and experiences*. Smashwords.

Book Chapters

Coggins, C. (1989). Preferred learning styles and their impact on completion of external degree programs (Reprint). In M. Moore & C. Clark (Eds.), *Readings in distance learning and instruction* (pp. 1–13). American Center for the Study of Distance Education.

Dahl, B., & Gibson C. (2012). Quality and community: Two key drivers for Lake Superior College, USA. In M. Mariasingam, T. W. Smith, & C. C. Gibson (Eds.), *Quality assessment and assurance in online learning* (pp. 65–87). Smashwords.

Gibson, C. (1993). Toward a broader conceptualization of distance education. In D. Keegan (Ed.), *Theoretical underpinnings of distance education* (pp. 80–82). Routledge (Also translated into Chinese in 1997).

Gibson, C. (1998a). The role of academic self-concept in distance learning. In C. Gibson (Ed.), *Distance learners in higher education: Institutional responses for quality outcomes* (pp. 65–76). Atwood Publishers.

Gibson, C. (1998b). Social context and the collegiate distance learner. In C. Gibson (Ed.), *Distance learners in higher education: Institutional responses for quality outcomes* (pp. 113–126). Atwood Publishers.

Gibson, C. (2000a). Distance education for lifelong learning. In A. Wilson & E. Hayes (Eds.), *Handbook of adult and continuing education* (pp. 423–437). Jossey-Bass Publishers.

Gibson, C. (2000b). The ultimate disorienting dilemma: The online learning community. In D. Evans & D. Nation (Eds.), *Changing university teaching: Reflections on creating educational technologies* (pp. 133–146). Kogan Page Publishers.

Gibson, C. (2003). Learners and learning: Theoretical foundations. In M. Moore, & B. Anderson (Eds.), *Handbook of distance learning* (pp. 147–160). Lawrence Erlbaum Assoc. Inc.

Gibson, C. (2005). Online learning: From high tech to high touch. In G. Kearsley (Ed.), *Online education: Personal reflections on the transformation of education.* Educational Technology Publications.

Gibson, C. (2007). From Chautauqua to correspondence to computers. In T. Evans, M. Haughey, & D. Murphy (Eds.), *International handbook of distance education* (pp. 259–277). Elsevier.

Gibson, C. C. (1990). Learners and learning: A discussion of selected research. In M. Moore (Ed.), *Contemporary issues in distance education in North America* (pp. 121–135). Pergamon Press.

Gibson, C. C. (2017). Distance education: Access for success. In A. B. Knox, S. C. O. Conceição, & L. G. Martin (Eds.), *Mapping the field of adult and continuing education: An international compendium* (Vol. 1, pp. 215–218). Stylus.

Gibson, C. C., & Gibson, T. (1997). Continuing education at a distance. In J. Fleming (Ed.), *An update on designing and implementing effective workshops* (New Directions for Adult and Continuing Education, No. 76, pp. 59–69). San Jossey-Bass Publishers.

Journal Articles

Becker, E. A., & Gibson, C. C. (1998). Fishbein and Ajzen's theory of reasoned action: Accurate prediction of behavioral intentions for enrolling in distance education courses. *Adult Education Quarterly, 49*(1), 43–55.

Becker, E. A., & Gibson, C. C. (1999). Attitudes among practicing respiratory therapists in a mid-western state toward completing a baccalaureate degree and toward distance education. *Respiratory Care, 44*(11), 1337–1352.

Coggins, C. (1988). Preferred learning styles of University of Wisconsin extended degree students and their impact on completion of external degree programs. *American Journal of Distance Education, 2*(1), 25–37.

Dillon, C., Confessore, S., & Gibson, C. (1992). Interaction in interactive satellite teleconferencing: Can it be increased? *The Journal of Interactive Television, 1*(1), 43–54.

Gallagher-Lepak, S., Scheibel, P., & Gibson, C. (2009). Integrating telehealth in nursing curricula: Can you hear me now? *Online Journal of Nursing Informatics, 13*(2). www.ojni.org/13_2/GallagherLepak.pdf

Gibson, C. (1990). One researcher's perspective: Questions and research strategies. *American Journal of Distance Education, 4*(1), 69–81.

Gibson, C. (1992à). Alphabet soup is coming your way (if it hasn't already!). *Lifelong Learning, 4*(2), 18–19.

Gibson, C. (1992b). Distance education: On focus and future [Essay review]. *Adult Education Quarterly, 42*(3), 167–179.

Gibson, C. (1996a). Academic self-concept – Its nature and import in distance education. *American Journal of Distance Education, 10*(1), 23–36.

Gibson, C. (1996b). Toward emerging technologies and distributed learning: Challenges and change. *American Journal of Distance Education, 10*(2), 47–49.

Gibson, C. (1997a). Distance education: Shifting paradigms in teaching and learning. *Open Praxis, 1*, 5–8.

Gibson, C. (1997b). Something old, something new, something borrowed, something blue. In *Facilitating learning at a distance* (pp. 7–11). SUNY Empire State.

Gibson, C. (2000). When disruptive approaches meet disruptive technologies: Learning at a distance. *Journal of Continuing Education in the Health Professions, 20*, 69–76.

Gibson, C., Boelter, L., Boyce, L., & LeFebvre, J. (1992). Can you teach consumer credit at home? *Journal of Extension, XXX*, 14–16.

Gibson, C., & Gibson, T. (1995). Lessons learned from 100+ years of distance learning. *Adult Learning, 6*(7).

Gibson, C., & Graff, A. (1992). Impact of adult's preferred learning styles and perception of barriers on completion of external baccalaureate degree programs. *Journal of Distance Education, VII*(1), 39–51.

Greer, E., & Gibson, C. (1994). Visual special effects in instructional video programs and their impact on adult learning: A review of the literature. *Journal of Applied Communications, 78*(3), 36–49.

Lee, J., & Gibson, C. (2003). Developing self-directedness through computer-mediated interaction. *American Journal of Distance Education, 17*(3), 173–187.

McDonald, J., & Gibson, C. (1998). Interpersonal aspects of group dynamics and group development in computer conferencing. *American Journal of Distance Education, 12*(1), 7–25.

Oehlkers, R., & Gibson, C. (2001). Learner support experienced by RNs in a collaborative RN-to-BSN program. *The Journal of Continuing Education in Nursing, 32*(6), 266–273.

Conference Presentations

Coggins, C. (1987a). *Learning styles and distance learners* [Paper presentation]. National conference of the American Association for Adult and Continuing Education.

Coggins, C. (1987b). Preferred learning styles of University of Wisconsin extended degree students and their impact on completion of external baccalaureate degree programs. In *Proceedings of the Midwest research to practice conference in adult, community and continuing education.* University of Michigan.

Coggins, C. (1988). Learners and learning: A discussion paper on selected research. *Proceedings: American symposium on research in distance education.* The Pennsylvania State University.

Davitt, M.,& Gibson, C. (1991). An analysis of humor in instructional videotape: Does it enhance learning? *Distance Education Online Symposium Research Forum.*

Gibson, C. (1991a). Musings: The distance education curriculum. In C. Dillon (Ed.), *Proceedings of the forum on the teaching of distance education.* Center for Research in Continuing, Professional & Higher Education, University of Oklahoma.

Gibson, C. (1991b). Recent research on learners and learning in distance education. In M. Moore (Ed.), *Discussion papers – 2nd annual research symposium on distance education.* American Center for Study in Distance Education, Pennsylvania State University.

Gibson, C. (1991c). Recent research on learning and characteristics of learners in distance education [Abstract]. In M. Moore, M. Thompson, & P. Dirr (Eds.), *The Second American Symposium on Research in Distance Education.* The American Center for the Study of Distance Education, Pennsylvania State University.

Gibson, C. (1992). Changing perceptions of learners and learning at a distance: Areview of selected recent research. In M. Moore (Ed.), *Distance education symposium papers* (Number 1, American Center for the Study of Distance Education Research Monograph Number 4, pp. 31–39). American Center for Study of Distance Education.

LeFebvre, J., & Coggins, C. (1988). Changing roles of teachers and learners in a non-credit distance education format. In *Proceedings of the Effective Teaching at a Distance Conference* (pp. 79–83). University of Wisconsin.

10
GLENNIE, JENNIFER (JENNY)

Photo of Jennifer (Jenny) Glennie contributed by Jennifer (Jenny) Glennie

> *My overarching goal has been to ensure that distance education supports the social justice and democratic project in sub-Saharan Africa.*

Jennifer (Jenny) Glennie has been a researcher, practitioner, and leader in her country of South Africa for many years. She obtained her Bachelor of Science Honours degree in Mathematics from the University of the Witwatersrand, South Africa in 1971. She went on to complete a Masters in Area Studies with a focus on education in Africa from the University of London, Institute of Education, and School of Oriental and African Studies (SOAS) in 1980.

When she returned to South Africa in 1974, Glennie became very involved with the South African Committee for Higher Education (SACHED), an anti-apartheid organization dedicated to providing quality education to all citizens of the nation. SACHED was very interested in distance education as a partial solution to the historical inequalities in South Africa. Glennie became entrusted with developing and managing distance education programmes from 1974 to 1979. She remained with SACHED for 15 years before moving on to becoming the founding director of the South African Institute for Distance Education (Saide) in 1992–1993. Under her leadership, Saide has developed into a sustainable NGO, which focuses not only on distance education and policy, but also on open educational resources (OER), as well as implementing new technologies into distance education in sub-Saharan Africa. She has initiated many projects over the years with Saide that include policy research, capacity building, and knowledge management.

Glennie's research interests are based on the South African scenario but would transpose to other developing countries as well. She is most interested in OER and quality/cost control of distance education in her region. Her publications are listed at the end of this chapter, along with an extensive list of her conference presentations and keynote addresses.

Jenny has received many awards over the years, but perhaps the most relevant ones are the Chancellor's Medal from the University of Pretoria for contribution to education in South Africa and the Honorary Fellow of the Commonwealth of Learning in recognition of an outstanding individual contribution to distance education.

Interview

Transcript Analysis Summary

Analysis of all interviews included in this volume led to the identification of 3,545 units of data. The mean of these collective units was 118 per pioneer, the median was 118.5, and the mode was 132. Individual interview units ranged from 59 to 217 units, yielding a spread of 158 units between all interviews. Jenny Glennie's interview generated 136 units, placing her interview in the lower end of the upper third of all interviews in terms of unit numbers.

A comparison of Glennie's interview to the interviews of all pioneers indicated that her interview profile shared no commonalities with the average interview profile (Figure 10.1). Her interview produced a greater-than-average number of units in the following areas: background, challenges, accomplishments, changes over time, goals, and career history. All these statistics are likely explained by the unique pioneering situation that Glennie found herself in. She began working in the field of DE at a time when black people in her country were, by law, systematically denied access to education. Glennie and her colleagues faced unimaginable hardships as they sought to provide equitable DE learning opportunities. Even after apartheid was officially dissolved, Glennie continued to battle against systematic injustices. This provides context for why Glennie's interview contained more than the average number of units in these areas.

Glennie's interview also produced a lower number of units than the average interview in the areas of benefits of DE, learning environment, research interest, interesting memories, early founders, others for the book, and final thoughts. The low number of units in the benefits of DE area could be explained by the fact that the interview questions did not ask about the benefits of DE. This topic was identified during the data analysis process. Glennie worked mainly as an administrator within DE-promoting organizations. Thus, her interview responses related to the description of her learning environment did not include the same kind or number of units that those who worked for educational institutions did. Also, her administrative position did not allow time to conduct her own research. Since Glennie was a founding pioneer in her country, she did not have much opportunity to meet other pioneers. Furthermore, her country received Internet access in recent years, so her

Glennie, Jennifer (Jenny)

Figure 10.1 All Respondents' Versus Jennifer (Jenny) Glennie's Parent Codes

ability to connect with other pioneers was quite limited for decades. These factors provide possible reasons for Glennie's low number of units in the areas of early founders and others for the book. It is not known why Glennie did not include final thoughts in her interview.

Link to recorded interview: tinyurl.com/Glennie-J

Transcript of Interview

Full Name: Jennifer (Jenny) Glennie
Institutional Affiliation: CEO and Founding Director of nonprofit organization Saide (South African Institute for Distance Education)
Key:

Regular font = Interviewee comments
Italicized font = Interviewer comments

Interview Questions

1. *What was your educational and experiential background before you became involved in distance education [DE]?*

   I became involved in distance education a very long time ago – some 40 years ago. Before that, for about 3 years, I was a university tutor and then a high school teacher in the area of mathematics. Since then, distance education has been a strong theme in all my work.

2. *In what year did you begin to look specifically into distance education [DE], and what were the circumstances in your world that initiated this interest in DE?*

   I began to look specifically into distance education in 1974, predominantly as an educational practitioner. I had been teaching secondary school mathematics in England after my university education in South Africa and wished to return home. This was the apartheid era, and I was given the opportunity to join an anti-apartheid education organization called SACHED [the South African Committee for Higher Education]. SACHED had a major interest in distance education for a number of reasons. Let me explain the context.

   At the time, a huge percentage of black South Africans had received only a rudimentary basic education, and only a small percentage had completed secondary school. Furthermore, black youths and adults of South Africa were being systematically denied the opportunity in the face-to-face system to further their education above certain levels. The apartheid state exercised extremely strong control over education, with all educational institutions segregated according to whether students were African, White, of Indian descent, or so-called Coloured. To this end, in 1959, the South African regime prevented Africans, Indians, and Coloureds from joining the big urban universities of South Africa unless they had special state permission. If you were African, you were required to attend designated universities in the so-called homelands of the time. If you were Indian or Coloured, you were required to attend the one Indian or Coloured university in the country. Furthermore, universities for Africans were designated for particular ethnic groups. Any organization wanting to provide educational opportunities to black South Africans needed official state permission, which could be withheld easily.

   However, there was one exception to this fierce segregation, and that was for distance education. So, for example, UNISA [University of South Africa] had always been able to accept students of all races and ethnicities. It was not that the different student groups were always treated the same, but they were allowed to enrol, so at that time, there were separate graduation ceremonies and, I believe, even separate examination venues.

   It was in this highly repressive context that SACHED, in accordance with its mission to provide opportunity for marginalized communities to pursue their educational aspirations, sought to exploit the space provided by distance education. We did this in two ways: First, we provided support to distance education students who were enrolled with UNISA, and second, SACHED set itself up as a distance education college for youth and adults wishing to pursue their secondary studies.

   I was also attracted to distance education because of its emphasis on interactive learning materials, particularly epitomized by the groundbreaking course materials of the British Open University. During my last year in England before returning to South Africa, I had been teaching in an impoverished school. My kids had a listening concentration span of about five minutes in any lesson period. So I moved very quickly into developing activity-based learning materials because this was the only way that I could hold the attention of my students. Ever since then, I have adopted a "resource-based learning" approach.

I was at SACHED for about 15 years. We were involved in a wide range of activities. Some of them were directly distance education, but some of them centred on providing high quality, contextualized, and interactive learning materials for wider use. So, for example, we ran a groundbreaking, innovative 24-page supplement, which had formal and non-formal educational materials of interest to a broad spectrum of South Africans. The supplement was in a mainstream newspaper, so it was distributed to over a quarter of a million readers.

3. *Which female researchers or female colleagues may have piqued your interest in DE?*

When I was coming back from England to South Africa, I had a brief period engaging with the National Extension College in order to try to understand how they were developing materials. Ros Morpeth was one of the leaders at that time. Later, I worked with Janet Jenkins of the International Extension College, whose work across Africa was influential.

I: You are a pioneer of DE in South Africa and a Founding Director of the South African Institute for Distance Education [Saide]. Could you please tell us a bit about what prompted you to initiate such undertakings?

Obviously, my background at SACHED ignited my interest in distance education and the important role that it could play. When Saide started in 1992–1993, we were moving into a new dispensation of a democratic South Africa and knew that we needed to transform the entire education system to serve the majority black population of our country. By that time, distance education was a strong element in the South African higher education sector. There were a number of distance teacher education colleges, with enrolments of nearly 23,000 students. UNISA at this stage had over 120,000 students, and Technikon SA, offering diplomas, had nearly 64,000 students.

Saide was conceptualized as a post-apartheid organization that would not offer direct support to students but would rather try to impact on the system as a whole to serve the needs of our new democracy. We would do that in two ways. One would be by having an impact on policy and systemic initiatives. The second would be through supporting educators and administrators involved in distance education to transform their practices.

One of Saide's first interventions was to organize an international review of distance education in South Africa. Raj [Gajaraj] Dhanarajan, who later became the president of the Commonwealth of Learning, led it and involved a number of other luminaries in distance education at the time, including Michael Moore, who is well known to you. Based on the review, we developed a range of recommendations on how one might pursue distance education to serve the needs of our emerging democracy.

The conclusions of the resulting review were quite a shock to the distance education community because there was considerable complacency among the key actors since they were able to say, as no other public provider in South Africa could say, that they had never denied access to black people. They had therefore asserted a moral high ground. However, the conclusions of the review were highly critical of their provision.

First, the review found that the completion rate among students was incredibly low. We had conducted what I think was one of the first cohort studies of distance education students. We traced students over a nine- or ten-year period to see how many of those who started actually completed. Completion rates varied between 6% and 15%. These results were quite horrifying to the institution. They had never thought about it in those terms as South Africa's university funding mechanism at the time rewarded students' success in individual courses, not in qualification completion. This concern for completion rates has been a particular emphasis of mine ever since, not only in South Africa but also internationally.

A second key finding was the preponderance of transmission modes of teaching, featuring a great deal of simple regurgitation and rote learning. The review concluded that "taken as a whole, distance education's contribution to the priorities for education and training in the [new] Policy Framework is variously marginal, inefficient and, in respect of the values sought for democratic South Africa, dysfunctional" [Saide, 1995, p. xxii in CHE, 2004, p. 142].

Given that the review was so critical of the state of distance education in the country, it was incumbent on us to identify the criteria for what could be considered good quality distance education. I prompted the reviewers to make a start in the final report. Then, together with our national department of education, we built on this to develop a suite of criteria with a detailed set of elements for each criterion. These were adapted and adopted in different parts of the world, including for Asian universities. A Saide staff member, with my involvement, led this work.

We continued to build on this initial work by leading the process with our National Association of Distance Education [NADEOSA] of developing case studies that exemplify good practice of the criteria. More recently, Saide produced *A Good Practice Guide for Distance Education in a Digital Age* for the Council on Higher Education's Higher Education Quality Committee. It has been widely acclaimed by the South African university community.

In the early days of our new democracy, Saide also conducted a review of teacher education at a distance. At that stage, one in three teachers in South Africa was involved in a distance education programme. In this instance, we found that there was a high completion rate, but the quality of provision was appalling. We found many examples of assignment and examination questions that simply asked students to regurgitate what was in the study guide. This was, of course, a major concern as teachers were being encouraged to perpetuate a system where students are not required to engage with or reflect critically on their study material.

My concern for distance education to provide both access and success to our students has been an ongoing theme of all Saide's work. To this end, I was extensively involved in setting up South Africa's new Higher Education Quality Committee. One of my contributions was to ensure that distance education should be an integral part of the higher education system and not treated, as occurs in some countries, as a system parallel to the dominant face-to-face one. I therefore worked to ensure that the criteria used in the quality assurance of higher education should apply to all modes of provision and should not assume a face-to-face context.

Since inception, Saide has developed in three major respects. The first is that we were set up to work in the South Africa. However, as we matured, we received a number of requests to extend our services beyond South Africa into sub-Saharan Africa. From 2008, we formally moved to work across the sub-Saharan region. The second development related to the growing opportunity for the use of educational technology. For example, we implemented a major initiative across seven universities in the region, developing institutional education technology strategies and then supporting them to give practical expression to strategies.

The third development has been around open education resources [OER]. Saide embraced this concept from early on, initiating "OER Africa," where we work with academics to increase awareness of the opportunities afforded by OER to develop skills in sourcing and integrating OER into practice. Furthermore, we supported academics to develop their own OER that reflected local contexts and practices so that Africa could be a contributor to the OER field, not just a consumer.

More recently, we developed a path-breaking initiative in the early childhood development sector, The African Storybook Initiative. Children's literacy levels across the region are extremely low. By way of an example, a recent study in South Africa has shown that only two out of ten children, having been at school for at least four years, can read for meaning. This has dire consequences for any child for future learning and for future employment. One of the contributing factors to these low levels of literacy is that there is very little for young children to read that is in their own language, reflects their context, and with which they can identify. Often one can count on one hand the number of books that might be available in a local language. We deployed technology and the concept of open educational resources to contribute to solving this problem. We now have a platform where you can create, translate, or adapt storybooks that will then be freely available for all to read, to download, or to print without the need to pay any licence fees. The platform now boasts over 1,000 unique stories and nearly 6,000 translations. Over 170 local languages of Africa are represented. In addition to appearing on our platform, African Storybook stories can be found on 18 different platforms, including the Global Digital Library and World Reader. We have reached about a million people already. In November 2018, we were awarded a prize from Google Impact South Africa of $125,000 to develop an offline story development app and a methodology to work with children to create their own stories.

4. *What are some of the goals that you strove to achieve in these geographic regions in the DE field?*

My overarching goal has been to ensure that distance education supports the social justice and democratic project in sub-Saharan Africa. To this end, I have promoted distance education provision as an integral part of the education system, governed by the same quality standards as other modes of provision. I have also worked with others to develop a clear concept of what constitutes quality distance education and to ensure that such a concept informs any quality assurance process.

I have then striven to promote the different components of quality distance education wherever possible. This included promoting student support that is not only remedial but also embraces learning as an interactive and social process, as well as a huge emphasis on the quality of learning materials (learner-centred, grounded in local context, activity-based, etc.). To this end, I have endeavoured to increase the pool of learning materials that meet these criteria for sub-Saharan Africa. This included supporting the development of OER.

Guided by a social justice agenda, student success has always been a central concern. Providing access is simply not enough, particularly for marginalized communities. I have promoted this agenda, wherever possible.

Finally, I set out to create a community of distance educators in South Africa who would be guided by a code of ethics and to support regional endeavours in this regard.

5. *What are some of your accomplishments in the field of DE that you would like to share?*

As a senior executive of both SACHED and Saide, I believe I have made a major contribution in changing the nature of distance education, particularly in South Africa, by ensuring that:

- There is innovative policy for distance education, open educational resources, and, more generally, about open learning that serves the transformation needs of our country. In particular, in South Africa I contributed extensively to a policy for university education for distance education and a chapter on open learning for the White Paper on Post Schooling to guide the department over the next ten or so years;

- There are explicit quality criteria for distance education and useful elements related to those criteria in place and that these are incorporated into national systems wherever possible;
- There is a growing supply of excellent open materials available to students, materials which are activity-based, contextualized for local context, and, where appropriate, purposively serve the outcomes of the learning programme. Examples of such materials under development currently include those for senior school management teams, educators in technical and vocational colleges, educators teaching reading, early childhood development educators, youth and adults who dropped out of school (we have huge numbers of such drop- or push-outs who wish to complete a new curriculum designed for this purpose), and political leadership;
- Student support is appropriately conceptualized and that the capacity of educators is built to offer such support. This could include workshops, print guides, and online courses;
- Student success becomes an essential element of what distance education should offer. It is an affront to equity to claim that distance education provides access, when it does so in a manner that does not provide for reasonable chances of student success. This concern has been across for all modes of provision. Over the last five years, I have been contributing to a Saide initiative working with five universities in South Africa centred on being systematic in pursuing improvement in student success rates. This goal is particularly important in a country like ours, where the state's spending on higher education needs to be as effective as possible; and that
- There is a vibrant distance education community. To this end, in 1996, I was the main instigator and founding president of our distance education organization, NADEOSA, in South Africa. I have continued to serve on the executive ever since and am proud that the association has both survived through some tough times and is thriving.

At an individual level, some of my accomplishments include:

- Being nominated by a variety of groups, including the Ministry of Education, as a long-standing member of the UNISA Council (its pinnacle governance structure), nudging it into a new future;
- Being appointed as the South Africa representative on the Commonwealth of Learning Board. I served there for eight years and was able to contribute to some major changes that occurred at the Commonwealth of Learning;
- Before I became a Board member at the Commonwealth of Learning, being recognized by the Commonwealth of Learning as a Fellow for my contributions to distance education;
- Being recognized for my contribution to education in general in South Africa by receiving a Chancellor's Medal from the University of Pretoria;
- Being asked by the Minister of Higher Education and Training to lead the founding council responsible for overseeing the development of Sol Plaatje University, one of the two universities created in the democratic era in South Africa. I continue to serve as the Deputy Chairperson of the council. It is now firmly established, an integral part of its community with committed staff and engaged students, and has one of the best student success rates in the country, despite the students having been medium to low achievers at school.

6. *What are some of the challenges that you faced over the years?*

In the early days when I was in SACHED, we were considered to be a threat to the South African state, so one of the challenges we faced was that several of our staff members and our projects were "banned" by the South African government. In short, this meant on the one hand that the staff members could not continue to work for us, and on the other that we had to cease the projects.

So in 1978, the director and one very senior staff member of SACHED were banned by the state, and two projects were closed. One was a teacher-upgrading programme, and the other was the newspaper project that I referred to earlier. It was believed that elements of these projects were undermining the apartheid state.

So, at a very young age, I was appointed as the Director of SACHED, tasked with stabilizing it, providing comfort to funders, initiating new projects, finding additional resources to continue with our work, and recruiting a permanent black director. I was able to do this in one and a half years and then resumed my plans to study further in the UK, retuning to SACHED in the early 1980s.

In this period, the political situation worsened, especially when a state of emergency was declared. Three of our branch offices experienced fires, and raids were carried out, documents confiscated, and staff detained.

Facing these challenges developed my resilience, including taking delight in working around obstacles when they arise!

Now, in a more democratic era on our continent, in pursuing the ongoing social justice agenda of transforming the education system so that it serves all students and not just the privileged few, our challenges include:

- Working in education systems that are poorly resourced, often with large classes and under-qualified educators,
- Finding innovative ways of meeting expectations within very constrained budgets,
- Working with poorly trained educators who often don't have the necessary pedagogical content knowledge,
- Understanding the achievement levels of our students rather than assuming the expected levels, and
- Ensuring that learners have access to contextually relevant learning materials.

A further challenge across the region is that while we now experience vastly improved, although sometimes patchy, connectivity at our university campuses, there is limited home connectivity and devices only for the elite. This makes it difficult to take advantage of educational technology.

7. *What was the "state of DE" when you first entered the field as opposed to DE in 2018?*

When I first entered the field in 1974, there was considerable innovation occurring internationally, led by the UK Open University and others such as the International and National Extension Colleges. In South Africa, the main distance education institution, which was UNISA, was caught in the academic boycott at the time. (This was a boycott that I certainly supported but had its implications for distance education provision in the country). This meant that South Africa, despite having had one of the first distance education universities in the world, dropped to being behind the times. The dominant distance education institution, UNISA, operated as a correspondence institution with very turgid study guides reflecting conservative and sometimes reactionary curricula, minimal student support, and little interaction with academics, except through four or so assignments in a full-year course. The nonprofit organization I joined, SACHED, was very deliberate in linking with developments abroad and innovating wherever we could. This was reflected in the learning materials we developed, the student support we offered, and the study groups that we organized. Wherever possible, we also developed innovative curricula that reflected the interests and needs of the marginalized groups we served.

At that time, there was, of course, no digital technology. It was purely print-based, with the occasional addition of video and audio, where distribution challenges could be overcome.

This situation has, of course, changed dramatically over the forty years. On our continent, the change in available technology is not as marked as in other more advantaged parts of the world. It was only four or five years ago when two new undersea cables were laid down the west and east coasts of Africa. These undersea cables then needed to be connected to underground cables across the different countries. Slowly, we have moved to a situation where the vast majority of universities experience reasonable broadband, although for some, this may be sporadic, especially when electricity is not available.

In the case of distance education, while there may be connectivity on the campus, students are not often, or at all, on the campus and can be scattered over a large geographical area. Institutions have created study centres that enjoy connectivity, but students often reside a long distance from these so may only visit once or twice per month. Distance education universities have to consider this context when planning. This certainly curtails the extent to which they can take advantage of the potential of technology.

So distance education providers work in the difficult environment of catering for two very different groups of students: those whose lives are digital and enjoy 24/7 connectivity and those who have access very seldom. Therefore, they still have to print study guides and submit their assignments via postal services. Often that means that study materials become "print behind glass," rather than being as interactive as might otherwise be the case if they could guarantee that their students were online more often.

For face-to-face colleges and schools, the technology provision is much worse than for universities. For example, when contacting some college staff, even now, one cannot rely on email because the recipient will not necessarily be in a position to check their email on a regular basis. With the penetration of smartphones, this context is changing, but data is still expensive.

This morning I was in a conversation about a course that we are developing for a leadership development institute across South Africa. We concluded [that] when the group is together with a facilitator, yes, we can use multimedia. However, we must assume that, for independent study tasks to be done at home, that students will have no Internet access, and, while they may have mobile phones, they are not likely to be smartphones, and where they are, we must remember that the data is expensive.

We have to remind ourselves constantly that there are very different worlds that our students live in – different contexts within in South Africa and across our region as a whole.

8. *What interesting stories would you like to share about where you started with DE and where you are now?*

An early story is about the first online course Saide offered. It was actually for distance educators. We asked everybody, "What's your email address?" All of the email addresses were supplied. What we did not ask, though, was, "How often do you access your email?" The reality was a horrible surprise! We learned very fast. Generally, our distance educators accessed their Hotmail account once a week at best. Therefore, we had to reorganize the course with that in mind.

Another memory was a fascinating debate that we had when I was a Council Member at UNISA. We were eager to take advantage of the increased connectivity in our country. We were also concerned that our graduates needed to be digitally literate. Initially, all of the student representative members who had iPads and smartphones supported the move. One major concern was that students would not have access to computers and connectivity. So a plan was made in this regard. Then the major concern emerged that staff might lose jobs when, for example, the whole printing and dispatch departments were considerably downsized. The students were eager to support the unions, so the process of adopting technology for all students was delayed for several years.

9. *What were your specific DE research interests, and have they changed/evolved over the years?*

I don't see myself as a researcher. I see myself primarily as a practitioner, so I will talk from that perspective.

From my early days, I was concerned about the notion of learner support and the extent to which it was often seen as something peripheral, not integrated and added subsequently, if at all! I have always understood learner support as something one plans for from the beginning of any learning design process. One has to withstand the pressure from bureaucrats to respond to any rise in costs by sacrificing support for the learning process.

The other important area has been open educational resources and the kind of impact that these can have on the educational sector, not only from a cost perspective but also on the quality of the teaching and learning process.

And the third has been the paramount importance of designing for student success. Even internationally, this is something that is not given enough attention in distance education. It is not enough to provide access; we have to provide a reasonable chance of success.

10. *Can you suggest names of other female pioneers in DE or online learning that you think we should include in the book?*

The only one that I thought that you might not have heard about, and she is more of a practitioner who was at UNISA, is Evie [Evelyn] Nonyongo. She worked for 20 years at SACHED, has contributed extensively to the Distance Education Association of South Africa [NADEOSA], and was key to its functioning for many years. She might also be able to give you further names.

One is a colleague of Evie's, Thandi Ngengebule. I would also include her. She was at SACHED and at UNISA. They were both important in the beginning of the transformation of South Africa.

Publications

Books

Glennie, J., Harley, K., Butcher, N., & Van Wyk, T. (Eds.). (2012). *Open educational resources and change in higher education: Reflections from practice.* UNESCO/Commonwealth of Learning.

Council on Higher Education. (2004). *Enhancing the contribution of distance higher education in South Africa.* Report of the investigation into distance education, Pretoria Council on Higher Education.

Book Chapters

Glennie, J. (1996). Toward learner-centred distance education in the changing South African context. In R. Mills & A. Tait (Eds.), *Supporting the learner in open and distance learning.* Pitman.

Glennie, J. (1997). Distance education: A way of providing cost-effective access to quality education. In H. Perold & J. Hofmeyer (Eds.), *Education Africa forum* (1st ed.). Education Africa.

Glennie, J., & Mays, T. (2019). Further perspectives on distance education in South Africa. In O. Zawacki-Richter & A. Qayyum (Eds.), *National systems in the era of global online distance education – Past, practice, prognosis.* Springer Open.

Glennie, J., & Welch, T. (2016). Open educational resources for early literacy in Africa: The role of the African storybook initiative. In F. Miao, S. Mishra, & R. McGreal (Eds.), *Open educational resources: Policy, costs and transformation.* UNESCO/Commonwealth of Learning.

Journal Articles

Glennie, J. (2006). Trends and issues in distance education: International perspectives (review) [Review of the book *Trends and issues in distance education: International perspectives*, by Y. L. Visser, L. Visser, M. Simonson, & R. Amirault, Eds.]. *The Review of Higher Education, 30*(1), 73–75. https://muse.jhu.edu/article/203462/pdf

Glennie, J. (2013). UNISA – Poised to realise its full potential. *UNISAWise*, July. Pretoria UNISA.

Glennie, J., & Mays, T. (2013). Rethinking distance in an era of online learning. *Internet Learning, 2*(2). doi:10.18278/il.2.2.10

Conference Presentations

Glennie, J. (1997). *Educational technology: Realizing the promise and diminishing the threat* [Keynote address]. Proceedings of the Commonwealth Conference on Educational Technology.

Glennie, J. (2013, May). *Convergence and difference between campus based and distance education: Trends in a digital age* [Presentation]. Senior Management Team at UCT.

Glennie, J. (2013, September). *Opening learning in universities/colleges/adult education* [Presentations]. Three Different DHET Assembled Groups.

Glennie, J. (2013, December). *Promoting open educational resources (OER)* [Keynote address]. Pan Commonwealth Forum, Abuja, Nigeria.

Glennie, J. (2014, July). *Distance education and the goals of the White Paper for post-school education and training*. Umalusi Conference on Distance Education.

Glennie, J. (2014, September). *Policy for the provision of distance education in South Africa Universities in the context of an integrated post-school system: Implications for UNISA*. UNISA Senior Management Team.

Glennie, J. (2015, July). *Online, open and flexible higher education for the future we want*. National Association for Distance Education and Open Learning in South Africa (NADEOSA) Conference.

Glennie, J. (2015, October). *Diverse modes of provision in South African higher education: Quality matters*. Council on Higher Education.

Glennie, J. (2016, February). *Making high-quality education a reality for all learners* [Panel presentation]. UNESCO Mobile Learning Week.

Glennie, J. (2016, October). *Can technology assist us in making university education more affordable?* Presidential Commission on University Funding.

Glennie, J. (2016, November). *OER contributing to early literacy in Africa: Evidence from Saide's African Storybook*. Pan Commonwealth Conference, Kuala Lumpur.

Glennie, J. (2017, July). *Dismantling challenges inhibiting post-school education and transformation through ODL* [Panel presentation]. Conference Celebration 25 Years of NADEOSA.

Glennie, J. (2017, September). *Open learning and the implementation evaluation of the NQF Act*. Department of Higher Education's Colloquium.

Glennie, J. (2017, September). *Using OER to address a fundamental educational challenge* [Plenary presentation]. UNESCO COL Summit on OER, Slovenia.

Glennie, J. (2018, February). *What have we achieved: Four years of Siyaphumelela?* [Panel presentation]. Achieving the Dream Conference, Nashville.

Glennie, J. (2018, September). *Moving forward with openness* [Closing address]. DEASA/NADEOSA Conference.

Glennie, J., & Mays, T. (2008). *Teacher education through distance education in Africa: Rising to the challenge* [Keynote Address]. African Council on Distance Education.

Glennie, J., & Welch, T. (2004). *Promoting quality in distance education* [Paper presentation]. All-Africa Ministers' of Education Conference on Open Learning and Distance Education.

11
GREGORY, SUE

Photo of Sue Gregory contributed by Sue Gregory

I don't think that we can even begin to think what the world is going to be like, but it is changing and we need to educate our students to be flexible to take on the change. Because what they learn here in five years' time won't be relevant.

Dr. Sue Gregory obtained all of her degrees from the University of New England in Australia. She began with a Bachelor of Arts, which was completed in 1985, and then moved on to finish a Masters of Education, focusing on computer education, in 2001. Her interests have enveloped the partnering of online learning with virtual world technology. Her years of experimentation with virtual worlds culminated in a PhD dissertation, *Exploring Authentic Learning Activities for Enhanced 2013 Learning Outcomes: Adult Learners and Their Perceptions of Learning in a Virtual World*, completed in 2013.

Dr. Gregory has held/holds a significant number of leadership roles in her field including:

- Head of School, Education at the University of New England, Australia;
- Australasian Society for Computers in Learning in Tertiary Education (ASCILITE) Executive, 2012 to present;
- ASCILITE Vice President (2015–2017, Acting President one month in 2016 and 2017);
- ASCILITE Spring into Excellence Research School – part of the facilitators and presenters for the inaugural school held in September 2017 at the University of Wollongong;
- ASCILITE Awards Chair (2013 to present);
- ASCILITE Community Mentoring Programme Chair (2014–2016; 2018 to present);
- ASCILITE Collaborative Community Mentoring Programme, Mentor, 2012, 2014, 2017;
- Experiential Learning in Virtual Worlds (ELVW) Steering Committee, 2011–2015;
- ELVW eBook editor, 2013, 2014 (*Experiential Learning in Virtual Worlds*);
- Chief Editor of three books on education in a virtual world (through Athabasca University Press, [AUP] 2016; NOVA, Science Publishers, Inc, 2015; and Springer Nature, 2018);
- Chief Editor of *Special Issue of Virtual Worlds Research*, 2016; and
- Chair, Australian and New Zealand Virtual Worlds Working Group, 2009 to present.

For the reader interested in virtual worlds and information and communications technology (ICT) use in online learning, Dr. Gregory's research listed at the end of this chapter will be of value.

Interview

Transcript Analysis Summary

Analysis of all interviews included in this volume led to the identification of 3,545 units of data. The mean of these collective units was 118 per pioneer, the median was 118.5, and the mode was 132. Individual interview units ranged from 59 to 217 units, yielding a spread of 158 units between all interviews. Sue Gregory's interview generated 138 units, which placed her interview in the top third of all interviews in terms of unit generation.

A comparison of Sue Gregory's interview to the interviews of all pioneers indicated that almost half of her interview was akin to the average interview in terms of units produced per thematic area (Figure 11.1). Six of the 14 thematic codes in her interview yielded a similar numbers of unit to the average interview. These included challenges, accomplishments, changes over time, others for the book, career history, and general gender-related comments. Gregory's interview yielded a greater-than-average number of units in four areas: background, learning environment, interesting memories, and final thoughts. Some of these units may be explained by Sue's early introduction to the field as a distance learning student. Other units focused on the unique area of distance learning that Sue eventually devoted much of her career to: that is, virtual world learning environments.

Gregory's interview generated a less-than-average number of units in the topic areas of benefits of DE, research interests, goals, and early founders. The lower number of units in benefits of DE should be understood from the point of view that this was not a topic that interviewees were asked to discuss. Rather, benefits of DE was identified as a theme during the data analysis process. Therefore, any references to the benefits of DE were initiated solely by the interviewees, which would help explain why Gregory did not mention this topic as much as some interviewees did. During her interview, Gregory stated that her research interests were devoted to studying virtual world learning, which provided reason for the limited number of units in this area. Lastly, due to the early state

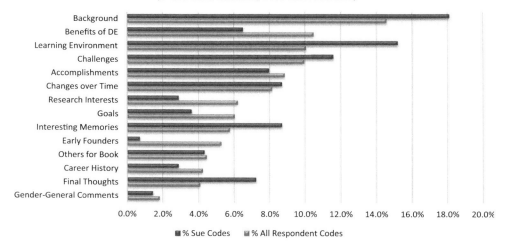

Figure 11.1 All Respondents' Versus Sue Gregory's Parent Codes

of virtual worlds in education at the time of her entry, Gregory could only recall one other virtual world female pioneer. This is why her interview had so few units in the early founders area.

Link to recorded interview: tinyurl.com/Gregory-S-2018

Transcript of Interview

Full Name: Sue Gregory
Institutional Affiliation: University of New England, Australia
Key:

Regular font = Interviewee comments
Italicized font = Interviewer comments

Interview Questions

1. *What was your educational and experiential background before you became involved in distance education [DE], online learning, mobile learning, and virtual world learning?*

    Interesting, my undergrad was in the early 1980s, and when I was finishing that, I finished it with distance education. That was when I received pieces of paper and cassettes in the mail to finish my study. Ever since then, all of my studies have been in distance education/online. Once I got into academia, our institution helped, but it was just a natural progression.

2. *In what year did you begin to look specifically into DE? Online learning? Mobile learning? Virtual world learning?*

    I would say in the 1990s when I was doing my master's. I did a master's of education in computer education. I was developing online packages in that. So that would have been when I started specifically looking into it. Because when I did my undergrad and grad diploma earlier, even though they were by distance, I wasn't actually looking at it in that way. So, it would have been in the late 90s.

    I: When did you begin to look at mobile learning?

    When mobiles became available. Whenever the first iPads came out, two colleagues and I got a little research grant so that we could buy the first iPads. We looked at it from three perspectives. One of us was a student, one of us was a lecturer, and the other one (which was me) was looking at it in relation to apps that you could use without spending money. So whenever iPads first came out, that is when I started researching mobile learning.

    Virtual world learning was in 2007, when someone said to me, "Sue, you need to do a PhD."

    I said, "I don't know what. Maybe I'll do it on wikis, blogs, and things like that."

    And they said, "Whatever it is, think about it as something that you have to immerse yourself in for the next six years."

    I said, "Ah, well, wikis and blogs won't do it!"

    Then someone suggested virtual worlds, and I said, "What's that?" So I went searching, and they grabbed me. I still think that they're the best educational tool available. So that was 2007.

3. *What were the circumstances in your world that initiated this interest in DE and online/mobile/virtual world learning?*

    I think mostly because I was a distance education student, I wanted to create an experience for students that was more engaging than listening to someone talk, reading .pdf documents, or receiving pieces of paper. I wanted to explore ways that you could engage with your colleagues, your peers, and your lecturers and enjoy the learning rather than being a sole learner. So that is what I think initiated my interest, to make it more exciting. It was totally boring back then. Sorry.

4. *Which female researchers or female colleagues may have piqued your interest in DE and online/mobile/ virtual world learning?*

    When I read that question, it was interesting because two people suggested virtual worlds, and they are both males. I had never heard of them [virtual worlds] at that stage. I didn't know what they were.

    But once I got into virtual worlds, eventually, about after a year, one of my supervisors, who is now pro vice chancellor at RMIT [Royal Melbourne Institute of Technology], Belinda Tynan, she was my mentor. She had delved into virtual worlds a little, but I found after not very long that I surpassed her knowledge.

A lot of people I met online were females that I aspired to know more about. One was Jo Kay. She is now in Canberra. Sarah Ball also did a lot in the US. The people I was following (this happens all the time), they got other jobs, and they started going out of virtual worlds. There are not that many people who've had that sustained time in virtual worlds as an educator. They start, and people go, "Aw, you're fantastic. Here, do this job." And suddenly they find that they're not doing so much anymore. I am the chair of the Australian Virtual Worlds Learning Group, and I can think of two people who've had a sustained time in virtual worlds in the past ten years. The rest have been plucked away to do other things. I find that very sad.

5. *Who would you identify as the early female leaders/founders in the field of DE? Online learning? Mobile learning? Virtual world learning?*

I should have gone and done some research on this one. There's Sarah Ball, and she's since gotten married [now Sarah Robbins], from the US; she was definitely a founder in virtual worlds because she wrote the *Second Life for Dummies* book. She doesn't even do anything in virtual worlds anymore. Again, I find that very sad.

In distance education, I find it interesting because, like Athabasca [University], we've been in distance education. We're coming up for our 65th year next year, with about 50 years in distance education.

One of my colleagues, Chris Redding, who was also one of my PhD supervisors, she was a great flag flyer for distance education for our rural students. There are so many. Helen Farley is a big one; she's been plucked away to another field. Who else? Well, even if we go over to New Zealand, there is Meryl Hearns, who's been doing fantastic things in virtual worlds. She's at Manukau Polytech [Manukau Institute of Technology] over in New Zealand and doing some great work. So a lot of these people are doing amazing things in virtual worlds.

If we go back to distance education, I can't specifically identify anyone. You just quote so many people along the way, and I never really found someone that I go, "Okay, I love exactly what you do, and I follow that." Now I grab bits and pieces off other people or just invent it myself.

6. *What are some of the goals that you strove to achieve in the field of DE? Online learning? Mobile learning? Virtual world learning?*

The biggest thing is people taking it up. I have struggled with this, and I know that I'm not the only one. Ever since working in this area [I learned that] you get people on board, you got to be passionate, you got to know that it takes time to learn, and it takes time to keep up the momentum, and people don't want to put in the time, I think. So I've found that I've been really lucky with the institution that I'm at, the University of New England, that they have supported me. It's almost ten years now that they have supported paying for our Second Life island. Every year, I think, "I've got to ask for money for that to be paid, and now they have." So that's been great. But to get people to actually teach in the virtual world has been really hard work.

When I first started, I was by myself. I did a lot of presentations and slowly started to get people on board. Then I did get one person on board for about five years. That was fantastic, but then she retired. I had another person coming on board, and she's also retired. This just happens. But there needs to be a lot more. There's so much that you can do in there! I now don't have the time to be mentoring people, holding their hand. They will have to take on the initiative. That's been something that I've been striving to achieve. So the very last time when someone said, "We will pay for the virtual life island," they said, "But we have to present this, have a workshop, and get people on board."

And I said, "Of course, I will do that." I haven't done that yet because this has only just happened, but I've had about 50 people come through, yet not one single person has continued on with that. So I think, "Okay, it's a lot of work." But I think that we all get busy in what we know. People need time to think about doing some things slightly different than what they do.

7. *What are some of your accomplishments in the field of DE/online/mobile/virtual world learning that you would like to share?*

There are a few things I think I've done. When I started teaching online in the virtual world, that was 2008. So in 2007, the idea was given to me, and I developed the space. Then in 2008, I was given some units that I could teach and coordinate and take my students into the virtual world. So that was a lot of learning on my behalf and the students'. The biggest accomplishment with that was that I found after every course there would probably be three or four people who would return the next year to go through the whole session again, even though they were no longer a student, to either keep learning or to assist me. That was fantastic.

One year we had more than 80 people try to participate. I didn't know at the time that we could only have a maximum of 50. So my marketing was really good.

I've received a lot of grants from this area. Let me think – probably up to close to a million [Australian dollars] in grants on it. I have written about 80 publications on virtual world learning. So I think those accomplishments are reasonably good. But the biggest non-accomplishment is that I'm not doing it at the moment. I'm still flying the flag, and it's still in my units, but I'm not teaching it. Every time that it is being taught at the moment, that little bit has to be taken out. That's the reverse accomplishment.

8. *What are some of the challenges that you faced in these areas of learning over the years?*

I think I've already said a few of them. Institutions taking it on board; like I said, I've been lucky, but other universities haven't. They've seen their spaces in the virtual world come and go. Always paying for it; people who are interested in universities will put up a building for millions of dollars, but they won't spend two thousand dollars on a virtual one, so always having to get that. Having people carrying on with the teaching of it; I always find that is a challenge. But I think that the biggest one is that people move on, and that space isn't filled. You really need within the one institution several people doing this sort of work so that there is momentum, and it keeps going.

9. *What was the "state of DE" when you first entered the field as opposed to DE in 2018?*

Well, I think I've already said that one. It was pieces of paper and cassettes, and now it's all online. You know, people can do amazing things online, so it's really an exciting space.

I was thinking of a unit designed like "Choose your own journey," so you can choose to read things, you can choose to watch things or listen to things, you can choose to use augmented or virtual reality, and then you can choose to go into a virtual world. You can work alone, you can listen or look, or you can have that interaction with technology in augmented or virtual reality, or you can go online and be totally immersed with something and interacting with other people. You can do that through other online tools, but it's almost like where we are now in online distance education. There is still a way to go. Artificial intelligence is getting there, but there is still a long way to go. The things I want to develop, I think it will take technology about 20 years to do that.

10. *What interesting memories would you like to share about the beginning of online, mobile, and virtual world learning?*

I find this very interesting, so . . . Back in 2006 or 2007 was when I started thinking about doing this. I set up my avatar, and I went into the virtual world. I looked around, and I didn't know what to do. I had teenage kids, so I said, "I've got this avatar. I don't know how to make them move . . ."

Anyway, they said, "You do this to make them walk, and this to make them move left and right, and this is how you can make them talk . . ."

And I went, "Ohhh, okay." So then I could talk to people and move around. Then for about a week or two, I thought, "This is all very nice," but I thought, "But I don't know what to do here." So I just left it.

Then a couple months later, I thought, "Right. Okay, if I am going to make this work, I need something else to do besides 'I can talk, and I can walk'; that's not that educational." So what I did was I went to a lot of classes, and I learned how to build and interact with people and create things. So I created my own online room where we would have tutorials and things like that. And then I was gone. Suddenly, I was in there all day and all night, trying to set up this environment. It totally immersed me. That was a memory for me in that I started, stopped, I needed something to do for my students to make me be there, but the thing was when I got my students in, I couldn't get rid of them. They wouldn't leave. This was over the years. I started with a two-hour session for something like seven p.m. to nine p.m., and they would stay until midnight, and because I was collecting data for my PhD, I would be staying there.

By the time I finished my PhD and got it all, and I was still teaching in there, after one hour I'd say, "Okay, it is eight p.m., I'm going, and I'll see you." How things changed. But the students still stayed there. You get so immersed. Time just flies.

Here's one memory. . . . I always tell my students, "You can come into the virtual world, but when you are with me, you have to have a human avatar." Because you can be anything; you can be an animal, a tree, or a car, whatever. So I said to them, "You must be a human, and (because they were in education) you must be presented as if you were teaching." I would always tell them that the reason was that I went to an online conference. There was a group of people. They were all talking and discussing things, and then this dog started talking. I said, "Who are you? You shouldn't be talking. You're a dog." I realized then that I was not taking any interest in what this dog was saying because he was a dog. He shouldn't be talking.

I can't have me responding like that to my students. So they had to be humans. I thought this dog was a real good eye-opener for me on what I thought people should be – *people* [emphasis in the original], not anything else. But they've all come as people. When they go away, they can do whatever they like.

11. *What were your specific DE/online/mobile/virtual world learning research interests, and have they changed/evolved over the years?*

The main interest has been student engagement in a virtual world, and it hasn't really evolved; evolved maybe in how I do things, but I'm still interested in student engagement and the comparisons in what they might get in a learning management system. In a learning management system, they might have (and you can do lots in them nowadays), but before it might be reading texts and etc., etc. Wikis, blogs, webinars, online quizzes – all of those sorts of things, in comparing them to what students are getting in virtual worlds; I've always had that interest.

One interesting result in part of my PhD was looking at two and a half thousand students and their results in the IT [information technology] education units that I taught in. I compared their grades. Anyone who was a distance education student who volunteered to use the virtual worlds, they mostly got an HD or D, that's 75% or greater, compared to other students who chose not to; they got a much lower grade. I don't put that down to my teaching at all, and most of the time, I wasn't the marker, so there wasn't any bias there. I put it down to the types of people that chose to go into a virtual world to learn because they are probably the more motivated. They are the ones who want to know about different ways of teaching and learning. So that's always been my thing is engagement and the differences between a virtual world and other technologies in learning.

12. *Could you please describe the learning environment that you currently work in (e.g., geographic and institutional setting, student demographics)?*

I am currently the Head of School, Education, and Professor at University of New England, Australia. We are based in Armidale, New South Wales, Australia. That is halfway between Sydney and Brisbane, about a six-hour drive to each. We are 1,000 meters up and about 200 kilometres from the coast.

We have about 24,000 students. Our university has about 80% online students, and 20% on campus. In our School of Education, 92% are distance learners, so we don't have a lot on campus (about 100 each year) and about 5,000 in our school.

In our school, we have about 55 full-time academic staff. That has plummeted a bit; we're actually recruiting at the moment. We use Moodle, which is a learning management system.

I use Second Life for my virtual world; it has five classrooms. The thing I love about a virtual world is that it doesn't have to be real. When I take students on, we go to places, and I go, "Look at this lecture theatre; I don't get why there a lecture theatre, because you don't need a lecture theatre. You could just have a crowd standing up."

However, I have been in a conference with someone who said, "I need to sit my avatar down because she's getting tired." That was kind of different.

But I have replicated real life; because I'm in education, we needed classrooms so students can practice their teaching. So I have replicated classrooms in the virtual world. There's whiteboards, even interactive whiteboards, cork boards, books that made the pages change, all that sort of stuff. So that's the learning environment. There are lots of real interactive tools in that environment. We are on an island called Australis for Learning, and it's shaped like Australia.

Back in 2009, our UNE (that's University of New England) joined with two other institutions, so we had a third of the island each. Since then both of them pulled out. Neither of the groups of people that I worked with back then do virtual worlds anymore, so UNE owns the whole island, but that's good. Now we have a hospital, we've got a shop for accounting, we've got a pharmacy. We've got three levels, so you can teleport up levels. We've got a lot of classrooms that a particular button may change. We have a little farm there with sheep, cattle, and a variety of animals. So interesting little themes, depending on what we are teaching at the time. We have a little school and classroom playground. So a lot of tools that you would find in a typical playground are found in these playgrounds, and they are interactive. So they make your avatar move when you're doing things like playing in the sand or on a swing, etc.

I: When you talk about some students being on campus, are they also engaged in some distance learning? Is it sort of like blended learning going on?

It is. We try not to because they actually choose to be here on campus, but sometimes, unfortunately, we have no choice, so there is blended learning. Yes, absolutely. But we do attempt as much as possible to give them an on-campus experience. However, having said that, in the first year of our undergraduate degree, the first practicum is an online practicum. Instead of going into the classroom to observe teaching, they do that online. So we have blended, yes.

Our institution is one of the earliest distance education institutions in Australia. We could probably say that we were the only one, but a lot of institutions are now getting in that space, so now that is no longer so. We do like to think of ourselves as the best, but we're not. I can't even say who the best is; a lot of people are doing this now. Some of the universities have a lot more money than us, so they do things differently and perhaps better, but it's arguable. I do think that we are doing well at UNE, and we know that everyone else is getting in this space, so we are trying to work out how we can stay number one and do things slightly different and better engage our students.

Our biggest thing is, because we are smaller than a lot of the universities, we get to know our students. So I think that's our number one thing here. Even though they are distance [learners], we know them. They're not just a student, not just a number; they're a person. So that's our big thing.

13. *Is there anything else you [would] like to address?*

I would like to see AI [artificial intelligence] developed. . . . I have this idea in my head, and I have talked to so many people, but at the moment, we just can't do it. In ten years, they will be able to do what I want.

In the 90s, I was developing web pages for companies. I thought to myself, "Well, that's the Internet. That's everything I need to know. There's nothing else." And how wrong was I?

So I don't think that we can even begin to think what the world is going to be like, but it is changing, and we need to educate our students to be flexible to take on the change. Because what they learn here in five years' time won't be relevant.

I don't teach the first-year undergrad IT unit here now, but when I did, I remember them coming back in four years, saying, "Ah, Sue, can you help me with this? This is something new that wasn't taught back when you were teaching."

I actually used to say, "Yes, it was. We did teach that." Like, for instance, interactive whiteboards were a big thing back then.

They'd go, "I've gone into a classroom where there's an interactive whiteboard, and I don't know how to use it."

And I would think, "Now, did I just waste a lecture and a couple workshops on that?" because they'd completely forgotten.

So even if it does exist in five years, they forget what they learned five years before.

Yes, AI, virtual reality, augmented reality, virtual worlds, holographics are all things that will make big changes.

I remember when they were creating web pages a few years ago where you could get in – it wasn't just a web page; it was more interactive. But it didn't take off. So things will come and go. Some things will take off, and some won't. It's hard to know. I don't know.

And in relation to me, I'll be forgotten. Definitely in 50 years, I will not be remembered, except when people are doing their tree of their family histories.

14. *Can you suggest names of other female pioneers in DE, online, mobile, and/or virtual world learning that you think we should include in the book?*

Anyone else to suggest . . . well, you've already talked to Helen [Farley], so there you go. She's amazing. She's so good.

I should open up my Virtual Worlds Working Group list and go, "All of these people."

Belinda Tynan is one that you should talk to down at RMIT. She's very good. She will be excellent in the distance education and online stuff, and she will know a little bit about virtual worlds. So she's very good.

Lisa Jacka up at Southern Cross University; she's early in her career, but she's done a lot of work in virtual worlds. She might be worth talking to. She's just converted her PhD into a book, so that's all good.

Meryl Hearns, up at Manukau Polytech in New Zealand; she hasn't finished her PhD yet, but she's done amazing work in virtual worlds.

I could tell you lots of guys, but you probably don't want them.

I will go through my list. A lot of people have gone on to other things, but I'll look.

Publications

Books

Gregory, S. (2013). *Exploring authentic learning activities for enhanced learning outcomes: Adult learners and their perceptions of learning in a virtual world* [Thesis]. University of New England, Armidale, Australia. https://epublications.une.edu.au/vital/access/manager/Repository/une:13869

Gregory, S., Jerry, P., & Tavers-Jones, N. (Eds.). (2014). *At the edge of the rift*. Inter-Disciplinary Press.

Gregory, S., Lee, M. J. W., Dalgarno, B., & Tynan, B. (Eds.). (2015). *Virtual worlds in online and distance education: Cases and applications*. NOVA: Science Publishers, Inc.

Gregory, S., Lee, M. J. W., Dalgarno, B., & Tynan, B. (Eds.). (2016). *Learning in virtual worlds: Research and applications*. Athabasca University Press.

Gregory, S., & Wood, D. (Eds.). (2018). *Authentic virtual world education: Facilitating cultural engagement and creativity*. Springer Nature.

Jerry, P., Tavers-Jones, N., & Gregory, S. (Eds.). (2013). *Riding the hype cycle: The resurgence of virtual worlds*. Inter-Disciplinary Press.

Book Chapters

Dalgarno, B., Lee, M. J. W., Gregory, S., & Tynan, B. (2016a). Conclusion. In S. Gregory, M. J. W. Lee, B. Dalgarno, & B. Tynan (Eds.), *Learning in virtual worlds: Research and applications* (pp. 295–306). Athabasca University Press.

Dalgarno, B., Lee, M. J. W., Gregory, S., & Tynan, B. (2016b). Introduction. In S. Gregory, M. J. W. Lee, B. Dalgarno, & B. Tynan (Eds.), *Learning in virtual worlds: Research and applications* (pp. xix–xxvii). Athabasca University Press.

Gregory, S. (2011a). Rethinking teaching and learning through Machinima professional development on Sloodle. In P. Jerry & L. Lindsey (Eds.), *Experiential learning in virtual worlds: Opening an undiscovered country* (1st ed., pp. 221–232). Inter-Disciplinary Press.

Gregory, S. (2011b). Teaching higher education students with diverse learning outcomes in the virtual world of second life. In R. Hinrichs & C. Wankel (Eds.), *Transforming virtual world learning, cutting-edge technologies in higher education* (Vol. 4, pp. 333–362). Emerald Group Publishing Limited.

Gregory, S. (2012). Learning in a virtual world: Student perceptions and outcomes. In K. Moyle & G. Winjnaards (Eds.), *Student reactions to learning with technologies: Perceptions and outcomes* (Vol. 1, pp. 91–116). IGI Global.

Gregory, S. (2013a). Comparison of students' learning in a virtual world. In P. Jerry, N. Tavares-Jones, & S. Gregory (Eds.), *The hype cycle upswing: The resurgence of virtual worlds* (pp. 123–134). Inter-Disciplinary Press.

Gregory, S. (2013b). Engaging classes in a virtual world. In K. Bredl & W. Bösche (Eds.), *Serious games and virtual worlds in education, professional development, and healthcare* (pp. 126–144). IGI Global.

Gregory, S. (2013c). Higher education professional development on virtual worlds through machinima of SLOODLE (linking Moodle with second life). In M. Childs & G. Withnail (Eds.), *Experiential learning in virtual worlds* (pp. 91–114). Inter-Disciplinary Press.

Gregory, S. (2014a). Student perceptions of learning from a distance through a virtual world. In S. Gregory, P. Jerry, & N. Tavares-Jones (Eds.), *At the edge of the rift*. Inter-Disciplinary Press.

Gregory, S. (2014b). Sustainability of virtual worlds in education: A review of assessment through midwifery programs. In S. Kennedy-Clark, K. Everett, & P. Wheeler (Eds.), *Cases on assessment in scenario and game-based virtual worlds in higher education* (pp. 26–35). IGI Global.

Gregory, S. (2014c). Taking the distance out of learning for students through a virtual world. In A. Hebbel-Seeger, T. Reiners, & D. Schäffer (Eds.), *Synthetic worlds: Emerging technologies in education and economics* (Vol. 33, pp. 205–231). Springer Science+Business Media New York.

Gregory, S., Bannister-Tyrrell, M., Charteris, J., & Nye, A. (2018). Heutagogy in postgraduate education: Cognitive advantages for higher degree online students. In F. F. Padro, P. Danaher, & E. Ronel (Eds.), *University development and administration: Post-graduate education in higher education* (pp. 189–209). Springer.

Gregory, S., Brown, T., & Parkes, M. (2013). A preliminary evaluation of the iPad as a tool for learning and teaching. In B. Tynan, J. Willems, & R. James (Eds.), *Outlooks and opportunities in blended and distance learning* (pp. 154–168). IGI Global: Information Science.

Gregory, S., Jerry, P., & Tavers-Jones, N. (2014). Virtual worlds (reality) at the edge of the rift. In S. Gregory, P. Jerry, & N. Tavares-Jones (Eds.), *Virtual worlds (reality) and the new marketplace*. Inter-Disciplinary Press.

Gregory, S., & Masters, Y. (2012). Comparison of role-plays in a virtual world. In P. Jerry, Y. Masters, & N. Tavares-Jones (Eds.), *Utopia and a garden party: Experiential learning in virtual worlds*, At the Interface: Cutting Edge Research (pp. 45–56). Inter-Disciplinary Press.

Gregory, S., Reiners, T., & Tynan, B. (2010). Alternative realities: Immersive learning for and with students. In H. Song (Ed.), *Distance learning technology, current instruction, and the future of education: Applications of today, practices of tomorrow* (pp. 245–271). IGI Global.

Gregory, S., Reiners, T., Wood, L. C., Teräs, M., & Teräs, H. (2015). Gamification and digital games-based learning in the classroom. In M. Henderson & G. Romeo (Eds.), *Teaching and digital technologies: Big issues and critical questions* (pp. 127–141). Cambridge University Press.

Gregory, S., & Smith, H. (2010). How virtual classrooms are changing the face of education: Using virtual classrooms in today's university environment. In W. Halloway & J. Maurer (Eds.), *International research in teacher education: Current perspectives* (pp. 239–252). University of New England.

Gregory, S., Tavares-Jones, N., & Jerry, P. (2013). The hype cycle upswing: The resurgence of virtual worlds. In P. Jerry, N. Tavares-Jones, & S. Gregory (Eds.), *Riding the hype cycle: The resurgence of virtual worlds* (pp. xi–xiv). Inter-Disciplinary Press.

Gregory, S., Tynan, B., Lee, M. J. W., & Dalgarno, B. (2015). Prologue. In S. Gregory, M. J. W. Lee., B. Dalgarno, & B. Tynan (Eds.), *Virtual worlds for online learning: Cases and applications*. NOVA: Science Publishers, Inc.

Gregory, S., Willems, J., Wood, D., Hay, L., Ellis, A., & Jacka, L. (2013). Learning and teaching in second life: Educator and student perspectives. In B. Tynan, J. Willems, & R. James (Eds.), *Outlooks and opportunities in blended and distance learning* (pp. 219–240). Information Science (an Imprint of IGI Global).

Gregory, S., & Wood, D. (2018). Conclusion. In S. Gregory & D. Wood (Eds.), *Authentic virtual world education: Facilitating cultural engagement and creativity* (pp. 199–203). Springer Nature.

Lee, M. J. W., Dalgarno, B., Gregory, S., Carlson, L., & Tynan, B. (2013). How are Australian and New Zealand higher educators using 3D immersive virtual worlds in their teaching? In B. Tynan, J. Willems, & R. James (Eds.), *Outlooks and opportunities in blended and distance learning* (pp. 169–188). Information Science (an Imprint of IGI Global).

Masters, Y., & Gregory, S. (2011). Second Life and higher education: New opportunities for teaching and learning. In P. Jerry & L. Lindsey (Eds.), *Experiential learning in virtual worlds: Opening an undiscovered country* (1st ed., pp. 137–146). Inter-Disciplinary Press.

Masters, Y., & Gregory, S. (2013a). Second Life: A novice/expert teaching and learning tale. In B. Tynan, J. Willems, and R. James (Eds.), *Outlooks and opportunities in blended and distance learning* (pp. 204–218). Information Science (an Imprint of IGI Global).

Masters, Y., & Gregory, S. (2013b). Virtual worlds enhancing student learning in higher education. In M. Childs & G. Withnail (Eds.), *Experiential learning in virtual worlds* (pp. 3–26). Inter-Disciplinary Press.

Masters, Y., Gregory, S., Dalgarno, B., Reiners, T., & Knox, V. (2012). Branching out through VirtualPREX: Enhancing teaching in Second Life. In P. Jerry, Y. Masters, & N. Tavares-Jones (Eds.), *Utopia and a garden party: Experiential learning in virtual worlds,* At the Interface: Cutting Edge Research (pp. 57–69). Inter-Disciplinary Press.

Masters, Y., Gregory, S., Dalgarno, B., Reiners, T., & Knox, V. (2015a). Branching out through VirtualPREX: Enhancing teaching in Second Life. In S. Gregory, M. Lee, B. Dalgarno, & B. Tynan (Eds.), *Virtual worlds for online learning: Cases and applications.* NOVA: Science Publishers Inc.

Masters, Y., Gregory, S., Dalgarno, B., Reiners, T., & Knox, V. (2015b). VirtualPREX: Providing virtual professional experience for pre-service teachers. In S. Gregory, M. J. W. Lee., B. Dalgarno, & B. Tynan (Eds.), *Virtual worlds for online learning: Cases and applications* (pp. 3–24). NOVA: Science Publishers, Inc.

Masters, Y., Gregory, S., Reiners, T., Knox, V., & Dalgarno, B. (2014). VirtualPREX: Developing teaching skills in Second Life. In C. A. DeCoursey & S. Garrett (Eds.), *Teaching and learning in virtual worlds* (pp. 69–94). Inter-Disciplinary Press.

Reiners, T., Gregory, S., & Knox, V. (2016). Virtual bots: Their influence on virtual worlds, and how they can increase interactivity and immersion through VirtualPREX. In S. Gregory, M. Lee, B. Dalgarno, & B. Tynan (Eds.), *Learning in virtual worlds: Research and applications* (pp. 167–190). Athabasca University Press.

Reiners, T., Wood, L. C., Gregory, S., & Teräs, H. (2015). Gamification design elements in business education simulations. In M. Khosrow-Pour (Ed.), *Encyclopedia of information science and technology* (3rd ed., pp. 3048–3061). IGI Global.

Reiners, T., Wood, L. C., Teras, M., Teras, H., Gregory, S., Chang, V., & Steurer, M. (2018). Selfguided exploration of virtual learning spaces. In S. Gregory & D. Wood (Eds.), *Authentic virtual world education: Facilitating cultural engagement and creativity* (pp. 61–78). Springer Nature.

Tynan, B., Gregory, S., Dalgarno, B., & Lee, M. J. W. (2015). Epilogue. In S. Gregory, M. J. W. Lee., B. Dalgarno, & B. Tynan (Eds.), *Virtual worlds for online learning: Cases and applications.* NOVA: Science Publishers Inc.

Wood, D., & Gregory, S. (2018). The affordances of virtual worlds as authentic, culturally diverse learning environments. In S. Gregory & D. Wood (Eds.), *Authentic virtual world education: Facilitating cultural engagement and creativity* (pp. 1–7). Springer Nature.

Journal Articles

Al Lily, A., Foland, J., Stoloff, D., Gogus, A., Erguvan, I., Awshar, M., . . . Schrader, P. (2016). Academic domains as political battlegrounds: A global enquiry by 99 academics in the fields of education and technology. *Information Development,* 1–19. https://doi.org/10.1177/0266666916646415

Bannister, B., Cornish, L., Bannister-Tyrrell, M., & Gregory, S. (2015). Creative us of digital technologies: Keeping the best and brightest in the bush. *Australian and International Journal of Rural Education, 25*(1), 52–65.

Charteris, J., & Gregory, S. (2018). Snapchat and digitally mediated sexualised communication: Ruptures in the school home nexus. *Gender and Education, 32*(6). https://doi.org/10.1080/09540253.2018.1533922

Charteris, J., Gregory, S., & Masters, Y. (2016). "Snapchat," youth subjectivities and sexuality: Disappearing media and the discourse of youth innocence. *Gender and Education,* 1–17.

Charteris, J., Parkes, M., Gregory, S., Fletcher, P., & Reyes, V. (2018). Student-initiated Facebook sites: Nurturing personal learning environments or a place for the disenfranchised? *Technology, Pedagogy and Education, 27*(4) 459–472.

Colferai Boton, E., & Gregory, S. (2015). Minimizing attrition in online degree courses. *The Journal of Educators Online, 12*(1), 62–90.

Cruz-Lara, S., Gregory, S., Fragoso, S., Albrecht, U.-V., & Lueg, C. (Eds.). (2014). The journal of virtual worlds assembled (2014). *Journal of Virtual Worlds Research, 7*(2).

Dalgarno, B., Gregory, S., Knox, V., & Reiners, T. (2016). Practising teaching using virtual classroom role plays. *Australian Journal of Teacher Education, 41*(1), 126–154.

Dalgarno, B., Lee, M. J. W., Carlson, L., Gregory, S., & Tynan, B. (2011). An Australian and New Zealand scoping study on the use of 3D immersive virtual worlds in higher education. *Australasian Journal of Educational Technology, 27*(1), 1–15.

Gregory, S. (2014), Authentic and engaging virtual practice teaching for rural and remote preservice teachers. *Australian and International Journal of Rural Education, 24*(3), 15–27.

Gregory, S. (2015). Discussion boards as collaborative learning tools. *International Journal of Continuing Engineering Education and Life Long Learning. 25*(1), 63–76.

Gregory, S. (Ed.). (2016). Assembled 2016 (Part 1). *Journal of Virtual Worlds Research, 9*(1), 1–157.

Gregory, S., & Bannister-Tyrrell, M. (2017). Digital learner presence and online teaching tools: Higher cognitive requirements of online learners for effective learning. *Research and Practice in Technology Enhanced Learning, 12*(18), 1–17.

Gregory, S., Jacka, L., Hillier, M., & Grant, S. (2015). Using virtual worlds in rural and regional educational institutions. *Australian and International Journal of Rural Education, 25*(2), 73–90.

Gregory, S., & Masters, Y. (2012). Role-play in a virtual world – real thinking with virtual hats. *Australasian Journal of Educational Technology, 28*(3), 420–440.

Gregory, S., Scutter, S., Jacka, L., McDonald, M., Farley, H., & Newman, C. (2015). Barriers and enablers to the use of virtual worlds in higher education: An exploration of educator perceptions, Attitudes and experiences. *Education Technology & Society, 18*(1), 3–12.

Masters, Y., Gregory, S., & Grono, S. (2015). PST online: Meeting the need for teaching innovation for virtual schools. *International Journal of Learning, Teaching and Educational Research, 14*(2), 1–16.

McDonald, M., & Gregory, S. (in press). Third generation virtual worlds in education: The way forward. *Journal of Virtual Worlds Research*.

Muwanga-Zake, J., Parkes, M., & Gregory, S. (2010). Blogging at university as a case study in instructional design: Challenges and suggestions towards professional development. *(IJEDICT) International Journal of Education and Development Using Information and Communication Technology, 6*(1).

Parkes, M., Gregory, S., Fletcher, P., Adlington, R., & Gromik, N. (2015). Bringing people together while learning apart: Creating online learning environments to support the needs of rural and remote students. *Australian and International Journal of Rural Education, 25*(1), 66–78.

Reyes, V., Gregory, S., Reading C., & Doyle, H. (2014). ICT teaching practices from a TPACK perspective – A view from a regional Australian University. *PLS Working Papers, 12*, 1–14.

Reyes, V., Reading, C., Ritz, N., & Gregory, S. (2016). An exploratory analysis of TPACK perceptions of pre-service science teachers: A view from a regional Australian perspective. *Journal of Computers in Education: Special Issue on Professional Learning, 12*(4). https://doi.org/10.4018/IJICTE.2016100101

Reyes, V. C. J., Reading, C., Doyle, H., & Gregory, S. (2017). Integrating ICT into teacher education programs from a TPACK perspective: Exploring perceptions of university lecturers. *Computers & Education, 115*, 1–19.

12
GUNAWARDENA, CHANDRA

Photo of Chandra Gunawardena contributed by Chandra Gunawardena

All of my colleagues came and told me, 'Why do you want to go to the Open University? It's like a correspondence school. There's no quality. There's no acceptance in the country. So, you better stay [here].

DOI: 10.4324/9781003275329-13

Dr. Chandra Gunawardena is an established researcher from Sri Lanka. She obtained her General Arts Degree in 1962 from the University of Ceylon in Peradeniya, Sri Lanka. She then completed a Post-graduate Diploma in Education in 1969 from the same institution. In 1977 she completed a Master of Arts in Education from the University of Sri Lanka. It is interesting to note that all these degrees were from the same institution, as Ceylon changed its name in 1972 to Sri Lanka. Gunawardena then spent time in Australian completing her PhD at La Trobe University, Melbourne, in 1980.

At present, Gunawardena is Emeritus Professor of Education at the Open University of Sri Lanka (OUSL), in Nawala, Nugegoda. She also holds a Doctor of Letters (Honoris Causa) awarded by the Open University of Sri Lanka. Over the span of her career, Gunawardena has also held many leadership roles. She has been Dean and acting Vice Chancellor of the Open University of Sri Lanka. She has also worked with and published for both UNESCO and the Commonwealth of Learning during her career.

Dr. Gunawardena's research interests include comparative education and sociology of education, with special reference to higher education and women's studies, particularly in developing countries. Her publications found at the end of this chapter focus on research of online learning pedagogy and quality assurance in developing countries, as well as gender issues in online learning.

There is a significant "brain drain" in developing countries, and many nationals who obtain graduate and tertiary degrees tend to move to developed countries. It is commendable that Dr. Chandra Gunawardena chosen to remain in her country of origin and work to improve education and access to education for those in the region. Her contribution to open and distance learning (ODL) and gender equity are significant.

Interview

Transcript Analysis Summary

Analysis of all interviews included in this volume led to the identification of 3,545 units of data. The mean of these collective units was 118 per pioneer, the median was 118.5, and the mode was 132. Individual interview units ranged from 59 to 217 units, yielding a spread of 158 units between all interviews. Chandra Gunawardena's interview generated 96 units, which was a noteable number of units, given that she completed the interview in a foreign language.

A comparision of Gunawardena's interview to the interviews of all pioneers indicates that her conversations yielded a similar number of units in relation to the average interview in four of the identified parent themes: accomplishments, interesting memories, early founders, and final thoughts (Figure 12.1). Her interview produced a significantly larger number of units than average in the areas of learning environment, challenges, and research interests. Most of the units found in the learning environment category focus on comparing other f-2-f institutions in her country to the uniqueness of OUSL, which extended its reach across 25 districts in the country and offered a blend of on-campus and distance learning opportunities. Some discussion on the challenges that Gunawardena faced over the years focused on changing the perceptions of educational stakeholders, including government, on the value and quality of DE. Another primary challenge was to encourage administrative colleagues and faculty to engage in more research initiatives. The high number of units in Gunawardena's research interests section spoke to her passion and devotion to research.

Gunawardena did not generate many units when discussing her goals, although she did detail three main goals during her career. First, she focused upon the development of quality learning materials when DE was print-based and delivered by mail. Second, she was also concerned about the level of English language competency among her colleagues. Finally, Gunawardena strove to improve engagement with research activities among her colleagues. She did not offer many units in

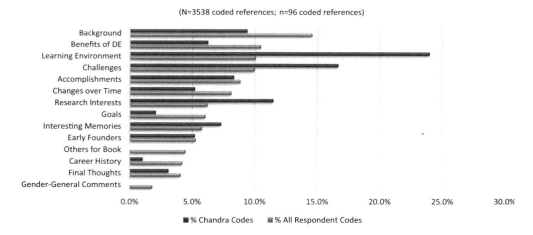

Figure 12.1 All Respondents' Versus Chandra Gunawardena's Parent Codes

the area of career history, either. This was most likely because Gunawardena devoted most of her career to two institutions.

Link to recorded interview: tinyurl.com/Gunaward-C

Transcript of Interview

Full Name: Chandra Gunawardena

Institutional Affiliation: Emeritus Professor, Open University of Sri Lanka; also Director for the Centre for Women's Research Organization

Key:

Regular font = Interviewee comments
Italicized font = Interviewer comments

Interview Questions

1. *What was your educational and experiential background before you became involved in distance education [DE] and online distance learning [ODL]?*

   I did my bachelor's degree and the post-graduate diploma in education at the University of Peradeniya (that was the most prestigious university at that time), and also the master's. I went for my PhD at La Trobe University in Melbourne.

   I was an Assistant Lecturer at Peradeniya University for two years. Then I joined as a permanent Assistant Lecturer at the University of Colombo in the Faculty of Education. I worked there for 21 years. Then I decided to apply for a professorship and started working with the Open University of Sri Lanka as the Professor of Education.

2. *In what year did you begin to look specifically into DE? ODL?*

   In 1993, a long time ago.

3. *What were the circumstances in your world that initiated this interest in DE and ODL?*

   At the time that I was working in the University of Colombo, there were only one or two professorships. Then when the Open University of Sri Lanka (OUSL) advertised a professorship, I decided to apply as it was a career improvement for me. So that was why I decided. I had been doing lectures for 21 years at the University of Colombo. They were only face-to-face lectures. And, of course, I did a lot of research. But at the time, I felt tired of these lectures, and I thought that I could try my hand at something else. That was really the reason why I applied.

4. *Which female researchers or female colleagues may have piqued your interest in DE and ODL?*

   The professor who retired before me from the OUSL was my teacher in the conventional university for a long time. She said, "Why don't you try your hand at open and distance learning?" And I decided to do so. Her name is Professor Elsie Kotalawala.

5. *Who would you identify as the early female leaders/founders in the field of ODL?*

   In Sri Lanka, she [Professor Elsie Kotalawala] was, of course, the first female professor. After that, there was one professor in English language teaching, and a few others since, in the science faculty, especially one professor, Uma Coomaraswamy, who became the vice chancellor later. She has worked very close with the Commonwealth of Learning, and they are the predominant distance education women leaders. But at the time that I joined the OUSL, I did not know them.

6. *What are some of the goals that you strove to achieve in the field of DE? ODL?*

   My first concern was that in distance education what was done at that time was mostly the development of course materials. That was given priority. I found that the academics tended to get outdated very quickly, especially because at that time, Internet was not available. And of course, some of our staff, even academic staff, were not that competent in the English because they could study up to their bachelor's degree in the mother tongue. That was a concern. Also, because I had participated in a lot of research studies earlier at the University of Colombo, I found that in the Open University the academics were not engaging much in research. They were only engaged in teaching and writing course materials. There was also this other concern that they were expected to sign in and sign off at work. They had to be at the university every day of the week, which did not give them much time for research. So I was concerned about this, though I could understand the reason. OUSL had a very large number of students, and we had a network of centres all over the country. So coordination was very important and very difficult. This is why they had to do teaching, writing course materials, and coordination more than research. That, I thought, was a major concern.

7. *What are some of your accomplishments in the field of DE and ODL that you would like to share?*

Our Department of Education was part of the larger Faculty of Humanities and Social Sciences, earlier. It was only a department, but I became the Dean of that faculty. That helped me to motivate academics to engage more in distance education research and also to participate in conferences and contribute to publications. Even after retirement, I am doing the same thing even now.

Therefore, I sort of mentored the university academics, made them participate in professional organizations, and to improve the credibility of the Open University as a quality institution because, at the time that I joined, the Open University of Sri Lanka was considered a low-quality university. People thought, "Who would want to join the university?" because the quality is very low. So I thought that if the quality was to be improved, they have to engage in research and make a name for themselves. So I did that. And especially because I was a Dean in the Faculty of Humanities and Social Sciences, and later in the Faculty of Education, I could do that without much difficulty.

Also, I was working very closely with the University Grants Commission [UGC], which overlooks all universities in Sri Lanka. I could apply for the Department of Education to be elevated to faculty status, and it was done. We could establish two other new departments of study also.

Later, after I retired, I became the Team Leader of the Distance Education Partnership Programme of Sri Lanka, which was sponsored by the Asian Development Bank. With the other academics in that organization, I could introduce and develop other academics in conventional universities and professional organizations that were conducting external degree programmes to develop their interest and competencies in distance education. So that was a major achievement, I thought.

8. *What are some of the challenges that you faced in the field of DE and ODL over the years?*

Even now I think these concerns continue. One challenge was the motivation; the inclination of academics was to be contented with teaching and coordination, without any interest in updating themselves or engaging in other interests. You are getting a monthly salary, you go and do the teaching and coordinating that is allocated to you, and that's that. They are not much interested in engaging in research or even in updating themselves. So, in the latter years, we could get sponsorship for them to go overseas for their doctoral studies. Most of them have gone to Canada, Australia, or the UK. But the other issue is that some of them do not come back. They come and work for a few years and then go back again. "Brain drain" is what they called it. So that is a challenge. So after the government pays for their education overseas and approve leave, still they don't feel that they are obliged to come back. Some of them are forced to pay back the money.

Secondly, you had to work with university administrators, especially the vice chancellors. Some of them could not understand why I am trying to motivate junior academics to work like this. They thought it was only to promote my stature. But they did not understand that the improvement of the quality of academics and the university was very important.

Sometimes we have to attend meetings of the Senate and the Council. If you are articulate in these meetings, some statements might not be perceived positively. But I believed strongly that I had to talk about what I felt. I thought that I was not struggling for my own personal gain, but for the benefit of the university.

I: Did you encounter some challenges in the reports that you presented to government and faculty?

Not exactly; perhaps they didn't want to read these documents, the university authorities or at the government level. But no, there was no concern about publishing these [documents].

I: It seemed that your reports may have indicated that [those whom] the Open University was working the hardest to reach were still the most under-represented group in the Open University. That was the people in very remote or isolated geographical location. Was this correct?

Not exactly; the Open University was the only university to have centres. Centres for the Open University are in every district in the country. There are 25 districts. All districts have a centre, where there is an office, and there are directors managing the offices. We enrol students from all of these districts. Our programmes are conducted in all three media. Of course, if there are no students for English, those programmes will not be conducted in the centre. They have to come to Colombo to participate in the day schools. But otherwise, all three media and all programmes are conducted all over the country. They may not have sufficient library facilities to go in and work there. And sometimes, as I said earlier, if we don't have enough academics with expertise in certain areas, the students will be forced to come to Colombo, which is our capital city, or to regional centres. But we also provide them with accommodation. They can apply, and if there is enough space, they can stay there, participate in the classes, and get back. Because it is an Open University, they don't have to come throughout the year, so they come mostly for weekend classes. Therefore, that's not a major concern, especially, for example, in the North. In the Jaffna District, the students are very much interested in our programmes. We also get other academics in the universities in the area to help us, to support us.

I: So, your university is able to reach students who might not otherwise . . .?

Of course. We are the only university doing that in the country.

9. *What was the "state of DE" when you first entered the field as opposed to DE and ODL in 2019?*

At that time, I was a Senior Lecturer at the University of Colombo, so when I was selected, all of my colleagues came and told me, "Why do you want to go to the Open University? It's like a correspondence school. There's no quality. There's no acceptance in the country. So you better stay."

In fact, one of my colleagues, who was next to me at the same level, said to me, "I won't apply for the next professorship if you stay here. I will give it to you."

I said, "No, I want to try out my hand at distance education." It was earlier considered as passing out of distance education materials and having exams: a correspondence school. But now it is the university with the largest student enrolment from all districts in the country. Now we are no longer restricted to print materials. We use blended education, we use virtual education, and we use OER [open educational resources]. Of course, we have got support, especially from the Commonwealth of Learning, and other academics from the international arena – especially Australia, Canada, and India. They were the people who supported us in the beginning. The University of Athabasca was supporting our nursing degree programme some time ago when we first started.

10. *What interesting memories would you like to share about the beginning of ODL?*

It was the perception that an Open University of Sri Lanka was not a quality university. This was accepted even by the University Grants Commission [UGC]. Now every year, our student numbers increase, so we apply so that we can obtain support [for] the hiring of new colleagues.

I remember attending a UGC meeting. That night I had to leave for a conference overseas, but I still went to the meeting. I said we need more funding. But UGC produced incorrect information. I challenged UGC, saying, "This is wrong. Take the information that I sent you." Finally, somehow, I could make them approve new funds for us. You have to have ready information, accurate information when you go for these meetings.

And I was also a member of the UCG subcommittee for the development of a course on university teaching and management. Later on, when quality assurance initiatives were started by the University Grants Commission, I was a member of those committees. I was a resource person for most universities, not only the Open University. So this is why you don't work just [to] improve a university for its own sake, but to get recognition from all of the others in the sector. That I think I managed, especially as I was a Dean three times – two times in humanities and social science and once in education. I was able, through those positions of authority, to help the university. This was the reason why my expertise or my work was not restricted only to the Open University of Sri Lanka. I participated on several boards in conventional universities, and I was invited to conduct research on issues in the entire university sector. I conducted staff development initiatives for universities, even the faculties of medicine and management in conventional universities. So much so that by 2015, there were no misgivings about the acceptance of ODL by Sri Lankan conventional universities. So we have to prove that what we are saying is correct. Otherwise they won't believe what we are saying.

Also, personally, I benefited a lot from the Commonwealth of Learning. They have these Pan-Commonwealth Forums every two years in different parts of the world. I participated in the first six. After that, due to health issues, I could not go. They got me involved in areas like multigrade teaching, child-friendly schools, and teacher education. At that time, I was no longer the Dean, but we developed a programme called the "Master of Arts in Teacher Education," an international programme that was supported by the Commonwealth of Learning [COL]. It was an innovative programme. This programme was bestowed an international award by COL. This led to further developments later on.

Now the present dean is very much interested in integrating technology and OER into our programmes. So this is how we have to work hard and prove that we are able to do what we are trying to achieve. And I think we have succeeded in this endeavour.

11. *What were your specific DE and ODL research interests, and have they changed/evolved over the years?*

As I said, at the University of Colombo, I was doing a lot of research studies with various organizations, which were accepted. But they were mostly related to social science education, which included teacher education, social study certification, employment, and gender. Some of these interests still continue. Also, I have been able to motivate some staff to undertake innovations of their own programmes. You know, how their student teachers look at these programmes to identify what difficulties they have and to improve them. That has been done.

I am also working for the Centre for Women's Research, so I do a lot of research on gender for them, with funding from international organizations like UNICEF, UNFPA, UN Women, and ILO.

I have done studies on distance education, but I can find and send them later.

For the university, the vice chancellor invited me to develop the role functions of Open University academics: what they are supposed to do at different levels from assistant lecturer to the professor level in different areas, like teaching, research, and collaboration with others.

Also, tracer studies of OUSL graduates: how the students who pass out [of the programmes] perform later on, scenario-based learning, gender, reflective practice in distance education, and we have done some case studies on distance higher education. Recently, I did a study on quality and equity in higher education in Sri Lanka, focusing on the Open University in Sri Lanka. So those are some of the studies.

I retired ten years ago, so I am unable to engage in research, even in distance education. I'm on the Board of the Faculty of Education, which meets every month, so I try to motivate others – the dean and the heads of departments and the staff to undertake research relevant to ODL. Mostly, that's what I can do.

12. *Could you please describe the learning environment that you currently work in or have most recently worked in (e.g., geographic and institutional setting, student demographics)?*

The headquarters of the OUSL is in a place called Nugegoda. It is very close to the capital of the country, Colombo. Nawala, Nugegoda, is where it started. It has really prospered, with a large number of buildings being constructed. The entire area is devoted to the Open University. We have five faculties – engineering, science, health science, humanities and social sciences, and education – and a large number of departments.

The Faculty of Education has the largest number of students. We conduct programmes from certificates (that is the lowest) to PhD. Some of the other faculties also do that. Now, for example, there is a vibrant Department of Law. The only Faculty of Law in the University of Colombo and the two Departments of Law are in the Open University and the University of Peradeniya. We had the only Health Science Faculty in the entire university system at that time. There may be one or two added later, but I'm not sure about that. Faculty-wise, it is only at the Open University of Sri Lanka.

We don't ask students for their formal education qualifications when they join a programme. Some of them who are young, who have not performed well at their first public examination, for example, can also get enrolled in the university programmes, but at the level that is called "foundation programme, foundation learning." There they are supported to develop their formal education competencies. Then they can join certificate programmes and do a one- or one-and-a-half-year programme. Now one programme offered by our faculty is the Certificate in Early Childhood Education, which prepares preschool teachers, early child-care people. After completing those, they can go further up and up until they can do the masters or even the PhD.

The Faculty of Engineering is also like that. They have a large number of departments. So this is why it is important. This is providing adult education not only for those who are formally qualified, but for those who are interested.

Of course, as you would expect, the number of drop-outs can be high if they don't have formal qualifications, unlike in the conventional universities, but most of them continue their education. They persevere and get higher qualifications. The formal qualifications from the Open University are recognized by any institutions. So they cannot say, "No, no, no, you did a university degree at the OUSL. We cannot consider you. That is not possible." So this is how we create credibility for the university.

Age does not matter. In fact, at one convocation/graduation, there was a father and a daughter, both of whom were awarded bachelor of law degrees. So there is no discrimination at all. Similarly, of course, in the Faculty of Education, and Humanities and Social Sciences, we have more women than men. In the Science and Engineering, especially in Engineering, the number of men enrolled in programmes is much higher. That is the system; the entire system in the country is like that. Only about 25% of engineering graduates are females. So that's the situation, and that has not changed much, even at the Open University.

The students who complete the programmes get hired by the labour market, which is very important. In fact, the tracer studies that I did of our graduates show that most of them are happy with what they got, and they have been able to get employment. Employment is a critical issue in our country. Graduates pass out [of programmes], but especially in the arts, humanities, and social sciences, they find it very difficult to get jobs. So that is one strength with the Open University.

We have the largest enrolment [in the country]. About three months ago, I was told that we have 45,000 students. Some universities have only about 10 or 15,000 because the universities in our countries are very small. Students have to sit for competency examinations and pass. We also have a mechanism called "district quota" to support students who come from underprivileged districts. As a result, some of the students who are in urban areas, even if they perform very well, may not be able to get into conventional universities through this system. But the OUSL gives them a chance to enrol in a programme that they are interested in.

I went for a meeting last week where the vice chancellor said we have the largest student number. It may be 40 to 50,000.

13. *Is there anything else you [would] like to address?*

For example, I mentioned the inadequacy of English language competency of the academic staff. Now, for the last 10 or 15 years, universities were expected to offer courses in English and their mother tongue, bilingual education. That is happening mostly in the case of Science, Engineering, and the Medical Faculties, not so much in the Arts and Humanities. The reason is that the students coming in for those faculties [i.e., Arts and Humanities] are coming in from the rural, disadvantaged areas. They may not have had good English teachers in their schools. So they have this issue. Those who perform well can get into university positions, but I think to undertake research or to even to write course materials, their English may not be good enough, and also their research competencies may be lacking.

Every university has staff development centres; the Open University also has a centre. To get promotions, the academics have to show that they have participated in a staff development course and completed it. The concern is that people do research, but their actual interest in research is very low. They do this because they have to get promotions; they have to go up the scale for career development, but not to enable universities to contribute to the country's economic and social development. At least when I was working, I found that it not only the evaluation of a particular course that is important. You have to see how it will contribute to the social development of the country. Why are some students not performing well when others can perform better? Those things are not researched carefully today. I have mentored some younger academic staff. They become co-authors with me for publications. Most of the work actually may be done by me, but they gain by being part of the research study. So this is what is important.

I think that the issue of the English language might not be an issue for all countries. For example, I have been working with India and Pakistan. Their academics' English, and even their students' English competency, is quite high compared to ours. That is not the issue across their countries.

I am also working with a government organization called the National Science Foundation. I am in the social sciences group there. We get articles published in our social sciences journal, but most of them come from other countries. Very few come from our own country. I don't know if I should actually talk about this, but that's a concern. Why? Because maybe our people are not interested in publishing their research. Or maybe they think that because we are a local journal, and we do peer review, that they cannot get their marks for promotion. That may be the reason that they have not really looked at it carefully enough. So that is a major concern because it [conducting research] is not only to improve your CV [curriculum vitae], but you can see how it can contribute to the country's economic and social development. That has to be transmitted to all university staff, including Open University staff.

The Open University publishes a magazine called the *Open Quarterly*. That should be on the web. I think about three or four months ago, I was interviewed by the dean, so you can learn a little more about me from that also, if you get the time.

14. Can you suggest names of other female pioneers in DE or ODL that you think we should include in the book?

One is Professor Uma Coomaraswamy. She is an emeritus professor. She was the former vice chancellor of the Open University.

I can also recommend a younger person: Professor Shironica Karunanayaka, professor of educational technology. She is the incumbent Dean of the Faculty of Education at the Open University. She has introduced so many new things to the system. She is quite competent in the area of technology. She's using MOOCs [massive open online courses], OER; she's using technologies to improve the quality of open education programmes. So you can perhaps try to contact her; talk to a younger person. Earlier on, she was the dean, and now again the Dean of the Faculty of Education.

Publications

Books

Davies, L., & Gunawardena, C. (1992). *Women and men in educational management: An international inquiry* (IIEP Research Report No. 95). International Institute for Educational Planning.

Gunawardena, C. (1991). *Comparative education (U.K., U.S.S.R., U.S.A., and Japan).* (Sinhala) Shiksha Mandira Prakashana.

Gunawardena, C. (1992). *Comparative education (Tanzania, China and SAARC countries).* (Sinhala) Shiksha Mandira Prakashana.

Gunawardena, C. (1995). *Social factor in education* (Sinhala) Sara Prakashana.

Gunawardena, C. (Ed.). (2005). *Not adding up: Looking beyond numbers – Gender equity in higher education in Sri Lanka.* Nawala Open University Press.

Gunawardena, C. (2016). *Gender and development in Sri Lanka: Implications for policy and practice – Thematic report based on census of housing and population, 2012.* United Nations Population Fund (UNPFA).

Gunawardena, C., & Ekanayake, M. B. (2009). *Inclusive Education in Sri Lanka.* National Education and Research Evaluation Centre, University of Colombo. (Sponsored by UNICEF).

Gunawardena, C., & Ekanayake, M. B. (2010). *Tracer study of OUSL graduates of 2009.* Open University of Sri Lanka.

Gunawardena, C., & Gamini, L. P. S. (2011). *Tracer Study of OUSL Graduates of 2010.* Open University of Sri Lanka.

Gunawardena, C., & Jayaweera, S. (2008). *Gender Mainstreaming: How does it happen in education in South Asia?* UNICEF Regional office for South Asia United Nations Girls' Education Initiative (UNGEI).

Gunawardena, C., & Jayaweera, S. (2013). *Marginalization and social exclusion of out of school children: Towards inclusivity.* UNICEF (Sri Lanka) & Colombo Centre for Women's Research.

Gunawardena, C., Kwesiga, J., Lihamba, A., Morley, L., Odejide, A., & Shackleton, L. (2004). *Gender equity in Commonwealth higher education: Emerging themes in Nigeria, South Africa, Sri Lanka, Tanzania and Uganda.* University of London Institute of Education.

Gunawardena, C., & Lekamge, D. (2004). *Sectoral review of general education: An evaluation of the implementation of the junior secondary school curriculum in two districts – Ratnapura and Kalutara* (Study Series No. 10). Colombo National Education Commission.

Gunawardena, C., Lekamge, D., & de Zoysa, S. (2014). *Trafficking of children for organized begging: A study of child beggars in Sri Lanka*. Colombo Centre for Women's Research.
Gunawardena, C., Lekamge, D., Dissanayake, S., & Bulumulle, K. (Eds.). (2009). *My son, my daughter: Socialization for gender roles in Sri Lanka*. Deepani Printers and Publishers.
Gunawardena, C., Lekamge, D., Karunanayake, S., & de Zoysa, S. (2009). *An in-depth study to identify the best practices among teachers for development of higher order cognitive skills in students*. Deepani Printers and Publishers.
Gunawardena, C., Lekamge, D., Karunanayake, S., & de Zoysa, S. (2016). *Changing academic profession in Sri Lanka: Roles, functions and perceptions of academics*. Open University Press.
Gunawardena, C., & Swarna, J. (2007). *Social inclusion: Gender and equity in education: SWAPs in South Asia – Bangladesh/ Nepal/Sri Lanka case study*. Kathmandu Regional Office for South Asia United Nations Girls' Education Initiative (UNGEI).
Gunawardena, C., Wijetunga, S., & Perera, L. (2004). *Sectoral review of general education: An evaluation of the effectiveness of the implementation of educational reforms at secondary school level*. Colombo National Education Commission.
Jayaweera, S., Gunawardena, C., & Edirisinghe, I. (2008). *Beyond the glass ceiling: Participation in decision making in the public domain*. Colombo Centre for Women's Research.
Morley, L., Gunawardena, C., Kweisiga, J., Lihambam, A., Odojide, A., Shackleton, L., & Sorhaindo, A. (2006). *Gender equity in Commonwealth higher education: An examination of sustainable interventions in selected Commonwealth universities*. DFID/Institute of Education, University of London.

Book Chapters

Gunawardena, C. (1987). Women and education in Sri Lanka. In G. Pearson & L. Manderson (Eds.), *Class, ideology and women in Asian societies* (pp. 66–80). Asian Studies Monograph Series.
Gunawardena, C. (1991). A career appraisal of women teachers in Sri Lanka. In S. Jayaweera (Ed.), *Gender and education: Women, work and schooling*. Colombo Centre for Women's Research.
Gunawardena, C. (1994). Psychological aspects of integration. In G. Moonesignhe (Ed.), *Sri Lanka: Towards nation building*. Shramaya Publications.
Gunawardena, C. (1995). Training of teachers through distance education in Sri Lanka: Problems and possibilities. In H. H. Kizilbash (Ed.), *Developing the ultimate resource* (pp. 205–212). Ali Institute of Education.
Gunawardena, C. (1996). School as a social system. In *The handbook on educational psychology* (Vol. 2, pp. 247–272). Ministry of Education.
Gunawardena, C. (2002a). Emerging global trends in teacher education. In *Hope for the future: Teacher education and development*. Department of Education, University of Peradeniya.
Gunawardena, C. (2002b). Quality assurance practices in teacher education programmes in the Open University of Sri Lanka. In K. Rama & M. Menon (Eds.), *Innovations in teacher education: International practices of quality assurance* (pp. 155–166). National Assessment and Accreditation Council (India), and The Commonwealth of Learning.
Gunawardena, C. (2002c). Youth and education. In S. T. Hettige & M. Mayer (Eds.), *Sri Lankan youth: Challenges and responses* (pp. 89–118). Freidrich Ebert Stiftung.
Gunawardena, C. (2005a). Conclusion. In C. Gunawardena (Ed.), *Not adding up: Looking beyond numbers – Gender equity in higher education in Sri Lanka*. Open University Press.
Gunawardena, C. (2005b). Women in university education: A statistical overview. In C. Gunawardena (Ed.), *Not adding up: Looking beyond numbers – Gender equity in higher education in Sri Lanka*. Open University Press.
Gunawardena, C. (2005c). Women's representation in The University of Colombo. In C. Gunawardena (Ed.), *Not adding up: Looking beyond numbers – Gender equity in higher education in Sri Lanka*. Open University Press.
Gunawardena, C. (2007). Interpreting university women's voices: Voluntary rejection or organizational micropolitics? In S. Jayaweera (Ed.), *Gender, education and socialization* (pp. 97–115). Department for International Development.
Gunawardena, C. (2008). Improving adult literacy. In *Education for all: Mid-decade assessment report- Sri Lanka* (pp. 109–130). Columbo Ministry of Education.
Gunawardena, C. (2009a). Best practice case studies in distance higher education: MATE(I) Programme: Transforming teacher educator development. In *Quality assurance tool kit*. Commonwealth of Learning, UNESCO and Distance Education Modernization Project (Sri Lanka).
Gunawardena, C. (2009b). Introduction. In C. Gunawardena (Ed.), *My son, my daughter: Socialization for gender roles in Sri Lanka* (pp. 1–9). Deepani Printers and Publishers.
Gunawardena, C. (2009c). Socializing for equitable roles. In C. Gunawardena, D. Lekamge, S. Dissanayake, & K. Bulumulle (Eds.), *My son, my daughter: Socialization for gender roles in Sri Lanka* (pp. 87–90). Deepani Printers and Publishers.

Gunawardena, C. (2009d). The study. In C. Gunawardena, D. Lekamge, S. Dissanayake, & K. Bulumulle (Eds.), *My son, my daughter: Socialization for gender roles in Sri Lanka* (pp. 10–19). Deepani Printers and Publishers.

Gunawardena, C. (2014). Underscoring the role of ICT and OER in curriculum renewal in higher education programmes in Sri Lanka. In S. Karunanayake & S. Naidu (Eds.), *Integrating OER in educational practice: Practitioner stories*. Faculty of Education, Open University of Sri Lanka.

Gunawardena, C. (2015). Higher education. In *Review of the implementation of Beijing Platform for Action in Sri Lanka – 1991–2015* (pp. 107–127). UNFPA and Centre for Women's Research.

Gunawardena, C. (2017). Quality and equity in higher education in Sri Lanka: Case study of the Open University of Sri Lanka. In *Tribute to a pioneer in Social Sciences at OUSL, Emeritus Professor Upali Vidanapathirana* (pp. 21–40). Dept. of Social Studies, Faculty of Humanities and Social Sciences, The Open University of Sri Lanka.

Gunawardena, C. (no date). Education and the future of Muslims with special reference to higher education. In *Challenge for Change: Profile of a Community* (pp. 99–112). Muslim Women's Research and Action Front.

Gunawardena, C., & Bulumulle, K. (2005). Gender equity: Interventions on access in the University of Colombo. In C. Gunawardena (Ed.), *Not adding up: Looking beyond numbers – Gender equity in higher education in Sri Lanka*. Open University Press.

Gunawardena, C., de Silva, W. A., & Kularate, N. G. (1997). Interventions to improve literacy in selected deprived communities in Sri Lanka. In *Case studies in education research and policy*. Asian Development Bank.

Gunawardena, C., & de Soysa, P. (1998). The right to growth and development. In S. W. E. Goonasekera, C. Gunawardena, & N. G. Kularatne (Eds.), *Child rights: The Sri Lankan experience*. The Open University of Sri Lanka.

Gunawardena, C., & Jayaweera, S. (2007). Access, equity and efficiency in education in Sri Lanka. In A. D. V. de S. Indraratne & D. Hirimuthugodage (Eds.), *Inequity, poverty and development* (pp. 85–116). Sri Lanka Economic Association.

Gunawardena, C., & Jayaweera, S. (2012). Poverty, education and conflict: A study of selected districts of Sri Lanka. In *New horizons in human rights*. Centre for the Study of Human Rights, University of Colombo.

Gunawardena, C., Naidu, S., Menon, M., Lekamge, D., & Karunanayaka, S. (2007). How scenario-based learning can engender reflective practice in distance education. In J. Michael Spector (Ed.), *Finding your online voice: Stories told by experienced online educators* (pp. 53–72). Lawrence Erlbaum Associates.

Journal Articles

Gunawardena, C. (1979). Ethnic representation, regional imbalance and university admissions in Sri Lanka. *Comparative Education*, *15*(3), 301–312.

Gunawardena, C. (1980). A six-year old adapts to her new environment. *The Educational Magazine*, *38*(1), 14–16. Victoria, Australia: Education Department.

Gunawardena, C. (1982). Matching education with employment opportunities in Sri Lanka. *Higher Education Review*, *15*(3), 58–71.

Gunawardena, C. (1984). Assessment-oriented learning and adult work: An international study. *Higher Education in Europe*, *9*(1), 63–71.

Gunawardena, C. (1985). Student learning orientations and adult work: The SLOG Project – Report of a collaborative study. *International Journal of Educational Development*, *5*(3), 217–222.

Gunawardena, C. (1987). Women in higher education in Sri Lanka. *Higher Education Review*, *19*(3), 8-23.

Gunawardena, C. (1989). Community oriented education programmes of University of Colombo. *Bulletin: A Twice Yearly Review of University Adult Education*, *2*(2), 54–56.

Gunawardena, C. (1990). Access to higher education in Sri Lanka. *Higher Education Review*, *23*(1), 53–63.

Gunawardena, C. (1991a). A consensual role for universities in Sri Lanka. *Perspectives in Education*, *7*(4), 265–276.

Gunawardena, C. (1991b). Brief encounter: 7 months as students in a British secondary school. *Education Now*, *11*(8–9).

Gunawardena, C. (1991c). Linking education with the world of work in Sri Lanka: The experience of two decades. *Educational Review*, *43*(1), 79–88.

Gunawardena, C. (1992). Employer expectations and equity in education in Sri Lanka. *International Journal of Educational Development*, *13*(2), 125–30.

Gunawardena, C. (1997). Problems of illiteracy in a literate developing society: Sri Lanka. *International Review of Education*, *43*(5), 599–609.

Gunawardena, C. (1999). Using technology for quality improvement of teacher education in OUSL: Problems and possibilities. *Indian Journal of Open Learning*, *8*(1), 73–78.

Gunawardena, C. (2003). Gender in Higher Education in Sri Lanka: A mismatch between access and outcomes. *McGill Journal of Education, 38*(3), 437–451.

Gunawardena, C. (2008). Gender equity in higher education in Sri Lanka [Special issue on gender equity in higher education]. *International Studies in Education, 9*, 17–22.

Gunawardena, C., & Lekamge, D. (2000). Estimation of study hours in relation to selected courses in the PGDE Programme of the OUSL. *Indian Journal of Open Learning, 9*(2), 217–229.

Gunawardena, C., & Lekamge, D. (2003). Status and issues of teacher education in Sri Lanka. *Anweshika, Indian Journal of Teacher Education*, 92–103.

Gunawardena, C., Lekamge, D., Karunanayake, S., Naidu, S., & Menon, M. (2007). Professional development of teacher educators with collaborative learning designs and networking. *Indian Journal of Open Learning, 16*(2), 101–112.

Gunawardena, C., Rasanayagam, Y., Leitan, T., Bulumulle, K., & Abeyasekera-Van Dort, A. (2006). Quantitative and qualitative dimensions of gender equity in Sri Lankan higher education. *Women's Studies International Forum, 29*(6), 562–571.

Yatigammana, M. R. K., Gapar, M. D., Johar, M. D., & Gunawardena, C. (2013a). Post-graduate students' perceived e-learning acceptance: Model validation. *International Journal of Asian Business and Management, 4*(3), 51–60.

Yatigammana, M. R. K., Gapar, M. D., Johar, M. D., & Gunawardena, C. (2013b). Postgraduate students' perceived e-learning acceptance model using SEM validation method. In *Technological Solutions for Business Practice in Asia*. Premium Research Papers, IGI-Global.

Yatigammana, M. R. K., Gapar, M. D., Johar, M. D., & Gunawardena, C. (2014). Comparison of e-learning acceptance among postgraduate students in Sri Lanka and Malaysia. *Journal of South Asian Studies, 2*(2), 165–176.

13
GUNAWARDENA, CHARLOTTE NIRMALANI (LANI)

Photo of Charlotte (Lani) Gunawardena contributed by Charlotte (Lani) Gunawardena

One of my initial goals was bridging the digital divide and providing access and looking at access in terms of different types of access; not only the physical access to technology, but also the psychological access, the comfort level, how we bridge the different types of distances in learning environments.

Charlotte Nirmalani (Lani) Gunawardena was born in Sri Lanka, where she completed her undergraduate degree in English at the University of Sri Lanka in 1976. She completed her graduate studies in the United States at the University of Kansas, firstly a Master of Education in 1982 and then a PhD in Curriculum and Instruction in 1988. Gunawardena is currently a Distinguished Professor of Distance Education and Instructional Technology at the College of University Libraries and Learning Sciences, University of New Mexico, Albuquerque, USA. She has been a Fulbright scholar working in Morocco and Sri Lanka.

Dr. Gunawardena has extensively worked on culture and distance/online learning; social technologies, online learning, and socially mediated meta-cognition; social presence theory; social context of digital learning; and social construction of knowledge in online learning communities. She has extensively consulted internationally: the prestigious Star Project for the US Department of Education, National American Research Centre for Health, World Bank, Asian Development Bank, and in many other projects, countries, and agencies. She served on the Army Education Advisory Committee appointed by the US Secretary of Defense. She won the prestigious Charles A. Wedemeyer Award in DE and has been consistent in leading, mentoring, and facilitating aspiring, talented, and committed young scholars in distance education, online learning, and instructional technology. Moreover, she has devoted herself to the cause of DE for over three decades. She has also occasionally contributed to distance learning in the Asian region, especially India and Sri Lanka. References included at the end of this chapter reflect her research interests.

Interview

Transcript Analysis Summary

Analysis of all interviews included in this volume led to the identification of 3,545 units of data. The mean of these collective units was 118 per pioneer, the median was 118.5, and the mode was 132. Individual interview units ranged from 59 to 217 units, yielding a spread of 158 units between all interviews. Lani Gunawardena's interview generated 217 units, placing her interview at the top of all interviews in terms of number of units produced.

A comparison of Gunawardena's interview to the interviews of all pioneers indicated that her interview profile shared numerous commonalities with the average interview profile (Figure 13.1).

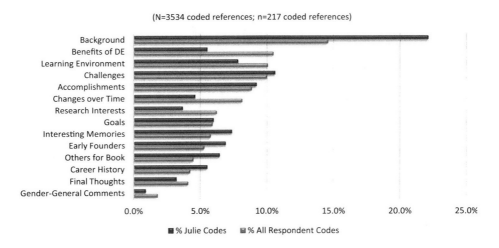

Figure 13.1 All Respondents' Versus Charlotte (Lani) Gunawardena's Parent Codes

Her interview yielded a similar number of units in 10 of the 14 topic areas: learning environment, challenges, accomplishments, goals, interesting memories, early founders, others for the book, career history, final thoughts, and general gender-related comments. A significantly larger-than-average number of units were generated in her conversations related to her educational and experiential background. Examination of this phenomenon indicated that Lani had learned and worked in a variety of international contexts.

Gunawardena's interview yielded a less-than-average number of units in three areas: benefits of DE, changes over time, and research interests. The smaller number of benefits units was most likely caused by the fact that the interview questions did not ask respondents to talk about the benefits they perceived DE to offer. This topic arose naturally among most interviewee conversations. Although Gunawardena was actively engaged in research throughout her career, she chose to talk broadly about three main research areas of interest. This could provide a reason for the relatively low number of research interest units in her interview.

Link to recorded interview Part A: tinyurl.com/Gunaward-L-A

Link to recorded interview Part B: tinyurl.com/Gunaward-L-B

Transcript of Interview

Full Name: Charlotte Nirmalani (a.k.a. Lani) Gunawardena
Institutional Affiliation: University of New Mexico, Albuquerque, New Mexico
Key:

Regular font = Interviewee comments
Italicized font = Interviewer comments

Interview Questions

1. *What was your educational and experiential background before you became involved in distance education [DE]?*

I began with English literature and English language as my focus of interest for my academic career soon after I graduated from high school. For my bachelor's degree at the university where I studied in Sri Lanka, currently called Kelaniya University, I selected to do English Honours, which means that you get a four-year degree instead of a three-year degree; Honours means that. So I really focused on English literature and English language as my areas. After I graduated with my BA [bachelor of arts], I taught English for three years at a high school in Sri Lanka called Museus College from grades 6 to 12. I also taught beginning French for grade 12. Then after three years of teaching, I moved on to become a research assistant at the University of Colombo. It was there that I realized that I would like to continue my education. I applied for a scholarship through the American Association of University of Women and got a place at the University of Kansas to pursue my master's degree in the teaching of English as a second language. At that time, I had not thought about distance education seriously, and also it wasn't a known field at that time. So I completed my master's in teaching of English as a second language.

I was going to go back to Sri Lanka when the civil war in Sri Lanka was beginning, and there was unrest in the universities. This was in 1982. One of my professors and eventually my dissertation chair, Dr. Robert Ridgway, called me to his office, expressed his concern about the situation in Sri Lanka, and encouraged me to pursue a doctoral programme instead of going back. I wasn't sure whether I was capable of doing the doctorate, and I had no funds left, yet decided to try it. I got in the doctoral programme in curriculum and instruction at the University of Kansas and started actually trying to get my degree in education.

While I was studying towards my degree, I became increasingly interested in media and how media could actually provide more access to education. One day, I had a long chat with my father, who was an educator. He was a principal for a long time in a school for the blind, the visually impaired. I was having a chat with him, and he said, "Television has just come to Sri Lanka. Why don't you really look at how television can support the learning process? That might be a good area for you to work on when you come back to Sri Lanka."

So that was at the back of my mind, and that's how I got into thinking about how media really might influence learning. My projects for my doctoral degree were based on that. I also did a minor in instructional television in the journalism and television department. That made me more interested in how to produce television. So at that time, that's how I really became interested in the utilization of media.

Even at the University of Kansas as a doctoral student, I was working for the Applied English Centre as a research assistant, helping them develop course materials for teaching English, and specifically with my prior background in teaching English for specific purposes, like English for the sciences, law, engineering, and etc. My master's thesis was really on focusing on English for scientific writing. So I had that background in English literature and English language and was now beginning to look at media as well in my work within my dissertation research

2. *In what year did you begin to look specifically into DE?*

   I think it was perhaps between 1985 and 1986. I was in my doctoral programme at that time.

3. *What were the circumstances in your world that initiated this interest in DE?*

   So let me carry on with my story about how I got really interested in distance learning. One of these interests was about those who could not get into traditional educational institutions in Sri Lanka. Things like this have really inspired me in terms of looking at distance learning, as my passion was to provide access because, at that time, there were very few opportunities for students who get through high school to actually proceed to the universities. The universities are government-run, and only about may be 15% of those who pass their advanced-level exam get into traditional higher education institutions. The institutions are full. Many of my fellow friends who completed high school and who did extremely well in their advanced-level exam could not get into a traditional university. There were not many other opportunities to pursue an academic career at that time.

   This always prompted me to look at how to find access to education for those who may not get into traditional education. At that time, this was an interest that was generated because of my background and heritage in Sri Lanka. Also, I told you my father's advice to look at media as a way to really enhance education was at the back of my mind. These two motivations, and the fact that my father was himself a distance learner who obtained his bachelor's degree from the University of London, led me to seek an internship at the Division of Continuing Education at the University of Kansas, which was the department handling distance learning at that time. My mentor there was Dr. Barbara Watkins. I said, "I would really like to intern with you because I really want to understand how you provide continuing education."

   Of course, it was mostly correspondence at that time, but they had one course, Brain, Mind and Behaviour, which was a psychology course that was utilizing a PBS [Public Broadcasting Service] programme as a video component to assist learning in the correspondence course.

   She said, "Why don't you study this because you are interested in media study? How is this really impacting students, and what do they think about the course because this is the only course that we have right now that utilizes a television component?"

   So I was given the opportunity to evaluate this course for them. That really led me to get in touch with the students who were taking the course. I had these great interviews where they told me about how the television component helped them learn. Then I really was hooked on the idea that maybe I needed to study this further. How do people learn? How do people learn from video, from television? That was the media at that time. So therefore, I began to look at distance education as a dissertation topic: a topic that blended education and media. My dissertation was on how the new communications technologies, specifically TV-related technologies, could be used for designing learning environments that really enhanced the learning process. That internship really spurred me on to look at how media was being utilized at that time and how I could use media for education.

4. *Which female researchers or female colleagues may have piqued your interest in DE?*

   Dr. Barbara Watkins in the Division of Continuing Education at KU, who provided me the internship to study how video influenced learning in a correspondence course, and Dr. Aletha

Huston, who was conducting a series of research studies on the influence of television on children, were the two female colleagues who piqued my interest in the use of television for DE. Both served on my dissertation committee and mentored me throughout the process. In addition, one of my committee members, Dr. Phil McKnight, showed me how to explore the relationship between television and learning. In the early days, I have to tell you the person who really helped me by providing resources for my dissertation was Dr. Tony Bates from the Open University. I just wrote to him because when I was looking at the research, it was just the Open University that was publishing the research on television and how it was enhancing the learning process. They had several papers. These were mostly Open University papers. He was so good about sending me a huge stack of their papers. That became a significant foundation for my review of the literature.

After I graduated with my PhD degree, I was very happy to know that my dissertation won the Charles Wedemeyer Award for book-length manuscripts in the field of DE, an award given by the National University of Continuing Education Association [NUCEA]. The award was made in 1988. It was my mentor, Barbara Watkins, at the Department of Continuing Education, who nominated me for this award.

Barbara was really a female mentor for me because she helped me with my dissertation research topic in terms of actually getting me into the field, and then with this [Wedemeyer] award, I got some recognition for my dissertation. I defended my dissertation in 1988, and one of the concerns of my committee was this word that I was using called *distance education* in the title of my dissertation because they said, "Who is going to know what distance education is?" I said, "You wait and see. People will know what it is pretty soon." Of course, before [the] 80s, it was correspondence.

Once I started my career, I moved on to the University of Oklahoma as a Kellogg Post-Doctoral Research Fellow at the Oklahoma Research Center for Continuing Professional and Higher Education, where I would be engaged in research on distance education. It was at that point that I now got connected with female researchers in the field. My initial contact there was Dr. Connie Dillon. She was a faculty member aligned and associated with the centre, but she was also teaching graduate-level classes. She undertook a study of the state of Oklahoma's distance education system, which was predominantly an instructional television–based system. Connie and I did an extensive evaluation of this system. That is where I really got into issues like learner support, how television was influencing students in the learning process, and also thinking through how to evaluate a distance education project because this was a statewide project that required quite a lot of energy to conduct the evaluation. So Connie and I wrote several papers on the findings. Mostly, our findings reflected the importance of learner support in terms of integrating learner support into distance learning. We also wrote another paper on evaluation research in distance learning, which was published in the *British Journal of Educational Technology*. So I consider Connie Dillon as one of my initial mentors in distance education research.

Subsequently, I moved to the University of New Mexico [UNM] as an Assistant Professor in the Training and Learning Technologies Programme hired to develop the graduate emphasis in distance education in the programme. This was a dream job for me to actually have the opportunity to develop my career in distance education. This is when I started developing graduate-level courses on distance education.

At the same time, I began attending the Distance Teaching and Learning Conference at the University of Wisconsin–Madison. There I met several other women researchers who were also beginning to research distance learning and teach about distance learning. We became a collaborative group, sharing our experiences and bouncing ideas off each other. The group included Connie Dillon; Chere Gibson at [the University of] Wisconsin-Madison, who was an organizer of the conference, but was also teaching about distance learning; Karen Murphy, who was an instructional designer at the University of Wyoming at that time; and Fred [Farhad] Saba from San Diego State University,

We began to brainstorm how we could connect our classes electronically. At that time, computer technology was just beginning to become available. The listservs were just beginning at that time; this was in 1989. I undertook to set up a project called the GlobalEd [Global Education] Project. The purpose of GlobalEd was to connect graduate students in several universities to collaborate on distance education research. This became a pretty popular project among those of us teaching about distance education. Other faculty, Landra Rezabek and John Cochenour from the University of Wyoming, and Marina McIsaac from Arizona State University, who was in Turkey at that time on sabbatical, joined GlobalEd. Marina connected her Turkish students into the GlobalEd Project. So this became an international project, a huge collaboration between predominantly women researchers and women teachers of distance learning. These colleagues were a major influence in my initial research on distance learning because we wrote several papers on the GlobalEd Project and looked at several factors that impacted distance education. Fred Saba has been very good in terms of working with us. He was one person who really collaborated with us on research. So it was good to have a male in our group as well.

I would also like to mention that during this time, Linda Harasim published a book on online education. I think that it was in 1990. This was a foundational piece on distance learning that really influenced some of my later research. For example, I'm working with learning analytics now. Some of the initial concepts of learning analytics were actually discussed in this book in a chapter by [Levin, Kim, and Riel], who looked at different types of analysis of interactions. Her work was really instrumental in some of my early work.

Another researcher who really influenced me was Robin Mason from the British Open University. She was also writing about online learning, and we later on collaborated on editing a special issue of the distance education journal that comes out of Australia. These are some of the female colleagues who piqued my interest in distance learning.

5. *Who would you identify as the early female leaders/founders in the field of DE?*

So, let me again repeat that some of the early founders that I feel were important in the field were [1] Connie Dillon from the University of Oklahoma. She was on the editorial board for the *American Journal of Distance Learning*; [2] Chere Gibson from the University of Wisconsin-Madison; she founded the distance teaching and learning conference and was one of the initial researchers who looked at learners. Chere's research focused a lot on learners and how to support learners. I wrote a chapter for her book on learning and learners; [3] Marina McIsaac, who was looking at the issue of culture and how culture influences the learning process; [4] Karen Murphy, who was doing research on online interactions and online learning; [5] Linda Harasim, with her book on online education; [6] Robin Mason from the British Open University, with her work in open and distance learning and computer mediated communication.

Then some of the other early researchers that I have met at the ICDE [International Council for Open and Distance Education] international conference on distance learning were [1] Liz Burge (again, I cannot remember the institution that she was from, but she is Canadian); [2] Ellen Wagner; I think Ellen was at the University of Northern Colorado at that time. She was researching how to define interaction; and [3] Sally Johnston, who later headed up the Western Interstate Commission for Higher Education [WICHE]. They were some of the early leaders in distance learning.

Looking at the international scene, I would like to mention a Sri Lankan colleague of mine, Gayathri Jayatilleke, with whom I have conducted research from the early years, since about 1995, I think. Gayathri was the Director of Educational Media at the Open University of Sri Lanka. I have collaborated with her quite a lot. I still collaborate on research projects with her because I do quite a bit of work in Sri Lanka as well. She's one person that I know who started fairly early. She got her doctorate in distance education from the British Open University and has been working at the Sri Lanka Open University since then, leading efforts to incorporate interaction and inquiry-based learning in learning designs.

In 2007, when I went to Sri Lanka as a consultant to the Ministry of Higher Education to develop a nationwide distance education network, I was fortunate to work with an authority in the field of distance education, Chandra Gunawardena, who was one-time Dean of Education at the University of Colombo. Chandra has conducted research on various topics on distance education, including the role of women and drop-out[s].

In the Australian context, Katherine McLaughlin has published creative work in distance education. I have enjoyed reading her work on culture and distance education.

But let me think through any other international folks. . . . Oh, I'm not sure when she began, but another person that you may want to look at is Insung Jung. We co-edited a book on culture and online learning. She is currently in Japan, but she's Korean. She may not be an early researcher, but I feel that she is another important person in this field who is writing from an Asian perspective.

6. *What are some of the goals that you strove to achieve in the field of DE?*

One of my initial goals was bridging the digital divide and providing access and looking at access in terms of different types of access, not only the physical access to technology but also the psychological access, the comfort level, how we bridge the different types of distances in learning environments. It can be social distance; it can be cultural, etc. So providing access is critical; I work in New Mexico. This is a state where a lot of the communities are separated by huge mountain ranges, very rural communities, and they hardly have any access to education. The moment you actually use expensive technologies, even at that time, like television, that really – if they don't have access to it – is difficult for them to participate in the learning process. I have to say that the University of New Mexico is a pioneer in distance learning. When I joined as an Assistant Professor in 1989, they already had distance teaching, mostly instructional television through satellite. This was a nursing programme that went throughout the state, and even eastern Arizona and southern Colorado. They also had an engineering programme through the College of Engineering that went predominantly to companies around Albuquerque, the main city, using Instructional Television Fixed Service [ITFS].

The nursing programme was interesting for me because of how they overcame the challenges. They had to make so many arrangements with hospitals in rural communities for these learners, who happened to be nurses working in those hospitals, to really access the satellite signal. They would meet at homes of their fellow nurses, or they would meet in hospitals to get the signals. So the one thing that was a great interest of mine initially was the issue of access and how to provide access to rural communities through distance learning, and the nursing programme was a good example of how it can be done.

Another area that has really influenced my work is how to develop a conducive social environment for distance learning, whether it is television or online. How do we actually develop a social environment? The socio-technical environment or a social environment mediated by technology? Because education is a social process, but sometimes when we use technology, we forget the social aspect of learning. So how can we make that learning environment conducive? So my research on social presence and how to generate that presence that connects you to others is one strand of research that has tried to address the social environment.

My research on culture and how culture influences the learning process and how it marginalizes some learners, the issue of language and English as a second language being sometime a difficulty for those whose first language is not English – all of these areas have led me to really examine the issue of culture, language, and even gender in online learning. So the social environment; how to design a conducive social environment and how to research it has been a predominant interest of mine, and culture is part of that social environment.

Another interest is how does learning happen online? How does learning happen in networked learning environments? Because I think that when computer-mediated communication came into the scene as a later-generation technology for distance learning, the real asset of that technology was that it could connect people together for a long period of time. So how do you develop these learning communities that engage in learning? So the learning community development, which is a social aspect, as well as how do they learn? And how do we know that they learn from the interactions with each other has been an interest of mine. This led me to my area of research in social construction of knowledge and the development of the interaction analysis model [IAM model], as well as looking at how people learn in different cultural contexts. So not only studying my context here at the University of New Mexico in the United States, but also understanding learning from the context of different cultures. I felt that this perhaps is where I really got a lot of motivation to study more and more.

7. *What are some of your accomplishments in the field of DE that you would like to share?*

I will talk about my accomplishments in three areas. The first accomplishment is my contributions to research in the fields of distance and online learning. [This includes] some of my early work on the social construction of knowledge and the development of the interaction analysis model [IAM] that has been one of the most often used models for analyzing interactions in collaborative learning. I have expanded this research now to utilizing newer analysis techniques, such as social network analysis and social learning analytic methods, to supplement the social component that is missing from IAM. I have a team of researchers here at UNM working on this line of research. A colleague, Nick Flor, from the Anderson School of Management; two of my former students, Damien Sanchez and David Gomez; as well as current doctoral students Yan Chen, Jasmine Desiderio, Monica Jean Dorame, Austin Megli, Dayra Fallad-Mendoza, and Megan Tucker (quite an internationally diverse team), and I are looking at how to analyze online interactions using a combination of interaction analysis, social network analysis, and social learning analytics so that we can have a more complete picture of how people interact, collaborate, and learn online.

Another area of research where I have made a contribution is my studies on social presence. I have looked at social presence from many angles and recently started examining how culture impacts social presence. The scale we developed in 1997 in the article I co-authored with Zittle to assess social presence through online surveys is still being used by researchers. I'm glad that my social presence research really did have an impact.

My research on how cultural factors influence communication and learning online is the third area where I have made an impact. I have written on globalization, culture and distance learning, identity, gender and language in synchronous cybercultures, and cross-cultural e-mentoring. I have also examined how culture influences the knowledge construction process as knowledge is constructed through the interaction of diverse voices. My co-authored book with Insung Jung on *Culture and Online Learning: Global Perspectives and Research*, published by Stylus, synthesizes some of my research on culture and online learning, and provides international perspectives on the topic. To summarize, my contributions in research are in examining social construction of knowledge online through interaction analysis and social learning analytic methods, social presence, and cultural factors that influence online communication and learning.

The second accomplishment I think is my design work: not only designing courses at UNM, but also designs for other cultural contexts. I recently produced a book, *Culturally-Inclusive Instructional Design: A Framework for Building Online WISDOM Communities*, with two of my former students, Casey Frechette and Ludmila Layne, to put our notions on how to design online environments out so that designers can use them. We were honored with the Best Book Award for this book by the Distance Learning Division of the Association for Educational Communications and Technology [AECT] at the 2019 convention. We have developed a companion website for this book, www.colectivo.io, where we want to develop an international community of instructional designers who share their designs that support cultural inclusivity. So I feel that one area that I have contributed is in the area of how to make designs more culturally inclusive, taking into account the different cultural and language factors that impact the learning process.

I have also reflected on my own learning as a teacher, an online teacher, as a distance teacher. Very early on, I think in 1990 or 1992, I published an article, "Changing Faculty Roles for [Audiographics and] Online Teaching," in the *American Journal of Distance Education*, which has been used quite a bit by other researchers (because I know from the permission requests that they send me). So the second area is on design and my reflections on designs and teaching.

The third area is the international projects that I have undertaken and contributed to. My students and I developed a mobile and e-learning solution for training physician assistants in Ghana. In fact, this was an interesting project because this Ghanaian physician was at a conference in Albuquerque that I was presenting at. He came back after the presentation and said, "You know what? I think you can help me develop an e-learning solution for the physician assistant programme that I have in Ghana because I can only train physician assistants who come on campus. I cannot take it out to the rural communities. Perhaps you have ways of doing that."

So my students worked on this over many semesters. After about three years, we wrote a grant to Grant Challenges Canada. It was a Canadian grant that my students wrote, and we got it. They were the initiators who wrote the grant. Then we went and implemented this project in Ghana. From that, I learned a lot about how to negotiate cultural spaces online and cultural spaces in international projects.

Also, I have worked in my country of birth, Sri Lanka, as a consultant for the Asian Development Bank–funded project called the National Online Distance Education System, housed within the Ministry of Education, where they were actually going to implement a national distance education online system. I was initially hired as a consultant by the Canadian organization that held the contract to train faculty and professionals on how to tutor and mentor online. Subsequently, I also went as a consultant for instructional design. So, again, I have not only contributed in terms of designing and training internationally, but I have also learned and shared these learning experiences with my students. Currently, I am working as a World Bank consultant to the Ministry of Health in Sri Lanka, helping them to design and assess online training courses for primary care physicians.

I think those are my contributions.

8. *What are some of the challenges that you faced in the field of DE over the years?*

Initially, it has been difficult to convince administrators that distance education can teach as well as traditional education and even better. This was so even in my own department, although I was hired as the faculty member to develop distance education as a graduate emphasis area. When we initially set up a project to teach courses at the Los Alamos Graduate Centre, which is situated in the mountains, it was difficult for me to negotiate with my supervisors on how this should be done because they really did not understand how distance education would work. So I set up an audiographics system because there was no room for our department in UNM's ITV system. Their television studios were occupied all of the time. And I also felt that television instruction was a one-way medium where students were more passive. They can ask questions, but it's not really interactive. I felt that audiographics using telephone lines – one for video and one for audio – would probably be more interactive. So I did set it up and finally got my department to support me in this effort, but it was a lot of convincing that I had to do. At that time, most of the people in charge were traditional face-to-face educators, predominantly male, and they had been flying in these little planes up to Los Alamos to teach face-to-face. It was difficult for them to figure out how distance learning could be a very effective medium. So that was my major challenge initially.

I have overcome so many challenges that there are too many to recall, but I will also talk a little bit about issues related to developing policies that are conducive to distance learners. At my own institution, I was on the distance education policy committee from my initial stepping into this university. One of the real difficulties we had was to make distance education as equitable as face-to-face: so, to develop policies that supported distance learners. We had to charge them extra, due to the delivery fee. There were also policies about learner support. We fought for the libraries to be more accessible. So developing those policies initially that were student friendly was a big challenge, but we've overcome them, I think.

Now I see another type of challenge. This is when institutions are really looking at utilizing distance learning as a money-making tool or as a tool where they are competing for students. We recently instituted a programme called the managed online programme. The university selected certain departments (ours was one of them) to teach certain programmes at a distance. All of the courses for the degrees had to be totally online, but we also had to undergo a review process. Some of the review process criteria were based on quality matters, but most of the criteria that they were using to evaluate the courses that would be part of the managed online programme were very behaviouristic. When my courses went up for review, I had to point out to them, "You know what? I really can't fit into your rubric because I teach from the social cultural and social constructivist perspective, and sometimes learning objectives emerge as I teach."

This was really difficult for them to handle. Of course, my courses, because they were well-designed, were accepted, but at the same time, there were these emphases on managed online programmes. We also had to have it in an eight-week format. All sixteen-week courses had to be crammed into an eight-week format, which is really difficult for students. In online learning, when you want to develop learning communities online, eight weeks is not enough. Students haven't even gone through that process of norming, storming, and performing when the eight weeks are done. That was really difficult for them, so to redesign, I had to remove modules. It's definitely not the sixteen-week course; it's a reduced format.

I'm really concerned about the quality of the learning experiences we offer our students when institutions buy into these managed online programmes. So that's my more recent pet peeve against administrators who don't really think through how learning happens online.

9. *What was the state of distance education when you first entered the field as opposed to distance education in 2018?*

When I first entered the field, correspondence education was pretty well entrenched. There were divisions of continuing education that were offering correspondence education. They were just beginning to look at television. Some of them were offering instructional television programmes, and some of them were utilizing video-based instruction. My dissertation was about how to enhance video-based instruction by utilizing some of the learning principles. For example, Gagne's nine events talked about how to integrate these principles to enhancing the learning people got from television because usually a television signal goes out, and then you expect to learn, and that doesn't happen. So TV was just beginning, and now, as you can see, the focus is on online and also mobile technologies.

The field has changed as the waves of technologies come and go. You also see different ways that we are adapting to technology. My main concern is that sometimes people adopt new technologies without really looking at how people learn and how to design for that learning utilizing the technologies. Now, with the online world, all the media – audio, video, and text – are all integrated in one online channel. I also feel that not only asynchronous, but also the synchronous, like the chat that we are having right now, is important for distance learning. When programmes discourage synchronous meetings, like our managed online programme does, I think we take away from learning experiences that certain students benefit from.

What interesting memories would you like to share about the beginning of online DE?

I talked a little bit about the GlobalEd project that I did when I initially started as a faculty member here [UNM], where we connected graduate students through a listserv. We connected them through a listserv that I established here at UNM and developed collaborative research experiences across universities. That was one of my wonderful memories.

Also, one of my initial memories was coming to UNM and setting up the audiographic system. So when I was hired, I was hired to set up the graduate emphasis area in distance education. At that time, our programme was teaching our master's degree in training and development at the Los Alamos Graduate Centre, which is a two-and-a-half-hour drive up the mountains. It was quite an isolated community. This is also where the Los Alamos National Lab is, and most of our students were employees of that lab. The model was to fly out in a small plane, teach, and come back. Sometimes I had to teach at seven o'clock at night, which meant that I was there until nine-thirty and I would get home really late. When the weather was bad, there was no flying, which was difficult. I had to stay overnight. So when I set up this audiographic system, I felt that we were beginning to look at distance learning in a more creative way and looking at interactive distance learning, rather than one-way delivery of distance learning.

The other thing that I have really good memories of was when I came here to UNM, there was a faculty member in my programme, Jack Gittinger, who was already running two bulletin board systems. One was called ENAN [Education Native American Network], which was funded by the BIA [Bureau of Indian Affairs]. It was connecting teachers from Native American schools to engage in collaboration with each other after they do their teacher training. The other one was called Cisco Net, which linked science teachers throughout New Mexico to do science projects. I studied these two examples of early bulletin board systems and did a video that I presented at a nationally broadcast distance education conference that Oklahoma State University was putting on at that time.

So these early bulletin board systems that already existed when I came here were also some of my very early memories of doing distance learning. That was in 1989. So from 1990 to 1992, these were my initial memories.

What were your specific DE research interests, and have they changed/evolved over the years?

In fact, one area that has evolved over the years is my interest in looking at culture and online learning. When we initially set up distance learning systems, we had really not thought about this influencing factor. I brought that in from my early experiences in the studying language and teaching of English as a second language. We also studied how different cultures utilize language and how languages can influence worldviews. When I started having challenges in my own online teaching early in my television teaching, I realized that there were issues that I didn't understand. What were they, and how can we describe them? That's how I got into my interest in culture, which really blended this passion I had for understanding culture with my passion for distance learning, which evolved really well. That area has really changed. Every day I learn something new about culture, and so I felt that is one area that has really evolved.

Another research area that has evolved is my understanding of how people learn online, and how people interact and create knowledge. I have always been interested in knowledge creation, rather than knowledge dissemination, and understanding how those interactions happen. Initially, we looked at it more qualitatively because the interaction analysis model actually analyzes the quality of the interactions. Now we are looking at how we can automate the interaction analysis model because it is difficult to get the time to analyze large amounts of interactions that occur in learning environments such as MOOCs [Massive Open Online Courses]. We are also combining more qualitative methods of analyses with more quantitative ones, such as social network analysis and social learning analytics – not the learning analytics institutions used to predict enrolment, but social learning analytics on how group dynamics support the online learning process, because we can do things like cluster analyses and see how the groups cluster, who are key players, etc., in the learning process. So that has evolved from more qualitative analyses of online interactions to incorporating more quantitative methods, such as social network analysis and social learning analytics, to support what we do qualitatively.

The understanding of social presence has also evolved. When I initially did research on social presence, I really didn't understand the influence of culture on social presence. Now, with more understanding of how cultural dynamics work, I realize that social presence is also culturally determined, especially when I did a recent study with Mexico. I understood from that study that social presence in Mexico is preferred in a different way than in the US. In Mexico, because it is a collectivist culture and also because it is a culture in which there is greater distance in power, the [Mexican] students really didn't want to know each other's backgrounds in detail. They said, "We really like to make up our minds about others and our connection with others by what they write, not so much because of who they are." So then I began to really look at this aspect. I was a Fulbright researcher in Morocco and Sri Lanka in 2004. I learned a lot about how dynamics there influence the learning process. I realized that social presence is also culturally determined. So my understanding has evolved over the years.

10. *Could you please describe the learning environment that you currently work in (e.g., geographic and institutional setting, student demographics)?*

I am at the University of New Mexico. UNM is considered to be a Hispanic-serving institution. It is one of the institutions around the country that has a large Hispanic population because that is the population New Mexico represents. New Mexico is considered a minority-majority state. We have a large Hispanic population as well as a large Native American population. So this university is considered the university that accepts and honours Native American traditions as well as Hispanic traditions. It's not that we are doing it very well, but we are very aware of the diversity of the students that we work with.

In addition to that, UNM also has a large international population. We have several refugee groups in the city that also attend the university.

New Mexico is one of the poorest states in the United States. Very often, fellow Americans don't understand that this is part of the United States. We often get confused with Mexico. It is also a mountainous state, because the Rocky Mountain range runs through the state. So communities are dispersed in rural locations. Albuquerque, where I am, is the largest metropolitan centre. Our capital is Santa Fe, which is also a city, but is smaller in size than Albuquerque.

What is an interesting demographic is that in a short geographic distance from Los Alamos to Albuquerque and south to Las Cruces, which is considered the Rio Grande research corridor because the Rio Grande flows that way, you have the highest concentration of people with PhDs anywhere in the United States. Yet the rest of the state lacks a lot of resources. I have Native American students who sometimes have difficulty getting electricity in their rural locations. They work with generators. Some of them cannot afford computers, even doctoral students. So we work with a lot of challenges. I think that UNM as an institution has learned that in order for education to really reach our students, we have to go out from our metropolitan centres and provide education to our rural communities. This is where distance learning has been a huge asset. We now have an undergraduate degree in training and instructional technology in our programme, Organization, Information, and Learning Sciences, that goes out to the entire state of New Mexico. That is a growing programme.

Our master's degrees are predominately online, but the doctorate is still face-to-face.

11. *Is there anything else you would like to address?*

I would definitely like people to read my book, *Culturally-Inclusive Instructional Design: A Framework for Building Online WISDOM Communities*. The reason I say this is because, throughout my years of teaching distance learning and designing distance learning environments, I really feel that a conducive learning environment, where diverse students can feel connected, can produce amazing learning experiences. It is difficult to do that. It is something that many instructors don't want to engage in because it is a lot of work to do that, to build a learning community. I really do believe that wisdom is an important goal to strive towards. It is different than intelligence. We have always focused on intelligence as the hallmark of an individual's merit. For me, wisdom, the understanding to work towards the good of others, for the common good, to be culturally humble – those characteristics of wisdom are very important. Actually, we discuss ten characteristics of wisdom in this book. Those are important values and qualities that we should develop in our distance learners while they also learn the content of whatever discipline that they are learning.

Sometimes in online learning we forget the social aspect, we forget the value systems and the skills that we need to develop in students, and I feel that this book is about developing those value systems in learners and how to be very cognizant of the cultural makeup of an online class because we don't see each other. This is especially so in the large-scale learning systems, such as MOOCs, because if you are going to go large scale, this is something that is going to be forgotten. Therefore, I think that I would like people to read my book on this.

Also, my research on the social construction of knowledge, the interaction analysis model – how to understand interactions online, as well as our combination of social learning analytics and social network analysis to do so – those might be areas that may be most important to future researchers in the field.

I feel that I was very fortunate to get into this field when I did. I think that it is a field that can really provide more access to education if it is designed well.

12. *Can you suggest names of other female pioneers in DE or online learning that you think we should include in the book?*

I've already mentioned Marina McIsaac, Chere Gibson, Connie Dillon, and also I gave you the name of one person from Sri Lanka and Insung Yung. I don't know how early Insung Yung was, but Gayathri Jayatilleke was pretty early. I will have to think about this a little bit more internationally.

Chandra Gunawardena is in Sri Lanka; she has the same last name as me. I would include her as a pioneer. I'm not too sure when she started with online learning. She came from the education field, but I don't know when she shifted to distance learning. When I worked with her on the Asian Development Bank project in Sri Lanka in 2007, she was considered one of the pioneers in distance learning there. She has been an educator most of her life.

I think very highly of Shironica Karunanayaka; she is also in education. She has done some very interesting work focusing on the use of OER [open educational resources], and she is also supervising doctoral students there. I was an external examiner for one of her student's dissertations. You might want to check on that, because I don't know when she started. She is really a big figure in Sri Lanka, but I don't know the point when she joined distance learning. It would be great to include her; she is a wonderful person.

Another person is Grainne Conole from Britain. Again, like Shironica, I don't know when she got into the field, but she has been a really big name. She published this book on designing for learning in an open world. I had her email address at one time. . . . I am looking at her book. She was at the University of Leicester when she wrote this book.

I'm sure that you have picked up a few people from Australia because Australia was a pioneer in distance learning. I remember one person. I think her first name is Kay; her last name is Sudweeks. She used to host conferences on cultural attitudes towards technology and education. She is also one whom I consider to be quite a pioneer in Australia.

There are folks in the Latin American countries that do distance learning perhaps we should look at.

Another person I remember is Marie-Noelle Lamy. I think that she may be part French. She is at the British Open University. She wrote a book on learning cultures in online education. She would also be a good person because I think that she has consistently done research. I wrote for her book, so I know her.

If you are looking at people in the Spanish-speaking world, people at the Open University of Catalonia, like Elena Barbera, are important distance education researchers. It is a fairly new institution. If you are looking for pioneers as such, I have to spend some time thinking about that. I will get back to you on it.

Publications

Books

Gunawardena, C. N., Frechette, C., & Layne, L. (2019). *Culturally inclusive instructional design: A framework and guide for building online wisdom communities.* Routledge.

Jung, I., & Gunawardena, C. N. (Eds.). (2014). *Culture and online learning: Global perspectives and research.* Stylus.

Book Chapters

Carabajal, K., La Pointe, D., & Gunawardena, C. N. (2003). Group development in online learning communities. In M. Moore & B. Anderson (Eds.), *Handbook of distance learning* (pp. 217–234). Lawrence Erlbaum.

Gunawardena, C. (1990). The integration of video-based instruction. In D. R. Garrison & D. Shale (Eds.), *Education at a distance: From issues to practice* (pp. 109–122). Krieger.

Gunawardena, C. (1995). Nuevos caminos en el aprendizaje: nuevas formas de evaluar (L. Bueno, Trans.). In *Cuadernos de educacion a distancia 3, Enfoques sobre evaluacion de los aprendizajes en educacion a distancia II*. Universidad de Guadalajara.

Gunawardena, C. (2004). Designing the social environment for online learning: The role of social presence. In D. Murphy, R. Carr, J. Taylor, & T. Wong (Eds.), *Distance education and technology: Issues and practice* (pp. 255–270). Open University of Hong Kong Press.

Gunawardena, C. N. (1993a). Collaborative learning and group dynamics in computer-mediated communication networks. *Research monograph of the American Center for the Study of Distance Education, 9*, 14–24. The Pennsylvania State University.

Gunawardena, C. N. (1993b). Inter-university collaborations: Factors impacting group learning in computer conferencing. In B. Scriven, R. Lundin, & Y. Ryan (Eds.), *Distance education for the twenty-first century* (pp. 248–251). Queensland University of Technology Press.

Gunawardena, C. N. (2001). Reflections on evaluating online learning and teaching. In E. J. Burge & M. Haughey (Eds.), *Using learning technologies: International perspectives on practice* (pp. 115–124). Routledge Falmer.

Gunawardena, C. N. (2003). Researching online learning and group dynamics: Models and methods. In Y. Fritze, G. Haugsbakk, & Y. T. Nordkvelle (Eds.), *Dialog og noerhet* (pp. 94–108). Hoyskoleforlaget AS- Norwegian Academic Press.

Gunawardena, C. N. (2004). The challenge of designing inquiry-based online learning environments: Theory into practice. In T. Duffy & J. Kirkley (Eds.), *Learner centered theory and practice in distance education: Cases from higher education* (pp. 143–158). Lawrence Erlbaum.

Gunawardena, C. N. (2013). Culture and online distance learning. In M. G. Moore (Ed.), *Handbook of distance education* (3rd ed., pp. 185–200). Routledge.

Gunawardena, C. N. (2014). Globalization, culture, and online distance learning. In O. Zawacki-Richter & T. Anderson (Eds.), *Online distance education: Towards a research agenda* (pp. 75–107). Athabasca University Press.

Gunawardena, C. N. (2017a). Cultural perspectives on social presence. In A. L. Whiteside, A. G. Dikkers, & K. Swan (Eds.), *Social presence in online learning: Multiple perspectives on practice and research* (pp. 113–129). Stylus.

Gunawardena, C. N. (2017b). Forward. In A. L. Whiteside, A. G. Dikkers, & K. Swan (Eds.), *Social presence in online learning: Multiple perspectives on practice and research* (pp. xiii–xv). Stylus.

Gunawardena, C. N., Idrissi Alami, A., Jayatilleke, G., & Bouacharine, F. (2009). Identity, gender, and language in synchronous cybercultures: A cross-cultural study. In R. Goodfellow & M. N. Lamy (Eds.), *Learning cultures in online education* (pp. 30–51). Continuum.

Gunawardena, C. N., & La Pointe, D. K. (2003). Planning and management of student assessment. In S. Panda (Ed.), *Planning and management in distance education* (pp. 195–205). Open and Distance Learning Series. Kogan Page.

Gunawardena, C. N., & LaPointe, D. K. (2007). Cultural dynamics of online learning. In M. G. Moore (Ed.), *Handbook of distance education* (2nd ed., pp. 593–607). Lawrence Erlbaum.

Gunawardena, C. N., & LaPointe, D. K. (2008). Social and cultural diversity in distance education. In T. Evans, M. Haughey, & D. Murphy (Eds.), *International handbook of distance education* (pp. 51–70). Emerald.

Gunawardena, C. N., & McIsaac, M. S. (2004). Distance education. In D. Jonassen (Ed.), *The handbook of research on education communications and technology* (2nd ed., pp. 355–395). Lawrence Erlbaum.

Gunawardena, C. N., Plass, J., & Salisbury, M. (2001). Do we really need an online discussion group? In D. Murphy, R. Walker, & G. Webb (Eds.), *Online learning and teaching with technology: Case studies, experience and practice* (pp. 36–43). Kogan Page.

Gunawardena, C. N., Wilson, P. L., & Nolla, A. C. (2003). Culture and online education. In M. Moore & B. Anderson (Eds.), *Handbook of distance learning* (pp. 753–775). Lawrence Erlbaum.

Gunawardena, C. N., & Zittle, R. H. (1995). An examination of teaching and learning processes in distance education and implications for designing instruction. *Research monograph of the American Center for the Study of Distance Education, 12*, 51–63. The Pennsylvania State University.

Gunawardena, C. N., & Zittle, R. H. (1998). Faculty development programmes in distance education in American higher education. In C. Latchem & F. Lockwood (Eds.), *Staff development in open and flexible learning* (pp. 105–114). Routledge.

Lowe, C., & Gunawardena C. (2004). Methods for evaluating interface design for online learning environments. In D. Murphy, R. Carr, J. Taylor, & T. Wong (Eds.), *Distance education and technology: Issues and practice* (pp. 160–169). Hong Kong: Open University of Hong Kong Press.

McIsaac, M. S., & Gunawardena, C. N. (1996). Distance education. In D. H. Jonassen (Ed.), *Handbook of research for educational communications and technology* (pp. 403–437). Simon & Schuster Macmillan.

Sanchez, I., & Gunawardena, C. N. (1998). Understanding and supporting the culturally diverse distance learner. In C. Campbell Gibson (Ed.), *Distance learners in higher education: Institutional responses for quality outcomes* (pp. 47–64). Atwood Publishing.

Journal Articles

Barberà, E., Layne, L., & Gunawardena, C. N. (2014). Designing online interaction to address disciplinary competencies: A cross-country comparison of faculty perspectives. *The International Review of Research in Open and Distance Learning (IRRODL), 15*(2), 142–169. www.irrodl.org/index.php/irrodl/article/view/1892/2896

Boverie, P., Gunawardena, C. N., Lowe, C. A., Murrell, W. G., Zittle, R. H., & Zittle, F. (2000). Designing satellite instruction for elementary students: Importance of the classroom teacher. *International Journal of Educational Telecommunications, 6*(2), 107–122.

Dillon, C. L., & Gunawardena, C. N. (1992). Evaluation research in distance education. *British Journal of Educational Technology, 23*(3), 181–194.

Dillon, C. L., Gunawardena, C. N., & Parker, R. (1992a). Learner support: The critical link in distance education. *Distance Education, 13*(1), 29–45.

Dillon, C. L., Gunawardena, C. N., & Parker, R. (1992b). Learner support in distance education: An evaluation of a statewide telecommunication system. *International Journal of Instructional Media, 19*(4), 297–311.

Duphorne, P. L., & Gunawardena, C. N. (2005). The effect of three computer conferencing designs on critical thinking skills of nursing students. *The American Journal of Distance Education, 19*(1), 37–50.

Frechette, C., Gunawardena, C. N., & Layne, L. (2016). How to design culturally inclusive online learning experiences (Yiwei Peng trans.). *Journal of Distance Education in China, 12,* 5–14. doi:10.13541/j.cnki.chinade.20161216.001

Gunawardena, C. N. (1989). The present perfect in the rhetorical divisions of biology and biochemistry journal articles. *English for Specific Purposes Journal, 8*(3), 265–273.

Gunawardena, C. N. (1990). Integrating telecommunication systems to reach distance learners. *The American Journal of Distance Education, 4*(3), 38–46.

Gunawardena, C. N. (1991). Current trends in the use of communications technologies for delivering distance education. *International Journal of Instructional Media, 18*(3), 201–213.

Gunawardena, C. N. (1992). Changing faculty roles for audiographics and online teaching. *The American Journal of Distance Education, 6*(3), 58–71.

Gunawardena, C. N. (1993). Videoconferencing and the adult learner. [Review of the book *Videoconferencing and the adult learner* by J. Dallat]. *Open Learning, 8*(2), 66.

Gunawardena, C. N. (1995). Social presence theory and implications for interaction and collaborative learning in computer conferences. *International Journal of Educational Telecommunications, 1*(2/3), 147–166.

Gunawardena, C. N. (1998). Designing collaborative learning environments mediated by computer conferencing: Issues and challenges in the Asian socio-cultural context. *Indian Journal of Open Learning, 7*(1), 105–124.

Gunawardena, C. N. (2005). Social presence and implications for designing online learning communities. *Open Education Research, 11*(5), 54–60. (Published in PRC and in Chinese Social Science Citation Index).

Gunawardena, C. N. (2020). Culturally inclusive online learning for capacity development projects in international contexts. *Journal of Learning for Development, 7*(1), 5–30. https://jl4d.org/index.php/ejl4d/article/view/403

Gunawardena, C. N., & Duphorne, P. L. (2000). Predictors of learner satisfaction in an academic computer conference. *Distance Education, 21*(1), 101–117.

Gunawardena, C. N., Flor, N. V., Gomez, D., & Sanchez, D. (2016). Analyzing social construction of knowledge online by employing interaction analysis, learning analytics, and social network analysis. *The Quarterly Review of Distance Education, 17*(3), 35–60.

Gunawardena, C. N., Hermans, M. B., Sanchez, D., Richmond, C., Bohley, M., & Tuttle, R. (2009). A theoretical framework for building online communities of practice with social networking tools. *Educational Media International, 46*(1), 3–16.

Gunawardena, C. N., Jayatilleke, B. G., & Lekamge, G. D. (1996). Learning styles of the Open University students of Sri Lanka (International Review). *Educational Technology Research & Development, 44*(1), 115–120.

Gunawardena, C. N., Jennings, B., Ortegano-Layne, L., Frechette, C., Carabajal, K., Lindemann, K., & Mummert, J. (2004). Building an online wisdom community: A transformational design model. *Journal of Computing in Higher Education, 15*(2), 40–62.

Gunawardena, C. N., Linder-VanBerschot, J. A., LaPointe, D. K., & Rao, L. (2010). Predictors of learner satisfaction and transfer of learning in a corporate online education program. *The American Journal of Distance Education, 24*(4), 207–226.

Gunawardena, C. N., Lowe, C. A., & Anderson, T. (1997). Analysis of a global online debate and the development of an interaction analysis model for examining social construction of knowledge in computer conferencing. *Journal of Educational Computing Research, 17*(4), 395–429.

Gunawardena, C. N., Nolla, A. C., Wilson, P. L., López-Islas, J. R., Ramírez-Angel, N., & Megchun-Alpízar, R. M. (2001). A cross-cultural study of group process and development in online conferences. *Distance Education, 22*(1), 85–121.

Gunawardena, C. N., Ortegano-Layne, L., Carabajal, K., Frechette, C., Lindemann, K., & Jennings, B. (2006). New model, new strategies: Instructional design for building online wisdom communities. *Distance Education, 27*(2), 217–232.

Gunawardena, C. N., Walsh, S. L., Gregory, E. M., Lake, M. Y., & Reddinger, L. E. (2005). Cultural perceptions of face negotiation in online learning environments. *Electronic Journal of Communication/ La Revue Electronique de Communication, 15*(1&2). www.cios.org/www/ejc/v15n12.htm

Gunawardena, C. N., & Zittle, R. (1997a). Distance learning and K-12 education in the United States. *Open Praxis, Bulletin of the International Council of Distance Education, 1*.

Gunawardena, C. N., & Zittle, F. (1997b). Social presence as a predictor of satisfaction within a computer mediated conferencing environment. *The American Journal of Distance Education, 11*(3), 8–25.

Hillman, D. C. A., Willis, D. J., & Gunawardena, C. N. (1994). Learner-interface interaction in distance education: An extension of contemporary models and strategies for practitioners. *The American Journal of Distance Education, 8*(2), 30–42.

Hollifield, M., Hewage, C., Gunawardena, C. N., Kodituwakku, P., Bopagoda, K., & Weerarathnege, K. (2008). Symptoms and coping in Sri-Lanka 20–21 months after the 2004 tsunami. *The British Journal of Psychiatry, 192*, 39–44.

Jayatilleke, B. D., & Gunawardena, C. (2016). Cultural perceptions of online learning: Transnational faculty perspectives. *Asian Association of Open Universities Journal, 11*(I), 50–63. http://dx.doi.org/10.1108/AAOUJ-07-2016-0019

Jayatilleke, B. G., Kulasekara, G. U., Kumarasinha, M. B., & Gunawardena, C. N. (2017). Implementing the first cross-border professional development online course through international e-mentoring: Reflections and perspectives. *Open Praxis, 9*(1), 31–44.

Knight, E., Gunawardena, C. N., & Aydin, C. H. (2009). Cultural interpretations of the visual meaning of icons and images used in North American web design. *Educational Media International, 46*(1), 17–35.

LaPointe, D. K., & Gunawardena, C. N. (2004). Developing, testing and refining of a model to understand the relationship between peer interaction and learning outcomes in computer-mediated conferencing. *Distance Education, 25*(1), 83–106.

Lucas, M., Gunawardena, C., & Moreira, A. (2014). Assessing social construction of knowledge online: A critique of the interaction analysis model. *Computers in Human Behavior, 30*, 574–582.

Palalas, A., Berezin, N., Gunawardena, C. N., & Kramer, G. (2015). A design-based research framework for implementing a transnational mobile and blended learning solution. *International Journal of Mobile and Blended Learning, 7*(4), 57–74.

Walsh, S. L., Gregory, E. M., Lake, M. Y., & Gunawardena, C. N. (2003). Self-construal, facework, and conflict styles among cultures in online learning environments. *Educational Technology Research and Development, 51*(4), 113–122.

Conference Presentations

Frechette, C., Gunawardena, C. N., & Layne, L. (2020). From theory to platform: Designing software to support online wisdom communities. *Proceedings of the 2019 ICDE World Conference on Online Learning, 1*, 272–281. http://dx.doi.org/10.5281/zenodo.3804014

Gunawardena, C., Jayatilleke, G., Kulasekara, G., & Kumarasinha, M. (2020). Distributed co-mentoring as a means to develop culturally inclusive online learning communities. *Proceedings of the 2019 ICDE World Conference on Online Learning, 1*, 389–400. http://dx.doi.org/10.5281/zenodo.3804014

Gunawardena, C. N., Moore, S. L., Barril, L., & Thabotharan, K. (2020, November 18). *Online assessment methods for student-centered learning: Active learning, collaboration, and application with authentic assessment* [Panel presentation]. Sponsored by the United States-Sri Lanka Fulbright Commission, Colombo, Sri Lanka. https://digitalrepository.unm.edu/ulls_fsp/156

Gunawardena, C. N., & Premawardhena, N. C. (2020, October 28). *Online course design for student centered learning* [Presentation]. Sponsored by the United States-Sri Lanka Fulbright Commission, Colombo, Sri Lanka. https://digitalrepository.unm.edu/ulls_fsp/152

Sanchez, D., Flor, N., & Gunawardena, C. (2020). Employing social learning analytic methods (slams) to reimagine the social dynamic of online learning collaborations. *Proceedings of the 2019 ICDE World Conference on Online Learning, 1*, 817–832. http://dx.doi.org/10.5281/zenodo.3804014

14
HENRI, FRANCE

Photo of France Henri contributed by France Henri

> *I developed in my PhD thesis a method to analyze computer conferencing content. It was the first "theoretically based" method meant to analyze what was going on in computer conferencing: types of content shared by students, the way they were interacting, level of participation, etc. This method became "the" reference to analyze computer conferencing. It has been largely applied. Many researchers referred to "Henri's method" in their work to improve this type of analysis, to expand it, or even to create a new method.*

Dr. France Henri was a prolific researcher and leader during the early years of online learning, particularly in the Canadian province of Quebec. She was one of a group of female leaders who created the Women's International Network (WIN) organization, which was rooted in the early International Council for Distance Education (ICDE) conferences.

Henri obtained a BA in History and Political Science from the University of Montreal, Canada, in 1969, and her MA in French Canadian History from McGill University, Canada, in 1971. She became interested in educational technology and obtained a second MA in that field at Concordia University, Canada, in 1974. She completed her PhD in Educational Technology at Concordia University in 1990.

Currently, Dr. Henri is an Associate Professor, Télé-université (TÉLUQ) and a regular researcher at the LICEF Research Centre at TÉLUQ. TÉLUQ is part of the University of Quebec institution and is unique in that it is the only French-speaking distance education university in North America. Its offices and centres are located in Quebec City, Canada.

Among Henri's many accolades is her recent nomination by the Minister of Education of Quebec as a member of the "Ordre d'excellence en Éducation" of Québec. Henri also currently holds the position of Honorary Research Professor at the LICEF Research Centre at TÉLUQ, which she has held since 2014.

Henri led and participated in numerous research projects that enhanced the field of online learning. She was very involved in early e-learning course design and how to support online students. She initiated the first online course at TÉLUQ that involved collaborative work. This was a new concept for many universities, which she and her team helped establish as a viable inclusion in online course design.

Much of Dr. Henri's research is published in the French language. We are hoping that some readers may be bilingual, or, as our technology progresses at such warp speed, that it will not be long before we are able to find translations of most research into the reader's first language. Some of her work has been published in English, as a perusal of her list of publications at the end of this chapter indicates.

Interview

Transcript Analysis Summary

Analysis of all interviews included in this volume led to the identification of 3,545 units of data. The mean of these collective units was 118 per pioneer, the median was 118.5, and the mode was 132. Individual interview units ranged from 59 to 217 units, yielding a spread of 158 units between all interviews. France Henri's interview generated 72 units, which placed her interview in the bottom fifth of interviews in terms of unit generation. There were two possible explanations for the low number of units. First, Henri completed the interview in English, which was a second language for her. The second reason was because she chose to complete the interview in asynchronous text-based, rather than in synchronous audio format.

A comparision of Henri's interview to the interviews of all pioneers indicated that, generally speaking, her interview yielded a similar number of units to that of the average interview (Figure 14.1). She produced significantly more units than the average interview in three areas: accomplishments, research interests, and goals. The number of units in these areas could be eplained by the breadth and depth of research aims and resultant activities that Henri was involved in during her career. While her interview had a comparable number of units to the average interview in the area of benefits of DE, her interview included far fewer challenge units. In fact, she identified only two challenges: student engagement in collaborative learning and the transmission model of education that typified early online learning delivery. The typical interview tended to yield slightly more benefit than challenge units. No explanation is offered for why Henri chose to share few interesting memories or final thoughts beyond her use of a second language and asynchronous, text-based responses for the interview.

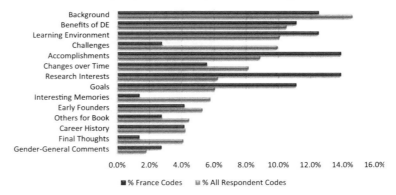

Figure 14.1 All Respondents' Versus France Henri's Parent Codes

Link to recorded interview Part A: tinyurl.com/Henri-F-A

Link to recorded interview Part B: tinyurl.com/Henri-F-2019

Transcript of Interview

Full Name: France Henri
Institutional Affiliation: Télé-université (TÉLUQ)
Key:

> Regular font = Interviewee comments
> *Italicized font* = Interviewer comments

Interview Questions

1. *What was your educational and experiential background before you became involved in online distance learning [ODL]?*

Educational experience

MA in Canadian history, McGill University (1971)

I chose to register to this MA in Canadian history simply by interest in the discipline. I had no idea of what the career opportunities might be after this MA. However, I knew at the end that I did not want to be an "historian" and work as a university professor. At that time, historians and professors used to work alone in their office, door closed, with little interaction with other historians, doing their own research mainly in libraries, digging through documents. However, things have changed today. The keywords in the educational milieu and in research are *collaboration, teamwork, international network, successful partnership*, and so on.

MA in Educational Technology, Concordia University (1974)

During my last year at McGill, I heard of a new programme at Concordia University. The first one in Canada: an MA in Educational Technology with Dave Mitchel as director. They were looking for MA graduate in any discipline. It was a condition to be accepted in the programme. Their logic was that those who wanted to use technology as educational support had to be specialized in a discipline. One could not exploit educational technology resources without being knowledgeable in a domain. I thought that this MA was designed for me. I was dreaming of doing documentary films at National Film Board. When you say, "film production," it means teamwork.

PhD in Educational Technology, Concordia University (1989)

Early work experience

1974 Université du Québec in Hull. One year as Head of the Audiovisual Service, mainly assisting professors in their use of AV resources. Not a challenging job.

1975–1976 Canadian government, Department of Communication, Educational Technology Branch. The mandate of this newly created Ed Tech Branch was to document and evaluate "technologies in education," and to offer advice on their implementation. I was hired as "Evaluation Officer" and spent two years in this very stimulating job.

Educational technology was in its infancy. It was a new domain that the Canadian government wanted to promote, develop, and implement into educational systems. Since "education" was a matter under provincial jurisdiction, the Department of Communication could not directly offer provincial education systems counselling, advice, and support for efficient use of technology in education. The strategy was to reach schools "indirectly" through libraries. We offered advices and support to librarians and school librarians on creating, implementing, and managing media libraries (*médiathèque*). Librarians would then be prepared to promote to teachers the effective use of technologies in their classes.

The Ed Tech Branch was also expected to reach higher education. They started with military college aimed at offering some courses in French to Francophone military students outside Québec. Under this mandate, I was involved in a very exciting and inspiring project aimed at the development of a "remote-teaching system." The team project was composed of engineers and educational technology specialists. An experiment between Collège Militaire de Saint Jean in Québec and Royal Military College of Canada in Kingston was planned to broadcast live instruction using a "slow scan television system." I was involved in the design and evaluation of this experiment, both from the technological and pedagogical points of view. It was very exciting. We were aware at that time that we were at the forefront and that the "remote teaching" approach had a real future.

In 1976, the Educational Technology Branch was abolished. Provincial governments challenged its existence in the sense that education was under provincial jurisdiction. They demanded that the resources invested by the Canadian government through the Ed Tech Branch be redistributed to the provinces. The Educational Technology Branch of [the] Communication Department was dissolved, and I was offered a position at Transport Canada Training Institute.

1977–1978 Canadian Government: Transport Canada Training Institute.

I was hired as an ed tech specialist to join the team working at the Francization of air controller training. For the team, Francization was a perfect opportunity to rethink and renew teaching strategies and explore the possible use of media and technology. Our room for maneuver was not very great since air traffic controller training must comply with very strict regulation and flawless use of complex technologies. Also, among the trainers, a well-anchored idea was that good teaching would generate good learning. Individual characteristics of learners were not a factor. When working with trainers, we tried to introduce a new training design approach based on a "learner-centred" training philosophy.

1979–1980 Years dedicated to my family.

1981–2014 Télé-université, Université du Québec (TÉLUQ). Working at TÉLUQ has been 32 challenging and exciting years. At that time, TÉLUQ was an institution at the forefront of technology and at the cutting edge of pedagogical innovation. As faculty member, I have developed many courses with the collaboration of most competent course teams. Course teams consisted of specialists from several fields: educational technology, student support, content expert, graphic designers, media specialists, linguistic reviewers, etc. Our main concern was "the student." I appreciated a lot the skills and expertise of the course teams' members I have worked with. They were very competent, sensitive to, and concerned by students' success. They defended the student's point of view. They were willing to implement all they could to support and facilitate learning; they were determined to induce changes in the system when it was necessary. If institutional practices or rules would not benefit the student, all did what they could to change or circumvent them.

Here is an example of what we could do to hold to our commitment towards "the student." At TÉLUQ, I did the first course based on [a] collaborative learning scenario. It meant that students would work together to solve a problem, complete a task, create a product, or carry out a project. For that, students had to be gathered in teams. But the notion of "group" or "team" did not exist in the TÉLUQ system.

Students were enrolled individually. After enrollment, they would receive the course material and the name, address, and phone number of their tutor. They were then ready to start the course, alone, without any possibility to communicate with other students enrolled in the same course. We bypassed this system's inability to offer students the opportunity to engage in collaborative learning. We asked the registration clerks to "manually" group students into teams of six to ten students. The same tutor would then be assigned to each "individual" student grouped "manually" to form a team. These "individual" students would start their course at the same time. To gather them, a forum would be opened for each group created "artificially," and the tutor assigned to these students would act as the forum moderator. Soon, the institution recognized that collaborative learning should be supported by the system. The practice of collaborative learning developed fairly quickly, and the registration system was modified accordingly.

At TÉLUQ, in 1992, I was among the founding members of the Laboratoire d'Informatique Cognitive et Environnements de Formation (LICEF). In 1995, LICEF got the status of research centre. Over the years, my main research topics were distance learning, computer conferencing, collaborative learning, communities of practice, and pedagogical design/pedagogical engineering.

2. *In what year did you begin to look specifically into DE? ODL? What were the circumstances in your world that initiated this interest in DE and ODL?*

As mentioned previously, as soon as 1976, I participated in a "remote teaching" experimentation at Transport Canada Training Institute.

3. *Which female researchers or female colleagues may have piqued your interest in DE and ODL?*

I met Thérèse Lamy at Concordia University in 1971. We were both enrolled in the Master's programme in Educational Technology. We became very good friends. Later on, we became colleagues at TÉLUQ. In fact, when I applied at TÉLUQ in 1981, she was with John Daniel on the jury who interviewed me.

I mentioned earlier (question 1) that I appreciated a lot the skills and expertise of the course teams' members I have worked with at TÉLUQ. They were "Very competent, sensitive to and concerned by students' success. They defended the student's point of view. They were willing to implement all they can to support and facilitate learning; they were determined to induce changes in the system when necessary. If institutional practices or rules would not benefit the student, all did what they could to change or circumvent them." This description corresponds to what Thérèse was.

I was very lucky to have Thérèse as [a] colleague at TÉLUQ. She was my coach, my mentor. She helped me to understand the system, how it worked, and what the stakes were. She was very good at depicting quickly problematic situations and reacting to them. Very active, highly dedicated to her work and to student achievement; this is what I appreciated so much from her. I admired her for her leadership, her team spirit, her respect for others, her strength of conviction, and, of course, for the quality of her work. For her, there was no problem without a solution. She could devote all her energy to defend a good cause and for changes to be made. She did not hesitate to go back even to the highest ranks of the institutional hierarchy to obtain changes. She was highly respected by her colleagues and by the hierarchy. She was a model for me.

4. *Who would you identify as the early female leaders/founders in the field of DE? ODL?*

Diana Laurillard.

I visited the OU many times between 1985 and 1995. I could see that the OU was a man's world. (This may have changed since. . .) Diana started as lecturer in 1981 and in 1995, she became pro vice chancellor for learning technologies and teaching at the OU. She made her way in its huge and "not so easy" institution. She became a high-ranked institutional manager, she was forward thinking (*avant-gardiste*), interested in technology and promoting collaborative learning. She received many academic honours and served in several international organizations, including UNESCO.

As a researcher and author, her "conversational framework" is an important contribution. It is a reference for the design of learning environments and for the adoption of a pedagogical strategy in which the learner has their place. In her vision, based on discussion, adaptation, interaction, and reflection, teachers and learners are becoming partners.

Rethinking University Teaching, the title of her 1993 book, is still inspiring. It clearly suggests that we should not hesitate to question our institutions, to promote flexibility of their structures, and to aim for innovation.

5. *What are some of the goals that you strove to achieve in the field of DE? ODL?*

I would mention three goals.

To promote distance education as:

- An effective and rewarding learning model;
- A source of personal growth that gives the learner the feeling of self-confidence and the satisfaction of being able to learn by oneself; and
- An opportunity for students to become independent learners, which is a competence required to engage in lifelong learning.

To convince all actors of education systems, including decision makers, that the questions to ask are not:

- "What are we going to teach?" but "What do they need to learn?"
- "How will we teach?" but "How will they learn what they need to learn?"

To convince all actors of education systems, including decision makers, that the finality (purpose) of education:

- Is not just about acquiring knowledge and skills related to a discipline or to a field.
- Is also about giving all students the opportunity to become independent learners in order to be able to engage in a process of lifelong learning.

5. *What are some of your accomplishments in the field of DE and ODL that you would like to share?*

The Minister of Education of Quebec recently nominated me as a member of the "Ordre d'Excellence en Éducation" of Québec. It is a recognition of my work that has touched me a lot.

Accomplishments in research

Distance education:

Henri, F., & Kaye, A. (Éd.). (1985). *Le savoir à domicile. Pédagogie et problématique de la formation à distance*. Québec: Presses de l'Université du Québec.

This book was the first book published in French on distance education, with Tony Kaye as co-editor. We started the work in 1983, and the book was published in 1985.

There were few books published in France on "*enseignement par correspondence.*" As you know, this type of "remote teaching" had nothing to do with DE or ODL. The book was a success in France and here in Québec. It describes organizational aspects and the general philosophy of DE, but especially the open approach to learning.

The cover of the book was created by the TÉLUQ's graphic designer team. They were very enthusiastic about doing this cover page, and I was very happy about it and proud of it. In fact, the design translated into an image [of] what TÉLUQ is all about: "reaching the students where they are" and offering them the learning resources and learning support they need. On the image, there is a telephone on the table. [The t]elephone was widely used to provide individual support to students.

Support was also provided via teleconferencing calls, bringing together students to socialize and discuss course content and difficulties. It was expected that students would also find motivational support during teleconferencing meetings. At that time, teleconferencing was kind of an innovation in distance education practices, meant to overcome distance and to provide social, cognitive, and educational presence and support.

Computer conferencing content analysis:

I developed in my PhD thesis a method to analyze computer conferencing content. The method was published in a NATO book edited by Tony Kaye. It was the first "theoretically-based" method meant to analyze what was going on in computer conferencing: types of content shared by students, the way they were interacting, level of participation, etc. This method became "the" reference to analyze computer conferencing. It has been largely applied. Many researchers referred to "Henri's method" in their work to improve this type of analysis, to expand it, or even to create a new method.

Henri, F. (1992). Computer conferencing and content analysis. In A. Kaye (Ed.), *Collaborative learning and computer conferencing*. Pays-Bas: Springer-Verlag.

Henri, F. (1992). Integration of computer-mediated communication in mass distance education: Should we rush into it? In D. Sanderson (Ed.), *Electronic networks in organizations: Issues and research perspectives*. Canada: Canadian Workplace Automation Research Centre, Government of Canada.

Collaborative learning:

In 2001, I published with Karin Lundgren-Cayrol a book on distance collaborative learning. I must say that there were not very many books on that subject. Collaboration with Karin was very productive and rewarding. I think we've done a great job defending and promoting collaborative learning and demonstrating that it can be implemented at a distance in virtual environments. The book is a mix of theory, conceptual definitions, and practice that underlie collaborative learning, such as virtual learning environments, spaces and structure of virtual environments, collaboration models and resources, and dynamics of collaborative learning. This book was also a success here in Québec, as well as in France.

Henri, F., & Lundgren-Cayrol, K. (2001). *Apprentissage collaboratif à distance. Pour comprendre et concevoir des environnements d'apprentissage virtuels*. Sainte-Foy, Quebec: Presses de l'Université du Québec.

Unfortunately, the cover page of the book was not designed by TÉLUQ's designer team. It was designed by the editor, Presses de l'Université du Québec. Not inspiring at all! (I mean the cover page.)

Learning with technologies:

Charlier, B., & Henri, F. (Éd.). (2010). *Apprendre avec les technologies*. Paris, France: Presses Universitaires de France.

As editors, Bernadette Charlier (University of Fribourg, Switzerland) and I published a book on learning and technologies. The themes addressed in this book are the analysis, design, and evaluation of technologies and resources for learning that constitute the essence of this book. It introduces concepts such as pedagogical design and scenario, network and community, training devices, and technology as a cognitive instrument. The book provides a synthesis of recent research on the transformations that technologies induce in teaching and learning. The authors of the chapters come from the fields of educational sciences, communication sciences, and computer science.

Cognitive modelling:

As researchers, we need to base our research work on relevant, well-constructed problems, on sound methodologies, and on the use of efficient tools. On this particular aspect, at the LICEF Research Centre, I had the opportunity to familiarize myself with cognitive modeling and the use of graphical modeling software (MOT and GMOT) developed by my colleague, Gilbert Paquette, and his research team. Graphic cognitive modeling was, and still is for me, highly precious for the design of course content, of learning scenarios, and at all steps of research projects to share and discuss our cognitive representations and to support group work.

MOOCs [Massive Open Online Courses]:

Currently, beside[s] my research aiming at renewing pedagogical engineering methods, I am working on MOOCs.

I participated in the research project entitled *Cours de masse en ligne et apprentissage personnalisé: le défi pédagogique des CLOM* (In English, MOOC and personalized learning: Pedagogical challenge). It was funded with a SSHRC [Social Sciences and Humanities Research] Grant 2014–2017 and involved Gilbert Paquette, France Henri, Josianne Basque, [and] Neila Mezgani.

Accomplishments in teaching

As mentioned previously, at TÉLUQ, I did the first course based on collaborative learning scenario. It meant that students would work together to solve a problem, complete a task, create a product, or carry out a project.

For the design of my courses, and especially for the design of learning scenarios, I applied the "MISA" pedagogical engineering method, which was developed at LICEF by my colleague, Gilbert Paquette, and his team. (LICEF stands for Laboratoire d'Informatique Cognitive et Environnements de Formation. This *"laboratoire"* was recognize as a research centre soon after its creation in 1992.) This method, based on cognitive engineering and modeling of knowledge, allows systematic design of the various "objects" that make up learning environments.

Using this method, I have tried to apply in my courses the ideas conveyed in my books and in my research. Essentially, I was promoting collaborative learning practices using stimulating learning scenarios supported by appropriate use of technologies. According to my definition, a "learning scenario" is made of a sequence of activities. There are various types of activities: cognitive, metacognitive, motivational, socialization, management (control) of learning, etc. Conceptually, an "activity," including [a] learning activity, is articulated around three components: 1) resource (any kind of input to the process); 2) process (a series of actions in order to achieve a particular end); and 3) output (result of the process, a reified object).

Learning activity = Resource (input) → process (series of actions) → result (output).

For instance, asking students to "read chapter 3" is not a learning activity by itself. But asking students to "read Chapter 3 to understand and analyze its content in order to develop a personal opinion" is a learning activity. Chapter 3 is the resource (or input); to read, understand, and analyze is the process; and to develop a personal opinion is the output (the learning). The result (output) can be in the form of a written document or a participation in an opinion debate or any other "reified object." For the student, it must be clear that the "product" contributes to the construction of their knowledge or to the development of their competencies. This approach tends to support metacognitive capacities and learner control of [their] learning.

The "Resource → process → output" model appears simple and most obvious. But it would be interesting to use this model to analyze activity guidelines in online courses. The results could be surprising...

6. *What are some of the challenges that you faced in the field of DE and ODL over the years?*

   The first challenge I faced was dealing with students who refused to engage in collaborative learning activities. They were not numerous, but I had to understand their resistance. These students knew only one model of distance learning: learning alone at one's own pace. Collaboration with other students disrupted their way of learning. They complained about the fact that they had to negotiate the work to be done, the work schedule, the method, the pace of work, and the availability of everyone to hold meetings. To communicate and to share was a problem.

   To meet the challenge, the first action was to explain very clearly right at the beginning in the course description and in the learning material what collaboration was all about and what competencies it required. I was advocating the fact that acquiring collaboration competencies was part of the learning within the course and that these competencies were expected for workers in today's work market.

   The second action was to allow students to choose their collaborators. They were invited to participate in computer conferencing to introduce themselves and to form teams. The idea was to let them choose the teammates with whom they had affinities.

   The learning scenarios would include individual activities, but only one collaborative activity. At the end of the course, there was always an individual activity inviting students to make a return on the experience of collaboration that they had lived and on the learning that they had been able to withdraw. Of course, there were no wrong answers for this activity.

   A second challenge for distance education in general was the "book model" that was embedded as the model of learning in the structure of online course platforms, such as Moodle. Platforms have evolved over time to focus more on learning than the transmission of knowledge.

7. *What was the "state of DE" when you first entered the field as opposed to DE in 2018?*

   Distance education was meant mainly to overcome spatiotemporal distance. The notion of "distance" was enriched by the concept of transactional distance (dialogue and structure) and by the social, cognitive, and educational "distance" or "presence."

   Student support was a real concern. There was a team of researchers at TÉLUQ that devoted its work [to] this issue. Practices of designers, of tutors, and of interveners with distance students were questioned. Interesting and productive research were conducted on this problem, trying to identify and analyze the representations and practices of learners in order to better understand "learning at a distance" (what it means for the student to learn at a distance). Practices of designers, tutors, or interveners with distance students were questioned. Results were intended to develop better support services for students and to design learning material that would be better adapted to students' needs.

   Learner autonomy was also a real concern, but to my knowledge, there was no well-structured research programme on the issue of distance learner autonomy as it is today in the perspective of lifelong learning.

8. *What interesting memories would you like to share about the beginning of ODL?*

   I would mention only one memory that gave a deep meaning to my professional and personal life and which is a kind of reward.

The greatest emotion that I felt during all these years at TÉLUQ was that aroused by the testimony of the women who had completed the studies programme in which they had committed themselves. These were extremely touching testimonials from women who recognized that they had gained valuable knowledge throughout their studies. They wanted to stress that what was most important to them, what they were most proud of, despite the discouragement they felt at the beginning of their studies in distance education, was that they had learned to learn by themselves. They did not regret the efforts made to combine studies, family life, and their professional work. They had courageously undertaken these studies for their personal development and to progress in the labour market. They also told us that were aware they had become a role model for their children.

These testimonies were made publicly at the graduation ceremony. The families were present (husband, children, cousins, aunts. . .), and all were very proud of the perseverance that their loved one had shown over the years to obtain this diploma.

9. *What were your specific DE and ODL research interests, and have they changed/evolved over the years?*

Main research topics and problems that I addressed over the years were:
- Distance education as a system: organizational aspects and values,
- Use of learning technologies,
- Computer conferencing and content analysis,
- Computer mediated communication,
- Collaborative distance learning,
- Virtual communities/community of practice,
- Personal learning environments (PLEs),
- MOOCs,
- Development of learner autonomy and lifelong learning, and
- Renewing pedagogical engineering methods to include the development of autonomy as a finality and the impact of this new logic on learning systems.

My research initially focused on distance education systems: values, organization, pedagogy, student support, technology, etc. Afterwards, my interest focused more specifically on the learner and the development of their autonomy. In this perspective, I have been working on personal learning environments (PLEs) and MOOCs. This led me to question and to criticize pedagogical engineering methods used to design learning environments. The need to renew these methods seemed to me urgent and unavoidable.

The problem is that pedagogical engineering methods focus solely on the development of knowledge and skills related to disciplines or knowledge domains. The autonomy of the learner is not taken into consideration. Renewed methods must aim at developing the autonomy of the learner "throughout their path," even and especially at higher level[s] of education. Development of autonomy is, nowadays, very closely interrelated to the capacity to use technology in an effective manner. Students must become "professional learners" to be adequately prepared to lifelong learning.

Here is a reference to a recent publication that clarifies my current epistemological posture:

Henri, F. (2019). Nouveau paradigme et nouvelle logique de formation. In Dans B. Albero, S. Simonian, & J. Eneau (Éds.), *Des humains & des machines. Hommage aux travaux d'une exploratrice*. Dijon: Raison & Passions.

10. *Could you please describe the learning environment that you currently work in (e.g., geographic and institutional setting, student demographics)?*

    I retired from TÉLUQ in 2014. But I am still active as [a] researcher at LICEF Research Centre. I supervise students (Master and PhD), and I participate in research projects.

11. *Is there anything else you [would] like to address?*

    No . . . Hope I have said enough.

12. *Can you suggest names of other female pioneers in DE or ODL that you think we should include in the book?*

    Margaret Haughey:

    Margaret Haughey is the author of several publications on distance education. She is engaged in the promotion of open distance learning, focusing on the needs of students, on transformative learning, and on empowerment of the students. She was editor of the *Journal of Distance Education*. Also, there is the Margaret Haughey Award presented to the authors of the best master's thesis or graduating paper in the area of educational administration and leadership completed at a Canadian university.

    Judy Roberts:

    She was the kingpin of Contact North. In no time, she did an outstanding job for the creation of Contact North. She had a team spirit and a great leadership. She managed to reconcile the highly political aspects of this project with the real needs of regions, of the various institutions, and of the population. She knew how to deal with cultural differences. She was dynamic and concerned about what people had to say, applying a bottom-up approach and a remarkable openness.

Publications

Books

Charlier, B., & Henri, F. (Éd.). (2010). *Apprendre avec les technologies*. Presses Universitaires de France.

Henri, F., & Kaye, A. (Éd.) (1985). *Le savoir à domicile. Pédagogie et problématique de la formation à distance*. Presses de l'Université du Québec.

Henri, F., & Lamy, T. (1989). *La formation à distance: Choix technologiques et practices and priorities*. Athabasca University & Canadian Society for Studies in Education.

Henri, F., & Lundgren-Cayrol, K. (2001). *Apprentissage collaboratif à distance. Pour comprendre et concevoir des environnements d'apprentissage virtuels*. Presses de l'Université du Québec.

Book Chapters (Chapitres de Livre)

Henri, F. (1992a). Computer conferencing and content analysis. In A. Kaye (Ed.), *Collaborative learning and computer conferencing*. Springer-Verlag.

Henri, F. (1992b). Integration of computer-mediated communication in mass distance education: Should we rush into it? In D. Sanderson (Ed.), *Electronic networks in organizations: Issues and research perspectives*. Canadian Workplace Automation Research Centre, Government of Canada.

Henri, F. (1995). Distance learning and computer-mediated communication: Interactive, quasi-interactive or monologue? In C. O'Malley (Ed.), *Computer supported collaborative learning* (pp. 145–161). NATO ASI Series, Springer-Verlag.

Henri, F. (2001). Des cours web à l'université. In T. Karsenti (Éd.), *Les TIC . . . au cœur des pédagogies universitaires* (pp. 117–143). Presses de l'Université du Québec.

Henri, F. (2003). Les campus virtuels, pourquoi et comment? In B. Charlier & D. Peraya (Éds.), *Technologie et innovation pédagogique* (pp. 71–78). De Boeck.

Henri, F. (2010). Collaboration, communautés et réseaux: Partenariats pour l'apprentissage. In B. Charlier & F. Henri (Éds.), *Apprendre avec les technologies*. Presses Universitaires de France.

Henri, F. (2019). Nouveau paradigme et nouvelle logique de formation. In B. Albero, S. Simonian, & J. Eneau (Éds.), *Des humains et des machines. Hommage aux travaux d'une exploratrice*. Raison & Passions.

Henri, F., & Basque, J. (2003). Concevoir des activités de collaboration en mode virtuel. In C. Daudelin & T. Nault (Éds.), *Collaborer pour apprendre et faire apprendre* (pp. 29–53). Presses de l'Université du Québec.

Henri, F., Charlier, B., Daele, A., & Pudelko, B. (2003). Evaluation for knowledge: An approach to support the quality of learners' community in higher education. In E. Stacey & G. Davies (Eds.), *Quality education @ distance* (pp. 211–221). Kluwer Academic Publishers.

Henri, F., Gagné, P., & Maina, M. (2005). Étude d'usage du téléapprentissage en vue de la conception d'une base de connaissances sur le domaine. In S. Pierre (Éd.), *Développement, intégration et évaluation des technologies de formation et d'apprentissage* (pp. 31–61). Presses Internationales Polytechniques/Polytechnic International Press.

Henri, F., & Maina, M. (2007). Pratique de design pédagogique et instrumentation du concepteur. In D. Guin & L. Trouche (Éds.), *Environnements informatisés et ressources numériques pour l'apprentissage: Conception et usages, regards croisés* (pp. 78–121). Hermès.

Henri, F., & Pudelko, B. (2002). La recherche sur la communication asynchrone: De l'outil aux communautés. In A. Daele & B. Charlier (Éds.), *Les communautés délocalisées d'enseignants* (pp. 12–44). Maison des Sciences de l'Homme.

Henri, F., & Pudelko, B. (2006). Le concept de communauté virtuelle dans une perspective d'apprentissage social. In B. Charlier & A. Daele (Dir.), *Les communautés virtuelles d'enseignants* (pp. 105–127). L'Harmattan.

Henri, F., & Ricciardi Rigault, C. (1996). Collaborative distance learning and computer conferencing. In T. T. Liao (Ed.), *Advanced educational technology: Research issues and future potential* (pp. 45–76). NATO ASI Series, SpringerVerlag.

Jeunesse, C., & Henri, F. (2013). L'autoformation au sein des réseaux ou l'autodidaxie 2.0. In P. Cyrot, D. Cristol, & C. Jeunesse (Dir.), *Les aspects sociaux de l'autoformation* (pp. 159–215). Éditions Chronique Sociale.

Pudelko, B., Daele, A., & Henri, F. (2006). Méthodes d'étude des communautés Virtuelles. In B. Charlier & A. Daele (Dir.), *Les communautés virtuelles d'enseignants* (pp. 127–155). L'Harmattan.

Pudelko, B., Henri, F., & Legros, D. (2003). Entre la conversation et l'écriture: Les deux faces de la communication asynchrone. In A. Taurisson & A. Senteni (Éds.), *Pédagogies.NET* (pp. 263–288). Presses de l'Université du Québec.

Journal Articles and Blog Postings (Articles de Revues et Billets de Blog)

Bejaoui, R., Paquette, G., Basque, J., & Henri, F. (2017). Cadre d'analyze de la personnalisation de l'apprentissage dans les cours en ligne ouverts et massif (CLOM). *Revue STICEF*, 24. http://sticef.univ-lemans.fr/num/vol2017/24.2.2.bejaoui/24.2.2.bejaoui.html

Charlier, B., & Henri, F. (2004). Pour une démarche d'évaluation en soutien à l'émergence de communautés de pratique dans un contexte de formation. *Revue Suisse des Sciences de l'Éducation*, 26(2), 181–204.

Charlier, B., & Henri, F. (2016). Rechercher, comprendre et concevoir l'apprentissage avec la vidéo dans les xMOOC. *Revue internationale des technologies en pédagogie universitaire*, 13(2–3), 36–45. www.ritpu.ca/fr/articles/view/285

Deschênes, A. J., Henri, F., & Lebel, C. (1993). Learning support in an international distance education course. *Media and Technology for Human Resource Development*, 6(1).

Henri, F. (1988). Formation à distance et communication assistée par ordinateur. *UNESCO Perspectives*, 18(1).

Henri, F. (1992a). Formation à distance et téléconférence assistée par ordinateur: Interactivité, quasi-interactivité ou monologue? *Revue de l'enseignement à Distance*, 7(1).

Henri, F. (1992b). Processus d'apprentissage à distance et téléconférence assistée par ordinateur: Essai d'analyze. *Canadian Journal of Educational Communication*, 21(1).

Henri, F. (1993). Formation à distance, matériel pédagogique et théorie de l'éducation: La cohérence du changement. *Revue de l'éducation à distance*, 8(1).

Henri, F. (1995). Formacion a distancia y teleconferencia asistada por ordenador: Interactividad, cuasi-interactividad o monologo. *Revista Educacion a Distancia* (6), 61–78.

Henri, F. (1996). L'autoformation assistée dans des environnements souples informatisés. *Les Sciences de l'Éducation Revue Internationale*, 29(1 & 2), 43–66.

Henri, F. (2012). Où va la distance? Est-ce la bonne question? *Distances et Savoirs*, 9(4), 619–630.

Henri, F. (2014). Les environnements personnels d'apprentissage, étude d'une thématique de recherche en émergence [Numéro spécial de la revue STICEF]. *Les EPA: Entre description et conceptualisation*, 21. http://sticef.univ-lemans.fr/num/vol2014/16-henri-epa/sticef_2014_NS_henri_16.htm

Henri, F. (2020, 25 mars). Le e-learning et la formation à distance ne conviennent qu'à un type d'étudiant en particulier" ou . . . l'art de rejeter la faute sur les autres! [Web log post]. INFOX#1 www.lip-unifr.ch/2020/03/25/infox1-le-e-learning-et-la-formation-a-distance-ne-conviennent-qua-un-type-detudiant-en-particulier-ou-lart-de-rejeter-la-faute-sur-les-autres/

Henri, F., Compte, C., & Charlier, B. (2007). La scénarisation dans tous ses débats. *Revue internationale des technologies en pédagogie universitaire*, 7(2), 14–24. www.ritpu.org/spip.php?rubrique46?lang=fr

Henri, F., Gagné, P., Maina, M., Gargouri, Y., Bourdeau, J., & Paquette, G. (2006). Society [special issue]. *Collaborative Distance Activities: From Social Cognition to Electronic Togetherness.* https://doi.org/10.1007/s00146-005-0021-6

Henri, F. Peraya, D., & Charlier, B. (2007). La recherche sur les forums de discussion en milieu éducatif: Critères de qualité et qualité des pratiques. *Revue Sciences et Technologies de l'Information et de la Communication pour l'Éducation et la Formation*, 14, 155–192. http://sticef.univ-lemans.fr/num/vol2007/18-henri/sticef_2007_henri_18.htm

Henri, F. et Pudelko, B. (2003). Understanding and analyzing activity and learning in virtual communities. *Journal of Computer Assisted Learning*, 19, 474–487. https://hal.archivesouvertes.fr/file/index/docid/190267/filename/Henri-France-2003.pdf

Lamy, T., & Henri, F. (1983). Télé-université: Ten years of distance education in Québec. *Programmed Learning and Educational Technology*, 20(3).

Paquette, G, Bourdeau, J., Henri, F., Basque, J., Léonard, M., Maina, M. (2003). Construction d'une base de connaissances et de ressources pour le domaine du téléapprentissage. *Sciences et Technologies de l'Information et de la Communication pour l'Éducation et la Formation*, 10(17).

15
HERRING, SUSAN

Photo of Susan Herring contributed by Susan Herring

> *My early CMC research had a real impact in debunking the popular belief at the time that computer-mediated communication was gender blind.*

Dr. Susan Herring comes from a background in linguistics. Her early work reflects her interest in languages and linguistic literature. She obtained her Bachelor of Arts in French from the State University of New York, Potsdam in 1976, then completed her Master of Arts in Linguistics at the University of California, Berkeley, in 1982. She remained at the University of California, Berkeley, to complete her PhD in Linguistics in 1991.

Her interests changed when she completed her tertiary degree, and the Internet was beginning to evolve. She became very interested in online discourse analysis and also the gender implications that she began to notice when analyzing online discourse.

Herring is currently the Director, Center for Computer-Mediated Communication, Indiana University, Bloomington, and has been in this position since 2014. She has held many important positions and been honored by several institutions. Most recently, she has been:

- Visiting Researcher, University of California, Santa Cruz, 2015–2016; Summer 2017; Summer 2018;
- Association for Information Science & Technology (ASIS&T) 2013 Research Award winner for research on computer-mediated communication;
- Fellow, Center for Advanced Study in the Behavioural Sciences (CASBS), Stanford, CA, 2012–2013;
- Visiting Fellow, Cornell University, Department of Communication, Fall 2008;
- Vice Chancellor's Visiting Fellow, La Trobe University, Australia, August 2001;
- Visiting Fellow, Centre for Communication Research, Auckland University of Technology, New Zealand, July-August 2001; and
- Visiting Fellow, Växjö University, Sweden, April 2000.

Dr. Herring's research on discourse analysis in computer-mediated communication has resulted in some seminal works. Her publications listed at the end of this chapter can also be found at http://info.ils.indiana.edu/~herring/pubs.html, where links to these publications are also provided.

Interview

Transcript Analysis Summary

Analysis of all interviews included in this volume led to the identification of 3,545 units of data. The mean of these collective units was 118 per pioneer, the median was 118.5, and the mode was 132. Individual interview units ranged from 59 to 217 units, yielding a spread of 158 units between all interviews. Susan Herring's interview generated 185 units, which placed her interview second from the top of all interviews in terms of unit generation.

A comparison of Susan Herring's interview to the interviews of all pioneers indicated that almost half her interview was akin to the average interview in terms of units produced per thematic area (Figure 15.1). Six of the 14 thematic codes in her interview yielded a similar numbers of units to the average interview. These included challenges, changes over time, goals, interesting memories, others for the book, and career history. There were three areas where Herring's interview captured more units than the average interview did: research interests, accomplishments, and general gender-related comments. Her interview produced nearly five units for every one unit in the average interview in research interests. This was because Herring pursued (and continues to pursue) a myriad of human-technology research topics. These research endeavours also explained why her interview possessed more accomplishment and general gender-related comments, the latter being one topic that prompted some of Herring's research activities.

Dr. Herring's interview contained a less-than-average number of units in the areas of benefits of DE, learning environment, early founders, and final thoughts. While a leader in the field of computer-mediated communication, Herring never perceived herself to be a DE practitioner. This information, coupled with the fact that there was no research question that asked

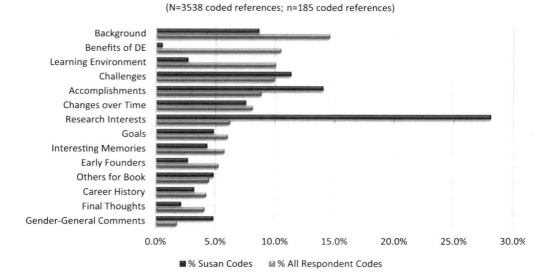

Figure 15.1 All Respondents' Versus Susan Herring's Parent Codes

interviewees to discuss the benefits of DE, offered two reasons there were few units assigned to the benefits of DE and early founder areas in Herring's interview. The low number of units in the category of learning environment was the result of Herring providing a very succinct response to that question, which did not include elaboration on such topics as the age, size, and geographic reach of her institition; specifics about the delivery modes; or student profiles. Finally, while she did offer detailed discussion in her final thoughts, she focused her conversation on four main points. One unit was assigned to each main point, which expalined the low number of units in this topic area.

Link to recorded interview Part A: tinyurl.com/Herring-S-A

Link to recorded interview Part B: tinyurl.com/Herring-S-B

Transcript of Interview

Full name: Dr. Susan Herring
Institutional Affiliation: Department of Information and Library Science, School of Informatics and Engineering, Indiana University
Key:

Regular font = Interviewee comments
Italicized font = Interviewer comments

Interview Questions

1. *How do you define "distance education," and how is it different from computer-mediated communication?*

I see distance education as a part of or a subset of online learning generally, because nowadays, distance education is all online, but not all online learning is distance education; some takes place outside formal learning contexts. Computer-mediated communication is centrally involved in online learning, both formal and informal. Quite a few students in my computer-mediated communication courses come from the School of Education, and most are interested in online learning or distance education. I've done a few research collaborations with them looking at online learning using methods of computer-mediated communication analysis.

I: What area(s) of computer-mediated communication [CMC] were you a pioneer in?

I would say there are three areas. I'm probably best known for my research on discourse and language use in online communication. Some people say that I am the founder of that area, maybe even the leading person in the world in that area. Maybe I can say that now because I'm getting old, and I've been doing it for a long time.

The second area is I was one of the first people to study gender differences and gender patterns in computer-mediated communication. That was where I started; actually, it was my very first CMC research.

I think that I have also pioneered in developing methodologies for analyzing computer-mediated communication, specifically computer-mediated discourse. I developed a paradigm called computer-mediated discourse analysis, or CMDA, that is used by people in universities in other places in the world. I've also worked on a paradigm for doing content analysis on the web, although I haven't spent as much time developing that as I have developing CMDA. I'm currently working on developing methodologies for analyzing multimodal online discourse – that's been the focus of my research for the past five years or so. Specifically, I've been developing new ways of analyzing how graphical means of communication are incorporated into CMC. Lately I've done a lot of research on emoji, for example: on stickers, gifs, image memes, that kind of thing. I have also been studying telepresence robots and how people use them to mediate human-to-human communication. I conceptualize all of that – graphics, telepresence robots – as part of computer-mediated communication in a broader sense, computer-mediated communication as inherently multimodal. So I would say that I am pioneering in that area, too, in multimodal computer-mediated discourse analysis. For example, I believe I'm the first person to study telepresence robots from a language and discourse perspective.

I: Can you please share your story about founding and directing the Center for Computer-Mediated Communication at the Indiana University Bloomington? For example, what prompted you to found the centre, what were the early years like, and how has the centre changed over the years?

I would trace my interest in developing a CMC research centre to around 2001–2002. I had previously spearheaded a proposal involving my school – at the time that we were a school, rather than a department. And at the time, there was a separate School of Informatics. I authored a proposal that involved both of our schools to fund a much larger centre at the university level, with a new faculty line and post-docs and all. We wrote up a proposal and a budget and submitted it. It was not funded; it came in as being fairly competitive, but it was not funded. I would have resubmitted the proposal the following year, but I was in a car accident in 2003, and I became physically disabled. After that, I scaled back my activities quite a bit. But years later, I was still interested in the idea of having a centre, so in 2014, I founded a more modest centre based in my department, rather than the university as a whole, although it involves people from all over the university. My motivation for doing it, in both cases, was to bring together the research expertise that I saw at Indiana University in different departments, both in our faculty and in our graduate students who are researching communication on the Internet, social media, and other forms of digital technologies. We have a very well-known male scholar in the School of Business, Alan Dennis, who has been working as long as I have on CMC. We have people who research social media in the telecommunications department, [which has] since merged into a media school. We have people in informatics, journalism, education, and linguistics, as well as some of the foreign language departments and other fields. So I thought that it would be a good idea to bring all of these people together. That's what I've done.

The centre currently has fellows from 11 departments, I think. There are 33 faculty and PhD student fellows at IU, and we also have affiliates – about 47, the last time I counted – affiliates from 15 or 16 different countries. These are people who spent time at Indiana University in the past or who otherwise have a strong connection to Indiana University – maybe they got their PhDs here – and who are scholars in the area of CMC and social media communications.

In terms of how the centre has changed over time, we initially focused on sharing our own research among ourselves because one of my goals was to create a community of scholars with shared interests. So we did things like we held research symposia where, for an entire day, the faculty fellows would present their research, and for another entire day, the PhD student fellows would present their research. Another time, we had a CMC speed-dating event, where fellows would pair up for five minutes and describe their current research activities, then they would switch to a new partner and do it again and so forth, until they had shared one-on-one with everyone in the room. That was a lot of fun.

This last year, the centre started to bring in scholars from outside of Indiana University. This has been a little difficult to do because we don't really have a budget, but we've been able to piggyback on and take advantage of some opportunities. Last year, we brought in a woman from the University of California, Berkeley, who is studying Chinese emoji. We were also able to sponsor a talk by a scholar from Germany, who I would say is one of the leading scholars in computer-mediated discourse in Europe, because our university brought him in for another event.

The centre also organized a panel last semester, where we incorporated some of our affiliates via distance technology, together with a couple of local experts. The panel was on the theme of authenticity, believability, and deception, and it dealt with fake news and other timely topics right before the mid-term elections here in the United States. We invited two of our affiliates as panelists, one in Pennsylvania and one in Italy, and we also had affiliates listening in via distance technology.

So our future goal – this is something that we have been talking about for a while – is to organize a conference where we apply for funding to bring some of our affiliates to Indiana University and make them more a part of our community, be able to interact face-to-face as well as online. We had the idea of maybe doing the conference to celebrate the fifth anniversary of the centre, which is going to be in 2019, although that might be a little short notice. So it might not be this year, but the year after that.

I: You were also a founder of the (We)blog Research on Genre (BROG) project. Could you please share your story about the founding and development of this project?

That project started back in 2002–2003. Blogs were just starting to attract media attention then. Several students actually brought them to my attention; I had not been aware of them before. Students in a couple of my classes expressed interest in studying blogs, maybe collecting data from them for a research project in the class. So I proposed a group project. At first, there were three students and myself. We set out to do just one research study, and it was so interesting that we decided to do a couple more research projects, and then we added another person when one of the original students graduated, and we added somebody else. Over the years, we completed five or six studies. At one time, there were as many as nine people, including another faculty member and a visiting scholar from Spain, on the project team. So it was active project that continued until the time, I would say, when blogs were no longer on the cutting edge. People were starting to talk about social networking sites and so on, and at that time, my interests started to shift away from blog studies. But for about five years, it was a very active research group.

Part of what attracted outside attention to that project was that the first paper that we wrote debunked some commonly held views of what blogs were and who was blogging. The popular media at that time were writing about male bloggers who were blogging about political activities, news stories, or other external events, and how their blogs were being influential. The popular view of blogs was that people were blogging about events that were not so much personal as external to the bloggers, politics in particular . . . politics, religion, and technology, of course. Technology bloggers were getting in the news. There was no mention of the fact that we had discovered that the majority of bloggers were actually female. The largest demographic of bloggers was young females. And they were writing different kinds of blogs; they were writing more about their personal experiences and their own lives. So that was one of our early findings, that blogs were not, as some people were describing them, all about linking to Internet content and being – not exactly content repositories, but content directories, if you will, filtering the content of the web and pointing people to interesting web content. Whereas what we discovered when we randomly sampled a large number of blogs was that the majority of blogs were more like personal journals, almost like diaries, and really quite a different animal [from the popular view]. That was how we got started, and that was something new and something that hadn't been noticed about blogs at the time.

2. *What education and experience did you have before you became involved in your area(s) of specialty?*

Well, I actually started off studying foreign languages. I was a French major as an undergraduate. I spent a year in France and travelled around Europe, picking up a bunch of other languages, a little bit of this, a little bit of that. I ended up studying 12 different languages, so I guess you could say that I was a language person. I went to grad school for linguistics, and my interest in linguistics was languages. When I was a PhD student, we were required to take one year of a classical language; it could be Greek, Latin, or Sanskrit. I thought, "Lots of linguists do Greek and Latin," so I chose Sanskrit. I've always liked to do things that were different from what other people have done.

So I studied Sanskrit for a year. My Sanskrit instructor had spent a lot of time in the south of India, in Tamilnadu. He told wonderful, colourful stories about Tamilnadu, and then our university offered courses in Tamil. And they were offering fellowship money; if you studied Tamil, you could get scholarship money. And I said, "I will study any language for money. You don't have to twist my arm." So I started studying Tamil. I studied it for a couple of years at UC Berkeley, and then I had an opportunity to study Tamil in India. I did that for a year, and then I thought, "Well, I did all of this, I've come this far," so I got a Fulbright fellowship, went back to India, and did my dissertation research on oral storytelling, storytelling in Tamil, particularly the use of time expressions in narrative. It was something completely different from what I ended up doing later on.

3. *What events in your life made you interested in your area(s) of specialty?*

How that worked out, I was studying at UC Berkeley to get my degree in linguistics, so I came back to Berkeley after I'd been in India for a couple of years and wrote my dissertation. But at that time, and this was the late 1980s, the Internet was starting to become more widely available. I was a relatively early Internet adopter. Around 1985, I was using email and other forms of computer-mediated communication because my university was on one of the original backbones of the Internet, so we had servers and we had Internet access. My ex-husband was a research assistant in the cognitive science programme; they had a server. He got an account on that server, and he got me an account. I had already been using early forms of CMC – email, and there was a real-time chat feature called Talk on UNIX platforms at that time. The problem then was that I knew almost no one else who had that access, so I couldn't really talk to many people online. But by the late 1980s, CMC was really expanding, and in particular, email mailing lists – or listservs as they were called then – were starting to come into use in academic disciplines. The field of linguistics started up an email list in the fall of 1990, and there were a couple other academic lists that started up in the late 80s, 1988–1989. So because of that, when I got back to the US and finished my dissertation, I thought that I would do just one little study looking at this very interesting new phenomenon of how people were communicating online. That's another story.

If you like, I can tell you about what got me specifically interested in my specialty, but in terms of my background and training, I would just also mention that I had an interest in historical linguistics, particularly in historical discourse grammar. My research area was the study of discourse grammar in the Tamil language, and I had also done a historical study of it. Part of my dissertation was comparing ancient storytelling with modern storytelling. I was looking at the grammar of time expressions and how that had evolved over time. I mention this because I have an abiding interest in language change over time and have applied that interest also to CMC.

I: I would like to hear more about the events in your life that made you interested in CMC, please.

As I mentioned, I got back from India the second time (I think it was in 1988) and these listservs were starting to take off. In the fall of 1990, the Linguist List was formed by the Linguistic Society of America as one of these email distribution lists. I was a member of that society, and what happened was they subscribed all of the members of the society to the list. I didn't have to do anything. All of a sudden, I started getting these emails – because it was a push technology – from the distribution list. And I started immediately observing interesting gender patterns. There was what was later to become known as a "flame war." The term wasn't really in use yet, but a conflict broke out in the group between linguists from one area of the field and linguists of another type. Basically, it was followers of Noam Chomsky, whom you might have heard of, and his generative linguistic paradigm on the one hand and researchers who looked more at the social, contextual, and psychological aspects of language on the other hand. The argument was about who "owned" the term *cognitive linguistics*. Who was most associated with that term? The generativists said it was Chomsky, and the other linguists said no. These others – George Lakoff was one of those people – said that "Cognitive linguistics is what we do here in our field [of cognitive semantics]."

What was interesting was that the topic, I thought, was of fairly broad interest to linguists in general, but virtually only men were participating. It was also a conflict-ridden discussion. So I asked myself, "Why are you not contributing to this discussion? You have some interest in this topic." Immediately, all of these excuses came to mind. "I'm too busy. People have already made the points that I would make," etc. But I also felt like it was an intimidating discussion because people were really kind of going at each other, you know. So I decided to study it empirically, to just ask people, "Why did you participate or not participate in this discussion? What did you think of this discussion?"

I devised a questionnaire, a survey, and I distributed it through the list, and because I am a discourse analyst by training, I also collected all of the logs, the transcripts of the conversation. This discussion had been going on for some time. There were three months of messages where people were arguing with each other about cognitive linguistics. So I conducted a discourse analysis of the transcript. I was inspired by the work of Deborah Tannen, in particular, who had done a lot of analysis of men's and women's spoken language. She had identified a number of features that tended to be characteristic of men's and women's speech. I had read that literature and was seeing some of the same patterns in the online data.

The survey responses were really interesting, too. Everybody agreed that it was a pretty contentious discussion, but when I asked why they didn't participate, the emphases of the men and women were very different. The men said things like, "Well, they were throwing flames and arrows, but it was actually rather entertaining because they weren't directed at me." Another man said, "Well, I didn't participate, but it wasn't so bad." And "If you think this is bad, you should see the philosophy list," or "You should see the artificial intelligence list," which were also very male-dominated groups. And other comments of that nature. The men found the contentiousness of the discussion entertaining, normal, or okay, as long as it wasn't directed at them, whereas the responses from the women were very different in nature.

One woman, for example, said, "I found it very off-putting. It made me want to avoid that conversation and not participate." Another woman said, "I was so turned off by this that it made me want to unsubscribe from this list." Yet another woman said, "I dislike people who are like this. It made me not want to be a linguist." In other words, she had extrapolated from the tone of the discourse the moral character of the people. It was very strong aversion.

I thought, "Wow! What's going on here?" That was how I got involved in the first place. Later I followed up with other survey studies and a lot more discourse analysis studies of online groups. It was not something that I intended to make a career out of, though. I had just finished my dissertation on this completely different topic of time expressions in Tamil narrative discourse, and I just wanted a break. I was interested in doing something new. I thought, "I will just do this one little paper and present it."

I presented that first paper at the Linguistic Society of America Conference in January of 1992, and the reaction that I got was quite interesting. A senior woman in the field, whom I respect quite a lot, came up to me, and she had read my abstract for the talk. She said, "I read your abstract." Then she kind of paused. I looked at her expectantly, and then she said (in a skeptical voice), "It's interesting . . . but is it linguistics?" That was kind of the response that I got at first. People didn't really think that studying online communication was linguistics because it was somehow more associated with popular culture, and linguists don't usually analyze popular culture. Maybe they thought, "That's something that people in communications do, but not us." I don't know, but I got that response from linguists.

Another interesting response that I got at that conference was from a woman who was more my peer (at that time, I was an Assistant Professor). She came up to me and said, "I read your abstract. You are very brave."

I said, "Oh?"

And she said, "You know some of those people that you are talking about [in your abstract] who were behaving badly" because what I had found in the transcripts that I analyzed was some men were behaving in very aggressive ways. I didn't name anyone by name, but this woman was also on the Linguist List, and she knew who I was talking about. She said, "You know, some of those people are here at the conference." Actually, the first thing that she asked me was, "Do you have tenure yet?"

I said, "No."

And then she said, "You are *very brave*" [emphasis in the original].

In fact, those male scholars, who were senior scholars, would not have deigned to come to a little sociolinguistics talk by an unknown junior female scholar. They didn't even bother to come to my talk, so as it turned out, I didn't have to face them directly.

That was the first study. I intended on only presenting the one paper, but it got so much attention. It got much more attention than the other work that I was doing at the time on Tamil.

Another funny story: You may not have heard about this event, but I was working in Arlington, Texas, in the mid-90s, and there's a town south of there called, Waco, Texas. Around that time, there was a man named David Koresh who founded a cult. This cult was living in a barricaded compound that was eventually stormed by the US government because they were heavily armed, and they had women and children in there, and they were not letting people leave the compound. So the Bureau of Alcohol, Tobacco, Firearms, and Explosives tried to get Koresh and these people to leave the compound. There was a showdown; gunfire was exchanged. The compound ended up catching fire and exploding, and a number of people were killed. It was a big event in the mid-1990s. Their cult was called the Branch Davidians, after the founder's first name, David.

Well, Tamil belongs to a language family called, "Dravidian," spelled with an *r*. And in 1995, I believe it was, I had been invited to give a keynote lecture at a historical linguistics conference in England, and I was talking about the ancient history of Tamil going back to BC times. I was talking about proto-grammar in Tamil. I joked in my talk that when I told people that I was studying gender differences in Internet communication, I would get a lot of excited interest – in fact, I was interviewed for a cover story about it on *Newsweek* (which is a major news publication in the United States) in 1993. But when I told people that I was working on a Dravidian language, they would say, "Oh, is that that compound that blew up in Texas?" Honestly, people didn't know what Dravidian languages were. I had to explain where Tamil was spoken. It was very obscure, whereas the gender and Internet work was starting to attract a lot of attention.

Throughout the 1990s, I was carrying out research in both areas. I was pursuing the line of research that I had started with my dissertation because I was teaching in a linguistics department, and that was part of what I was supposed to be teaching. But at the same time, I was continuing my research on Internet communication. I really felt schizophrenic for most of that decade, until I was offered a job here at Indiana University in information science in 2000. At that time, I made the decision to leave linguistics and move into a more technology-focused area.

4. *Were there any women who may have helped you become interested in your field? Who would you say are the other early female leaders/founders in your field?*

I was very influenced to start researching CMC by two articles written by women. One of them was an article on the social-psychological effects of computer-mediated communication by Sara Kiesler and her colleagues at Carnegie Mellon University. That was published back in 1984, in the mid-80s. It's just an excellent article; it's a classic article. I don't know if I ever met Sara Kiesler, but I've followed her work over the years. That was one of my early inspirations.

The other was the late Kathleen Ferrara. She was a linguist at Texas A&M University. She died young, in her 50s, but I had the opportunity to meet her because we were in Texas together at the same time. She had done an early pioneering study of the language that people used when they were communicating through a chat platform. It was an experimental study, a "Wizard of Oz" study, where the participants thought that they were interacting with a computer, but in fact, it was another human acting like a computer. They were supposed to be making travel arrangements using this platform. Kathleen looked at how they used language: how they used abbreviations and how their grammar became sort of telegraphic in the chat platform. She co-authored a paper about that. Since I was a linguist, I was very interested in that work as well. That paper was published in 1991.

Those women were true pioneers in CMC. When I started in the early 1990s, there was very little research that was published at that time. Those two papers in particular inspired me.

5. *What are some of the goals that you strove to achieve in your field?*

I have always been interested in bringing people together and creating community, not just for the social benefits, but also to grow the field. From the beginning, I was very consciously trying to develop language-focused CMC into an area that involved other people, that brought researchers together, so that we could see what had been done, what was known, what needed to be done, and what gaps needed to be filled.

I started by organizing panels and workshops in the early 90s. These panels led to collections that I edited, with the idea that they would enhance the visibility of this new, emerging area that people were starting to work on and that was inherently interdisciplinary. I was bringing together scholars from all kinds of disciplines who had an interest in online communication. I think that has always been one of my goals, and that's why I started the Center for Computer-Mediated

Communication here as well: to bring people together, to have a community to benefit ourselves, and, at the same time, to raise the profile of the work so that others on the outside would see that this area of computer-mediated communication that I was developing was a field – that there are people doing this, there is a body of literature about it.

And in the case of the centre, so that people on the outside would say, "This is a strength of Indiana University. Look at all of the people there who are working in this area."

6. *What are some of your accomplishments in your field that you would like to share?*

My early CMC research had a real impact in debunking the popular belief at the time that computer-mediated communication was gender blind. In the early days of the Internet, there was this popular view that because CMC was just text on a screen, that it was only your typing ability or your rhetorical skills in writing that mattered. You could be as influential as anyone, regardless of your gender, regardless of your social standing. As a man posted in one of the groups that I was studying in the early 1990s, "You could be a university president or a janitor, and we wouldn't know. Online, it's your ideas that matter, not who you are."

A famous cartoon was published in the *New Yorker* in 1993, of a dog sitting at a computer. You may have seen it. The dog is typing on the computer, saying to a doggie friend on the floor, "On the Internet, nobody knows that you're a dog." Well, that dog was a metaphor for women, for people of colour, for people with disabilities, poor people, people who would normally be stigmatized if their real identities were known. So there was this kind of utopian discourse that was going around, especially with regard to gender.

What I was seeing in my research on online discussions was that, first of all, the Internet was not a level playing field as much as people were claiming it was for men and women, and part of the reason was because gender was still visible in many cases. I discovered this in the early 90s. I got so excited when I saw this; I could see it so clearly. Men and women were using distinct discourse styles online, even professional linguists. I could tell in many cases, based on their language use, who was a man and who was a woman, or at least I could make a very good guess. Then I thought, "Well, I know a lot of these linguists; I know if they are men or women." So then I started looking in areas where I didn't know people, and I could still tell in a lot of cases. So that was the discovery. I thought I better publish it quickly, because pretty soon everybody was going to notice it. It seemed so obvious to me. That was why I was so eager to give that first talk at the Linguist Society of America in 1992. I was eager to be the first person to say this, and I was. I published quite a bit about gender and online communication after that. I think that work really had an impact. It changed the way people understood and wrote about gender communication online.

I think also with the BROG project that the early work that our project team did was effective in debunking popular misconceptions about blogs and bloggers: both the nature of the blogs and the gender and demographics of who was blogging.

Another accomplishment – one that I am probably best known for, actually – is creating the computer-mediated discourse analysis paradigm, which is a methodological tool kit that can be used to analyze online discourse from a variety of language-focused perspectives. I drew from my linguistic background in creating the paradigm, starting in 1994. I adapted methods of linguistic analysis to the specifics of different kinds of online communication. I use that paradigm a lot in my research, and I teach it to students. It's also used by people in other places, including in other countries.

Also, I was editor of the *Journal of Computer-Mediated Communication*, or *JCMC*, between 2004 and 2008. I inherited the journal from Margaret McLaughlin – Peggy McLaughlin – who was another pioneer. She founded the *Journal of Computer-Mediated Communication* in the mid-1990s, together with Sheizaf Rafaeli in Israel, but I think Peggy McLaughlin was the main mover and shaker. She became the first editor. It's an online journal; it was one of the early online journals. It has become quite successful; it is now the premiere journal in the field of computer-mediated communication, and I think I can say that I had something to do with raising the status of the journal from the online journal that Peggy founded. When I was editor, the impact factor of the journal went up quite a bit, along with its visibility. I worked hard as editor of *JCMC*, and that's something I am proud of.

More recently, in my current work (I hope that it will prove to be an accomplishment), in one of the projects that I mentioned earlier, telepresence robotics, I am actively engaged in introducing telepresence robotics and robot-mediated communication to other fields – to the field of linguistics, for example. I'm not the first person to study robot-mediated communication – Leila Takayama at UC Santa Cruz is the real pioneer in that area – but I've been giving lectures; I just gave a lecture yesterday via distance technology to people in the communications department at the University of Zürich. Often when I talk about my research, it's the first time that people are learning about telepresence robots. They sometimes come up to me afterwards and say that it was eye-opening, that it was not something that they were aware of before. I'm not exactly evangelical about it, but this is research that I'm engaged in, and I think it's really interesting. So I'd like to think that I am contributing in this area as well.

7. *What were some of the challenges that you encountered over the years in your field?*

One of the challenges is one that I have already mentioned. When I first starting researching CMC as a linguist, I encountered what I would characterize as a lack of support and even resistance from linguists. I mentioned before that a senior linguist whom I admired communicated quite clearly to me that she didn't think that what I was doing in CMC was really interesting or relevant to linguistics. Because of comments like that, I ended up deciding that if linguists did not appreciate that CMC was language and that it was of interest to linguistics, if I couldn't bring CMC to them, then I would bring linguistics into CMC. And that is what I consciously did in developing the CMDA [computer-mediated discourse analysis] paradigm, was to say, "Okay, let's take linguistic methods and linguistic questions and apply them to online communication." When I did that, indeed some linguists became more interested in what I was doing. But, paradoxically, I got more interest outside of linguistics. I started to get interest especially from education, people who were interested in distance education and online learning. I started to get interest from people in information science, in human-computer interaction, people who were interested in how these systems were designed and how they affected human communication behaviour. That was why I eventually ended up switching over into information science, because I realized I was getting more interest from outside linguistics than from within linguistics in what I was doing, even though I had trained for many years and had gotten a PhD in linguistics. That's why I ended up shifting from linguistics into information science. I have no regrets about that. Obviously, I'm still a linguist, and I still use my linguistic training in the work that I do now, but I feel like my research and teaching have benefitted and grown over the years from being in an environment where people are studying technology and where people are looking at the platforms from technological perspectives. I have collaborated with computer scientists, for example, and I find that very intellectually stimulating.

Another challenge that I have been grappling with for well over a decade, maybe 15 years now, is the challenge of analyzing CMC as it becomes increasingly multimodal. The CMDA paradigm that I developed was based on text because that was what there was in the 90s: chat, email, discussion forums, MUDs [multi-user dimensions] and MOOs [MUDs, object oriented], blogs, text messaging – all primarily text. But CMC has changed a lot. In the early years, there were different varieties of CMC, each requiring different clients or points of access. People would have their email client. If they wanted to go to a public chatroom, they would have to telnet to a special server. And then there were MUDs and MOOs; you had to telnet to a different server if you wanted to access those. And if you wanted to read newsgroups, you had to download a special reader. It wasn't like it is now where you can access many different forms of CMC through a browser very readily. Most people weren't aware of all the different forms that were available. It was much more "siloed," if you will. And web pages were not originally considered CMC by CMC researchers because they were more static and less interactive. But the web gradually became dynamic and more interactive, especially with the evolution of weblogs. Blogs were important in that process, as were social network sites.

Now the web is fully interactional and fully dynamic, and so it's been incorporated into CMC. It's also brought with it all of the multimodality of the web. We not only have images; we have audio conferencing and video conferencing, and now there are all of the different kinds of graphics that I mentioned earlier, like emoji, stickers, animated GIFs, and image memes. So the challenge for me, as someone who developed this methodological paradigm, is how to adapt the CMDA paradigm, or do we need a new paradigm as CMC changes? More generally, what methods should we use to analyze multimodal communication, and how do we integrate multimodal communication into our understanding of CMC? Starting around 2000, I was feeling increasingly that the text that I was analyzing – I was artificially separating it from the rest of what was going on. This is more of a scientific challenge than an external challenge, but it's something that I have struggled with. I've approached it from different perspectives; I've advanced different proposals to try to account for multimodality in CMC. A few years ago, the idea came to me to reconceptualize CMC itself as inherently multimodal and mediated by different kinds of "computer" technologies. Thus, we have text mediation, which gives us email, chat, blogs, and so forth. We also have mediation by audio, such as Skype in the early days before Skype had video. Video conferencing, of course; video is another mediating technology. Then, to this list, I've added graphics-mediated communication and robot-mediated communication. It is an open list. I envision it as a kind of an umbrella diagram, with each mediating technology arrayed below the highest node of multimodal CMC.

Another new CMC phenomenon that I am starting to look at with one of my doctoral students involves smart speakers like the Amazon Echo and Google Home. This is another kind of mediating technology because people are using them to communicate with other people, making calls and sending short messages. So now we have what I'm calling "smart speaker communication," which also falls under the rubric of CMC.

This is my current conceptual approach to grappling with the challenge of analyzing multimodal CMC, and I've argued that the CMDA paradigm can still be used to analyze these different kinds of mediated communication.

8. *What was your field like when you first entered it as compared to the state of it in 2018?*

Well, it was very small. It wasn't even a field then, but rather the seed of a field. I would say that CMC in the early 90s was beginning to emerge as a field. There were just a few people here and there who were studying aspects of CMC from different disciplinary perspectives. There was Sara Kiesler in social psychology; there was Kathleen Ferrara in linguistics; there was Shoshana Zuboff in business: a few scholars in different places. It was very much like exploring a new frontier. Almost everything was uncharted territory.

Another thing about that period, because the available literature was so small, it was almost possible to read everything that had been written about CMC in the early days. But interest in CMC grew very quickly, and of course, it soon became impossible to do that.

9. *What interesting memories would you like to share about the beginning of CMC?*

When I look back on that time, one of the things I reflect on is how slow the modems and Internet connections were. We had dial-up modems. I started off using a 300-baud modem and then I used a 900 baud-modem before we had cable access. So it was very slow to go online, and yet it didn't seem slow to us. Now, of course, it would seem painfully slow; we couldn't tolerate it. And connection speeds kept getting faster over time. We were like, "Wow, it's so fast now." We were impressed with the technology.

There was a tremendous amount of enthusiasm and excitement among those of us who were starting to work in this field. We were early adopters, well educated, mostly white and middle class, a restricted demographic, mostly men, but there were women as well. I would say there was a lot of enthusiasm, despite the limited technologies that were available.

I already mentioned how the different modes of CMC were located on different platforms and required separate modes of access. A lot of people who were into email in the early days did not know about chatrooms. People who were into chatrooms didn't necessarily know about newsgroups. People who were into using newsgroups didn't necessarily know about chatrooms or MUDs and MOOs. There were separate communities of practice, or communities of use, in these different modes. Over the years, though, it started to converge. Convergence has been one of the major trends in CMC over the decades, but CMC was fragmented and separated in the beginning.

10. *What were your research interests in CMC, and have they changed over the years?*

I can summarize that fairly concisely. My research interests in CMC shifted from a focus on gender online to online language use more broadly and then to the use of other semiotic systems – for example, graphical icons, what I call "graphicons," like GIFs, emoji, stickers, image memes, and so forth.

Most recently, the scope of my research has expanded to include any digital technology that mediates communication between human beings. This has allowed me to include under the umbrella of CMC mediating technologies like telepresence robots and smart speakers.

A brand-new project that I just started with several doctoral students is analyzing iPhone users' identity performances through "Animoji," which are emoji that are animated by your facial expressions. They are like masks that you can communicate through and record messages to send to your friends. Currently, Animoji are only available on the Apple iPhone X. There's a special camera in the phone that maps a grid onto your face. As you move your eyebrows, your head, your mouth, and so forth, the Animoji is animated and follows your movements. The iPhone provides some Animoji to start with that are mainly animals, so right now, sending Animoji is sort of a cute and playful thing, but it is going to expand in the future. I see it as something that people are going to use to communicate, for example, in real-time video conferencing. It won't just be these cartoonish images; you can also use photographic images and modify them and then animate them with your facial expressions; there are programmes that allow you to do that already. It's not something you can do with the iPhone now, but you can do it on your laptop; you can create these kinds of avatars, if you will, and communicate through them, and the technology that enables this is becoming more and more realistic.

Several years ago, scholars from the Information School at the University of Washington created a video of President Barak Obama speaking in what sounded like Obama's voice. It was a video representation that they had made of him, and they had synthesized his voice to have him say things that he never said. It was a completely realistic representation of Barak Obama saying something that he had never said. This is what is called a "deep fake," and I think this technology is going to converge eventually with user-friendly technologies like Animoji, and it will enable you to present yourself any way that you want online. You'll be able to present different versions of yourself, and you'll be able to modify them in various ways.

From a larger point of view, what is especially interesting about this is [that] people say that we're living in a post-truth era because of fake news and alternative facts and so forth, especially in US politics. I think that we may also be moving toward a post-authenticity world, where you can no longer trust the evidence of your eyes and ears in online communication. It looks like, it sounds like a real person, a specific person, but maybe it's really not. So right now, we are just starting with the Animoji research, just getting in on the ground floor.

We are interested in how people change their voice quality and their personality when they're speaking through these different kinds of Animoji masks. I think this has some interesting implications for the future of CMC.

Speaking of future predictions, I should mention one more thing. One of the ways that I suppose my research made a pioneering contribution was back in the early 90s, as kind of an offshoot of the research that I was doing on the linguistic styles of women and men. I noticed that there were contexts in which women were being harassed because of their gender, and I wrote several papers about that. Over the years, online harassment of women has become more common and much more misogynistic, with rape threats and death threats. The Gamergate thing a few years ago is what I think brought it into popular awareness, but it is now a really common thing. Female journalists, especially if they write about gender issues, report *routinely* [emphasis in the original] that they receive threatening and sexually degrading messages from men. I published a short piece in the *New York Times* a few years ago about why women were not contributing to Wikipedia. Even though the *New York Times* moderates its comments, I received a number of flaming comments from men, including accusing me of being a "feminazi" and so forth. So this is a reality for women who speak up online. Way back when I was first observing this phenomenon and studying it, my analysis was that its prevalence was related to the libertarian ideology of the early hackers who designed the Internet, who had the idea that the Internet should be free of centralized control and that it should be self-regulating. What I argued at the time was that that kind of setup favoured people who were more aggressive, basically people who were bullies, and it tended to favour men over women. Any complaints about abusive speech were met with accusations of "censorship." I think that same ideology has persisted as a thread throughout the history of the Internet until today because if anybody so much as suggests that there should be limits on the kind of hostile discourse – for example, hate speech – that can be expressed online. We see this on Facebook and Twitter and especially Reddit; there is a lot of discourse that is actively hateful and misogynistic, that is allowed to be expressed under the label of free speech, absolute freedom of speech, which is another idea that I think favours bullies. But any time there is a proposal that there should be any kind of limits on this kind of speech, there's a very strong counterreaction of accusations that this is censorship; this is not the way the Internet should work. Just the other day, I saw that someone had commented on Facebook that Susan Herring had foreseen this many years ago. It wasn't so much that I foresaw it, but that I saw that it was happening, and I described it back in the early 90s. Online abuse and harassment have gotten worse, sadly.

I: You were recently given the Association for Information Science and Technology Research Award. Could you please tell us a bit about the award and what contributions you were recognized for?

The association's website says, "This award recognizes an individual or organization for outstanding research contributions in the field of information science." I was given it for my contributions to CMC research. The award is for a contribution over a period of years.

11. *Could you please describe the learning environment in which you currently work?*

I work in the Department of Information and Library Science at Indiana University. My department offers two professional master's degrees: a master's in library science and a master's in information science. We also have a PhD programme in information science. I mostly teach and advise students in the PhD programme because it is mostly doctoral students who take my courses, although the courses also attract students from elsewhere in the university because CMC is such an interdisciplinary area. I am very fortunate to teach courses in my areas of specialization. I teach methods courses, and a lot of the doctoral students enrol because they want to learn methods of analysis, methods they might use in their dissertation research.

12. *Can you suggest the names of some female pioneers in DE, online learning, or CMC that you think we should include in our book?*

I mentioned some names of CMC pioneers before, but now that you ask about online learning, I would definitely add to my list Roxanne Starr Hiltz. She was a very early pioneer. In 1978, she and her husband, Murray [Turoff] wrote a book, which was probably the first study of CMC. They didn't call it CMC then, I don't think, but something else – computer conferencing or networked communication. Starr Hiltz has gone on to work in the area of distance education quite a bit over the years. I would definitely cite her as one of the very earliest.

Sara Kiesler, I mentioned. She's not in online learning, though; she's in social psychology. Margaret McLaughlin is in communications; she was another early one. Nancy Baym started a little later than me; she's a communications scholar who has become very well published and influential. Denise Murray was one of the very early scholars. She wrote her dissertation in the mid-80s on how people were using different modes of CMC in a business context – I think, IBM. She is an applied linguist, so she certainly has an interest in online learning and teaching. She's in Australia, I believe, although I think that she's moved on, maybe into administration. She'd be quite old now, so she may have retired. I tried to reach out to her on a couple occasions. She didn't seem to want to be part of what we were doing with CMC here in the United States. She sort of kept to herself, but her work has been important. She published a couple of books in the 90s following up from her dissertation research.

Let me think some more about distance education. I may be able to come up with some more names. Roxanne Starr Hiltz's name comes immediately to mind as being extremely important. I believe that she is still alive.

13. *Is there anything else you [would] like to address?*

I have been an active journal editor in addition to editing collections of volumes. As I mentioned, I was the editor of the *Journal of Computer-mediated Communication*, which is, I think, now the premiere journal in the field of CMC research. I currently edit the online journal *Language@Internet*.

I've also been the Co-PI [Co-Principal Investigator] on a couple of National Science Foundation [NSF] grants that touch on distance education. One of them was a project about 18 years ago that was out of the School of Education here, called the Quest Atlantis Project. It involved developing a 3D virtual world to teach science concepts to children between the ages of 9 to 12. I was in charge of a part of the project to maintain blogs by fictional characters that we had created in this world of Quest Atlantis. The characters were young people who were blogging about different topics that we wanted to get children involved in talking about online, like bullying and personal agency. There was that asynchronous component, and then there was the synchronous component of the 3D world.

Later, I was involved in a project to study the experiences of women in IT departments over time in five universities in the United States. That wasn't specifically about online learning. We did some of the data collection online, but we interviewed people; we did site visits and tried to find out as much as we could about what the experiences of women were in computer science as compared with management information systems, which is out of business schools; informatics, which was a new field; instructional technology, in schools of education; and information and library science. I was one of the Co-PIs on that project as well.

For the past several years, I've been a consultant on a NSF-funded project out of Cornell University, investigating the use of telepresence robots for distributed teamwork. We currently have another grant proposal pending to improve the ability of remote individuals to use telepresence robots to engage in informal work and social activities.

Although most of my connection to distance education is through CMC, which is a set of technologies that are very important in distance and online learning, I have also collaborated to some extent on research focused on online learning specifically, with students from the School of Education who take my courses. Because of that, I have several publications that are specifically about online learning. But the majority of my research is focused on CMC more generally, and especially CMC and language use.

Publications

Books

Demata, M., Heaney, D., & Herring, S. C., (Eds.). (2018). *Language and discourse of social media. New challenges, new approaches* (Special issue). *Altre Modernità*, I–X, 1–168.

Danet, B., & Herring, S. C. (Eds.). (2007). *The multilingual Internet: Language, culture, and communication online*. Oxford University Press.

Herring, S. C. (Ed.). (1996). *Computer-mediated communication: Linguistic, social and cross-cultural perspectives*. John Benjamins.

Herring, S. C., & Paolillo, J. C., (Eds.). (1994). *UTA working papers in linguistics* (Vol. 1.). University of Texas at Arlington: Program in Linguistics.

Herring, S. C., Stein, D., & Virtanen, T., (Eds.). (2013). *Handbook of pragmatics of computer-mediated communication*. Mouton.

Herring, S. C., van Reenen, P., & Schøsler, L. (Eds.). (2000). Textual parameters in older languages. *Current Issues in Linguistic Theory Series*. John Benjamins.

Book Chapters

Dainas, A., & Herring, S. C. (2021). Interpreting emoji pragmatics. In C. Xie, F. Yus, & H. Haberland (Eds.), *Internet pragmatics: Theory and practice*. John Benjamins. Prepublication version: http://ella.ils.indiana.edu/~herring/Interpreting_Emoji_Pragmatics.pdf

Herring, S. C. (2019). Grammar and electronic communication. In C. Chapelle (Ed.), *The concise encyclopedia of applied linguistics*. Wiley-Blackwell.

Herring, S. C. (2018). The co-evolution of computer-mediated communication and computer-mediated discourse analysis. In P. Bou-Franch & P. Garcés-Conejos Blitvich (Eds.), *Analysing digital discourse: New insights and future directions* (pp. 25–67). Palgrave Macmillan.

Herring, S. C. (2017). Introduction to "Pragmatics and the law: Speech act theory confronts the First Amendment." In L. Sutton (Ed.), *Context counts: Papers on language, gender, and power* (pp. 309–313). Oxford University Press.

Herring, S. C. (2016). Epilogue. In C. Lee (Ed.), *Multilingualism online* (pp. 137–146). Routledge.

Herring, S. C. (2016). Robot-mediated communication. In R. A. Scott, M. Buchmann, & S. M. Kosslyn (Eds.), *Emerging trends in the social and behavioral sciences: An interdisciplinary, searchable, and linkable resource* (pp. 1–16). John Wiley & Sons.

Herring, S. C. (2015). New frontiers in interactive multimodal communication. In A. Georgapoulou & T. Spilloti (Eds.), *The Routledge handbook of language and digital communication* (pp. 398–402). Routledge.

Herring, S. C., & Androutsopoulos, J. (2015). Computer-mediated discourse 2.0. In D. Tannen, H. E. Hamilton, & D. Schiffrin (Eds.), *The handbook of discourse analysis* (2nd ed., pp. 127–151). John Wiley & Sons.

Herring, S. C., & Kapidzic, S. (2015). Teens, gender, and self-presentation in social media. In J. D. Wright (Ed.), *International encyclopedia of social and behavioral sciences* (2nd ed., pp. 146–152). Elsevier [Winner of two PROSE awards for Excellence in Reference Works and for Multivolume Reference – Humanities & Social Sciences].

Herring, S. C. (2014). Language and the Internet. In W. Donsbach (Ed.), *The concise encyclopedia of communication*. Wiley-Blackwell.

Herring, S. C. (2014). Research: Computer-mediated communication. *ASIS&T Bulletin*, *40*(3).

Herring, S. C., & Stoerger, S. (2014). Gender and (a)nonymity in computer-mediated communication. In S. Ehrlich, M. Meyerhoff, & J. Holmes (Eds.), *The handbook of language, gender, and sexuality* (2nd ed., pp. 567–586). John Wiley & Sons, Ltd.

Koh, H., & Herring, S. C. (2014). Ebooks, ereaders, and ebook device design. In M. Khosrow-Pour (Ed.), *The encyclopedia of information science and technology* (3rd ed.). IGI Global.

Herring, S. C. (2013). Relevance in computer-mediated conversation. In S. C. Herring, D. Stein, & T. Virtanen (Eds.), *Handbook of pragmatics of computer-mediated communication* (pp. 245–268). Mouton.

Herring, S. C., Stein, D., & Virtanen, T., (Eds.). (2013). Introduction to the pragmatics of computer-mediated communication. In *Handbook of pragmatics of computer-mediated communication* (pp. 3–31). Mouton.

Dresner, E., & Herring, S. C. (2012). Emoticons and illocutionary force. In D. Riesenfel & G. Scarafile (Eds.), *Philosophical dialogue: Writings in honor of Marcelo Dascal* (pp. 59–70). College Publication.

Herring, S. C. (2012). Grammar and electronic communication. In C. Chapelle (Ed.), *Encyclopedia of applied linguistics*. Wiley-Blackwell.

Zhang, G., & Herring, S. C. (2012). Globalization or localization? A longitudinal study of successful American and Chinese online store websites. In M. Strano, H. Hrachovec, F. Sudweeks, & C. Ess (Eds.), *Proceedings of cultural attitudes towards technology and communication 2012* (pp. 430–445). Murdoch University.

Herring, S. C. (2011). Commentary. In C. Thurlow & K. Mroczek (Eds.), *Digital discourse: Language in the new media* (pp. 340–347). Oxford University Press.

Herring, S. C., Johnson, D. A., & DiBenedetto, T. (2011). Participation in electronic discourse in a "feminist" field. In J. Coates & P. Pichler (Eds.), *Language and gender: A reader* (2nd ed., pp. 171–182). Wiley-Blackwell.

Herring, S. C. (2010). Digital media. In P. Hogan (Ed.), *The Cambridge encyclopedia of the language sciences*. Cambridge University Press.

Herring, S. C. (2010). Web content analysis: Expanding the paradigm. In J. Hunsinger, M. Allen, & L. Klastrup (Eds.), *The international handbook of Internet research* (pp. 233–249). Springer Verlag.

Herring, S. C. (2008). Foreword. In S. Kelsey & K. St. Amant (Eds.), *Handbook of research on computer-mediated communication*. Idea Group, Inc.

Herring, S. C. (2008). Language and the Internet. In W. Donsbach (Ed.), *International encyclopedia of communication* (pp. 2640–2645). Blackwell Publishers.

Herring, S. C. (2008). Questioning the generational divide: Technological exoticism and adult construction of online youth identity. In D. Buckingham (Ed.), *Youth, identity, and digital media* (pp. 71–94). MIT Press.

Herring, S. C. (2008). Virtual community. In L. M. Given (Ed.), *Encyclopedia of qualitative research methods* (pp. 920–921). Sage.

Herring, S. C., & Zelenkauskaite, A. (2008). Gendered typography: Abbreviation and insertion in Italian iTV SMS. In J. F. Siegel, T. C. Nagel, A. Laurente-Lapole, & J. Auger (Eds.), *IUWPL7: Gender in language: Classic questions, new contexts* (pp. 73–92). IULC Publications.

Dainas, A., & Herring, S. C. (2021). Interpreting emoji pragmatics. In C. Xie, F. Yus, & H. Haberland (Eds.), *Internet pragmatics: Theory and practice* (pp. 107–144). John Benjamins. https://doi.org/10.1075/pbns.318.04dai

Danet, B., & Herring, S. C. (2007). Introduction: Welcome to the multilingual Internet. In B. Danet & S. C. Herring (Eds.), *The multilingual Internet: Language, culture, and communication online* (pp. 3–39). Oxford University Press.

Danet, B., & Herring, S. C. (2007). Multilingualism on the Internet. In M. Hellinger & A. Pauwels (Eds.), *Language and communication: Diversity and change. Handbook of applied linguistics 9* (pp. 553–592). Mouton de Gruyter.

Panyametheekul, S., & Herring, S. C. (2007). Gender and turn allocation in a Thai chat room. In B. Danet & S. C. Herring (Eds.), *The multilingual internet: Language, culture, and communication online* (pp. 233–255). Oxford University Press.

Ahuja, M., Ogan, C., Herring, S. C., & Robinson, J. C. (2006). Gender and career choice determinants in information systems professionals: A comparison with computer science. In F. Niederman & T. Farrat (Eds.), *IT workers: Human capital issues in a knowledge-based environment* (pp. 279–304). Information Age Publishing.

Herring, S. C., Ogan, C., Ahuja, M., & Robinson, J. C. (2006). Gender and the culture of computing in applied IT education. In E. Trauth (Ed.), *Encyclopedia of gender and information technology*. Information Science Publishing.

Herring, S. C., Scheidt, L. A., Kouper, I., & Wright, E. (2006). A longitudinal content analysis of weblogs: 2003–2004. In M. Tremayne (Ed.), *Blogging, citizenship, and the future of media* (pp. 3–20). Routledge.

Ogan, C., Robinson, J. C., Ahuja, M., & Herring, S. C. (2006). Gender differences among students in computer science and applied information technology. In W. Aspray & J. McGrath Cohoon (Eds.), *Women and information technology: Research on the reasons for under-representation* (pp. 279–300). MIT Press.

Cunliffe, D., & Herring, S. C. (2005). Introduction to minority languages, multimedia and the Web. *New Review of Multimedia and Hypermedia, 11*(2), 131–137.

Herring, S. C. (2004). Computer-mediated discourse analysis: An approach to researching online behavior. In S. A. Barab, R. Kling, & J. H. Gray (Eds.), *Designing for virtual communities in the service of learning* (pp. 338–376). Cambridge University Press.

Herring, S. C. (2004). Computer-mediated communication and woman's place. In R. Tolmach Lakoff and M. Bucholtz (Eds.), *Language and woman's place: Text and commentaries* (pp. 216–222). Oxford University Press.

Herring, S. C. (2004). Content analysis for new media: Rethinking the paradigm. In *New research for new media: Innovative research methodologies symposium working papers and readings* (pp. 47–66). University of Minnesota School of Journalism and Mass Communication.

Herring, S. C. (2004). Online communication: Through the lens of discourse. In M. Consalvo, N. Baym, J. Hunsinger, K. B. Jensen, J. Logie, M. Murero, & L. R. Shade (Eds.), *Internet research annual* (Vol. 1, pp. 65–76). Peter Lang.

Herring, S. C., Kouper, I., Scheidt, L. A., & Wright, E. (2004). Women and children last: The discursive construction of weblogs. In L. Gurak, S. Antonijevic, L. Johnson, C. Ratliff, & J. Reyman (Eds.), *Into the Blogosphere: Rhetoric, community, and culture of weblogs*. University of Minnesota.

Herring, S. C. (2003). Gender and power in online communication. In J. Holmes & M. Meyerhoff (Eds.), *The handbook of language and gender* (pp. 202–228). Blackwell Publishers.

Herring, S. C. (2001). Computer-mediated discourse. In D. Schiffrin, D. Tannen, & H. Hamilton (Eds.), *The handbook of discourse analysis* (pp. 612–634). Blackwell Publishers.

Herring, S. C. (2001). Foreword. In C. Ess & F. Sudweeks (Eds.), *Culture, technology, communication: Towards an intercultural global village*. SUNY Press.

Herring, S. C. (2000). Poeticality and word order in Old Tamil. In S. Herring, P. van Reenen, & L. Schøsler (Eds.), *Textual parameters in older languages*. John Benjamins.

Herring, S. C., van Reenen, P., & Schøsler, L. (2000). On textual parameters and older languages. In S. Herring, P. van Reenen, & L. Schøsler (Eds.), *Textual parameters in older languages* (pp. 1–31). John Benjamins.

Herring, S. C. (1999). Posting in a different voice: Gender and ethics in computer-mediated communication. In P. A. Mayer (Ed.), *Computer media and communication: A reader* (pp. 241–265). Oxford University Press.

Herring, S. C., Johnson, D. A., & DiBenedetto, T. (1998). Participation in electronic discourse in a "feminist" field. In J. Coates (Ed.), *Language and gender: A reader*. Blackwell.

Herring, S. C. (1996). Bringing familiar baggage to the new frontier: Gender differences in computer-mediated communication. In J. Selzer (Ed.), *Conversations* (pp. 1069–1082). Allyn & Bacon.

Herring, S. C. (1996). Bringing familiar baggage to the new frontier: Gender differences in computer-mediated communication. In V. Vitanza (Ed.), *CyberReader* (pp. 144–154). Allyn & Bacon.

Herring, S. C. (1996). Gender and democracy in computer-mediated communication. In R. Kling (Ed.), *Computerization and controversy: Value conflicts and social choices* (2nd ed., pp. 476–489). Academic Press.

Herring, S. C. (1996). Introduction. In S. C. Herring (Ed.), *Computer-mediated communication: Linguistic, social and cross-cultural perspectives* (pp. 1–10). John Benjamins.

Herring, S. C. (1996). Posting in a different voice: Gender and ethics in computer-mediated communication. In C. Ess (Ed.), *Philosophical perspectives on computer-mediated communication* (pp. 115–145). SUNY Press.

Herring, S. C. (1996). Two variants of an electronic message schema. In S. C. Herring (Ed.), *Computer-mediated communication: Linguistic, social and cross-cultural perspectives* (pp. 81–108). John Benjamins.

Herring, S. C., Johnson, D. A., & DiBenedetto, T. (1995). 'This discussion is going too far!' Male resistance to female participation on the Internet. In M. Bucholtz & K. Hall (Eds.), *Gender articulated: Language and the socially constructed self* (pp. 67–96). Routledge.

Herring, S. C., & Paolillo, J. C. (1995). Focus position in SOV languages. In P. Downing & M. Noonan (Eds.), *Word order in discourse* (pp. 163–198). John Benjamins.

Herring, S. C. (1994). Afterthoughts, antitopics, and emphasis: The syntacticization of postverbal position in Tamil. In M. Butt, T. King, & G. Ramchand (Eds.), *Theoretical approaches to word order in South Asian languages* (pp. 119–152). Stanford University Center for the Study of Language and Information.

Herring, S. C. (1992). Men's language: A study of the discourse of the LINGUIST list. In A. Crochetière, J-C. Boulanger, & C. Ouellon (Eds.), *Les langues menacées: actes du XVe congrès international des linguistes* (Vol. 3, pp. 347–350). Les Presses de l'Université Laval.

Journal Articles and Blog Postings

Allendorfer, W. H., & Herring, S. C. (2015). ISIS vs. the U.S. government: A war of online video propaganda. *First Monday, 20*(12). http://dx.doi.org/10.5210/fm.v20i12

Barab, S. A., Zuiker, S., Warren, S., Hickey, D., Ingram-Goble, A., Kwon, E-J., Kouper, I., & Herring, S. C. (2007). Embodied curriculum: Relating formalisms to contexts. *Science Education, 91*(5), 750–792.

Callahan, E., & Herring, S. C. (2011). Cultural bias in Wikipedia articles about famous persons. *Journal of the American Society for Information Science and Technology, 62*(10), 1899–1915. https://doi.org/10.1002/asi.

Callahan, E., & Herring, S. C. (2012). Language choice on university websites: Longitudinal trends. *International Journal of Communication, 6*, 322–355.

Cunliffe, D., & Herring, S. C. (Eds.). (2005). Minority languages, multimedia and the web [Special issue]. *New Review of Multimedia and Hypermedia, 11*(2).

Danet, B., & Herring, S. C. (2003a). Introduction: The multilingual Internet. *Journal of Computer-Mediated Communication, 9*(1).

Danet, B., & Herring, S. C. (Eds.). (2003b). The multilingual internet: Language, culture, and communication in instant messaging, email and chat [Special issue]. *Journal of Computer Mediated Communication, 9*(1).

Das, A., & Herring, S. C. (2016). Greetings and interpersonal closeness: The case of Bengalis on Orkut. *Language & Communication, 47*, 53–65.

Demata, M., Heaney, D., & Herring, S. C. (2018). Introduction. Language and discourse of social media. New challenges, new approaches [Special issue]. *Altre Modernità*, I–X.

Dresner, E., & Herring, S. C. (2010). Functions of the non-verbal in CMC: Emoticons and illocutionary force. *Communication Theory, 20*, 249–268.

Fox Tree, J. E., Whittaker, S., Herring, S. C., Chowdhury, Y., Nguyen, A., & Takayama, L. (2021, July). Psychological distance in mobile telepresence. *International Journal of Human-Computer Studies, 151*. https://doi.org/10.1016/j.ijhcs.2021.102629

Ge, J., & Herring, S. C. (2018). Communicative functions of emoji sequences on Sina Weibo. *First Monday, 23*(11).

Goh, D., Ogan, C., Ahuja, M., Herring, S. C., & Robinson, J. C. (2007). Being the same isn't enough: Impact of male and female mentors on computer self-efficacy of college students in IT-related fields. *Journal of Educational Computing Research, 37*(1), 19–40.

Herring, S. C. (1992). *Gender and participation in computer-mediated linguistic discourse*. ERIC Clearinghouse on Languages and Linguistics, document ED345552.

Herring, S. C. (1993a). Functional stability in language change: The evolution of tense and aspect in Tamil. *Studies in Language, 17*(2), 313–341.

Herring, S. C. (1993b). Gender and democracy in computer-mediated communication. *Electronic Journal of Communication, 3*(2).

Herring, S. C. (1993, June). Sex of LINGUISTs: Results of survey. *LINGUIST List, 4.517*.

Herring, S. C. (1995). Freedom of speech or freedom of harassment? *The College* (magazine of the UTA College of Liberal Arts), *1*(1), 8–9.

Herring, S. C. (1996). Linguistic and critical research on computer-mediated communication: Some ethical and scholarly considerations. *The Information Society, 12*(2), 153–168.

Herring, S. C. (Ed.). (1997a). Computer-mediated discourse analysis [Special issue]. *Electronic Journal of Communication, 6*(3).

Herring, S. C. (1997b). Ethics in cyber research: To cite, or not to cite? *The College* (magazine of the UTA College of Liberal Arts), *1*(2), 18–23.

Herring, S. C. (1998). Die rhetorische Dynamik geschlechtsbezogener Belästigungen in Online-Kommunikation. *Mitteilungen des Deutschen Germanistenverbandes*, *3*(98), 236–281.

Herring, S. C. (1998, March). Le style du courrier électronique: variabilité et changement. *Revue d'aménagement linguistique (formerly Terminogramme)*, *84–85*, 9–16.

Herring, S. C. (1999a). Interactional coherence in CMC. *Journal of Computer-Mediated Communication*, *4*(4).

Herring, S. C. (1999b). The rhetorical dynamics of gender harassment on-line. *The Information Society*, *15*(3), 151–167.

Herring, S. C. (2000). Gender differences in CMC: Findings and implications. *Computer Professionals for Social Responsibility Journal (formerly Computer Professionals for Social Responsibility Newsletter)*, *18*(1).

Herring, S. C. (2001). *Gender and power in online communication*. Center for Social Informatics Working Papers, no. WP-01–05.

Herring, S. C. (2002a). Computer-mediated communication on the Internet. *Annual Review of Information Science and Technology*, *36*, 109–168.

Herring, S. C. (2002b). Cyber violence: Recognizing and resisting abuse in online environments. *Asian Women*, *14*(Summer), 187–212.

Herring, S. C. (2003a). Media and language change: Introduction [Special issue]. *Journal of Historical Pragmatics*, *4*(1), 1–17.

Herring, S. C. (2003b). Review of Naomi Baron (2000), Alphabet to email: How written English evolved and where it's heading. *Journal of Historical Pragmatics*, *4*(1), 153–158.

Herring, S. C. (2004a). Intaanetto Tsuushin: Seisa/Seisabetsu no Koozoo to Minshuka no Kanoosee. In K. A. Reynolds & H. Nagahara (Eds.), *Jendaa no Gengogaku* [Current topics in the study of language and gender] (pp. 145–166). Akashi Shoten (Japanese translation of: Gender and democracy in computer-mediated communication, *Electronic Journal of Communication*, *3*(2), 1993.)

Herring, S. C. (2004b). Slouching toward the ordinary: Current trends in computer-mediated communication. *New Media & Society*, *6*(1), 26–36.

Herring, S. C. (2007). A faceted classification scheme for computer-mediated discourse. *Language@Internet*, 4.

Herring, S. C. (Ed.). (2010a). Computer-mediated conversation: Introduction and overview, Part I [Special issue]. *Language@Internet*, 7.

Herring, S. C. (2010b). Who's got the floor in computer-mediated conversation? Edelsky's gender patterns revisited. *Language@Internet*, 7.

Herring, S. C. (Ed.). (2011). Computer-mediated conversation, Part II [Special issue]. *Language@Internet*, 8.

Herring, S. C. (2011, February 4). A difference of communication styles [Where are the women in Wikipedia?] *The New York Times*.

Herring, S. C. (2015, October 19). Should you be capitalizing the word 'Internet'? *Wired*.

Herring, S. C. (2018). Emergent forms of computer-mediated communication and their global implications. *LinguaPax Review 2017. World Language Diversity: Old and New Frontiers, Emerging Scenarios*.

Herring, S. C., & Dainas, A. R. (2020.) Gender and age influences on interpretation of emoji functions. *ACM Transactions on Social Computing*. [Special Issue on Emoji Understanding and Applications in Social Media], *3*(2), 1–26. https://doi.org/10.1145/3375629

Herring, S. C., Dainas, A. R., Lopez Long, H., & Tang, Y. (2020). Animoji performances: "Cuz I can be a sexy poop." *Language@Internet*, 18, article 1. www.languageatinternet.org/articles/2020/herring/

Herring, S. C., Das, A., & Penumarthy, S. (2005). *CMC act taxonomy* [Online document].

Herring, S. C., & Demarest, B. (2017). "I'm the first video Voicethread – it's pretty sweet, I'm pumped": Gender and self-expression on an interactive multimodal platform. *ALSIC: Apprentissage des langues et systèmes d'information et de communication*, *20*(1).

Herring, S. C., Job-Sluder, K., Scheckler, R., & Barab, S. (2002). *Searching for safety: Managing "trolling" in a feminist discussion forum*. Center for Social Informatics Working Papers.

Herring, S. C., Job-Sluder, K., Scheckler, R., & Barab, S. (2002). Searching for safety online: Managing "trolling" in a feminist forum. *The Information Society*, *18*(5), 371–383.

Herring, S. C., & Marken, J. (2008). Implications of gender consciousness for students in information technology. *Women's Studies*, *37*(3), 229–256.

Herring, S. C., & Martinson, A. (2004). Assessing gender authenticity in computer-mediated language use: Evidence from an identity game. *Journal of Language and Social Psychology*, *23*(4), 424–446.

Herring, S. C., & Paolillo, J. C. (2006). Gender and genre variation in weblogs. *Journal of Sociolinguistics*, *10*(4), 439–459.

Herring, S. C., Scheidt, L. A., Bonus, S., & Wright, E. (2005). Weblogs as a bridging genre. *Information, Technology & People*, *18*(2), 142–171.

Herring, S. C., & Zelenkauskaite, A. (2009). Symbolic capital in a virtual heterosexual market: Abbreviation and insertion in Italian iTV SMS. *Written Communication, 26*(1), 5–31.

Kapidzic, S., & Herring, S. C. (2011). Gender, communication, and self-presentation in teen chatrooms revisited: Have patterns changed? *Journal of Computer-Mediated Communication, 17*(1), 39–59.

Kapidzic, S., & Herring, S. C. (2014). Race, gender, and self-presentation in teen profile photographs. *New Media & Society, 17*(6). https://doi.org/10.1177/1461444813520301

Koh, H. L., & Herring, S. C. (2016). Historical insights for ebook design. *Library Hi Tech, 34*(4), 764–786.

Koh, H. L., Herring, S. C., & Hew, K. F. (2010). Project-based learning and student knowledge construction during asynchronous online discussion. *The Internet and Higher Education, 13*, 284–291.

Konrad, A., Herring, S. C., & Choi, D. (2020). Sticker and emoji use in Facebook messenger: Implications for graphicon change. *Journal of Computer-Mediated Communication, 25*(3), 217–235. https://doi.org/10.1093/jcmc/zmaa003

Maestre, J. F., Herring, S. C., Min, A., Connelly, C. L., & Shih, P. (2018). Where and how to look for help matters: Analysis of support exchange in online health communities for people living with HIV. *Information, i*, xx, 5. https://doi.org/10.3390/infoxx010005.

Osman, G., & Herring, S. C. (2007). Interaction, facilitation, and deep learning in cross-cultural chat: A case study. *The Internet and Higher Education, 10*, 125–141.

Panyametheekul, S., & Herring, S. C. (2003). Gender and turn allocation in a Thai chat room. *Journal of Computer-Mediated Communication, 9*(1).

Paolillo, J. C., & Herring, S. C. (2005). Hyperlink obsolescence in scholarly online journals: JCMC reply. *Journal of Computer-Mediated Communication, 10*(3), article 17.

Souza, F. (2015). Interview with Susan Herring, University of Indiana [sic]. *Palimpsesto, 21*(July–December), 347–353.

Tang, Y., Hew, K. F., Herring, S. C., & Chen, Q. (2021). (Mis)communication through stickers in online group discussions: A multiple-case study. *Discourse & Communication, 1*(5). https://doi.org/10.1177/17504813211017707

Zhang, G., & Herring, S. C. (2013). In-game marriage and computer-mediated collaboration: An exploratory study. *Selected Papers of Internet Research, 14.0*.

Zhu, M., Herring, S. C., & Bonk, C. (2019). Exploring presence in online learning through three forms of computer-mediated discourse analysis. *Distance Education, 40*, 205–225. http://ella.ils.indiana.edu/~herring/zhu.et.al.2019.pdf

Conference Presentations

Abdul Mageed, M. M., & Herring, S. C. (2008). Arabic and English news coverage on aljazeera.net. In F. Sudweeks, H. Hrachovec, & C. Ess (Eds.), *Proceedings of cultural attitudes towards technology and communication 2008 (CATaC'08)*. Murdoch University Press.

Ahuja, M., Herring, S., Ogan, C., & Robinson, J. (2004). Exploring antecedents of gender equitable outcomes in IT higher education. *Proceedings of the 2004 SIGMIS Conference on Computer Personnel Research: Careers, Culture, and Ethics in a Networked Environment*, 120–123.

Allendorfer, W. H., & Herring, S. C. (2015, October). *ISIS vs. the U.S. Government: A war of online video propaganda*. Selected Papers of Internet Research 16: The 16th Annual Meeting of the Association of Internet Researchers.

Bourlai, E., & Herring, S. C. (2014). Multimodal communication on Tumblr: "I have so many feels!" *Proceedings of WebSci'14, June 23–26, Bloomington, IN*.

de Siqueira, A., & Herring, S. C. (2009). Temporal patterns in student-advisor instant messaging exchanges: Individual variation and accommodation. In *Proceedings of the forty-second Hawai'i international conference on system sciences (HICSS-42)*. IEEE Press [Nominated for a HICSS Best Paper prize].

El Mimouni, H., Fussell, S. R., Herring, S. C., Neustaedter, C., & Rode, J. (2018). SIG on telepresence robots. In *Extended abstracts of the 2018 CHI conference on human factors in computing systems*. ACM.

Emigh, W., & Herring, S. C. (2005). Collaborative authoring on the Web: A genre analysis of online encyclopedias. In *Proceedings of the thirty-eighth Hawai'i international conference on system sciences (HICSS-38)*. IEEE Press.

Freeman, G. Z., Bardzell, J., Bardzell, S., & Herring, S. C. (2015, March). Simulating marriage: Gender roles and emerging intimacy in an online game. *Proceedings of CSCW 2015*.

Herring, S. C. (1993). Aspectogenesis in South Dravidian: On the origin of the 'compound continuative' KONTIRU. In H. Aertsen & R. Jeffers (Eds.), *Historical linguistics 1989: Papers from the proceedings of the IXth international conference on historical linguistics* (pp. 167–185). John Benjamins.

Herring, S. C. (1994a). Discourse functions of demonstrative deixis in Tamil. In *Proceedings of the 20th annual Berkeley linguistics society (BLS-20). Parasession in Honor of Charles F. Fillmore*.

Herring, S. C. (1994b). Politeness in computer culture: Why women thank and men flame. In *Proceedings of the third Berkeley women and language conference* (pp. 278–294). Berkeley Women and Language Group.

Herring, S. C. (1995, November). Men's language on the internet. *Proceedings of the 2nd Nordic Language and Gender Conference. Nordlyd, 23*, 1–20.

Herring, S. C. (1998, July). *Ideologies of language use on the Internet: The case of "free speech"* [Paper presentation]. 6th International Pragmatics Conference, Reims, France.

Herring, S. C. (1999a). Interactional coherence in CMC. In *Proceedings of the 32nd Hawai'i international conference on system sciences (HICSS-32)*. IEEE Computer Society Press (HICSS Best Paper award).

Herring, S. C. (1999b). Pedagogical implications of synchronous computer chat: Coherence or equality? In *JILA'99: Journées internationales de linguistique appliquée*. Faculté des Lettres Arts et Sciences humaines de l'Université de Nice-Sophia Antipolis.

Herring, S. C. (1999, August). *Actualization of a counter-change: Contractions on the internet* [Paper presentation]. 14th International Conference on Historical Linguistics, Vancouver, Canada.

Herring, S. C. (2003). Dynamic topic analysis of synchronous chat. In *New research for new media: Innovative research methodologies symposium working papers and readings*. University of Minnesota School of Journalism and Mass Communication.

Herring, S. C. (2013). Discourse in Web 2.0: Familiar, reconfigured, and emergent. In D. Tannen & A. M. Tester (Eds.), *Georgetown university round table on languages and linguistics 2011: Discourse 2.0: Language and new media* (pp. 1–25). Georgetown University Press.

Herring, S. C. (2013, November). Telepresence robots for academics. *Proceedings of ASIST 2013, Montreal, Canada*.

Herring, S. C., & Chae, S. (2021). Prompt-rich CMC on YouTube: To what or to whom do comments respond? *Proceedings of the Fifty-fourth Hawai'i international conference on system sciences (HICSS-54)*. http://ella.ils.indiana.edu/~herring/HICSS.2021.herring.chae

Herring, S. C., & Dainas, A. R. (2017). "Nice picture comment!" Graphicons in Facebook comment threads. In *Proceedings of the fiftieth Hawai'i international conference on system sciences (HICSS-50)*. IEEE.

Herring, S. C., & Dainas, A. R. (2018). Receiver interpretations of emoji functions: A gender perspective. In S. Wijeratne, E. Kiciman, H. Saggion, & A. Sheth (Eds.), *Proceedings of the 1st international workshop on emoji understanding and applications in social media (emoji2018)*. Stanford University Press.

Herring, S. C., & Dainas, A. R., Lopez Long, H., & Tang, Y. (2020a). Animoji adoption and use: Gender associations with an emergent technology. *Proceedings of the 3rd international workshop on emoji understanding and applications in social media (emoji2020)*. https://doi.org/10.36190/2020.03 http://workshop-proceedings.icwsm.org/abstract?id=2020_03

Herring, S. C., Dainas, A. R., Lopez Long, H., & Tang, Y. (2020b). "If I'm close with them, it wouldn't be weird": Social distance and Animoji use. *HCI international 2020 proceedings: Late breaking work*. Springer. Prepublication version: http://ella.ils.indiana.edu/~herring/HCII2020.pdf

Herring, S. C., Dainas, A. R., & Tang, Y. (2021). "MEOW! Okay, I shouldn't have done that": Factors influencing vocal performance through Animoji. *Proceedings of the 4th international workshop on emoji understanding and applications in social media (emoji2021)*. http://ella.ils.indiana.edu/~herring/Emoji2021.herring.dainas.tang.pdf

Herring, S. C., & Demarest, B. (2011, October). *Mode choice in multimodal comment threads: Effects on participation and language use* [Paper presentation]. Internet Research 12.0, Seattle, WA.

Herring, S. C., & Estrada, Z. C. (2004). Representations of indigenous language groups of North and South America on the world wide web: In whose voice? *Proceedings of Cultural Attitudes Towards Technology and Communication 2004 (CATaC'04)*, 377–381.

Herring, S. C., Fussell, S. R., Kristofferson, A., Mutlu, B., Neustaedter, C., & Tsui, K. (2016). The future of robotic telepresence: Visions, opportunities and challenges. In *CHI'16 extended abstracts*. ACM.

Herring, S. C., & Ge, J. (2020). Do emoji sequences have a preferred word order? *Proceedings of the 3rd international workshop on emoji understanding and applications in social media (emoji2020)*. https://doi.org 10.36190/2020.05

Herring, S. C., Johnson, D. A., & DiBenedetto, T. (1992). Participation in electronic discourse in a 'feminist' field. In *Proceedings of the 1992 Berkeley women and language conference* (pp. 250–262). Berkeley Women and Language Group.

Herring, S. C., Kouper, I., Paolillo, J. C., Scheidt, L. A., Tyworth, M., Welsch, P., Wright, E., & Yu, N. (2005). Conversations in the blogosphere: An analysis "from the bottom up." In *Proceedings of the thirty-eighth Hawai'i international conference on system sciences (HICSS-38)*. IEEE Press.

Herring, S. C., & Kurtz, A. J. (2006). Visualizing dynamic topic analysis. In *Proceedings of CHI'06*. ACM Press.

Herring, S. C., Kutz, D. O., Paolillo, J. C., & Zelenkauskaite, A. (2009). Fast talking, fast shooting: Text chat in an online first-person game. In *Proceedings of the forty-second Hawai'i international conference on system sciences (HICSS-42)*. IEEE Press.

Herring, S. C., Martinson, A., & Scheckler, R. (2002). Designing for community: The effects of gender representation in videos on a Web site. In *Proceedings of the 35th Hawai'i international conference on system sciences*. IEEE Computer Society Press (HICSS Best Paper award).

Herring, S. C., & Nix, C. G. (1997, March). *Is "serious chat" an oxymoron? Pedagogical vs. social uses of internet relay chat* [Paper presentation]. American Association of Applied Linguistics Annual Conference, Orlando, FL.

Herring, S. C., Paolillo, J. C., Ramos Vielba, I., Kouper, I., Wright, E., Stoerger, S., Scheidt, L. A., & Clark, B. (2007). Language networks on LiveJournal. In *Proceedings of the fortieth Hawaii international conference on system sciences*. IEEE Press.

Herring, S. C., Scheidt, L. A., Bonus, S., & Wright, E. (2004). Bridging the gap: A genre analysis of weblogs. In *Proceedings of the 37th Hawai'i international conference on system sciences (HICSS-37)*. IEEE Computer Society Press.

Honeycutt, C., & Herring, S. C. (2009). Beyond microblogging: Conversation and collaboration via Twitter. In *Proceedings of the forty-second Hawai'i international conference on system sciences (HICSS-42)*. IEEE Press [Nominated for a HICSS Best Paper prize.]

Ishizaki, H., Herring, S. C., Hattori, G., & Takishima, Y. (2015, March). Understanding user behavior on online music distribution sites: A discourse approach. *Proceedings of iConference 2015*. www.ideals.illinois.edu/bitstream/handle/2142/73466/96_ready.pdf?sequence=2

Kim, Y., & Herring, S. C. (2018). Is politeness catalytic and contagious? Effects on participation in online news discussions. In *Proceedings of the fifty-first Hawai'i international conference on system sciences (HICSS 51)*. IEEE.

Koh, H., & Herring, S. C. (2007). Is interactivity important in information literacy tutorial sites? Comparison between highly-rated and randomly-selected online tutorials. *Proceedings of SITE 2007*.

Kutz, D. O., & Herring, S. C. (2005). Micro-longitudinal analysis of Web news updates. In *Proceedings of the thirty-eighth Hawai'i international conference on system sciences (HICSS-38)*. IEEE Press. (HICSS Best Paper award.)

Ogan, C., Herring, S. C., Ahuja, M., & Robinson, J. C. (2005). *The more things change, the more they stay the same: Gender differences in attitudes and experiences related to computing* [Paper presentation]. Annual meeting of the International Communication Association, New York.

Stoerger, S., Herring, S. C., & Kouper, I. (2007). "Great job, Quester!" Assessing language skills on Quest Atlantis. *Texas Linguistics Forum, 50*.

Venolia, G., Erickson, T., Tang, J., Lau, T., & Herring, S. C. (2014, February). Lifestyle teleworkers speak out! *Proceedings of CSCW 2014*, Baltimore, MD.

Zelenkauskaite, A., & Herring, S. C. (2006). Gender encoding of typographical elements in Lithuanian and Croatian IRC. In F. Sudweeks & C. Ess (Eds.), *Proceedings of cultural attitudes towards technology and culture 2006 (CATaC'06)*. Murdoch University Press.

Zelenkauskaite, A., & Herring, S. C. (2008a). Gender differences in personal advertisements in Lithuanian iTV SMS. In F. Sudweeks, H. Hrachovec, & C. Ess (Eds.), *Proceedings of cultural attitudes towards technology and communication 2008 (CATaC'08)*. Murdoch University Press.

Zelenkauskaite, A., & Herring, S. C. (2008b). Television-mediated conversation: Coherence in Italian iTV SMS chat. In *Proceedings of the forty-first Hawai'i international conference on system sciences (HICSS-41)*. IEEE Press.

Zytko, D., Freeman, G. Z., Grandhi, S., Jones, Q., & Herring, S. C. (2015, March). Enhancing evaluation of potential dates online through paired collaborative activities. *Proceedings of CSCW 2015*.

16
HILTZ, STARR ROXANNE

Photo of Starr Roxanne Hiltz contributed by Starr Roxanne Hiltz

One of the chapters in Network Nation, *which was finished in late '77, is on education, just the beginnings of the thoughts about whether we could build educational structures and we could have whole degree programmes online.*

Dr. Starr Roxanne Hiltz completed her undergraduate studies at Vassar College in 1963, with a major in sociology. She went on to complete a Master's in Sociology at Columbia University in 1964. She remained at Columbia University to obtain a PhD in Sociology in 1969.

Dr. Hiltz's research interests are numerous, as reflected in her publications listed at the end of this chapter. They include computer-mediated communication, information systems for emergency management, information systems evaluation-methodology, asynchronous learning networks, computer-supported cooperative work, group decision support systems, virtual teams, human-computer interaction, technology and society, pervasive information technologies, computers and education, and information systems and aging.

Hiltz is well known for co-authoring *The Network Nation*, which received the 1978 TSM Award from the Association of American Publishers for the Best Technical Publication of 1978. It was also nominated for an award as the best book in information science for 1978. The fourth printing of the paperback edition was in 1983. A revised edition was published by MIT Press in 1993. *The Network Nation* predicted the possibilities of the Internet and the World Wide Web and preceded her early work on one of the first longitudinal studies of online communities.

Hiltz has worked with the New Jersey Institute of Technology (NJIT) in the information systems department since 1985. Today, she holds the position of Professor Emeritus with NJIT. Hiltz has also been invited to work and conduct research with many universities, most recently as a Fulbright Fellow at the University of Salzburg, and Distinguished Chair in Media and Communication (2008–2009), University of Hawaii, as well as universities in Romania and Finland (2010–2011), and a visiting research professorship at the Catedra de Excelencia, at Carlos III University of Madrid.

In 2010, Dr. Hiltz was recognized by the Sloan-C fellowship (Online Learning Consortium): "For conceiving the idea of Virtual Classrooms and for scholarship related to the design, implementation, and verification of effective online education over multiple decades" (Sloan-C presentation statement, 2010).

Interview

Transcript Analysis Summary

Analysis of all interviews included in this volume led to the identification of 3,545 units of data. The mean of these collective units was 118 per pioneer, the median was 118.5, and the mode was 132. Individual interview units ranged from 59 to 217 units, yielding a spread of 158 units between all interviews. Starr Roxanne Hitlz's interview generated 158 units, which placed her interview near the top of all interviews in terms of unit generation.

A comparision of Hiltz's interview to the interviews of all pioneers indicated that nearly half her interview was akin to the average interview in terms of units produced per thematic area (Figure 16.1). Six of the 14 thematic codes in her interview yielded a similar numbers of units to the average interview. These included background, benefits of DE, challenges, accomplishments,

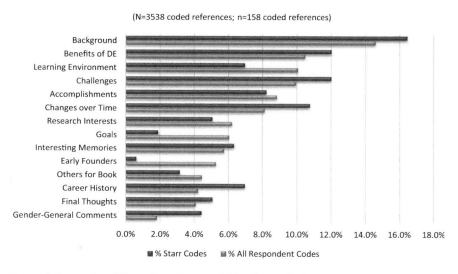

Figure 16.1 All Respondents' Versus Starr Roxanne Hiltz's Parent Codes

research interests, interesting memories, and final thoughts. Her interview produced somewhat more units in the areas of changes over time, career history, and general gender-related comments. Changes over time and career history units may be related to Hitlz's long career in the field, which made her privy to the transition from traditional snail mail correspondence to the modern era of online learning. Lastly, a number of the general gender-related comments reflected her experience as a female student who was discouraged from pursuing her academic dreams because of her gender.

Link to recorded interview: tinyurl.com/Hiltz-S

Transcript of Interview

Full Name: Starr Roxanne Hiltz
Institutional Affiliation: Distinguished Professor Emeritus, New Jersey Institute of Technology
Key:

Regular font = Interviewee comments
Italicized font = Interviewer comments

Interview Questions

1. *What was your educational and experiential background before you became involved in computer-mediated communication [CMC] and online and distance learning [ODL]?*

I went to a public high school, Baldwin High School on Long Island [New York, USA]. At the time, it was really excellent for those who were "gifted," as they called it. They had a whole set of courses for gifted and talented. So I actually took enough advanced courses to pass chemistry and math. For better or for worse, I got advanced placement in things because the high school was so good.

I started out liking science, but what I liked most was physics. But the physics professor was anti-female. Until another woman and I took physics, he hadn't had women. He did everything he could to discourage us. Then I talked to an uncle about it, who was a chemist, and he said, "You're right. In the natural sciences – and the harder they are, like chemistry is worse than biology, and physics is worse than chemistry – you will be discriminated against. You will never get promoted. You'll be somebody's lab assistant, do all of their work, and they will take all of the credit your whole life. Find something else." Which is sort of sad, but he was right.

It was that teacher and my uncle. He [my uncle] saw people in his labs. As I said, the women were not being promoted. [In high school] I had to take home ec [home economics]. I actually asked about shop. I wasn't allowed to take shop. I thought it might be neat to learn how to fix something, but no, no, I had to make some kind of flour and Crisco mix that I was supposed to make everything else out of. I wouldn't eat that slop anyway. The boys weren't allowed to take cooking.

So, I went to Vassar [College]. Vassar was all women at the time, and I think it was an excellent choice. Probably half of the faculty was female. They were wonderful role models. Most of them were not married, however, because it is really hard to be married, have kids, and work your way up in academia. Some of the ones who were the nicest to me were married. And basically, Vassar was saying, "It doesn't matter that you are women. Women can do anything they want to."

Nevertheless, I never took any more math and science. They excused me because of the advanced placement. I'm sorry about that now. I should have taken more math. I never did have calculus. Opting not to take them in college did hold me back from some of the more advanced mathematical techniques, still today.

I took almost all social sciences. I majored in sociology. I officially minored in economics, but I basically had a minor in anthropology and a minor in English also. I always liked to write. So, I was full of the social sciences where there were more women, and they were more accepted – not wonderfully accepted, but more accepted.

I went through in three years to catch up with my fiancé, which was kind of sad. Looking back on it, I didn't enjoy it as much as I would have if I wasn't taking seven courses a semester. In my third year, I was already married and commuting back and forth 80 or 90 miles from Poughkeepsie, New York [Vassar] to Troy [RPI]; wasn't too smart to do that, but I wanted to do it at the time – couldn't imagine waiting.

2. *In what year did you begin to look specifically into CMC and ODL? What were the circumstances in your world that initiated this interest in CMC and ODL?*

Well, with computer-mediated communication, in 1974. I had my first little projects going by 1975. As it says in the first chapter of *Virtual Classroom*, I was already starting to draft *The Network Nation* because we already had a system going up and data being collected, and field trials had gotten funding or were in the process of it. Actually, the field trials were with scientific research communities, which were very interesting, with the so-called invisible colleges. So I got to study other scientific communities, using literature from the sociology of science. All of my degrees were sociology.

With my PhD, I probably had the biggest data set that anybody had used up to that point. I was working for Prudential Insurance. First of all, when I did my thesis with this huge data set, I had to use the biggest computers there were at the time to do my runs on. So I had to learn how to run the programmes using really primitive things.

I was working at Prudential because I wanted to earn some money. I had not gotten chosen as a teaching assistant or funded after two years because I had followed my husband, who had gone into the army. So I wasn't around for any of that. I lost sponsorship at Columbia, so I needed somebody who was going to pay me to do my thesis. It turned out to be Prudential.

I had a wonderful boss there who said that he would get me what data and resources I needed, and he would give me one day out of five at the job to work on my thesis if I needed it. That was a pretty good deal. So he got me all of the data and had me learn to programme.

Actually, while I was there, I ended up training other researchers using some of the first really primitive statistical analysis programmes and things like that. I was becoming what some people thought was an expert in computer science because I knew a little more than the other people. I learned it on the job.

I had been doing research on widows because of Prudential. I was thoroughly sick of those depressing interviews, and Murray Turoff had just been hired at NJIT [New Jersey Institute of Technology]. Somebody that he knew from his research contacts was a colleague at Upsala College [East Orange, New Jersey], where I was chairing sociology, anthropology, and social work. He said that he was going to go back to California, but I could do the job Murray needed, which was social science research on users: see what they made of the systems he was inventing.

So I started working with him [Murray] in about '74 when he came to NJIT. For better or for worse, we hit it off. We both ended up getting divorced and got married to each other. I have been working with him ever since.

I got into computer-mediated communication in 1974–77; 1976–77 was actually quite important for me. I was a Visiting Fellow on an NSF [National Science Foundation] Faculty Fellowship at Princeton University. This was a life-saver for me. I was kind of drowning. I had a four-course load at Upsala; well, actually, since I was Chair, I had a three-course load. I was chairing a big department on two campuses. I had two kids. I had published everything that I had left from the research that I had done at Prudential. And I was thinking, "All right. How am I ever going to find the time and money to do something new and important in research?" So that NSF Faculty Fellowship was really important to give me a year to do reading, take some courses, and do some research and writing. I started *The Networked Nation* that year and doing some other research.

My sponsor at Princeton was Suzanne Keller, who was the first woman full professor at Princeton, I think. She had been one of my professors at Vassar who was very nice to me there. She let me take independent study so that I didn't have to commute another day to campus to get my last course. At Princeton, I was taking her course on the sociology of architecture, which is how architecture as a design of space affects the social interactions within it. Our final project was to design the classroom of the future. I was working on computer-mediated communication and starting to write *The Network Nation* about what was coming, so I realized that it didn't have to be a physical classroom. I could stop trying my pathetic attempt at architectural drawings, which weren't very good, and design cyber-spaces; a different structure for interaction for teaching and learning at the college level is how I saw it at the time. She saw it and said, "Oh, that is great! You should do that." So she encouraged it.

One of the chapters in *Network Nation*, which was finished in late '77, is on education, just the beginnings of the thoughts about whether we could build educational structures, and we could have whole degree programmes online.

I started looking for funding to do this. I tried several times. I didn't get it from NSF. They said, "We don't do education." But eventually, my name was given to a project officer at the Annenberg CPB [Corporation for Public Broadcasting] Project to expand access to college-level education. So they were funding things like *Sunrise Semester*. The project officer who started talking to me said, "Oh, that sounds great! You're going to build a virtual classroom. Write me a proposal."

So I got the money to build the first virtual classroom system and conduct the first classes online and conduct the first controlled field experiment, where we had the same courses offered online and face-to-face with the same instructor and the same syllabus. We compared what happened to the students. We had the faculty all write reports on how they found it different, challenging, better, worse.

3. Which female researchers or female colleagues may have piqued your interest in CMC and ODL?

None at the beginning. Linda Harasim read *The Network Nation*. She said that it just blew her away. She got in touch with me. She actually had one of her courses from Canada online on our virtual classroom system on EIES [Electronic Information Exchange System], the name of our system at NJIT. So she was in some of the original studies. Then she started designing her systems and writing her grants. And she ended up getting more money than I ever got. She became a colleague, and we did do a book together, two books together, I think. Now I have to remember. . . . How many books did I do with Linda? I guess it was only one. I don't see a second one [on my list of publications]. I think we did some chapters for each other's books. We did co-author *Learning Networks: A Field Guide to Teaching and Learning Online* in '95. It was nice to have her as a colleague and friend.

The other one who became a colleague and who went on to serve on one of my advisory boards later on, with the second virtual classroom set of grants from the Sloan Foundation, was Karen Swan. She was another valued colleague. We cheered each other on.

All three of us believed in collaborative learning online. We all don't approve of essentially computer-assisted learning that's drill and practice or things where there's no interaction. So we were all concerned with how, with software, with pedagogy, and with teachers setting up of activities through guidelines for interaction, to get the students actually teaching each other and learning from each other, as well as from the teacher or texts and other resources.

4. Who would you identify as the early female leaders/founders in the field of DE/CMC/ODL?

I've never been an expert on distance education per se. My impression when I first came into this was that distance education in 1977 or so was still correspondence. I had some friends and relatives who were still taking correspondence courses. They got stuff in the mail, and they worked on it and mailed it back. Or with *Sunrise Semester*, they watched videos at strange times of the day on television on PBS [Public Broadcasting Service], yet they were still getting packages in the mail to work on things and then send things back. I might have been wrong. There might have been some people doing something more interactive with distance learning, but I wasn't aware of it.

5. What are some of the goals that you strove to achieve in the fields of CMC and ODL?

Let's start with computer-mediated communication. We had some negative scenarios in *The Network Nation*, but they were few. We really thought things would turn out well, but take a look at Facebook. We saw CMC as a way to equalize access to information and people and resources and ability to participate. We saw working from home, learning from home, keeping in touch, socializing from home.

The original EIES system was for scientists, but we had some fun things in it. We had one conference where everyone wrote with pen names. It was devoted to writing an interactive novel online. Everybody would sort of write the next few paragraphs. Then somebody else picked up. It was kind of a sci-fi thing that took place in the future. It was a fun thing, too. And scientists like sci-fi things. We had a café, where it was just a place to drop in and chat about anything that interested you. We had online New Year's Eve parties. So we saw it as a place to socialize as well as to work. You could play as well as work.

I had hoped from the beginning that it would help women in particular who were stuck at home, or who might be working but, between work and families, didn't have time for much else to continue their education, to maybe be better able to balance work, family, continuing education, and socializing, to fit them in when the baby was sleeping or something like that.

I also had early interest in increasing access for those whom I called "handicapped" at the time, and that's not a good term now. I think it is "differently abled" or whatever the term is. I haven't kept up with that field, either, but I was very aware of people who had some limitations that most people didn't have, whether it was hearing or sight or mobility or whatever, that computer aids, along with computer-mediated communication, would enable them to do the equivalent of talking and listening. We worked there with a man who is no longer alive, Haig Kafafian, who had systems whereby you could type anything using a big electronic board; with a straw or your eyes, you could run this board. You were stopping on letters, so you were typing with whatever you had by blowing or blinking or twitching a finger, and you could compose a message online with what abilities you had. It was slow, but you could do it. So from the beginning, we tried to include online children with cerebral palsy, who had limited ability to type. They could use some of his equipment and be online. Nobody had to know that they had cerebral palsy. They could take as long as they needed to type their responses in an asynchronous system.

Other than increasing opportunities for those who need them, I thought it would improve democracy because I thought we'd get more people involved. They are involved, all right. They are involved in their little echo chambers, attacking the other side, reading what people just like them think and not anything else. I did not foresee that. I didn't foresee the Russians hacking and all of those things.

6. *What are some of your accomplishments in the fields of CMC and ODL that you would like to share?*

Well, *The Network Nation: Human Communication via Computer* was the first book to really describe the technical and social possibilities of what have become the World Wide Web and all of the systems that we have now. Working with one of the first large-scale operational systems, it was easy to see all of the things that could happen. So it was part technological forecasting and part based on my observations up to that date, which were not huge, but we had some data. We had observed some people and groups using the system that had been created so that we could try to project from that.

I spent a lot of time, now that I think may have been poorly spent, on something called "group decision support systems." The idea was there would be various kinds of voting, feedback tools, and structures for group collaboration that would help groups to make better decisions than they would make face-to-face without having to travel to face-to-face meetings. But it never totally succeeded. People, business men, like to have meetings. They get to drink and eat and travel to interesting places. They don't want to meet online for the most part.

I was also interested in online communities, which are communities of practice or interest that exist totally online and that persist over months to years. It's been nice watching them. There have been some in various medical areas for people who have the same condition. One of my colleagues in CMC was Jenny Preece. When she injured the meniscus in her knee in a skiing accident and was devastated because she couldn't ski for a while, she found an online community with these meniscus injuries of the knee where members shared what worked and what didn't work; stick with it, and some day you will be able to walk, and one day you will be able to run, and you will be able to ski. She found it helpful. So she started studying online communities. She wasn't in distance learning; she was in CMC. She was another colleague whom I visited with occasionally, although I don't think that I ever co-authored with her.

I think that is about it.

7. *What are some of the challenges that you faced in the fields of CMC and ODL over the years?*

In the beginning, everybody thought we were crazy. They said things like, "Why would anybody use an expensive computer to communicate with others when they can use a postage stamp or a ten-cent phone call? Makes no sense. You're crazy. Nobody will ever use this stuff. If you need to send a document, use fax." So people really did not see what we saw as the possibilities. The things we saw that would happen they thought would never happen.

The thing is that we were so early that we didn't put patents on anything. In fact, back at that time, you could not patent things that did not have some physical aspect. You could copyright code, but you could only copyright it in the language in which it was written. So I copyrighted all of the software capabilities for the virtual classroom, but anybody else could do it. They just had to do it in a different language, which they soon did. We were so early that we didn't realize it. We didn't do the Facebook thing and become a billionaire. We never took any money for anything or made any money on anything we invented. I'm a little sorry about that.

8. *What was the "state of DE" when you first entered the field as opposed to CMC/ODL in 2018?*

What I thought it was at the time was basically correspondence between some kind of mentor and you. You sent your stuff in, got it graded, and got your answers in the mail is my impression of what it was. With CMC, when we started it was just ARPANET [a Department of Defence network], and after that, the first private networks started. We actually started using some of those, too. They were expensive. That's one reason why we needed NSF funding – to get hundreds of scientists using our network. We had to pay for their connections because they were mostly academics. It was something like maybe $20 an hour. It was cheaper than long-distance phone calls, but people were spending 10, 20, or 30 hours a month online. That was too much to spend back then in the '70s on an academic salary. So CMC at that time was something that was done with funding. It couldn't pay for itself by charging users. It was too expensive because the computers were expensive, everything [was] expensive. The mini computers we were using to run EIES in the beginning cost like half a million [US dollars] each. Right now, your cell phone is more powerful.

So the computing power, the telecommunication hook-ups for CMC were expensive, few, and slow. When we first started, it was 300 baud, 300 bits per second – I don't know, whatever "baud" was. When it went up to 1,200 baud, people thought it was too fast. Right now, we're at 96,000 to 400,000 bits per second [bps] or more. So it was primitive, but the people who started using it thought it was really fascinating because they could easily communicate with people around the world, and they couldn't easily do that any other way.

9. *What interesting memories would you like to share about the beginning of your work in CMC/ODL?*

When I got the first grant from Annenberg CPB, I was still at Upsala College. I made it joint between Upsala and NJIT to have some humanities and social sciences courses at Upsala, and some computer and math courses at NJIT. At Upsala, the faculty heard about this because I sent around flyers. I recruited some of my colleagues who were pioneers and willing to take a chance. I told them, "If it's really a mess with these classes, you can go back to the classroom, right?"

They all tried the system, and it seemed to be stable. So I had flyers at registration for students to sign up for these classes, explaining what an online class was. It didn't meet at any particular time. It met seven days a week online, but they could sign on any time and place where they could get to a computer with a modem. We had a lab on campus that funding also paid for; I think it was seven Apple 2s or something with modems, and they could come there. If they got a device at home, they could use it there. Oh, we had to pay to keep the lab open, too. That's where some of the funding was: keeping it open on nights and weekends, as well as during days, so that there was definitely access.

Some of the other faculty saw this and said, "That's terrible! They're not meeting face-to-face. They won't get a good education." At a faculty meeting, they argued that I should not be able to do this. It should not be allowed. It would destroy education. It would harm the students. They wouldn't learn anything. I actually had a supportive dean who said, "That's not your choice. All faculty has the right to teach courses the way they want to with the permission of the dean, and I have given her permission. End of story. There will be no vote." But basically, some faculty members wanted to string me up as a witch or something. I don't know.

The other campus [NJIT] wasn't much friendlier. They didn't have a faculty meeting, but except for a few intrepid pioneers, most people thought, as I said, that I was crazy, that you couldn't teach this way, that it was bound to fail. So it was a bit of a slog uphill.

10. *What were your specific research interests, and have they changed/evolved over the years?*

I've always been interested in the social dynamics of computer-mediated communication in its various forms and how the structures for computer-mediated communication affect those dynamics. It goes back to the Suzanne Keller architecture seminar – how structures affect interaction. So I'm still interested in that.

I haven't been doing educationally related research since I went to emeritus status. I did for a couple years, but it's been like eight years. Since I'm not there anymore, I really can't do research on it so well anymore, and I don't have grants anymore.

The Sloan Foundation was very generous with grants for a number of years, but then Frank Mayadas, who was the programme officer who really liked asynchronous learning networks, or ALN as we called it, retired, and they stopped doing those grants. They said we don't need grants anymore. It's state of the art; everyone's doing it; they don't need grants to do it. Sloan doesn't need to fund that research anymore. I kind of disagreed. Just because everyone was doing it didn't mean that you didn't need to do some research on it. But anyway, I haven't been doing research on online distance learning recently.

Instead, besides general CMC dynamics, I went into the use of computer-mediated communication in social media in emergency response management and emergency response incidents from the public, partially because my husband, Murray Turoff, has always been interested in that. He was one of the co-founders of the International Network for Information Systems for Crisis Response Management (ISCRAM). We are both still active. I co-chair a social media and emergency response track pretty much every year. So I keep active with that research.

And with some of my former PhD students, I still do things of somewhat more general interest. For the last few years, one project has been fake news and to what extent people try to vet their sources, or they just believe whatever they read online.

Another project we just finished is what if the Internet goes out? What does it do to our lives? Because it's not impossible. Our former friends, the Soviets, or the Chinese or somebody could bring our Internet down. Cyber warfare, I think, is one of the biggest threats facing us. Right now, if all of our systems go down, it's not just getting to post things on Facebook that will be lost. A lot of our systems for gas stations, power plants, stores – you name it – are dependent on the Internet. If the Internet goes down, a lot of our civilization goes down for a while. So, I'm interested in that. It's not something that I anticipated back when we were saying how great the Internet systems were going to be: that we would make ourselves so dependent that if there was cyber warfare, it would be a way to wipe us out. You don't have to bomb us. You just have to get rid of all of our electricity, and we won't last long.

11. *Could you please describe the learning environment that you currently work in (e.g., geographic and institutional setting, student demographics)?*

With my teaching, I still do one or two courses online each year through NJIT in the information systems department, which has now been renamed informatics. I only teach at the PhD level now because I haven't the patience for undergraduates who don't want to take required courses that they aren't interested in.

The platform that we've been using is Moodle, which I find is pretty good; not as good as my own systems were, but they stopped working when all the funding ended. You need some kind of funding to keep things going – either venture capitalists or government – to keep large-scale software and the hardware to run it up to date.

NJIT is a technological university. Their students are quite good. It's one of the most diverse universities in the US in terms of the demographics of the student body; not just black and Hispanic, but India, China, Middle East, you name it; we get students from all over the world. That makes it fun to teach online.

12. *Is there anything else you [would] like to address?*

If you think you have a good idea and at first you don't succeed, try and try again. It took me many tries before I got anybody to believe that a virtual classroom was deserving of funding. For several years, we just did unfunded research. We put our own classes online. I did some questionnaires for the students and kept all the transcripts to describe what had happened so that I could begin to describe these possibilities with some empirical data under it.

Sometimes to do something that is really a breakthrough, you don't necessarily get funding right away. You might have to go without it.

I: What started you on this journey? What made you envision this in the first place?

Working with Murray Turoff. When I was first working with him, the system only existed in his mind, which was really peculiar. But he fairly soon got a bare-bones system up, and fairly soon he got a lot of his personal network on it. I found that I really liked getting on after dinner, putting the kids to bed, and having stimulating exchanges with my academic colleagues instead of watching something on what we called "the boob tube."

I also very early on got onto another system called Planet that was being run by the Institute of the Future. My former colleague from Upsala, Bob Johannsen, was involved in that. Even though these systems are asynchronous, there are always some people on them. One time, I had a meeting in about 20 minutes. There are ways for real-time chats for people who are on them at the same time. So I got in a real-time chat, and before I knew it, two hours were gone, and I missed the meeting. I obviously took to this form of communication and found it engaging from the beginning, to say the least.

13. *Can you suggest names of other female pioneers in DE, CMC, or ODL that you think we should include in the book?*

No, I can't, other than the names that you already have.

Publications

Books

Harasim, L., Hiltz, S. R., Teles, L., & Turoff, M. (1995). *Learning networks: A field guide to teaching and learning online*. MIT Press.

Hiltz, S. R. (1977). *Creating community services for widows: A pilot project*. Kennikat Press, National University Publications.
Hiltz, S. R. (1984). *Online communities: A case study of the office of the future*. ABLEX Publishing Corp., Human-Computer Interaction Series.
Hiltz, S. R. (1994). *The virtual classroom: Learning without limits via computer networks*. Ablex Publishing (Human-Computer Interaction Series). www.intellect-net.com
Hiltz, S. R., & Goldman, R. (Eds.). (2005). *Learning together online: Research on asynchronous learning networks*. Erlbaum.
Hiltz, S. R., & Kerr, E. (1982). *Computer-mediated communication systems: Status and evaluation*. Academic Press.
Hiltz, S. R., Pfaff, M. F., Plotnick, L., & Shih, P. C. (Eds.). (2014). *Proceedings of the 11th international ISCRAM conference*. ISCRAM.
Hiltz, S. R., & Turoff, M. (1978). *The network nation: Human communication via computer*. Addison Wesley Advanced Book Program.
Van de Walle, B., Turoff, M., & Hiltz, S. R. (Eds.). (2010). *Information systems for emergency management*. In V. Zwass (Series Ed.), *Advances in management information systems monograph series*. M. E. Sharpe Inc.

Book Chapters

Hiltz, S. R. (1978). Widowhood: A roleless role? In M. Sussman (Ed.), *Marriage and the family*. Haworth Press (Reprinted from *Marriage and Family Review*, 1(5).
Hiltz, S. R. (1980a). Experiments and experiences with computerized conferencing. In R. Landau & J. Bair (Eds.), *Emerging office systems* (pp. 187–222). Ablex.
Hiltz, S. R. (1980b). Operational trials of the electronic information exchange system: Feedback from the members. In *AAAS Symposium Series*. Westview Press.
Hiltz, S. R. (1986). Teleconferencing: Recent developments in computer-mediated communication and other technologies. In A. E. Cawkell (Ed.), *The international handbook of information technology and office systems*. North Holland.
Hiltz, S. R. (1990). Evaluating the virtual classroom. In L. Harasim (Ed.), *On-line education: Perspectives on a new medium*. Praeger/Greenwood.
Hiltz, S. R. (1992a). Constructing and evaluating a virtual classroom. In M. Lea (Ed.), *Contexts of computer-mediated communication* (pp. 188–208). Harvester Wheatsheaf.
Hiltz, S. R. (1992b). The virtual classroom: Software for collaborative learning. In E. Barrett, (Ed.), *Sociomedia: Multimedia hypermedia, and the social construction of Knowledge* (pp. 347–368). MIT Press.
Hiltz, S. R. (2004). The virtual classroom. In A. DiStefano, K. E. Rudestam, & R. J. Silverman (Eds.), *Encyclopedia of distributed learning* (pp. 470–472). Sage.
Hiltz, S. R., & Arbaugh, J. B. (2003). Studies of the effectiveness of ALN: Improving quantitative research methods. In J. Bourne & J. C. Moore (Eds.), *Elements of quality of online education*. SCOLE.
Hiltz, S. R., Arbaugh, J. B., Benbunan-Fich, R., & Shea, P. (2004). ALN research: What we know and what we need to know about contextual influences. In J. Bourne & J. C. Moore (Eds.), *Elements of quality online education* (Vol. 5). Sloan-C.
Hiltz, S. R., Dufner, D., Fjermestad, J., Kim, Y., Ocker, R., Rana, A., & Turoff, M. (2013). Distributed group support systems: Theory development and experimentation. In B. M. Olsen, J. B. Smith, & T. Malone (Eds.), *Coordination theory and collaboration technology* (Original work published 2001.)
Hiltz, S. R., Fjermestad, J., Ocker, R., & Turoff, M. (2006). Asynchronous virtual teams: Can software tools and structuring of social processes enhance performance? In D. Galletta & P. Zhang (Eds.), *Human-computer interaction in management information systems: Applications* (Vol. II, pp. 119–142). M. E. Sharpe, Inc.
Hiltz, S. R., & Turoff, M. (1980). More inequality? An exploration of the potential impacts of EFT on social stratification in American society. In *Computers and banking, electronic funds transfer systems*. Plenum. (Reprinted from *Telecommunications Policy*, March 1978).
Hiltz, S. R., & Turoff, M. (1992a). Structuring computer-mediated communication to avoid information overload. In D. Marca & G. Bock (Eds.), *Groupware: Software for computer-supported cooperative work* (pp. 384–393). IEEE Computer Society Press.
Hiltz, S. R., & Turoff, M. (1992b). Virtual meetings: Computer conferencing and distributed group support. In R. Bostrum, S. Kinney, & R. Watson (Eds.), *Computer augmented teamwork* (pp. 67–85). Van Nostrand.
Hiltz, S. R., Turoff, M., & Harasim, L. (2007). Development and philosophy of the field of asynchronous learning networks. In R. Andrews & C. Haythornthwaite (Eds.), *Handbook of e-learning research* (pp. 55–72). Sage.
Hiltz, S. R., Turoff, M., & Zhang, Y. (2002). Studies of effectiveness of learning networks. In J. Bourne & J. C. Moore (Eds.), *Elements of quality of online education* (pp. 15–41). SCOLE.

Shen, J., Hiltz, S. R., & Bieber, M. (2005). Collaborative assessment in asynchronous learning networks: Research in progress. In J. C. Moore (Ed.), *Elements of quality online learning: Engaging communities: Wisdom from the Sloan Consortium* (pp. 85–96). SCOLE.

Turoff, M., Foster, J., Hiltz, S. R., & Ng, K. (1990). The TEIES design and objectives: Computer mediated communications and tailorability. In E. Nahouraii & F. Petry (Eds.), *Object-oriented databases*. IEEE Computer Society Press (Reprinted from *Proceedings of the twenty-second annual Hawaii international conference on system sciences*, *3*, 403–411. IEEE Computer Society).

Turoff, M., & Hiltz, S. R. (1978). Computerized conferencing: A review and statement of issues. In Elton et al. (Eds.), *Evaluating new telecommunications policies*. Plenum.

Turoff, M., & Hiltz, S. R. (1979). Teleconferencing. In J. Belzer (Ed.), *Encyclopedia of computer and information science* (Vol. 13). Marcel Dekker.

Turoff, M., & Hiltz, S. R. (1980). Meeting through your computer. In W. C. House (Ed.), *Electronic communications systems* (Original works printed in 1977).

Turoff, M., & Hiltz, S. R. (1995). Computer-based Delphi processes. In M. Adler & E. Ziglio (Eds.), *Gazing into the oracle: The Delphi method and its application to social policy and public health* (pp. 56–88). Jessica Kingsley Publishers.

Turoff, M., & Hiltz, S. R. (2001). Effectively managing large enrollment courses: A case study. In J. Bourne & J. C. Moore (Eds.), *Online education: Learning effectiveness, faculty satisfaction and cost effectiveness* (Vol. 2, pp. 55–80). Sloan Center for Online Education.

Turoff, M., Hiltz, S. R., Fjermestad, J., Bieber, M., & Whitworth, B. (2001). Computer-mediated communications for group support: Past and future. In J. Carroll (Ed.), *HCI in the new millennium* (pp. 279–302). Addison Wesley.

Turoff, M., Hiltz, S. R., Li, Z., Wang, Y., & Cho, H-K. (2004). The Delphi process as a collaborative learning method. In J. Bourne & J. Moore (Eds.), *Elements of quality online education: Into the main stream – Wisdom papers*. Sloan-C.

Turoff, M., Hiltz, S. R., & Mills, M. (1991). Telecomputing: Organizational impacts. In S. Nagel & D. Garson (Eds.), *Advances in social science and computers* (Vol. 2, pp. 233–251). JAI Press.

Journal Articles

Banuls-Silvera, V. A., Turoff, M., & Hiltz, S. R. (2013). Collaborative scenario modelling in emergency management through cross-impact. *Technological Forecasting and Social Change*, *80*(9), 1756–1774.

Benbunan-Fich, R., & Hiltz, S. R. (1999a). Educational applications of CMCS: Solving case studies through asynchronous learning networks. *Journal of Computer-Mediated Communication*, *4*(3).

Benbunan-Fich, R., & Hiltz, S. R. (1999b). Effects of asynchronous learning networks: A field experiment. *Journal of Group Decision and Negotiation*, *8*, 409–426.

Benbunan-Fich, R., & Hiltz, S. R. (2003). Mediators of effectiveness of online courses. *IEEE Transactions on Professional Communication*, *46*(4), 298–312.

Benbunan-Fich, R., Hiltz, S. R., & Turoff, M. (2003) A comparative content-analysis of face-to-face vs. Asynchronous group decision making. *Decision Support Systems*, *34*, 457–469.

Bieber, M., Engelebart, D., Furuta, R., Hiltz, S. R., Noll, J., Preece, J., Stohr, E. A., Turoff, M., & Van de Walle, B. (2002). Toward virtual community knowledge evolution. *Journal of Management Information Systems*, *18*(4), 11–36.

Cho, Y., Im, I., Fjermestad, J., & Hiltz, S. R. (2003a). The impact of product category on customer dissatisfaction in cyberspace. *Business Process Management Journal*, *9*(5), 635–651.

Cho, Y., Im, I., Fjermestad, J., & Hiltz, S. R. (2003b). The impact of e-services and customer complaints on electronic commerce customer relationship management. *Journal of Consumer Satisfaction/Dissatisfaction and Consumer Behavior*, *16*, 106–118. https://jcsdcb.com/index.php/JCSDCB/article/view/78

Cho, Y., Im, I., Hiltz, S. R., & Fjermestad, J. (2002). The effects of post-purchase evaluation factors on online vs. offline customer complaining behavior: Implications for customer loyalty. *Advances in Consumer Research*, *29*(2002), 318.

Coppola, N. W., Hiltz, S. R., & Rotter, N. (2002). Becoming a virtual professor: Pedagogical roles and asynchronous learning networks. *Journal of Management Information Systems*, *18*(4), 169–190.

Coppola, N. W., Hiltz, S. R., & Rotter, N. (2005). Building trust in virtual teams. *IEEE Transactions on Professional Communication*, *47*(2), 95–104.

Czaja, S., & Hiltz, S. R. (2005, October). Digital aids for an aging society. *Communications of the ACM*, 43–44.

Deek, F. P., Hiltz, S. R., Kimmel, H., & Rotter, N. (1999, July). Cognitive assessment of students' problem solving and program development skills. *Journal of Engineering Education*, 317–326.

Deek, F., McHugh, J. A., & Hiltz, S. R. (2000). Methodology and technology for learning programming. *Journal of Systems & Information Technology, 4*(1), 25–37.

Dezhi, W., Bieber, M., & Hiltz, S. R. (2008). Engaging students and increasing learning with constructivist participatory examinations in asynchronous learning networks. *Journal of Information Systems Education, 19*(3).

Dezhi, W., Bieber, M., & Hiltz, S. R. (2009). Asynchronous participatory exams: Internet innovation for engaging students. *IEEE Internet Computing, 13*(2), 30–36.

Fjermestad, J., & Hiltz, S. R. (1998). An assessment of group support systems experimental research: Methodology and results. *Journal of Management Information Systems, 15*(3), 7–150.

Fjermestad, J., & Hiltz, S. R. (2000). Group support systems: A descriptive evaluation of case and field studies. *Journal of Management Information Systems, 17*(3), 112–157.

Gimenez, R., Hernantes, J., Hiltz, S. R., & Turoff, M. (2017). Improving the resilience of disaster management organizations through virtual communities of practice: A Delphi study. *Journal of Contingencies and Crisis Management, 25*(3). https://doi.org/10.1111/1468-5973.12181

Han, H. J., Hiltz, S. R., Fjermestad, J., & Wang, Y. (2011). Does medium matter? A comparison of initial meeting modes for virtual teams. *IEEE Transactions on Professional Communication, 54*(4), 376–391.

Hiltz, R. S. (1971a). Black and white in the consumer financial system. *American Journal of Sociology, 76*(6).

Hiltz, R. S. (1971b). The working wife: Impact on the life insurance industry. *CLU Journal, 25*(2).

Hiltz, R. S. (1971c). Why black families own less life insurance. *The Journal of Risk and Insurance, 38*(2).

Hiltz, R. S. (1974). Evaluating a pilot social service project for widows: A chronicle of research problems. *Journal of Sociology and Social Welfare, 1*(4).

Hiltz, R. S. (1975). Helping widows: Group discussions as a therapeutic technique. *The Family Coordinator, 24*(3), 331–336.

Hiltz, R. S. (1977). The impact of a new communications medium upon scientific research specialties. *Journal of Research Communication Studies, 1*, 111–124.

Hiltz, R. S. (1979). Using computerized conferencing to conduct opinion research. *Public Opinion Quarterly, 43*(4), 562–571. https://doi.org/10.1086/268555

Hiltz, S. R. (1978). The human element in computerized conferencing systems. *Computer Networks, 2*, 421–428.

Hiltz, S. R. (1982). The impact of a computerized conferencing system on the productivity of scientific research communities. *Behavior and Information Technology, 1*(2), 185–195.

Hiltz, S. R. (1986). The virtual classroom: Using computer-mediated communication for university teaching. *Journal of Communication, 36*(2), 95–104.

Hiltz, S. R. (1988). Productivity enhancement from computer-mediated communication: A systems contingency approach. *Communications of the ACM, 31*(12), 1438–1454.

Hiltz, S. R. (1993). Correlates of learning in a virtual classroom. *International Journal of Man Machine Systems, 39*, 71–98.

Hiltz, S. R. (1994). Teaching in a virtual classroom. *International Journal of Educational Telecommunications, 1*(2), 185–198.

Hiltz, S. R. (1997). Impacts of college-level courses via asynchronous learning networks: Some preliminary results. *Journal of Asynchronous Learning Networks, 1*(2).

Hiltz, S. R. (2005). Creating and sustaining effective ALNs. *Journal of Asynchronous Learning Networks, 9*(2), 11–15.

Hiltz, S. R., Benbunan-Fich, R., Coppola, N., Rotter, N., & Turoff, M. (2000). Measuring the importance of collaborative learning for the effectiveness of ALN: A multi-measure, multi-method approach. *Journal of Asynchronous Learning Networks, 4*(2).

Hiltz, S. R., & Czaja, S. (2006). Introduction, special issue on information systems for an aging society. *ACM Transactions on Human-Computer Interaction, 13*(3), 309–312.

Hiltz, S. R., Diaz, P., & Mark, G. (2011). Introduction: Social media and collaborative systems for crisis management. *ACM TOCHI, 18*(4).

Hiltz, S. R., Dufner, D., Holmes, M., & Poole, S. (1991). Distributed group support systems: Social dynamics and design dilemmas. *Journal of Organizational Computing, 2*(1), 135–159.

Hiltz, S. R., & Johnson, K. (1989). Measuring acceptance of computer- mediated communication systems. *Journal of the American Society for Information Science, 40*(6), 386–397.

Hiltz, S. R., & Johnson, K. (1990). User satisfaction with computer-mediated communication systems. *Management Science, 36*(6), 739–764.

Hiltz, S. R., Johnson, K., & Turoff, M. (1991). Group decision support: The effects of designated human leaders and statistical feedback in computerized conferences. *Journal of Management Information Systems, 8*(2), 81–108.

Hiltz, S. R., & Meinke, R. (1989). Teaching sociology in a virtual classroom. *Teaching Sociology, 17*, 431–446.

Hiltz, S. R., Shea, P., & Kim, E. (2007). Using focus groups to study ALN faculty motivation. *Journal of Asynchronous Learning Networks, 11*(1), 107–124.

Hiltz, S. R., & Turoff, M. (1981). The evolution of user behavior in a computerized conferencing system. *Communications of the ACM, 24*(11), 739–751.

Hiltz, S. R., & Turoff, M. (1985). Structuring computer-mediated communication systems to avoid information overload. *Communications of the ACM, 28*(7), 680–689.

Hiltz, S. R., & Turoff, M. (1991). Computer networking among executives: A case study. *Journal of Organizational Computing, 1*(4), 357–376.

Hiltz, S. R., & Turoff, M. (2002). What makes learning networks effective? *Communications of the ACM, 45*(2), 56–59.

Hiltz, S. R., Turoff, M., & Johnson, K. J. (1989). Experiments in group decision making: Disinhibition, deindividuation, and group process in pen name and real name computer conferences. *Decision Support Systems, 5*, 217–232.

Hiltz, S. R., Turoff, M., & Johnson, K. J. (1986). Experiments in group communication via computer: Face-to-face vs. computer conferences. *Human Communication Research, 13*(2), 225–252.

Hiltz, S. R., & Wellman, B. (1997, September). Asynchronous learning networks as virtual communities. *Communications of the ACM*, 44–49.

Jia, S., Hiltz, S. R., & Bieber, M. (2008a). Collaborative online examinations: Impacts on interaction, learning, and student satisfaction. *IEEE Transactions on Systems, Man and Cybernetics, 36*(6), 1045–1053. https://doi.org/10.1109/TSMCA.2006.883180

Jia, S., Hiltz, S. R., & Bieber, M. (2008b). Learning strategies in online collaborative examinations. *IEEE Transactions on Professional Communication, 51*(1), 63–78.

Kim, Y., Hiltz, S. R., & Turoff, M. (2002). Coordination structures and system restrictiveness in distributed group support systems. *Group Decision and Negotiation, 11*(5), 379–404.

Mayer, J., Jones, Q., & Hiltz, S. R. (2015). Identifying opportunities for valuable encounters: Towards context-aware social matching systems. *ACM TOIS, 34*(1).

Ocker, R. J., Fjermestad, J., Hiltz, S. R., & Johnson, K. (1998), Effects of four modes of group communication on the outcomes of software requirements determination. *Journal of Management Information Systems, 15*(1), 99–118.

Ocker, R. J., Hiltz, S. R., Turoff, M., & Fjermestad, J. (1996). The effects of distributed group support and process structuring on software requirements development teams: Results on creativity and quality. *Journal of Management Information Systems, 12*(3).

Ocker, R. J., Huang, H., Benbunan-Fich, R., & Hiltz, S. R. (2011). Leadership dynamics in partially distributed teams: An exploratory study of the effects of configuration and distance. *Group Decision and Negotiation, 20*(3), 273–292.

Ocker, R. J., Kracaw, D., Hiltz, S. R., & Rosson, M. B. (2009). Enhancing learning experiences in partially Distributed teams: Training students to work effectively across distances. *ACM Transactions on Computing Education, 1*(1).

Osatuyi, B., Hiltz, S. R., & Passerini, K. (2016). Seeing is believing (or at least changing your mind): The influence of visibility and task complexity on preference changes in computer-supported team decision making. *Journal of the Association for Information Science and Technology, 67*(9), 2090–2104.

Palen, L., Hiltz, S. R., & Liu, S. (2007). Citizen participation in emergency preparedness and response. *Communications of the ACM March*, 54–58.

Plotnick, L. L., & Hiltz, S. R. (2016). Barriers to use of social media by emergency managers. *Homeland Security & Emergency Management, 13*(2).

Plotnick, L. L., Hiltz, S. R., & Burns, M. (2013). You've been warned? Public perceptions of outdoor sirens and their alternatives for tornadoes. *IJISCRAM, 5*(3), 37–62.

Plotnick, L. L., Hiltz, S. R., & Privman, R. (2016). Ingroup dynamics and the effectiveness of partially distributed teams. *IEEE Transactions on Professional Communications, 59*(3), 203–229.

Plummer, M., Plotnick, L., Hiltz, S. R., & Jones, Q. (2008). A wiki that knows where it is being used: Insights from potential users. *The DATABASE for Advances in Information Systems 13, 39*(4), 13–30.

Privman, R., Hiltz, S. R., & Wang, Y. (2013). In-group (us) vs. out-group (them): Dynamics and effectiveness in partially distributed teams. *IEEE Transactions on Professional and Technical Communication, 56*(1), 33–48.

Saltz, J., Passerini, K., & Hiltz, S. R. (2007). Visualizing online interaction to increase participation in distance learning courses. *IEEE Internet Computing, 11*(3), 36–44.

Schultze, U., Hiltz, S. R., Nardi, B., Renneker, J., & Stuckey, S. (2008). Using synthetic worlds for work and learning. *Communications of the AIS, 22*, 351–370.

Shen, J., Bieber, M., & Hiltz, S. R. (2005). Participatory examinations in asynchronous learning networks: Longitudinal evaluation results. *Journal of Asynchronous Learning Networks, 9*(3), 93–113.

Swan, K., Shen, J., & Hiltz, S. R. (2006). Assessment and collaboration in online learning. *Journal of Asynchronous Learning Networks, 10*(1), 45–62.

Turoff, M., Chumer, M., Hiltz, S. R., Klashner, R., Alles, M., Vasarhelyi, M., & Kogan, A. (2004). Assuring homeland security: Continuous monitoring, control and assurance of emergency preparedness. *JITTA, 6*(3), 1–24 [Special issue].

Turoff, M., & Hiltz, S. R. (1982a). Computer support for group versus individual decisions. *IEEE Transactions on Communications, 30*(1), 82–90.

Turoff, M., & Hiltz, S. R. (1982b). The electronic journal: A progress report. *Journal of the American Society for Information Science, 33*(4), 195–202.

Turoff, M., & Hiltz, S. R. (1995). Software design and the future of the virtual classroom. *Journal of Information Technology for Teacher Education, 4*(2), 197–215.

Turoff, M., & Hiltz, S. R. (1998, July). Superconnectivity. *CACM*, 116.

Turoff, M., & Hiltz, S. R. (2005, October). Education goes digital: The evolution of online learning and the revolution in higher education. *Communications of the ACM*, 59–64.

Turoff, M., & Hiltz, S. R. (2008). Assessing the health information needs of the emergency preparedness and management community. *Journal of Information Services and Use, 28*, 269–280.

Turoff, M., Hiltz, S. R., Bahgat, A. N. F., & Rana, A. (1993, December). Distributed group support systems. *MIS Quarterly*, 399–417.

Turoff, M., Hiltz, S. R., Banuls-Silvera, V., & Van Den Eede, G. (2013). Multiple perspectives on planning for emergencies: An introduction to the special issue on planning and foresight for emergency preparedness and management. *Technological Forecasting and Social Change, 80*(9), 1647–1656.

Turoff, M., Hiltz, S. R., White, C., Plotnick, L., Hendela, A., & Yao, X. (2009). The past as the future of emergency preparedness and management. *International. Journal of Information Systems for Crisis Response and Management, 1*(1), 12–28.

Wellman, B., & Hiltz, S. R. (2004). Sociological Rob: How Rob Kling brought computing and sociology together [Invited paper]. *The Information Society, 20*(2), 91–95. https://doi.org/10.1080/01972240490422969

White, C., Plotnick, L., Hiltz, S. R., & Turoff, M. (2009). An online social network for emergency management. *International Journal of Emergency Management, 6*(3/4), 369–382.

Wu, D., & Hiltz, S. R. (2004). Predicting learning from asynchronous online discussions. *Journal of Asynchronous Learning Networks, 8*(2), 139–152.

Wu, D., Hiltz, S. R., & Bieber, M. (2010). Acceptance of educational technology: Field studies of asynchronous participatory examinations. *Communications of the Association for Information Systems (CAIS), 26*.

17
JUNG, INSUNG

Photo of Insung Jung contributed by Insung Jung

Another challenge is that when I talk with younger scholars or scholars from other disciplines who have been involved in MOOCs or OER, they don't seem to understand the base or root of ODL.

Dr. Insung Jung is a Korean researcher with an impressive publication record and international presence.

Dr. Jung completed her Bachelor and Master's degrees in Education at Seoul National University, Korea, in 1982 and 1984, respectively. She went on to study at Indiana University, Bloomington, United States, and graduated with a PhD in Instructional Systems Technology in 1988. Her dissertation was entitled *Development and Testing of Motivational and Instructional Devices (MIDs) for Instructional Text Development*.

Jung has been a Professor in the Department of Education and Language Education at the International Christian University (ICU) in Tokyo, Japan since 2003. She has also held many administrative positions, the most current being Chair (2016–2018) of the Department of Education/Language Education, ICU, as well as Director (2013–2014) of the Institute of Education Research and Service (IERS), ICU.

Dr. Jung is a reviewer for many international journals and sits on several boards of educational and technical journals and/or organizations. She is the Series Editor (2016–present) for *SpringerBriefs in Open and Distance Education*; an Editorial Board Member (2016–present) for the *International Journal of Educational Technology in Higher Education* (Springer); a Scientific Editorial Board Member (2013–2015) with the *Universities and Knowledge Society Journal* (RUSC), Spain; a Board Advisor (2012–present) for the International Board of Standards for Training, Performance and Instruction (www.ibstpi.org; USA/Global); and Co-editor in Chief (2007–present) for the *International Journal for Educational Media and Technology, Japan Association for Educational Media Studies*, and *Korean Association for Educational Information and Media*.

Her extensive list of publications, listed at the end of this chapter, represent her varied interests in online learning from supporting students to online design and quality assurance. Her more recent work focuses on new technologies and open practices, such as open educational resources (OER) and massive open online courses (MOOCs) and how they might enhance online learning.

Interview

Transcript Analysis Summary

Analysis of all interviews included in this volume led to the identification of 3,545 units of data. The mean of these collective units was 118 per pioneer, the median was 118.5, and the mode was 132. Individual interview units ranged from 59 to 217 units, yielding a spread of 158 units between all interviews. Insung Jung's interview generated 109 units, placing her interview in the lower end of the middle third of all interviews in terms of unit numbers. This is remarkable, given that Jung used a foreign language, English, to participate in the interview process.

A comparision of Jung's interview to the interviews of all pioneers indicated that her interview profile was, generally speaking, unique to that of the average interview profile (Figure 17.1). Her

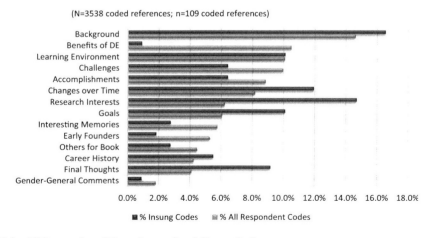

Figure 17.1 All Respondents' Versus Insung Jung's Parent Codes

interview produced a similar number of units to the average interview in the areas of background, learning environment, and career history. Her interview contained more than the average number of units in the areas of changes over time, research interests, goals, and final thoughts. Many of these units could be understood within the context of Jung's passion for research.

Insung Jung's interview also generated fewer than average units in the following areas: benefits of DE, challenges, accomplishments, interesting memories, and others for the book. The low number of units in these areas could, in part, be explained by the fact that Jung left the field in 2000 so that she might have more time to focus on research interests. The lack of benefits of DE units would also be because no interview question asked about the benefits of DE; this topic arose organically from the data analysis process.

Link to recorded interview: tinyurl.com/Jung-I-2019

Transcript of Interview

Full Name: Insung Jung
Institutional Affiliation: Professor, International Christian University, Tokyo, Japan
Key:

Regular font = Interviewee comments
Italicized font = Interviewer comments

Interview Questions

1. *What was your educational and experiential background before you became involved in online distance learning [ODL]?*

I would like to begin with my undergraduate experience. I majored in education at the Seoul National University [SNU] in Korea. In the programme, I gained the knowledge and skills needed to tackle various issues in K–12, higher education, and adult learning and participated in teaching practice in a high school context. After graduation, I went to the United States to study educational technology. Our department name was Instructional Systems Technology at the Indiana University of Bloomington [USA]. I studied there from 1984 to 1988. After that, I came back to Korea and was hired as a Senior Researcher first, and then later I became a Professor at the Korea National Open University [KNOU], which is a dedicated open and distance teaching university. I worked there for over ten years, and it was during this time that I really devoted myself to open and distance learning [ODL].

In 2000, I was invited to serve as the Director of the Multimedia Education Institute as well as an Associate Professor at the Department of Educational Technology by Ewha Womans University which, I believe, is the largest women's university in the world. Over 30,000 female students study there. The institute was later renamed as the Institute for Teaching and Learning. They tried to make online courses for female leaders around the world as well as their own students. After working there for three years, I became really interested in resuming my research, which was almost impossible in the busy Ewha Womans University work environment. Because of that, I felt lucky to be given the opportunity to come to Japan and join the International Christian University [ICU].

Japan is one of the closest countries to Korea geographically, but I think emotionally, it is farthest from a Korean's perspective. But the working environment there [International Christian University] is very peaceful and quiet. It is a small liberal arts college. ICU emphasizes teaching, although I have ample time to do international research with international scholars. At ICU, I have worked closely with many scholars with an ODL background, as well as scholars from liberal arts colleges. It's been more than 15 years at ICU, and I am still working there today.

2. *In what year did you begin to look specifically into ODL?*

I would say it was about 1985 or 1986 when I began to think about my doctoral dissertation topic. At that time, ODL was not really mainstream, especially when I think about the Korean situation. It was far from the mainstream education and was considered as second-rate education. As [Charles] Wedemeyer said, it was definitely a back-door education at that time.

I was interested in the self-directed study of adult learners who were learning at a distance, so my dissertation was on instruction and motivational design for distance learners.

3. *What were the circumstances in your world that initiated this interest in ODL?*

It was when I went back to Korea. As you may know, the education fever in Korea is very high. People who couldn't finish their higher education wanted to continue to study after work. To meet this need, several night schools were established at the traditional universities, and the Korean National University was founded in 1972 by the Korean government.

My interest was in how we could support distance learners in self-directed study. In the early 1990s, the textbook used at KNOU was very similar to any regular textbook used by traditional university students. It wasn't designed for the self-directed learners. It was full of text without any workbook integration and scaffolding strategies. Considering that the textbook was the primary medium for distance learning at that time, I mostly wanted to improve KNOU textbooks by integrating effective self-directed learning and motivational strategies into the textbook design. I think that was the motivation for why I wanted to begin my career as a scholar in ODL – to develop the textbook combining content, case studies, scaffolding advice, self-learning and evaluating activities, and worksheets. I wanted to improve the textbook for the distance learners.

4. *Which female researchers or female colleagues may have piqued your interest in ODL?*

I'm not sure if you are familiar with or know Robin Mason. She passed away in 2008 or 2009. I think she began her career in the UK [United Kingdom] at almost the same time as I began my career in Korea. We met on several occasions and several conferences. We talked about our study areas and several issues. I think she was the one who motivated me to do really serious research in ODL

Another person is Debra Perry. She is not in the field of ODL, but she was interested in non-formal education through museum design. She designed museums in a way so that people could fully interact with exhibitions. So I thought those principles could be integrated into ODL. She is the one who motivated me to look for non-formal education settings, not just formal education settings.

Another person who gave me the opportunity to move not just within open and distance education institutions, but also to look at how conventional universities could integrate ODL as well was the president of the Ewha Womans University at the time. Her name is Sang Jang. She was the first female scholar nominated for the position of the prime minister (PM), but unfortunately, she could not be appointed as the PM due to some personal matters. She was the one who believed in me to expand online education and integrate online education within the conventional university. When I was the Director of the Multimedia Education Institute there, the Institute was given full support to create a virtual campus for Ewha Womans University students, online certification programmes for women in the business and e-learning fields, and online courses on Korean studies for those students who were studying abroad. I think the president, Sang Jang, was the person who gave me the opportunity to actually experiment with various things in online learning.

5. *Who would you identify as the early female leaders/founders in the field of ODL?*

I think Robin Mason is one of them, as well as Betty Collis. Betty used to work at the University of Twente in the Netherlands. She is now an emeritus professor of the University of Twente. She published a book on tele-learning in a digital world. She also talked about flexible learning. I worked with her on one or two chapter publications.

Another person who is still active is Lani Gunawardena. Lani is another person who has been influential in my career. I worked with her on an edited book on culture and online learning. She is an expert on collaborative learning and culture in ODL.

Those three people come to my mind now.

6. *What are some of the goals that you strove to achieve in the field of ODL?*

From the early 1990s until 2000, for about a decade when I was working at the Korean National Open University, I tried to be involved in national policy making. This is because at that time, even if a KNOU student graduated with a four-year bachelor's degree, it wasn't really accepted as equal to a four-year degree earned from a traditional university. So they were at a disadvantage when going to a graduate school because that was considered to be a two-year education at the beginning. Even for promotion, the degree that they earned at the KNOU was not accepted. That's why I became interested in nondiscrimination policy. This was not a big movement, but I formed a group of people who were working in the government, in our school, and in other fields and worked together to improve the national policy on ODL. Finally, we were able to see no policy discrimination between distance learning and traditional learning, at least in the public sectors. In the public sectors, the KNOU degree was considered as the same full degree as the ones from the conventional universities.

After that, I was interested in quality assurance because one of the reasons for why people's distance education degrees were not fully valued was related to quality assurance. The KNOU was not evaluated and accredited through the same agency as conventional universities; they had a different track. Even though they may have a different track for accreditation, they should have the same kind or level of vigorousness as a four-year college. For this reason, I was actively involved in quality assurance in distance education in collaboration with other ODL scholars from different parts of the world and UNESCO offices in Bangkok and Paris.

One of the main points in quality assurance was integrating knowledge that we accumulated in instructional design. Instructional design was one of the most important topics that I tried to research and also develop the skills for open and distance teachers to create materials.

After I moved to the Ewha Womans University in 2000, I tried to integrate online and distance learning in the conventional university. At that time, ODL was not popular. These days, almost all universities have an online component, but at that time, it was not the case. So one main goal at Ewha was to explore and experiment various ways to blend ODL with face-to-face education.

I found online education to be a great way to continue lifelong learning, learning about topics in various areas, especially for women. Women tend to have more roles to play in a traditional society compared with men. Oftentimes, they don't have time to grow, to learn new stuff for themselves. At Ewha, I became interested in ODL for women, especially working moms and the women in business sectors as the business sector is more difficult for women time-wise compared to teaching in university.

But then since I came to ICU in Japan in 2003, I have developed interest in instructional design, individual factors and cultural factors that affect adoption of ODL, and various technologies in traditional higher education. My research interest in cultural factors affecting online education is related to the fact that our university is very international. We have students from many different countries. They seem to have different understandings of online discussion. When I integrate online discussion in my face-to-face classes, some students enjoy talking online, and they are not afraid of sharing their opinions, while other students really hate participating online. That is not just individual differences. There are, in fact, cultural variances. Most of the Japanese students do not seem to enjoy online discussion, whereas students from Western cultures enjoy it. So that was the time that I began to be interested in cultural aspects.

Recently, I am more interested in open educational resources [OER] and MOOCs [massive open online courses] because I go with their philosophy of openness in education. Another topic that I am interested in is ODL theories that are theoretical foundations of empirical ODL research. As you may know, our field has several theories, but compared to other fields, we still need more theories and new theories which could explain recent technology developments and pedagogical changes in ODL. Theories are very important for meaningful research so that we do not repeat the same research again and again, but instead create new research with meaningful questions from new theoretical paradigms. That is why I have been revisiting foundational ODL theories and exploring new ODL theories for the digital era with other ODL scholars from different regions. The result of this effort will be published as a book in 2019 by Springer.

7. *What are some of your accomplishments in the field of ODL that you would like to share?*

This is a difficult question. First, among several books that I published and edited, I would like to share two books on quality assurance specifically. One is on quality assurance in distance education and e-learning in a global context. It talks about models, policies, and research on quality assurance in ODL. It was published in 2011, but much of the content still explains ODL these days. Another book on quality assurance focuses on Asia. It specifically looks into the problems of quality assurance, or accomplishments of quality assurance, in distance education and e-learning in an Asian context. These two books are the ones I would like to share with your audience.

Another book is on culture. To my knowledge, this is one of the few books on culture in online learning. Lani [Gunawardena] and I worked together on this book. We talk about various aspects of culture in online learning and how culture, new culture, is created in online learning. It is a very interesting topic and gives useful ideas for research related to culture and online learning.

Another accomplishment is that I created a model of online learning, called the Model of Extended Teaching and Learning Spaces. When we look at online learning, we know that our teaching and learning spaces are extended, so I focus on extended teaching and learning spaces and how this concept can be applied in various types of online learning. I introduced the model in the BJET [*British Journal of Educational Technology*]. I focused on spaces mostly, but time is another factor that I would like to integrate into this model. This model of online learning could be one of my accomplishments in the field.

I also created a SpringerBrief series on open and distance education in 2016. Routledge, a well-known publishing company in the field of ODL, has had a series in ODL for many decades. They have published many excellent books in this field, but it is hard for young researchers or scholars from different fields, non-English-speaking countries especially, to have their books published with Routledge. Quantity-wise, it is overwhelming for people who want to write a book for the first time or need to have a book published rather quickly. That's why I created a series of briefs with Springer. These briefs are half or a little over half of a regular book in the number of pages. It is an academic book, but it can be published much more quickly. It has been two years since my series was created and Olaf [Zawacki-Richter], a leading scholar from the University of Oldenburg of Germany, is working with me as the co-editor of this series. Volume-wise, it is shorter. Time-wise, it can take less time than a regular book. But quality-wise, I would say it is very high. We already published four books.

The first one is about ODL in non-formal education by Colin Latchem, who used to be a co-editor for this series and my closest friend and colleague. The second one is on MOOCs, published by Allison Littlejohn from OUUK with a young scholar, Nina Hood, from the University of Auckland. Another two are by Olaf Zawacki-Richter, Adnan Qayyum from Penn State University of the United States, and many other prominent ODL leaders. We are going to have three more books on ODL theories, AI in open education, and OER in the next two years.

8. *What are some of the challenges that you faced in the field of ODL over the years?*

The first challenge was that ODL was a marginalized field in the 1980s and 1990s. Even when I was studying at Indiana University, my advisor advised me not to put "distance education" in the title of my dissertation. I was quite shocked. He said that distance education was not a well-established field (or something like that). He valued open and distance education, but he said it was not good for my dissertation title, and I could hide it inside. It was kind of a bias that people had when I studied distance education. They would ask, "Why do you want to study distance education? Why not study instructional design?"

Yes, I studied instructional design, but it was instructional design for distance education. It was quite a difficult situation, even when I came back to Korea. There were no colleagues who studied or were really interested in distance education. But thanks to the Internet and thanks to the online technologies, now many people are studying e-learning and online education. I now have many colleagues who are studying the field.

Another challenge is that when I talk with younger scholars or scholars from other disciplines who have been involved in MOOCs or OER, they don't seem to understand the base or root of ODL. They think MOOCs and online education are totally new. As you know, distance education has a long history. During this time, there have been many kinds of research on why people drop out, why people do not accept that type of technology, why learners have a difficult time in keeping their motivation while they are studying in distance education, etc. Those kinds of topics have already been studied. But when I look at recent papers, authors do not seem to understand such knowledge base in ODL. I think they focus mainly on reading about recent online education and ignore what has been researched in older media-based distance education. It was kind of a challenge for me to share some of the traditional, well-established knowledge in our field.

9. *What was the "state of DE" when you first entered the field as opposed to ODL in 2019?*

When I began my career in ODL, it was a marginalized area. Not many researchers from educational technologies or other fields were interested in distance education studies. But now there are more researchers from different fields, like computer science, who are studying open and distance learning, which is very promising because we can have different and fresh views in studying ODL.

I observe changes in research topics. When I first entered the field, even though there were not many researchers in the field, the research topics were quite diverse, like the adoption issues and learner support – how we could support learners who could not follow the open and distance learning pace. Course effectiveness was another topic and, of course, course development – textbook design, workbook design, TV programmes, radio, and all different types of media were all major research topics. When I attended conferences, participants would share knowledge around these areas. But these days, the topic seems to focus mainly on micro-level design issues in online education or advanced technology-supported learning settings. Of course, in the developed world, online is the most common form of ODL, but in developing countries and less developed parts of the world, videos and textbooks are still the major media of ODL. We don't see any serious research on these topics. It has just stopped. Even those scholars from developing countries talk about high technologies, like virtual reality and all of those latest technologies in ODL. They are experimenting with those technologies, but the main one is still textbooks, and open and distance learners are still suffering. They are not very successful in terms of completing the courses. Maybe today's distance learners have different types of learning difficulties. Those topics are not seriously researched these days. Fortunately, I see some changes in ODL research topics, as well as positive changes in the status of ODL, which is very promising.

10. *What interesting memories would you like to share about the beginning of ODL?*

When I was working at the KNOU, I was able to attend various international conferences, like AAOU [Asian Association of Open Universities] or ICDE [International Council of Distance Education] conferences. I met various people there from the developing countries who were trying to build or establish open universities.

I have a very interesting story from one of those international conferences. Bangladesh Open University was founded in 1992, I think. The Bangladesh academics mainly from traditional universities came to a conference in the early 1990s, around the time their university was established. Someone made a presentation on open universities in different countries. One of the audience members raised his hand and asked, "What is the feature of an open university?" And then he shared his understanding. He said, "Is it that the main gate of the university is open? Are the doors open, or are there no doors? Or is there no roof?" He was very serious. He was thinking of physical differences on campus. For him, an open university shouldn't have any doors or a gate, maybe no roof. Maybe because the weather in Bangladesh is very hot; I don't know.

I thought that was a very interesting understanding: a physically open structure. That was his point. The concept of an open university was not very clear in the beginning for those people who did not have an understanding or had not heard of openness in education.

11. *What were your specific ODL research interests, and have they changed/evolved over the years?*

At the beginning of my career, I was interested in instructional and motivational design in developing a course, with the course referring to TV programmes, radio programmes, and textbooks for open and distance education.

And then I saw some of the problems with learner support and interaction. Even if you design a course in such a way that it helps the learner to be motivated and be able to, step by step, complete one chapter at a time, there are still problems with helping students understand and with learner motivation, so learner support was a very important part of open and distance education. It still is, but in the early-mid-1990s, when there was no online communication or instant communication by mobile devices, it was a more serious problem. How can you promote interaction between learner and instructor and among learners? Learner-to-learner interactions were more difficult when there were no online discussion spaces or no network. That's why I became interested in interaction. After that, I became involved in quality assurance and policy issues. And then, in the mid-2000s, my focus shifted to cultural differences: how culture plays a role, and what kind of new online culture has emerged. Now I am interested in openness in education. The concept of openness has changed, from open access to open choice. Now we are talking more about open content through sharing the content or using OER and MOOCs. The concept of openness in education and theory-building, based on my experience, are very challenging yet exciting tasks for me now.

12. *Could you please describe the learning environment that you currently work in or have most recently worked in (e.g., geographic and institutional setting, student demographics)?*

I mentioned briefly that I am now working at ICU, a liberal arts college in Tokyo. It is a very beautiful and small campus with about 2,800 undergraduates, 200 graduate students, and over 150 faculty members. Some of the faculty members live on campus. It is a typical liberal arts environment. We don't have any fully online courses, but since I moved to this university, I have been asked to give some workshops for faculty members and help the Centre for Teaching and Learning to integrate technology into our courses. Many of our courses are blended. But the purpose for using technology for blending is a little bit different than open and distance education. It is to use IT [information technology] for critical thinking, creativity, and collaborative learning, or how to promote liberal arts values using technology, whereas maybe in ODL, we are more interested in access. Widening access is one of the very critical elements of ODL. And, of course, distance teaching institutions also like to promote critical, creative, and interactive education. ICU does not want to transition to a fully online environment, but, interestingly, these days, we are talking about integrating some of the online courses for the teachers' in-service training programme, a master's programme. So I think we may see some of those online courses in the not-too-distant future.

We have many young students – 17, 18, 19 years old – but there [are] some adult learners who are studying as well. Around half of them are Japanese students, and the other half are from different countries, so it is very international. ICU is actively involved in Japanese open courseware to share its courses with [those] other than ICU students. It is also developing some OER. But unlike big universities, ICU doesn't have many resources, so I guess the development of OER and open courseware focuses only on a few selected courses, not at the whole university level.

13. *Is there anything else you [would] like to address?*

I think that it is very important for young researchers in ODL to read some of the books published in our open and distance education series, the Routledge and SpringerBrief series, because they cover important topics in this area. You can see how history in ODL research and practice has changed over the years.

Another source for deeper understanding and inspiration would be *IRRODL* [*International Review of Research on Open and Distributed Learning*]; it is a very high-quality journal. It is important to not simply pick the topic that you are interested in, but also to develop a knowledge base or root understanding of that topic as well. A root understanding will help you to broaden your perspective in your research field. Like if you are interested in how to integrate a collaborative learning aspect in an online course, it doesn't have to be a distance online course. Even in the old days when there was no online component, we were talking about collaboration, student interactions. So you may want to go back to not just recent technologies, but the old, lower-technology theories and research findings.

Another suggestion for younger generations is to remember that open and distance education can make you very busy. When I was working at the Korean National Open University and the Ewha Womans University and developing and offering online courses, I was really busy every day. Everybody wanted me to come, and I was a committee member of government and institutional organizations, so there was no time to really think seriously about issues or problems or gaps in open and distance learning. You could easily become a busy practitioner. Time-wise, you don't have time to sit down, reflect on your practice, and then do the research. You really have to make time for research. The social demand for ODL has been always very high and will be even higher as we live in a lifelong learning society. Maybe because of that, ODL scholars do not have time to create many theories. We have a few of our own theories, but many of them are borrowed from other fields. I would say that the next generation of researchers really needs to make time to do research and separate themselves from their busy practice. Yes, you are involved in ODL practice, but you have to train yourself to separate yourself from the practice and try to see the practice as a third person. Otherwise, you tend to advocate and justify and not criticize.

Working at a liberal arts college, I have the disadvantage of not teaching fully open and distance courses, but because I am not directly involved in ODL practices, that gives me the advantage of being more objective. I can have a more critical mind looking at ODL development and OER and MOOCs. When you create and teach an open and distance course, it would be difficult to do critical research on your own course. Of course, you can do it. But at least you should be able to separate yourself from the practice. Does that make sense?

14. *Can you suggest names of other female pioneers in distance education or ODL that you think we should include in the book?*

Do you know Tian Belawati? She was the president of the Indonesian Open University and elected as the president of the ICDE. She was also involved in a quality-assurance project with me for many years. She didn't have time to do research while she was in office, but she contributed to the development of a quality-assurance system in Asia and beyond. She edited a book with Jon Baggaley and another book with me. I will send you her email.

Another person is Zoraini Wati Abas. She is now the vice president or the vice rector of the Wawasan Open University, a private open university in Malaysia. She used to be a professor at the Open University of Malaysia.

What about a female scholar from Israel? Gila Kurtz is the one who has been involved in ODL research. She presented many papers in several ODL conferences, including the European distance education conferences, so I will send her email as well.

Publications

Books

Beaudoin, M., Kurtz, G., Jung, I. S., Suzuki, K., & Grabowski, B. (2013). *Online learner competencies: Knowledge, skills and attitudes for successful learning in online and blended settings (The ibstpi series)*. Information Age Publishing.

Jung, I. S. (1991). *Practical instructional methods*. Educational Science Publications.

Jung, I. S. (1996). *Videoconferencing*. Park Young Rul Publications.

Jung, I. S. (1999). *Understanding distance education*. Educational Science Publications.

Jung, I. S. (Ed.). (2019). *Open and distance theory revisited: Implications for the digital era*. Springer.

Jung, I. S., & Choi, S. H. (2002). *Effective learning strategies for adult learners in a knowledge society*. Educational Science Publications.

Jung, I. S., & Gunawardena, C. L. (Eds.). (2014). *Culture and online learning: Global perspectives and research*. Stylus.

Jung, I. S., Kubota, K., Rha, I., & Terashita, T. (2006). *Distance education and e-learning*. Kitaoji Press (In Japanese).

Jung, I. S., Kubota, K., & Suzuki, K. (2008). *OPTIMAL instructional design model for e-learning/blended learning*. Tokyo Electronics University Press (In Japanese).

Jung, I. S., & Latchem, C. (Eds.). (2011). *Quality assurance and accreditation in distance education and e-learning: models, policies and research*. Routledge.

Jung, I. S., & Rha, I. (1989). *Current instructional design theories*. Educational Science Publications.

Jung, I. S., & Rha, I. (1992). *Current instructional design theories* (2nd ed.). Educational Science Publications.

Jung, I. S., & Rha, I. (2004). *Distance education*. Educational Science Publications.

Jung, I. S., et al. (1997). *Education in an information age*. Park Young Ryul Publication.

Jung, I. S., Nishimura, M., & Sasao, T. (Eds.). (2016). *Liberal arts education and colleges in East Asia: Possibilities and challenges in the global age*. Springer.

Jung, I. S., Wong, T. M., & Belawati, T. (Eds.). (2012). *Quality assurance in distance education and e-learning: Challenges and solutions from Asia*. Sage Publications.

Kim, J. W., & Jung, I. S. (2002). *Implementing distance education*. Korea National Open University Press.

Kim, Y. L., & Jung, I. S. (1994). *Development of multimedia package for distance learning*. Educational Science Publications.

Latchem, C., & Jung, I. S. (2009). *Distance and blended learning in Asia*. Routledge.

Park, S. I., Rha, I., Jung, I. S., Kang, M. H., & Kim, D. S. (1997). *Software design theories*. Korea National Open University Press.

Rha, I., & Jung, I. S. (1990). *Development and use of CAI*. Educational Science Publications.

Rha, I., & Jung, I. S. (1996) *Educational technology*. Educational Science Publications.

Book Chapters

Collis, B., & Jung, I. S. (2003). Uses of information and communication technologies in teacher education. In B. Robinson & C. Latchem (Eds.), *Teacher education through open and distance learning* (pp. 171–191). RoutledgeFalmer.

Jung, I. (2015). MOOCs pedagogy: Critical analysis and future models. In I. Rha (Ed.), *Massive open online courses (MOOCs) in the age of global learning* (pp. 47–73). Hakjisa.

Jung, I. (2016). Insung's voice: Great people, boundless opportunities, and meaningful changes. In A. Donaldson (Ed.), *Women's voices in the field of educational technology* (pp. 87–92). Springer.

Jung, I. S. (1997a). Information society and institutionalization of lifelong education. In Christian Academy (Ed.), *Information society, choice of education*. Daehwa Press.

Jung, I. S. (1997b). New information technology and education. In Y. S. Kim, M. H. Kang, & J. S. Jung (Eds.), *Theory and practice in educational technology toward 21st century* (pp. 143–158). Educational Science Publications.

Jung, I. S. (1999a). Design models of web-based instruction. In I. Rha (Ed.), *Web-based education*. Educational Science Publications.

Jung, I. S. (1999b). Virtual education in Korea. In G. M. Farrell (Ed.), *The development of virtual education: A global perspective*. The Commonwealth of Learning.

Jung, I. S. (2000). *An annotated bibliography on Internet-based learning environment*. Online monograph. American Center for the Study of Distance Education, Penn State University.

Jung, I. S. (2001). Open and distance education in Korea. In O. Jegede & G. Shive (Eds.), *Open and distance education in Asia Pacific region* (pp. 103–130). Open University of Hong Kong Press.

Jung, I. S. (2003a). Cost-effectiveness of online education. In M. G. Moore & W. G. Anderson (Eds.), *Handbook of distance education* (pp. 717–726). Lawrence Erlbaum Associates, Publishers.

Jung, I. S. (2003b). Cost-effectiveness of web-based corporate training. In I. Rha, C. Lim, & I. Lee (Eds.), *Foundations of corporate education* (pp. 369–390). Educational Science Publications.

Jung, I. S. (2005a). *Innovative and good practices in open and distance learning in the Asia-Pacific region*. A report of the study commissioned by UNESCO, Bangkok.

Jung, I. S. (2005b). Quality assurance survey of mega universities. In C. McIntosh (Ed.), *Perspectives on distance education: Lifelong learning and distance higher education*, (pp. 79–96). Commonwealth of Learning & Paris: UNESCO.

Jung, I. S. (2008a). Costing virtual university education. In W. J. Bramble & S. Panda (Eds.), *Economics of distance and online learning: Theory, practice and research* (pp. 148–161). Routledge.

Jung, I. S. (2008b). Quality assurance and continuous quality improvement in distance education. In T. Evans, M. Haughey, & D. Murphy (Eds.), *International handbook of distance education* (pp. 609–624). Emerald Group Publishing Limited.

Jung, I. S., & Sasaki, T. (2004). *A report on teacher training system and ICT integration in China, Indonesia and Korea*. 1st year COE report.

Jung, I. S., & Sasaki, T. (2005). *E-moderating strategies and their effects on interaction*. A report of the study supported by Matshushita AV Education Foundation Research Fund.

Jung, I. S., & Suzuki, K. (2006). Blended learning in Japan and its application in liberal arts education. In C. Bonk & C. Graham (Eds.), *The handbook of blended learning environments: Global perspectives, local designs* (pp. 267–280). Jossey-Bass/Pfeiffer, A Wiley Company.

Jung, I. S., Kim, J. W., & Kim, D. W. (2002). *Criteria for the establishment of a distance graduate school within a conventional university context*. A policy report supported by Ministry of Education and Human Resource Development, Korea.

Jung, I. S., Kudo, M., & Choi, S. (2015). Towards effective and less stressful online collaborative learning: Strategies to promote engagement while minimizing unnecessary cognitive load and stress. In B. H. Khan & M. Ally (Eds.), *International handbook of e-learning* (Vol. 1). Routledge.

Jung, I. S., Sanderson, S., & Fajardo, J. C. (2018). The core curriculum: An analysis of liberal arts colleges in Asia, North America and Europe. In M. Nishimura & T. Sasao (Eds.), *Doing liberal arts education: Global case studies* (pp. 7–19). Springer.

Jung, I. S., e al. (2003). *E-learning white paper*. (Future directions in e-learning development). Ministry of Commerce, Industry, and Energy & Korea Cyber-Education Association.

Kawashima, T., et al. (2008). *A study on Korea's university entrance examination system and the relationship between the Common Test (CSAT) results and academic performance in the university*. Report: Supported by Japanese Ministry of Education (In Japanese).

Latchem, C., & Jung, I. S. (2011). The blind men and the elephant: Differing realities of flexibility in Asian higher education. In E. Burge, C. C. Gibson, & T. Gibson (Eds.), *Flexible pedagogy, flexible practice: Notes from the trenches of distance education*. Athabasca University Press.

Littlejohn, A., Jung, I. S., & Broumley, L. (2003). A comparison of issues in reuse of resources in schools and colleges. In A. Littlejohn (Ed.), *Reusing resources for networked learning*. Routledge.

Park, J. H., & Jung, I. S. (1997). Production and utilization of teaching-learning materials. In *Theories and teaching methods of open education* (pp. 521–548). KNOU Institute of Lifelong Education.

Suzuki, K., & Jung, I. S. (2011). Instructional design and technology in an Asian context: Focusing on Japan and Korea. In R. A. Reiser & J. V. Dempsey (Eds.), *Trends and issues in instructional design and technology*. Allyn & Bacon.

Journal Articles

Anzai, Y., & Jung, I. S. (2011). Exploring potentials of a wiki in English writing. *Educational Media Studies*, *17*(1), 23–36.

Bozkurt, A., Jung, I. S., et al. (2020). A global outlook to the interruption of education due to COVID-19 pandemic: Navigating in a time of uncertainty and crisis. *Asian Journal of Distance Education*, *15*(1), 1–126. www.asianjde.org/ojs/index.php/AsianJDE/article/view/462

Choi, H. S., Lee, Y., Jung, I. S., & Latchem, C. (2013). The extent of and reasons for non-re-enrolment at the Korea National Open University. *The International Review of Research in Open and Distance Learning*, *14*(4). www.irrodl.org/index.php/irrodl/article/view/1314/2624

Duggan, J. M., Fajardo, J. C. C., Figueroa Jr., R., Yassin, E., Dawson, W., & Jung, I. S. (2021). K-12 education responses to COVID-19: A comparison of five countries. *International Journal for Educational Media and Technology*, *15*(1). https://jaems.jp/ojs/index.php/ijemt/article/view/330

Figueroa Jr., R. B., Fajardo, J. C., Tan, S., & Jung, I. S. (2020). Developing and evaluating a website as an OER for faculty development. *International Journal of Open and Distance e-Learning*, *6*(1). http://ijodel.com/wp-content/uploads/2020/07/002_Figueroa_et_al.pdf

Garcia, G., & Jung, I. S. (2020). Understanding immersion in 2D platform-based online collaborative learning environments. *Australian Journal of Educational Technology*, *37*(1). https://doi.org/10.14742/ajet.6106

Han, E. J., & Jung, I. S. (2002). Barriers to students' participation in web-based Instruction (WBI) and differences in barriers according to level of students' prior experience with WBI: A factor-analytic study. *Journal of Korean Association of Educational Information and Broadcasting*, *8*(4), 119–142.

Hong, S., & Jung, I. S. (2011). The distance learner competencies: A three-phased empirical approach. *Educational Technology Research and Development*, *59*(1), 21–42.

Hwang, D. J., Kim, J. W., Jung, I. S., & Bang, M. S. (1997). *A study on the design of virtual university for the 21st century*. Ministry of Education in Korea Policy Paper.

Jung, I. S. (1991). A study on the development of CAL for distance education. *Journal of Educational Technology*, *7*(1).

Jung, I. S. (1992). Introducing computer-assisted instruction to distance education. *Journal of Distance Education*, *6*(1), 55–128.

Jung, I. S. (1993a). Adult learning methods in the future. *Journal of Adult Learning*, *18*.

Jung, I. S. (1993b). Constructivistic courseware design for ill structured knowledge acquisition. *KACU Journal*, *16*, 655–674.

Jung, I. S. (1993c). Educational TV chart development and computer. *Journal of Distance Education*, *7*(3), 135–172.

Jung, I. S. (1993d). Improving the economics of budget allocation in distance education. *KACU Journal*, *17*, 561–573.

Jung, I. S. (1994). Use of computer-mediated communication system in higher distance education. *Korean Journal of Educational Technology*, *9*(1), 131–145.

Jung, I. S. (1995a). Analysis of cognitive-social factors in designing computer network. *Korean Journal of Educational Technology*, *11*(2), 219–233.

Jung, I. S. (1995b). Conceptual development of a dialectic curriculum model for non-formal education. *KNOU Journal*, *20*. Korea National Open University.

Jung, I. S. (1996a). Analysis of educational effects of computer-mediated communication system in an open and distance learning environment. *Korean Journal of Distance Education*, *9*, 5–36.

Jung, I. S. (1996b). Computer network and distance education. *Korean Journal of Educational Broadcasting*, *1*(2), 153–171.

Jung, I. S. (1997a). Development of a model for online virtual university from a constructivistic view. *Korean Journal of Educational Technology*, *13*(2), 315–338.

Jung, I. S. (1997b). *Instructional use of Internet*. KNOU Manual for Staff Development.

Jung, I. S. (1998a). Educational functions of internet. *Korean Journal of Distance Education*, *11*, 161–184.

Jung, I. S. (1998b). Virtual university and change in distance teaching universities. *KNOU Journal*, *25*, 777–796.

Jung, I. S. (1999). A strategic design for introducing distance education at the primary and secondary school level. *Korean Journal of Educational Technology*, *15*(1), 355–373.

Jung, I. S. (2000a). Internet-based distance education: Annotated bibliography. *Educational Technology International*, *2*(1), 139–171.

Jung, I. S. (2000b). Korea's experiments with virtual education. *Technical Notes Series*, *5*(2). World Bank.

Jung, I. S. (2000c). *Singapore's approach to preparing new teachers to use technology in the classroom*. Teacher Training and Technology Series, World Bank.

Jung, I. S. (2000d). Technology innovations and the development of distance education. *Open Learning*, *15*(3), 217–231.

Jung, I. S. (2001a). Building a theoretical framework of web-based instruction. *British Journal of Educational Technology*, *32*(5), 531–540.

Jung, I. S. (2001b). Issues and challenges of providing online In-service teacher training: Korea's experience. *International Review of Research in Open and Distance Learning*, *2*(1).

Jung, I. S. (2001c). Policy formulation and implementation in the use of information technology for distance education: A case of Korea. *Journal of Communications of the Korea Information Science Society*, *19*(9), 12–21.

Jung, I. S. (2002a). Development and management of ICT training program with reference to Korea. *Journal of APEC Studies, 4*(1), 39–56.

Jung, I. S. (2002b). Exploring success factors of virtual education at the tertiary level based on the analysis of experiences in virtual education worldwide. *Korean Journal of Educational Technology, 18*(1), 215–234.

Jung, I. S. (2002c, April–June). Virtual education at the tertiary level. *TechKnowLogia,* 26–30.

Jung, I. S. (2003a). A comparative study on the cost-effectiveness of three approaches to ICT teacher training. *Journal of Korean Association of Educational Information and Broadcasting, 9*(2), 39–70.

Jung, I. S. (2003b). Issues of cost-effectiveness in open and distance learning. *Distance Education in China, 196,* 26–32 (English written, Chinese translated).

Jung, I. S. (2003c). Online education for adult learners in South Korea. *Educational Technology, 43*(3), 9–16.

Jung, I. S. (2004). Convergence and diversity of quality assurance systems in distance education. *The SNU Journal of Educational Research, 13,* 75–106.

Jung, I. S. (2005a). A review of policy and practice in virtual education: In the context of higher education in S. Korea. *Educational Studies, 47,* 111–123. Institute for Educational Research and Service. International Christian University.

Jung, I. S. (2005b). Cost-effectiveness of online teacher training. *Open Learning, 20*(2), 131–146. http://journalsonline.tandf.co.uk/link.asp?id=n05855313g450559

Jung, I. S. (2005c). Discussion on quality in distance education. *Journal of Lifelong Learning Society, 1*(1), 1–24.

Jung, I. S. (2005d). ICT-pedagogy integration in teacher training: Application cases worldwide. *Educational Technology and Society, 8*(2), 94–101. www.ifets.info/issues.php?id=27

Jung, I. S. (2005e). Training ICT-competent teachers. *Educational Technology Research, 28*(1–2), 45–52.

Jung, I. S. (2007a). Approaches to quality assurance in distance education: With respect to cross-border higher education. *Journal of Lifelong Learning Society, 3*(1), 89–103.

Jung, I. S. (2007b). Editorial: Changing faces of open and distance learning in Asia. *International Review of Research in Open and Distance Learning, 8*(1). www.irrodl.org/index.php/irrodl/article/view/418

Jung, I. S. (2009a). Ethical judgments and behaviours: Applying a multidimensional ethics scale to measuring ICT ethics of college students. *Computers & Education, 53*(3), 940–949.

Jung, I. S. (2009b). Internet integration strategies of public educational TV stations. *Journal of Lifelong Learning Society, 5*(1), 199–218.

Jung, I. S. (2009c). The emergence of for-profit e-learning providers in Asia. *TechTrends, 53*(2), 18–21.

Jung, I. S. (2010a). Implications of brain research for adult open and distance learning in Asia. *Educational Studies, 52,* 121–129.

Jung, I. S. (2010b). Toward a systemic approach to quality assurance in e-Learning: An ecological perspective. *Educational Technology International, 11*(2), 25–41.

Jung, I. S. (2011). The dimensions of e-learning quality: From the learner's perspective. *Educational Technology Research and Development, 59,* 445–464.

Jung, I. S. (2016). MOOCs: What have we learned so far? *Journal of Cyber Education, 10*(2), 1–11.

Jung, I. S., & Choi, K. A. (1998). Analysis on media selection and utilization in distance education. *Korean Journal of Distance Education, 11,* 127–160.

Jung, I. S., & Choi, K. Y. (1997). *Analysis of instructional media selection and utilization process at the Korea National Open University.* KNOU Policy Paper.

Jung, I. S., & Choi, S. H. (1999). Factors affecting effectiveness of virtual training. *Korean Journal of Educational Research, 37*(1), 369–388.

Jung, I. S., & Choi, S. W. (1995). *Online multimedia hypertext design for distance learning.* Korea National Open University Policy Paper.

Jung, I. S., & Choi, S. W. (1997). Web page design for online learning. *Korean Journal of Distance Education, 10,* 55–90.

Jung, I. S., & Choi, S. W. (1998). Open and distance education and new information technology. *Korean Journal of Educational Technology, 14*(1), 163–186.

Jung, I. S., Choi, S. W., Choi, S. H., & Oh, I. K. (1997). *Analysis of two web-based virtual training courses.* Samsung HRD Center Evaluation Paper.

Jung, I. S., & Chung, H. S. (1993). Computer-mediated communication in Korean distance education. *Media and Technology for Human Resource Development, 6*(1), 49–59.

Jung, I. S., Ho, C., & Suzuki, K. (2013). YouTube use in colleges in Japan and USA: A comparative look. *Journal of Educational Media Research (Research Notes), 19*(2), 11–24.

Jung, I. S., & Hong, S. C. (1992). Educational TV production adopting course-team approach. *Journal of Distance Education, 6*(4), 63–103.

Jung, I. S., & Hong, S. Y. (2014). An elaboration model of student support to allow for gender considerations in Asian distance education. *The International Review of Research in Open and Distance Learning, 15*(2). www.irrodl.org/index.php/irrodl/article/view/1604/2829

Jung, I. S., & Hong, S. Y. (2016). Faculty members' instructional priorities for adopting OER. *The International Review of Research in Open and Distance Learning, 17*(6). http://dx.doi.org/10.19173/irrodl.v17i6.2803

Jung, I. S., Kudo, M., & Choi, S. (2012). Stress in Japanese learners engaged in online collaborative learning in English. *British Journal of Educational Technology, 43*(6), 1016–1029.

Jung, I. S., & Latchem, C. (2007). Assuring quality in Asian open and distance learning. *Open Learning, 22*(3), 235–250.

Jung, I. S., & Latchem, C. (2011, January). A model for e-education: Extended teaching spaces and extended learning spaces. *British Journal of Educational Technology, 42*(1), 6–18.

Jung, I. S., & Lee, D. S. (1993). Improving interactivity in distance education through computer-mediated communication. *Journal of Distance Education, 7*(4), 127–226.

Jung, I. S., & Lee, D. S. (1994a). A study on the role of system operator to improve interactivity in computer network system. *Journal of Distance Education, 8*(1), 131–159.

Jung, I. S., & Lee, D. S. (1994b). Analyzing use of computer networks as a student support system in distance education. *Journal of Distance Education, 8*(1), 95–130.

Jung, I. S., & Lee, J. H. (2019). The effects of learner factors on MOOC learning outcomes and their pathways. *Innovations in Education and Teaching International, 57*(5), 565–576. https://doi.org/10.1080/14703297.2019.1628800

Jung, I. S., & Lee, J. H. (2020). A cross-cultural approach to the adoption of open educational resources in higher education. *British Journal of Educational Technology, 51*(1), 263–280. https://doi.org/10.1111/bjet.12820

Jung, I. S., & Lee, K. J. (1997). *Design and evaluation of video conferencing system at the Korea National Open University*. KNOU Policy Paper.

Jung, I. S., & Lee, O. H. (2001). Development of team teaching models in a web-based teaching environment. *Journal of Korean Association of Educational Information and Broadcasting, 7*(2), 27–49.

Jung, I. S., & Lee, Y. (2015). YouTube acceptance by university educators and students: A cross-cultural perspective. *Innovations in Education & Teaching International, 52*(3), 243–253.

Jung, I. S., & Leem, J. H. (1999). Design strategies for developing web-based training courses in a Korean corporate context. *International Journal of Educational Technology, 1*(1), 107–121.

Jung, I. S., & Leem, J. H. (2000). *Cost effectiveness analysis of web-based virtual course*. Korean National Open University Policy Paper.

Jung, I. S., & Leem, J. H. (2001). Comparing cost-effectiveness of conventional distance education course and web-based course. *Korean Journal of Educational Technology, 17*(1), 131–164.

Jung, I. S., Leem, J. H., & Choi, J. K. (2000). *Cost effectiveness analysis of Web-based virtual course*. Korea National Open University Policy Paper.

Jung, I. S., Lim, C. I., Choi, S. H., & Leem, J. H. (2000). *Development of Web-based education program for lifelong learning environment*. Korea Research Foundation.

Jung, I. S., Lim, C. I., Choi, S. H., & Leem, J. H. (2002). The effects of different types of interaction on satisfaction and learning in Web-based instruction. *Innovations in Education and Teaching International, 39*(2), 153–162.

Jung, I. S., Lim, J. H., & Choi, K. A. (1998). *Design of virtual education system in a context of Korea National Open University (KNOU)*. KNOU Policy Paper.

Jung, I. S., & Oh, C. H. (1998). Development of evaluation index for educational TV Program. *Korean Journal of Educational TV, 4*(1).

Jung, I. S., Omori, S., Dawson, W., Yamaguchi, T., & Lee, S. (2021). Faculty as reflective practitioners in emergency online teaching: An autoethnography. *International Journal of Educational Technology in Higher Education, 18*(30). https://doi.org/10.1186/s41239-021-00261-2

Jung, I. S., & Rha, I. (2000a). A virtual university trial project: Its impact on higher education in South Korea. *Innovations in Education and Training International, 38*(1), 31–41.

Jung, I. S., & Rha, I. (2000b, July–August). Effectiveness and cost-effectiveness of online education: A review of literature. *Education Technology, 40*(4), 57–60. https://www.jstor.org/stable/44428629

Jung, I. S., & Sasaki, T. (2008). Toward effective and efficient e-moderation for blended learning. *Journal of Educational Media Research, 14*(2), 55–76.

Jung, I. S., Sasaki, T., & Latchem, C. (2016). A framework for assessing fitness for purpose in open educational resources. *International Journal of Educational Technology in Higher Education, 13*(3). https://doi.org/10.1186/s41239-016-0002-5

Jung, I. S., & Seo, Y. (2007). Gender and cultural differences in attitudes toward and use of ICT: Focusing on high school students in Korea and Japan. *Media Education Studies*, *13*(2), 15–26.

Jung, I. S., & Shim, H. S. (1996). Comparative study of usage patterns of computer network in distance education. *Korean Journal of Distance Education*, *9*, 37–64.

Jung, I. S., Sohn, J. G., Kang, B. W., & Youn, T. S. (1995). *Distance learning and national information superhighway*. Korea National Open University Policy Paper.

Jung, I. S., & Suzuki, Y. (2015). Scaffolding strategies for wiki-based collaboration: Action research in a multicultural Japanese language program. *British Journal of Educational Technology*, *46*(4), 829–838.

Jung, I. S., Wong, T. M., Chen L., Baigaltugs, S., & Belawati, T. (2011). Quality assurance in Asian distance education: Diverse approaches and common culture. *The International Review of Research in Open and Distance Learning*, *12*(6), 63–83.

Jung, I. S., & Yoo, M. (2014). An analysis of Asia-Pacific educational technology research published internationally in 2000–2013. *Journal of Asia Pacific Education Research*, *15*(3), 355–365.

Kim, K. H., & Jung, I. S. (1993). *A study on computer-mediated communication*. Korea Air and Correspondence University Research Paper.

Latchem, C., Jung, I. S., Aoki, K., & Ozkul, A. E. (2008). The tortoise and the hare enigma in e-transformation in Japanese and Korean higher education. *British Journal of Educational Technology*, *39*(4), 610–630.

Lee, J. H., & Jung, I. S. (2021). Instructional changes instigated by university faculty during the COVID-19 pandemic: The effect of individual, course and institutional factors. *International Journal of Educational Technology in Higher Education*, *18*(52). https://doi.org/10.1186/s41239-021-00286-7

Leem, J. H., & Jung, I. S. (1998). Participatory analysis of web-based instruction. *Korean Journal of Educational Technology*, *14*(2).

Lim, B., Leem, J., & Jung, I. S. (2003). Current status of cyber-education in Korean higher education and quality control: The year of 2002. *Korean Journal of Educational Research*, *41*(3), 541–570.

Mendoza, G., Jung, I. S., & Kobayashi, S. (2017). A review of empirical studies on MOOC adoption: Applying the unified theory of acceptance and use of technology. *International Journal for Educational Media and Technology*, *11*(1), 15–24.

Park, Y., Jung, I. S., & Reeves, T. (2015). Learning from MOOCs: A qualitative case study from the learners' perspectives. *Educational Media International*, *52*(2), 72–87.

Rha, I., & Jung, I. S. (1996). *Strategic training plan for the Daewoong Management Development Center*. Daewoong Policy Paper.

Rha, I., Kwak, D. H., Jung, I. S., Hwang, D. J., & Cho, Y. H. (1996). *Analysis and evaluation of videoconferencing system in distance higher education*. Seoul National University. Ministry of Information and Communication Evaluation Paper.

Shih, T. K., Antoni, G. D., Arndt, T., Asirvatham, A., Chang, C.-T., Chee, Y. S., Wang, Y.-H. (2003). A survey of distance education challenges and technologies. *International Journal of Distance Education Technologies*, *1*(1), 1–21.

Zawacki-Richter, O., et al. (2020). Elements of open education: An invitation to future research. *International Review of Research in Open and Distributed Learning*, *21*(3). https://doi.org/10.19173/irrodl.v21i3.4659

Conference Presentations

Jung, I. S. (1997a). *Information and interaction design for instructional web pages* [Paper presentation]. Asian Association of Open Universities Annual Conference and Exhibition. Selangor, Malaysia.

Jung, I. S. (1997b). *Search for a virtual teacher training* [Paper presentation]. Fifth international distance education workshop, Korea National Open University.

Jung, I. S. (1997c). *Design of a virtual university in a Korean context* [Paper presentation]. ED-MEDIA/ED-TELECOM97 World conference on Educational multimedia/ Hypermedia, World conference on Educational Telecommunications, Calgary, Canada.

Jung, I. S. (1996, December) *Videoconferencing system of KNOU* [Paper presentation]. Korean Society for Medical Informatics Annual Conference, Walker Hill Hotel, Seoul.

Rha, I., & Jung, I. S. (1997, June). *Making connections: Interactive video conferencing technology in distance education* [Paper presentation]. ED-MEDIA/ED-TELECOM97 World conference on Educational multimedia/ Hypermedia, World conference on Educational Telecommunications, Calgary, Canada.

18
KANWAR, ASHA

Photo of Asha Kanwar contributed by Asha Kanwar

> *If the Sustainable Development Goals are to be achieved by 2030, we will have to go beyond the "business as usual" approach and brick-and-mortar solutions. We will have to turn to distance education to help us to achieve development goals.*

Dr. Asha Kanwar obtained her Bachelor of Arts in 1971 from Panjab University, India. She continued her studies at Panjab, where she completed a Master of Arts in 1973 and a Master of Philosophy in 1983. She completed a Doctor of Philosophy in 1986 at the University of Sussex, England.

Dr. Kanwar's research interests and expertise are in open and distance learning, technology-enabled learning, open educational resources (OER), gender studies, quality assurance, and organizational development.

Kanwar has received numerous honours and awards for her research and leadership in open and distance learning, the most recent being:

2016:

- Doctor of the University conferred by the Open University, UK;
- DLitt (honoris causa) conferred by the Open University of Sri Lanka;
- DLitt conferred by Wawasan Open University, Malaysia; and
- DLitt conferred by the University of Swaziland.

2014:

- DLitt (honoris causa) conferred by the KK Handiqui State Open University, India; and
- Asian Association of Open Universities (AAOU) Meritorious Service Award.

2012:

- DLitt (honoris causa) conferred by Vardhman Open University, Kota, India.

Dr. Kanwar was a Professor with Indira Gandhi National Open University (IGNOU) from 1992 to 2009. She has also held many important positions with large institutions and organizations such as:

- Director, School of Humanities, IGNOU, New Delhi, India (1995–1998);
- Pro Vice Chancellor, IGNOU (1999–2000);
- Consultant, UNESCO-BREDA, Dakar, Senegal (2002–2003);
- Education Specialist: Higher Education and Policy Development, Commonwealth of Learning, Vancouver, Canada (2003–2006); and
- Vice President, Commonwealth of Learning, Vancouver, Canada (2006–2012)

Currently, Dr. Kanwar is the President and CEO of the Commonwealth of Learning, based in Vancouver, Canada.

Interview

Transcript Analysis Summary

Analysis of all interviews included in this volume led to the identification of 3,545 units of data. The mean of these collective units was 118 per pioneer, the median was 118.5, and the mode was 132. Individual interview units ranged from 59 to 217 units, yielding a spread of 158 units among all interviews. Asha Kanwar's interview generated 116 units, which nearly matched the mean and median statistics for all interviews.

A comparision of Kanwar's interview to the interviews of all pioneers indicates that, generally speaking, her conversations produced a unique number of units in over half the identified thematic areas in relation to the average interview (Figure 18.1). This may be because, unlike most pioneers, she has held a number of administrative positions at an international organization for much of her

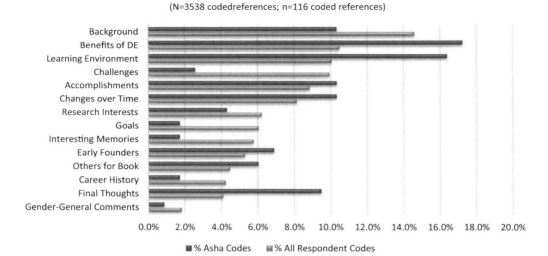

Figure 18.1 All Respondents' Versus Asha Kanwar's Parent Codes

career. In these positions, she would be acutely aware of the distance learning benefits that her organization has brought to many developing countries and marginalized people across the globe. This would also explain why her interview produced more units than the average interview in discussions on the learning environment that she worked in. The number of units Kanwar generated in the thematic area of final thoughts may, in part, also reflect her years of experience with the COL and a desire to pass on some of these insights to future generations of DE stakeholders. It is interesting to note that Kanwar did not speak about challenges as much as the average interviewee did. Perhaps this echoes her optimistic outlook on what she and her organization have to offer through their initiatives across the globe.

Link to recorded interview: tinyurl.com/Kanwar-A-2019

Transcript of Interview

Full name: Asha Kanwar

Institutional Affiliation: President and Chief Executive Officer, Commonwealth of Learning (COL)

Key:

Regular font = Interviewee comments
Italicized font = Interviewer comments

Interview Questions

1. *What was your educational and experiential background before you became involved in distance education [DE]?*

   I was doing my bachelor's degree in India. In our family, we had a tradition of girls getting married off at a very young age. So before I had completed my third year, I was married off, but I was good at my studies and wanted to continue. I wanted to do my master's like the rest of my classmates. So I had no choice but to become an external student. I did my master's, which was a two-year programme at the university, at a distance. So I had a first-hand experience of being a distance learner.

2. *In what year did you begin to look specifically into DE, and what were the circumstances in your world that initiated this interest in DE?*

   I went on a scholarship to the University of Sussex [England] to do my DPhil [Doctorate in Philosophy]. As a researcher, I went to interview Professor Arnold Kettle at the Open University, UK. I asked him why he had left a campus university to teach at an open university, and he said that on campus, he was just reaching a few students every year. But at an open university, he could reach large numbers of students, unlock their imaginations, and widen their horizons. I found that very inspiring.

   After I completed my DPhil, I went back to India. I was looking for a job, and a new open university had just been set up. I applied and got the job. That's how my journey in open and distance education began.

3. *Which female researchers or female colleagues may have piqued your interest in DE?*

   Those days, when we started out in the Indira Gandhi National Open University [IGNOU] as distance educators, we had come from research universities. So in the beginning, we were skeptical about how efficient the distance learning system was. Janet Jenkins from the Open University, UK, gave us intensive training in the different aspects of distance education, and from then on, she became a mentor and friend.

   And there was a Women's International Network in those days, which was part of the International Council for Distance Education [ICDE]. Liz Burge, Gisela Pravda, and Christine von Prümmer were at the forefront of research on women and distance education at the time and influenced many younger colleagues.

4. *Who would you identify as the early female leaders/founders in the field of DE?*

   Well, I have already mentioned some of these names. If you look at some of my colleagues in India, Dr. Neela Jagannathan, a librarian, was very impressive. The other people who made substantial contributions to distance education are Professor Uma Coomaraswamy from Sri

Lanka and Professor Brenda Gourley, the former vice chancellor of the Open University, UK. I think Dr. Caroline Seelig, who heads the Open Polytechnic of New Zealand, has contributed by promoting distance education and blended approaches for skills development.

5. *What are some of the goals that you strove to achieve in the field of DE?*

In countries like India, where we had a tradition of correspondence education, there was a negative perception that distance education was second rate, second choice, second chance, and not at par with the campus system. So quality assurance was a priority for us. In fact, in India, the quality-assurance system in higher education developed first in distance education when the Distance Education Council was set up in 1991. The establishment of the National Assessment and Accreditation Council in 1994 led to the expansion of the system to campus institutions. My primary interest was to strengthen the quality of the distance learning system, not just for parity of esteem, but for a better learning experience for our students.

6. *What are some of your accomplishments in the field of DE that you would like to share?*

I am heading an organization, the Commonwealth of Learning, which promotes distance and technology-enabled learning around the 53 member states of the Commonwealth. Advocacy for harnessing the potential of distance education, not just for enhancing access to formal education, but for non-formal and informal learning, is a major achievement. The formal system is important, as the 31 open universities in the Commonwealth are opening up access to millions who would otherwise not have had the opportunity. The open schools in 27 Commonwealth countries substantially increase the transition rates from primary to secondary school. COL is promoting the use of distance education for lifelong learning and for achieving development outcomes. If the Sustainable Development Goals are to be achieved by 2030, we will have to go beyond the "business as usual" approach and brick-and-mortar solutions. We will have to turn to distance education to help us to achieve development goals.

I have also tried to work on women and distance education. My Australian colleague, Margaret Taplin, and I did a report called *Brave New World: How Distance Education Changed Women's Lives* (2001), featuring case studies of women distance learners in Bangladesh, China, India, Hong Kong SAR, and Sri Lanka. *Speaking for Ourselves: Women in Distance Education in India* (1995) was edited by me and Dr. Neela Jagannathan. More recently, I brought out a book with my colleagues, Frances Ferreira and Colin Latchem (who is no more now), on *Women and Leadership in Open and Distance Learning and Development* (2013). This reflects on "becoming a leader," "being a leader," and "helping others to become leaders" and makes several recommendations for future leadership training for women. Based on these, we have been organizing workshops for training mid-career women academics from around the Commonwealth in leadership skills.

7. *You were the recipient of numerous awards over the years. One was the International Council for Distance Education Prize for Individual Excellence in 2009. Could you please tell us a bit about why you were selected for this award and any other acknowledgment of merit that you would like to mention?*

The ICDE Prize for Individual Excellence recognizes outstanding contributions to the theory and practice of open and distance learning. I have been fortunate to have the opportunities for contributing to the field in Asia, Africa, and around the Commonwealth, which covers all regions of the globe. I am also very proud of the Asian Association for Open Universities Meritorious Service Award.

It has been an honour to receive honorary doctorates from the Open University, UK; the Open University of Sri Lanka; Wawasan Open University, Malaysia; and two open universities in India: the University of ESwatini and the Open University of Mauritius.

8. *What are some of the challenges that you faced in the field of DE over the years?*

   The growing demand for tertiary education has led to the establishment of several open universities in Asia and Africa. These institutions have grown very quickly to cater to the need, but may not have the systems in place to provide the services at scale. For me, I think the biggest challenge was learner support – and it continues to be a challenge even today.

9. *What was the "state of DE" when you first entered the field as opposed to DE in 2019?*

   When I started in 1987 in IGNOU, we were looking at an industrial model based on a division of labour. There were teams that developed course materials, which included print and multimedia, and others who were responsible for the editing. And there were teams which did the printing and delivery, while others took care of tutoring and counselling.

   In 2019, we find a much more networked model. In the past, the "family silver," so as to speak, was the high-quality course materials developed by open universities. Today, we live in a world full of quality open educational resources [OER], potentially a sound staple for developing courses. There is much more collaboration across jurisdictions and time zones. The tutor is not the sole support for the learner, who can reach out to their peers for learning. The main difference is the transition from a 20th-century to a 21st-century model of distance education.

10. *What interesting memories would you like to share about the beginning of online DE?*

    IGNOU had introduced computers and connectivity for all staff members, but nobody really knew what to do with the technology. The vice chancellor initiated a programme called IT TRAP, which was a training programme for all personnel, from top to bottom, including the vice chancellor himself. Everyone had to undergo training for five days. This kind of holistic approach, which includes capacity building, was critical to the success of the initiative.

11. *What were your specific DE research interests, and have they changed/evolved over the years?*

    I started with quality assurance at the beginning of my career and then found myself more interested in how to create cultures of quality within institutions. I brought out an edited book in 2006 with Professor Badri Koul, one of the stalwarts of open and distance learning, on creating cultures of quality, where we looked at cases from different parts of the Commonwealth and what people have done, even if they are resource poor, to create cultures of quality. The other area has always been on the impact of distance education on the lives of Asian women, and now the focus is on women and leadership.

12. *Could you please describe the learning environment that you currently work in (e.g., geographic and institutional setting, student demographics)?*

    As you know, I work for the Commonwealth of Learning, or COL, which is an intergovernmental organization set up by Commonwealth heads of government. We are funded by contributions from member states. There are 53 member states, right from the Caribbean; Canada is a member; to Europe, Africa, Asia, and the Pacific. We are supporting open and distance learning around the Commonwealth. Most recently, we supported the transition of the Botswana College of Distance and Open Learning into the Botswana Open University by developing policies, setting up systems, and providing technical advice for technology requirements, costing, and workloads for faculty and staff.

    We are also helping with the establishment of open schools. The most recent examples are in Belize and Trinidad and Tobago. We are using open, distance, and blended learning to support technical and vocational education, particularly in the Pacific and in Africa. But we are also deploying distance learning methodologies for our Lifelong Learning for Farmers project in eleven countries, and training girls in skills for livelihoods in remote and marginalized communities in five countries. This gives you a flavour of the contexts in which we work.

13. *Is there anything else you [would] like to address?*

Open and distance education institutions have a wealth of experience and expertise in pedagogy, course development, and instructional design, but because of their focus on achieving parity of esteem with campus institutions, they have not provided the leadership that they could have in the development of MOOCs, which came from research institutions. So I think we need to think about the future, think about our niche and where we can make a difference. We need to become risk takers and leaders, rather than followers. That's the first thing that I would like to say.

Distance education is something that needs to address lifelong learning because, as populations age, they will need opportunities for learning at different stages of their lives. Even younger generations will need to prepare for the several career changes that they will face during their lives. I think that distance education is a tried and tested approach that can enhance opportunities for lifelong learning.

And distance educators have to keep a finger on the pulse of who the learners are: what they want, how they learn, and the technologies that work. Are we ready to offer shorter courses, micro-credits, alternative credentials?

14. *Can you suggest names of other female pioneers in DE or online learning that you think we should include in the book?*

I suggest Brenda Gourley, Caroline Seelig, Abtar Kaur. Sushmita Mitra, Cindy Gauthier, Jessica Aguti, and Madhulika Kaushik are other inspiring women who have made substantial contributions to the field.

Publications

Books

Bennett, B., Sareen, S. K., Cowan, S., & Kanwar, A. (Eds.). (2009). *Of Sadhus and Spinners: Australian encounters with India.* HarperCollins Publishers.
Kanwar, A. (1989). *The novels of Virginia Woolf and Anita Desai.* Prestige.
Kanwar, A. (1990). *Fictional theories and three great novels.* Prestige.
Kanwar, A. (Ed.). (1991). *Renu Gurnani's reflections.* Allied Press.
Kanwar, A. (Ed.). (1993). *The unforgetting heart: An anthology of short stories by African American women writers.* Aunt Lute (Reprint 1995).
Kanwar, A., Ferreira, F., & Latchem, C. (Eds.). (2013). *Women and leadership in open and distance learning and development.* Commonwealth of Learning.
Kanwar, A., & Jagannathan, N. (Eds.). (1995). *Speaking for ourselves: Women and distance education in India.* Manohar.
Kanwar, A., & Prakash, A. (Eds.). (2000). *Aphra Behn's the rover.* Worldview Books.
Kanwar, A., & Taplin, M. (Eds.). (2001). *Brave new women: How distance education changed their lives.* Commonwealth of Learning.
Kanwar, A., & Vats, S. (Trans.). (1991). *Ngugi wa Thiongo, Matigari.* Atma Ram Press.
Koul, B. N., & Kanwar, A. (Eds.). (2006). *Towards a culture of quality.* Commonwealth of Learning.
Marshall, S., Brandon, E., Thomas, M., Kanwar, A., & Lyngra, T. (Eds.). (2008). *Foreign providers in the Caribbean: Pillagers or preceptors?* Commonwealth of Learning.

Book Chapters

Balaji, V., & Kanwar, A. (2015). Changing the tune: MOOCs for human development – A case study. In C. J. Bonk, M. M. Lee, T. C. Reeves, & T. H. Reynolds (Eds.), *MOOCs and open education around the world*. Routledge.

Daniel, J., & Kanwar, A., & Uvalić-Trumbić, S. (2008). From innocence to experience: The politics and projects of cross-border higher education. In M. Field & J. Fegan (Eds.), *Education across-borders II: Politics, policy and legislative action*. Springer.

Dhanarajan, G., & Kanwar, A. (2003). Open and distance learning in Sub-Saharan Africa – Practice, policy and partnerships. In J. Shabani, et al. (Eds.), *Open and distance learning in Africa*. UNESCO.

Kanwar, A. (1989). Teaching literature to distance learners. In I. Khan (Ed.), *Teaching English through distance education*. Manohar.

Kanwar, A. (1991a). Raghunath Rao: A pioneering theoretician. In G. Gupta & O. P. Singhal (Eds.), *Anuvad Chintan Ke Saidhantik Ayam*. Bhartiya Anuvad Parishad.

Kanwar, A. (1991b). Virginia Woolf and Anita Desai. In R. K. Dhawan (Ed.), *Indian women novelists*. Prestige.

Kanwar, A. (1995). The joys of motherhood or the sorrows of motherhood. In H. Narang (Ed.), *Mightier than machete*. Wiley Eastern Ltd.

Kanwar, A. (1999). Zora Neale Hurston [Special issue]. *University News*. AIU.

Kanwar, A. (2001). Zora Neale Hurston: Literary matriarch and black magic: The works of Toni Morrison. In R. K. Dhawan (Ed.), *Afro-American literature*. Prestige.

Kanwar, A. (2003). Distance education for Asian women. In W. Zhang (Ed.), *Global perspectives: Philosophy and practice in distance education* (Vol. 1). China Central Radio and Television University (In English and Chinese).

Kanwar, A., & Clarke, K. (2011). Quality assurance in open universities around the world. In I. Jung & C. Latchem (Eds.), *QA and accreditation in distance education and eLearning*. Routledge.

Kanwar, A., & Daniel, J. (2008). Distance education and open universities. In P. Peterson, E. Baker, & B. McGaw (Eds.), *The international encyclopedia of education* (3rd ed.). Elsevier. https://doi.org/10.1016/B978-0-08-044894-7.00866-6

Kanwar, A., & Koul, B. (2007). Quality assurance and accreditation of distance higher education in the Commonwealth of Nations. In *Higher education in the world: Accreditation for quality assurance: What is at stake?* Palgrave Macmillan.

Kanwar, A., & Pillai, C. R. (2001). Distance education in India. In O. Jegede & G. Shive (Eds.), *Open and distance education in the Asia-Pacific Region*. Open University Press.

Kanwar, A., & Uvalic-Trumbic, S. (Eds). (2011). Neil Butcher. *Basic guide to open education resources (OER)*. UNESCO/COL.

Kanwar, A., & Vats, S. (Trans.). (1991). *Happy birthday, Toni Cade Bambara*. Akshara.

Mishra, S., & Kanwar, A. (2015). Quality assurance for open educational resources: What's the difference? In C. J. Bonk, M. M. Lee, T. C. Reeves, & T. H. Reynolds (Eds.), *MOOCs and open education around the world*. Routledge.

Journal Articles

Balasubramanian, K., Thamizoli, P., Umar, A., & Kanwar, A. (2010). Using mobile phones to promote lifelong learning among rural women in India. *Distance Education, 31*(2).

Daniel, J., Kanwar, A., & Uvalic-Trumbic, S. (2005). Who's afraid of cross-border higher education? A developing world perspective. *Higher Education Digest, 52*. Open University.

Daniel, J., Kanwar, A., & Uvalic-Trumbic, S. (2006, July–August). A tectonic shift in global higher education. *Change, 38*(4), 16–23. https://doi.org/10.3200/CHNG.38.4.16-23

Daniel, J., Kanwar, A., & Uvalić-Trumbić, S. (2007). Mass tertiary education in the developing world: Distant prospect or distinct possibility? In *Europa World of Learning* (Vol. 2). Routledge.

Daniel, J., Kanwar, A., & Uvalić-Trumbić, S. (2008). The right to education: A model for making higher education equally accessible to all on the basis of merit. *The Asian Society of Open and Distance Education, 6*.

Daniel, J., Kanwar, A., & Uvalić-Trumbić, S. (2009, March–April). Breaking higher education's iron triangle: Access, cost & quality. *Change, 41*(2), 30–35. https://doi.org/10.3200/CHNG.41.2.30-35

Kanwar, A. (1987b). An interview with Arnold Kettle. *Social Scientist 15*(7), 54–61. https://doi.org/10.2307/3517267

Kanwar, A. (1988a). A literature of their own: An experiment in feminist pedagogy. *Literature alive*. Madras.

Kanwar, A. (1988b). Raymond Williams and the English novel. *Social Scientist, 16*(5), 46–58. https://doi.org/10.2307/3517297

Kanwar, A. (1988c). *Women and theatre down the ages*. Tribune.
Kanwar, A. (1989). *F. R. Leavis, scrutiny and the great tradition*. Panjab University Research Bulletin, Chandigarh.
Kanwar, A. (1990). Distance education for women's equality: An Indian perspective. *Journal for Distance Education*, 5(2), 49–58.
Kanwar, A. (1992). *Motherlands* [Review]. Committee on South Asian Women's Bulletin.
Kanwar, A. (1994). Possessing the secret of joy [Review of the book *Possessing the secret of joy*, by A. Walker]. *English Association Journal*. L. N. Mithila University.
Kanwar, A. (1997). Malashri Lal's, "The law of the threshold" [Review of the book *The law of threshold (Women writers in Indian English)*, by M. Lal]. In *Summerhill*. IIAS.
Kanwar, A. (2016). Leadership and innovation for the future of ODL. *Open Education Research, 6*, 16–20.
Kanwar, A., Balasubramanian, K., & Umar, A. (2010). Towards sustainable OERs: A perspective from the global South. *The American Journal of Distance Education, 24*(2).
Kanwar, A., & Sahgal, S. (1990). *Problems in the sociology of literature*. Occasional Papers, Chandigarh.
Kanwar, A., & Vats, S. (Trans.). (1990, September–October). Guthera', Ngugi wa Thiongo. *Vipasha, 34*, Simla.
Smiley, J. (1993, March). *An interview by A. Kanwar*. Iowa Review, Iowa City, and Span.

Conference Presentations

Kanwar, A. (1999a). *Issues in course development: The experience of IGNOU in India*. Proceedings of Pan-Commonwealth Forum, Brunei.
Kanwar, A. (1999b, October). *Women, technology and distance education*. Proceedings of AAOU Conference, Beijing, China.
Kanwar, A. (2017). *Can open learning transform society?* [Paper presentation]. Developmental Interventions and Open Learning for Empowering and Transforming Society, Presen Krishna Kanta Handique State Open University (KKHSOU) Guawahati, India.
Kanwar, A., & Ramanujam, P. R. (1998). *Higher education in India*. Proceedings of the Jacques Delors Seminar, New Delhi, NIEPA.

19
KEOUGH, ERIN M.

Photo of Erin Keough contributed by Erin Keough

There was always somebody, or some group that was willing to say "yes" when they could have said "no" or were willing to take a risk on relatively untested technologies when they could have said, "We have always done it this way."

Erin Keough holds a Bachelor of Science in Chemistry from the University of Toronto, Canada, and a Master of Political Science in Public Policy from Memorial University of Newfoundland, Canada.

Keough's research focuses on public and private policies to enhance distance education and communication, as listed at the end of this chapter.

Contributions in early innovation and leadership were described in detail during Keough's interview. She was one of the early members of a team that worked in Newfoundland on the Telemedicine Project, beginning in 1982, which successfully brought collaboration, courses, professional development, and connectivity to rural and outlying regions of Eastern Canada through the Hermes Satellite. It was a joint project between the Medical Department and the Educational Department at Memorial University. It also brought secondary school courses to students in small communities. The success of this project rippled out nationally and internationally to help educators, institutions, and governments put broadband in place to provide connectivity to many.

Keough became Director of Telemedicine and Co-Director of the Telemedicine and Educational Technology Resource Agency (TETRA) at Memorial University in 1987 and worked in these positions through to 1995. During this period, the Telemedicine network doubled in size and developed a substantial role in distance education.

Keough very much pioneered and led early trials in satellite communication and the adoption and creation of virtual connectivity in Canada and internationally through her work with Telemedicine and TETRA.

Her recent roles include:

- 2006–2007 – Project director of Atlantic Consortium of Research Networks – Newfoundland and Labrador (ACORN-NL). ACORN-NL is the NL regional portion of the Canadian National Advanced Research and Education Network (CANARIE);
- 2009–2011 – Executive Director of Women in Resource Development Inc. (WRDC), a not-for-profit organization that works to promote the economic equality of women in Newfoundland and Labrador.

Interview

Transcript Analysis Summary

Analysis of all interviews included in this volume led to the identification of 3,545 units of data. The mean of these collective units was 118 per pioneer, the median was 118.5, and the mode was 132. Individual interview units ranged from 59 to 217 units, yielding a spread of 158 units between all interviews. Erin Keough's interview generated 147 units, which placed her interview in the upper third of interviews in terms of unit generation.

A comparision of Keough's interview to the interviews of all pioneers indicates that her interview yielded a unique profile to that of the average interview in terms of units produced per thematic area (Figure 19.1). Her profile generated a similar number of units to the average interview in four areas: learning environment, accomplishments, goals, and interesting memories. Keough's integral role in bringing social services and education to remote locations via satellite communications gave her profound insight into the benefits of DE. This would explain the significant number of units that her interview produced about the benefits in DE.

Keough's interview did not yield many units in the following areas: background, challenges, changes over time, research interests, career history, final thoughts, or general gender-related comments. The low number of units in the background area might be explained in two ways. First, Keough came into the field from an unrelated educational background. Second, once she began working in the field, her sole aim was to provide social services to those who did not have ready access to such services. The minimal number of units in the area of research interests is explained by Keough's declaration that she did not engage in research but chose instead to use others' research for her work. No explanations are offered as to why she produced few units in the remaining topic areas.

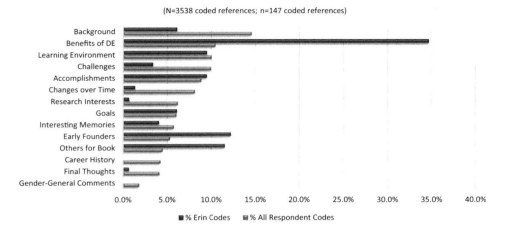

Figure 19.1 All Respondents' Versus Erin Keough's Parent Codes

Link to recorded interview Part A: tinyurl.com/Keough-E-A

Link to recorded interview Part B: tinyurl.com/Keough-E-B

Transcript of Interview

Full Name: Erin M. Keough

Institutional Affiliation: Memorial University of Newfoundland and Government of Newfoundland

Key:

Regular font = Interviewee comments
Italicized font = Interviewer comments

Interview Questions

1. *What was your educational and experiential background before you became involved in distance education [DE] and the development of your consortium model?*

    When I joined the Telemedicine group, I had an undergraduate degree [in] science [Chemistry]. I had worked for a few years at the Faculty of Medicine as a research assistant in a gastroenterology research lab. I realized at the time that if I wanted to progress in the science area, I was going to have to get a PhD, and, in truth, I did not think I would be interested in that path. The Faculty of Medicine and the Faculty of Education had recently been selected as one of the 14 Canadian research trials to test the Hermes Satellite. [See Question 2b.] I was intrigued with the possibility of the technology to make services (e.g., health, education) more accessible to people working and living in rural and remote places. I was lucky enough to be selected for a research assistant position in that trial. As I became more senior in the organization, I realized I needed a greater understanding of how institutions, bureaucrats, large corporations, [and] governments worked, so I completed a Masters in Political Science, focusing on public policy, particularly in the telecommunications area. In hindsight, I had really found my calling – helping making access to public services and resources more equitably available.

2. *In what year did you begin to look specifically into the consortium model? When did you begin to develop DE opportunities through this model?*

    I am going to tell you more than you will likely want to know about the network consortium and how it grew as I believe that this was our unique contribution to the expansion of DE and telehealth in our province and internationally, and perhaps nationally.

    The concept of a partnership-collaboration-consortium began with the Hermes Satellite trial in the mid-1970s, the operational phase of which was in 1977–1978. It was enlarged upon until the post-trial provincial private network, containing some 220 locations in 150 communities, could offer four programmes simultaneously and supported programmes for some 200 different agencies. When I left my position as Director in 1995 to provide direction to the Open Learning and Information Network [see Question 13], there were 8,000 hours of programmes offered by the user consortium annually; at its peak a few years later, there were 13,000 hours of programmes offered annually.

    In the mid-1970s, the Federal Department of Communications (DOC) undertook a national consultation to identify groups that would be interested in testing a new type of communications satellite for social purposes. Previously, satellites were used for data and transmission. During the initial consultations, 20+ groups in Newfoundland and Labrador [NL] expressed interest. Ultimately, two groups persevered to the end of the consultation process, Educational Television [ETV], a division of the School of Continuing Studies, and the Faculty of Medicine [CME], under the direction of the assistant dean of Continuing Medical Educations. They were one of 14 groups chosen for the Hermes Satellite trial.

From the mid-1960's, the Faculty of Medicine had been providing continuing medical education (CME), consulting, and other services to rural physicians through sending specialist[s] to secondary-level hospitals on "regional course tours." In 1965, the School of Continuing Studies in the Faculty Education had begun offering correspondence courses throughout the province, initially to help teachers practicing in rural communities to upgrade to degree status. It oversaw a network of 45 learning centres located in Memorial's Corner Brook Campus, the 17 Colleges of the North Atlantic campuses (the "College"), and a variety of other locations in the other communities. The programming was a correspondence model using mail and courier to deliver materials (print and video tape, examinations), regional tutors, and mail for interaction between the students and their professors. The school had its own production facilities, including a television facility, a graphics and print shop, and associated skilled technical staff, producers, graphic artists, etc.

The Hermes trial allowed both agencies to explore many aspects of the use of telecommunications (the trial format was one-way video/two-way audio) for remote delivery that could enhance their current activities. All the programmes during the three-month operational trial phase were health-based (continuing education for physicians and other allied health professionals, meetings of clinical staff, programmes for pregnant mothers, and transmission of x-rays from one rural hospital). ETV provided all the technical support. They worked in conjunction with DOC to operationalize the satellite ground stations, provided the production studio and trained staff, and were the broadcast/ communications hub. We learned much about technical, programme design, and client support during that trial. However, equally importantly, we confirmed our expectation that, in this largely rural province with a small population, no one group would be able to support this on its own and that we would not for the foreseeable future (if ever) be able to afford satellite as a primary delivery system.

So, from the very onset, it was collaboration between the DE people at the Faculty of Education and the Faculty of Medicine, with its clinical and continuing education needs.

The post-trial network:

Following the 1977 Hermes broadcasts and evaluation, Memorial developed a nine-community, 11-site audio-teleconference system [TCS] based in hospitals and two Memorial campuses, which began programming in September 1979. The business model that would make it sustainable was to use the network for health applications in the daytime and for credit courses at night. As time passed, weekend uses evolved, which tended to be less formal groups: for example, committees of associations, support groups, etc. The relationship between Telemedicine and distance learning, which began with the 1977 trials, moved into an ongoing operational partnership. Based on this approach and increasing the partners to other education and pubic organization, the TCS grew to 250 sites in 150 communities and, at its peak, supported 13,000 of programmes a year.

These sites were connected by a dedicated [private] four-wire, ground-based telecommunications network with interfaces that allowed us to link to other networks (national and international) on an ad hoc basis to participate in programmes or to add guest speakers. The dedicated network provided: a) a secure system for meetings, student discussions, meetings of health and education professionals, patient activities including medical data transfer; b) a consistent telecommunications speed and quality with oversight from the network hub now located in the Faculty of Medicine; and c) a predictable annual cost that could be shared among all the users. The four-wire system allowed outgoing communications (for example, a lecturer's voice and data) to transmit on one set of wires and voice/data from students on the other. Similarly, transmit medical tests (EEGs, ECGs, x-rays) could be sent from a remote location in one set of wires and discussed via other wires with the use of a centrally located specialist who was key to the Telehealth applications.

Administrators at the original 11 locations saw the benefits that education programmes and other activities would be to their organizations and communities, so they agreed to provide free access to any participant in network activities to three rooms in their buildings, which were wired into the network. All necessary conferencing equipment, including telewriters [stand-alone interactive data-sharing units], VCR units, and audio equipment, were provided on portable trollies and moved between rooms as needed. The host organization also appointed a staff person to coordinate activities at their site.

As years progressed and both digital-end equipment and networks became available, application specific equipment (e.g., the telewriters) was replaced by computer applications. As compression algorithms improved, more video conferencing was introduced, primarily for meetings, medical consultations (e.g., tele-oncology and tele-psychiatry), and a few specific programme groups.

The network turned up in September 1979 and, over time, became known simply as the teleconference system [TCS].

During the first three operational months (September–December 1979), programming was primarily in health fields (shared hospital rounds, continuing health education for physicians and nurses, and a few allied health groups, distributed meetings, etc.). By January, we were convinced that the network was reliable enough that we could be confident to schedule the twice-weekly teleconference sessions at preset times that were required for the 13-week university term. The School of Continuing Studies offered its first course (January–April term, 1980). By the fall 1980 term, they had converted three more courses to this format, and it went on from there. They did not convert all their courses to this format, as many adults preferred more independent study. By the late 1980s or early 90s, they were able to add email into the mix for some students. (Remember that the first widely available PC [personal computer], the Commodore 64 with 64 KB [kilobytes] of RAM and 20 KB of memory on the hard drive and modem speeds of 19.2 kbs [kilobytes per second], was not available until 1982. Even then, it was expensive by standards, the rural networks were not digital, and by and large, a telephone line could be quite noisy, playing havoc with data transmission.)

Telemedicine and Educational Technology Resource Agency (TETRA) 1987–1995 and onward:

Funding from the Atlantic Canada Opportunities Agency (ACOA) allowed the two partners (ETV – now Education Technology and Telemedicine) to build new space for a small staff that could concentrate on expansion activities (health and education) provincially and internationally, without impacting the already-substantial work of the existing DELT (formerly Continuing Studies) and Telemedicine staffs. A virtual design centre was created within the agency to facilitate transition to online activities in education and health.

During this period: a) the TCS provincial network increased in geographic spread and number of sites; b) more digital formats/equipment were integrated (e.g., at the headend, the print and editing suites were digitized, and at the sites, telewriters were replaced by computers); and c) Continuing Studies and Telemedicine/TETRA increased the range and number of programmes and services in distance education and health, including diagnostic consulting services (e.g., EEG, nuclear medicine, radiology), continuing professional education for a variety of health groups, and high school and post-secondary distance education programmers. The centre also implemented or expanded a number of international research projects during that period (Uganda [using low earth orbit satellites for programme delivery], University of the West Indies, the Philippines, Thailand, and Japan).

Open Learning and Innovation Network (OLIN), 1995–2005:

OLIN consisted of a staff of four and was responsible for three major activity areas: a) facilitating the redevelopment of 27 degree/diploma programmes into online learning format; b) developing and implementing international contracts in distance learning and telehealth in partnership with local SMEs, and c) developing a business plan and obtaining consensus on creation of a single high-speed network to support the activities of all provincial health and education networks. OLIN was created to facilitate partnerships among the many public agencies involved in development and delivery of telehealth and tele-learning services and small private sector tele-learning firms that wanted to expand their product base, as well [as] partner with the public sector groups to expand into the international setting. Most of the public sector agencies had substantial international experience; therefore, partnerships with small and medium enterprises (SMEs) were meant to give the SMEs initial exposure and provide credibility in the new endeavour. [See Question 13 response for additional information.]

The model:

So, based upon our first experience and that of all the partners in the consortium, the following was the model:

Every user agency was responsible for the development of its own programmes. Any group that required assistance with design, production, or delivery was helped by the instructional designers and technical staff from the School of Continuing Studies, Telemedicine, and, subsequent to 1987, TETRA. Every user also contributed an annual user fee to support ongoing operations of the network and its services (that is, the Telemedicine Centre) and later, TETRA. TETRA had a standalone unit attached to the university that was self-funded though user fees and in-kind contributions.

Telemedicine (and later, TETRA) was responsible for:

- Administration, coordination, and scheduling of the network programmes;
- Operation and maintenance of the network and end equipment;
- Assistance with programme design and instructor/student-user training for distance learning (particularly for health and non-education groups) and Telemedicine activities;
- Applied research and development in areas and technologies related to distance education and telehealth;
- Consulting with users to identify network and equipment working with the telecommunications providers to expand the reach of the network; and
- Identifying funding for all expansions.

School of Continuing Studies/ETV – later Educational Technology – was responsible for:

- Designing and producing all university credit and continuing education courses offered using this network;
- Working together with Telemedicine in identification and testing of equipment as technology changed, particularly in the first 10–15 years; and
- Helping to train new groups (particularly education groups) in appropriate instructional design as the user consortium expanded.

NOTE: Continuing Studies (later DELT) had numerous other responsibilities at the university, including designing and offering credit courses in all other formats, offering lifelong learning programmes, covering and broadcasting convocations, and operating audio-visual services for the St. John's campus.

Agencies with sites on the network were responsible for:

- Providing access for all TCS users to the appropriate rooms in the buildings free of charge. (This meant that Memorial students could attend their courses at hospitals, and members of associations could participate in their provincial meetings though a school or college site.);
- Paying an annual fee roughly based on the use pattern that covered telecommunication and operations costs of the network. All user agencies (including Memorial's faculties of education and medicine) paid this fee. All of the operational revenues were generated this way; and
- Providing a contact person, who made sure that the equipment was set up for any conference booked for that site and worked with Telemedicine to troubleshoot problems with equipment.

3. *What DE opportunities did this consortium model initially offer? Have these DE opportunities evolved over the years?*

As I mentioned above, the founding members initially offered university credit courses and a variety of health activities to support professionals practicing in rural communities, including continuing health education programmes. The university credit courses crossed a number of faculties – arts, science, nursing, business, education, and social sciences.

On the health education side, there were continuing education programmes for a variety of health professionals; there were less formal programmes offered like Grand Rounds (noon on Thursdays) and Pediatric Rounds (Tuesday mornings). We helped the various presenters reformat their presentations to include those attending by teleconference. Any health professional could participate from any network site. These types of sessions helped reduce professional isolation by regularly putting professionals in touch with their peers and, equally importantly, provided rural physicians and nurses with an opportunity to collect continuing education credits, which are required to maintain licences.

The user consortium grew organically. Within a few years, people who had taken part in courses, continuing education programmes, health, or education meetings brought ideas pertinent to their organizations forward, and we worked with them to address those needs (e.g., social workers who participated in association meetings started a support group for single mothers). Indigenous people who had taken part in a course on the network began using it for meetings of the joint councils. And so it went.

Some larger initiatives included:

1977 to date: Memorial's School of Continuing Studies/DELT maintained a major presence in DE and continued to expand their programmes within this consortium and other modalities. By 2012, they had 400 credit courses in operation and numerous full programmes, the first of which was the business degree. Memorial University of Newfoundland (MUN) used a variety of delivery modes from correspondence to eventually completely online for their offering, so it would be best to check with them about their total numbers. However, very soon after TCS started, MUN was offering courses from 6:00 to 10:00 p.m., Monday to Thursday on all four circuits – usually two to three programmes per time slot for the fall and winter terms. There was some use of the 4:00 to 5:50 p.m. slots and a few offerings in the spring terms as well. Learners were primarily adults either starting degree studies later in life or taking courses for general interest. Some, however, were with traditional learners who were taking face-to-face degrees at the campus but were using DE to take courses that could not be obtained in a timely manner on the campus.

1985: Department of Education used TCS to introduce the advanced high school curriculum in ten small rural high schools. This led to an ongoing programme called STEM-Net, which offered science, technology education, and math – the prerequisites for university entrance, which were often not available in small schools due to the lack of specialized teachers. The teachers for the programme were housed in the TETRA Centre and taught from 9:00 a.m. to 3:30 p.m. This very successful programme led to the evolution of the Centre for Distance Learning and Innovation, which now serves all provincial small schools on a digital broadband network using a learning management system [LMS]. The programme base was expanded as well to include courses like languages. All provincial schools were connected by 1994 (in part with funding from School Net).

1998: Memorial University cooperated with the College to offer a full first-year programme at a distance at all 17 college sites.

1990: The Marine Institute [MI] offered TCS-based programmes to fishers in coastal communities in Labrador. MI now has an extensive distance learning programme using the Internet and an LMS. Programmes attract national and international students.

1987–1995–2005: Expansion of international programme through the TETRA and OLIN Initiatives occurred. [See TETRA description under Question 2d, Post-Trial Network, and Question 13, OLIN response.] A number of these international projects dealt with distance learning or were in part distance learning oriented.

1995–2004: On the direct distance education side of things, OLIN funding facilitated the redevelopment of 27 degree/diploma distance learning programmes to online learning format and programme development support to local education-oriented SMEs in online development. In the subsequent phase, we worked with evolving distance learning SMEs to develop an international market for their products and services. The public sector groups had some depth of international experience; inclusion in international projects leant credibility to the small firms and supported their initial international efforts. [See Question 13 for additional information on OLIN.]

Late 1990s to early 2000s: Expanded video conferencing services to support initiatives of the government of Newfoundland and Labrador [GNL]: advanced education, health, justice, etc.). As an example, in 2001, TETRA partnered with Smart Labrador in a pilot to place video conference units in remand centres in coastal communities in Labrador to speed up the initial process of people charged while allowing the person to remain in his/her community and not have to fly to Goose Bay. By 2005, all courts in the province had video conference installations to allow these and other applications. TETRA provided training on using video conferencing and technical support. Applications in health that used video conferencing exclusively for remote patient consultations were oncology and psychiatry.

2002–2012: Although not directly distance education, broadband networks [BB] became an essential technical foundation as agencies moved to use more information technologies in their offerings. OLIN and members of its telehealth/tele-learning consortium partners helped to create the business case for the carriers to expand BB throughout the province. In 2002, BB was really only accessible in major communities. By 2012, it was accessible to 98% of the population.

What were the circumstances in your world that initiated this interest in developing the consortium model and the DE opportunities that it offered?

I think the phrase is "Necessity is the mother of invention." We were in a province with a small, very far-flung population. Five hundred thousand people, a hundred thousand of them in St.

Johns, hundreds of small coastal communities, schools everywhere, not a lot of money in any one single organization, and vision on behalf of the people who first said, "We have to find a way to provide better services despite all this." Memorial is the only university and, as such, has a social contract to help make its resources available to the citizens of the province and not just be an isolated institution of higher learning.

These were the initial drivers behind the development and expansion, being able to deliver more public and social services to the whole province instead of having it just concentrated in St. Johns or the 20 or so larger communities. Teachers needed to upgrade, and physicians needed access to sufficient continuing education so that they could maintain their credentials. Government and provincial institutions were interested in providing these types of services to support recruitment and retention.

4. *Which female researchers or female colleagues may have piqued your interest in the development of the consortium model and its DE initiatives?*

There weren't, and still are not, that many groups that use such a broadly-based consortium model. We were a bit of a poster child. In truth, early in my career, I had more contact with women who used telecommunications to address various social needs, and I can assure you they were few and far between. Doris Jelly was one such person who worked [in] the Communications Research Centre (DOC) in the area of satellites for health and education. Also Anna Casey-Stahmer, who worked for the Ontario government and who researched and wrote many articles in the early 1980s on the path from the satellite experiments to affordable operational programmes/network for education and health. And, of course, last, but certainly not least, the woman who hired me for that research assistant job, Judy Roberts, who was the research associate on the Memorial Hermes trial and remained with Telemedicine as assistant director through the development of the initial 11-site network. In 1982, she took a position as the senior founding staff person in the Telemedicine for Ontario Network and then moved again to be the senior founding staff person for Contact North, another collaborative network between Laurentian and Lakehead Universities and the pubic community colleges in Northern Ontario. I think both initiatives benefitted from her work here.

Louise Moran (I think when I knew her first when she was with the Open University UK) was a distance educator and researcher. She wrote extensively on collaborating in various distance learning environments. Her work was interesting and helpful. Louise would be in Australia now.

Someone who was likely at the same stage in her career path as me was Christine Marrett, of the University of the West Indies (UWI). Around the same time that Memorial was establishing its programmes and consortium, UWI was in the early stages of developing a satellite and ground-based audio network. I had been engaged by Johns Hopkins, in the early 80s, to go to UWI to look at their network and specifically at how their Telemedicine programme was progressing. They had a distributed university, three main campuses (Jamaica, Barbados, and Trinidad) and, if memory serves, fourteen smaller ones on the smaller islands. Not all programmes were available on all campuses: for instance, medicine was only available in Jamaica. They were in the early stages, establishing a network that would make more programmes available to more campuses. We secured a Canadian International Development Agency [CIDA] grant, through which we worked together for several years. This project was the foundation for an ongoing partnership between our two agencies.

5. *Who would you identify as the early female leaders/founders in the field of DE?*

There were many women who were doing foundational work in the programme, teaching, and instructional design areas as evolving technologies created new opportunities and challenges in the field. Some that come immediately to mind are:

- Thérèse Lamy at the Open University of Quebec, Université TÉLUQ, and her colleague, France Henri. We were on the Canadian Association of Distance Education (CADE) Board together.
- Kay Rogers was an early innovator and a source of support and inspiration to those of us coming to the field. She was at Carlton University in my day.
- Margaret Haughey – she was at the University of Alberta [U of A].
- Judith Tobin was with TV for Ontario [TVO]. She is currently conducting a contract for Contact North on its Pockets of Innovations project. At the moment, this often takes her out of the country.
- Other people in the mix of the day: Lucille Pacey, who was with the Open Learning Agency [British Columbia] and Betty Mitchell. While [they were] in distance education, they were trying to move that network piece forward, so they were the people I knew reasonably well.
- Liz Burge, originally from Australia and has returned to Australia now, was at University of New Brunswick [UNB] for a while and, before that, was at Ontario Institute for Studies in Education [OISE]. I looked to her for work around the learners: learner support, learning styles, etc.
- Joan Collinge from Simon Fraser University [SFU] was instrumental in early development and expansion of the programme at SFU. I believe she started with the SFU distance learning group in 1988.
- Louise Moran has already been mentioned.
- Jane Brindley is in British Columbia now but did a stint up Athabasca [Alberta] way, among other places.
- Anna Zawicki from University of Prince Edward Island [UPEI].
- Christine von Prümmer was also pretty instrumental. She was at the FernUniversität [Germany].

6. *What are some of the goals that you strove to achieve in the development of your consortium model and its DE offerings?*

Our overarching goal was to make public resources (education, health, justice, etc.) available in the main centres, and particularly St. John's, more accessible to everybody. With this, we hoped to improve conditions for citizens and decrease the feeling of isolation of professionals and others living in small or remote communities and thus encourage people to stay there longer. That was really our driving force. The education component, whether credit courses or continuing health education programmes, was key for health professionals because most of them are required to participate in a certain number of hours of professional development each year to maintain their credentials.

Another goal was to increase the availability of specialist services in health. Very few health specialists would practice outside major centres, and, indeed, it was expensive to fund the centres and teams to support them. From the outset, therefore, we were interested in medical data transmission to support to diagnosis and follow up. The type of equipment varied, and the number and types of specialist services grew as more digital and video applications became available.

Having developed the model from the health and education base, it was our intention to support many other public groups that needed to make their resources more widely available to their clients as well. Some groups, like social services, used the network and its established sites for their activities. Others, like the justice system, made use of our expertise to set up their video network, our training, and our bridging services. If there was a public good to offer and we could help, that group could join the consortium. Some groups came just to use our facilities because they were pretty unique in the day.

Memorial's experience and constant message was "Keep it needs driven, simple, affordable, and accessible" – a message well received by public institutions and developing countries.

7. *What are some of your accomplishments that you would like to share?*

The consortium's accomplishments were generated by the efforts of many people at many levels. There was always somebody or some group that was willing to say "yes" when they could have said "no" or were willing to take a risk on relatively untested technologies when they could have said, "We have always done it this way." Among those people back in the 1970s and 80s, were the president of the university, the ministers for health and education, and the senior administrators of schools and colleges. Funders, national and local, like Atlantic Canada Opportunities Agency [ACOA], were receptive to the model, as it was self-sustaining and produced benefits to many people and communities which, in turn, would assist community development. So, in the longer term, they were able to find ways to help fund local initiatives and contribute to international work.

I think that I have really touched on our accomplishments already. That being said:

We did grow that consortium from 2 groups to 200, a few sites to groups of 250, a handful of programmes to 8,000 (in my day), ultimately resulting in 13,000 hours of programmes annually by 2012 and Lord knows how many individuals.

We were privileged to carry out many interesting international projects that we all feel quite proud about. For example, I feel we made a difference in Uganda. Pediatricians at Memorial's Faculty of Medicine were among a group of Canadian physicians who were assisting the medical school at Makerere University in Kampala to recover, as it had been devastated by the upheaval caused by the dictator, Idi Amin. Physicians from Canadian medical schools were taking turns to give lectures, introduce new technologies, and help the various departments re-establish. The physicians came to us to establish a satellite link between Memorial and Makerere's medical school and to use our interface to link to the other Canadian medical schools in eastern Canada for additional expertise. We worked with carriers to provide the Canada/Africa link, trained all necessary staff on the use of site equipment, and ran the Canadian-African programmes from our headend. We also helped Makerere establish a network with the medical school in Nairobi, Kenya, for ongoing support. We trained them on network matters, use of end equipment for education, and medical data transmission. On a remote island, in a remote province in the Philippines, the first four telephones ever installed and I arrived on the same day. Four physicians served 50,000 people in the only hospital. Like physicians everywhere, they needed to keep their continuing medical education [CME] credits up to date in order to maintain their licence. As you can imagine, leaving that island for continuing education was a challenge. We helped them establish a link to the medical school in Manilla and provided technical and programme delivery/development training on both ends so the physicians could take part in some programmes being offered in Manilla.

We took part in many international partnerships with newly industrialized or industrialized countries like the Caribbean or Japan, but somehow the ones with less developed countries seemed more rewarding. A little help seemed to go a long way. I would include that kind of work in my accomplishments, my bit of something left to the world at large when they close the cover on the coffin.

The OLIN initiative that encouraged partnerships between the larger public sector agencies with a well-established international presence and relatively new SMEs in distance learning who wanted to bring their online learning products to an international market was a successful endeavour. A number of the companies were able to establish clients outside of Canada for their products. This was a good thing for the province.

As I indicated in Question 3 [2002–2012], my involvement in contracts to expand broadband networking to reach 98% of the NL population was both an accomplishment and a significant learning experience.

8. *What are some of the challenges that you faced in developing and implementing your consortium and the DE opportunities that it offered over the years?*

Let me see, challenges. What is a job without challenge? Just another boring day at the office. Challenges, if there were any:

- The state of rural telecommunications infrastructure certainly presented challenges at the beginning, but a slow and steady rollout allowed us to work with the carriers to create that private network. Having such a substantial customer allowed them to be comfortable making investments in infrastructure.

- Establishing a mutually satisfactory working relationship with the telephone company was interesting at first. Salespeople talked to customers, just like they do when you buy a car, but we really needed to talk to technicians and engineers. We wanted them to design a "new car!" Soon enough, the engineers were a common sight in our control centre. They also frequently came with us on international projects as, among other things, their presence gave us credibility when holding meetings with carriers in other countries.

- Trying to find funding for all of the expansions and ongoing technical changes and the cost of expanding the physical space we occupied as we grew also presented challenges. I am sure we shared this challenge with everyone else. When you are attempting something new or pushing boundaries, it is not easy for funders (private foundations, international agencies like CIDA or the World Bank, or various government departments) to place your request/interest within their establish[ed] guidelines. Not that people were unwilling; it was sometimes a challenge, that's all.

- As networks became more sophisticated, trying to get broadband out to rural and remote areas was not without difficulty. Not directly DE, but certainly fundamental to its expansion. This is why I ended up working on contracts for the government of Newfoundland and Industry Canada on their broadband rollout. The more sophisticated the networks and uses became, the more difficult it was for a telephone carrier to make a business case and the broader the set of groups that had to buy in to help them make that case. Trying to get broadband Internet to remote areas so that everybody could have education and health programming at their individual desks is a significantly larger undertaking than getting networks out there that are contained to specific agency sites.

But what's a job without a challenge? And, again, it wasn't that people were obstructionist. The more complex that it became, the more people there were that had to understand and agree to buy in and act. Left foot, right foot. ☺

9. *What was the "state of learning opportunities and DE" in your geographical area when you first entered the field as opposed to these learning opportunities in 2018?*

   I honestly think that the only groups involved in distance learning when we started were those at Memorial. The College had a distributed campus system. The university had a division complementary to Continuing Studies, Extension Services, which worked directly with and in communities carrying out community development work. There was not a correspondence programme at the high school level.

   As I mentioned earlier, in 1965, the university started its distance education programme based out of the 45 learning centres to upgrade teachers. The university also offered a six-week intersession in the summer that was designed so teachers could complete one or two courses in the summer break. By 2012, Memorial had four hundred courses being offered in various terms so that students could complete degrees. I imagine that Memorial offerings and approaches were similar to other dual-mode universities in the 1970s.

10. *What interesting memories would you like to share about the beginning of online DE?*

    I think that the interesting things are covered by the answers to your previous questions, but I will tell you a story or two that added a little intrigue or lighted the journey now and again.

    During one early international project, we were working with the University of the West Indies network [UWIDEC] to help expand their network and programmes on the island of Jamaica, which was the network hub. CIDA had funded the partnership. Our engineer partners from the Newfoundland Telephone Company, Jamaican Telephone Company, and us were just finished the design and had placed the necessary hardware in the telephone towers in Jamaica when Hurricane Gilbert [a Category 5 storm] hit. It blew every communications tower on the island down. CIDA was very forgiving. A year later we were able to restart. . . . Left foot, right foot.

    On the other end of the weather continuum, I called the Newfoundland Telephone Company in a "bit of a tone" one day because of the miserable quality of the Labrador programme circuit. They sent me a picture of what looked like a very large Abominable Snowman with two heads looking in different directions and other appendages heading in various directions. The helicopter had been dispatched to a high coastal hill in Nain [northern Labrador], which was carrying a number of men with sophisticated axes and some fancy heaters. The wind and sleet (freezing rain to you mainlanders) had deposited two and a half to three feet of ice all over the microwave tower, doing not much for the clarity of transmission. I would have my network back within the day, I was told in a long-suffering tone. The weather gods are not always kind.

    Princess Anne visited us sometime in early 1990. She was very interested and gracious and chatted to one of the groups on the network. However, for a week, we had security checking out the whole centre and everyone in it. On the day of her visit, there were formal-looking Royal Canadian Mounted Police [RCMP] officers with guns around; the whole path through the medical school from the door to our unit closed to any people. Dogs were sniffing for bombs in the unit just before she came. Don't entertain royalty is my advice; I can only imagine what it would have been like if it had been the Queen.

    When I was in the Philippines and was walking around a remote island with the hospital administrator, an ever-increasing collection of young children (five- to six-year-olds) was following, pointing at me, and giggling behind their hands. Eventually, I asked what was so funny. The administrator said that while they had heard of white people, most children on the island would never have seen one. However, it was not the colour of my skin that they found so funny; it was the colour of my hair. They thought that this mop of medium-brown hair with many red undertones, which really could look quite red in the bright sun (a gift from my grandmothers), was the strangest thing they had ever seen.

One of the earlier course offerings on the network was first-year physics. Couse materials were circulated, including the bits and pieces to do some rudimentary lab work (probably in the kitchen). One day at the end of term, the instructor received a call from the main post office in St. John's saying that there was a package up there addressed to him; it was ticking, and he was to come up and deal with it. It was a portable clock that had not had the battery removed. ☺ I guess today a bomb squad would be called.

What's a journey without a story, eh?

11. *What were your specific research interests, and have they changed/evolved over the years?*

I was not a researcher per se; I would consider myself to be a practitioner. I (we) quite shamelessly used the results of other peoples' research to produce our programmes. We did evaluate our various efforts and reported on them in conferences and some publications.

As time went on, my work became more focused on policy and governance models for agencies and networks. Also, as you can tell from my CV, I used my experience to work with governments (federal and provincial) to help create the case for, and monitor, the transition to digital broadband networks in rural areas of the province. While not distance learning or telehealth, neither of these activities was going to be able to continue without the new broadband. I felt my contribution to the teams (from years of experience) was to be the middle person between the technical teams and the bureaucrats who, in turn, had to keep the ministers informed and on board, as they made the funding decisions.

12. *Could you please describe the learning environment that you last worked in (e.g., geographic and institutional setting, student demographics)?*

While I will describe the last learning environment in which I worked, I reiterate that I feel that the post-OLIN contracts that I undertook with Industry Canada and the government of Newfoundland and Labrador to work with carriers to extend broadband networks to all communities was an important and increasingly necessary technical support to distance and online learning. When I finished my work on those contracts, broadband communications networks were within reach of 98% of the provincial population.

However, to the question, the last learning environment in which I worked was OLIN. This agency built on and expanded the previous work of TETRA and informally on the work of all the public distance education agencies in the province that offered distance learning opportunities. Given OLIN's small staff – four, including myself – we were facilitators, trainers, and mentors for the most part, although we did take part directly in some projects as we were responsible for three major activity areas:

a) Facilitating the redevelopment of 27 degree/diploma programmes into online learning format.

The programmes chosen for this activity had to i) be in some distance learning mode and easily moved to online format, ii) be of benefit to the province, and iii) have some potential for being used in the international market. Programmes from Memorial, the Marine Institute, the College, the K–12 sector (specifically, French being offered by the STEM-Net group), and one private training college dealing with construction were included in the mix. The SMEs in our alliance [See b following] were involved in the redevelopment. Some examples of programmes were i) a business programme, ii) creation of an e-learning repository for business innovation and growth and associated training created under an existing Irish-Newfoundland partnership (Memorial/the College), and iii) a Labourers' Educational Technical Assessment, which was a blueprint-reading module (the College).

OLIN's instructional designer took the lead on this objective.

b) Developing and implementing international contracts in distance learning and telehealth that included public institutions and local SMEs.

OLIN engaged two firms to review local programmes that were market ready [see earlier in this interview) and assess the international experience of the public sector groups and the additional skills in the SMEs. They then developed a marketing strategy that included suggestions for likely countries of interest for market development activities. We marketed ourselves as the Distance Learning Alliance. There were four public sector agencies – Memorial, the College, the Marine Institute, and STEM-Net – and 11 SMs with various foci – multimedia, instructional design, network development, evaluation, etc. During our marketing efforts, we also looked for potential co-funders to broaden the potential impact of our endeavours. Under this initiative, we developed projects in South America (Chile and Brazil), the Caribbean (Dominica and St. Vincent/the Grenadines), Sub-Saharan Africa (Senegal, South Africa, Tanzania, and Uganda, co-funded by the Acacia Project of the Canadian International Development Research Centre [IDRC]), the USA training for World Bank staff, and also funded work in India and building on the existing Irish-Newfoundland partnership (Ireland). I was the lead on the development of this objective.

c) Developing a business plan and obtaining consensus on the creation of a single high-speed network to support the activities of all provincial health and learning networks.

OLIN worked with all the networks in health and education (TETRA, the various provincial health and school boards, the College, Memorial high-speed network, etc.) to create and agree upon a technical definition document on organizational structure, governance and costing models, network description, and a business case for a single health and education network. This document was presented to [the] government. OLIN's computer networking engineer took the lead on the objective.

To fund these activities, including monetary contributions to programme redesign and international activities, OLIN was the implementing agency for an $11 million portion of a federal/provincial funding agreement between 1996 and 2002. As Executive Director, I collaborated with the Provincial/Federal Implementation Committee of the Economic Renewal Agreement in articulating and implementing the programmes under this portion of the overall agreement.

At the time I was housed at Memorial, but I reported to the Council of Higher Education. My direct report was through a working group of the council, which was comprised of the administrators of post-secondary, the Vice President [VP] of Academic at Memorial, and the VP of Academic at the College of the North Atlantic. OLIN also had an operational board that included representatives of other interested parties, such as the executive director of Operation ONLINE, an agency tasked to grow the information technology [IT] sector in the province. So in the ten years before I moved into the broadband initiative, this was my brief.

13. *Is there anything else you [would] like to address?*

I think I have covered pretty much everything I can think of, except to say in closing to anyone who might be considering this or a similar path, "The journey has its own rewards. Make sure you notice them as you go along."

14. *Can you suggest names of other female pioneers in DE or online learning that you think we should include in the book?*

You know, in fairness, in addition to the people I mentioned earlier, I would think it would be a good thing to interview Doreen Whalen here in St. John's because she was the woman in charge of the Memorial credit courses through the major growth period. She is no longer with Memorial, but if you need some contact information for her, I can easily find it. To miss out on her story would be to miss out much of the really significant work that the Faculty of Education did over the decades to further distance education in this province. She, I think, would have her own challenges and stories to bring to this discussion.

Publications

Books

Roberts, J. M., & Keough, E. M. (Eds.). (1995). *Why the information highway? Lessons from open & distance learning*. Trifolium Books, Inc.

Book Chapters

House, A. M., & Keough, E. M. (1988). Experiences in distance education and telemedicine between Canada, Kenya, Uganda and the West Indies. In R. Magarick & R. Burkman (Eds.), *Reproductive health education and technology issues and future direction* (pp. 166–174). Johns Hopkins University.

Keough, E. M. (1988). Atlantic Canada perspective: Memorial University of Newfoundland. In K. Faith (Ed.), *Toward new horizons for women in distance education* (pp. 109–121). Routledge.

Keough, E. M. (1990). Distance education at Memorial University of Newfoundland. In *Experiences in distance education*. Commonwealth of Learning and The University of West Indies.

Keough, E. M., & Pacey, L. (2003). Public policy and structures: strategic implementation. In M. G. Moore & B. Anderson (Eds.), *Handbook of distance education*. Lawrence Erlbaum Associates, Inc.

Roberts, J., Keough, E. M., & Pacey L. (2001). Public and institutional policy interplay: Canadian examples. In E. J. Burge & M. Haughey (Eds.), *Using learning technologies: International perspectives on practice* (pp. 26–37). Routledge.

Journal Articles

Burge, E. J., Smythe, C. L., Roberts, J. M., & Keough, E. M. (1993). The audioconference: Delivering continuing education for addictions workers in Canada. *Journal of Alcohol and Drug Education, 39*(1), 78–91.

Chambers, L. W., Neville-Smith, C., House, A. M., Roberts, J. M., Canning, E. M., O'Reilly, B., & O'Neill, M. (1981). Serving the needs of hearing impaired preschool children in rural areas. *Canadian Journal of Public Health, 72,* 173–180.

Haughey, M., Keough, E., & Roberts, J. (1997). Trends in Canadian post-secondary education: Their impact on distance education. *Open Praxis, 1,* 22–25.

House, A. M., Keough, E. M., & Hillman, D. (1987). Into Africa: The telemedicine links between Canada, Kenya and Uganda. *Canadian Medical Association Journal, 136,* 398–400.

House, A. M., Roberts, J. M., & Canning, E. M. (1981a). Telemedicine provides new dimensions in CME in Newfoundland and Labrador. *Canadian Medical Association Journal, 124,* 801+.

House, A. M., Roberts, J., & Canning, E. M. (1981b). Comparison of slow scan television and direct viewing of radiographs. *Journal of the Canadian Association of Radiologists, 32,* 114-117.

Keough, E. M. (1997). Distance education: Thoughts on current policy directions and their impact. *Communiqué, The Distance Education Practitioner's Magazine, 12*(3/4), 3–6.

Roberts, J. M., Canning, E. M., Chambers, L. W., House, A. M., Cox, M., & Neville-Smith, C. (1976). The role of physicians in caring for preschool deaf children in rural Newfoundland and Labrador. *Newfoundland Medical Association Newsletter, XVIII*(6), 5–8.

Roberts, J. M., House, A. M., McNamara, W. C., & Keough, E. M. (1993). Report on Memorial University of Newfoundland's experimental use of the communications satellite Hermes in telemedicine. *Journal of Distance Education/Revue de l' éducation à distance, VIII*(1), 34–42.

Conference Presentations

House, A. M., & Keough, E. M. (1989a). Memorial University of Newfoundland international distance education and telemedicine projects. In R. Sliwa & B. Battrick (Eds.), *Proceedings of the Olympus utilisation conference* (pp. 327–330). ESA Publications Division.

House, A. M., & Keough, E. M. (1989b). Telemedicine and distance education: The Memorial University of Newfoundland experience. *Proceedings of the IEEE conference on communication* (pp. 10.2.1–10.2.4). IEEE Communications Society.

House, A. M., & Keough, E. M. (1992). Distance health systems – collaboration brings success: The past, present and future of telemedicine in Newfoundland. In *Proceedings of second international conference on information technology and community health* (pp. 5–11). University of Victoria Press.

House, A. M., Keough, E. M., & Mooney, M. (1984). Application of Anik B telephone channels to meet health and education needs in remote areas. In *Proceedings of the Canadian Satellite Users Conference* (pp. 91–94). Queen's Printer.

Keough, E. M., Moran, L., Roberts, J., & Spronk, B. (1997). *The converging classroom: Are your policies ready?* [Paper presentation]. Eighteenth World Conference of the International Council for Distance Education, Penn State University, University Park, PA.

Keough, E. M., Roberts, J. M., Lawrence, E., & Fuchs, R. (1995). Networking for rural development. In D. Sewart (Ed.), *One world, many voices: Quality in open and distance learning* (Vol. 1, pp. 295–298). Selected papers from the Seventeenth World Conference of the International Council for Distance Education, Birmingham UK. Oslo, Norway.

Roberts, J. M., Lamy, T., Keough, E. M., Stahmer, A., & Helm, B. (1993). Issues for distance education in immigrant language learning: A Canadian case study. In *Selected readings from the eighth annual conference of the Canadian association for distance education* (pp. 187–200). Commonwealth of Learning.

Taylor, S., & Keough, E. (1993). Empowerment through teleconference making connections: Distance education for the 21st century. In B. Sorvin, R. Lunden, & Y. Ryan (Eds.), *Selected readings from the sixteenth annual conference of the international council for distance education* (pp. 225–230). ICDE and Queensland University of Technology.

Taylor, S., & Keough, E. (1995). Women's economic network. In D. Sewart (Ed.), *One world, many voices: Quality in open and distance learning* (Vol. 1, pp. 355–358). Selected papers from the Seventeenth World Conference of the International Council for Distance Education, Birmingham UK. Oslo, Norway: ICDE.

20
KOROIVULAONO, THERESA

Photo of Theresa Koroivulaono contributed by Theresa Koroivulaono

The Republic of the Marshall Islands is comprised of 70 square miles of land and 750,000 square miles of ocean, so we need to reconfigure our education model to suit our context, if we are truly student centred.

Dr. Theresa Koroivulaono studied at the University of Auckland, New Zealand, and completed a Bachelor of Arts degree in English in 1997. She went on to complete a Master of Arts degree in 1998. In 2010, she obtained a PhD in English. She also obtained a Graduate Certificate in Tertiary Teaching at the University of the South Pacific, Fiji, in 2012.

Koroivulaono was Acting Director of the University of the South Pacific (USP) from 2011 to 2015. USP is headquartered in Suva, Fiji. The university services 12 countries and 14 campuses spread across a vast area.

From 2015 to the present, Koroivulaono has been President of the College of the Marshall Islands. The College of the Marshall Islands serves the entire Micronesia region, which includes thousands of small islands as well as the five sovereign Federated States of Micronesia, Palau, Kiribati, the Marshall Islands, and Nauru.

Koroivulaono's mandate to offer quality higher education to a vast region is described in detail during her interview. Distance education and evolving new technologies have given her institution the tools to improve education throughout the Pacific region. She is proud of her recent accomplishment of planning, coordinating, and implementing the first Australasian Council on Open Distance and eLearning (ACODE) workshop at USP in June of 2013.

Koroivulaono's research interests include enhancing online learning designs, interactive and best practices in learning, and identifying the challenges of timely delivery of learning resources. Publications generated from these research interests are listed at the end of this chapter.

Koroivulaono's mandate to bring quality learning to a vast and isolated region of the South Pacific while working to lessen the isolation through advancing technology, is a challenge well suited to online learning.

Interview

Transcript Analysis Summary

Analysis of all interviews included in this volume led to the identification of 3,545 units of data. The mean of these collective units was 118 per pioneer, the median was 118.5, and the mode was 132. Individual interview units ranged from 59 to 217 units, yielding a spread of 158 units between all interviews. Theresa Koroivulaono's interview generated 132 units, which placed her interview just within the top third of all interviews in terms of unit generation.

A comparision of Theresa Koroivulaono's interview to the interviews of all pioneers indicated that half her interview was comparable to the average interview in terms of units produced per thematic area (Figure 20.1). Seven of the 14 thematic codes in her interview yielded a similar numbers of unit to the average interview. These included benefits of DE, challenges, accomplishments,

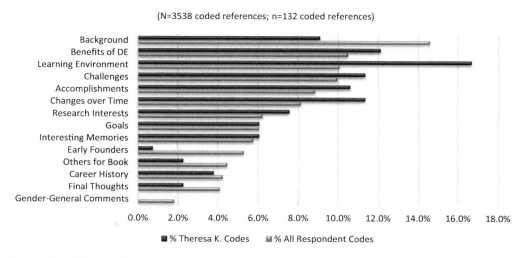

Figure 20.1 All Respondents' Versus Theresa Koroivulaono's Parent Codes

research interests, goals, interesting memories, and career history. Koroivulaona's interview contained significantly more units in the area of learning environment and a fair number more units in the area of changes over time as compared to the average interview. These extra units were produced from her detailed description of the composition and geographic reach of her institution, which provided education to diverse learners throughout the Marshall Islands, and the profound changes that occurred as a result of this massive undertaking.

Theresa's interview yielded fewer units than the average interview in her conversations about her background, early founders, others for the book, final thoughts, and general gender-related comments. The small number of units in most of these areas was related to the recent development of open online learning in her geographic location. Finally, it was not expected to find many units in this topic area, since general gender-related conversations arose organically during some interviewees' discussions.

Link to recorded interview: tinyurl.com/Koro-T-2018

Transcript of Interview

Full name: Violet Theresa Koroivulaono (commonly called Theresa)
Institutional Affiliation: President of the College of the Marshall Islands
Key:

    Regular font = Interviewee comments
    Italicized font = Interviewer comments

Interview Questions

1. *In what year did you begin to look into distance education [DE]?*

    Well, it was 2002. It wasn't here in the Marshall Islands. It was Fiji, in the South Pacific.

2. *What education and experience did you have before you became involved in DE?*

    In terms of my educational experience in distance education, none at all, but in terms of education, I had lived for almost 30 years at the time in Auckland, New Zealand, and I was relocating back to my home country of Fiji, and I was looking to secure employment. So I had no experience in distance education, but I had a master's in English and thought that I'd have a look at the newspaper and see what would come up there.

3. *What events in your life made you interested in DE?*

So I saw some positions that were being advertised at the University of the South Pacific [USP] at the Laucala Campus, Suva, Fiji. It is a regional university with its headquarters in Suva, Fiji. They have 12 countries and 14 campuses as part of the area of delivery. So because I was going back home, and my family lived in Suva, I wanted to look for employment opportunities there.

What I saw was a whole lot of lecturing positions and, of course, other administrative positions. What caught my eye was an area called Design and Development of Distance Learning Materials, and it was an instructional designer position. So I applied for that position over the others.

I: Were there any other life events that led you to the field of distance education, or would you say that was the main reason?

That was the main reason. The main reason was that I needed to move back home to be with my family. My parents were still alive at the time. My father had become ill and subsequently died before I could move back. My mother was still alive at the time. So I made that decision to move back home to be with my parents and my family. And as I said, I was looking for employment. The one area that really piqued my interest was when I read that particular part of the advertisement saying that an instructional designer was needed to design and develop distance learning materials for the South Pacific. I really had no idea what that meant. I did find out. I googled and found things out, and as I did that, I thought that this looked like something that I really wanted to become involved with.

4. *Were there any women who may have helped you become interested in DE?*

Not initially. Not initially, but certainly after starting work, I would recognize my fellow designers at the time, and that was from 2002 to 2014, nearly 12 years altogether, and in particular, I want to recognize my Head of Section and the Director for Flexible Learning where I was working, Dr. Helen Lentell. She had come from the Commonwealth of Learning in Canada to take the position as director of our unit, our department.

There was another colleague, Dr. Jennie Evans. She was the head of the Centre of Education, like a deputy director in the same section. I also recognize her considerable contribution to my education in DE.

5. *Who would you say are the early female leaders/founders in the DE field?*

Professor Asha Kanwar. She is the CEO of the Commonwealth of Learning, which is headquartered in Canada.

6. *What are some of the goals that you worked to achieve in the DE field?*

The biggest one for me, particularly coming from these large ocean states or small island developing states, is equitable educational opportunity. So, the opportunity to create learning experiences despite the many learning challenges that we have here, particularly with regard to natural resources and the continuity of those resources. A boat or a plane can be scheduled to fly out with the kinds of materials that the students need to advance their learning or to even engage in their learning, but there is no guarantee that the boat or the plane will actually make it in time. We train teachers at this college for this country. We have an Associate of Science in Elementary Education. Last year we were approved for our first baccalaureate at this college. It is in education: a Bachelor of Arts in Elementary Education. We also have a learning designer now, and that is one of the major initiatives at the College of the Marshall Islands to ensure the best possible DE learning designs. Taking quality education out to our outer island and atoll students is a major goal. The Republic of the Marshall Islands is comprised of 70 square miles of land and 750,000 square miles of ocean, so we need to reconfigure our education model to suit our context if we are truly student centred.

So it is those kinds of initiatives that we look at to be able to meet that goal of creating the most equitable of opportunities for particularly our outer-island remote students.

7. *What are some of your accomplishments in the field of DE that you would like to share?*

That's a difficult one to answer, because . . . I need to explain something here. Our cultures in the Pacific are based very firmly on humility. Just like every single island nation in this Pacific Ocean, North and South Pacific and Central Pacific, we share this belief, this practice. That's why it is hard for me to say that these are *my* [emphasis in the original] accomplishments. They're more *our* [emphasis in the original] accomplishments. The instructional design team that I worked with through the University of the South Pacific and now working as the President of the College of the Marshall Islands – there is a whole team that makes things happen here, from building structures to designing to making sure that the resources are maintained and sustained. So, having explained that, I will now talk about the accomplishments that we have made together.

At the University of the South Pacific [USP], there were many, many, many accomplishments: many of them first-time-round accomplishments and were continuations of what others had started before us. What we looked at, again, if I go back to this goal from the North to the South Pacific, the goal hasn't changed. It remains the same. You will notice that I didn't use the word *equal*. There is a very good reason that I didn't use that. I would love to use the word *equal*. However, we live in a very highly resource-challenged area because, both in the North and in the South Pacific, our economies are classified as developing countries. So there are always competing interests. I know that all of us are confronted with this. I think there are degrees; there are levels at which we are placed on a continuum of resources and sustainability of those resources over time. Our certainty of whether or not we are going to be at the same level is always something that we need to build into the kind of planning that we do.

So, in terms of accomplishments, one of the things that we engaged very heavily at the USP Centre for Flexible Learning as instructional designers was the area of research. I think that they still are, as we were then, a non-academic unit. So they were what we call a learning support unit. So, although research was not as prominent in our requirements for the conditions of our employment as they were with our academic colleagues, we felt that we needed to do the research because, while there was a whole lot of research in, say, neighbouring Australia or New Zealand – certainly in Canada, the US, and the UK – the kind of research that we needed to inform our positions in the Pacific wasn't as plentiful as we would have hoped. So we started to apply internally for funding that was available primarily to our faculty colleagues at the university for research.

One in particular that comes to mind. . . . We went out, and for instance, we tested the connectivity right up to Kiribati. Kiribati is an island nation on the equator in the Central Pacific. It's also a member country of the University of the South Pacific, or USP, as we call it. We worked our way around. We did tests in Vanuatu, in the Solomon Islands, [and] Fiji itself at different locations. I think there were also teams that went out to Tuvalu and Samoa. We tested the connectivity in the campuses and in the countries because we needed to inform ourselves about the kind of learning designs and the learning models we were developing to know whether the design worked, say, in a country like Kiribati, and what connectivity there was, whether it was satellite-based or whether it was fibre optic-based. What other kinds of factors impacted on students' learning? For instance, did they have a personal mobile device? Or did they have to come into campus because campus was always Internet-enabled. They are all Internet-enabled in the University of the South Pacific campuses and centres. So that particular research project was instrumental in informing us as designers about the suitability of the learning designs [that] we were producing as a community of practice and being directly informed by the student profile. The student profile, in terms of what they can and they can't do, given where they are located, was one of the fundamentals that informed our learning design.

8. *What were some of the challenges that you found in the field of DE?*

One of the big challenges, and I think this goes across boundaries, but particularly where we are as large ocean states, is the continuity. Take myself as an example: moving out after 14 years, being able to retain the kind of professionality that could build very good capacity on the ground to enable this service of design and development of distance learning materials to continue. So, in the first instance, retaining adequately and suitably qualified learning and teaching professionals: for example, learning designers, multimedia specialists, [and] learning management system specialists. That is very difficult when you are competing in the same areas with young professionals who want to improve their lifestyles. They look in the paper and go online for jobs advertised in Australia, New Zealand, and all of that, and so they go, or they stay for a little bit, and then they move on. So that is one challenge.

The next big challenge is training: being able to train properly and sustainably so that the work that needs to be done for delivery – and by delivery, I also mean for our academics – is done at the right time and available for follow-through questions and activities. So how do you train so that the person uses your learning materials from the learning design perspective in alignment with learning outcomes? We worked, as you may understand, with subject matter experts, with the academics. So being able to understand that distance should not be a challenge: the training, the distance, of course, but that the distance is not a challenge, that there are ways around this, and to treat the student who is learning at a distance just as if they were sitting right here beside you, that's what I found was one of the biggest challenges.

And, of course, there is always a stigma. You know, the age-old stigma, which I think continues to this day, although I am encouraged by the ubiquity of the Internet, which seems to have impacted somewhat in the way that distance education is perceived as second rate or, you know, not as good as face-to-face education. That's another stigma that I think we continue to battle as distance educators as well.

9. *What was DE like when you first entered the field as compared to DE in 2018?*

Huge differences. In principle, not a lot, but in the actual operations and the practice – and again, I referred to it just a few seconds ago – the Internet has made a vast world of difference even here where, when you look at the map, you can't see us. You can see a whole lot of water, and then you can see the names of our countries more than you can see our islands and atolls. So, even here, the Internet really does level a lot of those challenges.

When I first started in 2002, I was hired as an instructional designer of print materials. We were designing and developing print materials that we could package and send out. Now, when I look at what a learning designer does . . . In fact, what we have done here at the College of the Marshall Islands, we've just employed our first learning designer. And it's new not just to this college and to this country, but to this whole region. I don't think that there is a learning designer in Micronesia. (This is the area in which I live now.) So, having to train him because we are developing him internally, and again, that was another challenge. So, I talked about the

University of the South Pacific and the challenges there. Those challenges are magnified here at the College of the Marshall Islands. We interviewed for this position. We had two rounds of interviews, and we failed to get someone. We actually got people who said, "Yes, we are interested," and then when we got down to getting the contract sorted on how they needed to get here, because these were actually all off-island hires, they backed out. And that is understandable. So we decided to develop capacity internally. In the design for the training of our internal colleague, I'm seeing a lot of the differences, even though we are developing a course design blueprint, which is what I did when I was first an instructional designer in 2002; the blueprint now looks a lot different in terms of the kinds of components that we've needed to build into it because we have connectivity out in the islands. And where we don't, of course, we still have to go back to offline materials. But the biggest impact has been the Internet.

10. *What interesting memories would you like to share about the beginning of online DE?*

I think my one big one . . . When I went to work at USP, I walked into my office, and I thought, "What do I do? I don't know anything about this job that I've just been given. Where do I start?" I also know that I felt a constant sense of amazement every time that I picked up a book or had a meeting or a discussion with one of my colleagues, most of whom had been there for a while. It was like a fairy tale for me because they opened up this whole world of knowledge and experience that I found fascinating. I thought it was amazing; it was fascinating that we could be based in Suva, Fiji, and we were designing and developing materials that would be completed in six months' time that would be delivered to the equator, to Kiribati and, of course, the Marshall Islands where I now live, that were also part of USP. And to be sending materials that far: The area of delivery, if I remember correctly, is 33 million square kilometres of ocean – that's the area of delivery for USP – I was incredibly fascinated by that. Here, I can say the same thing; it continues. That same fascination and engagement with these challenges that sound so awfully passé, but it's true, you know; those challenges, if we could just nail a couple of the opportunities that those challenges present, and because we are so small, we are not economies of scale; we can actually have a huge impact very quickly.

11. *What were your DE research interests, and have they changed over the years?*

Ah, yes, I think that they have. In the beginning, I wondered about learning styles. I, myself, am a visual learner. Although I am an English graduate in all of the degrees that I've undertaken and now have, I prefer to learn through images and experientially. You know, to get into a situation, like scenario learning or problem-based learning. So that, to me, speaks a lot to the kind of the design and development of materials that I speak to, that I am interested now in sharing with my colleagues here.

As well, my geographical area of work here, every single island that I know here in the South and North Pacific, we are still living oral cultures. So, in parallel to what we do in our literate worlds, as we step back outside into our Indigenous communities, we are expected to conform and to be a Fijian, or a Marshallese, or someone from Kiribati. That, to me, is a very interesting area that I have never had the time to research properly, and I hope that, perhaps in retirement, that's an area that I can go back into, because the way that you learn in oral culture is by seeing and doing. In the academy, we go to the library, we get books, we substantiate, [and] we provide evidence by referencing another source that is usually in a book form or something similar to the written word, as opposed to how we live our lives outside of the academy.

So, learning styles is the first area that I found incredibly fascinating. I used a whole lot of videos and a lot more images in books that I was developing. Over time, in recent times, and up here now, I'm interested in open educational resources [OER], which I did a lot of work in before I came here. The kind of flexibility in terms of resources. . . . Here at the College of the Marshall Islands, we are a college of 1,000 students – that's the higher end of our enrolments – with about 175 employees. It costs sometimes hundreds of thousands of dollars a year to bring books in. That's a substantial amount of money that we perhaps could be using more creatively somewhere else like, for example, e-books, OER. So that kind of move away from, as I said, learning styles to, instead, the business of matching funding to the resources that I talked about earlier: that kind of challenge of matching funding with what's out there and what's best for the college and, of course, our mission. There are three key words in our mission: *quality, student-centred* [emphasis in the original] education. To match all of those, that's a constant battle. But, I think, therein lays the re-engagement, the re-ignition of passion that those of us here at the college have for facing these head on every day. And then thinking, on the other hand now, if we are truly student centred, what does this require us to do so that our students in Jaluit, which is about 40 minutes by plane, and Wotje, which is about an hour by plane, and Ebeye, that's about an hour by plane . . . what do they want? They are hungry for knowledge and for learning. What can we give them so that we know that it is especially relevant to them out there and not just for them and their families but for the atolls and their economy?

12. *Could you please describe the learning environment in which you currently work?*

Over 90% of our students are Marshallese, so they are from here. The Marshall Islands have a Compact of Free Association agreement with the United States. So Marshall Islanders can travel to the States without a visa and go to school, work, and live there. They can transfer easily as long as the national scholarships board is able to finance them to move on to a university education because they do, of course. The college offers certificates, diplomas, associate degrees, and one baccalaureate programme.

The students are mainly young, our school-leavers, but at the same time, they come in with 1.5 children. So, while they are young, they are also young parents.

We are very fortunate here in the Marshall Islands; because of the two military bases that the US has here, we are connected by fibre optic – not everywhere, but particularly in the main centres. So, in Ebeye, where one centre is located, we are connected by fibre optic cable. So we are able to leverage that opportunity in terms of the learning. We actually teach also using Zoom [an online video conference application]. Our instructors teach through Zoom to deliver lecture-type classes. And then we normally try to get them over to meet their students at least once a semester, and, ideally, they should stay in that distance education centre for at least a week. And the other distance learning centre, which is Jaluit (so that is Ebeye, which is northwest, and Jaluit, which is southwest) – that's the newer centre that we had opened last year in June. They [Jaluit] are not connected by fibre optic, but we are connected by satellite. In fact, just in the last two months, their satellite was down; the connections were down. So we have a very innovative coordinator out there who was able to access quite a lot of sites and apps working with our National Telecommunications Authority out there, who, of course, still remained connected, but he had that inside connection, so [he] was able to download a lot of stuff that we could use offline. Of course, again, in terms of copyright, we're also very aware of that, and that's why, again, I take you back to OER.

In terms of the kind of funding that's available for students, our students have access to what is called the Pell Grant, which means that they need to be enrolled in a US-accredited institution. We are a US-accredited institution as well, which enables us to use that facility for our students.

I'm not sure whether or not I mentioned this, but this college was initially established to train teachers and nurses for the country [the Republic of the Marshall Islands]. We've branched out into liberal arts, into selected vocational studies – we have a maritimes programme because we are an ocean environment. The biggest and perhaps the only industry here is fisheries: specifically, the tuna industry. In these areas, we need Marshallese citizens on the tuna boats (they are owned by foreigners), to keep an eye on the catch, to monitor the kind of catch that is being taken out by overseas fishing companies.

We only have two vocational studies programmes running. The other is carpentry, basic carpentry. We also have a Science Department, a STEM Department, and a Business Department. In most recent times, we have also opened a Marshallese Studies Department.

Our students mainly enter the college at the development education level. They are second-language speakers of English. We have a large component – in fact, the largest component of students that come in at that level, developmental education. So that's non-credit.

13. *Is there anything else you [would] like to address?*

Perhaps if I talk about the aspirations of the college?

I: Sure.

As part of those aspirations, we have just developed our first-ever Education Master Plan, and in there, we have five goals. One of them is open learning. We are focusing very decisively in that area. So when you talk about accomplishments, my accomplishments, our accomplishments are: being able to move that [open learning] to the centre stage here of our considerations for the future of our students, and for this country to be able to focus on the learning delivery and learning model that we need to develop even more strongly now, particularly since, in 2023, the Compact for Free Association is up for renegotiation. So we are not sure what kind of economic package will be available to the country and, hence, to the college. So we do need to keep building the networks and our partnerships in these areas so that we at least have possible avenues and options to turn to if we are to think about prioritizing even more the kinds of, particularly, financial resources that we have at the college. Again, I go back to our geographical profile to underline this focus on open learning. We are 70 square miles of land in 750,000 square miles of ocean. We need to keep revisiting our education model to ensure that it fits our country and student profile as much as possible, given our resources.

Our first strategic plan was in 2015, which coincided with my starting here at the college. It was my first key performance indicator because there had been one that was being developed for four or five years, so I think that the Board of Regents really wanted to see one. So we agreed that that would be one of my major key performance indicators. We completed the plan, and it was implemented in 2016. It ended in December 2018.

Our next strategic plan is under development. It will be from 2019 to 2023. Again, in there we decided to look at that strategic plan in terms of how it was structured in themes, rather than with goals, as one would normally expect. The themes are sustainability, innovation and creativity, and collaboration and partnerships. Again, that has so many anchors in the reasoning and the rationale of those kinds of thematic areas also in relation to our Education Master Plan and open learning.

So, for the future, I see the college developing and refining a model that, of course, takes in the experience and the knowledge that we've all contributed, both in our training and our continued conference attendances and interactions with other people (from our communities of practice off island). But this will definitely include infusing and embedding all of this knowledge and experience with a definite grounding in the Marshallese context in terms of how we design, develop, and deliver distance education materials.

14. *Can you suggest any names of other female pioneers in DE that you think we might include in our book?*

    Dr. Helen Lentell – I mentioned her name before – and Dr. Jenny Evans. I think that they both live in England now, but they were instrumental at USP in 2004 to 2008 for introducing new initiatives to keep abreast of the rapid changes in distance education, like adopting Moodle for the first time in 2007 as the USP learning management system. They were also responsible for the implementation plan of the activities required across the university for a successful rollout, like training and customizing Moodle for the USP environment and membership with the relevant communities of practice.

I: How did you manage to collaborate and connect with other people between the islands, and between the college and the other institutions on the islands? How did you start that, and how did you sustain that over the years?

This is really a good example of what I said before about turning a challenge into an opportunity. The challenge always for us was to be able to find adequate funding to be able to, say, for instance, showcase one of the research projects that we were doing or what we thought was an innovative practice, you know, how we were using Moodle. . . . One of our educational technologists had designed an orientation programme for students in a new course. It was a game that he designed as an icebreaker. The value systems that he used were the traditional value systems of the different islands. So, shell money in the Solomon Islands, stone money in Palau, and things like this. We wanted to share what we were doing with the rest of the world, and we were finding it difficult sometimes to find the kind of funding that we needed, so we reached out to colleagues, especially in New Zealand and Australia, because they were very close to Fiji, and they would then say, "Hey, you know what? We would like to come and do research in a certain area – say, for instance, in video conferencing – and what tool you are using? Because we have one here in the outback of Australia called React," which, of course, USP adopted through those kinds of connections.

There's an association called ACODE. They would be very good to get ahold of because they have many distance education champions. It's the Australian Council on Open, Distance, and e-Learning. We became members of those types of organizations and communities of practice and forums. So, because we became members, we were able to say to our university, "We are now members. We have access to these people and these kinds of learning resources, ideas, knowledge, and everything else." Through that, we were able to convince people that we could also access funding and other resources that were available through these channels.

So those were the kinds of initiatives that we came up with to be able to showcase the work that we were doing, and also because we wanted to go out there to engage with new learning opportunities as well, to see what people were doing and what we might find that could be used or adapted in our places of work.

Publications

Book Chapters

Chandra, R., Hazelman, V., & Koroivulaono, T. (2011). Leveraging technology for tertiary education in the South Pacific. In M. Martin & M. Bray (Eds.), *Tertiary education in small states: Planning in the context of globalization* (pp. 215–232). UNESCO International Institute for Educational Planning (IIEP).

Crump, S., Twyford, K., & Koroivulaono, T. (2020). Remote and rural education. In *Oxford Research Encyclopedia*. Oxford University Press. https://doi.org/10.1093/acrefore/9780190264093.013.516

Journal Articles

Koroivulanono, T. (2000). The third degree. *Journal of Doctoral Candidates Workshops and Seminars English Department 'Written Froze Spoken.'* University of Auckland.

Koroivulaono, T. (2007). Fijian women as orators: Exceptions to tradition? *Pacific studies. Women writing Oceania: Weaving the sails of the Waka*. University of Hawaii.

Koroivulaono, T. (2014). Open educational resources: A regional university's journey. *RUSC. Universities and Knowledge Society Journal, 11*(3), 91–107. http://dx.doi.org/10.7238/rusc.v11i3.2121

Conference Presentations

Hazelman, V., & Koroivulaono, T. (2013, December). *What next? Progressing learning innovations in a regional university* [Paper presentation]. Seventh Pan Commonwealth Forum.

Koroivulaono, T. (2006, September). *Distance and flexible learning at the University of the South Pacific* [Paper presentation]. Asian Association of Open Universities (AAOU).

Koroivulaono, T. (2009). *Education-driven technologies* [Paper presentation]. Vice Chancellor's Learning & Teaching Forum, University of the South Pacific, Laucala Campus, Suva, Fiji.

Koroivulaono, T. (2010, December). *Repurposing OERs: The USP experience: Models to choose, adopt, adapt* [Paper presentation]. Sixth Pan Commonwealth Conference (PCF6), Kochi, Kerala, India.

Koroivulaono, T. (2012a). *Existing online resources* [Paper presentation]. International Conference on ICT & Oceanian Cultures, University of the South Pacific, Laucala Campus, Suva, Fiji.

Koroivulaono, T. (2012b). *OER by Theresa Koroivulaono* [Video file]. Paris, France. www.unesco.org/archives/multimedia/index.php?s=films_details&pg=33&id=2612

Koroivulaono, T. (2012c). *Open education resources at USP* [Paper presentation]. Vice Chancellor's Learning & Teaching Forum, University of the South Pacific, Laucala Campus, Suva, Fiji.

Koroivulaono, T. (2013a). *A snapshot of transformative pedagogies in a sea of islands* [Paper presentation]. Vice Chancellor's Learning & Teaching Forum, University of the South Pacific, Laucala Campus, Suva, Fiji.

Koroivulaono, T. (2013b). *Improving English language proficiency in the world's most linguistically complex region: A role for OERs* [Paper presentation]. Twenty-fifth ICDE World Conference, Tianjin, China.

Koroivulaono, T., & Kelly, L. (2012). *From sea level up . . . and beyond: Multimodal learning at the University of the South Pacific* [Paper presentation]. Asia-Pacific Innovations Conference.

Kotton, S., & Koroivulaono, T. (2015). *Annual report highlights* [Paper presentation]. JEMFAC, Honolulu, Hawaii.

Kotton, S., & Koroivulaono, T. (2017). *Annual report highlights* [Paper presentation]. JEMFAC, Honolulu, Hawaii.

Kotton, S., & Koroivulaono, T. (2018). *Annual report highlights* [Paper presentation]. JEMFAC, Honolulu, Hawaii.

21
KURTZ, GILA

Photo of Gila Kurtz contributed by Gila Kurtz

I was invited to be the head of a satellite unit at the Open University of Israel. There I saw the option of using the Internet providing live sessions to schools and homes. I was not sure where it would go to from there, but I understood something huge was happening.

Dr. Gila Kurtz began her studies with a Bachelor of Arts in Sociology and Anthropology from Tel-Aviv University, Israel, in 1980. Her Master of Arts in Public Policy was completed in 1987 at the same institution. In 1995, Kurtz obtained a PhD in Political Science from Bar-Ilan University, Israel.

DOI: 10.4324/9781003275329-22

Dr. Kurtz has been active internationally with various universities and organizations. Some of the most recent have been:

- 2000–2008 – Member, the Inter-University Centre for e-Learning (IUCEL), Israel;
- 2005–2008 – Member of the steering committee, the European Distance and E-Learning Network (EDEN);
- 2011 to Present – Member of international network activity, Sustaining a Global Perspective on Higher Education through International Collaboration, Intercultural Creativity and Networked Quality in Teaching and Learning Models, Danish Ministry of Science and Technology, Denmark;
- 2011 to Present – Scholarship of Teaching & Learning (SoTL) Mentor, International Journal for the Scholarship of Teaching and Learning, Georgia Southern University Statesboro, Georgia, USA;
- 2013–2015 – Board Member, the Inter-University Centre for e-Learning (IUCEL), Israel;
- 2013 – School of Education, University of California Berkeley, USA;
- 2014 – Instructional Design, Development, and Evaluation (IDD&E) Department, School of Education Syracuse University, USA; and
- 2015 – School of Education, University Roma, TRE, Italy.

Dr. Kurtz's research interests, reflected in her list of publications at the end of this chapter, include digital learning, future learning technologies, instructional design, and digital readiness.

Interview

Transcript Analysis Summary

Analysis of all interviews included in this volume led to the identification of 3,545 units of data. The mean of these collective units was 118 per pioneer, the median was 118.5, and the mode was 132. Individual interview units ranged from 59 to 217 units, yielding a spread of 158 units between all interviews. With 62 units, Gila Kurtz's interview generated the second lowest number of units

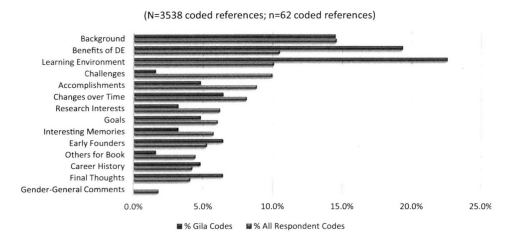

Figure 21.1 All Respondents' Versus Gila Kurtz's Parent Codes

among all interviews. This is likely due to the fact that Gila completed the interview in English, which was a foreign language to her.

A comparision of Kurtz's interview to the interviews of all pioneers indicated that her interview yielded a similar number of units to that of the average interview in five areas: background, changes over time, goals, early founders, and career history (Figure 21.1). Kurtz's interview produced significantly more units in the thematic areas of learning environment and benefits of DE. Many of the units found in the learning environment area related to her institutional work with emergent technologies for learning, which include recent robotic and artificial intelligence (AI) initiatives. It is interesting to note the disparity between the large number of benefits units and scarcity of challenge units in her interview. This does not fit the typical interview profile, which tends to have slightly more benefit than challenge units. The lower-than-average number of units in research interests is due to the fact that Kurtz's main research aim, human-technology interaction, had remained constant throughout her career.

Link to recorded interview: tinyurl.com/Kurtz-G

Transcript of Interview

Full name: Gila Kurtz
Institutional Affiliation: Holon Institute of Technology (HIT), Israel
Key:

Regular font = Interviewee comments
Italicized font = Interviewer comments

Interview Questions

1. *What was your educational and experiential background before you became involved in e-learning and online distance learning [ODL]?*

   I came from the social sciences. My undergraduate degree or BA [Bachelor of Arts] degree was in sociology, and then I moved to public policy. My doctorate work was in public policy, women within politics, but nothing in distance education.

   As a student I worked with the Open University of Israel as an instructor. There, I was exposed to the option of distance education [DE]. From there, it all started.

2. *In what year did you begin to look specifically into e-learning and ODL?*

When I finished my doctoral dissertation, I was invited to the University of Michigan in Ann Arbor [Michigan, USA]. This was a programme for young, promising researchers in social sciences. The year was 1995. When I got there, it was the first time I was exposed to the Internet. Looking at this channel where they sent us emails and I could write emails, I thought, "Whoa! The world is changing! You can change the world through the Internet."

When I came back to Israel, I was invited to be the head of a satellite unit at the Open University of Israel. There I saw the option of using the Internet, providing live sessions to schools and homes. I was not sure where it would go to from there, but I understood something huge was happening. I flourish in an environment where things are not clear. I like it when it is not clear, and you don't know what to do. But, you know, it was something big. I was there the first time to give a course by the Internet at the Open University of Israel and also in one of the campuses based in Israel at Bar-Ilan University, where I did my PhD. So I knew it was something big. I didn't know where it would go to, but I really wanted to go to be part of it.

3. *What were the circumstances in your world that initiated this interest in e-learning and ODL?*

I like to meet people; I like to meet students. I understood that using this DE and ODL [open and distance learning] offered me an opportunity to teach and learn from the best and to the best because we won't have any physical and time barriers.

Six years after I started e-learning, I was invited to teach in the Master of Distance Education and e-Learning programme at the University of Maryland University College [UMUC, Maryland, USA]. There I could teach and learn differently, meaning that it was different than face-to-face. (I love to teach face-to-face.) But teaching and learning at a distance provides you with a different mode of teaching and learning, mainly because of the option to reflect. I mean that it's not like now we are talking, I say something, and that's it. Think, pause, and move on. So there were a lot of new pedagogical options that I really paid attention to and thought, "Oh, I want to explore this."

4. *Which female researchers or female colleagues may have piqued your interest in e-learning and ODL?*

I would say that one in Israel is Professor Sarah Guri-Rosenblit from the Open University of Israel. She is one of the leaders in the DE field. She is one of the pioneers in Israel. She was one of the pioneers from the previous generation of the Open University, when it was correspondence, books, and so on. She laid the foundation for current way of using the Internet. She was one of the ones who influenced me. When I say influenced, I heard her, and I understood what was changing. She is one of the best. She has papers that I've read, classic papers.

From abroad, there are many, but I want to mention Gilly Salmon from England. She's one. I met her two months ago. She's still a leader. She looks ahead. There are others that influenced me, but she is one of the main characters. I really looked to her.

5. *Who would you identify as the early female leaders/founders in distance education, e-learning, and ODL?*

I read many papers, and I found that there are males, also, that influenced me. But I don't think that outside the two of them . . . Any new publication I rush to read because I really follow their work. There are others like Dr. Stella Porto, who was the head of the master's programme at the UMUC. We had a lot of talks and did research together. I still follow her.

6. *What are some of the goals that you strove to achieve in e-learning and ODL?*

Can I be honest? I wanted to make the world a better place for learning. I wanted to provide the best education to the rural areas either here in Israel or in the world, in Africa, and even the

USA where I was teaching – places that are really rural. I thought that this might be the way to do [it]. Otherwise, we might not be able to do it.

Another thing – I like to get to know new people, new environments. This was my option. Otherwise, I would teach face-to-face. This was a way to stay in Israel and welcome the global community.

7. *What are some of your accomplishments in e-learning and ODL that you would like to share?*

First of all, being in this industry, I was honoured to be invited to be a visiting scholar. So I travelled either to conferences or to teach. I was at the University of California Berkeley in the USA, the Syracuse University (USA), and also in Italy, and with the EDEN [European Distance Education Network] organization. I got an honour from EDEN, something like a Senior Fellow or the like. So I feel like people are really seeing my work.

I got a teaching recognition award from UMUC. But why I am saying this – I know I am a good teacher, but why I was really happy with this was to prove that my English was okay for teaching because I was afraid that I was not so clear with the English. It really touched my heart getting this teaching recognition award.

And most of all, getting to know people; I have a lot of friends through my work. Former students are colleagues now and my best friends. I am very humbled by this. So this is a main accomplishment – getting to know people.

8. *What are some of the challenges that you faced in e-learning and ODL over the years?*

I want to share with you my recent years of challenges or doubts, recent being five and less years. We know that e-learning doesn't suit everyone. But I do feel that nothing can replace the face-to-face – not because of the teaching and learning part, but because of the non-mediated connection. This brings me to my current job, which is Head of the Master's Programme at Holon Institute of Technology [HIT], and my previous job, where I was also Head of a Master's Programme on Information Communication Technology [ICT]. They are not fully online courses. I said, "Okay, we can teach this, but we need to add a face-to-face component" – as we say, "blended." I don't think that pure DE can work for everyone, but with blended, it might. I just have my doubts. Technology really keeps us apart. I can't really explain, but it's not like when we are face-to-face, the human touch.

9. *What was the "state of DE" when you first entered the field as opposed to e-learning and ODL in 2019?*

It was correspondence, books; and assignments were delivered via mail. I was the coordinator at the Open University [of Israel] when it was telephone office hours, and also at UMUC again, it was telephone. Later, we used Skype.

Now the technology reach allows me to do so many things, it can be really fast. It can be either real time, time delayed, and all of these options that we didn't have before.

10. *What interesting memories would you like to share about the beginning of e-learning and ODL?*

Because I am in the Middle East and I was an Adjunct Professor for ten years at UMUC, I taught American soldiers in Iraq because it was in the same time zone. We had live meetings. I don't know if you know this or not, but we are kind of enemies, Israel and Iraq. So for me, it was so exciting to see Baghdad because it was video conferencing. Here's the thing – my mother was born in Baghdad, and for her, telling her, "I see Baghdad through conferences that I have with the students," it was kind of heart touching for her and for me to close the circle by teaching to Iraq.

11. *What were your specific e-learning and ODL research interests, and have they changed/evolved over the years?*

    My main interest didn't change. It was the interaction between humans and technology. Technology for itself was not one of my interests. I just want to say to you right now my current research is on using social robots for learning. So this is all interaction: human-technology. What happens when humans interact with technology? This is my main interest. I think that technology is not just a means. It is something that changes the way we feel, we learn, we think. I'm not too sure that everybody agrees with me, but this is what I am looking for. Another example: a number of my publications are on using social media, like Facebook, as a learning platform, which is kind of strange because Facebook is not for this. You can see that first, you can use any technology for learning if you find the pedagogical excuse, and then you change the way you teach and the way you deliver, by the interaction in the class.

12. *Could you please describe the learning environment that you currently work in or have most recently worked in (e.g., geographic and institutional setting, student demographics)?*

    Right now, I am Dean of the Faculty of Instructional Technologies and Professor at HIT. Our main focus is on using technology for training in organizations. So this is kind of a change for me because my previous job was in the School of Education and the use of ICT in education, so this has changed my focus. So the students are coming from training management or instructional designers. They are in their 30s to mid-40s. They are very much technology oriented. They are coming mainly from the centre of the country, Tel Aviv, Jerusalem, those kinds of places. The focus is on the current state of use of technology within the organizational environment, but also trying to predict or look at the future of the use of learning technology within the institution.

    Our programme is face-to-face, but we have a number of courses that are blended or using different channels for learning. For example, we have a course that uses podcasts. They listen to the podcast and then come to class to discuss. It uses the "flipped-classroom approach." Another example is a MOOC [massive open online course] that has three face-to-face meetings through the semester.

    I have two main interests: research and teaching. One is on the impact of instructors' virtual presence on completion rates in MOOCs. The second one is the use of social robots within training. What we are doing is planning an escape room game activity. In this game, the workers are locked in the room, and they have to escape from it within a certain limited time by solving problems. This is team-based learning. You have challenges that you have to go over. What we do is put a human on the outside. We have a robot, whose name is NAO. He is the instructor and also sort of a peer. Are you familiar with Sophia, the robot?

    I: Yes.

    So, like Sophia, he can move, he can talk, and he has voice and face recognition. And by the way, I say, "he" because he is blue. We have one in red, and this is "she," which is funny. So we say, "NAO is escaping." I am so excited with this research. This is the new work that is coming in. The next generation of training and learning; this is what is really of interest to me. Artificial intelligence and IoT [the Internet of things] also, all of these things; this is what I am currently doing.

13. *Is there anything else you [would] like to address?*

    I have two suggestions or things that I would like to share with the young generation. The first one is "Don't be afraid to try something new," and "Don't stick to what you know. Think out of the box." This is how we progress. If we stay in our comfort zone, I don't think that we can progress. If you look, for example, at MOOCs, the intention was something else, and now it is moving, which is good. All the time we need to be thinking "How can we make it better?" When I say, "Don't stay in your comfort zone," I don't just mean embrace technology, but think again and again because the workplace is changing. Everything is changing. We need to lead. So don't be afraid to lead. This is one thing.

The other thing is "Go beyond your profession." For example, I am working now with scientists from the computer department and from mathematics, not social sciences. They give me an interdisciplinary way of thinking and working. It cannot be only us from the DE profession. It should be interdisciplinary because I think this is the best way to make progress and research.

I am very happy to give advice or help anyone, so would be very happy if you would share my details so that people can connect with me. I am here to help and also to learn.

14. *Can you suggest names of other female pioneers in DE, e-learning, or open and distance learning [ODL] that you think we should include in the book?*

Again, Sarah Guri-Rosenblit; I can connect you with her. I will look over some resources for you. I was mainly focused on Israel, which is why I have her name. And Stella Porto; I can give you her details if you think she suits.

Publications

Books

Arar, K., Kurtz, G., & Bar-Yishai, H. (Eds.). (2021). *Education as a complex system*. Tel-Aviv-Pardes (In Hebrew).
Beaudoin, M., Kurtz, G., Jung, I., Suzuki, K., & Grabowski, B. (2013). *Online learner competencies: Attitudes, knowledge, and skills for successful learning*. Information Age Publishing.
Chen, D., & Kurtz, G. (Eds.). (2011). *ICT, learning & teaching*. The College for Academic Studies (In Hebrew).
Kurtz, G. (1998). *Teaching with interactive television* [Research report]. The Open University of Israel (In Hebrew).
Kurtz, G. (2003). *Guidelines for learning through forums* [Research report]. Bar-Ilan University (In Hebrew).
Kurtz, G. (2014). *Uses of new interactive technologies between teachers, parents and students* [Research report]. The Israel Academy of Sciences and Humanities – Initiative for Applied Education.
Kurtz, G., & Chen, D. (2012). *Online learning: A digital toolkit for teachers*. The College for Academic Studies (In Hebrew).

Book Chapters

Beaudoin, F. M., Kurtz, G., & Eden, S. (2009). Experiences and opinions of e-learners: What works, what are the challenges, and what competencies ensure successful online learning, In Y. Eshet-Alkalai, A. Caspi, S. Eden, N. Geri, & Y. Yair. (Eds.), *Learning in the technological era*. The Open University of Israel.
Eden, S., Kurtz, G., & Mevarech, Z. (2011). The effect of meta-cognition teaching on student performances in an online course. In D. Chen & G. Kurtz (Eds.), *ICT, learning & teaching* (pp. 149–162). The College for Academic Studies (In Hebrew).
Kohen-Vacs, D., Kurtz, G., & Zaguri, Y. (2019). Requirement analysis: Towards the deployment of architecture incorporated with IoT for supporting work-based learning and training: On the threshold of a revolution. In I. Buchem, R. Klamma, & F. W. Wild (Eds.), *Perspectives on wearable enhanced learning: Current trends, research and practice*. Springer.
Kurtz, G. (2011). Integrating online technologies in Israel: Promises and challenges. In D. Chen & G. Kurtz (Eds.), *ICT, learning & teaching* (pp. 11–32). The College for Academic Studies (In Hebrew).
Kurtz, G. (2014). Students' perceptions of using Facebook group and a course website as interactive and active learning space. In Y. Eshet-Alkalai, A. Caspi, N. Geri, Y. Kalman, V. Zilber, & Y. Yair (Eds.), *Learning in the technological era* (pp. 65–73). The Open University of Israel (In Hebrew).
Kurtz, G. (2015). Integrating Facebook in an academic teaching context. In N. Notzer (Ed.), *How to succeed in academic teaching* (pp. 175–186). The College for Academic Studies (In Hebrew).

Kurtz, G., & Amichai-Hamburger, Y. (2008). Psychosocial well-being and attitudes toward e-learning. In Y. Eshet-Alkalai, A. Caspi, S. Eden, N. Geri, & Y. Yair (Eds.), *Learning in the technological era*. The Open University of Israel.

Kurtz, G., Meishar-Tal, H., & Pitterse, E. (2013). Implementing Facebook group as a learning environment in a higher education setting: A case study. In L. Rosemary, P. Goodyear, B. Grabowski, S. Puntambeker, J. Underwood, & I. Winters (Eds.), *Handbook on design in educational computing* (pp. 279–287). Routledge.

Kurtz, G., Teeni, D., Mevarech, Z., & Neuthal, T. (2006). The experience of implementing instructional technology in Israel higher education. In M. Beaudoin (Ed.), *Perspectives on higher education in the digital age* (pp. 153–164). Nova Science Publishers.

Meishar-Tal, H., & Kurtz, G. (2015). The laptop, the tablet, and the smartphone attend the lecture. In J. Keengwe & M. Maxfield (Eds.), *Advancing higher education with mobile learning technologies: Cases, trends, and inquiry-based methods* (pp. 183–193). IGI Global.

Porto, S., Blaschke, L. M., & Kurtz, G. (2011). Creating an ecosystem for life-long learning through social media: A graduate experience. In C. Wankel (Ed.), *Educating educators with social media* (pp. 107–134). Emerald.

Journal Articles

Beaudoin, F. M., Kurtz, G., & Eden, S. (2009). Experiences and opinions of e-learners: What works, what are the challenges, and what competencies ensure successful online learning. *Interdisciplinary Journal of E-Learning and Learning Objects*, 5, 275–289.

Frank, M., Kurtz, G., & Levin, N. (2002). Implications of presenting pre-university courses using the blended e-learning approach. *The Journal of Educational Technology & Society*, 5(4).

Gunn, C., Kurtz, G., Lauridsen, K., Maurer, T. W., & Steele, G. (2010). Evolution and engagement in SoTL: Today, tomorrow, and internationally. *International Journal for the Scholarship of Teaching and Learning*, 4(2).

Kantor, J., Kurtz, G., & Teeni, D. (2005). Learning financial accounting as a fully online course. *E-Business Review*, 5, 23–35.

Kurtz, G. (2013). Facebook group as a space for interactive and collaborative learning. *The International Journal of Social Media and Interactive Learning Environments*, 1(4), 406–418.

Kurtz, G. (2014). Integrating Facebook group and a course website: The effect on participation and perceptions on learning. *American Journal of Distance Education*, 28(4), 253–263.

Kurtz, G., & Peled, Y. (2016). Digital learning literacies – A validation study. *Issues in Informing Science and Information Technology*, 13, 145–158.

Kurtz, G., & Peleg, E. (2015). On the flip side of the coin: Thinking dispositions in learning blogs. *American Journal of Educational Research*, 3(2), 16–19.

Kurtz, G., & Sagee, R. (2004). From campus to web: The changing roles of on-class faculty to online teaching. *The Journal of Educators Online*, 1(1). https://www.thejeo.com/archive/2004_1_1~2/kurtz_beaudoin_sagee

Kurtz, G., & Sponder, B. (2010). SOTL in online education: Strategies and practices for using new media for teaching and learning online. *International Journal for the Scholarship of Teaching and Learning*, 4(1).

Kurtz, G., Amichai-Humburger, Y., & Kantor, J. (2009). Psychosocial well-being of Israeli students and attitudes toward open and distance learning (ODL). *The International Review of Research in Open and Distance Learning (IRRODL)*, 10(2).

Kurtz, G., Beaudoin, M., & Sagee, R. (2004). From campus to web: The transition of classroom faculty to online teaching. *The Journal of Educators Online*, 1(1).

Kurtz, G., Kochavi, E., & David, K. (2013). Teachers' perceptions of the use of the interactive whiteboard and its impact on their self-perceptions as ICT literate. *Journal of Modern Education Review*, 3(2), 155–161.

Kurtz, G., Sagee, R., & Getz-Lengerman, R. (2003). Alternative online pedagogical models with identical contents: A comparison of two university-level courses. *The Journal of Interactive Online Learning*, 2(1).

Kurtz, G., Tsimerman, A., & Steinar-Lavi, O. (2015). The flipped-classroom approach: The answer to future learning? *The European Journal of Open and Distance Learning*, 17(2). https://doi.org/10.2478/eurodl-2014-0027

Meishar-Tal, H., Kurtz, G., & Pitterse, E. (2012). Facebook groups as LMS: A case study. *The International Review of Research in Open and Distance Learning (IRRODL)*, 13(4).

Conference Presentations

Balas, T., Lehman-Wilzig, S., Cohen-Avigdor, N., & Kurtz, G. (2006). *Whose news is it anyway? Comparing the production and consumption of internet and TV news* [Paper presentation]. Thirty-seventh Conference of the Israeli Sociological Society, Israel (In Hebrew).

Beaudoin, M., & Kurtz, G. (2008). *Experiences and opinions of e-learning: What works, what doesn't and why?* [Paper presentation]. European Distance and E-Learning Network (EDEN) workshop, France.

Beller, M., Kurtz, G., & Or, E. (1996). *New technologies for distance learning: Ofek – interactive satellite courses* [Paper presentation]. Second International Science and Technology Education Conference, Israel (In Hebrew).

Beller, M., Kurtz, G., & Or., E. (1997). *Advanced technology in the service of higher education: OFEK – interactive distance learning via satellite* [Paper presentation]. Eighteenth International Council for Open and Distance Education (ICDE) World Conference, USA.

Blaschke, L. M., Kurtz, G., & Porto, S. (2010). *Assessing the added value of web 2.0 tools in e-learning: The MDE experience.* User generated content assessment in learning: Enhancing transparency and quality of peer production. The European Distance and E-Learning Network (EDEN) Publications.

Fienmasser, A., & Kurtz. G. (2000). *Integrative solutions for the changing training environment* [Paper presentation]. Sixteenth Conference on Computers in Education, Israel (In Hebrew).

Grabowski, B., Kurtz, G., Jung, I., Beaudoin, M., & Suzuki, K. (2011). *Online learner competencies: Results of a worldwide validation study.* E-Learn Conference, Honolulu, USA.

Kantor, J., Kurtz, G., & Teeni, D. (2005). *Learning financial accounting at a graduate level as a fully online environment* [Paper presentation]. European Distance and E-Learning Network (EDEN) Conference, Finland.

Kurtz, G. (1996). *The Internet in service of educational systems* [Paper presentation]. Thirteenth Conference on Computers and Education, Israel (In Hebrew).

Kurtz, G. (1998). *Satellite communication in the service of higher education: OFEK – interactive distance learning via satellite* [Paper presentation]. International Conference on Collaborative and Networked Learning, Indira Gandhi National Open University. India.

Kurtz, G. (2000a). *Distance learning and teaching via broadband infrastructure* [Paper presentation]. Fourth Internet Society Conference, Israel (In Hebrew).

Kurtz, G. (2000b). *Distance learning from class or home?* [Paper presentation]. Seventeenth Conference on Computers and Education, Israel (In Hebrew).

Kurtz, G. (2000c). *E2B: e-learning to business* [Paper presentation]. Seventh Training and Learning Conference, Israel (In Hebrew).

Kurtz, G. (2006). *From face-to-face teaching to online tutoring: Expectations, attitudes and practical implementations in a work-place* [Paper presentation]. First Chais Research Center for the Integration of Technology in Education Conference, The Open University of Israel (Hebrew).

Kurtz, G., & Amichai-Humburger, Y. (2008). Psychological well-being and attitudes toward e-learning. In *How do we learn: Where do we learn?* The European Distance and E-Learning Network (EDEN) Publications.

Kurtz, G., & Bar-Ilan, J. (2010). *The use of wiki application for collaborative learning* [Paper presentation]. Wikipedia Academy Conference, Israel (Hebrew).

Kurtz, G., Beaudoin M., & Sagee, R. (2004). *From campus to web: the transition of classroom faculty to online teaching* [Paper presentation]. European Distance and E-Learning Network (EDEN), Research Workshop, Germany.

Kurtz, G., & Beller, M. (1996). OFEK – advanced technology in the service of higher education. In *International Distance Education Symposium* [Symposium]. International Distance Education.

Kurtz, G., & Fayne, Z. A. (1999). *Successful concept of cooperation between a knowledge institution and a distance learning organization: The Israeli case* [Paper presentation]. European Open Distance Learning (ODL) Conference, Portugal.

Kurtz, G., & Friedman, B. (1999a). *A holistic, individual, technologically mediated learning environment at the Open University of Israel* [Paper presentation]. "The new educational frontier: Teaching and learning in a networked world" 19th Open Learning and Distance Education Conference, Vienna, Austria.

Kurtz, G., & Friedman, B. (1999b). *A holistic, individual, technologically mediated learning environment at the Open University of Israel.* The new educational frontier: Teaching and learning in a networked world" 19th Open Learning and Distance Education Conference, Vienna, Austria. (In Hebrew).

Kurtz, G., Friedman, B., & Privamn, M. (1999). *Computer mediated distance learning environment at the Open University of Israel* [Paper presentation]. Seventeenth Conference on Computers in Education, Israel (In Hebrew).

Kurtz, G., Friedman, B., Privamn, M., & Tal, E. (1998). *Integrating satellite communication and internet in the Open University of Israel* [Paper presentation]. Fifteenth Conference on Computers and Education, Israel (In Hebrew).

Kurtz, G., & Kohen-Vacs, D. (2020). *A team-based training game guided by a humanoid robot.* Knowledge Management Conference (KM 2020), Lisbon, Portugal. [Best Research Idea Award.]

Kurtz, G., & Kohen-Vacs, D. (2021). *SocialNAO – A personalized learning workshop for elderly guided by a humanoid robot.* Knowledge Management Conference (KM 2021), Leipzig, Germany. [Best Research Idea Award].

Kurtz, G., Neuthal, T., Teeni, D., & Mevarech Z. (2006). *The e-learning experience in Israel higher education: Current status and challenges for the future* [Paper presentation]. European Distance and E-Learning Network (EDEN) Conference, Austria.

Kurtz, G., Oved, R., Rosenberg, N., & Neuthal, T. (2007). *Toward online teaching: The transition of faculty from implementation to confirmation at Bar-Ilan University* [Paper presentation]. Second Chais Research Center for the Integration of Technology in Education Conference, The Open University of Israel (In Hebrew).

Kurtz, G., & Porath, N. (2012). *Higher order thinking strategies in learning blogs* [Paper presentation]. European Distance and E-Learning Network (EDEN) Conference, Porto, Portugal.

Kurtz, G., & Porto, S. C. S. (2006). Implementing live technologies to online teaching: An institutional perspective. *Research into online distance education and e-learning: Making the Difference*. The European Distance and E-Learning Network (EDEN) Publications.

Kurtz, G., & Privman, M. (1998, June). Integrating technologies into higher distance education: A theoretical perspective and empirical implementations. In K. Edwards (Chair), *Universities in a digital era: Transformation, innovation and tradition roles and perspectives of open and distance learning* [Symposium]. 7th EDEN Annual Conference, Paris, France. https://old.eurodl.org/?p=archives&year=1998&article=16

Kurtz, G., & Sagee, R. (2001). *Integrating e-learning technology in academic courses: A comparative study* [Paper presentation]. Eighteenth Conference on Computers in Education, Israel (In Hebrew).

Kurtz, G., Sagee, R., & Beaudoin M. (2004). *The changing roles of on-class faculty to online teaching: A comparative study* [Paper presentation]. Nineteenth Conference on Computers in Education, Israel.

Kurtz, G., & Sponder, B. (2011). *Learning styles and preferred web 2.0 applications as learning tools* [Paper presentation]. First MDE Conference, University of Maryland University College (UMUC), Washington, USA.

Kurtz, G., Sponder, B., Litto, F. M., & Oshima, J. (2011). *Using web 2.0 for fostering students' creativity and supporting diversity in online courses: Strategies and practices* [Paper presentation]. Twenty-fourth International Council for Open and Distance Education (ICDE) World Conference, Bali, Indonesia.

Meishar-Tal, H., Kurtz, G., & Pitterse, E. (2012). *Learning with Facebook groups* [Paper presentation]. European Distance and E-Learning Network (EDEN) Conference, Porto, Portugal.

Mevarech, Z. R., & Kurtz, G., (2006). Comparing e-Learning implementation within business vs. academic organizations: Two case-studies. In *Research into online distance education and e-learning: Making the Difference*. European Distance and E-Learning Network (EDEN) Publications.

Peleg, E., & Kurtz, G. (2013). On the flip side of the coin: Thinking dispositions in learning blogs. In *The Joy of Learning Enhancing Learning Experience – Improving Learning Quality* (pp. 85–92). The European Distance and E-Learning Network (EDEN) Publications.

Privman, M., Kurtz, G., & Walden, T. (1998). *The text component in the Ofek broadcast via distance learning lesson: Interactive satellite at the Open University of Israel* [Paper presentation]. Thirteenth Israeli Association for Literacy SCRIPT Conference, Israel (In Hebrew).

Shulz, T., Kurtz, G., Friedman, B., & Alberton, Y. (1997). *The use of technology to evaluate the technology: Theoretical and practical implications* [Paper presentation]. Eighteenth International Council for Open and Distance Education (ICDE) World Conference, USA.

22
LAMY, THÉRÈSE

Photo of Thérèse Lamy contributed by Thérèse Lamy

Education is important for people so that they can be free, can develop critical thinking, to be better people.

Dr. Thérèse Lamy studied at the University of Ottawa, Canada, where she completed a Bachelor of Arts in 1962 and a Master of Arts in History in 1964. In 1970, she completed an internship in

Cinema, Television and Psychology of Communication at Ryerson Institute of Technology, Canada. She completed a second Masters of Arts in Educational Technology at Concordia University in 1975, going on to obtain a PhD in Educational Technology at the University of Montreal in 1989.

Lamy's research interests include:

- New paradigms of educational communication in a context of distance learning,
- Vocational training and training of trainers in distance learning,
- Learning technologies and programme design for distance education, and
- Distance learning and international development.

Throughout her career, Lamy has maintained a teaching, research, and leadership role with Télé-Université, while also working as a consultant since 1989 with numerous educational institutions and government educational departments throughout Canada. The list of her publications at the end of this chapter does not include her many programmes, reports, handbooks and so on, created for particular departments and institutions throughout Canada.

Lamy has been an active member of the Association Canadienne de l'Enseignement à Distance (ACED) and the Association Internationale de Pédagogie Universitaire (AIPU), as well as being a founding member of the Conseil Québécois pour la Formation à Distance (CQFD), and was President of CQFD from 1997 to 1999. She was also actively involved in the International Association for Distance Education (ICDE) during the formation of the Women's International Network (WIN) and also the Canadian Association of Distance Education (CADE), which was an early organization that brought together people who were beginning to explore online learning and open and distance learning.

Interview

Transcript Analysis Summary

Analysis of all interviews included in this volume led to the identification of 3,545 units of data. The mean of these collective units was 118 per pioneer, the median was 118.5, and the mode was 132. Individual interview units ranged from 59 to 217 units, yielding a spread of 158 units between all interviews. Thérèse Lamy's interview generated 132 units, which placed her interview just within the top third of all interviews in terms of unit generation.

A comparison of Thérèse Lamy's interview to the interviews of all pioneers indicated that nearly half of her interview was comparable to the average interview in terms of units produced per thematic area (Figure 22.1). Six of the 14 thematic codes in her interview yielded a similar numbers of units to the average interview. These included background, accomplishments, changes over time, goals, interesting memories, and final thoughts. Lamy's interview generated a significantly greater-than-average number of units in the area of benefits of DE and a somewhat greater-than-average number of units in the early founders and others for the book categories. It was obvious from her interview that Thérèse Lamy was passionate about DE, which she saw as the means to offering education to those who could not otherwise obtain it. This passion translated into the collection of numerous units in this area. Given her early entry into the field, Lamy was able to offer the names of many of her colleagues and even a couple predecessors as well.

Lamy's interview produced fewer-than-average units in the learning environment, challenges, research interests, career history, and general gender-related comments areas. The lack of units in the learning environment and research interests areas were due to the fact that she was retired at the time of the interview. Although she discussed five specific challenges in her interview, these did not yield a great number of units in this topic area. Lastly, career history and general gender-related

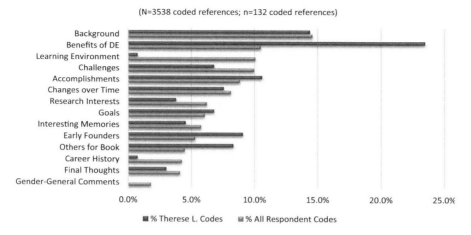

Figure 22.1 All Respondents' Versus Thérèse Lamy's Parent Codes

comments were not tied to any interview questions. These topics were identified during the data analysis process as being subjects that some interviewees brought up while providing answers to interview questions.

Link to recorded interview: tinyurl.com/Lamy-T-2019

Transcript of Interview

Full name: Thérèse Lamy

Institutional Affiliation: La Cité des Jeunes de Vaudreuil, Télé-université (TÉLUQ), self-employed in the field of distance education (DE)

Key:

Regular font = Interviewee comments
Italicized font = Interviewer comments

Interview Questions

1. *What was your educational and experiential background before you became involved in distance education [DE]?*

   I was a history teacher first of all in high school, Cité des jeunes de Vaudreuil. I worked there from 1964 to 1973. In that period, I worked as a history teacher, but also in the last two or three years, I was the director of the audiovisual service at the school. I finished that period as an agent working for the Ministry of Education, trying to implement in the province of Quebec, in the secondary schools working with the French language teachers to equip labs with audiovisual aids in teaching French. That period was before being involved in distance education [DE].

2. *In what year did you begin to look specifically into DE?*

   I would say that it was after a summer course at Ryerson University [Toronto, Ontario, Canada]. It was a course designed for teachers in Ontario, and they admitted teachers from other provinces. We had courses in cinema and television with faculty of the College of Communication. That was interesting how it linked with DE. The distance here was educational communication mediated by media. The link doesn't seem evident, but that was how my interest in media brought me to DE.

   The particular event was the opening of a job at Télé-université [TÉLUQ; Quebec, Canada] in 1975. They were looking for educational technologists, and I had done my Masters in Educational Technology at Sir George Williams [now Université Concordia; Montreal, Quebec] at that time. Télé-université specialized in DE.

3. *What were the circumstances in your world that initiated this interest in DE?*

   I was a history teacher for adolescents, and history wasn't very popular with most of them, so I was looking for ways to get students interested in history, in critical thinking, and looking at the facts. Also, I think I was interested in seeing how we could mediate learning more, and having a more learner-centred attitude and models of teaching. I found at Télé-université an orientation, which was mediated teaching, but also more learner-centred, learner-oriented. And also, a great interest for me was in educational communication because, of course, in DE, you necessarily have the need of educational communication with media, whatever they are.

4. *Which female researchers or female colleagues may have piqued your interest in DE and online distance learning [ODL]?*

   I'll talk to you about a pioneer and an administrator, Francine MacKenzie. She was the Director of Research and Development at Télé-université, sociologist, and the initiator of the first course by Télé-université. That was a success. They had 4,000 students, employees of Desjardins [cooperative financial group] and, therefore, adult students. It was largely print-based with animation face-to-face with the students by trained Télé-université tutors. So that was the first course. Francine developed in that course what became the basis of the model of Télé-université: that is, media-based autonomous learning using tutors with groups of students. Francine believed that the university was influenced by the [British] Open University. She also believed in a university without walls, a university without registered academics. She believed also in the necessity of bringing education to adults in the workplace and into their homes. She was also very creative, being a sociologist. She developed courses that tackled social issues in the Québec society at the time, with different teams at Télé-université. To give you some examples, in 1976, under her direction, we designed a course on sustainable development called

L'environnement un Bien Collectif Menace, a revolutionary topic at the time. Nobody was talking about the environment in society. No courses were given at universities. She initiated courses in human rights and civil liberties, First Nations, and so on. She was a driving force and socially very aware, and also a very innovative administrator with a futurist look and driving force in the political spheres to arrive at this model for Télé-université that was different from other universities, a very different model. That's why I picked her to answer your question because she was responsible for developing a very interesting model on which we lived for a while, although Télé-université then, like others, had some academics in place but kept largely some of the lines that were developed by Francine.

5. *Who would you identify as the early female leaders/founders in the field of DE and ODL?*

   From West to East, pioneers in DE that I recognized included Lucille Pacey, Margaret Haughey, Liz Burge, Judy Roberts, Judith Tobin, Erin Keough, France Henri, Sylvie Malaison, Denise Paquette-Frenette, Claudette Beaulieu, and Geneviève Jacquinot, who was a collaborator who worked with a lot of us in Quebec and a major contributor of DE in France.

6. *What are some of the goals that you strove to achieve in the field of DE and ODL?*

   My inspiration and guidance for my professional career came from an article written [by] Geneviève Jacquinot in which she tried to define DE. Translating it, it would be "tame distance and abolish absence." This, translated, means to provide access to knowledge and diplomas to those who are otherwise psychologically, physically, or economically, or socially, or geographically at a distance and change the teacher-oriented model to a learner-centred model, and doing all of this, of course, through user-friendly media, whatever they were.

7. *What are some of your accomplishments in the field of DE and ODL learning that you would like to share?*

   Some of them are breaking ground for social change, courses like environment, civil rights and liberties; working with new content in new fields, that was at Télé-université; inventing with my colleagues, and with all of our other colleagues throughout Canada, new pedagogical models to bridge the distance between the learners and content, and also trying to work with media so that they would give access to knowledge for students from wherever they came or wherever they were.

   Another accomplishment that I wish to point out was training teachers because I did a lot of that in my consulting work, training teachers in DE how to design courses that were particular to the field of DE and were very different from campus-based courses. Also, I was training teachers working at a distance with a variety of media and insisting on the learner-oriented models.

8. *What are some of the challenges that you faced in the field of DE and ODL over the years?*

   At the beginning, it was facing the skepticism from traditional universities and colleges towards the validity of DE. That was a Canadian problem.

   Training teachers in media courses for DE learning environments and changing their pedagogical model from a teacher-centred approach to a learner-centred approach was also a challenge. This comes up often for me because it was a major question. Also, designing media courses based on interaction and interactivity. The distinction between interaction and interactivity was a big issue at that time (but not so much anymore, I guess), but with interaction, we were talking about what was going on between the student and the knowledge, and interactivity referred to the technological aspects of whatever media. People were fascinated (and probably some still are) with the media itself. What we were trying to deal with at that time is that we wanted people not to be slaves to the machines or the technology, but that they would be interested more in what we could do with them.

9. *What was the "state of DE" when you first entered the field as opposed to ODL in 2019?*

   Technically, when I started, it was more print-based and audio-based, with some face-to-face meetings. Then after that, it had evolved. Media became more sophisticated and more individualized and user friendly also. The arrival of the Internet changed a lot of things in the support systems that we could offer to the students. And the online – for me, online learning is a bit of – how can I say that? I think I always referred to DE; whether it's online is more of a technical thing than referring to a model of some kind. But anyway, I think that technology permits a lot more flexibility for the students. It's easier to reach people through different modes. For students, it's also easier because technology is no longer a barrier anymore; it can be individualized; technology is definitely more user-friendly than it was at the beginning of my career in distance education. However, I think that the issues that we had for support services for student learning must still be present since I left in 2004. But at that time, it was still an issue – support services. How do you not only individualize the students' learning, but how do you support them? What does it mean? What services do you offer through the technology? Because, I guess, there is more to DE or online education than interaction with a machine. Technology today probably allows more interaction, more flexibility, and probably a friendlier approach. I hope it does.

10. *What interesting memories would you like to share about the beginning of ODL?*

    Well, there were quite a few moments, but since I had to choose, I chose one – the beginning of CADE [Canadian Association of Distance Education]. CADE was founded in 1982–1983 or thereabouts. That association was a national association. It allowed us, working mostly in adult education, to share our experiences in DE. At the beginning, we met by audio conferencing. Then after a while, we had some face-to-face meetings. I think it was every two years. Other meetings were online, by the phone, or video conferencing. So I think this association worked a lot to bring credibility to DE throughout Canada and also at the international level.

    The particular moment that I recall was the first face-to-face meeting of CADE, at York University [Toronto, Ontario, Canada]. After a few years of audio conferencing, we met face-to-face for the first time, and it was quite an occasion because, after two years of audio conferencing, we could put names to faces and faces to the names that we had heard for two years. For me, it was an important moment because it also showed the importance of this network of humans meeting face-to-face. And also, for all of us, I suppose, it was an example of how students could live through DE never meeting people, just being at a distance. So for us it provided an example of the particular challenges that the students had to face. So that was an interesting moment not only for the human interaction and friendships that it allowed us to build after a while, but it also strengthened the links and helped us to work to promote DE in Canada, and it also gave us a sensitivity to what the students were living at a distance.

    The second moment was probably teaching that international seminar in Montpellier [France] with people from all over the Mediterranean and trying to pass on our experience from Téléuniversité to these people about DE. People came from all over the Mediterranean for that seminar. The seminar lasted five weeks. Its contents were about DE, media, administration, support services, how to build a network, all the topics in the field.

11. *What were your specific DE and ODL research interests, and have they changed/evolved over the years?*

I was interested mainly in designing learning environments for DE using different communication tools. That was my main interest because I thought communication tools and communication in DE were the most important things for developing critical thinking and all of the other skills in distance learning. So how did it evolve? I guess maybe I didn't evolve. I guess I just tried to perfect that approach.

12. *Is there anything else you [would] like to address?*

I think perhaps 50 years from now, people will be asking, "Why did you do this? Why was it important to go into DE and invest money and do top research about that, since we had networks of universities, colleges, and schools in Canada?"

The answer to these questions were and are still are the issues of access to knowledge, bridging the gap of geographical, economic, social, physical, and psychological distance; designing mediated learning environments that allow autonomy and freedom for the learner. Education is important for people so that they can be free, can develop critical thinking, to be better people. I thought that the regular system in education couldn't offer all the possibilities to everyone. I still think that DE – and that's why the effort was done – offered all these possibilities. It was sort of a necessity to have this parallel system to the official structure.

13. *Can you please describe the learning environment that you currently work in or have most recently worked in (e.g., geographic and institutional setting, learner demographics)?*

I retired in 2004 from professional involvement in DE. However, the professional experience and the thirst for educational communication are still alive and well in my professional retirement. In 2011, I became a Municipal Councillor in Baie Saint-Paul. In that capacity, I use our public-televised meetings and other social media to explain different municipal issues to our fellow citizens.

14. *Can you suggest names of other female pioneers in DE, e-learning, or open and distance learning [ODL] that you think we should include in the book?*

Well, all of those I have already mentioned, except Geneviève Jacquinot, who is not there anymore. All of the others, I'm not in contact with except a bit with France and Judy Roberts. Sylvie Malaison lives in Quebec City. Sylvie Malaison is an interesting person because she worked for the Department of Education for Quebec, which was then called SMTE, which was a service that dealt with technology. The Ministry of Education was not interested in DE at that time. I'm talking about the 1970s. They started later. Sylvie worked with them for a while. They did courses for adults. Then she moved to Toronto and worked with TV Ontario. She lives in Quebec now.

Denise Paquette-Frenette [from Ontario] worked a lot with Contact Nord [also known as Contact North], like Judy Roberts, on the French side. She came to Télé-université to get her diploma in DE and worked in Ontario. I lost track of her. I don't know where she is. She lived in Toronto for quite a while. I guess she's still there.

Claudette Beaulieu was from New Brunswick. She was at the University of Moncton and was very, very important for DE at the University of Moncton. She was the director; DE was sort of based in the Adult Education department. She moved out of there. She's been out of there for quite a few years. I think she lives in Quebec somewhere, but I haven't got a trace of her.

The other names you know: Liz Burge, Margaret Haughey, Erin Keough, and Judith Tobin. Judith worked with us at CADE. I guess, I think most of her career was at TV Ontario, but in the educational sector and interested in doing DE somehow. Judy Roberts knows her very well. They are very good friends. Judy Tobin was with us in CADE, but I don't know if she did a lot of work in DE.

Publications

Books and Courseware

Lamy, T. (1995a). *Divers auteurs à la conception de 20 guides de cours pour le programme de Garde Educative à l'enfance*. Collège des Grands Lacs.

Lamy, T. (1995b). *La vidéocommunication pour apprendre et pour communiquer*. Centre d'Éducation permanente. Université Laurentienne.

Lamy, T. (1998). *Apprendre par la vidéo comprimée: Un échange convivial*. Chenelière\McGraw-Hill.

Lamy, T., Dao, K., & Patoine, L. (1987). *Le tissage des réseaux et la formation à Distance*. Actes du colloque des usagers du satellite.

Lamy, T., & Henri, F. (1989). *Les médias. La formation à distance maintenant*. Télé-Université.

Lamy, T., Henri, F., & Marchand, R. (1990). Développement d'une activité de formation à Distance. *La formation à distance maintenant*. Télé-Université.

Lamy, T., & Roberts, J. (1998). *Classes virtuelles: Apprendre sur l'inforoute*. Chenelière\McGraw-Hill.

Book Chapters

Lamy, T. (1985). La télématique, un outil convivial? In F. Henri & T. Kaye (Eds.), *Le savoir à domicile: Pédagogie et problématique de la formation à Distance*. Presses de l'Université du Québec.

Lamy, T., Gagné, P., & Sauvé, L. (1989). La technologie éducative dans l'enseignement à distance, son rôle et sa place, une étude exploratoire. In R. Sweet (Ed.), *Post-secondary distance education in Canada*. Athabasca University Press.

Lamy, T., & Henri, F. (1989). La formation à distance: Des choix technologiques et des Valeurs. In R. Sweet (Ed.), *Post-secondary distance education in Canada*. Athabasca University Press.

Lamy, T., & Pelletier, P. (1995). The Francophones of Canada: A global network. In J. Roberts & E. Keough (Eds.), *Why the information highway? Lessons from open and distance learning*. Trifollum Books Inc.

Journal Articles

Lamy, T. (1987). La Télé-Université, an open learning system. *Council for Educational Technology, 20*.

Lamy, T., & Daniel, J. (1976). The political evaluation of educational broadcasting: A Canadian case study. *Education Broadcasting International, 9*(1).

Lamy, T., & Henri, F. (1983). Télé-Université: Ten years of distance education in Québec. *PLET, 20*(3).

Lamy, T., & Marquis, C. (1979). Une école pour demain. *La Revue de l'Association Canadienne d'éducation de la Langue Française, 8*(3).

Conference Presentations

Lamy, T. (1994a). *Fragments d'incertitudes, allocution de clôture du congrès annuel du REFAD*. Actes du Colloque du REFAD.

Lamy, T. (1994b). *La formation à distance au Canada* [Paper presentation]. Congrès des Enseignants francophones de la Nouvelle-Ecosse.

Lamy, T. (1994c). *Stakes in distance education training in Canada* [Round table]. Materiel Management Training Centre, Ministère de la Défense National du Canada.

Lamy, T. (1996). *Les technologies d'information et de communication et la pédagogie* [Paper presentation]. Congrès des enseignants francophones du Nouveau-Brunswick.

Lamy, T. (1997). *L'entreprise privée et les TIC* [Paper presentation]. Congrès de l'ACED.

Lamy, T. (1998a). *L'interactivité et les technologies ou quelle sorte d'interactivité pour apprendre?* [Paper presentation]. Congrès de l'ACED.

Lamy, T. (1998b, September). *Les technologies nous rendent-elles stupides ou intelligents?* Colloque du Conseil Québécois de la formation à distance.

Lamy, T., & Bourdages, L. (1992). *La communication éducative, un élément de complicité en formation à distance* [Paper presentation]. Congrès de l'Aced, Ottawa, Ontario.

Lamy, T., Burge, L., Bizzocchi, J., Thomas, N., & Roberts, J. (1992). *A dialogue about dialogue in distance learning* [Paper presentation]. Congrès de l'Aced, Ottawa, Ontario.

Lamy, T., & Faille, C. (2000). *Table d'échanges et d'expertises et d'expériences pédagogiques en formation à distance.* REFAD.

Lamy, T., Léveillée, P., & Sauvé, L. (1990). *A la recherche du technologue de l'éducation dans la formation à distance au Canada.* Actes du colloque du Cipte.

Lamy, T., & Mayer. D. (1996). *Les technologies d'information et de communication: une formation nécessaire* [Paper presentation]. Congrès de l'ACED, Moncton, New Brunswick.

Lamy, T., & Richer, M. (2001). *Table d'échanges et d'expertises et d'expériences pédagogiques en formation à distance.* REFAD.

Lamy, T., & Richer, M. (2002). *Table d'échanges et d'expertises et d'expériences pédagogiques en formation à distance.* REFAD.

Lamy, T., & Richer, M. (2003). *Table d'échanges et d'expertises et d'expériences pédagogiques en formation à distance.* REFAD.

Lamy, T., & Richer, M. (2004). *Table d'échanges et d'expertises et d'expériences pédagogiques en formation à distance.* REFAD.

Lamy, T., & Richer, M. (2005). *Table d'échanges et d'expertises et d'expériences pédagogiques en formation à distance.* REFAD.

Lamy, T., & Roberts, J. (1996). *Videoconferencing: Learning with a new technology* [Paper presentation]. Congrès de l'Association des collèges communautaires du Canada, Toronto, Ontario.

Lamy, T., Roberts, J., Helm, B., & Keough, E. (1992). *New alliances: Serving immigrant needs through distance education techniques* [Paper presentation]. Congrès de l'Aced, Ottawa, Ontario.

Lamy, T., & Villardier, L. (1980). *Tutorship by teleconferencing in distance education, an evaluation report at Télé-Université.* Actes du colloque de l'Université du Wisconsin. University of Wisconsin.

23
MEEKS GARDNER, JULIA (JULIE)

Photo of Julia (Julie) Meeks Gardner contributed by Julie Meeks Gardner

> [T]rying to explain the vision of the Open Campus was greeted with so many naysayers who explained that this would never succeed. I found that really interesting because I thought it was such

a huge opportunity, and isn't it obvious if you have a dispersed constituency of 17 countries, that distance education was the way to share our offerings?

Julia (Julie) Meeks Gardner was born in the West Indies, where she completed both her undergraduate and graduate studies. She completed a Bachelors in Agricultural Science at the University of West Indies (UWI) in 1984 and went on to complete a PhD in Nutrition at UWI in 1994. She went on to carry out research for UWI at the Tropical Metabolism Unit, which became the Tropical Medicine Research Institute. She carried out research there for many years (1990–2002) on human nutrition and child development, while also involving herself in children's rights and issues. She then moved on to become head of the Caribbean Development Centre at UWI, which is based in the Open Campus. As head of the centre, she was also the first Director of the Consortium for Social Development and Research. The consortium was formed to create better opportunity for collaboration and cooperation and, in turn, a better base for research activities. She has been Deputy Principal of UWI's Open Campus since 2014, where she is also the Campus Coordinator for Graduate Studies and Research.

Meeks Gardner became focused on distance education in 2008. The focus is on 14 countries without traditional campuses. She became involved in structuring and piloting UWI's online programmes with the aim of providing high-quality tertiary education to all regions in the West Indies through online learning. She strove to ensure high quality by having very small tutorial groups and online participation in small groups. Meeks Gardner sees quality and relevance of programmes as very critical and has in place qualitative reviews of all programmes cyclically to ensure these aims are achieved.

Meeks Gardner's own interests in distance education have been focused on graduate work and managing research and research supervision online. References included at the end of this chapter reflect these and other academic research interests.

Interview

Transcript Analysis Summary

Analysis of all interviews included in this volume led to the identification of 3,545 units of data. The mean of these collective units was 118 per pioneer, the median was 118.5, and the mode was 132. Individual interview units ranged from 59 to 217 units, yielding a spread of 158 units between all interviews. Julie Meeks Gardner's interview generated 99 units, placing her interview near the top of the bottom third of all interviews in terms of number of units produced.

A comparision of Gardner's interview to the interviews of all pioneers indicated that her interview profile shared few commonalities with the average interview profile (Figure 23.1). Her interview yielded a similar number of units in three areas: accomplishments, goals, and career history. Significantly more than average units were generated in her conversations related to learning environment and final thoughts. These units may be explained by the fact that she played (and continues to play) an integral role in pioneering the spread of DE throughout the West Indies.

While Julie Meeks Gardner's interview produced fewer-than-average numbers of units for benefits of DE and challenges, her results still reflect the general tendency of the average interview to produce a few more benefit than challenge units. Lastly, her late entry into the field may explain Gardner's lower number of early founders and others for the book units.

Figure 23.1 All Respondents' Versus Julia (Julie) Meeks Gardner's Parent Codes

Link to recorded interview: tinyurl.com/Meeks-J-2018

Transcript of Interview

Full Name: Julie Meeks Gardner (a.k.a. Julie Meeks)
Institutional Affiliation: The University of the West Indies
Key:

> Regular font = Interviewee comments
> *Italicized font = Interviewer comments*

Interview Questions

1. *What was your educational and experiential background before you became involved in online and distance learning [ODL] at the Open Campus?*

I was in research at the Tropical Metabolism Research Unit, which became the Tropical Medicine Research Institute. I was part of the Child Development Research Group there for many, many years, where I worked in human nutrition and child development, and also many related areas of children's rights and children's issues generally.

Then I moved to become the Head of the Caribbean Child Development Centre, which had a more Caribbean focus, but still concentrating on many of the same children's issues, including nutrition and policy issues. The Caribbean Child Development Centre was, and still is, based in the Open Campus [of The University of the West Indies]. I was the Head of that Centre for ten years, during which time I was also the first Director of the Consortium for Social Development and Research, a consortium of four research departments within the Open Campus. We formed the consortium to have better collaboration and cooperation. Because we were actually quite small research institutes, we had a greater critical mass in joining interests in social development and could have a better base for research activities. After ten years or so of this, I was appointed Deputy Principal of the Open Campus in 2014. That has been my position since.

In addition to holding the Deputy Principal portfolio, I'm also what is called the Campus Coordinator for Graduate Studies and Research, which, on the three traditional campuses, is now a full Director's post, so I am basically wearing two full-time hats. I really enjoy the Graduate Studies and Research portfolio because that is where I have spent most of my academic time.

2. *In what year did you begin to look specifically into the Open Campus project? What were the circumstances in your world that initiated this interest?*

In 2008, the University of the West Indies created the Open Campus out of the former what they called Outreach Sector Departments. So there was a School for Continuing Studies, there was the Board for Non-Campus Countries and Distance Education, there was the UWIDEC, which was the University of the West Indies Distance Education Centre, and there was the Tertiary Level Institutions Unit. All of those were brought together into a structure very similar to the traditional campuses in terms of a Principal, a Deputy Principal, a Registrar, and the formal structure of the other campuses, with a particular remit to focus on the 12 or so countries that did not have a traditional campus [now 14].

So, Jamaica has a traditional campus, Barbados has a traditional campus, and Trinidad has a traditional campus. The Open Campus was to serve all other countries, [as] well as all of the underserved areas within Jamaica, Trinidad, and Barbados, which are further away from the campus. We focused on less traditional student populations, often more mature working people with families and so on.

All of our degrees are online, although many of them have courses that require a face-to-face exam assessment, so it's online/blended for the most part. We also offer, in addition to the online teaching, the ability to come into one of our centres around the region. [Throughout, *region* refers to the English-speaking Caribbean.] We have 42 centres across the 17 countries. If you have Internet difficulties, if you have computer access challenges, if you just want a small community to deal with your education, you can come to the centre. You can have somebody to talk to if you are having any difficulties, you can find other students, and you can have the technology support.

I am describing it to you instead of telling you how it came about, sorry. So, in 2008, we formed the Open Campus and my centre, which was part of the School of Continuing Studies, Just by history, it had nothing to do with distance education, but it did have a community outreach around child development issues and early childhood training in particular. Our sister research institutes also fell under the new structure of the Open Campus. Because UIWDEC online training was such a big part of this, I became very involved in the whole structure of online delivery: programme planning, course development, and delivery of online programmes. Then

I was given a number of tasks or portfolios to deal with, including graduate studies and research, from very early [on]. We started our graduate programmes, I think, about 2013. I was appointed the Campus Coordinator, so I was heavily involved in the planning and development of the programmes and piloting them through the quality assurance systems of the university, and then, in terms of delivery, I was quite involved in the delivery as well, particularly the research aspects, research projects, and theses and so on, to ensure that we had high quality, because the University of the West Indies certificates are very highly regarded. We did not want to be seen to be diluting the quality in any way.

3. *Which female researchers or female colleagues may have piqued your interest in your work with the Open Campus?*

That is very easy. It is Professor Hazel Simmons-McDonald. Professor McDonald was the first Principal of the Open Campus from 2008 to 2014. She is an incredible dynamo, who was just so extremely enthusiastic and positive and creative. She saw a vision of how, in our dispersed islands and dispersed communities, we could harness the Open Campus to provide the tertiary education for all regions. She's easily the inspiration for my doing what I am doing. She also really encouraged me to take up leadership roles when I was somewhat reluctant. I was really very happy as a quiet researcher. [Chuckles.] She insisted on my taking up leadership roles and getting involved in the nitty-gritty of distance education. So that's the person I would say who's had the most influence in terms of distance education and online learning.

4. *Who would you identify as the early female leaders/founders in the field of ODL?*

I don't have a strong background in online and distance education outside of the Open Campus experience. I don't really have a sense of the whole development and history outside of the region. Within the region, easily Professor Simmons-McDonald has been a major person who has led and encouraged its development within our region.

5. *What are some of the goals that you strove to achieve at the Open Campus and in the field of ODL?*

One of the things was ensuring very high quality. We know that, internationally, online learning has had a checkered history. There have been very excellent centres delivering online education. The Open University comes to mind, as well as your own institution, Athabasca [University], as beacons of very high quality. But there have also been some more questionable offerings. We did not want there to be any question about the degrees that we were offering online; so much so that our model of having very small tutorial groups and online participation in small group requirements has been seen as a model internationally. So the maintenance of the high quality has been very important, building in requirements for very high-quality assurance from inception right through delivery and ongoing through delivery, so we have qualitative reviews of all programmes cyclically. So quality and relevance have been very critical.

Even within our own institution the UWI, there has often been some hesitation in embracing what we are trying to do because it's unfamiliar, and people tend to be wary of the unfamiliar. People tend to have had their own education via face-to-face means, and when you start to talk about online, big questions are raised over everyone's head. So fighting the negativity, fighting even hostility, and just trying to get people to understand, both internally and externally, about what we are trying to do, about why it is not inferior to what is being offered on the traditional campuses; this has been perhaps most of what we have been striving to do.

I was so consoled and encouraged by a recent report that was done by our University Office of Planning, which compared the post-graduate experience on all four campuses (the three traditional campuses and the Open Campus), and in almost every single element of what was asked, the Open Campus was clearly ranked highest by all of the students in terms of the student experience. This was just released in October, and I am trying to share it very widely as a justification of what we are doing that at least our students recognize the high quality of what we are putting forward.

6. *What are some of your accomplishments in the field of ODL that you would like to share?*

When I say my accomplishments, I've done none of this single-handedly by any means. For my team, one of the big accomplishments that we have done is within the graduate programming. We offered graduate programming, mostly in education and business, since about 2013. These were Masters', MScs [Masters' of Sciences], and also a Master's of Arts in English and so on. They were going quite well. I was particularly pleased with how our research project aspects were managed. I had a particularly strong research coordinator, who ensured the students were matched with good research supervisors and that research supervisors underwent further training, not just in research supervision, but online research supervision.

More recently, we have developed an EdD, Doctorate in Education, for our Leadership in Education with two streams, both for higher education and for primary and secondary school. The first cohort of the EdD is now in the very last phase of doing their research projects. It has been quite a journey. It is the first time that an EdD was offered within the University of the West Indies. It took quite a bit of design to make it fit to meet all of the requirements. I am very proud of how that has been coming out. We've also seen that there has been a tremendous demand for it.

And finally, also within the graduate programming, we are offering the first research degree. It is an MPhil/PhD in Child and Youth Studies. It has not been done before within the University of the West Indies, that a research degree has been offered online. So the course content will be online, and the research supervision will be online. Allowing our researchers to stay in country, stay at home, and not have to travel to one of the countries with a traditional campus, we think this is going to quite revolutionize how research degrees are seen and utilized across the region.

Those are the biggest [accomplishments].

7. *What are some of the challenges that you faced in the field of ODL over the years?*

I had mentioned earlier overcoming some resistance internally with people understanding what we were trying to accomplish and how this would be helpful for all the region's development. We had difficulty in trying to explain that we were not targeting the same market of 18-year-old school leavers that the other campuses typically targeted. So we were not in competition; the perception of competition has also been a problem.

We have had a lot of difficulty (I think that I can say this) in terms of collection of receipts from all the governments and even from the students, but particularly from our governments. We support the students of the 17 countries and report to 17 governments. Some governments will, for example, support a number of students. The students come, finish their degrees, but the governments don't pay their tuition that they had promised to. So we have a great debt carrying, which is very challenging to operate in an environment where it is not that we are not producing and earning the funds, but we're not able to collect the funds. And so we have cash flow difficulties.

So the understanding of what we are trying to accomplish, as well as the operations in terms of the cash flow, have been our most difficult challenges to my mind.

8. *What was the "state of DE" when you first entered the field as opposed to ODL in 2018?*

   Back in 2008, distance learning was seen . . . The perception was much more of a niche, high-tech area that wasn't something for everybody. It was something over there, at least within the campus where I was situated.

   And now, it's very clear that it has a much, much broader reach. Basically, now everybody has access to Internet and a smartphone or a tablet; they are available in schools all over; they're so much more available, and [with] Internet penetration much higher, it is so much easier to access courses. So, it [online learning] has become so much more mainstream. Whereas in the early days, people saw it as something a few people "over there" are doing, now it is much more embraced generally, online education and what it can accomplish. There's much more interest in offering various courses and programmes online.

   That's the biggest thing I can think of.

9. *What interesting memories would you like to share about the beginning of ODL in the Open Campus?*

   When we were starting the Open Campus our then-vice chancellor, who was our CEO [chief executive officer], speaking to us internally within the School of Continuing Studies and within Distance Education, trying to explain the vision of the Open Campus, was greeted with so many naysayers who explained that this would never succeed. I found that really interesting because I thought it was such a huge opportunity, and isn't it obvious, if you have a dispersed constituency of 17 countries, that distance education was the way to share our offerings? The memory of the meeting where it was presented to us that we were going to become an Open Campus – and this is internal, now – not even internal within the university, but internal right within what became the Open Campus – there was so much negativity, much of which I am happy to say has been overturned. There is a lot more clarity of the importance and a lot more acceptance of the vision.

10. *What were your specific ODL research interests, and have they changed/evolved over the years?*

    My own research has not been focused on distance and online education. My own research has been focused on other academic areas.

    My work with online and distance education has been very operational, and I have to admit to following up with reporting these academic fora so that we can share and scrutinize what we've done. But my colleagues have, to a large extent; typically, we make a good showing of our work at various international conferences and so on about online education.

    My own interests have been focusing on the graduate work and managing research and research supervision online, but I have not reported these in an academic forum. (I should!)

11. *Could you please describe the learning environment that you currently work in (e.g., geographic and institutional setting, student demographics)?*

    Let me start with the geographical. The University of the West Indies is a multi-campus university based in the former British West Indies islands and countries. Of the four campuses, three are traditional campuses and one is called the Open Campus, which is both operating as distance online learning; we offer degrees up to the doctoral level online, and as well, we have face-to-face teaching at over 40 sites in 17 countries around the region.

    In 1948, when our university started (that was 70 years ago), the vision was that a university would serve what was then the British West Indian countries, or territories, as we were then. We were initially a college of the University College of London (called the University College of the West Indies, UCWI). By the early 1960s, we became a fully-fledged independent university, the University of the West Indies. In the 60s, we added the campuses in Barbados and Trinidad, and had students from all over the region attending these three traditional campuses. But back in 1948, when we originally started, we also started an Extramural Department where we were taking information from the university, both by radio and face-to-face seminars, short courses, workshops, and this was across the region. So that's how we started with having so many centres across the countries in many places. So, both in Barbados and Trinidad, we had Extramural Departments, even before we had the campuses there.

So now we are an institution with some 50,000 degree students. We have many more students doing short courses. Within the Open Campus, we have perhaps 6,000 students, or a little below that, who are pursuing degrees, and perhaps 10,000 students who are taking short courses, continuing professional education, or continuing education programmes.

We have a dispersed leadership as well. Our Principal resides in Barbados; our Registrar, myself as Deputy Principal, and our Chief Financial Officer are in Jamaica; our Campus Librarian and Campus IT [Information Technology] Officer are in Trinidad; our Director of the Country Sites is in Dominica – and we meet every day via technology: Zoom, Blackboard Collaborate, Skype meetings, and so on. So we have a highly dispersed environment where we have had to learn to work, meet, and talk; communicate generally.

Our students are drawn from the 17 countries, as well as many other countries from around the world. We have just finished formalizing our international students' office – that is, from countries outside of the Caribbean – and although we have always had a few students, we are focusing more on our international students now and organizing the administrative functions to better accommodate those students outside of the Caribbean.

Many of these students are Caribbean students who are living outside of the region or nationals from other countries who have a particular interest in Caribbean issues, so they will see programmes with a focus on Caribbean and want to join. And also, a number who join say it is because of the strong reputation of the University of the West Indies, and when they see that they could do online programmes with the University of the West Indies, they choose to do that.

We tend to have an older demographic for both our undergraduate and post-graduate students. They tend to be married, have children or to have other family responsibilities, like looking after elderly parents, and many are working. So we do have an older group in terms of our undergraduate population. They tell us that they are so happy to have this opportunity, either because they missed this opportunity when they were school leavers – they had to work, they had their family commitments, and so on – and so they were so happy to be able to come and join at this stage of their lives, at an older age, married or working and so on; they could study and stay at home in their island. Before that, they would have had to leave their country or home, have the funding to live in another country for three or four years to complete their undergraduate degree. Instead, they can continue in their jobs; they can continue to live with their families and maintain those commitments. They can do the courses part time as they can manage, both financially and time-wise, and complete their degrees.

Our graduations are such occasions of joy where the students tell us their stories of what they had to overcome to accomplish what they did. So, yes, our demographic is different than that of the traditional campuses.

12. *Is there anything else you would like to address?*

Our project has been not a simple one. We deal with 17 governments. We deal with – I think it is nine financial currencies. It's only three time zones in the region, but because we have international students, we have very many time zones. So we have complicated systems. We have had to work very, very hard to develop the support to manage these systems. We have made huge strides and are continuing to make huge strides.

Fifty years from now, I would not want someone to pick up this book and recognize the challenges we faced when all of these systems were not yet mature. We had to sit down, work out what was needed, talk with software vendors, talk with many people who have had similar challenges in dispersed environments, and try to work out how to get things done. I think that's what I'd like readers to know.

Thank you very much for including me and for including the University of the West Indies and our experiment. I think it has been a journey that would be of interest to other people. I hope that you and they may find it of interest.

13. *Can you suggest names of other female pioneers in distance education or ODL that you think we should include in the book?*

I am going to limit this regionally. There is a very important academic. Her name is Denise Gaspard-Richards out of Trinidad, who heads our Academic Programming and Delivery Division. She manages this very large division, which does all of our online programming from conception through to delivery. I think that she might be an interesting person to include. I can send you her email address if you like.

Publications

Books

Buzzi, G., Solimene, U., & Meeks Gardner, J. (1998). *A study of traditional Jamaican medicine*. The World Health Organization – Collaborating Centre for Traditional and Natural Medicine.

Henry-Lee, A., & Meeks Gardner, J. (Eds.). (2008). *Promoting child rights through research* (Vol. 1). Sir Arthur Lewis Institute of Social and Economic Studies, University of the West Indies.

Henry-Lee, A., & Meeks Gardner, J. (Eds.). (2010). *Promoting child rights through research* (Vol. 2). Sir Arthur Lewis Institute of Social and Economic Studies, University of the West Indies.

Meeks Gardner, J., Powell, C. A., & Grantham-McGregor, S. M. (2001). *A case-control study of aggression among Jamaican children*. Planning Institute of Jamaica: Kingston.

Book Chapters

Anaokar, P., Thomas, K., Thomas, J., Minott, C., Campbell, M., & Meeks Gardner, J. (2016). Preparing Jamaican children in state care for independent living: A situation analysis. In T. Islam & L. Fulcher (Eds.), *Residential child and youth care in a developing world: Global perspectives* (pp. 283–298). The CYC-Net Press.

Grantham-McGregor, S. M., Meeks Gardner, J., Walker, S., & Powell, C. (1990). The relationship between undernutrition, activity levels and development in young children. In N. Scrimshaw & S. Schurch (Eds.), *Activity, energy expenditure and energy requirements of infants and children* (pp. 361–384). Nestle.

Guerra, N. G., Williams, K. R., Meeks Gardner, J., & Walker, I. (2010). Case study: The Kingston YMCA youth development programme: An effective anti-violence intervention for inner-city youth. In L. Knox & J. Hoffman (Eds.), *Youth violence prevention around the world* (pp. 81–87). Praeger International Press.

Matthies, B., Meeks Gardner, J., Daley, A., & Crawford-Brown, C. (2009). Issues of violence in the Caribbean. In F. Hickling, K. Morgan, & B. Matthies (Eds.), *Caribbean psychology* (pp. 393–464).

Meeks Gardner, J. (1998). Activity and maternal-child interactions in undernutrition: Studies in Jamaica. In *Nutrition, health and child development: research advances and policy recommendations* (pp. 32–42). PAHO Scientific Publication No. 566.

Meeks Gardner, J. (2006). Children and violence: Interventions at school and at home. In *Children and adolescents growing up in contexts of poverty, marginalization and violence in Latin America* (pp. 93–106). CIESPI.

Meeks Gardner, J., & Chang, S. M. (2007). Studies of behaviour and aggression among Jamaican children. In *The tropical metabolism research unit, the university of the West Indies, Jamaica, 1956–2006: The house that John Built* (pp. 110–119). Ian Randle Publishers.

Meeks Gardner, J., Henry-Lee, A., Chevannes, P., Thomas, J., & Baker-Henningham, H. (2008). Violence against children in the Caribbean: A desk review. In A. Henry-Lee & J. Meeks Gardner (Eds.), *Promoting child rights: Selected papers from the Caribbean Child Research Conference 2006* (Vol. 1, pp. 3–29). Sir Arthur Lewis Institute of Social and Economic Studies.

Journal Articles

Bachrach, L. R., & Meeks Gardner, J. M. (2002). Maternal knowledge, attitudes, and practices regarding childhood diarrhea and dehydration in Kingston, Jamaica. *Pan American Journal of Public Health, 12*, 37–44.

Baddeley, A., Meeks Gardner, J., & Grantham-McGregor, S. (1995). Cross-cultural cognition: Developing tests for developing countries. *Journal of Applied Cognitive Psychology, 9*, S173–S195.

Baker-Henningham, H., Meeks-Gardner, J., Chang, S., & Walker, S. (2009). Experiences of violence and deficits in academic achievement among urban primary school children in Jamaica. *Child Abuse and Neglect, 33*, 296–306.

Baker-Henningham, H., Walker, S., Powell, C., & Meeks-Gardner, J. (2009). A pilot study of the incredible years teacher training programme and a curriculum unit on social and emotional skills in community preschools in Jamaica. *Child: Care, Health and Development, 35*, 624–631.

Black, M. M., Walker, S. P., Wach, T. D., Uluer, N., Meeks Gardner, J., Grantham-McGregor, S., Lozoff, B., Chutkan, M. E., Meeks Gardner, J., & Wilks, R. (2001). Concepts of obesity among Jamaicans. *Cajanus, 34*, 127–134.

Engle, P. L., Black, M., Behrman, J., Cabral de Mello, M., Gertler, P., Kapiriri, L., Martorell, R., Eming Young, M., & the International Child Development Steering Group (Grantham-McGregor, S., Lozoff, B., Meeks Gardner, J., Wachs, T., & Walker, S.). (2007) Strategies to avoid the loss of developmental potential among 200 million children. *Lancet, 369*, 229–242.

Engle, P. L., & Cabral de Mello, M. (2008). Policies to reduce undernutrition include child development. *Lancet, 371*, 454–455.

Ferguson, G. M., Fiese, B. H., Nelson, M. R., & Meeks Gardner, J. M. (2019). Transdisciplinary team science for global health: Case study of the JUS Media? Programme. *American Psychologist, 74*(6), 725–739. https://doi.org/10.1037/amp0000383

Ferguson, G. M., Meeks Gardner, J. M., Nelson, M. R., Giray, C., Sundaram, H., Fiese, B. H., Davis, B. K., Tran, S. P., Powell, R., & JUS Media? Programme Study Team. (2021). Food-focused media literacy for remotely acculturating adolescents and mothers: A randomized controlled trial of the "JUS Media? Programme". *Journal of Adolescent Health*. [Advance online publication.] https://doi.org/10.1016/j.jadohealth.2021.06.006

Ferguson, G. M., Muzaffar, H., Iturbide, M. I., Chu, H., & Meeks, J. M. (2017). Feel American, watch American, eat American? Remote acculturation, TV, and nutrition among Jamaican adolescent-mother dyads. *Child Development, 89*(4), 1360–1377. https://doi.org/10.1111/cdev.12808

Ferguson, G. M., Nelson, M. R., Fiese, B. H., Meeks Gardner, B. H., Koester, B., & The JUS Media? Programme Study Team. (2020). U.S. media enjoyment without strong media literacy undermines adolescents' and mothers' efforts to reduce unhealthy eating in Jamaica. *Journal of Research on Adolescence, 30*(4), 928–942. https://doi.org/10.1111/jora.12571

Fernald, L. C., Ani, C., & Meeks Gardner, J. (1997a). Aggressive behaviour in children and adolescents. Part I: A review of the effects of child and family characteristics. *West Indian Medical Journal, 46*, 100–103.

Fernald, L. C., Ani, C., & Meeks Gardner, J. (1997b). Aggressive behaviour in children and adolescents. Part II: A review of the effects of environmental characteristics. *West Indian Medical Journal, 46*, 104–106.

Fernald, L. C., & Meeks Gardner, J. M. (2003). Jamaican children's reports of violence at school and home. *Social and Economic Studies, 52*, 121–140.

Grantham-McGregor, S., Yin Bun, C., Cueto, S., Glewwe, P., Richter, L, Strupp, B., & the International Child Development Steering Group (Engle, P., Black, M., Meeks Gardner, J., Lozoff, B., Wachs, T., & Walker, S.). (2007). Over two hundred million children fail to reach their developmental potential in the first five years in developing countries. *Lancet, 369*, 60–70.

Kruszewski, K., & Meeks Gardner, J. M. (2005). Breastfeeding patterns among 6-week-old infants at the UHWI. *West Indian Medical Journal, 54*, 28–33.

Meeks Gardner, J. M., Grant, D., Hutchinson, S., & Wilks, R. (2000). The use of herbal teas and remedies in Jamaica. *West Indian Medical Journal, 49*, 331–336.

Meeks Gardner, J. M., Grantham-McGregor, S. M., & Baddeley, A. (1996). Trichuris trichiura infection and working memory in Jamaican school children. *Annals of Tropical Medicine and Parasitology, 90*, 55–63.

Meeks Gardner, J. M., Grantham-McGregor, S. M., Chang, S. M., & Himes, J. (1999). Behaviour and development of stunted and non-stunted Jamaican children. *Journal of Child Psychology and Psychiatry, 40*, 819–827.

Meeks Gardner, J. M., Grantham-McGregor, S. M., Chang, S. M., Himes, J., & Powell, C. (1995). Activity and behavioral development in stunted and non-stunted children and response to nutritional supplementation. *Child Development, 66*, 1785–1797.

Meeks Gardner, J. M., Grantham-McGregor, S. M., Chang, S. M., & Powell, C. (1990). Dietary intakes and observed activity of stunted and non-stunted children in Kingston, Jamaica. Part II: Activity. *European Journal of Clinical Nutrition, 44*, 585–593.

Meeks Gardner, J. M., Grantham-McGregor, S. M., & Powell, C. P. (2005). Effects of zinc supplementation on the growth, morbidity and behavioural development of undernourished Jamaican children. *American Journal of Clinical Nutrition, 82*, 399–405.

Meeks Gardner, J. M., & Powell, C. A. (2004). Aggressive youth and youth experiences of violence: Who is at risk in Jamaica? *Caribbean Childhoods, 2*, 71–81.

Meeks Gardner, J. M., Powell, C. A., & Grantham-McGregor, S. M. (2007). Determinants of aggression and prosocial behaviour among Jamaican schoolboys. *West Indian Medical Journal, 56*, 34–41.

Meeks Gardner, J. M., Powell, C. A., Thomas, J., & Millard, D. (2003). Perceptions and experiences of violence among Jamaican youth. *Pan American Journal of Public Health, 14*, 97–103.

Meeks Gardner, J. M., & Powell, C. P. (2003). Early childhood malnutrition, behaviour and maternal-child interactions. *Caribbean Childhoods, 1*, 1–10.

Meeks Gardner, J. M., Thomas, J., & McKenzie, N. (2009). Documenting interpersonal violence prevention programmes for Jamaican children. *Caribbean Childhoods, 4*, 52–63.

Meeks Gardner, J. M., Walker, S. P., Chang, S. M., Vutchkov, M., & Lalor, G. C. (1998). Undernutrition and elevated blood lead levels: effects on psychomotor development among Jamaican children. *Public Health Nutrition, 1*, 177–179.

Meeks Gardner, J. M., Walker, S. P., Gavin, K. A., & Ashworth, A. (2002). Weaning porridges in Jamaica are no longer of low energy density: an explanation. *Public Health Nutrition, 5*, 295–302.

Meeks Gardner, J. M., Walker, S. P., & Grantham-McGregor, S. M. (2003). A randomized controlled trial of the effects of a home visiting intervention on the cognition and behaviour of term low birth weight Jamaican infants. *Journal of Pediatrics, 143*, 634–639.

Meeks Gardner, J. M., Williams K. R., Guerra, N. G., & Walker, I. (2011). The Jamaica youth survey: Assessing core competencies and risk for aggression among Jamaican youth. *Caribbean Quarterly, 57*, 35–53.

Meeks Gardner, J. M., Witter, M. M., & Ramdath, D. D. (1997). Zinc supplementation: effects on the growth and morbidity of undernourished Jamaican children. *European Journal of Clinical Nutrition, 52*, 34–39.

Stephenson, D., Meeks Gardner, J., Walker, S., & Ashworth, A. (1994). Weaning food viscosity and energy density: Their effects on ad libitum consumption and energy intakes in Jamaican children. *American Journal of Clinical Nutrition, 60*, 465–469.

Wachs, T. D., Chang, S. M., Walker, S. P., & Meeks Gardner, J. M. (2007). Relation of birth weight, maternal intelligence and mother-child interactions to cognitive and play competence of Jamaican two-year old children. *Intelligence, 35*, 605–622.

Walker, S. P., Wach, T. D., Meeks Gardner, J., Lozoff, B., Wasserman, G. A., Pollitt, E., Carter, J., & the International Child Development Steering Group. (2007). Child development: Risk factors for adverse outcomes in developing countries. *Lancet, 369*, 145–157.

Wasserman, G. A., Xinhua, L., Factor-Litvack, P., Meeks Gardner, J., & Joseph, H., Graziano, J. H. (2008). Developmental impacts of heavy metals and undernutrition. *Basic and Clinical Pharmacology & Toxicology, 102*, 212–217.

White, V. O., & Meeks Gardner, J. (2002). Eating disorders in Jamaica. *West Indian Medical Journal, 51*, 32–34.

Williams, H., Younger, N., Campbell-Forrester, S., & Meeks Gardner, J. (2009). Correlates of aggressive behaviour: A re-analysis of the Caribbean Youth Survey. *Caribbean Childhoods, 4*, 1–18.

Zinc Investigators' Collaborative Group (Bhutta, Z. A., Black, R. E., Brown, K. H., Meeks Gardner, J. M., et al.). (1999). Prevention of diarrhea and pneumonia by zinc supplementation in children in developing countries: Pooled analysis of randomized controlled trials. *Journal of Pediatrics, 135*, 689–697.

Zinc Investigators Collaborative Group (Bhutta, Z. A., Black, R. E., Brown, K. H., Meeks Gardner, J. M., et al.). (2000). Therapeutic effects of oral zinc in acute and persistent diarrhea in children in developing countries: Pooled analysis of randomized controlled trials. *American Journal of Clinical Nutrition, 72,* 1516–1522.

Conference Presentations

Meeks Gardner, J., & Grantham-McGregor, S. M. (1994). Activity, child development and undernutrition. *Proceedings of the Nutrition Society, 53,* 241–248.

24
MORAN, LOUISE

Photo of Louise Moran contributed by Louise Moran

[F]or nearly a century, DE was widely considered a second-rate form of education because of the supposed desirability of a face-to-face connection between teacher and student.

Dr. Louise Moran completed her first degrees in Australia, with a Bachelor of Arts in History and Politics in 1968 from the Australian National University, before moving on to a Graduate Diploma in Educational Administration from Adelaide College of Advanced Education in 1980. Later she moved to Canada where she obtained a PhD in History and Policy in Distance Education in 1992 at the University of British Columbia.

DOI: 10.4324/9781003275329-25

Moran's research interests include:

- The history of non-traditional forms of education, especially in Australia, and the history of higher education more broadly;
- Collaboration as an educational strategy;
- The social and educational implications of electronic technologies; and
- Concepts and practice of distance and flexible learning.

Her publications reflect the aforementioned research interests, but also include:

- Concepts of distance education and flexible learning, and institutional and national policy frameworks to facilitate them;
- Use of information technologies in distance education and flexible learning;
- Planning and management of development and delivery systems, student support programmes, and staff development;
- Policy and politics of higher and distance education, including quality assurance, strategic alliances, and internationalization; and
- History of distance education and qualitative research methods.

Dr. Moran spent a great deal of her career working on national and institutional policy, which is reflected in her publications at the end of this chapter.

Moran also played a leading role in national professional organizations including:

- Open and Distance Learning Association of Australia – member of Executive Committee (1993–1995); Chair, Research Awards panel (1993–1995); and
- Australian Institute of Tertiary Educational Administrators – National Vice President (1984–1988), and Victorian State Vice President (1985–1986); Victorian Professional Development Sub-Committee (1979–1982); South Australian Executive Committee (1978–1979).

Interview

Transcript Analysis Summary

Analysis of all interviews included in this volume led to the identification of 3,545 units of data. The mean of these collective units was 118 per pioneer, the median was 118.5, and the mode was 132. Individual interview units ranged from 59 to 217 units, yielding a spread of 158 units between all interviews. Louise Moran's interview generated 120 units, placing her interview just over the middle of all interviews in terms of number of units produced.

A comparision of Louise Moran's interview to the interviews of all pioneers indicated that her interview profile held little in common with the average interview profile (Figure 24.1). Her interview yielded relatively similar numbers of units in 4 of the 14 topic areas: benefits of DE, changes over time, research interests, and general gender-related comments. Overall, Moran's interview produced a greater-than-average number of units in five areas: challenges, accomplishments, goals, interesting memories, and career history. Perhaps many of these units could be explained by the wide array of national and international DE initiatives that she was involved in throughout her career.

Moran's interview generated a lower-than-average number of units in the areas of learning environment, early founders, others for the book, and final thoughts. The lack of units related to the topic of learning environment would be explained by the fact that Moran was retired at the time that the interview was conducted. The interview questions related to final thoughts and suggestions

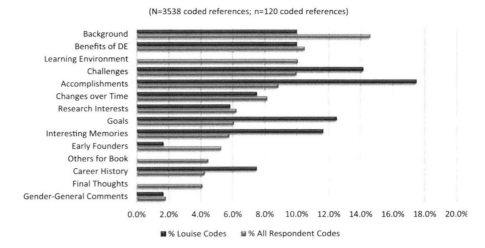

Figure 24.1 All Respondents' Versus Louise Moran's Parent Codes

for other book candidates were deleted from the final version of the transcript. Why this was done was not known.

Link to recorded interview: tinyurl.com/Moran-L-2019

Transcript of Interview

Full name: Louise Moran

Institutional Affiliation: Primarily: Deakin University, Victoria, Australia; secondarily: University of South Australia and its predecessor, the Adelaide College for Advanced Education. Also, ten years with her own consultancy, LifeLong Learning Associates (L3A)

Key:

Regular font = Interviewee comments
Italicized font = Interviewer comments

Interview Questions

1. *What was your educational and experiential background before you became involved in distance education [DE]?*

   There are two parts to that. The first is adult and continuing education. In the early 1970s, I worked at the Australian National University in Canberra in the Centre of Continuing Education [CCE], which took a very different approach from the traditional adult learning establishments. CCE focused on professional education and support to companies and institutions that were developing their organizational development programmes. That was a very good grounding for me in adult learning in its many forms and formats.

   I then moved into academic administration more broadly in the mid-1970s: student administration, academic policy development, curriculum development, and secretary-ships of the major academic committees, including Academic Board and the Council [board of governors] of the then–Adelaide College of Advanced Education. I had a very good, four-year training in those aspects of academic life before I moved more specifically into distance education [DE] in 1979.

2. *In what year did you begin to look specifically into DE?*

   I moved to Deakin University in 1979 to run the student side of the brand-new university and its DE programme, but in fact, I first got involved in DE in 1976 at the Adelaide College of Advanced Education. The college had originally been a teacher's college attached to the South Australian State Department of Education. In the mid-1970s, it became an independent degree-granting college focused on professional education in teacher education and other fields. The college was also responsible for administering not only its own DE programme, but also those of all other colleges in the state. Since teacher education throughout Australia was then moving towards a four-year degree qualification (from one-to-three-year courses), that meant teachers everywhere had to upgrade their qualifications, so DE became the chief method for doing so.

   The Curriculum Committee had oversight of the curriculum, assessment, and teaching methods of every course unit, major sequence, and degree programme the college offered. The Academic Policy Committee was responsible for the academic development and funding of the institution. As secretary of the college's Curriculum Committee and Academic Policy Committee, I was very closely involved in the planning of our DE offerings and in the development of new curriculum and its accreditation, experiences which stood me in good stead throughout the rest of my career.

3. *What were the circumstances in your world that initiated this interest in DE?*

   It wasn't until I moved to Deakin University in 1979 that I became involved in DE hands on. Deakin is based in Geelong, a city about an hour by road from Melbourne, the capital of Victoria. It was established in 1977 to teach on campus and had a particular mandate to teach nationally using a new model of DE adapted from the very successful British Open University [BOU] one. This was wildly different from anything that had gone before in Australia.

   My first role at Deakin covered student administration and support for our off-campus students. It was exciting and challenging as the growth was very rapid. Student numbers doubled each year in the early days, so the programmes to support them constantly required adaptation and expansion. A four-year Bachelor of Education degree piggy-backed on existing courses, but the brand-new Bachelor of Arts added new courses and majors each year. We introduced the world's first fully off-campus MBA in 1981, along with an equally innovative Graduate Diploma in Computing and, in succeeding years, added a number of other post-graduate professional qualifications. So, life was never peaceful!

4. *Which female researchers or female colleagues may have piqued your interest in DE?*

None, I am sad to say. When I read that question, I really, really searched my memory, but piquing my interest in DE, there was no one.

5. *Who would you identify as the early female leaders/founders in the field of DE?*

My own networks became peopled with women from Canada, the UK, and, in a couple of cases, from Germany, and their friendships are still important to me, though I'm now long retired. The most prominent female figure in the early days of DE in Australia was Renée Erdos [1911–1997]. Renée started teaching history in the 1940s in the New South Wales [NSW] technical education system. In the 1950, she went on to run the NSW College of External Studies. She was very active in the International Council for Correspondence Education and was its secretary for a number of years, becoming a much-respected international figure in the early days of modern DE.

In more recent times, a major figure was Margaret Cameron, the founding chief librarian at Deakin University, who was responsible for establishing a very innovative and effective library service for our distance students who were scattered all over a vast country, often a very long way from any library, let alone an academic one. Margaret instituted a system where librarians chose books based on a student's requests and posted them out with a prepaid parcel for returning them. The costs were not insignificant, but – unlike every other DE university's experiences – students kept to a rapid turnaround, and few books were lost.

6. *What are some of the goals that you strove to achieve over the years in the field of DE?*

One of the things I was most passionate about from the beginning was opening up access to higher education for people who have never had the opportunity before, or those who were seeking to either strengthen their expertise in a particular area or expand to new fields. That morphed extremely quickly into an interest in opening up access for women, particularly to the Bachelor of Arts programme at Deakin University, where a substantial number (about 33%) were mature age – i.e., they didn't have to have a qualification or previous study in order to enrol. We established an enrolment process in which applicants were asked not only the usual factual information, but also to write a letter explaining why they wanted to study. That taught me a lot about the aspirations and learning support requirements of women who had never had the chance to study after school and those for whom family or other opposition to them studying would continue to be a problem.

The second goal became important to me in the 1980s and sharpened into the focus of my PhD, and that was about achieving parity of esteem for distance versus face-to-face study. In Australia, DE was, with few exceptions, offered in "dual mode" – i.e., the qualification, its content, and assessment are the same, regardless of whether it is taught on or off campus, and mode of study is not recorded in the student's testamur. Today, with the ubiquity of online learning, the distinction has lost its meaning, but for nearly a century, DE was widely considered a second-rate form of education because of the supposed desirability of a face-to-face connection between teacher and student. So, for a new university like Deakin, teaching in dual mode meant it had to work hard to achieve acceptance by the conventional and older universities.

At Deakin, we set out to do this by adopting the BOU model, which put a premium on the quality of the distance learning materials themselves and on the teaching supports to them.

We went to a huge amount of trouble over an extended period of time to prove ourselves in the rather snooty university environment that prevailed then. I later took that up in my PhD in a Canadian setting. This was a study of the Open Learning Institute of British Columbia from its inception in the 1970s through to the mid-80s, when it was transformed into the Open Learning Agency, later the BC Open University, and now Thompson Rivers University. The focus of my PhD was "How did this most unusual and innovative institution achieve parity of esteem in the then–academically clique-y environment of the established British Columbia universities?" Their solutions were both similar and different from ours at Deakin, but equally involved the preparation of openly available, very high-quality course materials and the effective co-option of well-respected academics, together with substantial learning supports.

My third goal started in the early 1980s when I first visited Canada, and that was about collaborating with other DE institutions, not only in Australia but also internationally (particularly, for me, in Canada and in Hong Kong), to enable the exchange and/or sale of our course materials. There were a number of aspects to collaboration, a major one being about amortizing the high costs of course development and materials production. Plus, there were quite a number of us at Deakin and elsewhere who believed it made no sense to maintain intellectual silos between our institutions and that knowledge should be shared as readily as practicable. I wasn't very successful (the "Not Invented Here" factor being a strong deterrent to adopting another's course), but we made a sustained effort – for example, in exchanging course materials between Deakin and the Open Learning Institute and with the Open College of Hong Kong. We also bought some courses from the BOU in the early days, as did OLI. I co-published (with Ian Mugridge) a book on *Collaboration in Distance Education* in 1993; it was certainly my most successful publication, and interest in the issue persisted throughout my career.

My fourth goal was about improving the quality of materials. Before Deakin was established, the instructional design quality underpinning the content in most Australian DE programmes was very diverse because it depended entirely upon whether the academics concerned understood how to put a course together for effective learning. Some, of course, were splendid, others dire, most middling. Student support was often patchy, and students could be left to sink or swim on their own. Standards and resources for print production were often dismal (faded gestetner copies, anyone?). We set national benchmarks in all these aspects, and the resources we put into all of them reflected that. Regrettably, too many policymakers and funding bodies persisted in the belief that DE was a cheap form of education; that's still too often reflected in the resources provided for online learning.

A further goal for me arose in the 1980s as we moved from improving access for Australian students to higher education towards providing access also for overseas students. Until 1986, most students who came to Australia to study came under the Colombo Plan, an exceptionally good government-funded scholarship programme. I had had a quiet go, in the very early 1980s, at enabling Australian students who were overseas to enrol in some of our DE courses. It was a complete flop. Postal services were hopeless, and for students to find the necessary additional learning resources was just too hard in the out-of-the-way countries that they were living in.

In 1986, the Australian government opened access to our universities for fee-paying overseas students, a process which has now evolved into Australia's third-largest export "industry." That year, I started Deakin's international programme to bring overseas students to the campus in Geelong. By the 1990s, Deakin and other Australian universities were establishing campuses in mostly neighbouring Asian countries as well. DE materials and techniques have featured large in making such programmes work.

At about the same time, we started working with professional associations and large organizations in Australia to provide continuing professional education to students in their own work settings. In the 25 years since then, the face of higher education and training has been hugely transformed by information technologies, politics, and the sheer expansion in numbers.

7. *What are some of your accomplishments in the field of DE that you would like to share?*

I spent a great deal of my career working on institutional and national policy development using DE. That gave me a great deal of satisfaction. It was not something that many people identified as a major stream, if you like, in DE. Most of the emphasis in the literature and the way that people talked about themselves was as instructional designers, course developers, editors, learning advisers, and so on. Very few of us described ourselves as primarily a leader of a DE system or policy of a distinct kind, or sought to think and write about policy in a holistic way. That was my main academic interest in DE for most of my working life and was a logical extension of my earlier background in broader academic administration, as well as a long-time active involvement in the Australian professional body of academic administrators.

I was fortunate in having a position at Deakin that enabled me to influence the way in which our policies were developed, and to evolve and adapt the DE programme to meet demands for growth and change. I was responsible in the 1980s for coordinating the academic planning of the university's DE programme and negotiating with the faculties over allocation of resources from my centralized budget for course development and materials production. There was inevitably never enough money to do all we wanted, but I was able to reduce our costs by a third, which meant the faculties could continue to expand at a reasonable rate while we still maintained the standards we'd set. That was very satisfying. In the 1990s, with the advent of decentralized models at both Deakin and the University of South Australia, the challenge was more about defining *flexible learning* in such a way that it made sense in each of the different faculties and their fields of knowledge.

Another accomplishment that I am proud of was the success of Deakin University Press [DUP], which was created to capitalize on our DE publications in a commercial market. By the mid-1980s, Deakin was the largest educational publisher in Australia in terms of volume, rather to the chagrin of commercial publishers, because we provided most of that material directly to students rather than selling it. We realized there was also a market for the standalone monographs and essays that were part of many courses, and developed a good niche for DUP in Australia and overseas from the 1980s. In addition, we decided to publish a small number of discrete books outside the scope of our courses. The first such book – I hasten to say this decision was made before I became the DUP publisher! – was a history of nudism in Australia, written by a Deakin academic who was, himself, a nudist. It achieved extraordinary publicity, but failed miserably to find a commercial market because it was neither titillating enough for the soft porn market (the photos were all airbrushed, for example) nor genteel enough for the "family" market of commercial booksellers. I ultimately remaindered it to a dubious publisher based in Hawaii.

I would nominate as a special highlight of my career the broadening of access to higher education through DE, especially for women who hadn't had the opportunity to study beyond high school. Boys might be encouraged to go on to further education or training, but the girls left school at 15 or 16, became secretaries or shop assistants, married and had babies, and that was supposed to be that. There was a huge pent-up demand among so many of those women for an intellectual challenge, the idea that there were alternatives to that scenario. It was the reality behind the film *Educating Rita*. Every challenge Rita faced in studying for her BA at the BOU was encountered by our students – just not all of them by one person! I'm very proud of the support services we put in place at Deakin and the University of South Australia to help students learn how to learn and to overcome educational and personal obstacles to successful study.

I'd also nominate the international programmes that I was initially involved in in the 1980s at Deakin and then more broadly through the 1990s and 2000s. Having set up the initial framework for Deakin's international programmes from 1986, I later became something of an expert in Australia on international education, and it was a major plank in my later consulting career. That was very satisfying, too, because providing opportunities for people in countries where education was difficult, if not impossible, to access became a significant factor for me. In parallel with that international education focus, I was also very involved, over some 20 years, in using DE strategies to provide professional continuing education through professional associations, especially in the financial services sector.

Finally, I would nominate as a career achievement my involvement in the early adoption of information technologies. On the one hand, that was about helping create the policy settings for the implementation of computer-mediated communications in my two Australian universities and in Sweden. In particular, though, I was heavily preoccupied in the 1990s and 2000s with the development of national networks for using information technologies for various teaching purposes at school level, in the vocational education system, and at university level. Those early days were exciting, and trying to realize the potential of the new technologies was challenging but fascinating. It's ironic that it's all moved so fast that nowadays I am a complete ignoramus and something of a Luddite. Too much that worked well or better, like print, is being thrown out like the proverbial baby and bathwater.

Overall, I think my achievements lay in creating innovative policies and systems in higher education and training for people in many places and circumstances, and then changing and adapting those to meet new situations. It wasn't always easy, but I enjoyed the vast majority of my career, made some wonderful friends, and it was fun and intellectually stimulating.

8. *What are some of the challenges that you faced in the field of DE over the years?*

A sustained challenge was the opposition from traditional universities and traditional faculties to the idea that DE was a legitimate approach to teaching and learning, let alone one which could produce high-quality results. As I said earlier, the whole question of parity of esteem ran through pretty much everything we did. It was very good for us in a way because it sharpened how we thought, what we did, how we expressed what we did, how we proved ourselves through the quality of student outcomes – the qualifications they achieved and the way those powered their way into people's lives and workplaces. But the opposition was certainly very strong. I remember in the early days at Deakin University trying to get credit transfer arrangements in place so our students could move to one of the other universities in Victoria, established variously between the 1850s and 1960s. One initially refused point blank to accept any of our subjects for credit transfer. It took some years of arguing to get that accepted. The resistance has gone now, but I doubt the informal pecking order of universities will ever disappear. It was a very powerful incentive to try and achieve parity of esteem and influenced very much the way in which I approached my PhD.

Until the 1990s, I worked in largely centralized systems which I found – and still think – worked especially well for DE, with its heavy reliance on economies of scale and specialized expertise. That coloured the inevitable internal tensions and power plays on all sides. In the 1990s, much of the centralized infrastructure was dispersed to faculty control, and that created a new set of challenges. DE, done well, is not a cheap form of education, but that was often not well grasped by senior academics under constant pressure to do more with less.

The third challenge, and this extended over my entire career, was helping academics understand the importance of instructional design in their own work, regardless of teaching methods and sites of teaching and learning – in other words, both on and off campus and multimode forms of education. I don't know whether it applies now, but certainly at the time I retired, it was still unfortunately the case in higher education in Australia that academics were not required, as school teachers are, to learn formally how to teach, assess, and support their students, and how to make effective use of the technologies available, be they lecture theatres or computers. That meant that you had to rely far too much on serendipity, with some academics being absolutely wonderful teachers, and some academics being appalling, and everyone else in between.

In the 1990s, the federal government became increasingly interested in quality assurance, and put in place a number of programmes to try and "up" the quality of teaching and learning in universities. Academic staff development became a feature in every university, but it wasn't necessarily well done or accepted – a combination of the "Not Invented Here" factor and a common resistance by many academics to having anyone look inside their classrooms. Nevertheless, quality assurance became a major feature of academic planning, and the expertise of our instructional designers, editors, and others played a significant part in programmes both on and off campus. In a number of universities, including both of mine, the "distance education centre" was merged with academic staff development centres. Quality assurance, in one form or another, played a growing part in my roles in the 1990s, both within my universities and at national level.

9. *What was the "state of DE" when you first entered the field as opposed to DE in 2019?*

I can only answer up to about 2007, when I retired. One way to chart the changes is through the nomenclature, at least in Australia. When I first entered the field in the 1970s, it was called "external" or "correspondence study." Even now, in "What did you do in your career?" conversations, I sometimes get a puzzled look about "distance education," followed by "Do you mean correspondence study?" When the International Council for Correspondence Study changed its name to Distance Education in the early 1980s, it caused great consternation among the older generation. A decade later came "flexible learning," signalling the blending of on and off campus; 20 years later, it's "online learning." I take a certain melancholy pleasure in realizing that DE, as a discrete field, came and went in the course of my 30-year career. It's as foreign a field to today's teachers and administrators as paper card records of correspondence students' history were in my day.

Distance education in Australia started, arguably, in the 1880s, with technical training programmes for workers in country centres. (I delight in the notion that one of the very first courses was for sanitary inspectors in country NSW.) Fast forward a century, and it was a firmly established – if slightly disreputable – form of study at all levels of schooling, training, and university education. There were incremental improvements in technologies and communications along the way. Deakin's establishment in 1977 represented a profound paradigm shift. External study at university level then relied largely on lecturers' notes, limited correspondence during the semester, limited library services, and compulsory residential schools. In adapting the BOU model of dedicated course team, high production values, and extensive student learning supports, Deakin changed the way all Australian distance educators approached their work. Curiously, the BOU had adopted the Australian (University of New England) model of residential schools as part of their own search for parity of esteem. We decided to offer occasional voluntary workshops in some subjects, on the twin grounds that the learning materials should be self-sustaining, and that costs to students of travel and time away from work and family were unacceptably high. Even our on-campus students enrolled in the same courses had occasional tutorials but no lectures. Perhaps some of those ideas persist in different form today as universities replace classroom teaching with online learning.

10. *What interesting memories would you like to share about the beginning of online learning?*

In the late 1980s, the Dean of Education at Deakin, Professor Iain Wallace, tried to get the university to experiment seriously with the emerging information technologies. He was ahead of his time and little happened. I was very sceptical – and in some ways, still am. I remain to be convinced that a computer screen is preferable to print as an effective way to read and absorb complex ideas and data. Plus it's nowhere near as enjoyable as a book! When I returned to Deakin in 1992 after completing my PhD, the technology was still clunky. When Ian Mugridge and I were compiling our book on *Collaboration in Distance Education* in 1992–1993, he tried to send me chapters as attachments to email, but my screen kept freezing and sending the entire system into conniptions – very irritating and off-putting. That problem disappeared quickly, though, and the ability to exchange drafts and play with options has made collaborative writing infinitely easier.

It was email that made all the difference. Our approach at Deakin was particularly influenced by a clever instructional designer, Lyn Thompson, who developed a prototype computer-mediated communications system (CMC) to support teaching and learning on and off campus. In 1991, the university had merged with two other institutions, one a multi-campus college based across metropolitan Melbourne, the other a two-and-a-half-hour drive to the southwest. As degree programmes were redesigned to run across the campuses as well as nationally, CMC became a central tool for everyone. The early version rapidly evolved into a sophisticated cross-campus network, catering also to students all over the country as they gradually acquired computers and Internet connections. Lyn's work was instrumental in Deakin's leadership in this area through that decade.

That experience was mirrored, with increasing technological sophistication and practicability of application, in my time at the University of South Australia and then at Mid Sweden University in northern Sweden in 1997–1998, both being multi-campus universities seeking to use flexible learning strategies to teach on, across and off campus.

For my own part, I got involved in the design of national networks to support teaching and learning at all levels of education and training. Federal government involvement and funding helped drive change at system level through the next decade, and the take-up and effective use of information technologies became a prominent part of my consulting work through to 2007. To give two examples: I set up my consulting company, LifeLong Learning Associates, in 1998 on returning to Australia from Sweden, and soon was leading a project to design a national electronic network for teaching and learning in the school systems across the nation. I then partnered with KPMG to design an evaluation architecture and conduct the first evaluation phase of a government-funded $100 million, five-year programme (the Flexible Learning Framework) to establish the use of flexible learning technologies in the vocational education systems, both public and private. That programme had a huge transformative effect within the technical/vocational system and beyond.

11. *What were your specific DE research interests, and have they changed/evolved over the years?*

Early on, I was interested in the development of policy and processes to build DE programmes and run them. That evolved into an interest in DE as a policy of the state, as a mechanism for the provision of educational opportunities, most particularly in higher education and later on, also in vocational education. Then, because I have always been a historian (by inclination as well as training), I became interested in the history of DE, although I didn't publish in the area until I started on the PhD in the late 1980s. I contemplated writing a history of Deakin University, but it would have been too hagiographic; I was too closely involved to be able to write a considered, impartial history. However, I found the question of how such innovative institutions as Deakin achieved legitimacy in the academic firmament very intriguing, and so I tried to answer it by undertaking a history of the Open Learning Institute of British Columbia.

When I returned to Deakin in 1992, I thought it might be possible to write a different kind of history of the university and made a start on it, but it proved problematic, and I didn't persist. Instead, I started thinking about the history of DE in Australia, since we were among the earliest in the world to take up the challenges in a systematic way from the late 19th century. I began to address that in an address to the Open and Distance Learning Association of Australia in 1997 and to encourage my colleagues to think more historically about their own work. Most of the audience was familiar with one or another aspect of what I was describing, but no one was then working on a rigorous historical study of DE in Australia. For various reasons I didn't persist with that work – life intervened. Now that the era of "distance education" is over, I would like to think that the historical contexts will be explored by current or future researchers. I'm delighted that you are compiling this book because the voices of women are all too often not heard or recorded.

Since retiring, I have taken that question up in a different context as a member of the National Foundation for Australian Women, through participation in the Australian Women's Archives Project, which is now almost 20 years old. Our goal is to retrieve women's voices in Australian history in two ways: first, by preparing short biographies of Australian women of note, past and present, in virtually any field, which are then uploaded to the online Women's Register (www.womenaustralia.info). The register is linked to the National Library of Australia's wonderful information finding tool, Trove, and it is now a primary research tool for researchers on Australian women's history. Secondly, the project encourages women and collecting institutions to ensure women's papers are preserved and made available for future researchers. Otherwise, women's history is invisible and/or lost.

Returning to the history of DE, my history of the Open Learning Institute [OLI] of British Columbia was based on the records of OLI, which were then housed in their library in Richmond [British Columbia]. After I left, OLI moved to Burnaby, and in the process, all those files were destroyed. I only discovered this when I returned to British Columbia in 2005 as a consultant to the then-brand-new Thompson Rivers University in Kamloops, which was partly built on a merger with OLI's successor, the British Columbia Open University. I had been able to photocopy a great deal of material from the OLI records, and this was now the only record left of arguably one of the most innovative DE institutions ever. It took some time to happen, but I was thrilled (and relieved) to be able to give all those papers to Thompson Rivers University in 2017.

Publications

Books

Moran, L. (1990). Deakin University, Australia. In B. N. Koul & J. Jenkins (Eds.), *Distance education: A spectrum of case studies*. Kogan Page.
Moran, L., & Mugridge, I. (Eds.). (1993). *Collaboration in distance education: International case studies*. Routledge.
Moran, L., & Rumble, G. (Eds.). (2004). *Vocational training through distance education: A policy perspective*. Routledge.

Book Chapters

Latchem, C., & Moran, L. (1998). Staff development issues in dual mode institutions: The Australian experience. In C. Latchem & F. Lockwood (Eds.), *Staff development issues in open and flexible education*. Routledge.

Moran, L. (1993). Documentary and oral testimony in institutional research. In M. Crick & B. Geddes (Eds.), *Research methods in the field: Ten anthropological accounts*. Deakin University Press.
Moran, L. (1994). Quality assurance in distance education at Deakin University. In P. M. Deshpande & I. Mugridge (Eds.), *Quality assurance in higher education*. Commonwealth of Learning.
Moran, L. (1995). Education at the margins – studying at a distance. In J. Perry & J. Hughes (Eds.), *Anthropology: Voices from the margins*. Deakin University Press.
Moran, L. (1997). Flexible learning as university policy. In S. Brown (Ed.), *Open and distance learning in industry and education*. Kogan Page.
Moran, L., & Mugridge, I. (1993a). Policies and trends in inter-institutional collaboration. In L. Moran, & L. Mugridge (Eds.), *Collaboration in distance education: International case studies*. Routledge.
Moran, L., & Mugridge, I. (1993b). Collaboration in distance education: An introduction. In L. Moranm & L. Mugridge (Eds.), *Collaboration in distance education: International case studies*. Routledge.
Moran, L., & Myringer, B. (1999). Flexible learning and university change. In K. Harry (Ed.), *Higher education through open and distance learning*. Routledge.
Moran, L., & Rumble, G. (2004). Vocational education and distance learning. In L. Moran & G. Rumble (Eds.), *Vocational training through distance education: A policy perspective*. Routledge.
Rumble, G., & Moran, L. (2004). Towards a policy for vocational education and training in an electronic age. In L. Moran & G. Rumble (Eds.), *Vocational training through distance education: A policy perspective*. Routledge.

Journal Articles

Moran, L. (1985). Planning an off-campus program. *Currency*, *1*, Deakin University.
Moran, L. (1986). Collaboration and marketing of educational course materials. *Journal of Tertiary Educational Administration*, *8*(2).
Moran, L. (1990). Inter-institutional collaboration: The case of the Australian inter-university women's studies major. *Journal of Distance Education*, *6*(2), 32–48.
Moran, L. (1991). Review of Athabasca University: The evolution of distance education [Review of the book *Athabasca University: The evolution of distance education*, by T. C. Byrne]. *Historical Studies in Education*, *3*(1), 137–140. Moran, L. (1994). Guest Editor of *ODLAA Occasional Papers*, *1*(May).
Moran, L. (1993a). Genesis of the open learning institute of British Columbia. *Journal of Distance Education*, *8*(1), 43–70.
Moran, L. (1993b). Review of exploring open and distance learning [Review of the book *Exploring open and distance learning*, by D. Rowntree]. *Open Learning*, *8*(3), 60–61.
Moran, L. (1997). Review of WAIT to Curtin: A history of the Western Australian Institute of Technology [Review of the book *WAIT to Curtin: A history of the Western Australian Institute of Technology*, by M. White]. *History of Education Review*, *26*(1), 98–99.
Moran, L., & Edge, D. (1994). Performance of under/over 21-year-old students and implications for open campus delivery. *ODLAA Occasional Papers*, *1*, 20–29.
Moran, L., & Stanley, W. Croker. (1981). Take counsel with yourself. *Open Campus*, *3*(1).

Commissioned Reports

KPMG Consulting Australia & LifeLong Learning Associates. (2001). *Australian flexible learning framework – Evaluation of strategy 2000*. [Evaluation commissioned by Australian National Training Authority]. www.flexiblelearning.net.au
KPMG Consulting Australia & LifeLong Learning Associates. (2002). *Australian flexible learning framework – Phase 1 evaluation*. [Evaluation commissioned by Australian National Training Authority]. www.flexible learning.net.au
LifeLong Learning Associates. (1999). *Strategic analysis: Improving teaching and learning in Australian school education through the use of information and communications technologies*. [Report commissioned by the Schools Advisory Group of Education Network Australia]. www.edna.gov.au/publications/ict_schools/cover.html
LifeLong Learning Associates. (1999–2003). Multiple reports for the Australian Insurance Institute (professional body for the insurance industry) on professional continuing education courses and curricula, globalisation of training markets, and organisational change and development.
LifeLong Learning Associates. (2001). *Review of flexible learning at James Cook University*. [Commissioned by James Cook University].

LifeLong Learning Associates. (2003a). *An 'alumni' scheme for Victorian TAFE*. [Design of concept and pilot projects commissioned by Office of Training and Tertiary Education, Victorian Department of Education and Training]. Victorian Department of Education and Training.

LifeLong Learning Associates. (2003b). *Evaluation of the policy and research program of the Australian Flexible Learning Framework*. [Commissioned by Australian National Training Authority]. Australian National Training Authority.

LifeLong Learning Associates. (2003c). *Facilitating access to international markets for vocational education and training*. [Discussion paper commissioned by Australian National Training Authority]. Australian National Training Authority.

LifeLong Learning Associates. (2003d). *Operation of city and guilds in Australia*. [Report commissioned by Australian National Training Authority]. Australian National Training Authority.

LifeLong Learning Associates. (2003e). *The Australian quality training framework and globalisation of training markets*. [Report commissioned by Australian National Training Authority]. Australian National Training Authority.

LifeLong Learning Associates. (2004). *Export of education services from Victoria: Policy analysis for legislative review*. [Commissioned by Victoria Department of Education and Training]. Victoria Department of Education and Training.

Maclean, P., Moran, L., & Rowland, R. (1987). *The inter-university women's studies major: Evaluation of a model of inter-institutional collaboration in distance education*. [Report commissioned by Commonwealth Tertiary Education Commission. Geelong]. Deakin University.

Moran, L. (1988). *Australia's contribution to promoting distance education in the South Pacific and Southern Africa: Issues and options re the CHOGM Commonwealth of Learning initiative*. [Report commissioned by Australian International Development Assistance Bureau]. Deakin University.

Moran, L. (1995). *National Policy Frameworks to Support Integration of Information Technologies into University Teaching/Learning*. [Report commissioned by Dept. of Employment, Education & Training. Canberra].

Moran, L. (1996). Distance education, copyright and communication in the information society. [Commissioned by UNESCO for Committee of Experts on Copyright in the Information Society]. New Delhi, India, November (1996). Published in *Distance Education and Copyright*, UNESCO Copyright Bulletin Vol. 33, No. 2, April–June (1999). Paris: UNESCO Publishing.

Moran, L. (1998a). *Mid Sweden – A networked, flexible learning university*. [Educational concept and change management plan commissioned by Mid Sweden University]. Mid Sweden University.

Moran, L. (1998b). *The flexible learning action group project on Internet use – A formative evaluation*. [Commissioned by University of Technology, Sydney].

Moran, L. (1999). Advice to Charles Sturt University on provision of off campus courses on fraud investigation and prevention, followed by brokering of a partnership with the Australian Insurance Institute.

Moran, L. (2001). *Report to Commonwealth of Learning on forum for vice chancellors on best practice in open and distance learning*. Commonwealth of Learning.

Moran, L., Hont, J., Calvert, J., & Bottomley, J. (1993). *Electronic facilities network to enhance tertiary open learning services*. [Report of a project conducted for the Australian Department of Employment, Education & Training]. AGPS.

PhillipsKPA, & LifeLong Learning Associates. (2005). *Evaluation of the education services for Overseas Students Act 2000*. [A review commissioned by the Australian Department of Education, Science and Training of the effectiveness and efficiency of the Australian legislation covering services to students at all levels of public and private education and training, in all States and Territories, and intersection of the Act with the Migration Act]. Australian Department of Education.

Stewart-Rattray, J., Moran, L., & Scheuler, J. (2001). *Scope of flexible learning and implications for improved data collecting and reporting systems*. [Report commissioned by Australian National Training Authority]. National Centre for Vocational Education Research. www.flexiblelearning.net.au

Strategic Partners, & LifeLong Learning Associates. (2000). *Evaluation of the Rural Family Relationships Education Program*. [Commissioned by Commonwealth Department of Family and Community Services].

25
MURRAY, DENISE

Photo of Denise Murray contributed by Denise Murray

> *I did the first linguistic analysis of computer-mediated communication. It was seeing computer-mediated communication in both the email and the chat form that I saw potential for education. So that, for me, was a real light bulb experience.*

Dr. Denise Murray became a certified secondary English, history, and math teacher at Queensland Teachers' College in 1963. She obtained a Bachelor of Arts in English and History at Queensland University, Australia, in 1966 and a Master of Arts in Linguistics at Macquarie University in 1981. She went on to complete her PhD in Education: Second Language Education at Stanford University, United States, in 1986.

Dr. Murray is currently Professor Emerita at Macquarie University, Professor Emerita at San José State University, and Professor at Anaheim University.

Dr. Murray was Executive Director the AMEP Research Centre and the National Centre for English Language Teaching and Research (NCELTR) at Macquarie University from 2000 to 2006. She was founding Chair of the Department of Linguistics and Language Development at San José State University from 1990 to 2000.

Dr. Murray has also been active her entire career as a consultant for educational institutions, professional organizations, and government agencies. She has taken on leadership roles at universities and with professional organizations. She has worked internationally as guest speaker at numerous conferences. Dr. Murray visited Anaheim University Residential, Tokyo, Japan, in 2016 and Chulalongkorn University Language Institute, Bangkok, Thailand, in 2010, as an invited lecturer.

Murray's research interests include computer-assisted language learning, cross-cultural literacy, and the intersection of language, society, and technology, as well as leadership in language education. As demonstrated in her list of publications at the end of this chapter, her research began specifically with second-language learning and then evolved into the merging of this topic with new technologies and online education.

Interview

Transcript Analysis Summary

Analysis of all interviews included in this volume led to the identification of 3,545 units of data. The mean of these collective units was 118 per pioneer, the median was 118.5, and the mode was 132. Individual interview units ranged from 59 to 217 units, yielding a spread of 158 units between all interviews. Denise Murray's interview generated 95 units, which placed her interview in the lower third of interviews in terms of unit generation.

A comparision of Murray's interview to the interviews of all pioneers indicates that her interview yielded a unique profile to that of the average interview in terms of units produced per thematic area (Figure 25.1). Although the number of units that Murray's interview produced for benefits of DE and challenges superceded the number of units in the average interview, the pattern between these sets of interviews remained similar. That is, both sets of interviews generated slightly more benefits than challenges units. The higher-than-average quantities of units in the areas of benefits of DE, learning environment, challenges, and changes over time may have three primary reasons. First, Denise was one of the few interviewed pioneers whose background included a traditional post-secondary DE correspondence education. She then went on to complete her doctoral thesis on computer-mediated text analyses, making her among the first in the world to study this new phenomenon. Thus, Denise had a unique perspective on emerging technologies and the evolution of DE from the time of traditional correspondence to modern day. Two other possible reasons for Denise's higher-than-average number of units in these areas were the diversity of students and subject areas that she was involved with.

Murray did not generate as many units as the average interviewee did in the areas of accomplishments, goals, others for the book, career history, or final thoughts. When analyzing her accomplishment units, it was learned that most of this conversation focused on what teams that she worked with did, rather than what she accomplished. This type of response was found among many of the

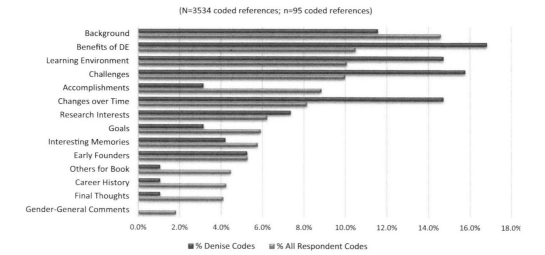

Figure 25.1 All Respondents' Versus Denise Murray's Parent Codes

pioneers' interviews, despite the fact that the interview question related to this topic specifically asked these women to discuss their personal accomplishments. Due to the prevalence of this tendency, further exploration of this phenomenon is presented in Part Two of this book. Discussion of her goals centred on one theme – how to generate productive conversations while reducing idle chatter among students in the online environment. At the time of her interview, Murray was aware that many of pioneers whom she knew had already been interviewed for the book; this would explain the number of units in this category. Career history was a topic that arose organically during some interviewees' conversations. It was not an overt interview question. Since she was not asked this question, Murray did not discuss this topic during her interview. No explanation is offered for the minimal units found in the final thoughts section.

Link to recorded interview: tinyurl.com/Murray-D-2018

Transcript of Interview

Full Name: Denise Murray
Institutional Affiliation: Emeritus Professor, Macquarie University; Anaheim University
Key:

Regular font = Interviewee comments
Italicized font = Interviewer comments

Interview Questions

1. *What was your educational and experiential background before you became involved in DE and online learning?*

   I consider distance learning as an area that I have a deep and abiding commitment to, largely because I completed my bachelor's degree by distance learning back in the day when it was by correspondence only. That was because I was a teacher already in a high school but hadn't completed my degree. If I wanted to complete it, I had to do it in my own time.

   Like Canada, Australia is a vast country. I was transferred from the capital city where I lived to teach in a high school which was 1,300 miles away. The only university in the state at that time was in the capital city, so there was no chance of me doing further education while I was stationed up in Atherton. So I did it by correspondence, which was paper-based, and then sent off to the library to mail books back to you.

   I have had a commitment my whole life to distance learning for people who are either in remote and rural areas or aren't able to access education otherwise. Of course, being Australian, it also comes from this almost-legendary School of the Air that's used in the outback of Australia for elementary children.

   Later in my career, as I moved from general high school teaching into teaching English as a foreign language, or English as a second language, I realized that there were also people who were unable to access education for other reasons. They were adults. They may have family obligations. They may have work obligations. So they are not able to attend a brick-and-mortar institution.

   So, in various stages of my career, I've been involved in different types of distance education. So for me, distance education has firm roots in trying to provide education for people who aren't able to do it in the more traditional classroom for whatever reason.

   In the early days, it was correspondence. Then it became tapes being sent back and forth, to CDs [compact discs], and so on. But with the advent of computer technology, I saw opportunities that were not available through other means. This was a way of teachers being able to interact, which was difficult to do otherwise.

   Although I had a couple pieces published in CALL [the journal *Computer-assisted Language Learning*], a lot of the work that I read about CALL conflates online language teaching with CALL. It is really important to separate those out. Online language teacher education, which is largely what I do, has its roots in distance education, rather than in the technology.

   CALL is rather different, because CALL started with traditional classrooms or with laboratories where students had extra practice, mainly drill and grill, in laboratories in the early days, and then more inventive tasks were created. Then, of course, we had interactive media and multimedia, which opened up the whole possibilities for CALL. But CALL covers a wider gambit and a wider clientele than does online education. Online education, to me, is a delivery mechanism, and there have been other delivery mechanisms for learning.

I haven't done online language learning. My online instruction has always been either in teacher education or something more associated with teacher education.

If we are also going to also focus on computer-assisted delivery, then the impetus for that while I was doing a doctorate at Stanford [University], I was doing a class in literacy with Shirley Brice-Heath. She asked us to do a small ethnography of literacy practices of someone we saw frequently. Of course, when you are married, the person you see most frequently is either your children or spouse. So I decided to follow my husband around. One night, he was in the study on the computer (he's a computer scientist), sitting in front of a black screen with green text. I brought him in a cup of coffee. I suddenly saw that the text was moving. He was typing, and he would read something, and then he was typing. I said, "What on earth are you doing?" I needed to know this because this was a literacy practice. And so he explained chat to me, and then email. Now this is back in 1985, when the only people who had email were a few universities and propriety companies, like IBM, which was who he worked for.

I was intrigued with this, so I focused most of that ethnographic report on his interactions, using both chat (or what we would now call "chat," which, of course, didn't exist as "chat" in those days) and email. So Shirley said, "Okay, that's your dissertation topic."

And I said, "No. I was going to do a study of the writing of Japanese writers of English." I was a TESOL [teaching English to speakers of other languages] professional.

She said, "No. This is really exciting work." And so I did the first linguistic analysis of computer-mediated communication. It was seeing computer-mediated communication in both the email and the chat form that I saw potential for education. So that, for me, was a real light bulb experience.

2. *In what year did you begin to look specifically into computer-mediated communication [CMC]?*

I was awarded my PhD in 1986, so I was doing it in 1985.

3. *What were the circumstances in your world that initiated this interest in CMC?*

I have always been interested in literacy as well. Not literacy as the ability to decode text, but the ability to make meaning from text – and by *text*, I use a very systemic linguistics picture of multimedia text. So that's always been an interest to me. That is why I was taking a class in literacy with Shirley Heath.

4. *Which female researchers or female colleagues may have piqued your interest in DE, online learning, or CMC?*

Well, clearly Shirley Heath, although she knew nothing about it at the time. They weren't colleagues, but people [whose work] I read, like Susan Herring, did far more work after I did on linguistic analysis of computer-mediated communication. Shirley Turkle's work is something that really struck me because I'm not a technophile. I feel very strongly that technology is something that enhances human abilities. If we don't look at it that way, we are prone to choose things that don't necessarily assist either education or human interaction. So I don't think that one should go down the line of "Oh, we've got this whiz-bang new CALL programme," or "There's this new social media. I want to use that with education," unless it really facilitates whatever the objective is in education. I think that Turkle's work has been really informative of how dangerous it can be to be so focused on the technology side of technology.

5. *Who would you identify as the early female leaders/founders in the field of online distance education [ODL]?*

Narrowing that further into the field of online language education, I would say David Nunan. He was instrumental in starting the master's degree at Anaheim University, which is a fully online university, back in the late 80s or early 90s, I think. All they were able to do was have discussion lists for students – there was nothing else available technologically – and chat. But the chat was very primitive, and the bandwidth was very low. I taught a couple of classes with him. You would be typing in, and the student would be coming back to you, and you still hadn't answered the previous student's question, which, of course, still happens today. Then there would be silence. You didn't know if the line had dropped, and they couldn't communicate with you, or whether they didn't know how to answer the question. There was this great unknown out there. So, it was really clunky and clumsy. But David persevered. As a result, when the new multimedia technologies came in, it became a lot more robust.

Now I work for AU [Anaheim University], teaching the occasional class. We use a conferencing programme, GoToMeeting, which is so much more robust for students and more user friendly. They can see faces, they can talk, they can put up documents; it's the same as Zoom.

I think that I need to go back. David's reason for being interested in Anaheim (it already had a degree in business) was because he, like me, was an Australian. He had been at Macquarie University before I had. While he was at Macquarie, there was a lot of distance education being done, the same as I did my bachelor's degree, by correspondence, because the university was 1,300 miles from where I was teaching. Macquarie University was one of the forerunners in Australia of universities that provided distance education. He and Chris Candlin started the Master's in Distance Education in Australia, and that was correspondence only, with them going to different outposts, maybe, and having classes with students if they could come into a centre. And then they graduated to CDs.

By the time I was at Macquarie, we were teaching truly online masters' and doctorates. But by then, we also knew that many of the students that we were interacting with had horror communications in terms of bandwidths in their own countries. So we always had backups of CDs that would be sent out to rural and remote areas where people couldn't stay online while we were doing anything that was live. That's a problem still today, I think. As you, yourself, have found, in remote areas, it is not always possible to keep some of these connections live for what is probably the most interactive and useful form of online learning for students.

I: *You talk about David. Can you think of any women who were involved in that era?*

Unfortunately, no.

6. *What are some of the goals that you strove to achieve in the field of ODL?*

My approach to education is you have objectives for the course, and then you work back to look at what is the best way for learners to achieve those objectives. If certain types of technology will help you achieve that, then use that technology. If it won't help you achieve it, then don't use it. That's the sort of frame that I always use. I find that discussion lists are very useful for students, but they need to be very carefully directed, because if they aren't, you'll have a monologue by one student who answers everything, and nobody has anything left to say. So, the sorts of assignments given on discussion lists need to be very skilfully crafted.

I know the Athabasca [University] work of Garrison and colleagues that talks about teaching, social, and cognitive presence, and I think their three-part analysis is very important for us to be thinking about when we are examining any instruction that we are going to be doing online.

We can't assume that students are thinking at high levels just because they are saying something on a discussion list or a chat list.

Chat is one of the things that I find the least useful. It's useful if a connection is lost, a video or something like that, a student can write and let you know. But I find that when students are chatting and having these independent conversations while there are other visual interactions going on, that I'm never quite sure whether they are really paying attention to the knowledge that is being discussed and the arguments that are being discussed because the research clearly shows that we cannot parallel process. People think [that] we can, and they keep saying that they're very good at multitasking. Well, it turns out that we're not. The research shows that for a brief moment, we stop what we are doing and do the other thing, and then we switch backwards and forwards. That turns out to be the least effective way of learning.

7. *What are some of your accomplishments in the field of ODL that you would like to share?*

I think some of my most recent work with my colleague from University of Utah, MaryAnn Christison. We're primarily teacher-educators. We've finished a large questionnaire study on online language teacher education. We think that our findings from that are truly important. It was funded by TIRF, the International Research Foundation for Teacher Language Education.

We followed this up with a commissioned piece for AQUEDUTO, which is headquartered in Britain. It's an online language education quality assurance organization that is relatively new but has a lot of potential. Because areas that MaryAnn Christison and I have investigated were quality and how varied quality is in online delivery.

If you look at a website, they will say that they're the best thing since sliced bread, but you have no way of proving that. Sometimes you can't even find who the instructors are to know what the quality of instruction might be.

So many of these short courses in online language teacher education, TESL [teaching English as a second language] in particular, that are fly by night; when you start looking for who they are accredited by, you'll find three or four schools all owned by the same company have this one accrediting agency that is owned by the same company.

When I first started doing this in my first piece of research with TIRF, I was just stunned at how duplicitous actually some of the claims being made on web pages by people who were offering particularly short courses in, you know, "In ten weeks you will be a perfect language teacher and travel around the world."

Being professional in TESOL, and having been president of the international association, I was outraged that people assumed that they could automatically set up as these experts because they happened to speak English.

So what we've done for AQUEDUTO is written a paper on what we know about research on best practice and quality in online language teacher education. While we don't know a lot, we do know quite a number of things. One of the points in that piece that we've written, which will eventually be available on their website, was that the Athabasca work on presence was really valuable as a framework, but you would also need to use the frameworks that have come from language teacher education in traditional settings because that has a background in language education, as opposed to a more general education. But in this piece, looking at all of the online language teacher education, we found that people conflate so many things, which is why I mentioned CALL, because people conflate CALL with online education.

When you read some of the research, people don't really tell you in detail whether their programme is a blended programme or if it's totally online, and that means two totally different things as far as I'm concerned in terms of social presence. If it is totally online, as an instructor, you have to somehow build the social presence among your learners and yourself through an online environment. If the class also meets face-to-face in a regular classroom and does group work, they may have already established social presence in a more familiar environment and maybe transfer that to an online discussion list, for example. We don't know the answer to that. But if an article or piece of research doesn't tell me that, there's really no way for me to know how to interpret their findings about something like social presence. So that was one of the things that sort of disturbed me. Research needs to be a lot clearer about defining terminology and being clear about exactly what type of instructional practice they had in the research that they're looking at, rather than just say, "I did this piece of work on a discussion list."

8. *What are some of the challenges that you faced in the field of ODL over the years?*

    Sadly, a drop-out rate that has nothing to do necessarily with the instruction or the technology or the motivation or the investment of the learners, but because most of the people who are doing distance education are doing it because they are in remote and rural areas or because they have commitments like family and work, often those other commitments take over and become overwhelming, and they are unable to continue.

    For people who are in distance situations, I remember when I was doing the correspondence course, I never even saw . . . I didn't even know who the professors were who were sending me this stuff. I didn't even have photographs of them. I had no way of contacting them other than by a letter, sort of typewritten because I was not a great typist. It would go in the mail, maybe come back in the mail; a very unsatisfying experience it can be. When people feel this remote, away from it, it is very hard to stay engaged. You can be highly motivated, but it's really hard to see what you're gaining out of the experience. So that's really the hardest thing.

    I think the other is the unfortunate direction that online learning has taken, where many universities in particular, plus these for-profit companies, have seen this as a way of money making. That, to me, is the second greatest challenge. In order to stay true to what I believe are the important motivators for doing online learning, the profit motive can't come into it because it is not cheaper. The fact that universities are putting more and more classes online, thinking this is the answer to their budgetary problems when provinces and states are reducing funding, is very misguided. It ends up giving online learning a bad reputation for quality when that, as I said, is the other issue that I think is really important. So I find it quite distressing that this has often been the case.

    The online network [Online Learning Consortium] that started examining online higher education learning in the United States, they've been very clear about quality and finances; you don't do it just to save money. Their measures of quality I find very, very useful for people who are looking at online education.

9. *What was the "state of DE" when you first entered the field as opposed to ODL in 2018?*

    Oh, primitive. Absolutely primitive! I do think with all of the new multimedia opportunities we have, it really has improved the experience for both learners and teachers. But I do still worry about university expectations that we can therefore teach 40 in a class, and it's easy. It's not.

10. *What interesting memories would you like to share about the beginning of ODL?*

    My research interests have been literacy in its broadest sense and educating teachers for ESL [English as a second language]. I don't do work in second language acquisition or anything like that. I'm very interested in what teachers do.

I've had a number of tangential issues. As you probably realized, I have a very strong sense of social responsibility, so I have done some work in that, too. I had a recent publication, nothing to do with what we're talking about, which was looking at English – who has access to it and who doesn't have access to it and what the drivers are in that access.

Access is one of the issues that I have written about since 1985: both access to education and also access to all this wonderful new technology. If you don't have access to it, it can be the most marvelous technology, but it is not going to necessarily help the people who don't have access to it.

When I was TESOL president back in the 90s, people were trying to do everything online. I kept saying, "The world still isn't there yet. Maybe those of us who teach in North America who are middle class, we have this access. But our students and our teachers in our field in remote Vietnam, in remote Cameroon, are they able to access this?"

One of the things that I have been recently doing some work in is cell phones and smartphones have become the go-to for everything. And yet studies in California have shown that, in many cases, children who are from poor families, immigrant families – they don't have computers at home. Yet the teacher is telling them [that] they have to do a project, go on the Internet, find all of these resources, and write up their report. I challenge anyone to do that on a smartphone. I'm reasonably tech savvy. Sure, smartphones can do everything that computers can do, but try and do a real project. I think that's really very difficult not just for the students, but for the teachers who are not taking into account these learners who don't have access to computers at home, or if they do, they don't have broadband, so they're trying to do it on a semi-smartphone because they usually have one that is many models previously. And now the teacher's expectation is that everybody can do this. I think that is really unfortunate.

There are wonderful examples (in fact, one is a colleague of mine in Cameroon) where teachers have used smartphones to interact with each other in professional development activities, but they've paid attention to the fact that their connections are always dying.

I'm very cognizant of this. My husband and I were teaching in a university in Thailand when I was finishing my master's degree. This was back in '79, so this was a long time ago. There was no word processor. There was only a mainframe computer, and because he was in the computer science department, we all had access to it as faculty. I was typing it up on the mainframe computer using a text-editing programme – that's all like coding in those days, not word processing, which was the most tedious thing, having to put in all of the codes for punctuation and stuff. (Thailand today still has power shortages all of the time.) Because I was not that tech savvy at the time, I kept forgetting to save everything. There was no autosave, of course. I would have done a whole pile of my dissertation, and we'd lose the power, and I would have to go back and do it all again. So I've had personal experience with a lot of this stuff that I'm talking about, which I guess is why I feel so strongly about access being number one. There is no point in trying to use a delivery methodology if the learners are not able to access it in a way that is transparent, easy to navigate, and reliable.

11. *What were your specific ODL research interests, and have they changed/evolved over the years?*

    I guess I was initially more interested in the language being used, but with more experience, I became more focused on issues, such as quality and access, and other educators' perceptions and experiences with online language teacher education.

12. *Could you please describe the learning environment that you currently work in (e.g., geographic and institutional setting, student demographics)?*

I occasionally do work for Anaheim University in classes in their doctoral programme only. It's a doctoral programme in TESOL. The students come from all over: Korea, Japan, Canada, all over the US, we've had somebody from Saudi, and I'm trying to think where else. Because we have live classes for an hour a week, we have found that there are some places where students don't sign up for Anaheim. They don't want to get up at two and three o'clock in the morning. Most of the classes work really well for Asia and the US. We have had some students from the Middle East; they've had a rather hard time getting on.

This programme hires faculty as people who already have a career, often have full-time jobs elsewhere. My colleague, MaryAnn Christison, who's from the University of Utah, she co-teaches with me in some of these classes. The faculty has already made a name in the field of TESOL through their other work. Several have been TESOL past presidents – people like Kathy Bailey.

We use GoToMeeting as our conferencing tool. And as I said, there is a live one-hour class and, depending upon who is teaching, faculty will give a PowerPoint presentation. We will have tasks for students to do. Because the classes are fairly small in the doctoral programme, we don't break them into separate rooms. While they are doing this, we keep them together, and they answer individually, either by voice or they can do it in the chat box. I prefer they do it in the voice, but that's because I have a hard time reading the chat box; it's so small. At the end of the hour, the students have a student-led discussion without the faculty present.

There is an online discussion list and we try to carefully craft the sorts of tasks that we give students. Because it's a doctoral programme, they tend to be highly motivated and do interact well together, and because they tend to be in many classes together, they tend to get to know each other very well, and there's a lot of support behind the scenes that we don't see as instructors where they interact with each other.

MaryAnn and I have co-supervised doctoral students with their dissertations – a wonderful one was from Canada, actually. The students are all currently teaching somewhere, often in intensive programmes. The ones overseas are usually at universities in Korea or Japan.

The institution's office is in Anaheim, California; that's where it's run from. But the people teaching on it are all over the place. One of the EdD [educational doctorate in TESOL] professors, Hayo Reinders, is in Auckland sometimes when he's not travelling. That's been one of the advantages for those of us who have other jobs, or people who are retired and do a lot of other consulting and aren't always necessarily in one place. You can actually do the class when you are somewhere else, if you have a good connection, of course. There have been times where MaryAnn Christison and I have taught something, and she was in a remote place like Guatemala where she wasn't getting a good connection, but co-teaching makes it really easy because we both can do it.

I think that's probably all you need to know about the programme. It's got the Certificate Programme, the Master's Programme, and the EdD in TESOL. It has other programmes that have nothing to do with language learning. One more thing about that programme: There is a residential [component]. Students are required to do two residencies during their degree programme. The residential is for a week. It is sometimes held in California. It has been held in Korea and in Japan. That is intensive; two or three faculty go and do intensive work with the students, particularly work around research and how to do research to help students with theses and dissertations.

13. *Is there anything else you [would] like to address?*

For me, the most important thing is the people. The technology is the facilitator. It is something that helps us to do something better, such as the glasses that I am wearing help me to see better. Sure, it has opened up a lot of ways of doing things that we never thought of before, and certainly things like AI [artificial intelligence] are going to perhaps change a lot of this. But when I was doing my doctorate at Stanford [University] back in the 80s, they were saying then that AI would be taking over the world in the next five years, and that's how many years ago?

So, yes, we have made great strides in AI, but again, I think that human beings should always be conscious of the fact that we use technology to advance our own knowledge, our own abilities. We've got to be very careful to think that technology answers everything without being very thoughtful about it. I'm using *technology* here in a very, very broad sense because this is true of all technology, not just the amazing things that are happening with voice recognition and speech recognition and all of this, but all of the technologies that science has developed for us over time need to be used with care

That would be always my message. Educational learning is about people interacting, learning from each, and learning to be with each other. We shouldn't lose sight of that no matter what whiz-bang technologies we have.

14. *Can you suggest names of other female pioneers in DE or online learning that you think we should include in the book?*

I don't know if you included MaryAnn Christison on the list. She has come to it late, but she has done some quite remarkable work at the University of Utah, putting their courses online. I think she has some really, really good insights into what it means to put a regular class online, what are some of the difficulties that you need to be made aware of and take care about and how to manage large classes (which she does) and how to manage, for example, practice teaching online. (That's something that we brought up in this recent article we did for AQUADUTO.) I think that she has some really useful insights. As I said, she's come to it much later than I have, but a pioneer is a pioneer if they are doing something new and useful for the field, rather than people who start the field, if you know what I mean. She is a multiply busy human being, but I would highly recommend talking to her.

Publications

Books

Murray, D. (1988). *CATESOL Directory of ESL teacher preparation programs in California and Nevada.* CATESOL.
Murray, D. (1991). *Conversation for action: The computer terminal as medium of communication.* John Benjamins.
Murray, D. (Ed.). (1992). *Diversity as resource: Redefining cultural literacy* (pp. xvii, 1323). TESOL Publications.
Murray, D. (2003). *Integrating citizenship content in teaching adult immigrants English: An evaluation of Let's Participate: A course in Australian citizenship.* NCELTR.
Murray, D. (Ed.). (2008). *Planning change; changing plans: Innovations in second language teaching.* University of Michigan Press.
Murray, D. (2013). A case for online language teacher education. *The International Research Foundation.* www.tirfonline.org/wp-content/uploads/2013/05/TIRF_OLTE_One-PageSpread_May20131.pdf
Murray, D., & Christison, M. A. (2009). *Leadership in English language education: Theoretical foundations and practical skills for changing times.* Routledge.
Murray, D., & Christison, M. A. (2011a). *What English language teachers need to know I: Understanding learning.* Routledge.
Murray, D., & Christison, M. A. (2011b). *What English language teachers need to know II: Facilitating learning.* Routledge.
Murray, D., & Christison, M. A. (2014). *What English language teachers need to know III: Designing curriculum.* Routledge.
Murray, D., & Christison, M. A. (2019). *What English language teachers need to know I: Understanding learning* (2nd ed.). Routledge.

Murray, D., Christison, M. A., & Anderson, N. (1998). *Leadership development: Expanding our professional skills.* TESOL.
Murray, D., Lloyd, R., & McPherson, P. (2006). *Teacher and learner use of new technologies in the AMEP.* NCELTR.
Murray, D., Master, J., & Lloyd, R. (2005). *Recruitment of volunteer home tutors for the AMEP home tutor scheme: Strategies to improve recruitment.* NCELTR.
Murray, D., & McPherson, P. (2002). *Using planet English with AMEP learners.* NCELTR.
Murray, D., & McPherson, P. (2003). *Communicating on the Net.* NCELTR.
Murray, D., & McPherson, P. (2004). *Using the Web to support language learning.* NCELTR.
Murray, D., & McPherson, P. (Eds.). (2005). *Navigating to read; Reading to navigate.* NCELTR.
Murray, D., Rew, L., & Walker, C. (1989a). *Lifeline Mac: A handbook for teachers in computer classrooms.* SJSU.
Murray, D., Rew, L., & Walker, C. (1989b). *Lifeline PC: A handbook for teachers in computer classrooms.* SJSU.
Murray, D., & Wigglesworth, G. (Eds.). (2005). *First language support in adult ESL in Australia.* NCELTR.

Book Chapters

Christison, M. A., & Murray, D. E. (2020). An overview of multilingual learners' literacy needs in the 21st century. In G. Neokleous, A. Krulatz, & R. Farrelly (Eds.), *A handbook of research on cultivating literacy in diverse and multilingual classrooms.* IGI Global Publishing. https://doi.org: 10.4018/978-1-7998-2722-1.ch001
Murray, D. (1985). Composition as conversation: The computer terminal as medium of communication. In L. Odell & D. Goswami (Eds.), *Writing in non-academic settings* (pp. 205–229). Guilford Press.
Murray, D. (1988). When the medium determines turns: Turn-taking in computer conversation. In H. Coleman (Ed.), *Working with language* (pp. 210–223). The Mouton.
Murray, D. (1989). Teaching bilingual students. In H. Guth (Ed.), *The Wadsworth manual: A practical guide for writing teachers* (pp. 66–79). Wadsworth.
Murray, D. (1990). The discourse structure of conversation for action. In M. A. K. Halliday, J. Gibbons, & H. Nicholas (Eds.), *Learning, keeping and using language* (pp. 283–298). John Benjamins.
Murray, D. (1992a). Collaborative writing as literacy event. In David Nunan (Ed.), *Collaborative learning and teaching* (pp. 100–117). Cambridge University Press.
Murray, D. (1992b). Unlimited resources: Learners' language, culture, and thought. In D. E. Murray (Ed.), *Diversity as resource: Redefining cultural literacy* (pp. 259–274). TESOL Publications.
Murray, D. (1993). Program evaluation: A simulation. In D. Freeman (Ed.), *New ways in teacher education* (pp. 112–115). TESOL Publications.
Murray, D. (1995). Knowledge machines: Language and information in a technological society. In *Language and social life series* (pp. xii, 1–202). Longman.
Murray, D. (1996). The tapestry of diversity in our classrooms. In K. M. Bailey & D. Nunan (Eds.), *Voices and viewpoints: Qualitative research in second language education* (pp. 434–448). Cambridge University Press.
Murray, D. (1997a). Changing the margins: Dilemmas of a reformist in the field. In C. Pearson Casanave & S. Schecter (Eds.), *Becoming a language educator* (pp. 179–186). Lawrence Erlbaum.
Murray, D. (1997b). On getting there from here. In C. Pearson Casanave & S. Schecter (Eds.), *Becoming a language educator* (pp. 209–212). Lawrence Erlbaum.
Murray, D. (2001a). New technology: New language at work? In A. Burns, D. Hall, & C. Coffin (Eds.), *Analysing English in a global context* (pp. 38–49). Routledge.
Murray, D. (2001b). Whose 'standard'? What the ebonics debate tells us about language, power, and pedagogy. In J. E. Alatis (Ed.), *Language in our time: Bilingual education and official English, ebonics and standard English, immigration and the Unz Initiative* (pp. 321–334). Georgetown University Press.
Murray, D. (2003a). Changing clients in the AMEP at the turn of the 21st century. In G. Wigglesworth (Ed.), *The kaleidoscope of adult second language learning: Learner, teacher and researcher perspectives* (pp. 19–28). NCELTR.
Murray, D. (2003b). Materials for new technologies: Learning from research and practice. In W. Renandya (Ed.), *Methodology and materials design in language teaching* (pp. 30–43). SEAMEO Regional Language Centre.
Murray, D. (2004a). New frontiers in technology and teaching. In C. Davison (Ed.), *Information technology and innovation in language education* (pp. 25–44). University of Hong Kong Press.
Murray, D. (2004b). The language of cyberspace. In E. Finegan & J. Rickford (Eds.), *Language in the USA* (pp. 463–479). Cambridge University Press.
Murray, D. (2004c). The role of assessment in performance-based standards. In G. Poedsoejoedarmo (Ed.), *Teaching and assessing language proficiency* (pp. 67–76). SEAMEO Regional Language Centre.
Murray, D. (2005a). Applied linguistics in Australasia and the Pacific. In K. Brown (Editor-in-Chief), *Encyclopedia of language and linguistics* (2nd ed., Vol. 1, pp. 342–349). Elsevier.
Murray, D. (2005b). Dell H. Hymes. In P. Strazny (Ed.), *Encyclopedia of linguistics* (pp. 484–485). Fitzroy Dearborn.

Murray, D. (2005c). ESL in adult education. In E. Hinkel (Ed.), *Handbook of research in second language learning and teaching* (pp. 65–84). Lawrence Erlbaum.
Murray, D. (2005d). L1 as a resource in adult learning settings. In D. E. Murray & G. Wigglesworth (Eds.), *First language support in adult ESL in Australia* (pp. 12–23). NCELTR.
Murray, D. (2007a). Creating a technology-rich English language learning environment. In J. Cummins & C. Davison (Eds.), *Kluwer international handbook on English language teaching* (pp. 747–761). Springer.
Murray, D. (2007b). Teaching and learning communicative competence in an e-era. In J. Liu (Ed.), *English language teaching in China: New approaches, perspectives and standards* (pp. 75–90). Continuum.
Murray, D. (2010a). Changing stripes – chameleon or tiger? In D. Nunan & J. Choi (Eds.), *Language and culture: Reflective narratives and the emergence of identity* (pp. 164–9). Routledge.
Murray, D. (2010b). Learning by doing: The role of data collection in action research. In G. Park, H. P. Widodo, & A. Cirocki (Eds.), *Observation of teaching: Bridging theory and practice through research on teaching* (pp. 49–62). Lincom Europa.
Murray, D. (2011). Vocational ESL. In E. Hinkel (Ed.), *Handbook of research in second language learning and teaching* (Vol. 2, pp. 65–84). Lawrence Erlbaum.
Murray, D. (2012). Financial planning and management of resources. In M. A. Christison & F. L. Stoller (Eds.), *A handbook for language program administrators* (2nd ed., pp. 243–262). Alta Book Center Publishers.
Murray, D. (2013a). Higher education constraints on innovation. In L. Wong & K. Hyland (Eds.), *Innovation and change in English language education* (pp. 186–199). Routledge.
Murray, D. (2013b). Technology and literacy. In C. A. Chappelle (Ed.), *The encyclopedia of applied linguistics* (pp. 186–199). Wiley-Blackwell.
Murray, D. (2017a). Should we offer a CALL course? In J-B. Son & S. Windeatt (Eds.), *Voices of CALL teacher educators* (pp. 169–183). Continuum.
Murray, D. (2017b). Variation in L2 learner speech. In J. Liontas (Editor-in Chief). *TESOL encyclopedia of English language teaching* (pp. 1–6). John Wiley & Sons.
Murray, D., & Christison, M. A. (2008). Strategic planning for English language teachers and learners. In C. Coombe, M. L. McClosky, L. Stephenson, & N. J. Anderson (Eds.), *Leading in English language teaching and learning* (pp. 128–140). University of Michigan Press.
Murray, D., & Christison, M. A. (2012). Understanding Innovation in English language education: Contexts and issues. In C. Tribble (Ed.), *Managing change in ELT* (pp. 61–74). British Council.
Murray, D., & Christison, M. A. (2017). Going online: Affordances and limitations for teachers and teacher educators. In L. Wong & K. Hyland (Eds.), *Faces of English* (pp. 215–230). Routledge.
Murray, D., & Christison, M. A. (2019a). Online language teacher education (OLTE). In H. Mohebbi & C. Coombe (Eds.), *Research questions in language education and applied linguistics*. Springer.
Murray, D., & Christison, M. A. (2019b). The Odyssey of professional excellence and quality assurance in TESOL: Looking ahead and facing challenges. In J. D. Martínez (Ed.), *Quality in TESOL and teacher education: From results culture towards quality culture*. Routledge.
Murray, D., & Christison, M. A. (2021). The shifting faces of English language teaching. In J. Quinn & G. Kleckova (Eds.), *Anglophone literature in second-language teacher education* (pp. 37–50). Routledge. https:// doi:10.4324/9780429288869-3-3
Murray, D., & Kuhlman, N. (2000). Current and future state of ESL instruction in the US. In M. A. Snow (Ed.), *Implementing the ESL standards for pre-K-12 students through teacher education* (pp. 33–47). TESOL.
Murray, D., & McPherson, P. (2006). Let's participate: Designing a civics course for adult migrants. In M. A. Snow & L. Kamhi-Stein (Eds.), *Developing a new program or curriculum for adults* (pp. 285–309). TESOL.
Murray, D., & Nichols, P. (1992). Vietnamese literacy practices and their effect on academic writing: Case studies. In F. Dubin & N. Kuhlman (Eds.), *Cross-cultural literacy: Global perspectives on reading and writing* (pp. 175–187). Prentice-Hall.
Murray, D., Nichols, P., & Heisch, A. (1992). Identifying the languages and cultures of our students. In D. E. Murray (Ed.), *Diversity as resource: Redefining cultural literacy* (pp. 68–83). TESOL Publications.
Murray, D., & Wigglesworth, G. (2005a). Implications for L1 use – where to now?. In D. E. Murray & G. Wigglesworth (Eds.), *First language support in adult ESL in Australia* (pp. 146–151). NCELTR.
Murray, D., & Wigglesworth, G. (2005b). Introduction. In D. E. Murray & G. Wigglesworth (Eds.), *First language support in adult ESL in Australia* (pp. viii–xii). NCELTR.

Journal Articles

Murray, D. (1987). Requests at work: Negotiating the conditions of conversation. *Management Communication Quarterly*, *1*(1), 58–83.
Murray, D. (1988a). Computer-mediated communication use within IBM. *Technical Communication*, 339–340.

Murray, D. (1988b). Computer-mediated communication: Implications for ESP. *English for Specific Purposes*, 7, 3–18.
Murray, D. (1988c). The context of oral and written language: A framework for mode and medium switching. *Language in Society*, 17(3), 351–373.
Murray, D. (1989). Social and functional uses of the present continuous. *The TESOL Recorder*, 22(4), 72–77.
Murray, D. (1990a). CmC. *English Today*, 6(3), 42–46.
Murray, D. (1990b). ESL in the California State University: Who are we? And where will we go? *CATESOL Journal*, 3(1), 105–108.
Murray, D. (1990c). Literacies as sociocultural phenomena. *Prospect*, 5(3), 55–62.
Murray, D. (1991). Computer conversation: Adapting the composing process to conversation. *Written Communication*, 8(1), 35–55.
Murray, D. (1992). Making it happen: An ESL professional organization's advocacy for teachers and learners. *ELT Journal*, 46(1), 92–95.
Murray, D. (1994). Using portfolios to assess writing. *Prospect*, 9(2), 56–69.
Murray, D. (1997a). Articulation or collaboration? *CATESOL Journal*, 9(1), 207–214.
Murray, D. (1997b). Is remediation an articulation issue? *CATESOL Journal*, 9(1), 175–182.
Murray, D. (1998a). An agenda for literacy for adult second language learners. *Prospect*, 13(3), 42–49.
Murray, D. (1998b). Ebonics – A case study in language, power, and pedagogy. *TESOL Quarterly*, 32(1), 144–146.
Murray, D. (1999). Access to information technology: Considerations for language educators. *Prospect*, 14(3), 4–12.
Murray, D. (2000a). Changing technologies, changing literacy communities? *Language, Learning and Technology*, 4(2), 43–58.
Murray, D. (2000b). Protean communication: The language of computer-mediated communication. *TESOL Quarterly*, 34(3), 397–423. https://doi.org/10.2307/3587737
Murray, D. (2003). Editorial. *Prospect*, 18(1), 1–4.
Murray, D. (2005). Technologies for second language literacy. *Annual Review of Applied Linguistics*, 25, 188–201.
Murray, D. (2008). From marginalization to transformation: How ICT is being used in ESL learning today. *International Journal of Pedagogies and Learning*, 4(5), 20–35.
Murray, D. (2018). The world of English language teaching: Creating equity or inequity? *Language Teaching Research*, 24(1). https://doi.org/10.1177/1362168818777529
Murray, D. E., & Christison, M. A. (2020). *Online language teacher education: A review of the literature* [Report]. Association for Quality Education and Training Online (AQUEDUTO). http://aqueduto.com/research/
Murray, D. E., & McPherson, P. (2005). *Navigating to read – Reading to navigate* [Report]. Macquarie University. www.ameprc.mq.edu.au/__data/assets/pdf_file/0005/240359/Teaching_in_Action-navigation.pdf
Murray, D. E., & Garvey, E. (2004). The multilingual teacher: Issues for teacher education. *Prospect*, 19(2), 3–24.
Murray, D. E., & McPherson, P. (2006). Scaffolding instruction for reading the Web. *Language Teaching Research*, 10(2), 131–156.
Murray, D. E., & Wigglesworth, G. (2007). Opening doors: Teachers learning through collaborative research. *Prospect*, 22(1), 19–36.

26
ROBERTS, JUDY

Photo of Judy Roberts contributed by Judy Roberts

Was there a way that communications technology, if properly used, could overcome that rural isolation and give people access to the educational opportunities that they needed?

Judy Roberts is from Northern Ontario, Canada, where isolated rural communities had little access to specialized educational resources. She completed an Honours Degree in Philosophy and Psychology at York University before going on to take a Master of Criminology at University of Toronto, Canada, in 1972. She became involved in distance education for evolving health professionals in the 60s and early 70s using the only available technology of the time, which were film and video tapes.

The Fogo Island Project, in partnership with the Donner Canadian Foundation; the National Film Board's Challenge for Change Program; and Memorial University's Extension Service provided support to remote health-care workers in Newfoundland.

Roberts was motivated to become more involved in the initiative and moved to Newfoundland, where she became Executive Secretary of the Royal Commission on Municipal Government. She involved herself in the Telemedicine Project, which used one-way video and two-way audio via satellite, and then a dedicated interactive telephony network.

The Telemedicine Project focused on professional development of health-care workers at four remote hospitals in Newfoundland. She was involved in the project from 1975 to 1982, after which she worked in delivering a distance education credit course for hospital workers wanting to access credited studies with the flexibility of working during hospital working hours and/or evenings.

This lack of access to specialized education and professional development drove her interest in using communication technology to reach communities too remote to access educational opportunities and develop materials for teachers and students for use in distance education.

Roberts went on to join Toronto General Hospital and the University of Toronto, through which the Canadian Association for Distance Education (CADE) was formed. At the time, distance education was further evolving to the use of tools and technology applicable to remote learning environments, which included audio cassette for both radio and audio conferencing. Lucille Pacey, president of CADE, was also involved in bringing in the use of satellite technology to provide further reach and access to education.

Roberts's goal was to provide improved access through expertise in instructional design, distance education pedagogy, and the use of technology for learning and the employment of technology experts to make it viable. Roberts wanted to create accessible materials for both educators and learners. This culminated in the publication of *Why the Information Highway: Lessons from Open and Distance Learning* (General Distribution Services, 1995).

Roberts's contributions to distance education helped evolve it from print-based correspondence and/or video tapes to professional conference presentations and, in turn, helped make online distance education a reputable approach. Her work contributed to making education more accessible to remote communities, and made the potency of communication technologies and how to adapt them to use in distance education a reality for learning communities she helped serve in Canada. She helped to write and publish accessible user-friendly materials for teachers that supported distance education for health services professionals in what continue today to be remote, inaccessible areas of Canada.

Roberts has been a member of the Canadian Association for Distance Education (L'association Canadienne de l'éducation à distance) since 1983.

References included at the end of this chapter reflect her interests in distance education.

Interview

Transcript Analysis Summary

Analysis of all interviews included in this volume led to the identification of 3,545 units of data. The mean of these collective units was 118 per pioneer, the median was 118.5, and the mode was 132. Individual interview units ranged from 59 to 217 units, yielding a spread of 158 units between all interviews. Judy Roberts' interview generated 118 units, indicating that the sum of her interview units matched that of the average interview.

A comparision of Roberts' interview to the interviews of all pioneers indicated that, despite possessing the same number of units as the average interview, her interview profile shared few commonalities with the average interview profile (Figure 26.1). Her interview produced a greater-than-average number of units in the following areas: background, accomplishments, interesting memories, early founders, and career history. Beginning her career in the 1960s, it is of little wonder that this pioneer had a lot to share with readers in these subject areas.

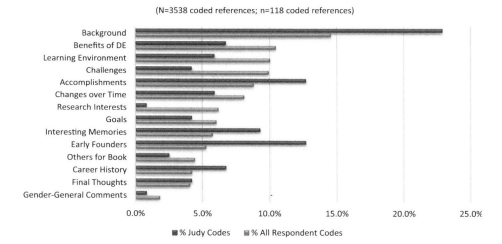

Figure 26.1 All Respondents' Versus Judy Roberts' Parent Codes

Roberts' interview generated lower-than-average numbers of units in eight areas: benefits of DE, learning environment, changes over time, challenges, research interests, goals, others for the book, and general gender-related comments. The lower-than-average number of benefits units could be explained by the fact that the interview did not ask respondents to talk about the benefits of DE. This was a topic that arose organically during discussions related to responses to interview questions. Roberts's interview also contained fewer-than-average challenges units. Although Roberts generated fewer units in benefits and challenges than the average interview, her unit profile in these two topic areas reflected the tendency of the average interview to have slightly more benefit than challenge units. Since Roberts held administrative and instructional design consulting positions during her career, she did not engage in research activities. This explains why there are so few units in this part of her interview. Finally, the theme of general gender-related comments, like benefits of DE, naturally arose during some interviewees' converations, so it is not surprising that Roberts's interview did not contain many general gender-related comment units.

Link to recorded interview Part A: tinyurl.com/Roberts-J-A

Link to recorded interview Part B: tinyurl.com/Roberts-J-B

Transcript of Interview

Full name: Judy Roberts

Institutional Affiliation: Memorial University, Newfoundland, Canada; Toronto General Hospital – University of Toronto, Canada; Contact North Network, Sudbury, Canada; Her own consulting company, Judy Roberts & Associates/Associés Inc., which worked nationally in Canada and internationally as well.

Key:

Regular font = Interviewee comments
Italicized font = Interviewer comments

Interview Questions

1. *What was your educational and experiential background before you became involved in distance education [DE]?*

   I have an Honours Degree in Philosophy and Psychology from York University. After working for the Donner Canadian Foundation [1968–1972], I did a Master's Degree in Criminology at University of Toronto.

2. *In what year did you begin to look specifically into DE?*

   Although it does not fit in the classic definition of DE, the Fogo Island Project in the late 1960s/early 1970s involved using film and video tapes, the only available technologies then, in community development. (The Donner Canadian Foundation, the National Film Board's Challenge for Change Program and Memorial University's Extension Service were the project's partners.) It's become known as the Fogo Island Process, and has been used both nationally and internationally.

   Motivated by my visits to the province, I moved to Newfoundland in 1972 and was hired as the Executive Secretary on the Royal Commission on Municipal Government. In 1974, I became involved in the Newfoundland component of a Canadian Government Hermes satellite initiative (one-way video, two-way audio) that became known as the Telemedicine Project, with a focus on continuing education for health professionals working at four rural hospitals in Newfoundland.

The continuing education programme was the first one that I would put under a very, very broad heading of DE; planning for the initiative began in 1974. We first used one-way video/two-way audio via satellite, and then used a dedicated interactive telephony network. I was involved in that project until 1982. One of your other pioneers in this book, Erin Keough, was a colleague that I worked very closely with; when I left in 1982, she took over my position with Memorial University's Telemedicine Project.

One of our close partners was the part-time studies programme at the university. The hospital-based professionals wanted their continuing education during hospital working hours; part-time credit studies served working adults and delivered their courses in the evenings. They had a track record of delivering courses using video tapes and paper-based correspondence for a number of years before the satellite project; led by Craig McNamara, they also partnered with the medical school in creating the dedicated telephony network. Partnering with them was my first experience delivering credit DE in a classic credit course application.

3. *What were the circumstances in your world that initiated this interest in DE?*

Having grown up in northern Ontario, I understood the challenge of having specialized educational resources in one central location and professionals in fairly isolated rural environments who did not have convenient access to those resources. So it was the lack of access in rural and remote communities that was the driver for looking at the question "Was there a way that communications technology, if properly used, could overcome that rural isolation and give people access to the educational opportunities that they needed?"

4. *Which female researchers or female colleagues may have piqued your interest in DE and online distance learning [ODL]?*

Well, unfortunately for the theme of this book, I have to say that the people who, in effect, introduced me to DE were men. It was the Dean of Continuing Medical Education Dr. Max House's vision that launched Memorial University's role in exploring what communication technology [i.e., the federal government's satellite, Hermes] could do to increase access to continuing education for rural health professionals. The university's educational television service and its part-time credit studies had been exploring video tape and print, and again, the leadership, Craig McNamara, was male. Erin Keough and I were probably the first two senior women that were hired.

However, I should note that two women were key members of the federal government's Hermes satellite initiative: Anna Stahmer and Doris Jelly. They were part of the group within the Department of Communications that went across the country in the early 1970s soliciting proposals for social and educational applications of the satellite. [A joint activity between the Canadian Department of Communications and NASA (National Aeronautics and Space Administration, USA), Hermes was initially driven by engineering requirements to test high frequency satellite technology.] Memorial University was interested in the initiative because it would get some "free" satellite terminals, some free time on the satellite, and one- and two-way audio.

Anna was the leader of the evaluation initiative in the Department of Communications. Each approved user had to have its own evaluation team, but Anna was responsible for a small, three-person team that did an evaluation across all projects so that the federal government had some sense of common lessons learned through the projects that it supported. Doris was a key member of the department's administrative team supporting all the projects.

When I came to the Toronto General Hospital and the U of T [University of Toronto] in 1982, I met women such as Liz Burge, Kay Rogers, and Arlene Zuckernick, who were forming the

Canadian Association for Distance Education [CADE]. Somewhere in the 1982-to-1985 time period is when I became aware of the fact that, in the university credit learning environment across Canada, there were a lot of women involved in DE leadership, particularly in instructional design, using whatever tools and technology were available in their environment.

As you may know, Kay Rogers was the founding president of CADE. Our very first conference was out at York University [Toronto, Canada]. I can remember a small band of us from across Canada meeting in the student residence and wondering if CADE would survive.

5. *Who would you identify as the early female leaders/founders in the field of DE and ODL?*

I would start my answer by mentioning Margaret Norquay, the founding director of Ryerson University's CJRT-FM Open College [Toronto, Canada]; it used radio to offer part-time credit courses. Liz Burge and I worked with her to write a handbook entitled *Listening to Learn: The Use of the Voice in Distance Education* and its companion piece, *À l'écoute du savoir: L'expression orale dans la formation à distance*; both were published in 1987, and contained print and audio cassette material about talking and listening that applied to both radio and interactive audio conferencing approaches.

In addition to Anna and Doris, Lucille Pacey in Vancouver [BC, Canada] was with the Knowledge Network when it used the Hermes satellite. She maintained a leadership role in that organization and its successor, the Open Learning Agency [BC, Canada]. She was also a president of CADE.

Judith Tobin at TV Ontario was a staunch supporter of DE and CADE and has recently completed a contract with Contact North/Contact Nord.

Margaret Haughey (Victoria), Jane Brindley (Vancouver), and Jennifer O'Rourke (not sure where she lives) were also key pioneers.

6. *What are some of the goals that you strove to achieve in the field of DE and ODL?*

I think it was the classic goal of providing access. Within that broad goal, although my role was more on the project management side, one of my core values was ensuring that core teams included expertise in instructional design, learning design – as we called it, "pedagogy." In addition to having the technical people to make the technology run, it was also really important to have a learning design expert who could make sure that any faculty that were going to be involved in teaching had support in terms understanding how they needed to modify their classroom techniques in order to make best use of whichever technology they were given.

Another goal was to create accessible support materials for both faculty and students. To that end, I worked with Liz Burge in writing *Classrooms with a Difference* [published by OISE in 1993]; co-editing with Erin Keough *Why the Information Highway: Lessons from Open and Distance Learning* [General Distribution Services, 1995], and editing a series of five manuals under the theme, Lifelong Learning on the Information Highway. [Funding for the series published in 1998 was provided by the federal government's Office of Learning Technologies, Human Resources Development Canada, with administrative support from the Knowledge Network in Toronto.]

7. *What are some of your accomplishments in the field of DE and ODL learning that you would like to share?*

I think that I learned more than I contributed, but if pushed, I would highlight three accomplishments:

I contributed project management services to three teams that launched trailblazing innovations in DE, ODL, and Telemedicine in Newfoundland and Labrador and Ontario and was supported in making presentations within and outside Canada sharing lessons learned from those projects.

I helped to write and publish the accessible user-friendly materials for teachers and learners described above.

I managed a successful independent consulting company in DE and ODL for almost 20 years. Clients came from public and private organizations, both within and outside Canada.

I would note that a lot of this initial innovation came from smaller institutions, such as Memorial University or Laurentian University and Cambrian College in Sudbury, Lakehead University, and Centennial College in Thunder Bay [Canada]. (Now that is a bit of a generalization, and there are certainly some examples that would go against that point.) They had a responsibility to serve isolated communities and therefore saw the potential of communication technologies and were prepared to learn whether and how they could use [them].

So certainly during most of my work in DE and ODL, including the consulting practice, most of my clients tended to be ones that had a mandate to outreach and, for various reasons, had come to wonder whether there was something that communications technology could offer. I had a greater or a lesser role as a consultant, such as helping clients do feasibility studies, environmental scans in what was already happening and, if they were going to do a pilot project, helping them to develop a project plan. In a couple of examples, I was hired to be the project manager on contract to help the institution run their pilot project and/or also help them design a benchmark study to see whether they had achieved their goals.

One of the interesting migrations was that, as time went by, especially in the consulting field, open and distance learning [ODL] became so "mainstream" that the kinds of work that I did in terms of "Is this a credible thing for you to be looking at?" became moot. I think that it's a tribute to the quality of work completed by the initial band of pioneers that DE/ODL became credible. And now almost everybody to some degree uses communication technology in both DE/ODL and is adopting the hybrid model, where technology is used in classroom learning.

8. *What are some of the challenges that you faced in the field of DE and ODL over the years?*

As I just implied, credibility was certainly an initial issue, which also meant that financing for pilot projects was sometimes challenging to find.

The quality and availability of technical equipment was also an issue until the business case for investing in hardware, software, and networks became feasible.

Underestimating the importance of instructional design and the need to modify classroom-based approaches was also a challenge.

9. *What was the "state of DE" when you first entered the field as opposed to ODL in 2019?*

One benchmark is that when we organized the first CADE conference, we figured that, if we got 20 to 30 people to come and managed to afford to rent a couple rooms at the York University campus, we could say that we were successful. Today, almost every professional conference has presentations related to ODL because it is considered to be an accepted approach.

When I first entered the field, DE was based on a self-study model based on print-based correspondence and/or video tapes. "Best efforts" were made to include some sort of tutoring in local study groups that would meet throughout a semester. Today, a wide variety of audio, computer, and video conference tools and networks are available that facilitate learner-to-learner and learner-to-teacher live or delayed interaction. I think the development of the interactive technology was a big influence in spreading ODL beyond a small group of people in extension/ part-time study services who tried to do their best with self-study techniques.

However, it is still a challenge to persuade people that successful teaching and learning is not just a question of learning which buttons to press for whatever technology tool that you are using, but it is also thinking about how you are going to modify the design of your teaching because even with a real-time interactive technology, you do need to give some thought about how you are going to adjust the teaching techniques that you are used to using in a face-to-face classroom.

10. *What interesting memories would you like to share about the beginning of ODL?*

I think that I've already talked about that very first conference of the CADE. When I look back [at] how fearful we were that nobody would come and what an enormous amount of work it was to pull it off, I am amazed. However, it was also a lot of fun hanging around the dormitory at York University at the end of each day, realizing that the conference was actually going well. I remain in contact with many of those pioneers today.

I also treasure memories of the colleagues in the more remote hospitals in Newfoundland and the northern Ontario communities in northern Ontario who made extraordinary efforts to make the Telemedicine and Contact North/Contact Nord Project successful. They were prepared to do whatever they needed to do in order to get better access to educational resources. And the learners were also prepared, within reason obviously, to take advantage and learn what they had to do in order to be successful in this new approach to education.

Other than that, I would spare you the tales of satellite surveys on Newfoundland hospital roofs in the dead of winter, and driving miles and miles to have a discussion with a community about where they want their Contact North learning centre to go. There are all kinds of war stories.

11. *What were your specific DE and ODL research interests and have they changed/evolved over the years?*

I have to take the fifth on this one because as a project manager, I never engaged in research as such. My concerns were more about what we needed to pull together as a document that we could submit to get the funding that we needed. And then making sure that we met all of the objectives and the budget requirements of the funding because all of them – Memorial University, Telemedicine, the University of Toronto, and the Contact North network – that was all soft money. None of it initially was hard money. If we did get research funding, the research was, to some extent, influenced by what the funding agencies required us to do.

For a long time, research focused on the question of whether DE [was] as effective as classroom education based on criteria such as the marks [of] distance learning students compared to the marks of classroom students. Marks were considered a key indicator that DE was credible. Fortunately, in my opinion, the mainstreaming of ODL means that the basic credibility question has been answered, and research has now shifted its focus to developing teaching and learning techniques appropriate to student needs and the content being learned.

12. *Can you please describe the learning environment that you currently work in or have most recently worked in (e.g., geographic and institutional setting, learner demographics)?*

As I implied above, as ODL became more mainstream, the kind of consulting work that I had been doing was no longer needed, and I shifted my focus to full-time employment at TELUS. I was physically based in Toronto and worked for a specialized group that sold high-end video conferencing equipment, Skype, WebEx, and customized touch panels to corporate, government, and educational institutions. My role involved developing customer training materials appropriate to the technology and offering training either remotely or in person.

Learners were all adults. Part of the product description of what we offered was small group training to maybe six or eight people maximum. One of the reasons for sticking strictly to that was that we were doing short, two-hour sessions, although we could repeat the session if there were multiple people at a company that needed to learn. I focused both on what buttons to press and tips on how to promote interaction and discussion. Depending on client needs, the tips related to either meeting management or teaching and learning.

If a manufacturer had a handout, which Telecom and Cisco did, we would distribute that, but I also wrote short and long quick reference guides and manuals that would be provided as custom reference material so that users would have something in the room that they could consult about how to use the equipment and tips on interaction.

13. *Is there anything else you would like to address?*

I very much appreciated the chance to become a faculty member in an online distance education master's programme that the University of Maryland University College [UMUC] and Oldenburg University in Germany offered. The founding co-directors and faculty were colleagues who had come to know one another well at ICDE conferences. That was another important impact CADE had; we came to know the ICDE. Going to the international conferences was an important source of enrichment and learning. I have also had the opportunity to teach a couple of courses in Athabasca [University] Master's of Distance Education.

I would also add that, however good it is to have the asynchronous means of communication, I think that there's no substitute for having some elements of synchronicity. For example, I found it challenging to know how to help some of the students who were struggling in the course I taught unless I had the opportunity to speak to them in real time. I found that talking to somebody and hearing their voice gave me the ability to read their emotional status and decide how much effort to invest in extra individual tutoring. For example, if somebody was struggling, talking to them in either a one-on-one telephone call or in a monthly group conference call enabled me to assess if they were really working hard and wanted help, or whether they were treating the course as a pretty casual thing and weren't likely to do a whole lot more than whatever they had to do to get by. I would adjust my approach accordingly. Maybe because the very first technology that I ever used extensively was the audio conferencing in Newfoundland, I'm a proponent of supplementing online asynchronous tools with synchronous tools.

I believe that any successful DE or ODL programme design should be based on the answers to two fundamental questions: 1) Who are my learners? and 2) What is the content that they will be learning? It may then be possible to assess 1) Which technology/ies (print, audio, video) is/are most appropriate in this context? and 2) Which attributes of this technology/ies are the key ones?

Let's look at what is probably an oversimplified version of a possible design thought process. If I am going to be relying a lot on writing as one of my technologies, would good old-fashioned print on paper be appropriate and for what activities? Or is the computer the best way to facilitate print-based activities? Do I need to use audio? Is it going to be synchronous or asynchronous? Is the audio on a computer going to meet the need? Or will using telephone calls [be] more reliable if I am serving remote rural learners? Do I need visual elements other than print? Do I need still video or moving video? Do I want the video to have sound, or do I want to create my own sound over some moving video images?

In other words, I believe that asking technology-neutral questions in the first phase of your planning is crucial to success: "Given what I want people to learn, what is the best way for them to learn it and why?" While the final business plan for a course or a programme will incorporate many other factors, I believe that learning design is the bedrock of any approach.

14. *Can you suggest names of other female pioneers in DE, e-learning, or open and distance learning [ODL] that you think we should include in the book?*

    Arlene Zuckernick. She lives in Victoria [British Columbia, Canada]. As one of the early presidents of CADE, she's definitely somebody that you need to have in the book.

    Two key Québec contacts are Thérèse Lamy and France Henri. Both were with the TéléUniversité. Thérèse is now in Baie Ste Paul, Quebec [Canada].

Publications

Books and Courseware

Burge. E. J., & Roberts, J. M. (1993). *Classrooms with a difference: A practical guide to the use of conferencing technologies*. Ontario Institute for Studies in Education.

Burge. E. J., & Roberts, J. M. (1998). *Classrooms with a difference: Facilitating learning on the information highway* (2nd ed.). Cheneliere/McGraw-Hill.

Burge, L., Norquay, M., & Roberts, J. (1987). *Listening to learn: Using the voice in distance education*. Instructional Resources Development Unit, OISE/CJRT FM-Open College. Print and audio cassette manual.

Lamy, T., & Roberts, J. (1998). *Classes virtuelles: Apprendre sur l'inforoute*. Chenelière\McGraw-Hill.

Roberts, J. M., Brindley, J. E., & Spronk, B. (1998). *A learner's guide to the technologies:(Lifelong Learning on the information highway)*. Office of Learning Technologies (OLT). Chenelière/McGraw-Hill.

Roberts, J. M., & Keough, E. (Eds.). (1995). *Why the information highway? Lessons from open and distance learning*. Trifolium.

Book Chapters

Haughey, M., & Roberts, J. (1996). Canadian policy and practice in open and distance schooling. In T. Evans & D. Nation (Eds.), *Opening education: Policies and practices in open and distance education* (pp. 63–76). Routledge.

Roberts, J., Keough, E. M., & Pacey L. (2001). Public and institutional policy interplay: Canadian examples. In E. J. Burge & M. Haughey (Eds.), *Using learning technologies: International perspectives on practice* (pp. 26–37). Routledge.

Journal Articles

Burge, E. J., & Roberts, J. (1984). Audio-teleconferencing in continuing education: A case study with implications. *Canadian Journal of University Continuing Education, 10*(2), 20–30.

Burge, E. J., Smythe, C. L., Roberts, J. M. & Keough, E. M. (1993). The audio-conference: Delivering continuing education for addiction workers in Canada. *Journal of Alcohol and Drug Education, 39*(1), 78–91.

Burge, L., & Roberts, J. (1992). Dialogue on dialogue. *International Journal of E-Learning and Distance Education, 7*(2), 89–94.

Chambers, L. W., Neville-Smith, C., House, A. M., Roberts, J. M., Canning, E. M., O'Reilly, B., & O'Neill, M. (1981). Serving the needs of hearing-impaired preschool children in rural areas. *Canadian Journal of Public Health, 72*, 173–180.

Haughey, M., Keough, E., & Roberts, J. (1997). Trends in Canadian post-secondary education: Their impact on distance education. *Open Praxis, 1*, 22–26.

House, A. M., Roberts, J. M., & Canning, E. M. (1981a). Telemedicine provides new dimensions in CME in Newfoundland and Labrador. *Canadian Medical Association Journal, 124*, 801+.

House, A. M., Roberts, J. M., & Canning, E. M. (1981b). Comparison of slow scan television and direct viewing of radiographs. *Journal of the Canadian Association of Radiologists, 32*, 114-117.

Roberts, J. M. (1987). Ontario government launches distance education network. *International Journal of E-Learning and Distance Education, 2*(2), 73–74.
Roberts, J. M. (1996). The story of distance education: A practitioner's perspective. *Journal for the Association for Information Science and Technology, 47*(11), 811–816.
Roberts, J. M., Canning, E. M., Chambers, L. W., House, A. M., Cox, M., & Neville-Smith, C. (1976). The role of physicians in caring for preschool deaf children in rural Newfoundland and Labrador. *Newfoundland Medical Association Newsletter, XVIII*(6), 5–8.
Roberts, J. M., Gallant, G., Keough, E. M., & Zuckernick, A. (2005). *CADE/ACÉD & AMTEC: Moving forward together* [Report to CADE/ACÉD & AMTEC Boards of Directors]. www.cade-aced.ca
Roberts, J. M., House, A. M., McNamara, W. C., & Keough, E. M. (1993). Report on Memorial University of Newfoundland's experimental use of the communications satellite Hermes in Telemedicine. *International Journal of E-Learning and Distance Education, 8*(1), 34–42.
Roberts, J. M., O'Sullivan, J., & Howard, J. (2005). The roles of emerging and conventional technologies in serving children and adolescents with special needs in rural and northern communities. *International Journal of E-Learning and Distance Education, 20*(1), 84–103.
Roberts, J. M., & Umbriaco M. (2007). CADE: Looking forward by glancing back. *International Journal of E-Learning and Distance Education, 21*(3), 167–213.

Conference Presentations

Keough, E. M., Moran, L., Roberts, J., & Spronk, B. (1997). The converging classroom: Are your policies ready? In *Conference Abstracts from the 18th World Conference of the International Council for Distance Education, The new learning environment: A global perspective* (p. 168). PennState University.
Keough, E. M., Roberts, J. M., Lawrence, E., & Fuchs, R. (1995). Networking for rural development. In D. Sewart (Ed.), *One world, many voices: Quality in open and distance learning* (Vol. 1, pp. 295–298). Selected papers from the 17th World Conference of the International Council for Distance Education, Birmingham, UK.
Lamy, T., Burge, L., Bizzocchi, J., Thomas, N., & Roberts, J. (1992). *A dialogue about dialogue in distance learning.* Congrès de l'Aced.
Lamy, T., & Roberts, J. (1996). *Videoconferencing: Learning with a new technology.* Congrès de l'Association des collèges communautaires du Canada.
Roberts, J. M. (1995). Towards excellence in distance education: National initiatives in the Canadian policy environment. In M. A. Koble (Ed.), *Towards excellence in distance education – A research agenda: Research conference discussion papers* (pp. 486–495). The American Center for the Study of Distance Education.
Roberts, J. M., Lamy, T., Keough, E. M., Stahmer, A., & Helm, B. (1993). Issues for distance education in immigrant language learning: A Canadian case study. In *Selected readings from the 8th annual conference of the Canadian association for distance education* (pp. 187–200). The Commonwealth of Learning.

27
SEELIG, CAROLINE

Photo of Caroline Seelig contributed by Caroline Seelig

The power and potential of open, distance, and flexible learning was the thing that I thought, "Good grief, this has got so much power!"

Dr. Caroline Seelig received her undergraduate degree in science from Smith University College of Swansea, UK, in 1985. She obtained a PhD in Biology from the aforementioned university. Then she went on to study at the University of Wales, where she obtained her Post-Graduate Certificate of Education, qualifying her as a secondary school science teacher in 1991.

Her interest in education was further enhanced while Academic Manager at Tai Polytechnic, NZ, and she went on to complete a Master of Educational Administration at Massey University,

NZ. While Deputy Chief Executive of Nelson Marlborough Institute of Technology, NZ, she enjoyed both the flexibility and the power of online learning. Her interests have since been in creating opportunities for lifelong learning that provide flexibility to the diverse and ever-changing needs within wider learner communities.

She has worked for four polytechnics in New Zealand. She started with a very small regional one in Greymouth called Tai Poutini Polytechnic. Then she went on to New Zealand's Eastern Institute of Technology, Hawke's Bay. Her position as Deputy Chief Executive at Nelson Marlborough Institute of Technology followed. Her fourth and current polytechnic is the Open Polytechnic of New Zealand.

As Chief Executive of Open Polytechnic of New Zealand, she has led the open polytechnic in a transformational vocational programme that has aimed to ensure that the institute remains at the forefront of applied technology to provide flexible support to students' learning within an open-learning context. This has involved developing a learning management system (LMS) that students can contextualize and customize and, in doing so, take ownership of it. She has aimed to develop an intuitive LMS from the perspective of both teachers and learners to ensure opportunities for social learning to take place and one that is visually as pleasing on a phone or tablet as on a laptop. Furthermore, the LMS system was, and continues to be, developed to handle big data analytics, as she feels this drives the quality experience of learners and allows for better intervention strategies to offer struggling students the support they need, when they need it.

Dr. Seelig was awarded an Honorary Fellowship by the Commonwealth of Learning for her services to the advancement of open and distance learning in 2013. References included at the end of this chapter reflect her interests in student choice, access, and flexibility in their studies, which she thinks is so much easier to do online than in face-to-face education.

Interview

Transcript Analysis Summary

Analysis of all interviews included in this volume led to the identification of 3,545 units of data. The mean of these collective units was 118 per pioneer, the median was 118.5, and the mode was 132. Individual interview units ranged from 59 to 217 units, yielding a spread of 158 units between all interviews. Caroline Seelig's interview generated 132 units, which was slightly more than the average interview had.

A comparison of Seelig's interview to the interviews of all pioneers indicates that her conversations yielded a similar number of units in relation to the average interview in half of the identified parent themes (Figure 27.1). Two areas where her interview produced significantly more units were the benefits of DE and her DE goals. As the head of a polytech institution in New Zealand, Seelig played a primary role in developing a system that offers open, distance, and flexible learning (ODFL) to traditional and non-traditional students, many of whom would not otherwise be able to gain an education. Moreover, she envisioned a future where her institution would continue to pioneer innovative ODFL initiatives that would lead the world into a new era of inclusive learning. Perhaps this is why Seelig's interview generated more units in these two areas.

Seeling's interview did not capture much information about changes over time; this may be due to the fact that she began to work for her institution just as it was beginning to adopt online learning intiativies. Seelig did not speak much about her accomplishments. In fact, part of the units coded to this theme contained conversation about the collective accomplishments of people at her institute. This may be in keeping with the findings that the mores in some cultures discourage discussion of individual or female accomplishments. (These findings are discussed at more length in Part Two of this volume.) Seeling was unable to provide many names of early female founders in our field; this

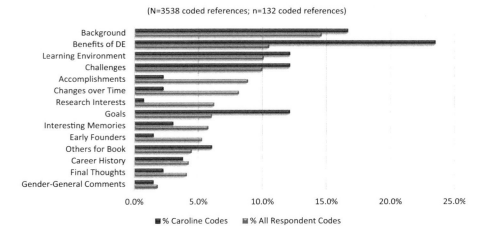

Figure 27.1 All Respondents' Versus Caroline Seelig's Parent Codes

would explain why her interview produced fewer units than the average interview did. Finally, in her role as the chief administrator at her institution, Seelig did not have the opportunity to conduct research; the only unit found in the research interest category records this fact.

Link to recorded interview: tinyurl.com/Seelig-C-2019

Transcript of Interview

Full Name: Caroline Seelig
Institutional Affiliation: The Open Polytechnic of New Zealand

Key:

Regular font = Interviewee comments
Italicized font = Interviewer comments

Interview Questions

1. *What was your educational and experiential background before you became involved in online distance learning [ODL]?*

   I started out as a biologist in research biology and then moved to education. This was when I was with the UK and trained as a secondary school teacher. I got this wanderlust and wanted to come to New Zealand, where I applied for jobs and got a job in the polytechnic sector.

   This is my fourth polytechnic in New Zealand. I started with a very small regional one in Greymouth called Tai Poutini Polytechnic. Then I went to Eastern Institute of Technology in Hawke's Bay. Then I got a position as Deputy Chief Executive at Nelson Marlborough Institute of Technology. My fourth polytechnic is this one, the Open Polytechnic of New Zealand.

2. *In what year did you begin to look specifically into ODL?*

   Probably about 14 years ago. I was at a regional polytechnic at the top end of the South Island of New Zealand, Nelson Marlborough Institute of Technology. It's a predominately a face-to-face regional vocational organization, but at that point, we were just starting to put predominately resources, but also some courses online. That was on a Moodle platform [learning management system; LMS]. I just started the process of enjoying the flexibility and power of online learning there.

3. *What were the circumstances in your world that initiated this interest in ODL?*

   At that point, it was predominately about student choice and flexibility of their study, which I think is so much easier to do online than you can face-to-face. You ask students what they want, and they do want flexibility, they want choice, and they want personalization. It was just those tentative steps to just getting much more flexible, which I found was interesting moving from a face-to-face organization that was trying to be more flexible. Then when I moved to Open Polytechnic, I totally embraced the idea of student-centric, learner-centric education. But in a face-to-face [environment] it was much harder because it goes against the very culture of what we were doing sometimes.

   I can talk a lot about that later when I talk about transformation. The power and potential of open, distance, and flexible learning was the thing that I thought, "Good grief, this has got so much power!" It's the anytime, anyplace, anyone, any pace; that sort of stuff really does challenge traditions in face-to-face organizations.

4. *Which female researchers or female colleagues may have piqued your interest in ODL?*

   I think probably there were two that were very significant. One is Shawna Butterfield, who was the Chief Executive of Open Polytechnic before me. Can I send you the details later?

   I: *That's wonderful. Thank you.*

   Not only was she a woman leader of a large polytechnic in New Zealand, but she was the woman leader of the open, distance one and very engaged with the open, distance movement. Going back about 20 years now, she was highly involved with the Commonwealth of Learning at the time, I think, when Sir John Daniel was the president there and she was on the board.

   I visited Open Polytechnic long before I had the aspiration of working here, and she was such an advocate, such a forceful advocate. And because she knew so much about open and distance learning, she modelled the Open Polytechnic on the Open University in the UK and put in place the infrastructures and policies that today, I can still see. She held rigidly to the philosophies of learner-centric; that's not a word, but you know what I mean. So that would be one.

The other one would be Asha Kanwar. I knew her when she was the deputy to Sir John at the Commonwealth of Learning: wonderful academic background that fully embraces the power and potential globally for open, distance, flexible learning. She carries that drive for equity, and the things that she has achieved in that organization and has achieved across the world are phenomenal.

I think it was the Commonwealth of Learning that I visited probably my first year at Open Polytechnic. They are doing some truly amazing stuff with some truly amazing people across the world. You see their influence. You go to conferences. One of the other people on RICE is someone that I met at the Commonwealth of Learning Conference in Namibia. The impact that they have and the leadership, whether it is in New Zealand or Australia, or it is a country that is developing very much, they have enabled them to leapfrog traditional organizations in terms of technology.

So, they are two of the people. Other people like Belinda Tynan, RMIT [Royal Melbourne Institute of Technology], but also came out of the Open University in the UK – really good academic record. She is very interested in the student voice and educational technology, done a lot of research, but also things like ICDE [International Council of Distance Education] and the Commonwealth of Learning; she's very involved.

One of the ones that I was mentioning before was one of the academic staff at Namibia, Maggy Beukes-Amiss. Have you got her on your list? She's the Director of the Centre of E-Learning and Interactive Multimedia. She's just a great advocate doing great things in Namibia.

Educational technology does allow you to leapfrog, doing things that organizations in Australia and New Zealand and UK and Canada would go, "Wow! That's impressive."

5. *Who would you identify as the early female leaders/founders in the field of ODL?*

That's harder, isn't it? I would still go certainly with Shawna and Asha. I've got my notes here. Let me look up to see when Shawna was here. She was here for 14 years. She finished in 2003. That would make it 1989 when she started here.

6. *What are some of the goals that you strove to achieve in the field of ODL?*

One of the bigger things that we tried to do was develop a learner management system that worked for ODFL [open, distant, and flexible learning]. We looked around for an appropriate system that would allow us to follow the traditional principles of ODFL but in our current-day situation. So we were looking to develop a learning management system that we could work with partners on, whether they were other universities or polytechnics, secondary schools, corporate partners, or NGOs [non-government organizations]. We developed a learning management system called iQualify, which we launched about five years ago. We developed principles of what we wanted in an LMS. We did want it to be labelled so that we could work with partners and so our partners could use it so that their students think it's theirs: that they can own it, contextualize and customize. We needed it to be very intuitive from both a teacher and a learner perspective if we wanted it to embrace social learning. It had to be mobile and responsive. It had to look as beautiful on your phone as it did on your laptop or your tablet. And it had to generate analytics (that's another thing that I'll come to), because big data and analytics is the thing that will drive the quality improvement and the improvement of the experience for learners. We developed this, and we continue to develop this. We have sort of 40 upgrades every month. And we probably have, I don't know, 50, 60 partners around the country who work with us on this platform. It is highly interconnectable, and it can link with all of the other data sets that we need it to. We are now beginning over the last year or so; we now think that we can get closer to our learners than you can face-to-face. We can almost see the engagement of our students in real time. We know when our students are struggling, when they are succeeding; we know when we need to intervene. We know when their experience with our digital courseware isn't as good as it should be, and we know when we need to improve our digital courseware. I could talk about that for hours, but getting that really good technology that integrates into our systems, which allows us to support our learners in a way that we never could. Because when I first came to Open Polytechnic, it was a paper-based correspondence organization. The limitations of paper in that you can't in real time know where your students are and what they are up to, when they need support or are struggling, or when they are flourishing and they need the next course; you can't see it. But now it is just amazing: totally excitable about that ability to support learners. And it does give us real insight.

Being a polytechnic, our students tend to be part time, older, on job, like lots of ODFL students, with huge commitments, whether that is family or jobs or community obligations, so they are always time pressed or time stressed. So that ability to support them when they need supporting, and allow them to travel at their speed with lots of motivation and support. So bringing in really good technology that worked for the learners and worked for our teachers and worked for the organization and our partners was very important and, from that, getting the data and analysis which is going to allow us to make huge step changes in the quality and service that we provide.

And assessment – I'm going to talk a little bit now about the transformation. For the last two years, we've been going through a very large transformation with the organization. That really was to go to the next step of student choice, flexibility, and personalization and really give students that anytime, anyplace, any device, any pace and allow them 365 [days of] admissions. The hard nut to crack is assessment. Through our transformation process, we separated assessment out of the traditional role of the academic staff member. We separated that out to sit alone so that we could do on-demand assessments, or we could do assessment-only study, or we could do commercial opportunities for assessment. That's been a really exciting journey to be able to do that. And, again, it gives us much, much more flexibility.

Now, in that transformation, we have one of the largest Australasian courseware developers. It's very project-oriented in quite a lean, agile way; we plan our product, we plan on how we are going to keep it relevant and current, and we build lots of courseware, and we keep it on a regime to keep it very current and very relevant.

I've gone off track slightly, but those are the big things that excite me. It's about learner success, I guess, ultimately.

7. *What are some of your accomplishments in the field of ODL that you would like to share?*

When I got here, we were a paper-based organization, and our qualification completions and our student retentions reflected that. I might come back to this when we come to the issues, the problems that we face. One of the problems that ODFL programmes face all over the country is that they have a similar cohort of students; they tend to be part time; they tend to be older, time stressed, and on jobs, and a lot of this gets in the way of study, so outcomes always look poorer in ODFL organizations than they do in face-to-face. That becomes a difficulty for some governments and their regimes for funding. But one of the things that I do would focus very much on that and how we could improve that.

Probably one of the achievements was that we brought our course completion, qualification completion, and course retention figures up to the level of face-to-face organizations. We have probably tripled our qualification outcome and probably ten percentage points up in course completion. That is a big movement for an ODFL organization. We are now considered a much more credible tertiary organization because of that. But it is a very unfair yardstick that they use to measure this, I think.

8. *What are some of the challenges that you faced in the field of ODL over the years?*

What I just alluded to is one: The way that ODFL is seen, and if governments measure your success according to formula-like completions, we tend not to stack up well against other organizations. So keeping the organization sustainable and viable has been a challenge. But we've met that challenge. I think that all public sector education is on a formula of reduced funding from government and ministries, and it is hard, very hard, for them to thrive. Also, we shift in demographic and economic cycles. It is quite hard to survive on the funding cycles that we get. So the reputation of ODFL is shifting, but in the early days that was very hard.

Let me see . . . other challenges – investment. We have to invest in educational technology. We have to invest and capitalize in courseware development, and it is hugely expensive. And again, as a public sector organization, that is difficult to find that investment, especially when you are building your own technology. Yes, it is difficult to find that [funding]; it is a challenge.

Perceptions by the rest of the education sector; they often feel quite threatened by distance learning. I think that's something we've seen across the world. Now competition, depending upon what government cycle you are in (we are in a national government cycle; they encourage competition). Within a small country, having dozens of organizations all developing distance learning materials is a principle government strategy. (We have to be careful what we write there.) But we now have a Labour government that is much more interested in collaboration, and that brings some quite exciting possibilities forward.

What have been some other challenges? Challenging some traditional cultures and perceptions of roles, especially in tertiary education; that is always a struggle. And the future may not look like it does now. There is a lot of work to do. As I said, separating out, and I have to be careful with these words, but some countries don't like unbundling, or desegregating, but that classic desegregated role of open, distance, and flexible learning is probably the one that will be most viable and sustainable. But the challenge of moving an organization to an unbundled and desegregated state is actually very, very difficult.

9. *What was the "state of DE" when you first entered the field as opposed to ODL in 2019?*

Distance education, when I look at when I first came to Open Polytechnic, it was very paper based until ten years ago, really. When I first came to Open Polytechnic, there were big printers, we had a warehouse that ran all of the logistics operation, and the warehouse was full of shelves from ceiling to floor where we had our course materials, which were copy-developed over – I don't know – one course could have taken a year to develop. It would be printed; it would be put on the shelf; changes would be very difficult. Our academic staff would predominately give feedback to students through marking of assessments and assignments. The majority of the work that students were doing was summative. There wasn't so much formative work that staff could give feedback on. And the courses were sent out in a lot of "pizza boxes," which were cardboard boxes full of materials, sent out all over the country – in fact, all over the world. It was an enormous postal bill. I'm trying to think what else. But it has all changed.

And probably the proportions of staff; we had a lot of staff in different positions. Now, if I look at my staff, I have a lot of education technologists. I've got staff with job titles that I wouldn't have thought of ten years ago. We have experience designers. We never had those ten years ago. We had education designers. It was quite different.

10. *What interesting memories would you like to share about the beginning of ODL?*

I think that the international connection of people who are leading and involved with ODFL was one of the things that I found illuminating and quite amazing, actually. I can remember ten years ago going to one of the workshops or conferences that the Commonwealth of Learning had organized, and they asked us to talk about our challenges. I talked about the challenges of funding and how our government would fund organizations on an arbitrary formula and not really understand, or not have a really good perception of, what ODFL does and its place in the network of learning. I was followed by colleagues from all over the world. They talked about the challenges in their countries. They talked about wars, and they talked about losing thousands of students in those wars, and they talked about [the] difficulties of training women in an environment where a male teacher could not be communicating with a female student. They talked about religious persecution, these issues that were actually much more significant than my funding one. I think that it was about that time that I really appreciated the power and potential of distance learning, and the way that distance learning can keep going, and it can keep moving with the student. It can move to where the learners are and what they do, and it can make them safe. You can't have a male teacher in a room with a female student, but you can have distance learning. If your country or your city is disrupted by war or by natural disasters, distance learning can keep going. It can move, and it can take different times, and it can be supported in different ways. It is one of those things that can persist and can flourish when other things are breaking down. I think that that global, international insight into a network of ODLF people was really quite inspiring. That probably sounds a bit rambling.

11. *What were your specific ODL research interests, and have they changed/evolved over the years?*

Leadership is a big one, and that is probably because some of the people that you will be talking to are researchers, and I'm a Chief Executive or a manager, and leadership of organizations to embrace digital technologies and education technology infrastructures is something that really interests me. Student outcomes and transformation, change, change within organizations interest me as well.

12. *Could you please describe the learning environment that you currently work in or have most recently worked in (e.g., geographic and institutional setting, student demographics)?*

I will also send you some stuff with information and figures.

The Open Polytechnic has been around for close to 75 years. We started after the Second World War. We were a training organization for returning service men and service women. Obviously, in those days, they were very trade-focused courses. They were paper-based modalities.

We are now an organization where everything is online. I have talked about some of the online stuff. We have 30,000 learners, which is about 25% of the country's polytechnic learners. They are from all over New Zealand. We tend to follow the national demographic. So, in terms of Auckland or Māori or the Pacific Island, we follow the national demographics there. We are based in Wellington, but really that is our headquarters. We don't have any students on our campus.

We are a specialist trainer in prisons, and we are doing a bit of research on how we can move that with the correction services to as online as we can, but obviously, we are still predominately paper-based in our prison-based deliveries. That is an area where we do get huge feedback, and we do change lives with education in prison.

We run programmes from pretty foundational to degree-level programmes. We've got about 120 programmes and about 1,200 courses, and they pretty much follow the traditional curriculum of

ODFL. We've got a number of blended programmes, which, when we talked about challenges earlier, we had to battle with central agencies and bureaucracies to do some of these blended programmes across New Zealand because there was a feeling that it wouldn't work well. They were things like social work, early childhood education, which are very successful programmes for us and provide students with opportunities that they wouldn't get otherwise.

I will send you data on Open Polytechnic. We don't have a big international market. We are predominately New Zealand–based. But we are starting to get partners offshore who are using our learning management system for their own students. And we partner with universities and organizations globally who use our LMS.

13. *Is there anything else you [would] like to address?*

    I think that it is a very fast-changing area to be involved with. I think the future for ODFL will be very exciting. Particularly in New Zealand, as we move from a paper-based environment to one which is going to be much more collaborative, I think there will be many, many more opportunities for learners if we can coordinate that well. A national ODLF in a mix of other organizations can have incredible potential for students. They can mix studies face-to-face, blended, online, anytime, within cohorts and semesters, move around the country in order to get that. . . . We can develop if we can work together to get that theory, modular, stackable curricula that can be structured in a way to enhance total student mobility almost. That does take a very coordinated sector, but I think that's where we're heading. I think we are heading to a place where we can embrace the power of ODFL within a network of providers. I think that will really benefit our students in the future. Because people say there's nothing special about ODFL now. I'm not sure if you've heard that everyone is doing it. But if you are pure ODLF, you can do it in a very systematic, smart way, and working with partners, I think that is where the future lies. I think it's very exciting.

14. *Can you suggest names of other female pioneers in distance education or ODL that you think we should include in the book?*

    Maggie, in Namibia, would be very interesting. You've probably got lots. Belinda Tynan. You have Asha. Shawna probably hasn't been involved probably for 15 years. Who else can I think of? Another Commonwealth of Learning person is Alison Mead Richardson; she's got some wonderful international, very rich stories of changes that have been made. She's recently left the Commonwealth of Learning, but I think she was there probably for a decade and has worked heavily in the Pacific, heavily in Africa. There is another expert in Namibia from the Commonwealth of Learning, Francis Ferreira. She would be good as well. She has a huge wealth of stories. Interestingly, when I think of the women who are in ODFL, like Asha, Alison, and Francis, they are on the ground in developing countries wherever the research is. I wonder if there is a difference there.

Publications

Book Chapters

Seelig, C. (2013). Being a leader in open and distance higher education. In A. Kanwar, F. Ferreira, & C. Latchem (Eds.), *Women and leadership in open and distance learning and development* (pp. 21–32). Commonwealth of Learning. http://oasis.col.org/handle/11599/24

Seelig, C., & Nichols, M. (2017). New Zealand: Open polytechnic. In C. Latchem (Ed.), *Using ICTS and blended learning models for transforming TVET* (pp. 103–116). United Nations Educational, Scientific and Cultural Organization (UNESCO) & Commonwealth of Learning. http://oasis.col.org/handle/11599/2718

Journal Articles

Seelig, C. (2013a). Being a leader in open and distance higher education. In A. Kanwar, F. Ferreira, & C. Latchem (Eds), *Women and leadership in open and distance learning and development* (pp. 21–32). Commonwealth of Learning.

Seelig, C. (2013b). The role distance learning has to play in offender education. *Journal of Learning for Development J4LD, 1*(1).

Seelig, C. (2018a). *Designing a digital experience to meet the demands of future learners and industry*. World Federation of Colleges and Polytechnics.

Seelig, C. (2018b). Learner analytics offer a promising pathway to increased learner success in ODFL. *Connections, 23*(2).

Seelig, C. (2019). Transformational change in delivery at Open Polytechnic New Zealand. *Journal of Learning for Development*.

Seelig, C., & Nichols, M. (2017). *Using ICTs and blended learning in transforming technical and vocational education and training (TVET)*. Commonwealth of Learning, NZ: Perspective Series, 103.

Seelig, C., & Rate, L. (2014). The role distance learning has to play in offender education. *Journal of Learning for Development J4LD, 1*(1). https://jl4d.org/index.php/ejl4d/article/view/20

Conference Presentations

Seelig, C. (2009). *A decade of distance education in the Commonwealth: Achievements and challenges*. Commonwealth of Learning Conference, Nigeria.

Seelig, C. (2010a). *Development and challenges of ODL and formal TVET* [Keynote Speaker]. The 6th Pan-Commonwealth Forum on Open Learning Skills.

Seelig, C. (2010b). *Developments in online and distance learning*. Higher Education Summit, Creating Education without Boundaries.

Seelig, C. (2012a). *Appropriate education performance indicators and the future of distance and online education*. Association of Open, Flexible and Distance Learning Conference, Auckland, NZ.

Seelig, C. (2012b). *The ITP sector in 10 Years*. New Zealand Institutes of Technology and Polytechnics Annual Conference, New Zealand.

Seelig, C. (2017). *Building an effective digital learning experience*. Digital Campus and Blended Learning Innovation Conference, Auckland, NZ.

Seelig, C. (2018a). *Designing a digital experience to meet the demands of future learners and industry*. World Federation of Colleges and Polytechnics, Australia.

Seelig, C. (2018b). *Open, distance, flexible learning best practice*. High level roundtable for Vice Chancellors & Heads of ODL Institutions, Malaysia.

Seelig, C. (2021a). *Is online education a thing?* [Keynote]. CITRENZ, Wellington.

Seelig, C. (2021b). *Leadership for responsiveness, Are we flexible enough?* Virtual ICDE Leadership Summit.

Cadwallader, A., Standring, D., & Seelig, C. (2019, September). *Transformation of open distance flexible learning at the intersection of national reform of vocational education and training* [Paper presentation]. Pan-Commonwealth Forum 9 (PCF9) Edinburgh, Scotland. http://oasis.col.org/handle/11599/3332

28
SIMMONS-MCDONALD, HAZEL

Photo of contributed by Hazel Simmons-McDonald

> *I'm certain that women who served in universities in earlier times contributed in some way to the promotion of distance education, but I think that this has not been recorded. With the exponential advances in technology, I think that we have an opportunity to do so, and it is imperative that women's contributions should be noted.*

Dr. Hazel Simmons-McDonald was born in the West Indies and began her post-secondary education at the University of the West Indies (UWI), where she completed an Honours Degree in English. Her interests at the time focused on English Literature and Linguistics, which led to her interests in distance education. She went on to complete a post-graduate diploma in English Teaching and returned to Saint Lucia where she taught English at the local Teacher's College, now a division of Sir Arthur Lewis Community College, St. Lucia. As her interests related to young learner language-acquisition issues of French Creole-speaking children, she went on to complete a Master of International Development in Education. On completion, she became an Adjunct Lecturer in the Use of English at the University of West Indies (UWI) for two years, before returning to Stanford to complete both a Master of Linguistics and a PhD in English Education. She has taught applied linguistics and carried out research in this field at UWI, Barbados. She moved full time into distance education at UWI as the Pro-Vice Chancellor and Principal of the Open Campus, where she taught and supervised post-graduate students. In 2006, she led an initiative to develop the Open Campus, integrating the outreach centres across regions of the West Indies, where students who could not attend a main campus (such as in Jamaica) could gain access to further education. These centres were integral to establishing the Open Campus in 2006. How well the centres related to the main campuses in terms of meeting educational needs of non-campus countries in the West Indies became a key interest of Dr Simmons-McDonald's, owing to first-hand experience with both on- and off-campus resources in the West Indies.

As distance education had existed in some form and developed into various forms from the onset of establishing UWI in 1947, it was proposed that all outreach and social departments be unified to take full advantage of advancements in both developing technologies and pedagogy in order to better serve locals in outlying communities in the region, especially in those countries without brick campuses. Dr Simmons-McDonald undertook this transformational task to integrate the various educational entities into an open and distance learning campus, providing technology-driven quality education throughout the Caribbean region.

Dr. Hazel Simmons-McDonald's research and interests in Education for both Distance, Linguistics and Culture are extensive. Her research in Distance Education has primarily focused on access, flexibility, learner-centredness, and enhanced learning management systems to bring geographically separate educational entities within existing infrastructures together to form a robust local and international standard of education for the West Indies.

Interview

Transcript Analysis Summary

Analysis of all interviews included in this volume led to the identification of 3,545 units of data. The mean of these collective units was 118 per pioneer, the median was 118.5, and the mode was 132. Individual interview units ranged from 59 to 217 units, yielding a spread of 158 units between all interviews. Hazel Simmons-MacDonald's interview generated 108 units, placing her interview in the lower middle third of all interviews in terms of unit numbers.

A comparison of Simmons-MacDonald's interview to the interviews of all pioneers indicated that her interview profile was, generally speaking, quite similar to that of the average interview profile (Figure 28.1). Her interview produced quite a few more units in two areas: benefits of DE and goals. Since Simmons-MacDonald played an integral role in bringing DE to all learners across the Caribbean, she was acutely aware of how DE improved the lives of individuals and their communities. This would help to explain why she extoled the virtues of DE during her interview. Given that her university was continuing to expand and develop its offerings at the the time of her interview, it would make sense that her interview also yielded a greater-than-average number of goal units.

Simmons-MacDonald's interview produced a lower-than-average number of units in reseach interests, others for the book, and final thoughts. As an administrator at her university, she did not have much time to devote to her own research endeavours. The low number of units produced in the area of others for the book was explained by her late entry into the field and her pioneering position in the Caribbean distance learning environment. It is not known why Hazel did not contribute final thoughts to her interview.

Figure 28.1 All Respondents' Versus Hazel Simmons-McDonald's Parent Codes

Link to recorded interview: tinyurl.com/Simmons-H

Transcript of Interview

Full name: Dr. Hazel Simmons-McDonald, Professor Emerita of Applied Linguistics
Institutional Affiliation: University of the West Indies
Key:

Regular font = Interviewee comments
Italicized font = Interviewer comments

Interview Questions

1. *What was your educational and experiential background before you became involved in distance education [DE]?*

    I will start from the time that I was an undergraduate. I studied at the University of the West Indies [UWI] Mona Campus. I pursued an Honours Degree in English, as that was my main interest at the time. The programme focused primarily on literature in English and introductory studies in linguistics.

I had decided that I wanted a career in teaching, so after getting my first degree and completing a year in teaching at a secondary school in St. Lucia, I returned to Mona to pursue a one-year post-graduate diploma in the teaching of English. I returned to Saint Lucia and taught English first at the Teacher's College, which is now part of the Sir Arthur Lewis Community College. After a couple years, I was transferred to teaching in the six-form division of the college.

I thought that I needed a broader study base because I was interested in issues related to language learning by children who spoke French Creole as a first language. So I went off to Stanford University in California for one year to pursue a Master's Degree in International Development Education. Subsequent to that, I accepted an adjunct lectureship in the Use of English Department at the University of the West Indies at Mona. I stayed there for two years before returning to Stanford, where I obtained a Master's Degree in Linguistics and then pursued a PhD in English Education. These qualifications set me off on my academic career at the Cave Hill Campus at the University of the West Indies in Barbados. I taught applied linguistics there and focused on research in that field for most of my career.

I was also required, as we all are usually, to give service in administration. I served as the Head of Department of Linguistics, as a Deputy Dean of Outreach, then as a Deputy Dean in Planning, and later as the Dean of the Faculty of Humanities and Education. I also served as the Head of the Language, Linguistics, and Literature Department when the university decided to merge selected departments into one department for efficiency purposes. I served in these various administrative positions over a period of roughly ten years. The post of Dean of the Faculty of Humanities and Education was the last administrative position I had before I was drawn full time into distance education at the university. I was offered the post of Pro-Vice Chancellor and Principal of the Open Campus, and I continued to teach during those years and supervised post-graduate students during my tenure as Principal.

I should say that during my years as an undergraduate, though, I had a bit of familiarity with the work of the University of the West Indies Extramural Department in St. Lucia, where I taught in the evening programme and where I used to volunteer during my August vacations when I returned home on holidays from study and when I also taught at the community college.

The Extramural Department is the arm of the university which provides opportunities for people on the various islands in what was then called the non-campus countries. Students get the opportunity to go these centres to pursue further education. These departments became an integral part of the University's Open Campus when it was established later. When I became Principal of the Open Campus, I found the experiences that I had working in the department in St. Lucia very beneficial.

2. *In what year did you begin to look specifically into distance education [DE]?*

I became involved on a full-time basis in distance education in 2006. That was the time that the Open Campus was being planned. At that time, I was offered the job, and I agreed. I was given the responsibility to lead the initiative at that time, and the groundwork began in September of that year. At that time, and for rest of that year, I was mostly in consultation with the then Pro-Vice Chancellor of Continuing Education Studies, Professor Lawrence Carrington. We focused on all of the entities that had existed as outreach entities in the university that I would have to consider in forming the Open Campus. So September 2006, I would say, is probably the definitive date.

3. *What were the circumstances in your world that initiated this interest in DE?*

The Caribbean comprises many islands from the Greater Antilles in the north; they arc from the south of the panhandle of Florida to the north of South America. When the university was established as the University College of the West Indies in 1947, the understanding was that it would serve the English-speaking countries of the region. The first "bricks campus" was established in Jamaica at that time. But from its inception, the mission of the university was that it would make provision for people in the countries dispersed across the Caribbean to have access to continuing education. The Extramural Departments were designed to bring the college to those people who could not go to the campus in Jamaica.

Campuses were later established at St. Augustine in Trinidad and Tobago, and at Cave Hill in Barbados, but even in these countries, Extramural Departments had been established earlier. All of these were integral to the distance education programme of the university. Resident tutors managed the centres. They offered programmes at different levels. For example, the University Certificate of Education courses as well as the General Certificate of Education [GCE] courses at the O and A level so that those who may not have got certification at secondary school had the opportunity for recovery through these courses. They also offered training in adult education and other programmes.

In a dispersed environment such as the Caribbean, these Extramural Centres sought to determine higher education needs of the people of the region and to offer them, through various forms of modalities, the hope of continuing education. This is where distance education became important. That is where I cut my teeth on DE service through the teaching of evening classes to people and so on. It was sort of a face-to-face situation in the non-campus countries as an arm of the university. That was my first experience with DE.

4. *Which female researchers or female colleagues may have piqued your interest in DE?*

My interest in DE began when I volunteered at the Extramural Centre in St. Lucia. At the time, the residential tutor was a former teacher called Mrs. Patricia Charles. She had introduced a range of programmes. She was a dynamic, energetic lady. She included a number of GCE courses and a vibrant menu of programmes, as well as a whole suite of creative arts programmes, which also involved public performances. So she gave me and other students who were returning home the opportunity to tutor in the evening programmes, participate in creative arts programmes, [and] attend sessions presented by members of faculty who came in from the campuses from time to time to teach at the centre. She was a mentor; I consider her to be an important mentor in my life, especially in respect to what can be done locally in the field to promote education. So I would say that she was the first person who piqued my interest in distance education through various things that were being done and by making me aware of how the centre related or did not relate, as the case may be, to the main campuses and what needed to be done to ensure that the people in the non-campus countries could have their educational needs met.

5. *Who would you identify as the early female leaders/founders in the DE field?*

It is easy to find references to the contributions of men made to the field of distance education in what we might refer to as the early years. Reference is often made, for example, to the Pitman shorthand course, which was one of the earliest, if not the earliest offered by distance. And I should say in St. Lucia and some of the other countries, that course was one of the earliest being taught.

When I became involved with the university's open and distance project, I found out more about women who were providing leadership in the field at the time, rather than early founders per se. In my work, I was fortunate to meet a few of those. I met Asha Kanwar, who had worked at the Indira Gandhi National Open University and had been a consultant in open and distance learning at UNESCO's regional office for education in Africa. At the time [that we met], she had joined the Commonwealth of Learning and had invited me to participate in a conference, which she had organized in Nigeria.

I also met Denise Kirkpatrick, who had worked at the Open University in the UK and who, at the time, held a leadership position at Adelaide. I met her at another conference. I was impressed with the concepts that these ladies presented on open and distance learning, and the contributions that they have made in the field attest to their understanding of the possibilities of ODL [open and distance learning] and their commitment to advancing the field.

Another person, whom I was impressed with the work that she had done, was Caroline Seelig. She was the CEO of the Open Polytech in New Zealand. I hadn't met her personally, but I had read about her in the course of doing my work.

Through the ICDE [International Council of Distance Education], I met a number of other women who are leaders in the ICDE. These stand out because of the interactions that I had with them.

I'm certain that women who served in universities in earlier times contributed in some way to the promotion of distance education, but I think that this has not been recorded. With the exponential advances in technology, I think that we have an opportunity to do so, and it is imperative that women's contributions should be noted. I think that in recent years, there are several women who have contributed in a significant way. Those that I mentioned did a lot of groundbreaking work. Perhaps not "early" in the sense that we might refer to Pitman, but really groundbreaking and innovative with respect to the concepts that they presented and their ideas for promoting distance education in the world.

6. *You are a pioneer and a founder of DE in the Caribbean/West Indies. Could you please tell us a bit about what prompted you to initiate such undertakings?*

Distance education in the Caribbean, I think, is as old as the University of the West Indies, which was established in 1947 as the University College of the West Indies in Jamaica. Because of the dispersed nature of the countries in our region, which the university serves, it had established early the Extramural Departments or Centres, and they were the links with the "brick" campuses. Since then, distance education has evolved based upon available resources in the region.

The university had established the Radio Education Unit on the Mona campus, which had made distance teaching possible. Later, it introduced the Challenge Examination Scheme through which students at a distance were given just the syllabus and the book list for relevant courses or courses for which they wanted to take an examination, and the centre in the non-campus countries sought to provide some assistance to the students who were going to take those examinations. So the support was really not substantial or even didn't exist for the students who thought that they might want to take a course from the university at the time. Occasional visits by lecturers from relevant faculties at the Mona Campus enhanced the experience for those in the centres who opted to take the challenge examination. The resident tutors did whatever they could to provide support.

The university then introduced the distance teaching experiment which, in 1985, was recast as the University of the West Indies Distance Teaching Enterprise [UWIDITE]. It was first an experiment; they got funding, and then they recast it as an enterprise. That utilized interactive audiographic teleconferencing, which allowed for interaction between the lecturer, who taught the course at the campus, and students, who would gather in the teleconferencing labs at the centres to participate in the classes and listen to the lectures.

I think that the university made a significant movement in its DE programme in 1996, when it implemented recommendations in the Renwick Report [Renwick et al., 1992], based on the Commonwealth of Learning Study, that it should become a dual-mode institution through the improvement of technologies offered by UWIDITE. This resulted in the establishment of the UWI Distance Education Centre [UWIDEC]. That establishment introduced tele-writers, which allowed for information to be written on these tele-writers and viewed instantly in the Distance Centres. And so there was better communication between students taking courses in these non-campus countries and the lecturer who might be teaching the course. The teleconferencing facilities at the centres were enhanced through the UWIDEC. Tutorial support was provided for the students at the centres, and print materials, in terms of the courses, the notes, also became part of that programme. So the students had not only the teleconferencing and print support but the possibility of tutorials through the teleconferencing improvements that had been made.

UWIDEC was the system that was in operation when I became involved with DE on a full-time basis. I should say (if I haven't said before), distance education was on an evolutionary trajectory from the time that it was introduced. I can't honestly say that I initiated the next phase. However, there were many entities existing at the time: for example, the UWIDEC, the Extramural Departments across the region (which had been rebranded as Centres), and various units which had been formed over time to extend the reach of the university to off-campus communities. Some of these – just to give you an example – were the Caribbean Child Development Centre, the Human Resources and Development Unit, the Social Welfare Training Centre, and the Trade Union Education Institute. At the time, the Vice Chancellor, Professor [Eon] Nigel Harris, and the Director of the School of Continuing Education Studies, Professor Lawrence Carrington, proposed that all of these outreach and social departments should be consolidated to take advantage of developing technologies and advances in pedagogy and andragogy to form an entity that would better serve people in rural, underserved communities of the region, especially in the countries with no bricks campuses.

So I was asked to undertake this task. That is where I came into the picture as a full participant in the DE enterprise. I was asked to undertake the task of merging and transforming the various entities into an open and distance learning campus that would provide high quality programmes and technology-driven education to people within the Caribbean region and elsewhere who wished to access education.

I believed firmly that the campus should provide open access to education, that it should harness the available technologies and resources to reach people, especially in rural and remote areas, who wished to access education. I also believed that it should be the conduit through which the bricks campuses could deliver their courses to the wider region so that there would be a unified, seamless presentation to the world of a one-look, one-feel high-quality online courses and programmes that the Open Campus would offer for the university.

At the time, different campuses were doing different things with competing courses, with the same title sometimes, on the market. So the Open Campus had a unique role to synchronize these processes and present to our clients quality courses that would actually represent the top quality that the university was supplying. I thought that would allow the university to have a more penetrating regional and international reach. So this was one of the ideas that I had at the planning stages as one of the things that the campuses in collaboration with the Open Campus could do: integrate and synchronize the university efforts and also expand the reach of providing distance to places that had not hitherto received access to this. To this end, we paid attention to the branding of the Open Campus, and we referred to it as "a campus for the times and for the future," and we used the phrases "online, on site, on demand" to define the thrust of our enterprise.

7. *What are some of the goals that you strove to achieve in these geographic regions in the DE field?*

I will refer to about five or six of them. One of the goals was to create a campus that was truly open and available to all who wished to reach their potential through access to education. So, to facilitate this, we sought to provide opportunities for those without qualifications to access programmes; those would be scaffolding courses and programmes that would prepare them for study at successively higher levels. In that sense, openness was very important. Whereas with the brick universities, you had to have certain qualifications to enter, a lot of people were marginalized because they couldn't enter. So we thought that we would provide access to them by giving them scaffolding courses that they needed, or what you might wish to call "access courses," that would help them to get to successively higher stages of education, and also give them access to better opportunities for work or opportunities to do further study at the brick campuses if they wanted or if they wanted to pursue further studies at the Open Campus. So we tried to have openness operating at that level, through the creation of those courses.

We also implemented prior learning assessment to facilitate entry by students with non-traditional backgrounds. That was important to us to really establish this concept of openness and to ensure that we were providing opportunities for a wide range of students.

Another goal was that we wanted to ensure the quality of teaching and learning experiences. So we focused on innovative pedagogic design; we set up a system to undertake relevant research and also tried to forge community partnership for successful delivery of programmes in multimodal ways. We had, for example, 44 existing sites across the Caribbean at the time that I was asked to form the Open Campus, with several of them existing even in countries that already had brick campuses, like Jamaica and Trinidad. We had to conceive of how we might use these sites for the benefit of people who perhaps did not have access to laptops and mobile phones. We also had teleconferencing facilities in some of the centres. We thought that we really had to think of ways that we could build on the technologies so that people could access first, top quality service in terms of the delivery of courses if they didn't have a laptop available to them. So the quality teaching and learning experiences had us focus on how we could use these inputs that were pre-existing to improve our delivery of distance education and to do it through the face-to-face, blended, and online learning mechanisms that we inherited in various ways. We sought to pull those together into a seamless system that would really provide top-quality service to people.

As the campus designated to manage ODL for the university, one of our objectives was to produce a top-quality online product and deliver it to learners in the region and beyond. Now this would really require some collaboration with the brick campuses and the Open Campus. We thought that was something that we should do to create this one-look, one-feel, top-quality product that could go out to the world as the University of the West Indies online suite of programmes. That turned out to be one of the challenges that we had to face, but it was an objective that we had. We thought that it would serve the university well if we could put in place the mechanisms that would assist the campuses with the creation of online courses of their own that could go out through the Open Campus so that the campus would be a conduit for all of the ODL material of the university. We devised a system whereby the campus where the course originated would be so recognized. This way, the unified effort of the UWI for promoting DE would be highlighted.

Another important objective was to procure quality services to provide necessary training so that our Open Campus would provide the training for ODL expertise for curriculum development, training of course facilitators, training of e-tutors to manage and facilitate online instruction, [and] assist the other campuses with training for online course development. All of this was necessary because the support that is needed for distance education, I think, is even more intense than simply going to a lecture and having a tutorial, which is what you get on a brick campus. You have to provide 24/7 support for learners who may need to speak to someone. So you have to train facilitators who will be connecting with students, listening to them, and giving that kind of support. We wanted to be able to set that up through the course requirements that we established, but also through a 24/7 help desk that would provide service for learner support.

We also wanted to develop a technological base and the services to deliver our programmes. So while the teleconferencing was fine, it was just an audio system, and there was probably, in some cases, just a small TV that was at the front of the room by which one might see the lecturer. But most of the time, it meant really listening and having to press the buttons at the centres to communicate. It wasn't that effective. So our goal was to enhance the conferencing facilities and to create state-of-the-art video conferencing facilities at all the centres. That was a major objective that would actually transform the whole learning experience into something enjoyable and, with the supports provided, make distance education something that was beneficial and enjoyable to students.

The last one, which I kind of alluded to earlier, was to have a UWI online brand that was characterized by excellence and would present the university more broadly as a provider of quality online programmes.

So these are the six that I mention here, but there were other minor ones that we focused on in terms of how to establish good collaborative principles between the departments, creating a structure that would actually serve the purpose of the university, of the Open Campus particularly, in relationship with the university. That also was a very important one, and we spent a lot of time figuring out what would work best.

So these are some of the ones that come to mind as I speak.

8. *What are some of your accomplishments in the field of DE that you would like to share?*

I will just speak to the ones that I became responsible for at the campus. The main one was the actual creation of the Open Campus. This formation, which incorporated the various entities of which I spoke in a collaborative, administrative structure that would have the purpose of producing and delivering programmes that would meet the needs of clients. I think that this is one of the things that we accomplished: setting up a unique and innovative structure that was able to serve these disparate clients and also connect with the traditional structures of the university in some ways.

Another one was the upgrading of the technological structure to state-of-the-art video conferencing centres and making [it] possible for students to access sessions as needed from their laptops, tablets, or mobile phones, wherever they could be. In other words, get the education to them wherever they were using the supports that they had. Also, trying to assist with the provision of laptops for students and making sure that because we had the existing sites, to build those video conferencing facilities at the sites so that people who haven't got a laptop, tablet, or cell phone could go into the centre at their convenience, sit in the lab, and participate in the class and the chatrooms, and have a more holistic educational experience. That was important.

I think that the renovation, refurbishment, and upgrading of the centres across the region to include those state-of-the-art video conferencing centres was important. We are talking about

44 of those at the time when I took over; having gone across and looked at some of them, it was imperative for us to change them, make them more learner-friendly environments for students. That was a big objective. I am very happy that we were able to transform a number of them, to move away from those small, crowded rooms and to set up labs and learning areas that were most pleasant for students. The transformation of these sites where students had to go to either meet with other students or to go on [a] video conferencing unit to try and access the information that they needed, that was a critical thing. I am happy that we were able to transform several of those. However, the work of transformation needs to continue to address the large number of sites for which the OC is responsible.

One important undertaking was the funding issue. We had to decrease our dependence on governments. The setup in the region was that all of the governments contributed to the university. When the Open Campus was formed, there was some concern that the university would be asking the governments for more money, and a lot of them dug their heels in [chuckles quietly] and were not very forthcoming in respect of wanting to give money for yet another campus, although the expectation was that they would see immediate transformations on the ground in their own countries. So that was a big issue for us. How could we decrease dependence upon government funding and increase our campus income-generating mechanisms as a means of achieving stability?

Over the years that I was there, we managed to increase our income and to decrease our dependence on the subventions that the governments gave. We then reached for the goals that we had set to be totally independent and fully dependent on our income, simply because you don't want to be increasing fees on students to the extent that it hinders them from even applying to you for courses. But we were able to reach a level that decreased that dependence. Our search for funding helped in that regard and I will speak to that a little later.

So these are some of the accomplishments that we actually achieved. With the funding, in order for us to achieve some of the developments in terms of the physical plant – that is, the video conferencing rooms, the online access by students at the sites, the improvement of access to library materials, and the development of additional courses – I had prepared a proposal, which was submitted to CIDA [Canadian International Development Agency] in Canada. I visited several universities and institutions in Canada at the time that I was trying to plan this because it was an unsolicited request, and I was asked to present myself to speak to why we wanted this. It was for a considerable sum. I have to say that we are very grateful to the Canadian government for even listening to us. They liked the ideas that we offered. In 2012, they approved a $20 million Canadian grant, which would help us improve our suite of courses – not just to improve the courses, but to develop many more courses – and to do some of the sorts of improvements that I was talking about moments ago with the types of technologies that would help us to deliver ODL more efficiently.

So the expansion of technological capabilities to reach people in remote regions is one of the things that we hoped that this grant would help us to do, and increasing the number of programmes in the undergraduate fields as well as the access courses, that helped us tremendously. We are grateful that the Canadian government came to our aid and provided these funds.

So the last few years, from 2014 until now, the actual rollout of the funds has been done. A lot of the projects that were earmarked have been undertaken. We are very grateful that this helped establish the Open Campus even further in terms of its goals.

Awards include:
- Award for Outstanding Contribution to Linguistics & Multidisciplinary Education. The University of the West Indies Institute for Gender and Development Studies. February 2019;

- Frank Collymore Literary Award for Collection of Short Fiction, 2018;
- Award for Outstanding Contribution to Education. Global Distance Learning Awards, World Education Congress, Mumbai, India. June 27, 2014;
- Order of the British Empire (OBE) by Her Majesty Queen Elizabeth II at her birthday honours in June 2011, for contribution to education. Investiture November 16, 2011; and
- Honorary Advisor, the Commonwealth of Learning [COL]. 2009–2014.

I: In 2014, you received an award for Outstanding Contribution to Education from the Global Distance Learning Congress. Could you please tell us a bit about this award and why it was given to you?

I don't know why it was given to me – I am speaking on a personal level – I don't know why it was given to me. I was actually very surprised when I received a letter saying that they were giving me an award. It came hard on the heels of having been given an OBE award [Office of the Order of the British Empire] in 2011 by the Queen [of England] for what was said to be a contribution to education. So I suppose that people were hearing about the establishment of the Open Campus, and because I happened to be the principal, they probably figured, "She's the one we should earmark for an award." I don't know that I deserved it any more than any of my other colleagues who were working on the project. We had a dedicated team, and the success of the campus is dependent as much on their efforts and commitment.

When the notice came, it came in the form of a letter I received from Oliver Warren, who was the Chair of the Awards and Academic Committee of the Congress. I just thought that I would quote some of the phrases that he said, and I guess that's their reason for giving it to me. He said, "[My] leadership and contribution to the field of education was well known. In the view of the Congress, [I] occupied the position they considered strategic and iconic." I suppose that was because I was establishing a new campus. They said that they were giving me the award because they considered me "to be a thinker and a doer, as well as a role model and believer in change."

So it was very unexpected. I hadn't thought of myself in those ways, really. I was just doing the work that I was asked to do. For me, giving service is important; I was just doing my job. But they rewarded me for it. I was extremely humbled by it, and I am very honoured, I have to say.

9. *What are some of the challenges that you faced over the years?*

With specific reference to distance education and the formation of the Open Campus, there were several, but I will cite four of the main ones that we faced in the first few years. One was the attempt to reshape the various outreach entities into a campus with a UWI government structure. There was need for innovation; there was need for difference in order to create a structure that would allow for ease of doing business. We encountered some resistance to this because we were asked at the same time, because we were part of the university, to conform to the traditional ways, but that was not going to serve our purposes. So that was one of the challenges that we had to deal with head on. We had to find creative ways to overcome that resistance and to argue for a system that would really position the Open Campus for success and allow it at the same time to participate fully in the work of the university.

Another was trying to obtain acceptance from the brick campuses to present online courses. At the time that the campuses were sending out their courses, there was no system for monitoring what was going on. So one would often find two campuses with online courses out there in the world with the same title, sometimes with different content, and so on. One thing that we thought we would do was to let the Open Campus be the conduit for one-look, one-feel, high-quality course for the university, and then the university could build on that image of having this suite of online, ODL programmes that represented it in its entirety on the campuses. We would work with the campuses to do that. In that respect, there was some resistance.

Trying to agree on a mutual income-sharing agenda also proved to be something of a challenge.

Another was financial and human resource constraints. There were lots of people in the system with UWIDEC before we formed the Open Campus. To have to retrain everybody to really meet the needs for an efficient ODL system, that was tremendous. We needed qualified people. We needed to train people, as I said – facilitators and tutors – academic content was needed. So the human resource constraints, that was one thing. This was costly. We had to have the financial support for it, and since we weren't getting the amount of funding to do it, we really had to find creative ways to meet the targets that we had set.

Managing expectations from governments who expected to see transformations in their local centres almost immediately after the Open Campus was formed was another one. So even though there was an increased quantum of interventions from the governments, we had to make do with the distance education continuing studies from before. But we were creating something new, something exciting, and that needed an infusion of funds to get it going. We weren't getting that increased infusion that we knew we needed, but at the same time, we were getting demands to show what we were producing, so we had to balance that very carefully.

I would say that these were some of the main ones that we faced at the time. There were several other little ones, but those were the big ones that we had to deal with.

10. *What was the "state of DE" when you first entered the field as opposed to DE in 2018?*

As I mentioned earlier, much of the distance education in the university comprised delivery through the UWIDEC system. Since the formation of the Open Campus, the course delivery systems have been considerably enhanced to include video conferencing facilities and other state-of-the-art techniques. So we tried to introduce and establish an efficient ODL system, which I can say has taken off, and that's been doing well. We had a very efficient technology team that helped to find state-of-the-art conferencing tools that we needed for course delivery, as well as communication tools. So we explored things like Blackboard, Collaborate, and Blue-Jeans with Zoom, and others to ensure that we got the best systems for facilitating meetings and for delivering the courses.

In addition to that, because students were all over the Caribbean, we needed a student management system, an Open Campus student management system that would really give us access to all of the information we needed about our students as they came in, as they proceeded through their studies with us, and as they left. This record system had to be efficient and accurate. I have to say that this was another big challenge that I didn't mention before, but trying to get that system to work by actually tapping into the resources that existed in far-flung countries was something that our IT team had to deal with. By the time that I left, they were able to create that OCSM system, which is the Open Campus Student Management system that helped them to keep track of the students coming into the campus. So that was a big thing.

Since then, too, it was a growth thing. Student enrolment has increased consistently over the years, as also have the number of programmes and courses. When we began, we had a handful of undergraduate and post-graduate courses. As the years proceeded, one of the units that we created in our structure was called Academic Programming and Delivery (APAD). It was the business of APAD to drive the delivery process of courses. We focused on getting the qualified people in that particular unit when we started so that they could focus on building the suite of programmes that we offered. That has paid off tremendously. Now the Open Campus offers a much broader suite of programmes and courses than we did in 2007. So that, again, is one of the differences.

And I would say the consistent upgrading of the technologies so that everything is now working in a really seamless, efficient fashion at that level.

All of these things that I mention are positive. There's just one thing – since we have managed to allow the Open Campus to be the conduit through which UWI would produce this suite of courses for the university, I think that there is an experiment to allow campuses to go back to what was before to create their own online courses. So I'm not sure what the effects of that might be, but I'm hoping that it is just an experiment and that the investment in the Open Campus will pay off and that the university will have that broader international and regional image as a top quality ODL provider. We had dubbed it a campus for the times, a campus for the future. I honestly believe still that this is what it could be for our people in the region because we are so spread out over the Atlantic and the Caribbean that the university and its promise of education is one of the things that can unite us and help us to develop as a people. I think the Open Campus has a big role to play in that, and, with its development over the years, it is trying to meet that particular mandate. I am sure that as we go through subsequent years, if it can do that even more efficiently, it will have served its purpose.

11. What interesting memories would you like to share about the beginning of online DE?

Should I say the excitement of planning the structure for the campus, long days and nights of collaboration, consuming coffee, and sitting around the table getting frustrated? All of those things bonded us together as colleagues and helped us to work for a common cause. Hopping to islands to determine the state of play there, going to very remote areas, places that I've never been before in the Caribbean, and looking at the places where the university was trying to reach people. Meeting the people themselves and seeing the need. Those are the things that I remember the most. And the collegial friendships that were formed, working for a common cause, working together, and sitting with people around a table, just brainstorming and working through things: the collegial camaraderie, the friendship, and the respect that emerged from these times. These are the things that have stayed with me: the respect and admiration for my colleagues, who worked extremely hard and who are all deserving of awards, believe me. And the people, the people whom we serve, the places where we serve them, and addressing their needs.

This was an eye-opener. I remember the first time I visited one place. I said, "As soon as we leave here, we are closing this down; we are closing the door." That was one of the first places where we had to open a new centre because it was inconceivable that we could even ask people to attend courses there, to sit around one older television. So these things, I think, are the things that remain with me, that give me hope. It was a good thing to be involved in the formation of ODL, the Open Campus. It may make some little difference. I don't know.

12. What were your specific DE research interests, and have they changed/evolved over the years?

I did not do much research in distance education. I had done a lot of research in my field of specialization, applied linguistics. I like to do empirical research, and I continue to do a lot of research in this field. In just taking on this massive job of trying to form the Open Campus, I could not participate in the kind of empirical research that was required. We had a research and development team that did a lot of the ground research for the campus. But I was asked to give papers and addresses because of the newness of the campus in the Caribbean, I suppose, and I had to write these papers, so I framed what I said based on the information that had been done in the empirical research that existed. I was able to use that to present a narrative about the Open Campus, its objectives, and some of the things that you are asking me about, to share that with groups like the ICDE, on lifelong learning and things like that. So the papers are more like invited addresses dealing with that, but to say that I did empirical research, I can't honestly say that I did that myself, but I did write some papers for the purpose of workshops and conferences where I was asked to speak. I had to rely on the work done by our research team in terms of the figures and numbers that they came up with.

So my research interests still remain quite a lot in the applied field, but I think that there is such an important thing that is possible, because of how we are set up in the region and because of the challenges that children who speak French Creole have, for example, or other language-learning difficulties; it might be that distance education can provide them with an opportunity. Through all of the systems that we have existing now, we can provide innovative ways for language learning that bring them into an exciting environment where they can really interface with native speakers through video conferencing or whatever. The Open Campus can play a role to enhance language-learning capabilities of our people to prepare them for successive education. That's the research project that I would like to work on if I had the chance. That would be the marriage of my former field and distance education in a way that might be beneficial.

13. *Can you suggest names of other female pioneers in distance education or ODL that you think we should include in the book?*

Professor Vivienne Roberts is one that I can think of. Professor Roberts was Deputy Principal when I was Principal. She drove the prior learning assessment aspect so could give you a good perspective on that.

Professor Julie Meeks Gardner was the leader of the Child Development Centre, an integral part of the Open Campus. She is Deputy Principal now. She came up from the formation days, so she would have a really good perspective on that as well.

I can send you their email addresses after. I will probably put in a couple other names and addresses for you when I send the information.

I: We were wondering if you might have any contact details for Vilma McLennan.

Yes, I can send that to you.

I: And Claudia Harvey?

I think Claudia has moved back to Barbados. I can find out for you. I think that I probably have her email; I will look for it and send it to you.

I: Thank you very much.

14. *Is there anything else you [would] like to address?*

Well, I think that the work that I've done . . . well, it was not just me; the importance of collaboration and willingness to collaborate for the success of an idea, an innovation that promised to change in a significant way, the work that we do so that it benefits people. It would be important for us to subdue our own wishes or whatever to ensure that we take the higher ground and perspective that will make it a success for everybody. I don't know how to say this, but it's like collegiality, collaboration, and promise of maintaining a vision, a vision for our people, the place where we live and we work, and the people that we serve so that, in 50 years' time, if we look back, we can say that what we did actually helped to improve our lot as a nation. For me, that's the importance of doing these things.

I'm not really sure why you asked me to do this, really, but thank you.

Publications

Book Chapters

Simmons-McDonald, H. (2019). *Symbols of solidarity and truth? Vernaculars in Literature*. In R. Blake & I. Buchstaller (Eds.), *The Routledge companion to the work of John R. Rickford* (pp. 409–419). Routledge.

Simmons-McDonald, H. (2020). Home language why it matters. In K. Belgrave & J. Jules (Eds.), *Transformative pedagogical perspectives on home language use in classrooms* (pp. 225–246). IGI Global.

Simmons-McDonald, H. (2021). West Indian English: An introduction to literature in selected varieties. In A. Kirkpatrick (Ed.), *The Routledge handbook of world Englishes* (2nd ed., pp. 355–370). Routledge.

Conference Presentations

Simmons-McDonald, H. (1984, May). *Monitoring and evaluating within the teaching system* [Paper presentation]. Consultative Conference on Teacher Education, St. Lucia.

Simmons-McDonald, H. (1992, March). *Comparative patterns in the acquisition of English negation by speakers of St. Lucian French Creole and Creole English* [Paper presentation]. Seminar Series of the Department of Language and Linguistics. University of West Indies, Cave Hill.

Simmons-McDonald, H. (1992, May). *Developing thinking and analytical skills in young children* [Keynote address], OAS Regional Workshop on the preparation of instructional packages for young children, Saint Lucia.

Simmons-McDonald, H. (1992, August). *The acquisition of English negation by native speakers of French Creole* [Paper presentation]. The 9th Biennial Conference of the Society for Caribbean Linguistics, University of West Indies, Cave Hill.

Simmons-McDonald, H. (1993, October 26). *Language and education policy: The place of vernaculars in formal education* [Paper presentation]. Symposium on Creole into the 21st Century, St. Lucia.

Simmons-McDonald, H. (1995, March). *Second/foreign language acquisition: problems encountered by Caribbean learners* [Paper presentation]. Secondary School Teachers of foreign languages at Erdiston College.

Simmons-McDonald, H. (1995, May). *Principles of first and second language acquisition* [Paper presentation]. Foreign Language Teaching Group, Erdiston College.

Simmons-McDonald, H. (1995, June). *Improving teacher competence and learner proficiency in bi-dialectal situations* [Paper presentation]. The OAS Seminar on Teaching English as a Second Language, St. Lucia.

Simmons-McDonald, H. (1995, October). *Standardising the French Creole: Implications for education* [Paper presentation]. Saint Lucian Student Society, University of the West Indies, Cave Hill Campus.

Simmons-McDonald, H. (1996, August). *Theoretical considerations on the relationship between aspects of classroom process and the development of proficiency in English* [Paper presentation]. 11th Biennial Conference of the Society for Caribbean Linguistics, St. Maarten.

Simmons-McDonald, H. (1996, November). *Instructed second language acquisition and learner proficiency in the Caribbean context* [Paper presentation]. Seminar series of the Department of Language, Linguistics and Literature. University of the West Indies, Cave Hill Campus.

Simmons-McDonald, H. (1997, October). *The Place of Creole in the development of Saint Lucia* [Paper presentation]. Conference on Creole and Language Development: Challenges for a New Century, Saint Lucia.

Simmons-McDonald, H. (1998, March). *Language policy in the Caribbean: The challenge of becoming literate* [Paper presentation]. School of Education, Ritter Hall, Temple University.

Simmons-McDonald, H. (1998, December). *Principals as agents for change* [Keynote address]. National Conference of School Principals, Saint Lucia.

Simmons-McDonald, H (1999, February). *The St. Lucian Media as Teacher: Bridging the Gap between the Traditional and the Modern* [Paper presentation]. Conference: Encounters of Excellence, St. Lucia.

Simmons-McDonald, H. (1999, July). *Is English a second language in Barbados?* [Paper presentation]. Frank Collymore Hall Public Lecture Series, Bridgetown.

Simmons-McDonald, H. (1999, August). *Ways of Learning: Language Education and the Vernacular speaker* [Paper presentation]. Colloquium on Language Education – the 13th Biennial conference of the Society for Caribbean Linguistics, Mona, Jamaica.

Simmons-McDonald, H (1999a). *Creolisation, culture and identity* [Paper presentation]. International Conference on Creoles, the Seychelles.

Simmons-McDonald, H. (1999b). *Educational politics and creole education: Issues of knowledge and power* [Public lecture]. The Seychelles.

Simmons-McDonald, H. (2001a). *Addressing imbalances in education: Explorations with a vernacular education model* [Paper presentation]. Islands in Between: Folklore, Literature and Languages of the Eastern Caribbean Conference, St. Lucia.

Simmons-McDonald, H. (2001b). *Cultural preservation and language reclamation: The St. Lucian paradox* [Paper presentation]. (Re)Thinking Caribbean Culture Conference, Cave Hill Campus.

Simmons-McDonald, H. (2001c). *Decolonizing English: The Caribbean counter-thrust* [Keynote address]. The Cultural Politics of English as a World Language Conference, Freiburg University, Germany.

Simmons-McDonald, H. (2001d). *Journeys* [Graduation address]. The Class of 2001 at the Sir Arthur Lewis Community College, Saint Lucia.

Simmons-McDonald, H. (2001e). *Vernacular literacy: Influencing policy through pedagogical experimentation* [Paper presentation]. Conference of the American Association for Applied Linguistics (AAAL), Missouri, USA.

Simmons-McDonald, H. (2002, March). *Vernacular education and the non-native speaker of English: Alternative pathways to literacy* [Paper presentation]. International Conference on Problems and Prospects of Education in Developing Countries, Barbados.

Simmons-McDonald, H. (2002, August). *The effects of vernacular instruction on the development of bi-literacy abilities of native speakers of French Creole* [Paper presentation]. 14th Biennial Conference of The Society for Caribbean Linguistics, University of West Indies, St. Augustine.

Simmons-McDonald, H. (2004a). *Creole influenced vernaculars and literacy* [Paper presentation]. Lucia Studies Conference, St. Lucia.

Simmons-McDonald, H. (2004b). *Evidence of a common cultural heritage in the French Creole proverbs of selected Caribbean territories* [Paper presentation]. Cultural Studies Conference, University of West Indies, St. Augustine.

Simmons-McDonald, H. (2004c). *In support of Afrogenesis: A study of St. Lucian French Creole Proverbs* [Paper presentation]. St. Lucia Studies Conference.

Simmons-McDonald, H. (2004d). *Teacher attitudes to Saint Lucian language varieties* [Paper presentation]. Fifteenth biennial conference of the Society for Caribbean Linguistics, Curacao.

Simmons-McDonald, H. (2005, May). *Using the native language to promote the acquisition of the second language* [Paper presentation]. Mico College Conference on Teacher Education. Jamaica Conference Centre.

Simmons-McDonald, H. (2006, August). *Language instruction and planning for Creole-influenced vernacular speakers – A study of Dominica* [Paper presentation]. 16th Biennial conference of the Society for Caribbean Linguistics, Dominica.

Simmons-McDonald, H. (2007, May). Language, identity and freedom – a creolist perspective [Paper presentation]. *Conference Trajectories of Freedom: Caribbean Societies – Past and Present.* University of West Indies, Cave Hill.

Simmons-McDonald, H. (2008, July). *Revisiting notions of 'deficiency' and 'inadequacy' in Creoles from a vernacular education perspective* [Keynote address]. The Joint Conference of the Society for Caribbean Linguistics and the Society for Pidgin and Creole Languages, Cayenne (French Guiana).

Simmons-McDonald, H. (2008, November). *Education in an innovative society* [Paper presentation]. Canada-Caribbean-Central America Education Partnership Forum, Canadian Bureau for International Education (CBIE), St. John's, Newfoundland, Canada.

Simmons-McDonald, H. (2009, May). *Developments in open and distance learning in the Caribbean: The UWI Initiative* [Paper presentation]. Commonwealth of Learning (COL) Forum: A Decade of Distance Education, Abuja.

Simmons-McDonald, H. (2011). *Creating a framework of strategic partnerships in a distributed environment: A Caribbean perspective.* The ACU Conference of Executive Heads. Hong Kong.

Simmons-McDonald, H. (2011a). *Education for capacity building and regional sustainability* [Public lecture]. Education the Gateway Series, St. Vincent and the Grenadines.

Simmons-McDonald, H. (2011b). *Role of the University of the West Indies in supporting lifelong learning* [Paper presentation]. Eastern Caribbean Governments/UNICEF End Cycle and Multi-Country Programme Action Plan 2012–2016 Meeting – Equity: Ensuring the Rights of All Caribbean Children, Accra Beach Conference Centre.

Simmons-McDonald, H. (2014, June). *Open and distance education: A pathway to the development and prosperity of small states in a dispersed environment.* The World Congress of Distance Education, Mumbai, India.

Simmons-McDonald, H. (2015, March). *Literature, culture and politics of deprivation* [Inaugural lecture]. The Kamau Brathwaite Lecture Series, Cultural Studies & Humanities Festival. University of West Indies, Cave Hill, Barbados.

Simmons-McDonald, H. (2015a). *Language, education and culture in Saint Lucia: Issues of identity* [Lecture]. Saint Lucia Students' Association, University of the West Indies, Saint Lucia.

Simmons-McDonald, H. (2015b). *Language, identity and the politics of cultural erosion.* The 6th Patricia Charles Memorial Lecture, Saint Lucia.

Simmons-McDonald, H. (2015, October). *Language, education and culture: Cultivating Caribbean identities*. The Annual Edward Leblanc Memorial Lecture, Dominica.

Simmons-McDonald, H. (2016, June). *Invited Lectures and Keynote addresses Culture, identity and language: Reclaiming the soul of an Island*. The Harold F. C. Simmons Memorial Lecture, Harold Simmons Folk Academy; Saint Lucia Studies Conference, Saint Lucia.

Simmons-McDonald, H. (2019, November). *Employability and lifelong learning* [Keynote address]. International Council of Distance Education, Standing Conference of Presidents (ICDE/SCOP), Spain.

References

Renwick, W., et al. (1992). *Distance education at the University of the West Indies. Report of an appraisal carried out on behalf of the Commonwealth of Learning Organisation for Economic Co-operation and Development (OECD)* (Report No. ISBN-1-895369-14-2). Commonwealth of Learning. https://files.eric.ed.gov/fulltext/ED364768.pdf

29
SPRONK, BARBARA

Photo of Barbara Spronk contributed by Barbara Spronk

We were really pioneering this whole notion in the very beginnings of Athabasca [University], and as pioneers, we lived under continual threat that this was an experiment, a pilot that might not go anywhere.

Dr. Barbara Spronk received her undergraduate degree and Master of Anthropology from the University of Alberta in Canada. Then she went on to obtain her PhD in Anthropology from the University of Alberta. Her PhD focused on housing condominiums and cooperatives as corporate groups.

During her career, Dr. Spronk held the following positions:

- June 1996–March 2002: Executive Director, International Extension College;
- April 1989–October 1989: Dean, Arts and Sciences (Acting), Athabasca University;

- April 1988–December 1993: Project Manager, CIDA-funded ILP project in Northeast Thailand with Ramkhamhaeng University;
- September 1988–August 1991: Project Manager, University Certificate in Health Development Administration (a collaborative project of Athabasca University and the Yellowhead Tribal Council);
- December 1981–December 1983: Director, Regional and Tutorial Services, Athabasca University, Edmonton, Alberta;
- May 1980–December 1980: Vice-President, Learning Services (Acting), Athabasca University, Edmonton, Alberta; and
- October 1978–April 1980: Head, Social Science, Athabasca University, Edmonton, Alberta.

Dr. Spronk has received many awards throughout her career, with the most recent being Honorary Life Member, Canadian Association of Distance Education, 2003. Her research interests include gender issues in distance education, and the use of new media and technologies for flexible learning. References included at the end of this chapter reflect these research interests.

Interview

Transcript Analysis Summary

Analysis of all interviews included in this volume led to the identification of 3,545 units of data. The mean of these collective units was 118 per pioneer, the median was 118.5, and the mode was 132. Individual interview units ranged from 59 to 217 units, yielding a spread of 158 units among all interviews. Barbara Spronk's interview generated 114 units, which was marginally less than the mean and median statistics for all interviews.

A comparison of Spronk's interview to the interviews of all pioneers indicates that, generally speaking, her conversations produced a unique number of units in over half the identified thematic areas in relation to the average interview (Figure 29.1). Perhaps some explanation for Spronk's

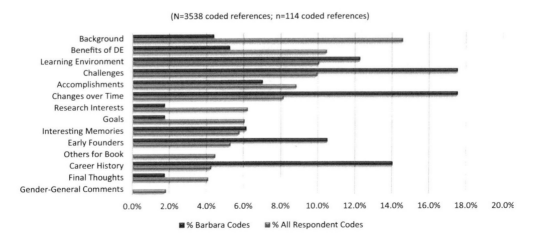

Figure 29.1 All Respondents' Versus Barbara Spronk's Parent Codes

unique interview profile comes from the myriad of founding intiatives that she was involved in during the span of her career. For instance, she played an integral role in developing the fledgling Athabasca University and some of its largest programmes, as well as its student service offerings. She also engaged in other groundbreaking initiatives in Mozembique and Sri Lanke. Another reason for her unique profile could be the sheer expanse of her career. She began working in the field at a time when DE was only delivered by snail mail correspondence. Significant challenges that she discussed during this time included lack of acceptance and understanding of DE, nonexistent student support services, and gender ratio disparities between face-to-face and DE learning environments. Spronk navigated numerous eras of emerging pedagogies and technologies in the field throughout her career in a breadth of learning environments, ending her career by tutoring 173 students online at a dual-mode institution in Guelph, Ontario.

Link to recorded interview: tinyurl.com/Spronk-B

Transcript of Interview

Full Name: Barbara Spronk
Institutional Affiliation: Retired Adjunct Professor, Athabasca University
Key:

Regular font = Interviewee comments
Italicized font = Interviewer comments

Interview Questions

1. *What was your educational and experiential background before you became involved in distance education [DE]?*

I had a Bachelor's and a Master's Degree in Anthropology from the University of Alberta. The Master's was awarded in Spring 1971, and at that point I registered as a PhD candidate, also at the University of Alberta. I had taught a couple of courses in anthropology as a graduate student. By the time that I had heard about distance education, I had had my first and second children, who were at the time 15 months and six weeks of age. No awareness of distance education whatsoever.

2. *In what year did you begin to look specifically into DE? What were the circumstances in your world that initiated this interest in DE?*

It was at the very beginning of 1975. My second child was six weeks old, and I received [a] phone call from a former colleague from graduate school who was leaving for a job at Memorial in Newfoundland and who wondered if I would be able to finish the job he had started at the newly fledged Athabasca University, where he was in charge of completing the foundation course in social science. I knew only as much about Athabasca University as I had read in the local paper. It looked interesting, but I knew nothing. There I was, nursing a six-week-old baby, and I said, "Dennis, you've got to be kidding!"

He said, "No, no, no. This is something that you can do mostly at home."

So I did take on the job of completing that first foundation course in social sciences for Athabasca. The university itself was only about three years old; it was still a pilot project. It didn't become a fully-fledged chartered university until, I think, 1978. Those were very early days.

Shortly after that, I also became one of Athabasca's first telephone tutors. Students weren't completing their courses (there were only three courses at the time). Student were registering but not getting anywhere, so the university implemented a system of telephone tutors; I was one of the first of those.

I then took on the job as Coordinator for the social science courses overall. We started developing a considerable number of additional courses in social sciences, and by 1978, I was a full-time faculty member in anthropology (and a full-time mom – my children were four, three, and two!). Then, in the spring of 1979, I became acting Vice President Academic for close to a year. The university had just been told it was to be moved to the town of Athabasca from the city of Edmonton. Things were in considerable disarray – the Vice President Academic had left for Concordia University, the President had resigned in high dudgeon over the government's actions, the VP Admin was made Commissioner for the move to Athabasca, and we were left with no executive officers. So there I was, only three years and a bit into my time with Athabasca, and I was acting VP Academic. It was a baptism of fire.

After that, in 1981, I was given a year of leave to complete my PhD and came back to the university in 1982 as Director of Regional and Tutorial Services. This was a fascinating job because we were charged not only with the oversight of the telephone tutors, but also setting up regional offices in Edmonton, Calgary, and Fort McMurray. Given the impending move to Athabasca, we realized that we were going to have to have these satellite operations, and I was in charge of setting those up. I was also at the time in charge of our collaborative programming with First Nations Tribal Councils in and around Edmonton, which enabled me to put my anthropological training to good use.

In 1984, with the move of the University to Athabasca, I returned full-time to the faculty as a professor of anthropology. During my time as a faculty member, I was President of the Faculty Association for a couple of terms.

In the 1980s, I became Director of Athabasca's first international project in Thailand. This was a CIDA-funded partnership project. (CIDA was then the Canadian International Development Agency, under the auspices of the federal government.) I continued work on supporting our First Nations programming. I was also becoming interested in distance education at large. I did a study tour in the UK, taking a look at the operations of the Open University there and, in particular, at how they managed their regional and student support services.

In the 1990s, I was on a partial secondment to the University of Calgary as a distance education advisor on their CIDA-funded Tier One project, which was a five-year project to develop a

Centre of Excellence in Participatory Development at the University of Calgary. In addition, I was becoming very involved on the board of the Canadian Association for Distance Education [CADE], where I served a term as President, and also with the International Council in Distance Education [ICDE] and the Women's International Network [WIN].

In 1996, I left Athabasca University to move to Cambridge in the UK, where I took on the job as Executive Director of the International Extension College. This was an organization that I had become aware of during my study tour in the UK. It was an NGO [non-governmental organization] devoted to the promotion of distance education and other innovative approaches to education in low-income countries of the global South. This job took me around the world, literally, to a number of countries (around 20 in total) where distance education was definitely a factor in developing the post-secondary education system. I couldn't have asked for a better opportunity to apply my background in anthropology, my passion for distance education and its possibilities, and also my consuming interest in distance education in contexts other than our own. It was a fabulous experience.

I left Cambridge in 2002 for Gabriola Island in BC, where I continued as a tutor in the MDE [Masters in Distance Education] at Athabasca. In 2004, under the auspices of the Commonwealth of Learning in Vancouver, I spent four months on a project in Mozambique that was training people from all over the country and a variety of agencies and institutions in how they could apply distance education techniques and processes to their own training initiatives.

In early 2005, I spent five months on a project in Sri Lanka that was under the auspices of the Association of Community Colleges in Canada. This project focused on developing a network for e-learning in Sri Lanka, quite a challenge in a country that was just recovering from the tsunami of December 26, 2004.

I came back to Canada, this time to Waterloo, Ontario, and in 2006, [I] took on a couple of courses tutoring online for the University of Guelph. This gave me some experience in a dual-mode setting, where so many of my CADE colleagues had been working.

So that was the story of my life in distance education up to about 2007. After that point, I spent about another five years tutoring online for Athabasca's Masters in Distance Education degree and also writing a course on approaches to international development for the Master of Arts Integrated Studies at Athabasca. My time at Athabasca formally ended in around 2012, and since then, I have been only an interested bystander.

3. Which female researchers or female colleagues may have piqued your interest in DE?

Since my attraction to distance education was more or less accidental – I really just fell into it – I think that I can answer that question best by just naming some of the women at Athabasca who were instrumental in helping to form my understanding of what was involved in distance education and how best to proceed. There was Dr. Gail Crawford, who was one of the first instructional designers at Athabasca. She taught me a great deal about instructional design and the needs of distance education students for clarity and consistency in educational materials design. Dr. Arlene Young was the first counsellor at Athabasca University. She taught me a great deal about the emotional needs of distance education learners. Carroll Klein was one of the first editors at Athabasca University, and she basically taught me how to write distance education materials for distance students. So I would really credit those three women for teaching me about what was involved in creating distance education materials and supporting distance education learners.

Once I got involved with the Canadian Association of Distance Education, and especially the International Council for Distance Education, I became exposed to some fabulous women who were, I'd say, a continuing source of inspiration. One of them was Ros Morpeth, who is still the Executive Director of the National Extension College in Cambridge in the UK, and Margaret Haughey, who was then at the University of Alberta and later spent a term as Vice President Academic at Athabasca. France Henri and Thérèse Lamy from TÉLUQ University I remember as being particularly provocative in their thinking about distance education. As Francophone educators, they had a different take on distance education than we did as Anglophones, and we had many fascinating and very challenging discussions.

And I can't resist mentioning another "woman," or at least character, with whom I became very involved as a distance educator. In 1982, Athabasca was a very tense and anxious place; staff at all levels were trying to come to terms with what a move to Athabasca would mean for them and their careers. Our Vice President Academic at the time, Dr. Ross Paul, a gifted and very funny guy, was doing his best to support us in this trying time, and for the post-convocation reception that year, he wrote and directed a musical revue spoofing distance education. An example of his deathless lines: "In distance education, it is so very rare/That you ever see a student, you wonder if they're there." Among the characters was a dyed-in-the-wool, curmudgeonly academic named Dr. Iva E. Tower, very old school, death on distance education. I took on that role. We performed the revue for both the local and then an international audience at the ICDE conference in Vancouver later that June, and after that, Dr. Tower took on a life of her own. Arrayed in her academic robes (mine), closed at the front with diaper pins, wearing a fright wig, spectacles held together with tape, ratty sneakers, and drooping socks and snorting into a grubby (former) diaper, she appeared at tutor conferences, the burial of the AU time capsule, at least one CADE conference, and, in her swan song, at an international conference on learner support in Cambridge. She had one rule: She would not agree to appear unless Ross Paul was in the audience. Just to make sure he continued to be held responsible for this horrible creation, I think! We needed a sense of humour to survive in distance education.

So that's a brief list; I could go on and on. I met so many really wonderful women in distance education through my work at Athabasca and nationally and internationally. It could be a very long list.

4. *Who would you identify as the early female leaders/founders in the field of DE?*

This is going back to my national and international experience. The women in the UK to whom I credit the beginnings of serious distance education in an institutional context were first, a woman named Jenny Lee, who was an MP in the Labour Government in the UK at the time of the founding of the Open University. She was instrumental in getting the Open University going in the UK – actually pushed it through, a very challenging job.

Shortly after I met her, Ros Morpeth became the Executive Director of the National Extension College, which was set up around the same time as the Open University in the UK and did a very similar job, on a much smaller scale and without government funding, in the college sector in the UK.

I would again mention France Henri and Thérèse Lamy at the TÉLUQ University in Canada as being instrumental in the beginning [of] distance education in the Francophone world in Canada. Those are the ones that come to mind.

5. *What are some of the goals that you strove to achieve in the field of DE?*

When I ponder this question, the first answer that comes to mind is "survival." We were really pioneering this whole notion in the very beginnings of Athabasca [University], and as pioneers, we lived under continual threat that this was an experiment, a pilot that might not go anywhere. So we were really making it up as we went along. We didn't have much in the way of models to follow. There was, of course, the Open University in the UK, but they were operating in a much different context on a national level with enormous funding, whereas we were operating with provincial funding, reaching out nationwide but certainly on a much more restricted scale than the Open University. With the challenges we were facing, we really felt like experimenters. So I would put survival as my first goal. We ended up not only surviving, but thriving.

I think overall what attracted me to distance education and fostered my passion for distance education was that, at least in its early days, it appeared to be striving to democratize post-secondary education. We really were working to make post-secondary education available for anyone who wanted to take it up, regardless of their educational background, regardless of where they lived, regardless of their circumstances and experiences. This was an opportunity I would not have had anywhere other than Athabasca. I certainly wouldn't have had the opportunity to work, for example, with First Nations communities, which is a challenge we took up at Athabasca as early as 1976, before we were even a full-fledged chartered university. The reason we could work as an institution with First Nations learners is that we were open; that is, we required no prior educational credentials. So it was not only distance education that attracted me, but the openness that distance education offered and made possible.

6. *What are some of your accomplishments in the field of DE that you would like to share?*

Through my work, both nationally and internationally, I helped promote Athabasca University's presence on the national and international scene through the Canadian Association for Distance Education and through the International Council for Distance Education. We were certainly pioneers in the field but still had a great deal to learn from the colleagues that followed us into distance education, especially those who are doing it on a dual-mode basis rather than the single-mode distance education model that Athabasca University was developing.

Another thing that I would list as an accomplishment was my promotion of the centrality of student support systems to distance education. It became clear to me very early on that without meaningful, consistent, and systematic student support processes – the human connection – students were going to fall like flies. That has continued to be the case from everything that I've been reading. People in various generations of distance education and online learning that have followed us in the field have kept rediscovering this. "Whoa! If they don't have student support, they're not going to complete! Got it!"

I also found it very satisfying to introduce my Canadian students to international perspectives on distance education, gender perspectives on distance education, and especially the cultural aspects of distance education and its implications for various aspects of distance education operations and institutionalization.

I was also able to make contributions to education projects in a large number of countries of the global South. The ones that come most immediately to mind, where I worked most intensively, are Guyana, Bangladesh, Sudan, Mozambique, and Thailand.

7. *What are some of the challenges that you faced in the field of DE over the years?*

In the very beginning, the biggest challenge was to explain distance education to mainstream practitioners. Our colleagues in mainstream universities found us puzzling. The whole terminology of distance education, the fact that we were not only doing all our work at a distance with students, but were also an open institution, was a combination they had never encountered before. It was one of our very early challenges as pioneers in the field.

Another challenge was to convince colleagues and students to take gender equity seriously. Women comprised probably two-thirds of our students, even in the early days at Athabasca University, but we weren't necessarily taking this into account, especially the fact that women tended to be mothers of often-young children, with limited mobility and very limited time. We had so many graduates who would tell us of their study hours being restricted to the hours after their children went to bed that our degrees became known as "midnight hour degrees" because that is when these women had the time to study. It really became a passion for me to research and to develop the factoring of gender and gender equity into our operations at all levels.

A further challenge was to open the minds of our students, especially to other and often competing perspectives on the material they were studying. I did this certainly as an anthropologist, but also as my experience with education in other contexts developed, including First Nations contexts.

Then, in my work internationally, one of my big challenges was to avoid what I came to call the "template trap." Many of my colleagues, as I did, were working at well-funded, single-mode institutions, and we came equipped with a definite mindset on how distance education institutions both do and should operate. This was a real limitation, I think, because only a few countries in the world – not even ours – can launch distance education on a national scale with the kind of funding that was at that time available to the Open University in the UK, for example. The OU was really the five-star hotel model of distance education in the world, and theirs was not a model that could be adapted very readily or appropriately to countries in the global South. The funding just wasn't there. These models were not sustainable. My biggest challenge became to push sustainability and adaptability. I'm not convinced that I really succeeded in this, but it was certainly a continuing challenge and passion.

8. *What was the "state of DE" when you first entered the field as opposed to DE in 2018?*

Distance education, as it operated in 1975, would look pretty primitive now. It was paper-based. Our contact with students was primarily by telephone. We did use media, but our media were television and radio. We also found the need in certain circumstances, especially in First Nations communities, to supplement that with face-to-face meetings.

Comparing that to what's available now, with this massive array of communication technologies and social media, it's like another universe. Everything now is electronic and digital, pretty much technology-driven. Even in the global South, things have changed incredibly since my work in these countries. A lot of support is offered by cell phones. Solar power, for example, enables much greater connectivity electronically than conventional sources of power did when I was working on these projects.

And, overall, I think there has been a movement from what we came to call the industrial model of distance education, which we practiced at Athabasca, to the more artisanal approach more characteristic of the instructor or professor in the classroom with a particular cohort of students. In the early days of electronic delivery, it struck me that we had moved very much to an artisanal model where a professor could correct and change as he or she went along, which was something that just wasn't possible in the more industrial or "Fordist" approach that we had been using at Athabasca.

I have been able to follow to some extent the waxing and waning of the massive open online course phenomena: the extent to which distance education on a mass basis has been developed by business-oriented and profit-oriented institutions, very much moving away, I think, from the initial vision that we had as pioneers at Athabasca. We certainly weren't doing it for a profit. We were doing it to open educational opportunities to students, and not just open these opportunities, but give students as great a prospect for completion and satisfaction as possible. This, as I said earlier, has had to be rediscovered by the folks that were behind the development of these massive open online courses. They, too, realized that students were taking them up in huge numbers, but they were getting completion rates of something like 3 and 5%. Without student support of the systematic nature, students weren't going to finish. But learner support costs money, and in the increasingly corporatized and profit-driven world of online learning, this is problematic, to say the least.

So, again, what has really struck me is that continuing rediscovery and reinvention of student support systems, regardless of the mode of delivery that is involved.

9. *What interesting memories would you like to share about the beginning of online DE?*

At Athabasca in the very early 90s, a couple of faculty members presented a seminar on something called Mosaic, which was a predecessor of the World Wide Web. We took a look at this and thought, "That's interesting; we can see maybe using it for research, but what real application or possibilities would it have for our students apart from its research prospects?"

Well, very quickly some faculty members at Athabasca took this whole thing on board and developed our Masters of Distance Education, which I think was one of the first graduate degrees ever offered in an online context. The challenges of developing that were considerable, first of all internally, because faculty members were suspicious of this model, and secondly, externally, persuading an eventual student population that they could complete a graduate degree entirely online without ever meeting face-to-face, except at convocation.

We felt like pioneers. Those were heady days of challenging discussions and downright fights at the faculty level at Athabasca over whether we were going to be able to attract sufficient numbers of students. Hah! Not a problem. It was, I think, 1995 when we first offered the Master's in Distance Education degree, but my memory is a bit hazy on that.

10. *What were your specific DE research interests, and have they changed/evolved over the years?*

I'm sure that they evolved to some extent, but I had a continuing passion for cultural perspectives in distance education. That came both, as I mentioned earlier, from my background as an anthropologist and as a practitioner of distance education on the national and international scene.

Some of my first publications with a distance education focus were on First Nations' distance education and the impact of First Nations' cultures on the whole process of teaching and learning. That eventually developed into a much broader concern with the culture-bound nature of teaching and learning in countries of the global South, and certainly my concern with culture-bound teaching and learning on how it impacts distance education on every level and in every aspect, from planning and development through delivery, evaluation, and graduation.

11. *Could you please describe the learning environment that you most recently worked in (e.g., geographic and institutional setting, student demographics)?*

I guess my most recent experience would be in Mozambique and Sri Lanka. Both of these were very challenging environments because, in Mozambique, we were working with trainees who, if they had English at all, it would have been their fourth or fifth language. Since Portuguese is the official language in Mozambique, we were working through interpreters in that language in doing our work.

In Sri Lanka we were working in 2005 immediately following the devastation of the tsunami. So we were working in an environment in which the development of online learning seemed to be, even to us, considerably down the list of priorities. The challenge was to see if we couldn't adapt the vision of the project to become something more realistic for the needs of Sri Lanka. I'm not convinced we succeeded.

When I got back to Canada from those projects, I was offered an opportunity to tutor online for the University of Guelph. That was, again, another context for me because I had never tutored online in a dual-mode setting. It was both fascinating and quite shocking because I had 173 students in my class. During my time at Athabasca University, we had never had cohorts of more than 30 students for any given tutor. Our contracts were written in such a way that no tutor was responsible for more than 30 students at a time. So, there I was, responsible for 173 students, with the assistance of a part-time TA. It was a shock, to put it mildly. The distance education unit organized computer conferences in such a way that students could at least talk to each other in small groups; they didn't have much opportunity to talk to me except through email, but we did give them as many opportunities as we could so that they could at least talk to each other and to work in groups to some extent. That was a challenge of a whole other kind! I left after a couple of years, not entirely convinced that it was actually working.

12. *Is there anything else you [would] like to address?*

Just to say that I feel a pioneer, and I'm both fascinated and somewhat terrified by the extent to which anyone working in the field now has to be creatively okay with the technologies and with social media. I would feel totally out of my depth to try to develop an online course now, given the wealth of platforms that are available, the extent to which I would feel required to include in my course development and delivery various aspects of social media and even gaming – especially with the cohort of students that might include Gen Xers [Generation X] and millennials who are using technology so much more as part of their daily lives than I am, certainly. I experienced this with the undergraduates at Guelph. When I asked them if they missed face-to-face contact, especially since the course was part of a communications credential, they said, "No. No, we don't miss face-to-face communication at all because we are communicating with each other mostly through social media."

So, I thought, "Okay, Barbara, this is when you officially begin to feel old."

Things have moved on, and I'm now watching all of this as an interested spectator, but [I] am certainly no longer a participant.

13. *Can you suggest names of other female pioneers in DE or online learning that you think we should include in the book?*

I was trying to think of the people who might still be available. So many of the people that I've worked with have either passed away or just disappeared.

Ros Morpeth, if you don't have her on your list. She is still the Executive Director at the National Extension College. She left the National Extension College for a time when it was taken over by a private, for-profit business, but that was a failing enterprise. Ros ended up once again resuscitating the National Extension College as a very viable, not-for-profit college. So I would certainly urge you to get in touch with her.

Margaret Haughey, of course, who I think is still in Alberta, although I'm not sure about that.

I think France Henri and Thérèse Lamy from the TÉLUQ University are retired but are probably still available, at least electronically. They were both Francophone pioneers in the Quebec context.

Those are the ones that come immediately to mind.

Publications

Books

Spronk, B., (1992). *Distance education: Practices and potential*. University of Waterloo, Cultural Management Centre, Cultural Leadership Development Project.

Spronk, B., Anderson, L., Thomas, E., Amsterdam, G., Glasgow, F., Henry, P., & Kartick-Lewis, S. (2002). *A gender and ICTs: Listen to the learners*. University of Guyana.

Spronk, B., & Assheton-Smith, M. (Eds.). (1993). *Women and social location: Our lives, our research/Nos vies, nos recherches: Reflet de notre societe*. Ragweed Press/Gynergy Books.

Spronk, B., Carunungan, M., Alisara Chuchat, & K. F., Kurtz, S. (1997a). *Reflections on participatory education in cross-cultural settings*. Division of International Development, University of Calgary.

Spronk, B., Roberts, J., & Brindley, J. (1998). *Learner's guide to the information highway*. McGraw-Hill/Chenelière.

Book Chapters

Spronk, B. (1988). Management by democracy vs. democracy by management: A housing co-operative and condominium compared. In J. Andre & D. Laycock, (Eds.), *The theory and practice of co-operative property* (pp. 131–144). Centre for Cooperative Studies, University of Saskatchewan.

Spronk, B. (1992). Wearing the WID label: A case study of unease. In P. J. Van Esterik (Eds.), *Gender and development in Southeast Asia*. Canadian Asian Studies Association.

Spronk, B. (1995). Appropriating learning technologies: Aboriginal learners, needs and practices. In J. Roberts & E. Keough (Eds.) *Why the information highway? Lessons from open and distance learning*. Trifolium Books Inc.

Spronk, B. (1998). Seeing the world through two pairs of eyes: Staff development issues in distance and open learning programmes for First Nations Peoples in Canada. In C. Latchem & F. Lockwood (Eds.), *Staff development in open and flexible learning*. Routledge.

Spronk, B. (2001a). Leadership beyond the mainstream. In D. Hanna & C. Latchem (Eds.), *Leadership in distance education*. Kogan Page.

Spronk, B. (2001b). Naming the issues in developing countries. In L. Burge & M. Haughey (Eds.). *Using learning technologies: International perspectives on practice*. Routledge.

Spronk, B. (2003). Open classrooms and globalisation: Connections and reflections. In J. Bradley (Ed.), *The open classroom: Distance learning in schools*. Kogan Page.

Spronk, B. (2004). Addressing cultural diversity through learner support. In J. Brindley, C. Walti, & O. Zawacki-Richter (Eds.), *Learner support in open, distance and online learning environments* (pp. 169–178). Bibliotheks- und Information system der Universität Oldenburg.

Spronk, B. (2007a). Critical issues: Naming the issues. *International Handbook of Distance Education*. Elsevier.

Spronk, B. (2007b). Culture, technology and making choices. In E. J. Burge (Ed.), *Flexible higher education: Reflections from expert experience* (pp. 141–148). Open University Press/McGraw-Hill.

Spronk, B., Anderson, L., Bradley, J., & C. Yates (2000). Basic education audiences. *Basic education at a distance*. Routledge.

Spronk, B., & Radtke, D. (1987). Distance education for native women. In K. Storrie, (Ed.), *Women, isolation and bonding: Readings in the ecology of gender*. Methuen/Garamond.

Spronk, B., & Radtke, D. (1988). Problems and possibilities: Canadian Native Women in distance education. In Karlene Faith (Ed.), *Toward new horizons for women in distance education: International perspectives*. Routledge.

Journal Articles

Spronk, B. (1969). Being and nothingness in anthropology. *Western Canadian Journal of Anthropology*, 1(3).

Spronk, B. (1973). Fieldwork symposium (Ed.). *Special issue of Western Canadian Journal of Anthropology*, 3(3).

Spronk, B. (1975). The real estate agent as middleman: The larger picture. *Western Canadian Journal of Anthropology*, 4(4), 53–55.

Spronk, B. (1981). Condominiums, cooperatives, and the home ownership dream. *Canadian Journal of Anthropology*, 2(2).

Spronk, B. (1994). Distance education for participatory development: A case study. *Canadian Journal of University Continuing Education*, 20(2).

Spronk, B. (1999). Dialogue: Nonformal education at a distance: A framework for discussion. *Caribbean Journal of Education*, 3(2), 172–179. https://www.mona.uwi.edu/soe/publications/jedic/article/604

30
VON PRÜMMER, CHRISTINE

Photo of Christine von Prümmer contributed by Christine von Prümmer

When I first worked at the FernUniversität, there were only male professors, not one woman.

Dr. Christine von Prümmer received her undergraduate degree in Sociology from Smith College in the USA. Then she went on to study at the University of Constance in Germany, where she obtained her Master of Sociology and Political Science. Her PhD focused on the sociological contexts of the educationally disadvantaged.

During her studies at Konstanz University, Christine participated in research in access to tertiary education and the socialization processes of university students from various academic disciplines.

This grounding in empirical research piqued her interest in pursuing further research in these vital areas of educational developments. She went on to Stuttgart as a sociological project leader of the government-funded study of the educational backgrounds of former students of Rudolf-Steiner Schools from 1974 to 1977. Her time in Stuttgart coincided with the 1970s second wave of feminism and contributed to the Women's Aid Movement in Germany. She became involved in the establishment of a refuge for battered women in Stuttgart and, on completion of the Steiner School project, Christine accepted a temporary research position in a Sheffield-based project that focused on the housing needs of battered women, which was funded by the Department of Environment and driven by the National Women's Aid Foundation.

She held the position of Institutional Researcher at the German FernUniversität, a single-mode distance teaching university from 1978 until her retirement. Her research has spanned a wide range of issues, such as access and exclusion, choice of studies, use of technologies, learning preferences, and the evaluation of courses and curricula. Since the early 1980s, her research and writing have focused on gender in distance education and gender issues in virtual, open, and distance learning environments.

Interview

Transcript Analysis Summary

Analysis of all interviews included in this volume led to the identification of 3,545 units of data. The mean of these collective units was 118 per pioneer, the median was 118.5, and the mode was 132. Individual interview units ranged from 59 to 217 units, yielding a spread of 158 units among all interviews. Christine von Prümmer's interview generated 107 units, ranking her interview moderately below the mean and median number of interview units.

A comparision of von Prümmer's interview to the average interview indicates a similar number of units were generated by both in four areas: benefits of DE, learning environment, goals, and interesting memories (Figure 30.1). What is interesting to note, however, is that while von Prümmer's interview yielded a similar number of units to the average interview when discussing the benefits of

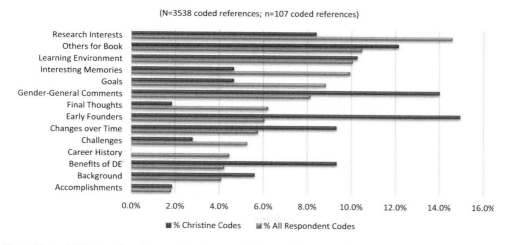

Figure 30.1 All Respondents' Versus Christine von Prümmer's Parent Codes

DE, her interview did not produce anywhere near the number of units as the average one did in the area of challenges. The reason for this is not known.

Christine von Prümmer's interview generated far more units than most other interviews in discussions on early female founders, others for the book, and general gender-related comments. These units can be explained by her early international experiences with colleagues, which led to her devotion to other pioneering female colleagues, as well as some of her research endeavours. It is understandable that her interview would produce more research interest units than the average interview, as she was employed as a researcher.

Dr. von Prümmer did not discuss many challenges, accomplishments, or final thoughts during the interview. The primary challenges that she identified were the lack of female administrators and colleagues at her university, as well as the under-representation of women in international DE organizational leadership positions and conference presentations. The potential reason for mentioning so few accomplishments could be related to cultural mores that discourage women from promoting themselves, a topic that is discussed at more length in Part Two of this volume.

Link to recorded interview: tinyurl.com/Prummer-C

Transcript of Interview

Full name: Dr. Christine von Prümmer
Institutional Affiliation: FernUniversität in Hagen, Germany (FeU; single-mode DE institution, 1978–2011)
Key:

Regular font = Interviewee comments
Italicized font = Interviewer comments

Interview Questions

1. *What was your educational and experiential background before you became involved in distance education [DE]?*

   I completed my secondary schooling in 1966 with the German *Abitur*, the equivalent of British A-Levels or American high school diploma, but also entitled me to enter a German University. Instead, I went to the United States on a full scholarship awarded to me by Smith College, a renowned women's college and one of the Seven Sisters. I majored in sociology and graduated with honours in 1969.

Returning to Germany, I enrolled in a four-year master's programme at the newly established University of Constance, where I could get at least some credit for courses taken toward my American degree. In those days, bachelor degrees were not known in Germany, and it took me until 1973 to do the requisite number of courses and complete my MA in Sociology and Political Science. I stayed on as a post-graduate student and research assistant. In 1974, I moved to Stuttgart as sociological project leader in a three-year empirical study on the educational biographies of former students of Rudolf-Steiner Schools. In 1978, I spent six months in Sheffield, England, carrying out the pilot phase of a research project into the housing needs of battered women.

2. *In what year did you begin to look specifically into DE?*

In 1978.

3. *What were the circumstances in your world that initiated this interest in DE?*

Actually, I had come into contact with distance education when my older brother took an engineering course with a private correspondence college. But that was while I was still at school. I also knew about the University of Maryland's courses for American soldiers and their dependents, who were stationed in my hometown Schweinfurt and got an education via correspondence courses. So I was very interested when one of my Stuttgart colleagues got a job as institutional researcher at the FernUniversität [FeU] in Hagen. It still seems like a fortunate coincidence that there was a job opening in her unit just as I was winding up my involvement in the Sheffield project. I did get the job and entered FeU in October 1978, where I worked as institutional researcher and evaluator until I reached the [compulsory] retirement age of 65 in June 2011.

4. *Which female researchers or female colleagues may have piqued your interest in DE?*

In the beginning I was mainly interested in the possibilities of redressing educational disadvantages through distance education and, of course, fascinated by the professional challenges and technological developments of the job. Gradually, I began to be concerned with the situation of women in distance education, specifically women academics like me who were grossly under-represented at FeU and, indeed, at other universities. Also, the question of sexist, non-inclusive language became increasingly important. With respect to distance education, women colleagues became important when I became engaged in international activities.

It wasn't so much my interest in distance education in general that was piqued by women colleagues, but my beginning to focus on gender issues in distance education. The main trigger to that was a four-month exchange stay at Athabasca University in 1983, when the AU was still in Edmonton. I met a lot of wonderful people there, and women who were feminists and active, introduced me to all sorts of things that I found very exciting. My "exchange partner" was Reinhild Rodrigues, at the time responsible for regional activities. Through her, I got to visit various regional centres and enjoyed a great two-week stay at the Blue Quills First Nations College near St. Paul, Alberta.

I found out that at the time about two-thirds of the students at Athabasca were women. People would ask me, "What is the percentage of women at your university?" I didn't know. When I found out it was 17%, I was very put out and started asking, "Why is there 17%, and what makes this difference in percentages?" And that was what got me started on doing this research, which for 30 years kept me busy on gender issues in distance education and virtual and e-learning. That was basically the event that got me started.

In Edmonton, I met women who were active in WIN, the Women's International Network. At the time, the colleagues that I worked with, whom you probably know at least by name, were Barbara Spronk, Gail Crawford, Jane Brindley, and Christine Nelson.

I: Is the Women's International Network still in operation today?

Unfortunately not; the origin of the Women's International Network was the ICDE conference in Vancouver [BC, Canada] in 1982, where the women who attended the conference became increasingly fed up and quite annoyed with the fact that the majority of people working and studying in distance education were women, but on the podiums and in the positions in this international organization, it was all men. So, they started the Women's International Network in 1985, creating an acronym – WIN – which is in itself a statement. WIN was "launched" at the next ICDE World Conference in Melbourne [Australia]. It had a big presence of women, and had special sessions and a keynote session that women designed and carried out and so on. That was basically the beginning of the network. From then on, women colleagues were represented on the board of ICDE [The International Council for Distance Education], which also provided money and support to WIN activities and networking.

So that was quite a powerful thing, supported by a lot of men, too, but basically the initiative of women. For me, it was very important to be part of the WIN network. The first product of the network was this Karlene Faith book, *Toward New Horizons for Women in Distance Education: International Perspectives*. That was the first time that an international cooperation happened with women, I guess, from all continents contributing to this book. It was really very, very important, and it was presented to the distance education world at the ICDE World Conference in 1988 in Oslo. The Oslo conference was an important milestone for WIN, and thanks to the Programme Chair David Sewart, women were more fairly represented in keynotes and sessions.

In the 1980s and 1990s, WIN was a strong presence at international conferences: namely, ICDE World Conferences, the annual conferences of the Canadian Association of Distance Education [CADE], and the Cambridge Conferences organized bi-annually by the OU UK's Alan Tait and Roger Mills. In 1993, Swedish colleagues organized an international WIN conference in Umeå, Sweden, on the theme of *Feminist Pedagogy and Women-Friendly Perspectives in Distance Education*. I was fortunate to be involved in these international activities, visit DE colleges and universities in other countries, and attend many of these conferences where I presented findings from our own research and could connect with, and learn from, colleagues in other countries.

5. *Who would you identify as the early female leaders/founders in the field of distance learning?*

Now, that is a question of whether you want names as far back as Naomi Mackintosh, for instance, or Judith A. Calder and Betty Swift of the OU UK, whose book *A Degree of Difference* was published in 1977. But people that I have actually met and remember from the time would be ... I am sure that there are more than just the ones who come instantly to mind. In Canada, it would again be Barbara Spronk, Gail Crawford, Jane Brindley; all of these were at AU [Athabasca University] at the time. And Liz Burge, who was in Toronto at that time and later in Fredericton; she's gone back to Australia since then.

In England, I would name Gill Kirkup of the OU UK because Gill Kirkup did a parallel study to my own project on the situation of women and men in distance education, and we collaborated closely for a long time. She has been working on gender issues for as long as I have known her. I think that she is now retired, too, but she was very active in the English network and internationally. Gill is an expert on gender issues and technology, and we did things together on women and e-learning, etc. She's a prolific writer. Other names that come to mind are Helen Lentell, Liz Manning (both OU UK), and Ros Morpeth of the National Extension College.

I can think of three names in Germany. One is myself, of course.

Gisela Pravda, who worked at a government institute [BIBB] and was responsible for approving and accrediting courses for vocational distance education courses, I think it was. She was very much interested in language issues because, with respect to gender inclusivity, German is a lot more difficult than English to get gender-inclusive language. Gisela spent years in Latin America – I think Colombia – and even managed to introduce gender-sensitive, gender-inclusive language into Spanish, which I think is quite something, even more difficult than German. Gisela is also committed to the equitable presentation of women in teaching and learning materials, and she developed guidelines and a code of practice for gender mainstreaming in distance education courses. She used to work together with Liz Burge. They were always teamed up at conferences and so on. So I think she would be considered influential for women in distance education.

And there's a colleague from the FernUniversität, Ulrike Schultz. Ulrike studied law originally and has done a lot to promote women in the law profession, as well as making the legal profession a better place to be for women lawyers. She works internationally as well, and is active in the Women and Gender in the Legal Profession group. She initiated a number of research and teaching projects, such as the online course programme Virtual International Gender Studies [VINGS]. You could find her on the Internet.

6. *What are some of the goals that you strove to achieve in the field of DE?*

To begin with, it was quite simply making it possible for people to get an education that they missed out on beforehand. Then it became more and more focused on the situation of women in distance education. In the beginning, it was, of course, finding out why there were so few women students at the FernUniversität compared both to Athabasca, but also to private distance education institutions in Germany.

At first people said, "Oh, it's to do with the fact that we've got these male-oriented subject areas at the FernUniversität," which I found out, through an analysis of student statistics and course enrollment patterns, was not a sufficient explanation. So, with my colleague, Ute Rossié, I looked into the situation of women and men, and we found out that it is a lot more difficult for women to study at a distance, mainly because they have what Cheris Kramarae later called "the third shift." In 2001, Cheris Kramarae wrote a book, *The Third Shift*, which is about women doing distance education or e-learning in the United States. I thought it was quite a good name for it because what we found was that women tend to take on more work once they start their distance education, and men do less. Like, for instance, if a man takes up studying at a distance, goes for a degree or whatever, his family or his wife or partner will take over his chores in the household and with the children, and she will support him, maybe do some research for him and what not. He can concentrate on studying. A woman who takes up studying tends to feel guilty and selfish and, through external as well as internal pressures, feels that she owes it to herself and her family to be perfect as a housewife, as a mother, and get good grades on top of it all. So she has a harder time because of what she feels, herself, that she has to do, but also from what her relatives and friends feel: that she shouldn't neglect her children, she shouldn't neglect her household or her partner, or take time and money for her own "hobby." She should just not study. And so it is much more difficult for her to get her education this way.

My professional self-conception is based on doing feminist research. This is reflected in both the research design and the handling of the findings. Therefore, what we did with our research once we found these mechanisms at work, we reported our results back to groups of women. They found that it's not their individual inability to cope with everything, but it's a structural thing that works against women. So the women students could get together and find out that it was legitimate to not be a perfect housewife and to take time away from their children, to do something for themselves. This interaction and feedback we gave the women, and the feedback that we got from the women on what we found and how we interpreted our findings was very fruitful, both for us as the researchers and also for the students. The FernUniversität now has over 40% women students, so I feel that we have achieved something. Others factors have been at work, too, of course, but I do feel that we made a contribution with our research and the sharing of the results.

7. *What are some of your accomplishments in the field of DE that you would like to share?*

When I first worked at the FernUniversität, there were only male professors, not one woman. (I'm not a professor. I'm just academic staff, lecturer level. I'm not even in teaching.) There were very few lecturers who were women, but no professors. Not just through my research, but also because I was active as a faculty representative on the *Personalrat*, which is sort of a cross of faculty committee and union. We worked toward having women professors and an adequate percentage of women on the academic staff. I was also active in our statewide network of female academics. We got the government of North Rhine-Westphalia to provide the funding for the establishment of designated women's professorships and gender-oriented studies. Eventually, in 1985, the FernUniversität had its first woman professor. Now I don't really know how many we have, but we now have a (what is it in England, a vice chancellor or president of the university?) *rektorin*, which I guess would be president of the university, who is a woman. And the chief of administration is a woman. So we actually have two women leaders, and I think that's quite a bit of progress, compared to what it was in the late 70s, early 80s. [Looking up the data on the internet, I find that currently 26 out of 86 professors are women. At 22.3%, that is still not enough. The ratio of male to female academic staff/lecturers at FeU is 469 to 217, or 45.3%.]

8. *What are some of the challenges that you faced in the field of DE over the years?*

Not being taken serious as a woman, especially asking for the gender-inclusive language. I could tell you some episodes that happened to me: for instance, when I had my first-ever presentation at a Cambridge conference. I think this must have been in 1987. You know how you are nervous when you do your first presentation and in a foreign language and so on. I was talking about the situation of women and how difficult it was and so on. When I had finished, this eminent professor from my own university got up, stood in front of me with his back to me, and said something about how this may be somewhere or other true but not at his university, and he didn't know what I was talking about. So some other colleagues, men as well as women, told him that he was demonstrating what I had been talking about, so . . . So that was just one instance of how women who were asking for women's rights in the university were treated by many male colleagues and professors. It was quite a challenge.

On the other hand, there were wonderful men and women in the field who supported me personally as well as the cause of women in distance education. It was great to have the network to be able to talk to people who felt the same way, and also to have men, such as Alan Tait of the OU UK and long-time editor of the DE journal *Open Learning* or Ross Paul of the AU. It wasn't only women who thought that the field of distance education would be enriched if women participated more fully. I'm thinking of David Sewart from the Open University [OU UK] who was president of the ICDE for some time [1988–1992]. He gave us the platform in Oslo to present the Karlene Faith book and so on. So that was quite interesting – lots of challenges.

And I don't think they are over yet, but I've been out of the university for a long time now, so I can't say what it is like now.

9. *What was the "state of DE" when you first entered the field as opposed to DE in 2018?*

I'm not so sure that this is a question that can be answered easily. The obvious thing was that it was all paper-based, and you were lucky if you could do telephone interviews, which was *very expensive* [emphasis in the original] at the time. We still had "dumb" terminals rather than PCs. I remember that our first PC had ten megabits of hard disc, so technology was not very advanced. It was quite exciting to be in the development of technology, and see some paths that didn't lead to anywhere and others that did.

I was in the Centre for the Development of Distance Education [ZFE] doing institutional research. In addition to course and system evaluation, we evaluated the new technologies, and so we got to see where the technologies led to dead ends, where they were overtaken by developments, and where they actually succeeded. It was quite exiting. And today, if they know that Zoom exists, people could do video conferences with it. [Which I did not know, so we are doing this interview by phone.]

For me, the major thing was the communication – being international. For instance, writing a paper with Gill Kirkup, even though she was in England, and I was here. In the beginning, when we were trying to prepare things for the 1985 conference in Melbourne, we had to fax things, and it took ages to organize this joint WIN session that we did. Nowadays, you just sit down and write an email and you add attachments, send your picture, and what not. It's really, really quite, quite wonderful, like talking to you right now.

10. *What interesting memories would you like to share about the beginning of online DE?*

I'm not so sure who would be interested. Well, it is putting your newly acquired knowledge of PowerPoint, for instance, to work creating a beautiful presentation with all kinds of moving things and what not. And getting to a place where they had Macintoshes instead of PCs to present it, and Apple didn't want my PowerPoint presentation. So they copied it to a PC and then did all sorts of transfers. In the end, it was a very sloppy thing because all of those beautiful, technical little things [that] didn't work. Ever since then, I have stuck to doing very simple presentations. No moving bits, no arrows shooting in or anything. So that was a bit funny.

And, of course, people who get their assistants to do their presentations and don't know much of what they are doing or just reading off of the screens and things. But I think that we all would have profited from having courses in how to prepare presentations.

I remember evaluating a multi-point video conference in 1998 when such events were prohibitively expensive and required complicated technical setup in the different locations. There were hundreds of business admin students in each of the lecture halls in Munich, Berlin, and Hamburg and in the FeU studio. Nearly twice as many students participated than had been the case when everyone had to travel to Hagen for these seminars. There were some funny moments when the professor forgot to face the camera and instead engaged in discussion with the students in the rom. Today, oral exams can be taken via video conferencing; the FernUniversität uses Moodle and offers a virtual campus, which students can access easily.

For me, doing research, online surveys made life a lot easier as once you construct your questionnaire, it saves the tedious inputting of the data, especially typing in the open-ended answers. Unlike some of the new colleagues, I steadfastly refused to create automated reports directly from the electronic database. Rather, I believe that figures in themselves are meaningless, may even be misleading, and that context and interpretation must remain with the researcher. Still, the things that you can do with SPSS and such is wonderful. I am sure that you have this, too.

11. *What were your specific DE research interests, and have they changed/evolved over the years?*

My job started out as an institutional researcher doing course evaluation at first. So that's what I did, and I got interested in looking at different aspects and so on. But until my interest in gender issues evolved, it was just more or less routine work. After that, my focus was on women and men in distance education. I was so fortunate in meeting Gill Kirkup at the Open University and getting her interested in doing a parallel study. It was absolutely amazing, the things that we found by comparing the two sets of data. I don't know if you have come across our very first joint paper, which was "Supports and connectedness: The needs of women distance education students," but I understand that this paper – though published in 1990 – is still being looked at today. It really got us started, convinced us that we were on the right path with looking at gender issues. It is not a deficit if women want to have contact and connections with other people. It's just another way of going about it. So that was really interesting. The concern with gender and technologies, the virtual university and e-learning evolved gradually as computers and the Internet became an increasingly important part of open and distance education.

Another important aspect of my research was the question of social mobility through distance education: i.e., did people from a working-class background utilize the FernUniversität to achieve a degree and, through this, a higher social position? So, in my part of the survey, because for reasons of data protection, we didn't get this kind of data from the files of the FernUniversität, unlike the OU, we included questions on mothers' and fathers' education and work. It became apparent eventually that we would not use this data, analyze it for the university, because there was never time enough or interest enough for this kind of analysis.

Eventually, I figured that it would be an absolute shame to let this data just rot in some data graveyard. I started looking at it and decided to do a PhD. That was at the time when the issue of women from a working-class background not getting higher education became prevalent again. As a feminist and sociologist, I decided to look into this. It took me eight years, but eventually I finished analyzing this data. I found that women (whose mothers and/or fathers, because that was the new thing, to look at mothers, too, not only working class fathers) had quite often not had the chance to do the straight education route and used their distance education degree studies as a means to achieve their own social mobility – to do it themselves, rather than through marriage as was the usual route. You know how sociologists usually compare father's position and husband's position and then extrapolate the woman's social mobility or not. In this case, it was the women themselves who counted.

So, in 1996 I got my PhD, just a few days before I turned 50. So that was my present to myself on my 50th birthday, and it was absolutely wonderful. My thesis, entitled *Frauen im Fernstudium: Bildungsaufstieg für Töchter aus Arbeiterfamilien*, was published (without the extensive appendix of tables) in 1997.

Then a few years later, I wrote an English language book. I thought it would simply be a translation of this PhD thesis, but I was advised by Alan Tait, editor of the Routledge Studies in Distance Education, to make it more international. So eventually I did this book, *Women in Distance Education: Challenges and Opportunities*, where the working-class social mobility stuff was just an example, but not the main book. That was changes in my research interests.

12. *Could you please describe the learning environment that you most recently worked in (e.g., geographic and institutional setting, student demographics)?*

I mentioned that I retired mid-2011. During the time that I worked at FeU, there had been all sorts of reorganizations and eventually evaluation: i.e., institutional research became part of the university administration. Since I wanted to continue as academic staff member, I was in my own little unit, working more or less independently on research into gender issues in virtual learning environments, but also doing a few projects with my colleague, Ute Rossié. We had been working together for over 20 years. Since I was then attached to the *rektor's* [the university president's] office, I did the evaluation of the ICDE conferences in Vienna in 1999 and in Düsseldorf in 2001, for which he was the programme chair. I also had a contract with a law professor for designing and carrying out an evaluation programme of the newly established Hagen Law School and its course programme for the certification of specialist lawyers and attorneys.

After retirement, I moved to Darmstadt, where my brother and his family live. In Darmstadt, there is a private distance education institution, which by now also set up a degree-conferring college. I had a contract with them to do the evaluation of various gender issues and other things. So I did that. I also had a contract with Olaf Zawacki-Richter at the Universität of Oldenburg. I was part of various research projects that he did, co-authored some papers, and did a few workshops with him. He works with Terry Anderson a lot.

For a few years, I kept on working as a freelance institutional researcher basically. But I haven't been doing so much lately because my health wasn't so good.

13. *Is there anything else you [would] like to address?*

Well, I think it is a wonderful idea that you are doing this book. Talking to you, I notice that even though you are doing this project, you haven't come across various names and developments of things, so I think it is a wonderful thing to preserve the memory of what a lot of women worked very hard at accomplishing for the field of distance education and in the field of distance education, which is going back to a point that I didn't get to before and which relates to WIN.

WIN is no longer functional. This happened in 1997 at the ICDE conference at Penn State when some woman came forward out of the woodwork and wanted to formalize the organization. But the whole point was that it was an informal network and it didn't want any statutes and what not. The conference at Penn State was also one where it was again men on the podium. Actually, Gisela Pravda went up on the podium and said she was going to just test if it would break down if a woman stepped on it, somebody other than a white Anglo-Saxon Protestant in a dark suit. So that was basically the end of WIN at that time. ICDE stopped funding. You do need funding for mailing and all sorts of things to keep up the work. Unless the woman chairing WIN had good enough standing and resources in her institution, it wouldn't work because ICDE wouldn't support it any longer. So that was basically very sad to see this go. But while it was in existence, it was absolutely wonderful.

In fact, the network struggled on informally. In 2001, we organized a pre-conference workshop in Hagen, which was attended by over 30 international colleagues interested in the theme of gender issues in virtual open and distance learning environments. This successful event extended into the main conference. Because of the costs associated with travelling to Hagen, a second workshop, not connected to an international conference, could not attract enough participants to make a recurrent event seem feasible. By now, of course, most of us oldies have retired and do no longer attend the international conferences, which played such a big role in meeting and networking. I think I would still make the effort to go to Cambridge for those lovely conferences organized by Alan Tait and Roger Mills. But, alas, they, too, have retired, and the Cambridge conferences with them.

I'm really looking forward to your book. Thanks for doing it.

Publications

Books

Hofmann, U., von Prümmer, C., & Weidner, D. (1981). *Bildungslebensläufe ehemaliger Waldorfschüler. Eine Untersuchung der Geburtsjahrgänge 1946 und 1947*. Pädagogische Forschungsstelle beim Bund der Freien Waldorfschulen. Stuttgart.

von Prümmer, C. (1997). *Frauen im Fernstudium. Bildungsaufstieg für Töchter aus Arbeiterfamilien*. Campus Forschung. ISBN 3-593-35721-6.

von Prümmer, C. (2000). *Women and distance education: Challenges and opportunities*. Routledge Studies in Distance Education. ISBN 0-415-23258-9

Book Chapters

Engler, S., & von Prümmer, C. (1993). Studienfach, geschlecht, "soziale Herkunft" – zum verhältnis von geschlecht und klasse an der hochschule. In A. Schlüter (Ed.), *Bildungsmobilität. Studien zur individualisierung von arbeitertöchtern in der moderne* (pp. 105–125). Deutscher Studien Verlag.

Ewert, J., Hauff, M., Mielke, W. H., & von Prümmer, C. (1998). Multipointvideokonferenzen in der lehre der FernUniversität – Erste erfahrungen mit einem innovativen lehrkonzept. In Gesellschaft der Freunde der FernUniversität (Eds.), *Jahrbuch* (pp. 25–38). FernUniversität.

Fandel, G., Bartels, J., & von Prümmer, C. (2006). Karriere- und einkommenseffekte der akademischen weiterbildung - dargestellt an absolventen des wirtschaftswissenschaftlichen zusatzstudiengangs für ingenieure und naturwissenschaftler am fachbereich wirtschaftswissenschaft der FernUniversität in Hagen. In M. Weiß (Ed.), *Evidenzbasierte bildungspolitik: beiträge der bildungsökonomie* (pp. 151–171). Duncker & Humblot.

Karsten, M. E., Groten, M., von Prümmer, C., & Sattel, U. (1986). Frauen-arbeit, frauen-studien, frauenförderung an der FernUniversität Hagen. In Gesellschaft der Freunde der FernUniversität (Eds.) *Jahrbuch 1986* (pp. 87–125). Hagen.

Nebert, D. G., & von Prümmer, C. (1997) . . . . and from Smith you can go anywhere! Das Frauen-College aus der Sicht von zwei Ehemaligen. In S. Metz-Göckel & F. Steck (Eds.), *Frauenuniversitäten. Initiativen und Reformprojekte im internationalen Vergleich* (pp. 245–258). Leske und Budrich.

Stöter, J., Bullen, M., Zawacki-Richter, O., & von Prümmer, C. (2014). From the back door into the mainstream: The characteristics of lifelong learners. In O. Zawacki-Richter & T. Anderson (Eds.), *Online distance education: Towards a research agenda* (pp. 421–458). Athabasca University Press.

von Prümmer, C. (1988). Gleiche chancen für frauen? Anmerkungen zu faktoren, die frauen den zugang und verbleib im fernstudium erschweren. In Gesellschaft der Freunde der FernUniversität (Eds.), *Jahrbuch 1988* (pp. 86–100). FernUniversität.

von Prümmer, C. (1989). Frauen im fernstudium: Auch ein thema für die studienzentren. In Gesellschaft der freunde des Studienzentrums Bad Hersfeld (Ed.), *10 Jahre Studienzentrum Bad Hersfeld* (pp. 39–42). Bad Hersfeld: Studienzentrum des Landes Hessen für Studierende der FernUniversität Hagen.

von Prümmer, C. (1990). Frauenpolitik an der hochschule als aufgabe der personalräte. In A. Schlüter, C. Roloff, & M. A. Kreienbaum (Eds.), *Was eine frau umtreibt. frauenbewegung – frauenforschung – frauenpolitik* (pp. 173–194). Centaurus.

von Prümmer, C. (1992). Zur sozialen herkunft von fernstudentinnen und fernstudenten. Fernstudium als nachholen von bildungschancen? In A. Schlüter (Ed.), *Arbeitertöchter und ihr sozialer aufstieg. Zum verhältnis von klasse, geschlecht und sozialer mobilität* (pp. 173–194). Deutscher Studien Verlag.

von Prümmer, C. (1993). Kommunikation im Fernstudium. In Gesellschaft der Freunde der FernUniversität (Eds.), *Jahrbuch, 1993* (pp. 179–197). FernUniversität.

von Prümmer, C. (1995). Frauen an der FernUniversität. Entwicklungen und trends der frauenanteile unter den studierenden und beschäftigten. In Rektor der FernUniversität (Ed.), *20 Jahre FernUniversität. Daten, fakten, hintergründe* (pp. 198–205). FernUniversität.

von Prümmer, C. (1998a). Evaluation von multimedia: Einige Beispiele aus der FernUniversität. In M. Hauff (Ed.), *media@uni – multi.media? Entwicklung – Gestaltung – Evaluation neuer Medien* (pp. 201–216). Waxmann.

von Prümmer, C. (1998b). Ohne die betreuung im studienzentrum hätte ich die zwischenprüfung nicht geschafft. zum stellenwert von mentorieller betreuung und studienzentren aus der sicht von studentinnen und studenten der FernUniversität. In Gesellschaft der Freunde der FernUniversität (Eds.), *Jahrbuch 1998* (pp. 121–138). FernUniversität.

von Prümmer, C. (1999). Medienevaluation als empirisch geleiteter reflexion. In K. Lehmann (Ed.), *Studieren 2000. Alte Inhalte in neuen Medien?* (pp. 221–237). Waxmann Verlag.

von Prümmer, C. (2000). Förderung von frauen durch monoedukation? Das beispiel des Amerikanischen Smith College. In A. Mischau, C. Kramer, & B. Blättel-Mink (Eds.), *Frauen in Hochschule und Wissenschaft – Strategien der förderung zwischen integration und autonomie* (pp. 113–124). Nomos Verlagsgesellschaft.

von Prümmer, C. (2002). Neue Medien und Lernen im Netz – Frauen und der Lernraum Virtuelle Universität. In Heinrich-Böll-Stiftung und Feministisches Institut (Eds.), *Feminist_spaces – Frauen im Netz. Diskurse – Communities – Visionen* (pp. 77–98). Ulrike Helmer Verlag.

von Prümmer, C. (2004a). Das Projekt VINGS als Beispiel für die evaluation des Lernraums Virtuelle Universität. In D. M. Meister, S.-O. Tergan, & P. Zentel (Eds.), *Evaluation von e-learning. Zielrichtungen, Zukunftsperspektiven, methodologische Aspekt* (pp. 184–195). Waxmann Verlag.

von Prümmer, C. (2004b). Gender issues and learning online. In J. Brindley, C. Walti, & O. Zawacki-Richter (Eds.), *Learner support in open, distance, and online learning environments* (pp. 179–192). Arbeitsstelle Fernstudienforschung, Carl von Ossietzky University.

von Prümmer, C. (2010). Frauen in fernstudium und e-learning: Zugangs- und studienbedingungen unter genderaspekten. In C. Bauschke-Urban, M. Kamphans, & F. Sagebiel (Eds.), *Subversion und intervention: Wissenschaft und geschlechter(un)ordnung* (pp. 201–218). Verlag Barbara Budrich.

von Prümmer, C. (2011). Distance education. In B. J. Bank, S. Delamont, & C. Marshall (Eds.), *Gender and education: An encyclopedia* (Vol. 1, pp. 163–170). Johns Hopkins University Press.

von Prümmer, C. (2021). ODDE and Gender. In O. Zawacki-Richter & I. Jung (Eds.), *Handbook of open, distance, and digital education*. Springer.

von Prümmer, C., & Rossié, U. (1988). Gender-related patterns in choice of major subject or degree course at the FernUniversität (West Germany). In K. Faith (Ed.), *Toward new horizons for women in distance education. International perspectives* (pp. 39–66). Routledge.

von Prümmer, C., & Rossié, U. (2001). Gender-sensitive evaluation research. In E. J. Burge & M. Haughey (Eds.), *Using learning technologies: Stories from practice* (pp. 135–144). RoutledgeFalmer.

von Prümmer, C., & Rossié, U. (2004). Evaluation im Fernstudium. In H. Müller (Ed.), *30 Jahre ZFE? Zukunft braucht Herkunf* (pp. 257–283). Zentrum für Fernstudienentwicklung (ZFE), FernUniversität.

Zawacki-Richter, O., & von Prümmer, C. (2013). Open universities und open learning: Offene hochschulen international. In A. Hanft & Katrin Brinkmann (Eds.), *Offene hochschulen. Die neuausrichtung der hochschulen auf lebenslanges lernen* (pp. 30–41). Waxmann Verlag.

Journal Articles

Han, P., Kortemeyer, G., Krämer, B. J., & von Prümmer, C. (2008). Exposure and support of latent social networks among learning object repository users. *Journal of Universal Computer Science*, *14*(10), 1717–1738.

Kirkup, G., & von Prümmer, C. (1990). Support and connectedness: The needs of women distance students. *Journal of Distance Education/Revue de l'enseignement à distance*, *5*(2), 9-31.

Kirkup, G., & von Prümmer, C. (1997). Distance education for European women. The threats and opportunities of new educational forms and media. *The European Journal of Women's Studies*, *4*(1), 39–62.

von Prümmer, C. (1986). Women at the FernUniversität: Gender related differences in students' choice of degree programs. *ICDE Bulletin*, *11*(May 1986), 42–50.

von Prümmer, C. (1990, April). Study motivation of distance students. A report on some results from a survey done at the FernUniversität in 1987/88. *Research in Distance Education*, 2–6.

von Prümmer, C. (1992). Women in education in Papua New Guinea and the South Pacific [Review of the book Women in education in Papua New Guinea and the South Pacific by E. Wormald & A. Crossley, Eds]. *Open Learning*, *7*(1), 71–72.

von Prümmer, C. (1994). Women-friendly perspectives in distance education. *Open Learning*, *9*(1), 3–12.

von Prümmer, C. (1998a). Evaluation of media and technology at the German FernUniversität. *Open Learning*, *13*(3), 59–65.

von Prümmer, C. (1998b). In my own skin. Dialogues with women students, tutors and counsellors. Researching reality, meaning, change and growth in Open University [Review of the book *Dialogues with women students, tutors and counsellors. Researching reality, meaning, change and growth in Open University*, by M. Heron]. *Open Learning*, *13*(2), 66–67.

von Prümmer, C. (2003a, October). Book review - e-Research: Methods, strategies, and issues [Review of the book *e-Research: Methods, strategies, and issues*, by T. Anderson & H. Kanuka]. *International Review of Research in Open and Distance Learning (IRRODL)* *4*(2). http://www.irrodl.org/index.php/irrodl/issue/view/16

von Prümmer, C. (2003b). Evaluation als Thema für die Personalräte. Hochschulevaluation unter den Bedingungen des HG NW. *Gewerkschaft und Wissenschaft. Hochschulpolitik mit der GEW, 1*(2003).

Von Prümmer, C. (2003c). The third shift: Women learning online [Review of the book *The third shift: Women learning online*, by C. Kramarae]. *Education, Communication & Information (ECI), 3*(3), 408–410.

von Prümmer, C., & Rossié, U. (1988). Gender in distance education at the FernUniversität. *Open Learning, 3*(2), 3–12.

Zawacki-Richter, O., & von Prümmer, C. (2010). Gender and collaboration patterns in distance education research. *Open Learning, 25*(3), 95–114.

Zawacki-Richter, O., von Prümmer, C., & Stöter, J. (2015). Open Universities: Offener zugang zur hochschule in nationaler und internationaler perspective. *Beiträge zur Hochschulforschung, 1*(2015), 8–24.

Conference Presentations

Demiray, U. (1995). Uzakt eğitimde cinsiyet bati alman açık üniversitesi'nde ögrenim gören kadınlar ve erkekler. In *Dünyada açıkögretim: Ilkerli, isleyisi ve örnekleriyle* (pp. 205-213). Eskişehir: Turkuaz yayıncılık. Turkish language translation of: von Prümmer, C. (1988). Gender in distance education: Women and men studying at the West German FernUniversität. In D. Sewart & J. S. Daniel (Eds.), *Developing distance education: Papers submitted to the 14th ICDE World Conference* (pp. 372–374). International Council for Distance Education.

Hauff, M., Kirkup, G., & von Prümmer, C. (1998). Frauen und neue medien: Nutzung und nutzen des internets am arbeitsplatz hochschule und im studium. *Beiträge zu einem Workshop der Arbeitsgruppe Frauen und neue Medien*. Frauenvorträge an der FernUniversität Nr. 25. Die Frauenbeauftragte der FernUniversität.

Kirkup, G., & von Prümmer, C. (1996, December). How can distance education address the particular needs of European women? In G. Fandel, R. Bartz, & F. Nickolmann (Eds.), *University level distance education in Europe. Assessment and perspectives* (pp. 33–50). Proceedings of a Workshop Jointly Organised by FernUniversität and EADTU, Hagen. Deutscher Studien Verlag.

von Prümmer, C. (1988, August). Gender in distance education: Women and men studying at the West German FernUniversität. In D. Sewart & J. S. Daniel (Eds.), *Developing distance education* (pp. 372–374). 14th ICDE World Conference, Oslo, Norway.

von Prümmer, C. (1993). Women-friendly perspectives in distance education [Keynote presentation]. *Feminist Pedagogy and Women-Friendly Perspectives in Distance Education. The Women's Studies Center of Umeå Series of Reports* (No. 4, 199, pp. 4–28). Umeå universitet.

von Prümmer, C. (1993a, June). *Papers presented at International WIN Working Conference*.

von Prümmer, C. (1993b, June). Women in distance education. A researcher's view [Keynote presentation]. *Research in distance education. Present situation and forecasts* (pp. 51–67). Umeå universitet. Report from a Nordic Research Conference, Umeå, Sweden.

von Prümmer, C. (1995a, July). Putting the student first? Reflections on tele-communication and electronic leading strings. In A. Tait (Ed.), *Putting the student first: Learner-centred approaches in open and distance learning* (pp. 260–265). Open University East Anglia. Collected Conference Papers of the Sixth International Conference on Open and Distance Learning, Cambridge, UK.

von Prümmer, C. (1995b, June). Communication preferences and practice: Not always a good fit for German distance students. In D. Sewart (Ed.), *One world many voices: Quality in open and distance learning* (pp. 292–295). International Council for Distance Education and Open University UK. Proceedings of the 17th World Conference for Distance Education, Birmingham, UK.

von Prümmer, C. (2004, March). Gender issues and learning online: From exclusion to empowerment. In U. Bernath & A. Szücs (Eds.), *Supporting the learner in distance education and e-learning* (pp. 474–480). BIS-Verlag. Proceedings of the Third EDEN Research Workshop, Carl von Ossietzky University, Oldenburg.

von Prümmer, C., Kirkup, G., & Spronk, B. (1988, August). Women in distance education [Keynote presentation]. In D. Sewart & J. S. Daniel (Eds.), *Developing distance education* (pp. 57–62). 14th ICDE World Conference, Oslo, Norway.

von Prümmer, C., & Rossié, U. (1990, November). Familienorientierung als erfordernis und als strategie. In A. Schlüter & I. Stahr (Eds.), *Wohin geht die frauenforschung?* (pp. 171–175). Böhlau Verlag. Dokumentation des gleichnamigen Symposions vom, Dortmund.

31
YOUNG, ARLENE M. C.

Photo of Arlene Young contributed by Arlene Young

I've had a lifelong interest in social justice.

Arlene M.C. Young comes from a background in educational psychology. She obtained her Bachelor of Arts at the University of Alberta in 1966 and later a Diploma in Educational Psychology through the Faculty of Education at the University of Alberta in 1984. In 1987, she completed a Master of Counselling Psychology at the University of Alberta; her thesis was entitled *The Effects of an Assertiveness Training Workshop for Women on Assertion and Self-Esteem*. Her PhD in Educational Psychology at the same institution resulted in her dissertation, *Making Sense of Women's Job Loss Experiences*.

Young had a long career with Athabasca University, Alberta, Canada. She began in administration as Supervisor in Personnel Services in 1975. In 1977, she became a Counsellor for the next 20 years. She held the roles of Acting Manager, Northern Regional Office, from 1987 to 1988 and also Senior Counsellor at the Northern Regional Office in 1984 and 1985 during this time.

Arlene became an Associate Professor at Athabasca University in 1997. She retired in 2003, but continues to tutor with Women's and Gender Studies (WGST) 266: Thinking Through Women's Lives at AU and also worked on the WGST 499: Applied Project from 2003 to 2015.

Young's research studies have focused on the challenges that women face within higher education and learning.

Interview

Transcript Analysis Summary

Analysis of all interviews included in this volume led to the identification of 3,545 units of data. The mean of these collective units was 118 per pioneer, the median was 118.5, and the mode was 132. Individual interview units ranged from 59 to 217 units, yielding a spread of 158 units among all interviews. Arlene Young's interview generated 125 units, which was just over the mean and median statistics for all interviews.

A comparison of Young's interview to the interviews of all pioneers indicates that, generally speaking, Young's conversations produced a similar number of units in ten of the identified thematic areas as most of the interviewed pioneers did (Figure 31.1). Young spoke more about the challenges that she faced and shared more interesting memories than most others did. Her focus on challenges was most likely due to the fact that she was a pioneer in human resources and social services, which were areas that, as she explains, garnered little attention, appreciation, and support from upper administration, who were struggling with other institutional growing pains and their own priorities. Young produced fewer units than most others did in two areas: accomplishments and research interests. It is not known why she did not talk more about her accomplishments. However, the single unit coded to research interests indicates that she did not declare any research interests during the interview.

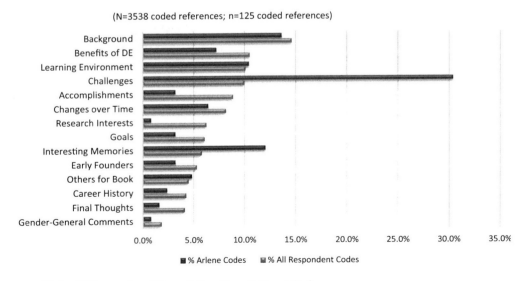

Figure 31.1 All Respondents' Versus Arlene Young's Parent Codes

Link to recorded interview: tinyurl.com/Young-A-2018

Transcript of Interview

Full Name: Arlene M. C. Young
Institutional Affiliation: Athabasca University
Key:

Regular font = Interviewee comments
Italicized font = Interviewer comments

Interview Questions

1. *What was your educational and experiential background before you became involved in distance education [DE] and online distance learning [ODL]?*

   I had a BA [Bachelor of Arts].

2. *In what year did you begin to look specifically into DE?*

   That's a really good question. I started at Athabasca University [AU] in 1975. When I first started at AU, I was not in a distance education position. I started off as a Supervisor of Personnel Services. What drew me to Athabasca University was that it was distance education and an open institution. So I really valued what they were trying to do, even though they didn't know what it was going to be.

3. *What were the circumstances in your world that initiated this interest in DE?*

   First of all, I think that I've had a lifelong interest in social justice, and this seemed to fit well into that as it was allowing students with life experience but not the educational background to get into university. I thought that was worthwhile.

   Also, I knew from my own experience, people living in remote locations really have little access to further education. I lived in small towns in Manitoba and Northern Ontario for a few years. Really, there was very little access, and what access there was was not clear to me and seemed to be pretty hands off. There wasn't much support for learning.

4. *Which female researchers or female colleagues may have piqued your interest in DE? Who would you identify as the early female leaders/founders in the field of DE?*

Colleagues certainly piqued my interest because, at that time, the university was very small. We were working out of one building. There were people from multi-disciplines talking about how they were going to bring this about. I may not have made much by the way of contribution, but I certainly heard a lot of the discussions, and believe me, those discussions were heated. At least they could be heated; they weren't always. So it was very interesting.

There were a lot of women. Gail Crawford, Sydney Sharpe, Muriel Skinner (that's not the name that she uses now; that was her married name); those are the ones who come to mind at the moment.

Oh, I know another one who is really important – Barbara Spronk. I would say that Barbara was one of the leaders, definitely.

5. *What are some of the goals that you strove to achieve in the field of DE?*

I think primarily I was concerned about student success because my first position working directly with distance education was as a student advisor and, later on, as a counsellor. My focus was on students learning, and learning effectively, so that they could achieve their goals. That was through information.

Later on, I did a lot of work with study skills and just trying to prepare them for the experience of distance education because there are some real challenges in distance education. And believe me, with the students now – I was just going over my records on whose contracts end this month, and the vast majority do not finish a course. I wish I could say otherwise, but that's how it is. Yet there are some that just move right along. In talking to them at the beginning of the course, I could not predict which ones would and which ones wouldn't. I find that really hard. I'm sure there is predictability, but I don't know what it is. Because some of the ones who are not completing have gone ahead and completed the first assignment really early in the course, so they were right on target, and yet they didn't go beyond that. I think that sometimes students don't realize that (a) it really is university-level study, and (b) they have to commit a lot of time to it. I think a lot of them don't understand that. But the ones who get it, even the ones who struggle, work really hard, and they get through.

I had one yesterday that I referred for a writing assessment, because I think she just doesn't know how to write an essay. That's a serious problem in this course. You really do need to do that. I work with students a lot on essay writing, but it's within the context of improvement, rather than teaching how.

So anyway, that's one of the difficulties that I encounter, and I feel badly about that. I'm tutoring now. I've been teaching since 1998, I believe.

In the MDE [Master of Education in Distance Education] programme, it was different because students were in a cohort. We were in touch online all of the time, so it was a different situation. And the students were doing a master's programme, so they were well oriented to university studies. There were still some who didn't get through for reasons I never really understood, nor should I. Sometimes it would be probing too deeply into their lives, and that's not my position. It's not a fair thing for me to do. They have a right to privacy.

6. *What are some of your accomplishments in the field of DE that you would like to share?*

Well, I think we worked really hard to develop a counselling programme that would work at a distance, and that's been developed even further since I was involved in counselling. We certainly did a lot of work over the phone, but we also wrote a lot of publications that were geared specifically to distance education and to counselling issues, and issues of motivation and success in learning.

7. *What are some of the challenges that you faced in the field of DE over the years?*

I don't think that all of the challenges that we faced were unique to distance education. There was a feeling – not universal, goodness knows – but a feeling within the administration of the university that counselling wasted money. If you aren't bringing cash in, you don't count. We were not bringing cash in. So the counselling was seen as being of little value, even though we self-consciously focused on strategies for learning and overcoming barriers to learning. That was our focus. We weren't dealing normally with personal counselling, although having said that, it's really hard to talk about barriers and not get into personal counselling. We did it to the extent that it was necessary in that situation, but that was not our focus.

At one time, student services, and counselling in particular, was eliminated. It was struck out of the budget. I can't remember what my position name changed to. I was still counselling students, but I was doing other things as well, doing evaluation reports and so forth, but I still did counselling.

I can remember one supervisor said to me, "How many students are you counselling?"

And I said, "Well, let me think about this for a moment. I'm not supposed to be doing any counselling, and you want me to give you statistics on how many students I'm counselling? Have I got that right?"

She looked sort of ashamed of herself, and she left. I thought, "Do you think I'm going to hang myself, for heaven's sakes? No, I'm not." I just kept on doing what I was doing, and the staff referred people to me for counselling anyway, so I just kept on doing it.

8. *What was the "state of DE" when you first entered the field as opposed to DE in 2018?*

First of all, it was very exciting because there were all sorts of ideas of how things could be done and should be done. Many of them were tried out in various courses. So there was certainly no sense of orthodoxy about how you do it. It was pretty much an open field.

Now, it became much more structured and an orthodox set of procedures. Probably the greatest change in that was when we started doing the courses online. To some extent, the demands of websites and so forth imposed that. That's not a complaint. It's just an observation that courses have become much more similar – not entirely, but because of the technological changes.

9. *What interesting memories would you like to share about the beginning of ODL?*

First of all, I was delighted when we started doing it because it seemed like the right thing to do. Not to take advantage of that technology would have been just plain foolish.

At first, we certainly didn't know how to use it well, but we tried. We still use, to a large extent, email communication and other messaging services. I have to say the one in the course format I just detest. I try to get my students to use email, and on the whole, that works reasonably well. I very rarely get a phone call, where that used to be pretty much the norm, but it isn't anymore.

The difficulty of that, as you know, is that it is easy for written phrases to be misunderstood. So I try to be really careful about how I phrase things, but even having done that, there are times when I know that it's not understood, or it doesn't go over well or whatever happens to be. So that's the difficulty.

We are still doing most of our work in writing. I don't think that's necessarily a bad thing, but it does impose a limitation.

In the MDE, one of the things that I found difficult was dealing with people in the various time zones. Now as long as we were doing asynchronous conferencing, it worked well. But I had one former student who was doing a degree in Australia and getting up at three in the morning because they didn't have asynchronous conferencing. Could you imagine getting up at three o'clock in the morning to participate in a conference? I just thought that was just stupid. Who would impose that on students? So I think that there are things to avoid in planning distance education programmes.

10. *What were your specific research interests, and have they changed/evolved over the years?*

Like I said, I came in with a BA with a focus on history and English, and while I was working at AU, I did a Master's Degree in Educational Psychology. Well, I did a Certificate in Educational Psychology and a degree in Counselling Psychology, and then I did a doctorate in Educational Psychology as well. So my learning was enhanced; I started to understand more about the theory of learning. The theory of learning is somewhat like the theory in counselling. Sometimes it works, and sometimes it doesn't, but one of the things that you have to learn as a practitioner is to analyze the situation and pull what you can out of your bag of tricks and use what seems appropriate at the time.

One of the difficulties in distance education is that sometimes it's hard to know. Your way of judging is limited by the communication technique because you are communicating in writing, and it's mostly asynchronous. Occasionally, students [will] phone me when they are running into some difficulties, and then I'm much better able to judge because it's an interactive process, and I can help them figure out what's needed more efficiently than I can otherwise. I don't mean that I can't do it by email, but it's certainly not as efficient.

11. *Could you please describe the learning environment that you currently work in (e.g., geographic and institutional setting, student demographics)?*

I work from my home, which is ideal, because I'm only working part time. That works for me. I can manage the other things that I am doing and work with the university quite well in working from home. The difficulty, of course, is that I don't have as much contact with my colleagues. That's okay. I think contact with my colleagues was much more important first of all, when I was full time and when I was very much involved with the Faculty Association and other things in the university. I learned a lot that way in collaboration with other people. Right now, I am quite prepared to let other people look after those things, and I will just deal with the course. By the way, if I encounter difficulty, I do raise that.

It's asynchronous teaching that I'm doing. My students are mostly in Canada by far. I have occasionally had students who were in Africa, in the Pacific Islands, and the Caribbean, but most of them are in Canada. The course is certainly very much geared towards Canada.

Yes, it is asynchronous. We don't have any online webinars or anything like that. I suppose we could, but we don't. Any experience I have had doing this with students in this course – and we have tried a few things over the years – they've not been very successful. Students want to work at their own pace.

12. *Is there anything else you [would] like to address?*

The one thing that I would like readers to know was that it was very exciting: the interaction of a whole lot of ideas on how you do it and why. There was certainly conflict over whether there should be entry requirements or not. There were mixed feelings in either direction on that. I think that open entry is important. I also understand that some students are simply not prepared for it. But I'd rather err on the side of openness. That's my own preference, so I'm okay with that. That was one of the issues that came up, and it was fairly rigorously debated, I would say. I couldn't characterize those on one side or the other as male or female, because I think that it was quite broadly discussed.

I think that probably my experience that was the most telling was the one in counselling. Counselling was always under siege at budget time. We were always being threatened with being cut. It took away from the main focus. It's the kind of difficulty you have in any organization: the difference between so-called line positions and staff positions. Staff positions are always questioned more. Why do we need them? What are they contributing? We really had to work very hard at expressing, first of all, what we were doing, why we were doing it, how we were doing it, and how we tried to make it more efficient by writing publications. I did a book on exam anxiety, for example. Well, I edited it; I didn't plan the programme. We wrote a pamphlet for students getting started that would take them through things they needed to think about. I'm not sure that it was very successful, but it was a stab at doing it. Virginia Nielson wrote a whole set of books on study skills that were really good. We just tried really hard. Now there is a whole lot of stuff online, which is really good.

So what we tried to do was to keep on doing the things that we were doing: that is, overcome barriers and develop techniques for doing that at a distance, and I think that's continuing to this day.

I: You talk about distance education as being an issue of trying to balance different aspects, different life roles, and requiring new sets of skills. Could you talk a little more about that?

Well, I think it requires a lot of balance with instructors and counsellors, but it also requires it with students. I think that students need excellent time-management skills to do distance education. They certainly need to read very well. If they can't, then they need to get some help with that. But managing time and setting goals is really important for students. Well, it's pretty important for me, too, come to think of it.

13. *Can you suggest names of other female pioneers in DE or ODL that you think we should include in the book?*

I think that I've already mentioned some of them. Jane Brindley was one that I worked with and was very influential, and Shannon Whelan.

Publications

Books and Reports

Young, A. (Ed.) (1990). *Coping with exam anxiety*. Athabasca University.
Young, A. (1986). *My experiences at an Open University summer school: An evaluation report for the London Regional Office*. Open University.
Young, A. (1998). *Student diary*. Athabasca University.
Young, A. (2000). *University certificate: Counselling women*. Progress Report.
Young, A. (2006). *Selected study skills books in the AU Library: An annotated bibliography* (2nd ed.). www.athabascau.ca/html/services/advise/ssbib.htm
Young, A., Hunter-Moffatt, R., & Oddson, L. (1994). The Sunrise Project's success in extending northern and First Nations' education: An evaluation report for Athabasca University.

Book Chapters

Cavanaugh, C., Ellerman, E., Oddson, L., & Young, A. (2001). Lessons from our cyberclassroom. In E. J. Burge & M. Haughey (Eds.), *Using learning technologies: International perspectives on practice* (pp. 61–71). Routledge/Falmer.

Young, A. M. C. (1988). A renewed emphasis on nurturing in the counselling of women. *Developing distance Education* (pp. 447–449). International Council for Distance Education.

Young, A. M. C. (2010). Telling stories to make sense of job loss. In L. R. Ross (Ed.), *Counselling women: Feminist issues, theory and practice*. Toronto Women's Press.

Journal Articles

Young, A. M. C. (1988). *The theme of nurturing in the counselling of women*. Women's International Network Newsletter.

PART TWO

This encyclopedia is divided into two parts. Part Two contains Chapter 32, Analysis of Interviews, which begins with a description of the qualitative research study used to gather and analyze the pioneers' collective interview data. The results of the thematic analyses are then presented before emergent themes and their possible interpretations are discussed. Where appropriate, this discussion also considers how these findings relate to existing literature. The final section of Chapter 32, Conclusion, summarizes the salient themes identified in the data and the limitations of the study. The concluding chapter, Final Thoughts, summarizes key implications that the content of this book may hold for policymakers, administrators, educators, historians, researchers, writers, and students who are interested in distance education and online learning.

32
ANALYSIS OF INTERVIEWS

Introduction

The purpose of this chapter is to provide researchers, educators, and students of distance education (DE), online learning, educational technology, and gender studies with comprehensive analyses, discussions, and conclusions drawn from the perceptions and lived experiences of the 30 pioneering women who contributed to this book. Preceding chapters devoted to each pioneer also contain a brief comparative analysis between the data generated from that pioneer's interview and the collective interview results presented in this chapter. It is hoped that this approach gives voice to these intrepid women and enables stakeholders to gain new insights into the individual and shared realities of these pioneers.

The chapter is presented in a primarily traditional research reporting manner. The first section, Research Methodology, provides an overview of the research method employed, research questions explored in the study, interviewee selection process, and data analysis procedures. Next, the Results section presents the findings of the study. The Discussion section then reflects on the themes emerging from these results and their possible interpretations and, where appropriate, considers how these findings relate to existing literature. The final section of this chapter, Conclusion, summarizes the salient themes identified in the data and discusses the limitations of the study. (Key implications for stakeholders and recommendations for future research are, however, reserved for the last chapter, Final Thoughts.) The chapter begins with the definition of key terms used in the study.

Discussion and Definition of Terms

Two clusters of terms are presented herein. The first cluster – distance education, CMC, ODL, and online learning – are terms that various participants used during their interviews. The second cluster, pioneers, includes three terms that the authors used to help in the selection of candidates for this study.

Distance Education, CMC, ODL, and Online Learning

When the authors began this study, they assumed that most of the identified pioneers for the project would consider themselves to be working within the field of distance learning. It was soon discovered, however, that some of the women identified their career paths as being largely, if not solely, related to CMC (computer-mediated communication), ODL (which meant open and distance learning or open and distributed learning, depending upon the interviewee's understanding of the acronym), ODel (open delivery), ODFL (open, distance, and flexible learning), open learning, and online learning. Most seemed to concur that *distance education* equated to a traditional, snail mail correspondence approach that was either exclusively print-based or primarily print-based and potentially supplemented with audio or audio-video tapes, CDs, or DVDs and, occasionally, radio or television broadcasts or teleconferencing. While some of the women tended to define their particular term according to the technologies being used (e.g., CMC), others appeared to view the term that they used according to access and inclusiveness (e.g., open to geographically isolated, non-traditional, and other marginalized learners).

It is no wonder that so many different terms were used in the process of gathering data from the interviewees. The topic of what the correct term for distance learning should be is one has generated a wealth of literature from dictionary and literary community definitions to entire books devoted to the subject. In his July 7, 2008 blog, "What do you mean by . . .?" Tony Bates offers one explanation for why scholars cannot seem to agree on the appropriate terms or definitions in our field. He says, "When using terms such as online learning and distance education, we are trying to describe a very dynamic and fast changing phenomenon, and the terminology often struggles to keep up with the reality of what is happening." In this blog, it is apparent that Bates subscribes to distance learning definitions based on the technologies used to deliver learning. (Those who are interested in a more exhaustive discussion on these terms may like to review the Quality Assurance Agency for Higher Education's [2020] article, "Guidance: Building a Taxonomy for Digital Learning.")

For the purpose of this study, the authors made no attempt to challenge respondents' use of their chosen term or to categorize the respondents' term according to any potential authority's view of the term. In short, the authors accepted whatever term (and understanding of the term) that respondents chose to use during their interviews.

Pioneers: Founders, Leaders, Researchers/Writers

To facilitate the selection of potential pioneers in distance and online learning, the authors selected three guiding terms: founder/trailblazer, leader, and researcher/writer. When reviewing any potential pioneer's available profile, the authors determined that the profile had to match one or more of these terms. Definitions for these terms are as follows:

> **Founder/Trailblazer:** Founders tend to be experts in a particular field of knowledge who initiate the genesis of a new organization. Driven by a vision or belief in what purpose or goals the organization may achieve, founders typically define the scale, scope, and initial operational processes of the organization. Consequently, founders tend to play a central leadership role in the organization, at least during the initial development and operation of the organization (Nelson, 2003; Schein, 1995). While trailblazers may often be founders, they also tend to be among the first people to explore, develop, or use a new idea, inquiry, innovation, enterprise, or space.
>
> **Leader:** Leaders encourage, influence, or otherwise motivate others to engage in certain actions that are intended to lead to the achievement of particular goals within certain settings or environments (Adeoye, 2009; Legacee, 2018; Ward, 2018). These may include activists and/or advocates for a particular cause.
>
> **Researcher/Writer:** Researchers actively conduct academically acceptable research in their field of expertise or areas of interest. Writers are scholars who have produced academic, peer-reviewed publications in journals, book chapters, or books in their field. They may also include editors of literary works in their field.

Research Methodology

A qualitative research methodology was selected to collect and thematically analyze data (Boyatzis, 1998; Gibbs, 2007) from 30 female pioneers of online learning. One research instrument, an interview script (Appendix A), was used in the study. This script was altered slightly for use with pioneers for whom English was a second language (Appendix B). Potential interviewees were provided with a copy of the interview script when they were invited to join the study. One participant was interviewed in person. Other interviewees chose to participate in a telephone or virtual meeting. All interviews were conducted at a time that was convenient for the interviewees and were digitally recorded with their consent. Transcriptions of the interviews were sent to the interviewees, who were instructed to edit their interviews as they liked. Final respondent-verified versions of the interviews were then used for data analysis purposes. (A copy of the verified interview for each participant is found in the preceding chapter devoted to them in this book.)

Research Questions

The study sought to capture the perceptions and lived experiences of women who were pioneers in distance learning initiatives that led to their engagement in online learning. To this end, these women were asked about the people and events motivating their interest in the field, the challenges that they faced, the learning environments that they worked in, the contributions that they made to the field, and any interesting memories or other thoughts that they wanted to share with other stakeholders. The aim was to provide a general framework to guide the study, while also giving the respondents the opportunity to tailor their responses, based on their unique histories and insights. To this end, the research questions were:

1. What was your educational and experiential background before you became involved in distance education (DE)?
2. In what year did you begin to look specifically into DE?
3. What were the circumstances in your world that initiated this interest in DE?
4. Which female researchers or female colleagues may have piqued your interest in DE?
5. Who would you identify as the early female leaders/founders in the field of DE?
6. What are some of the goals that you strove to achieve in the field of DE?
7. What are some of your accomplishments in the field of DE that you would like to share?
8. What are some of the challenges that you faced in the field of DE over the years?
9. What was the "state of DE" when you first entered the field as opposed to DE in 2018 (or 2019*)?
10. What interesting memories would you like to share about the beginning of online DE?
11. What were your specific DE research interests, and have they changed/evolved over the years?
12. Could you please describe the learning environment that you currently work in (e.g., geographic and institutional setting, student demographics)?
13. Is there anything else you would like to address?
14. Can you suggest names of other female pioneers in DE or online learning that you think we should include in the book?

One aim of the interview process was to provide consistency in questioning between interviews. Therefore, only one noteworthy change was made; the term *distance education* (DE) was replaced in

---

★ Some interviews were conducted in 2018; the remainder were completed in 2019.

interview scripts with whatever distance learning term the interviewee preferred. For example, some interviewees identified their contributions as being exclusive to CMC, ODL, or open learning.

Selection of Respondents

Two hundred potential respondent names were generated by employing a two-phase snowball sampling strategy (Cohen et al., 2011). In the first phase, the authors selected 42 candidates (or 21.0% of all potential respondents) from three sources: 1) the authors' own resources, 2) online literature searches, and 3) discussions with others who had a long history in the field. Candidates' online profiles were then compared to the three guiding terms established by the authors (i.e., founder/trailblazer, leader, researcher/writer, as defined in the Introduction; see Table 32.1). Candidates whose profiles did not match at least one of the guiding terms were excluded. Those who had not begun to work in the field of distance learning by 1980 were also excluded, unless they came from a country where distance learning was introduced in later years. Any remaining candidates who could not be contacted by email or telephone, were ill, or had passed away were also removed from the list. This exclusionary process left 23 (54.8% of all author-selected) candidates. Of these, 16 respondents (38.1% of all author-selected candidates) accepted the invitation to join the study, yielding a 69.6% positive response rate to the authors' invitation. One did not complete the interview process, yielding a total of 15 author-identified respondents in the study.

The second phase involved asking respondents during their interviews to provide the names of others whom they believed would fit the criteria for the study. A list of 158 names was collected (79.0% of all potential respondents). Fifty-seven duplicate names and four partial names were removed from this list, leaving 97 candidates. Fifteen more names were removed because these names were also on the authors' list. This left 82 unique names on the respondent-generated list (or 41.0% of the original potential respondent list). In the interest of completing the project in a timely manner, the authors processed candidate names in the order that they were received in during the interviews. This meant that the first 30 respondent-offered names were reviewed. Of those, 7 did not fit the study inclusion criteria and 8 declined the invitation to participate. The remaining 15 (50.0% of the 30) respondent-identified candidates joined the study. All in all, a

Table 32.1 Respondent Inclusion/Exclusion Criteria

Inclusion Criteria	Exclusion Criteria
Profile matched one or more of the following defining terms in the field of distance learning: 1. A founder/trailblazer, 2. Leader, *and/or* 3. Researcher/writer	Profile *did not match* any of the three defining terms in the field of distance learning: 1. A founder/trailblazer, 2. Leader, *and/or* 3. Researcher/writer
Began working in the field in 1980 or earlier (if from a country where distance learning was established by this period) *or* by 2000 or earlier (if from a country where distance learning was just becoming established)	Began working in the field in the field after 1980 (if from a country where distance learning was established by this period) *or* after 2000 (if from a country where distance learning was just becoming established)
Could communicate clearly with interviewer in English	Unable to communicate clearly with the interviewer in English
Was able to be contacted by the authors	Could not be contacted by the authors
Was physically and mentally able to participate	Was too ill to participate or was deceased

Analysis of Interviews

total of 30 participants from the first and second phases of the selection process completed the study.

Data Analysis Process

Coding: Respondent-verified interviews were coded using NVivo 12 Plus and NVivo Pro qualitative data analysis, as well as Excel 2019 software. Inter-coder reliability measures were used to establish coding protocols, clarify the meaning of codes, and ensure the ability of others to replicate the coding process; intra-coder reliability measures were used to confirm the primary coder's stability or accuracy of coding over time (Campbell et al., 2013; Krippendorff, 2004; Stemler, 2013). Both authors coded a total of 328 units, or 9.3% of all coded units included in this study (N = 3,534 total coded units; see Figure 32.1).

One author set up the initial coding framework. Then both authors co-coded 13 units while clarifying coding protocols and code definitions. During this process, the authors initially disagreed on approximately one-third (9 units or 30.8%) of the codes. Once the authors agreed on the changes that needed to be made, they then separately coded the rest of the first interview. Out of a resulting total of 125 coded units, the authors agreed on 108 units (86.4% of the total units). Further clarifications of definitions for codes resulted in the authors reaching 100% agreement on this first sample. A second interview was then randomly selected from the next six interviews (or 20% of the total number of interviews) to be coded separately by each author. Upon comparing the results,

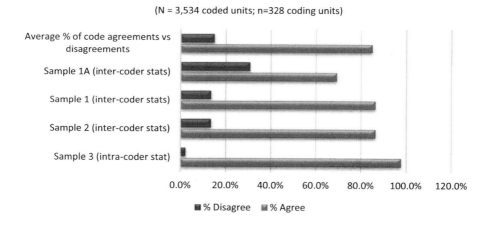

Reviewed Text	% Agree	% Disagree	% Total Units
Sample 3 (intra-coder stat)	97.7%	2.3%	100.0%
Sample 2 (inter-coder stats)	86.4%	13.6%	100.0%
Sample 1 (inter-coder stats)	86.4%	13.6%	100.0%
Sample 1A (inter-coder stats)	69.2%	30.8%	100.0%
Average % of code agreements vs disagreements	**85.0%**	**15.1%**	**100.0%**

Figure 32.1 Inter- and Intra-Coder Reliability Statistics

the authors learned that they had again achieved 86.4% agreement (51 out of a total of 59 units). Although no golden rule for what constitutes a good level of coding agreement has been established, some researchers have suggested that 70% agreement is acceptable, while 90% or higher is viewed as exceptional (Campbell et al., 2013; Fahy, 2001; Hodson, 1999; Hruschka et al., 2004; Krippendorff, 2004; Kurasaki, 2000; Wark, 2018). Since the authors had obtained 86.4% agreement on the last two samples, it was decided that the one author would continue coding alone.

To establish intra-coder reliability, the other author randomly selected one of the final six interviews (or the final 20% of all interviews) for the authors to code separately. This third sample had 131 units in all. The authors agreed upon 128 (or 97.7%) of the units, confirming that coding stability had most likely been maintained throughout the coding process.

Unit of analysis: According to Garrison et al. (2005), "the unit of analysis should fit with the research questions, theoretical framework, models, and methodology employed in the study" (Wark, 2018, p. 152). Moreover, the unit of analysis should be one "that multiple coders can identify reliably and simultaneously, one that exhaustively and exclusively encompasses the sought-after construct" (Rourke et al., p. 17). Given these recommendations, the authors determined that the most useful unit of analysis would be the thematic concept. For instance, when a respondent mentioned a particular award that they received when they were discussing their achievements, dialogue related to this award was coded to the name of the award.

Coding framework: The coding framework consisted of top-level thematic codes, or "parent" codes. Second-level, or "child" codes, were established under each of the parent codes. Third-level, or "grandchild" codes, were assigned beneath the child codes. Then fourth level, or "great-grandchild" codes, were generated for the next level of sub-themes and so on from there. To pick up on the previous example, if a respondent was discussing a particular award that they were given, the parent code would be "accomplishments," the child code would be "awards," and the grandchild code would be the name of the award that the respondent was discussing.

Some data was assigned to more than one code. To illustrate, when asked about which females may have piqued her interest in distance learning, one respondent replied, "Gail Crawford, Sydney Sharpe, Muriel Skinner (that's not the name that she uses now; that was her married name); those are the ones who come to mind at the moment." This quote was subsequently coded under each of the women's names, yielding a total of three codes for this unit of data.

Results

This section begins with a general report on the parent coding themes generated from this study. Respondents' collective responses to the research questions are then presented as categorized under nine parent coding themes. Three other parenting themes – benefits of distance learning, career history, and general gender-related comments – are not overtly tied to any of the research questions yet are identified as significant themes as well. Results related to these latter themes are also reviewed in this section. All reporting presents codes in order from the codes containing the most to the codes containing the least number of units. Results for child or grandchild codes that yielded less than 5% of the units for a higher-level code are reported herein but not expanded upon, due to the negligible impact their results have on this study.

Coding Themes

In all, 3,534 coded units were categorized in this study (Figure 32.2). Fourteen parent codes were identified. Arranged from most discussed to least mentioned, these include: background (516 units, or 14.6% of all units), benefits of distance learning (371 units; 10.5%), learning environment (356 units; 10.1%), challenges (353 units; 10.0%), accomplishments (313 units; 8.9%), changes over time

Analysis of Interviews

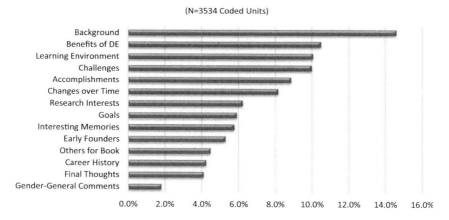

Figure 32.2 All Respondents' Interview Parent Codes

(288 units; 8.1%), research interests (220 units; 6.2%), goals (209 units; 5.9%), interesting memories (204 units; 5.8%), early founders (187 units; 5.3%), others for the book (158 units; 4.5%), career history (150 units; 4.2%), final thoughts (145 units; 4.1%), and general gender-related comments (64 units; 1.8%).

Background

Countries: While most respondents lived and worked in one country for most, if not all of their lives, some, like Liz Burge and Lani Gunawardena, worked in other countries for extended periods of time as well. For the purposes of this study, it was decided to only record the country where each respondent had spent most of her career (Figure 32.3).

Two out of five (twelve, or 40.0%) of the pioneers came from the North American continent. Seven (23.3% of all pioneers) came from Canada, three (10.0%) came from the United States, and two were from the West Indies. The Asian and Oceania continents were each home to seven pioneers (23.3%). Within Asia, two (6.7%) originated in Sri Lanka and one each (3.3%) came from China, India, Indonesia, Israel, and Korea. In the Oceania continent, five (16.7%) came from Australia, one (3.3%) worked in the Marshall Islands, and another one worked in New Zealand. Another two (6.7%) worked in Africa; one (3.3%) was from South Africa, and the other (3.3%) was from Namibia. One (3.3%) of the pioneers lived in South America; she was from Argentina. The final pioneer (3.3%) came from the European continent and the country of Germany.

*Number of Pioneers Interviewed by Country**

One			*Two*	*Three*	*Five*	*Seven*
Argentina	Indonesia	Namibia	Sri Lanka	USA	Australia	Canada
China	Israel	New Zealand	West Indies			
Germany	Korea	South Africa				
India	Marshall Islands					

* This chart indicates the primary country where each pioneer worked.

Analysis of Interviews

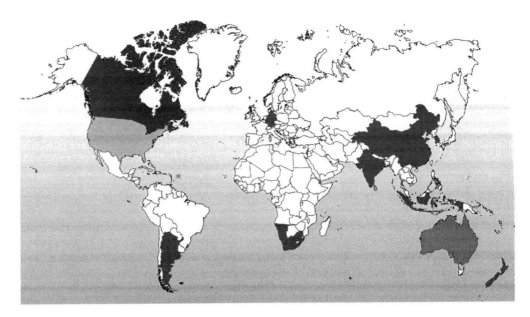

Figure 32.3 Locations Where Female Pioneers Worked

Collective responses to the first four research questions were sorted into the parent theme, background, and five main sub-themes: education, experience, year, initiating circumstances, and influencers. These four research questions were:

1. What was your educational and experiential background before you became involved in distance education (DE)?
2. In what year did you begin to look specifically into DE?
3. What were the circumstances in your world that initiated this interest in DE?
4. Which female researchers or female colleagues may have piqued your interest in DE?

Education: Eighty-seven (or 16.9%) of the coded units belonging to the parent code background were assigned to the child code education (Figure 32.4). Within the child code education, five sub-codes, or grandchild codes, were identified. These were, in order from most to least discussed: unrelated (34 of the 87 units coded to education, or 39.1% of the units coded to education), education (20 units; 23.0%), technology (17 units; 19.5%), distance learning (13 units; 14.9%), and undeclared (3 units; 3.4%).

Experience: Eighty-three units (16.1% of all units coded to the parent code background; Figure 32.5) related to the pioneers' educational background. Arranged in order from most to least discussed, these experiences were divided into the following child, or second-level codes: DE (26 units; 31.3% of background units), education (20 units; 24.1%), research (15 units; 18.1%), unrelated (12 units; 14.5%), and technology (10 units; 12.0%).

Year: Some respondents mentioned more than one year when asked about what year they began to look specifically into DE. Others talked about a specific year but mentioned that year at different times in the interview. This resulted in the generation of 40 units (or 7.8% of all background units) being coded to the child code year. Organized according to decades containing the most units to the least units, the decade from 1970 to 1979 contained 15 units (37.5% of the units coded to year),

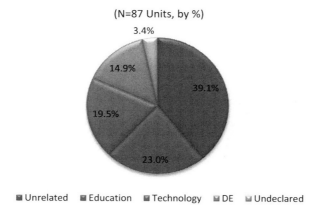

Figure 32.4 Pioneers' Educational Background by Field

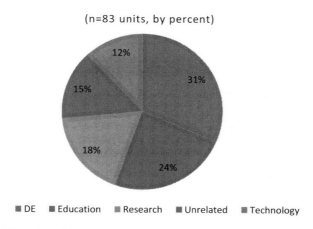

Figure 32.5 Pioneers' Experiential Background by Career Field

1980–1089 (11 units; 27.5%), 2000–2009 (7; 17.5%), 1990–1999 (4; 10.0%), 2010–2019 (2; 5.0%), and undeclared (1; 2.5%).

To produce a clearer picture of what year each respondent began to look into DE, a second statistical calculation was performed. This calculation considered only the earliest year that each respondent mentioned in their interview. Listed from the greatest to the least number of respondents for each decade, 12 pioneers (or 40.0% of all pioneers; Figure 32.6) began to look into DE between 1970 and 1979, 8 (26.7%) began between 1980–1989, 6 (20.0%) started somewhere between 2000 and 2009, 3 (10.0%) began between 1990 and 1999, and 1 (3.3%) did not state when she became involved in the field.

Initiating circumstances: One hundred forty-nine units (or 28.9% of all units assigned to the parent code background; Figure 32.7) were categorized as being among the initiating circumstances that led the pioneers in this study into this educational field. In order from the grandchild code with the most to the one with the least number of coded units, the following initiating circumstances

Analysis of Interviews

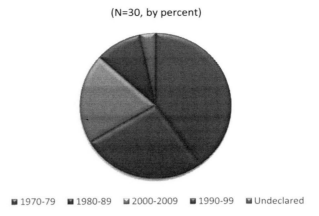

Figure 32.6 When Respondents Became Interested in the Field

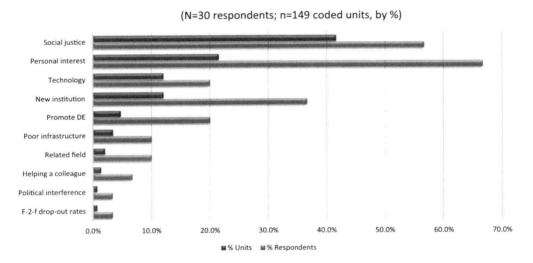

Figure 32.7 Initiating Circumstances: Respondents vs Coded Units

were cited: social justice (62 units; 41.6% of all initiating circumstances units), personal interest (32 units; 21.5%) technology and new institution (each had 18 units; 12.1%), promoting DE (7 units; 4.7%), poor DE infrastructure (5 units; 3.4%), working in a related field (3 units; 2.0%), helping a colleague (2 units; 1.3%), and finally, political interest or face-to-face (f-2-f) drop-out rates (1 unit each; 0.7% each).

The number of respondents who spoke at some length about particular circumstances were compared to the lesser conversations that some larger clusters of respondents had about other circumstances. Two-thirds of the respondents (20; 66.7%) indicated that they were drawn to the field by personal interest; such discussions netted one-fifth of the codes in this subsection. New institution and technology generated the same number of codes, yet only 6 participants (20.0%) discussed technology while 11 (36.7%) mentioned new institutions. Six respondents (20.0%) said that their desire to promote DE was also an initiating factor; however, they did not discuss this reason in much detail (7 units; 4.7% of all initiating circumstances.

Although some respondents spoke about social justice in a broad sense (yielding 10 units, or 16.1% of all social justice units), 7 other great-grandchild codes were also identified under this grandchild node. Organized from most to least spoken of, these 7 include: learner support (12 units; 19.4% of all social justice nodes), other marginalized groups (11 units; 17.7%), geographic isolation (10 units; 16.1%), adult learners (8 units; 12.9%), access to education (6 units; 9.7%), education for women (4 units; 6.5%), and life experience students (1 unit; 1.6%).

Influencers: Twenty-nine (96.7%) of the 30 interviewees provided responses to the question "Which female researchers or female colleagues may have piqued your interest in DE?" Twenty-five (83.3%) provided names of female colleagues, leaders, and mentors. Twelve (40.0%) mentioned organizations. Eleven (36.7%) indicated that there were few to none who piqued their interest in DE. Eight (26.7%) provided names of men in response. Lastly, three used terms that were non-gendered; these included *colleagues*, *team*, and *fellow designers*.

A total of 157 units (30.4% of all background units) were assigned to the child code influencers (Figure 32.8). Five great-grandchild codes were identified. Organized from those containing the most to those with the least number of units, these grandchild codes were: females (107 units; 68.2% of all influencer units), males (21 units; 13.4%), few to none (15 units; 9.6%), organizations (formal, mixed gender; 11 units; 7.0%), and no gender (3 units; 1.9%).

Five units (4.7%) of the grandchild code females included data that discussed female influencers in a general manner. A further 102 (95.3% of units coded to female) were separated into five great-grandchild code categories. These included, in order of most to least number of units: leaders (45 units; 42.1%), colleagues (36 units; 33.6%), mentors (12 units; 11.2%), Women's International Network (WIN; 5 units; 4.7%), and unnamed (4 units; 3.7%).

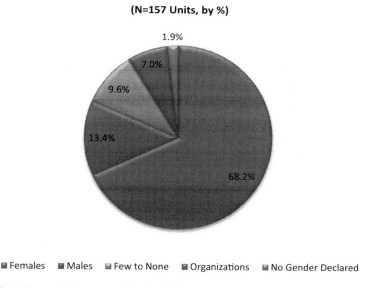

Figure 32.8 Who Influenced Pioneers to Join the Field

Learning Environment

The parent code containing the third most units (356 units; 10.1% of all codes) was learning environment. Units sorted into this parent code contained data that answered the 12th research question, "Could you please describe the learning environment that you currently work in (e.g., geographic and institutional setting, student demographics)?"

Learning environment units were divided into five thematic child codes. Listed in order from most discussed to least mentioned, these included: institutional description (211 units, or 59.3% of all learning environment units), student demographics (115 units; 32.3%), work specifics (15 units; 4.2%), consultant (11 units; 3.1%), and student support (4 units, 1.1%). Due to the negligible number of units generated from work specifics, consultant, and student support codes, only institutional description and student demographics data results are presented here.

Institutional Description: Twenty-six, or 86.7% of all respondents, offered institutional descriptions. Sorted from grandchild codes with the most to the least number of units, these descriptions dwelt upon: geographic sites (44 units; 20.9% of all institutional description units), instructional mode (39 units; 18.5%), education level (37 units; 17.5%), programme or course (34 units; 16.1%), age of institute (25 units; 11.8%), history of institute (11 units; 5.2%), access issues (8 units; 3.8%), intergovernmental and faculty (each yielded 4 units; 1.9%), dual mode (3 units; 1.4%), and quality issues (2 units; 0.9%). Grandchild codes containing over 5% of institutional description codes are elaborated on later in this chapter.

Geographic sites: Twenty-three (76.7%) of respondents provided geographic descriptions of the learning environments in which they worked. When discussing this geography, 11 (36.7%) of the respondents indicated that their institution was located on one site. Three (10.0%) said that their institution was spread across 2 to ten 10. Five (16.7%) worked at institutions that had 11 or more sites. Eight (26.7%) also provided details about the main campus of their institution.

Thirteen (43.3%) of respondents worked for national institutions. Six (20.0%) were employed with international institutions. Two (6.7%) described their institutions as having provincial jurisdiction. The final two (6.7%) who provided geographic descriptions did not declare whether their institutions were regional, provincial, national, or international in scope.

Instructional mode: Seventeen (56.7% of all) respondents discussed the instructional mode that their institution offered. Eleven (36.7% of all) respondents indicated that their institution offered a blended approach, with 5 (16.7%) saying that the approach was primarily DE and 3 (10.0%) indicating that their blended approach was primarily f-2-f. The final 3 (10.0%) did not elaborate on the balance between DE and f-2-f delivery. Five (16.7% of all) respondents worked at DE institutions; of these, 3 (10.0%) were employed at ODL institutions. Three (10.0%) described the mode of delivery at their DE institute as being asynchronous. One (3.3%) stated that her institution engaged primarily in synchronous delivery. The final respondent (3.3%) said that hers was an f-2-f institute.

Education level: Twenty-two (73.3% of all) respondents described the education level that their institution provided services for. Seventeen (56.7%) characterized their institution as being a university, three (10.0%) viewed their institution as a college, one (3.3%) described her institute as a K–12 open school, and the final one (3.3%) described her institute as being a lifelong learning one. Six (20.0%) individuals who saw their institution as being a university or college also described their institution as serving all levels of learners.

Programme or course: Fourteen (46.7%) of all respondents provided details about the programme or course that they were involved with at the time of the interview. Six (20.0%) described the programme or course as being DE in nature. Four (13.3%) described their programme or course as being learner-centred, blended, and/or f-2-f. Three (10.0%) said that the delivery was asynchronous, while two (6.7%) stated that their programme or course delivery was synchronous. Two (6.7%) said

Analysis of Interviews

that open educational resources (OER) were used, and one (3.3%) was engaged in a massive open online course (MOOC) at the time of the interview.

Age of institute: Although twenty (66.7% of all) respondents discussed the age of their institution, fourteen did not provide specific details about the year in which their institution was established. Of the remaining six, three indicated that their institutions were operational sometime between 1931 and 1950. One respondent's institution was underway between 1951 and 1970. Another respondent said that her institution was founded between 1971 and 1990. The final respondent who provided details about the age of her institution said that it was launched between 1991 and 2000.

Student demographics: Twenty-two (73.3% of all) respondents provided data on student demographics. Three grandchild codes were identified. The code containing the most units was student profiles, which was discussed by 19 (63.3% of all) respondents and generated 68 units (59.6% of all student demographic units). Seventeen (56.7%) respondents talked about geographic locations and, in doing so, produced 26 units (21.9%). Lastly, population size was mentioned by 19 (63.3%) of the respondents and included 21 units (18.4%).

Student profiles: Nineteen (63.3% of all) respondents generated 9 great-grandchild codes under the grandchild code student profiles. In order from the great-grandchild codes with the most to the least number of units, these include: age range (31 units; 45.6% of all student profile units), cultural issues (13 units; 19.1%), graduate level (8 units; 11.8%), undergraduate level (4 units; 5.9%), employed grads and no prerequisites (each had 3 units; 4.4%); merged levels and undeclared (each with 2 units; 2.9%), and lastly, perseverance and prepared (each had 1 unit; 1.5%).

Geographic locations: Seventeen (56.7% of all) respondents identified 3 great-grandchild codes when describing the profiles of their students. These codes were divided into: international students (14 units; 53.8% of units assigned to geographic locations), national students (11 units; 42.3%), and regional (1 unit; 3.8%).

Population size: Three great-grandchild codes were defined by 19 (63.3% of all) respondents under the grandchild code population size. The code containing the most units was undeclared, which yielded 12 units (57.1% of all population size units). Institution size produced another 7 units (33.3%). Lastly, class size generated 2 units (9.5%).

Challenges

The parent code with the third largest number of units related to specific research questions was challenges, which encompassed 353 units (10.0% of all coded units; Figure 32.9). The data arising from these units was generated in response to the eighth research question, "What are some of the challenges that you faced in the field of DE over the years?" All 30 respondents answered this question. Their responses were sorted into 25 child codes. Listed from the ones with the most units to the ones with the least units, these child codes included: acceptance-understanding (83 units; 23.5% of all units coded to challenges), institution growing pains (43 units; 12.2%), funding (38 units; 10.8%), technology (29 units; 8.2%), gender (28 units; 7.9%), faculty (21 units; 5.9%), cultural issues (18 units; 5.1%), student support (15 units; 4.2%), student attrition (11 units; 3.1%), human resources and quality (each yielding 10 units; 2.8%), sustainability (8 units; 2.3%), instructional delivery, research, successful students (each producing 7 units; 2.0%), adaptability, not unique to DE, and synchronous learning (each containing 3 units; 0.8%), colleague isolation and student collaboration (each having 2 units; 0.6%), and lastly, class size, general comments, and patents (each holding 1 unit; 0.3%).

Results from child codes containing more than 5% of the parent code units are further discussed here.

Acceptance/Understanding: Twenty-four (80% of all) respondents felt that the most significant challenge they faced during their career was acceptance and/or understanding of DE by others.

Analysis of Interviews

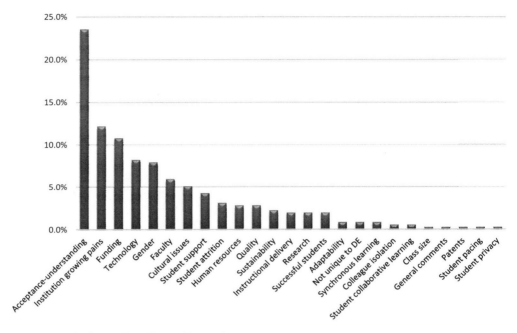

Figure 32.9 Challenges Identified by Respondents

Six child codes were identified within this broader theme. In order from most frequently to least frequently mentioned, these codes were: orthodoxy (30 units; 36.1% of all acceptance-understanding units), general comments (16 units; 19.3%), credibility (14 units; 16.9%), government expectations (11 units; 13.3%), DE not commonplace (10 units; 12.0%), and terminology (2 units; 2.4%).

Institution Growing Pains: Thirteen (43.3%) of all respondents cited institution growing pains as one of the challenges that they faced over the years. Beyond two units (4.7% of all challenge units) that contained general comments about the growing pains, sub-themes identified included: developing systems (18 units; 41.9%), debates (12 units; 27.9%), and skepticism (11 units; 25.6%).

Funding: Over half (17, 56.7%) of all respondents believed that funding was a challenge. Twelve units (57.9% of all funding units) contained general comments about this issue. More specific funding concerns included: student support (8 units; 21.1%), network (4 units; 10.5%), and the move to a corporate model of for-profit institutes (4 units; 10.5%).

Technology: Two out of five (13; 43.3% of all) respondents felt that technology was a challenge. Ordered from the most to least mentioned, specific technological concerns included: developing infrastructure (12 units; 41.4% of all technology units), limitations of technology (10 units; 34.5%), evolving technology and the need to place pedagogy before technology (each yielding 3 units; 10.3%), and lack of training (1 unit; 3.4%).

Gender: Twelve (40.0% of all) interviewees indicated that gender issues were a challenge. Female subordination was the most frequently expressed sub-theme (10 units; 35.7% of all gender units). Male dominance was the second most discussed theme (8 units; 28.6%). These were followed by debunking myths and equality; both generated 4 units (14.3%). No difference and supportive men were the least-mentioned gender issues (each yielding 1 unit; 3.6%).

Faculty: Almost one-third of the pioneers in this study (9; 30.0%) stated that faculty issues were a challenge. Eight of the nine women who discussed this topic indicated that the lack of skills among faculty was most vexing (11 units; 52.4% of all faculty units). Other faculty concerns included: motivation (5 units; 23.8%) and lack of research (2 units; 9.5%). The least-mentioned faculty concerns were brain drain, currency, and few publications (each garnering 1 unit; 4.8%).

Cultural Issues: One out of three (10; 33.3% of all) interviewees stated that cultural issues were also a challenge. Cultural issues related to social structures were most frequently cited (13 units; 72.2% of all cultural issue units). Language barriers (3 units; 16.7%) and other issues (2 units; 11.1%) were also recalled.

Accomplishments

The parent code producing the fourth most units directly bound to a research question answered the seventh inquiry: "What are some of your accomplishments in the field of DE that you would like to share?" All respondents offered answers to this question and, in doing so, provided 313 units of data (or 8.9% of all coded units; Figure 32.10), sorted into 21 child codes. Ordered from the child code containing the most to the least number of codes, these codes were: implementing new initiatives (58 units; 18.5% of all accomplishment units), literary contributions (43 units; 13.7%), DE advocacy and student learning (each containing 29 units; 9.3%), research (26 units; 8.3%), team accomplishments (24 units; 7.7%), international contributions (21 units; 6.7%), awards (19 units; 6.1%), student support (14 units; 4.5%), teacher education (11 units; 3.5%), networking (6 units; 1.9%), education while working (5 units; 1.6%), faculty development and institutional profile (each with 4 units; 1.3%), gender equity and instructional resources (each containing 3 units; 1.0%), sustainability (2 units; 0.6%), and general comments, government committee appointment, and student success (1 unit each; 0.3%).

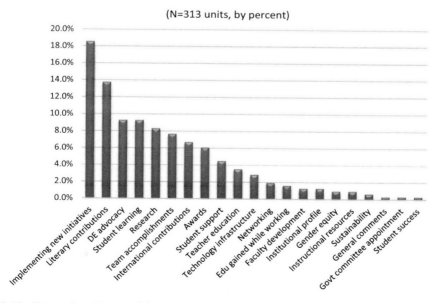

Figure 32.10 Respondents' Accomplishments

Arranged from most discussed to least mentioned, child codes containing more than 5% of the accomplishment units are reviewed here.

Implementing New Initiatives: Seventeen (56.7% of all) respondents discussed the implementation of new initiatives among their accomplishments. Listed from those containing the most to the least number of units, the grandchild codes generated from this child code were: new programmes and/or courses, and new systems (each with 13 units; 22.4% of all implementing new initiatives units), new network (10 units, 17.2%), new policies (7 units; 12.1%), new conferences (5 units; 8.6%), new funding structures (4 units; 6.9%), upgrading centres (3 units; 5.2%), new institution (2 units; 3.4%), and new centres (1 unit; 1.7%).

Literary Contributions: Ten (33.3%) of the pioneers counted literary contributions among their accomplishments. From those with the most to the fewest units, literary sub-theme contributions included: learning with technology (10 units; 23.3% of all literary contribution units); support (7 units; 16.3%); online learning (5 units; 11.6%); ODL learning theory (4 units; 9.3%); collaborative learning (3 units; 7.0%): collaboration with colleagues, culture, editor, and unrelated to DE (each containing 2 units; 4.7%); and lastly, DE in French, ethics, gender, publisher, quality assurance, and research (1 unit or 2.3% each).

DE Advocacy: Nine (30% of all) pioneers recounted DE advocacy initiatives among their accomplishments. Two-thirds of these women reflected upon their engagement in DE promotion, yielding 11 units, or 37.9% of all DE advocacy units. Nine units (31.0%) were assigned to access; four units (13.8%) contained data related to awareness of issues or technology integration. The final unit (3.4%) was on sustainability.

Student Learning: Accomplishments related to student learning were recounted by 11 (36.7%) of the women. Presented from the grandchild codes with the most to the least number of units, these included: cultural issues and prisoners (each with 5 units and 17.2% of all student learning units); learner-centred (4 units; 13.8%); DE system (3 units; 10.3%); cognitive modelling, cooperative learning, experiential learning, and gender issues (each with 2 units; 6.9%); and finally, health education, international perspectives, MOOCs, and user-friendly resources (each having 1 unit; 3.4%).

Research: Six (20%) of the respondents included research contributions among their accomplishments. Twenty-six units (8.3% of all accomplishment units) contained data about research accomplishments. Five women made general comments about their research, producing 9 units (34.6% of all research accomplishment units). Other research units included: gender issues (9 units; 30.8%), online discourse (6 units; 23.1%), robotics (2 units; 7.7%), and computer conferencing content analysis (1 unit; 3.8%).

Team Accomplishments: Eleven (36.7%) of the women mentioned team accomplishments, a topic that generated 24 units, or 7.7% of all accomplishment units. No grandchild codes were identified within this conversation area.

International Contributions: Fourteen (46.7%) of the respondents identified international contributions among their accomplishments, producing a total of 21 units (6.7% of all accomplishment units). Comments of a general nature or related to consulting each yielded 6 units (28.6% of all accomplishment units). Online learning model and quality assurance topics each included 2 units (9.5%). International Association of Distance Education (ICDE) President, ODL learning theory, ODL student support, and visiting scholar had one unit each (4.8%).

Awards: One-third of the women (10 women; 33.3%) listed awards among their accomplishments. Of the 19 award units (6.1% of all accomplishment units), 3 (15.8% of all award units) were assigned to honorary doctorates. Another 2 units (10.5%) were related to the AAOU Meritorious Service and Charles Wedemeyer awards. The ACDE, AIST Research, Chancellor, COL, ICDE, and institutional teaching awards each contained 1 unit (5.3%).

Analysis of Interviews

Changes over Time

All participants responded to the nineth interview question, "What was the 'state of DE' when you first entered the field as opposed to DE in 2018 (or 2019)?" The resulting discourse generated 288 units (8.1% of all interview units). Discussions about the early years included 133 units (46.2% of all changes over time units). Current years yielded 95 units (33.0%). Reflections on the greatest change over time produced 50 units (17.4%), while slow changes produced 8 units (2.8%). Finally, 2 units (0.7%) included discussion about personal changes over time. The results from the child codes containing more than 5% of the units from this parent code follow. These child codes are early years, current years, and greatest change.

Early Years: Everyone in the study discussed the early years of DE, producing 133 units (46.2% of all changes over time units). Ordered from the grandchild code with the most to the least number of units, these included: technology (65 units; 48.9%), DE not commonplace (20 units; 15.0%), industrial model (14 units; 10.5%), primitive (11 units; 8.3%), course materials and experimentation (each with 6 units; 4.5%), research (5 units; 3.8%), exciting (3 units; 2.3%), blended learning (2 units; 1.5%), and dual mode (1 unit; 0.8%).

Current Years: Twenty-four (80%) of the respondents discussed what the field was like at the time of their interview. This discussion netted 95 units (33% of all changes over time units). Arranged from most to least number of units, the grandchild codes included: technology (56 units; 58.9% of all current year units); network model (10 units; 10.5%); student support (7 units; 7.4%); experimentation (6 units; 6.3%); orthodox and research (each with 3 units; 3.2%); blended learning, managing growth, and MOOCs (2 units each; 2.1%); and lastly, artisan model, business model, new staff roles, and firmly established (each generating 1 unit, or 1.1%).

Greatest Change: Fifty units (17.4% of all changes over time units) were identified by 18 (60%) of the women in this study. Ordered from the grandchild code with the most to the least number of units, thematic discussions included: technology (21 units; 42.0% of all greatest change units), changing DE model (14 units; 28.0%), moving to online (10 units; 20.0%), acceptance-understanding (3 units; 6.0%), and research areas (2 units; 4.0%).

Research Interests

Everyone in this study responded to the 11th interview question, "What were your specific DE research interests, and have they changed/evolved over the years?" Responses generated a total of 220 units (6.2% of all study units; Figure 32.11). Fourteen sub-themes, or child codes, were identified. Organized from the child codes with the most to the fewest number of units, these were: technology (60 units, or 27.3% of all research interest units); social issues (48 units; 21.8%); evolved (209 units; 13.2%); distance education (26 units; 11.8%); support (14 units; 6.4%); quality assurance (8 units; 3.6%); institutional development (6 units; 2.7%); no research, retired now, sharing research, and student success (each having 5 units; 2.3%); learner autonomy and policy and governance (each possessing 4 units; 1.8%); and lastly, not related to DE (1 unit; 0.5%). Further results for the child codes that produced more than 5% of all research interest units are shared next.

Technology: Sixteen (53.3%) of the respondents were engaged in technology-related research. Of the 60 units (27.3% of all research interest units) categorized under technology, most were linked to CMC (i.e., 24 units, or 40.0% of all technology units). In descending order of unit numbers, other grandchild codes that were identified included: pedagogy and technology (7 units; 11.7%); social media (6 units; 10.0%); virtual worlds (5 units; 8.3%); OER (4 units; 6.7%); human-technology interaction, low technology, MOOCs, and robotics (each with 3 units; 5.0%); and haptic feedback (2 units; 3.3%).

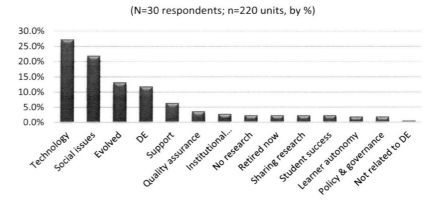

Figure 32.11 Respondents' Research Interests

Social Issues: The second most common technology research topic centred on social issues, producing 48 units (21.8% of all research interest units). Twelve (40.0%) of the women discussed research related to social issues. Data generated from these discussions yielded 18 units (37.5% of all social issues units) about gender issues, 11 units (22.9%) on social science education, 8 units (16.7%) on cultural issues, 7 units (14.6%) about access, and 2 units (4.2%) each related to literacy and social mobility.

Evolved: Twenty-four women (80% of all women included in the study) conducted DE research. Of these, 15 (62.5%) stated that their research interests had evolved over the years. Their responses generated 19 units, or 65.5% of the 29 units included in all of the evolved category units. Eight women (33.3%) indicated that their research interests had not changed; their responses produced 9 units (31.0%). The final pioneer who conducted research did not respond to this part of question 11. Her non-response was recorded as a single unit (3.4%) and sorted into the undeclared grandchild code.

Distance Education: Eleven (36.7%) of the women in the study discussed DE research activities in a broad sense, netting 26 DE units (11.8% of all research interest units). Of these, 10 units (38.5%) were identified as being related to instructional design, 7 units (26.9%) were about DE learning environments, 4 units (15.4%) were about DE research in general, 3 units (11.5%) involved DE as a system, and the final 2 units (7.7%) were about ODL theory.

Support: The last research interest area, support, was mentioned by 7 (29.2%) of the 24 women who conducted research. All 7 reported doing research related to student support, producing 10 units (71.4% of all support units). Two of the women also reported on faculty support research, yielding 3 units (21.4%). Lastly, one of the women said that she conducted general DE support research. This comment generated one unit (7.1%).

Goals

The parent code to generate the seventh-most units was goals (209 units, or 5.9% of all study units). Data sorted into this parent code came from all participants in response to the sixth interview question, "What are some of the goals that you strove to achieve in the field of DE?" These responses were further sorted into 16 child codes (Figure 32.12). Organized from those with the most to the least number of units, these child codes were: social issues (58 units; 27.8% of all goal units); support (33 units; 15.8%); student success (21 units; 10.0%); quality assurance (16 units; 7.7%); research (13

Analysis of Interviews

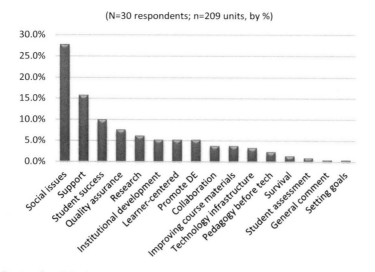

Figure 32.12 Respondents' Goals

units; 6.2%); institutional development, learner-centred, and promoting DE (each with 11 units; 5.3%); collaboration and improving course materials (8 units each; 3.8%); technology infrastructure (7 units; 3.3%); pedagogy before technology (5 units; 2.4%); survival (3 units; 1.4%); student assessment (2 units; 1.0%); and lastly, general comments and setting goals (1 unit each; 0.5%).

Child codes yielding more than 5% of all goal units and containing grandchild codes are elaborated upon next.

Social Issues: The most commonly shared goal among the interviewees was in addressing social issues; 16 of the women (53.3%) identified this as one of their goals, generating 58 units (27.1% of all goal units). Sub-themes identified within the social issues category included, in order from most to least discussed: access (31 units; 53.4%), decrease isolation (9 units; 15.5%), improve education (8 units; 13.8%), gender (5 units; 8.6%), improve communities (4 units; 6.9%), and general comments (1 unit; 1.7%).

Support: The child code support was mentioned by 13 (43.3%) of the respondents and yielded 33 units (15.4% of all goal units). Three grandchild codes were identified: learner support (15 units; 45.5% of all support units), faculty support (10 units; 30.3%), and technology support (8 units; 24.2%).

Student Success: Twelve (23.7% of all) respondents listed student success as one of their goals. Sub-themes included: better learning experience (16 units, or 76.2% of all student success units), providing information (3 units; 14.3%), and study skills (2 units; 9.5%).

Research: Research was mentioned as a goal for 6 (20%) of the women. Organized from those with the most to the least number of units, sub-topics included: cultural issues and ODL theory (3 units each; 23.1% of all research goal units); gender research (2 units; 15.4%); and faculty, general comments, MOOCs, OER, and sharing resources research goals (1 unit each; 7.7%).

Interesting Memories

Twenty-nine of the 30 respondents in this study responded to the tenth research question, "What interesting memories would you like to share about the beginning of online DE?" These responses

Analysis of Interviews

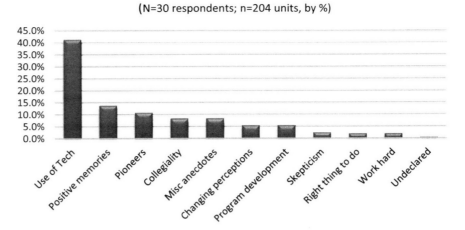

Figure 32.13 Respondents' Interesting Memories

yielded 204 interesting memory codes (5.8% of all study codes). Eleven child codes were identified (Figure 32.13). Organized from those with the most to the least number of codes, these were: use of technology (84 units; 41.2% of all interesting memories units), positive memories (28 units; 13.7%), pioneers (22 units; 10.8%), collegiality and miscellaneous anecdotes (each producing 17 units; 8.3%), changing perceptions and programme development (11 units each; 5.4%), skepticism (5 units; 2.5%), right thing to do and working hard (each with 4 units; 2.0%), and undeclared (1 unit; 0.5%).

Further details on child codes that possess grandchild codes and contain more than 5% of all interesting memories units are provided next.

Use of Technology: The use of technology was cited as an interesting memory by two out of three women (66.7%) in the study. Units relating to the use of technology were separated into seven sub-themes. Ordered from those with the most to the least number of units, these sub-themes included: types of technology (32 units; 38.1% of all use of technology units); limitations of technology (22 units; 26.2%); integrating technology (21 units; 25.0%); experimentation (6 units; 7.1%); and lastly, CMC analysis, digital research software, and training (each with 1 unit; 1.2%).

Positive Memories: Nineteen women (63.3% of all respondents) recounted positive memories when asked to share interesting memories. Four grandchild codes were identified. These included: excitement (18 units; 64.3% of all positive memory units), what DE offered (7 units; 25.0%), students meeting face-to-face (2 units; 7.1%), and women students (1 unit; 3.6%).

Pioneers: Of the 14 women (or 46.7% of all respondents) who talked about being pioneers in the field, 11 focused on the creation of new networks. Discussions on new networks produced 17 units (77.3% of all pioneer units). The remaining 5 units (22.7%) were more general comments about pioneering in DE.

Early Founders

All participants provided responses to the fifth interview question, "Who would you identify as the early female leaders/founders in the field of DE?" Twenty-six (86.7%) of the participants suggested one or more women's names, generating 157 units (84.0% of all early founder units). Twelve (40.0%) of the participants clarified that they were aware of few to no early female leaders or founders in this field; these comments generated 18 units (9.6% of early founder units). Ten units (5.3%)

Analysis of Interviews

were assigned to the child code organizations. These organizations included the Canadian Association of Distance Education (CADE), International Association of Distance Education (ICDE), and Women's International Network (WIN). The child code that yielded the fewest units was general comments, which produced 2 units (1.1%).

Others for the Book

When asked the 14th question, "Can you suggest names of other female pioneers in DE or online learning that you think we should include in the book?" 25 (83.3%) of all respondents offered at least one name. This generated 158 units (4.5% of all coded units in this study) or, in other words, a list of 158 female pioneers that the respondents felt might be good candidates for this book project. (After removing 57 duplicate and 4 partial names, 97 unique pioneering women's names were left on the list of potential candidates.)

Final Comments

The 13th interview question asked, "Is there anything else you would like to address?" to which 27 (90.0%) of the women in this study offered a reply. Ordered from the child code with the most to the least number of units, responses were categorized as follows: advice (90 units; 62.1% of all final comment units; Figure 32.14), overcoming barriers (25 units; 17.2%), positive memories (18 units; 12.4%), sharing work (5 units; 3.4%), comments about the book and the need for leadership (3 units each; 2.1%), and finally, 1 respondent stated that she had no comment (1 unit; 0.7%). Two child codes, advice and overcoming barriers, yielded a number of grandchild codes, which are discussed next.

Advice: Twenty-four (80.0%) of all respondents chose to end the interview with words of advice, producing 90 units (62.1% of all final comments included in the study). Thirteen grandchild

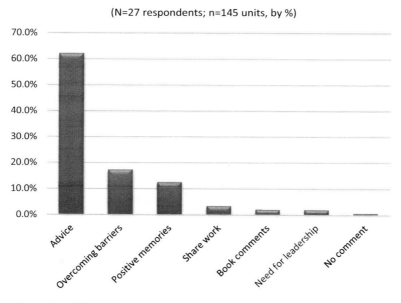

Figure 32.14 Respondents' Final Comments

Analysis of Interviews

codes were identified. Listed from those with the most to the least number of units, these are: remain current (21 units; 23.3% of all advice units); be learner-focused (18 units; 20.0%); think about the future of DE (16 units; 17.8%); the value of research (7 units; 7.8%); experiment and revise, take risks, and team-based approaches (5 units each; 5.6%); student support (4 units; 4.4%); network and put people first (3 units each; 3.3%); and lastly, enjoy the rewards of DE, use an interdisciplinary approach, and lifelong learning (1 unit each; 1.1%).

Overcoming Barriers: Fourteen (46.7%) of the women in this study included final comments about overcoming barriers. Nine overcoming barriers grandchild codes were found. Listed from those with the most to the fewest number of units, these were: perceptions (8 units; 32% of all overcoming barriers units); funding and systems development (4 units each; 16.0%); technological currency (3 units; 12.0%); work hard (2 units; 8.0%); and lastly, government issues, language barriers, numerous barriers, and time zones (1 unit each; 4.0%).

Emergent Codes

Three parent codes and two cross-category themes emerged from the data. None of these were overtly related to any interview script questions (Appendices A and B). The three emergent parent codes included benefits of DE, career history, and general gender-related comments; the two cross-category themes were technology and gender.

Benefits of DE: Even though respondents were not asked about the benefits of DE, all 30 of the respondents mentioned this topic during their interviews. This resulted in benefits producing the second highest number of units of all parent codes identified in the study (371 units; 10.5% of all study units). Twelve child codes were identified (Figure 32.15). Ordered from those with the greatest to the least number of units, these child codes include: social justice (179 units; 48.2% of all benefits of DE units), information communication technologies (ICT; 40 units; 10.8%), continuing education (37 units; 10.0%), openness (34 units; 9.2%), community development and flexibility (each with 20 units; 5.4%), socializing and superior (12 units each; 3.2%), economic (10 units; 2.7%), job opportunities (4; 1.1%), cohorts (2 units; 0.5%), and asynchronous learning (1 unit; 0.3%). One child code, social justice, yielded a number of grandchild codes as well.

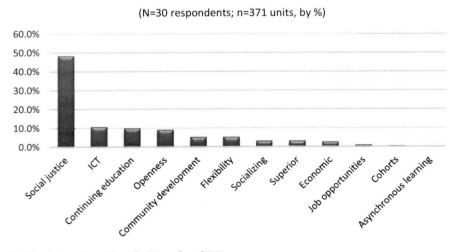

Figure 32.15   Respondent-Identified Benefits of DE

Social justice: The most prevalent sub-theme among the benefits of DE identified by the study respondents was social justice (179 units; 48.2% of all benefits units). Twenty-eight (93.3%) of all respondents mentioned social justice. Grandchild codes emerging from the social justice child code were: access to education (56 units; 31.3%), geographic isolation (24.6%), other marginalized groups (36 units; 20.1%), learner support (18 units; 10.1%), gender equality (13 units; 7.3%), life experience students (7 units; 3.9%), and general comments (5 units; 2.8%).

Career History: A second parent code to organically arise from the interview data was career history (150 units; 4.2% of all study units). Twenty-seven (90.0%) of the respondents discussed some aspect of their career history during the interviews. These discussions were sorted into four child codes: early career (65 units; 43.3% of all career history units), mid- and later career (41 units each; 27.3%), and unspecified (3 units; 2.0%).

Early career: Twenty-three (76.7% of all) respondents talked about their early career (65 units; 43.3% of all career history units). Nine grandchild codes were identified within this child code. Ordered from the ones with the most to the least number of units, these grandchild codes were: faculty member (20 units; 30.8% of all early career codes); researcher (15 units; 23.1%); administrative leadership (8 units; 12.3%); DE writer (7 units; 10.8%); educational technologist (4 units; 6.2%); course writer, programme developer, and student advisor/counsellor (3 units each; 4.6%); and lastly, tutor (2 units; 3.1%).

Mid-career: Seventeen (56.7% of all) respondents talked about their activities during the middle years of their career, generating 41 mid-career units (27.3% of all career units). Arranged from the grandchild codes with the most to the least number of units, sub-topics included: faculty (14 units; 34.1% of mid-career units), administrative leadership (11 units; 26.8%), advisor-consultant and instructional designer (each with 5 units; 12.2%), involvement in associations (4 units; 9.8%), and researcher (2 units; 4.9%).

Late career: Although late-career discussions produced the same number of codes as mid-career conversations did (i.e., 41 units, or 27.3% of all career history units), 19 women (63.3% of all respondents) mentioned late-career activities. Three grandchild codes were identified: administrative leadership (19 units; 46.3% of all late career units), faculty (12 units; 29.3%), and advisor-consultant (10 units; 24.4%).

General Gender-related Comments: The final parent code to emerge during the interviews was labelled general gender-related comments. Even though 18 (60.0% of all) respondents contributed to this parent code, it yielded the least number of units of all parent codes. Eight sub-themes were identified. Organized from the most to the least number of units, these sub-themes were: female subordination (27 units; 42.2% of all general gender-related comment units); male dominance (22 units; 34.4%); female grit (6 units; 9.4%); cultural segregation, debunking myths, general comments, and no difference (each yielding 2 units; 3.1%); and lastly, supportive men (1 unit; 1.6%).

Cross-category Themes: Two prevalent themes crossed most of the 14 parent categories established during the coding process. The cross-category theme with higher number of units was technology, and the one with fewer units was gender.

Technology themes: Technology was mentioned by all participants when responding to various interview questions. These sub-themes were categorized under 12 of the 14 parent codes identified in the study. The aggregation of all technology sub-theme results yielded a total of 721 units (20.4% of all study units), making technology the primary theme to emerge from this study. Figure 32.16 illustrates the number of units per parent category versus the number of respondents who mentioned technology within each parent category. Organized from the code with the most to the least number of units, technology sub-theme units were found in the following parent codes: changes over time (209 units; 29.0% of technology theme units), interesting memories (116 units; 16.1%), research interests (93 units; 12.9%), background (50 units; 6.9%), goals (48 units; 6.7%), accomplishments (44 units; 6.1%), benefits of DE (41 units; 5.7%), challenges and learning environment (each with

Analysis of Interviews

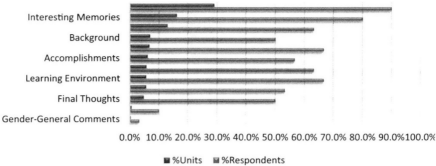

Figure 32.16 Technology Sub-Themes: Respondent vs Coded Unit

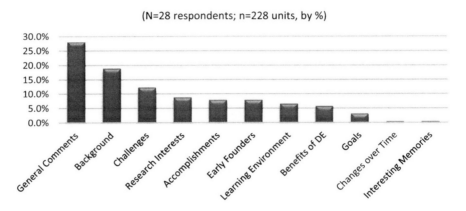

Figure 32.17 Respondents' Gender-Related Comments

40 units; 5.5%), final thoughts (34 units; 4.7%), career history (4 units; 0.6%), and general gender-related comments (2 units; 0.3%).

Gender themes: Twenty-eight (93.3%) of all respondents made references to gender-related topics within the context of 11 (or 78.6%) of all parent codes, yielding a total of 228 units (or 6.5% of all units included in this study). Ranked in order from the parent code with the most to the least units, these were: general gender-related comments (64 units; 28.1% of all gender theme units; Figure 32.17), background (43 units; 18.9%), challenges (28 units; 12.3%), research interests (20 units; 8.8%), accomplishments and early founders (18 units each; 7.9%), learning environment (15 units; 6.6%), benefits of DE (13 units; 5.7%), goals (7 units; 3.1%), and lastly, changes over time and interesting memories (each with 1 unit; 0.4%).

Discussion

Discourse on the results from the previous section, Results, begins with the 11 parent codes that were overtly tied to one or more interview questions. Three emergent parent codes and two

Background

Countries: One explanation for the geographic distribution of the selected pioneers was the authors' need to communicate in the English language. Most of the women in the study came from countries where English was commonly spoken. Even though English was not native to some respondents, such as Li Chen, Insung Jung, Beatriz Fainholc, and Christine von Prümmer, they willingly communicated in English. Despite the prevalence of English throughout Europe, and especially northern Europe, however, the authors were able to include only one pioneer from this continent. Three other well-known candidates had passed away; it is a tragedy that their stories – told in their own words – are lost forever.

It is also discouraging that, due to the authors' limited language abilities, so many other female pioneers from across the globe were unable to share their experiences and insights in this volume. Such contributions might have provided new perspectives on the lives of female pioneers around the world.

Education: Two out of five units coded to respondents' educational background were unrelated to distance learning, education, or technology. In fact, 20 (74.1%) of the 27 respondents who discussed their educational background said that they had educational backgrounds that were not connected to distance learning, education, or technology. This is what some had to say:

> [Respondent 1]: I had a Bachelor's and a Master's degree in Anthropology from the University of Alberta. The Master's was in 1971, and at that point, I registered as a PhD candidate, also at the University of Alberta. I had taught a couple of courses in anthropology as a graduate student. By the time that I had heard about distance education, I had had my first and second children, who were at the time 15 months and six weeks.

> [Respondent 2]: I completed my secondary schooling in 1966 with the German *Abitur*, the equivalent of British A-Levels or American high school diploma but also entitled me to enter a German university. Instead, I went to the United States on a full scholarship awarded to me by Smith College, a renowned women's college and one of the Seven Sisters. I majored in sociology and graduated with honours in 1969. Returning to Germany I enrolled in a four-year master's programme at the newly established University of Constance where I could get at least some credit for courses taken toward my American degree. In those days, Bachelor's degrees were not known in Germany, and it took me until 1973 to do the requisite number of courses and complete my MA in Sociology and Political Science.

> [Respondent 3]: When I joined the Telemedicine group, I had an undergraduate degree science (chemistry).

> [Respondent 4]: I came from the social sciences. My undergraduate degree or BA (Bachelor of Arts) degree was in sociology, and then I moved to public policy. My doctorate work was in public policy, women within politics, but nothing in distance education.

Given that the field of DE was beginning to blossom and online learning was nonexistent when many of these pioneers were students, it seems reasonable that few had any formal educational background in these areas. Similar logic could be used to explain why few had educational backgrounds with information and communication technologies, which were also just beginning to emerge in the realm of education. However, it is somewhat surprising to learn that more pioneers did not have schooling in the broader field of education. Examining the collective results of these pioneers' work experiences, the years in which they began to work in the field, the people who influenced them early in their careers, and other initiating circumstances may provide further insight into how these women became pioneers in this field.

Experience: While over half of the coded units (46 units; 55.4% of all units coded to experience) indicated that pioneers began their careers with some experience in DE and/or education and nearly one-third (25 units; 30.1%) began with backgrounds in research or technology, the remaining 14.5% of the units (12 units) indicated that some respondents had no experience in any of these areas when they began to work in DE or online learning. All in all, one out of three respondents stated that their experiential background was not related to any of these fields. Furthermore, only four respondents (13.3%) reported having had any experience as a DE learner before they began working in the field. These findings clearly underline the pioneering nature of the respondents, as defined in the Introduction of this chapter.

Year: Some respondents mentioned more than one year when asked the question "In what year did you begin to look specifically into DE?" To provide a clearer picture of when each respondent began to look into the field, the authors performed a second calculation, which considered only the earliest year that each respondent mentioned in their reply. In keeping with the authors' candidate selection process, discussed in the Selection of Respondents subsection of the Research Methodology section, two significant clusters were found (Figure 32.6). The first cluster, 1970 to 1989, included respondents who worked in countries where traditional DE was already established, and emergent educational technologies were either unheard of or were in their infancy. This cluster included 20 (or 66.7%) of all respondents. The second cluster spanned from 1990 to 2009 and comprised 9 (30.0%) of the remaining respondents. Respondents in this latter cluster either worked in countries where online learning was just beginning to emerge or were engaged in pioneering initiatives in their particular area of interest. Examples of such individuals include Li Chen, who was (and still is) a pioneer at the Beijing Normal University, the first DE institution in China; Helen Farley, who was integral to bringing DE to prisoners incarcerated in Australia and now New Zealand; Julie Meeks Gardner from the Open Campus, University of the West Indies; and Theresa Koroivulaono, President of the College of the Marshall Islands.

Initiating Circumstances: Over a quarter of the conversational units (28.9%) in the parent category background were devoted to the circumstances that initiated the pioneers' interests in this field. Even though two-thirds of these women indicated that they had been drawn to the field due to personal interests, discussion of these interests included only one-fifth of the units for the child category, initiating circumstances. On the other hand, when 56.7% of the participants cited catalysts related to social justice, these conversations generated twice as many units. Moreover, discussions surrounding personal interests did not produce any specific sub-themes, whereas discourse related to social justice yielded seven commonly-mentioned sub-themes. This may suggest that, although the majority of these pioneers had personal reasons for entering the field, they felt others would be more interested in learning about the social justice issues that motivated them. Regardless of what their reasons may have been, it remains clear that personal interests and social justice compelled most of these pioneers to pursue futures in this field. Perhaps one respondent sums it up best:

> My inspiration and guidance for my professional career came from an article written by Geneviève Jacquinot in which she tried to define DE. Translating it, it would be "tame distance and abolish absence." This translated means to provide access to knowledge and diplomas to those who are otherwise psychologically, physically or economically or socially or geographically at a distance and change the teacher-oriented model to a learner-centred model and doing all of this, of course. through user-friendly media, whatever they were.

Influencers: When asked the question "Which female researchers or female colleagues may have piqued your interest in DE?" a few respondents confessed that they had to think long and hard about the question:

> [Respondent 1]: None, I am sad to say. When I read that question, I really, really searched my memory, but piquing my interest in DE, there was no one.
> [Respondent 2]: That is a very difficult question. I cannot recall any particular name at this time; in my earlier years working in this field, it was mostly men in the literature.

Some respondents provided explanations for why it was hard to identify women who piqued their interest in DE. They said:

> [Respondent 1]: In general, no. The interest in DE and women studies did not exist at the faculty and in other social organizations. The traditional society did not perceive these issues: the traditional role of women had been naturalized, fixed as the ancestral interaction with men, the view of the everyday communication, the silence and subjacent violence and so on. The socialization in the cultural framework presented a strict psycho-political dissociation and a deep social differentiation between men and women, with women having a minor and prohibited participation in many areas, existing according to stereotypical expectations, first education of the children exclusively in their hands, etc. Also, it was reflected, obviously, in the educational sphere (in formal schooling and informal everyday life), including the teachers training in biased roles, and kept for many centuries until today. The habits, or the mentality, as it is known nowadays, fixes and consolidates the inferiority of women in any social groups and situations.
> [Respondent 2]: I have to say that at the time I joined AU, there were not that many women working in the field, but I was lucky to meet many of them who were really making a difference. . . . In the 1970s and 80s, when each country might have only one or two institutions that defined themselves through open and distance learning, practitioners looked beyond their borders to find colleagues working on similar challenges.
> [Respondent 3]: When I entered into this area at the beginning, I never met very many females, but I met a female leader who was leading the China Radio and TV Open University in China at that time.

Comments such as these verify results from the authors' exhaustive, albeit fruitless, search of the literature that was the impetus for this book. While countless books, journal articles, blogs, newscast interviews, and podcasts on male pioneers in the field were quickly amassed during the authors' literature review, only two journals offered articles on noteworthy females in the field. The first, *Journal of Learning for Development* (*JL4D*; https://jl4d.org/index.php/ejl4d), ran a series of articles in Volume 4, Issues 1–3 (2017), and Volume 5, Issue 1 (2018) on leaders in DE from across the globe. These articles included paragraphs featuring some female leaders and pioneers. The second, the *International Women Online Journal of Distance Education* (*intWOJDE*; www.wojde.org/; Demiray, 2012), initiated in 2012, also invited (and continues to invite) submissions on the history of DE.

Due to the lack of references to pioneering women in the literature, it was determined that the most likely research sampling strategy to employ was snowballing. This strategy proved to be much more productive, yielding a list of 60 unique names of women who influenced the pioneers in this study.

Despite the request to provide the names of females who had piqued their interest in the field, over a quarter of the participants (8 respondents; 26.7% of all respondents) offered a total of 11 male names as well. The provision of these names may offer further credence to interviewee claims and the authors' literature review findings that men historically dominated the field in the early years of DE.

Learning Environment

At the time of the interviews, 28 (93.3% of all) respondents were still actively engaged in the field at least to some extent. Two of the 28 (or 6.7% of all 30) respondents were still involved in volunteer duties. The remaining 26 (86.7%) were working full time as educators, administrators, and/or consultants, or were taking on lighter teaching and research roles as adjunct professors.

The broad parameters of the research question generating learning environment coding results (i.e., "Could you please describe the learning environment that you currently work in [e.g., geographic and institutional setting, student demographics]?"), coupled with the breadth of educational activities that the respondents were engaged in at the time of their interviews, led some respondents to dwell on certain themes while others selected different topics to discuss in their responses. Although the resultant array of answers is difficult to interpret, in part due to the reduced numbers of responses tied to each child code, some conclusions can still be drawn from the patterns of these responses.

Institutional Description: Geographically speaking, half of the employed participants providing responses worked for institutions that were located on a single site, while the other half worked for institutions that had two to ten, or more than eleven sites. Almost three-quarters (15; or 71.4% of the 21 who provided answers) worked for national institutions while slightly more than a quarter (6; 28.6%) worked for provincial or international institutions.

Of the 17 (56.7% of all 30) respondents who discussed the instructional mode of their institution, nearly two-thirds stated that their institution offered a blended approach. Almost one-third worked for a wholly DE/ODL institution. Only one worked at a f-2-f institution.

Over three-quarters of respondents who provided information about the educational levels offered at their place of employment characterized their institution as being a university. One-third of the respondents either described their universities as accepting pre-university level students, as delivering courses for all levels of education, or as offering lifelong learning opportunities.

Just under half (14, or 46.7%) of all respondents described the programme or course that they were involved with at the time of the interview. There appeared to be a nearly even split between the number of programmes or courses that were DE in nature versus those that were either blended, asynchronous, or synchronous. Just one was f-2-f.

Only six (20%) of all respondents offered the specific age of their institution. The founding of these institutions ranged from 1930 to 2000. Three institutions were operational by 1970. The other three were opened between 1971 and 2000. This span is explained by the two clusters of pioneers selected for this study. One cluster is represented by respondents who worked in countries where DE was established by the 1980s. The other cluster consists of respondents who were employed in countries where DE institutions were more recently founded.

Based on the trends noted here, it appeared that, regardless of the age of their institution, the number of campus sites that it had, or its geographical reach, most respondents appeared to be working for an open university that offered courses to students at all educational levels and embraced a lifelong, blended approach to learning.

Student Demographics: Conversations related to student demographics yielded one-third of the units under the parent code learning environment. Nearly three-quarters (22; 73.3%) of all women included in this study discussed some student demographics.

Student profiles were mentioned by two-thirds of the women and generated two-thirds of the student demographic units. Perusal of the great-grandchild coding results indicates that two-thirds of the women who provided information on student ages worked with students who were non-traditional. The women identified these students as older adults, working adults, parents, the geographically isolated, prisoners, or otherwise marginalized learners. The remaining third of the women who discussed student ages stated that they worked with traditional students. However, only one of the women in this group stated that the full-time students at her institution fit the traditional student profile (i.e., attending the institute shortly after high school graduation). Here is what some of the women had to say:

> [Respondent 1]: We have many young students, 17, 18, 19 years old, but there some adult learners who are studying as well.
> [Respondent 2]: Some are coming straight through from a baccalaureate degree, but many are adult students who have been working since graduating from their last degree and are re-entering university at the master's or doctoral level. They are often switching careers to go into a psychotherapy role or become a psychologist.
> [Respondent 3]: The students are mainly young, our school leavers, but at the same time, they come in with 1.5 children. So while they are young, they are also young parents.

One-third of the women who discussed their students' profiles indicated that they were involved in providing education to learners who were overcoming cultural barriers. These included those facing cultural isolation, gender issues, and racial discrimination; prisoners; and refugees. Some of the women engaged in these initiatives had this to share:

> [Respondent 1]: But we are also deploying distance learning methodologies for our Lifelong Learning for Farmers project in 11 countries and training girls in skills for livelihoods in remote and marginalized communities in five countries.
> [Respondent 2]: The real challenge here – well, there are a lot of challenges – but the real challenge here is that Māori are vastly over-represented. They are about 15% of the non-incarcerated population and 51% of the incarcerated population. So the Indigenous over-representation is huge in New Zealand. So there are all sorts of cultural considerations to take into account with that.

Just over half the women discussed where their students were geographically located; this discussion produced one-fifth of the student demographic units. One woman said that the students she worked with came from the local region. The remaining women were evenly split; half these women worked with national students, and the other half worked with students at the international level.

Although student population size units were recorded for two-thirds of the women, this topic produced less than a fifth of the student demographic units. Nearly two-thirds of the women who discussed population size did not offer a specific number. For instance, one respondent said, "But now, it is the university with the largest student enrolment from all districts in the country." Of the remaining women, most worked at institutions with student populations ranging from 20,000 to 50,000. One woman worked at an institution with a student population of 10,000. Another woman worked for an institution with less than 5,000 students. Two women discussed their class sizes; one worked with classes having more than 150 students; the other had classes with less than 30 students.

All in all, the data results suggest that the demographics of the students these pioneers were working with at interview time were difficult to define universally. Part of the problem was that only half to two-thirds of the working women provided information in this area. Nevertheless, a tentative summary of the data suggests that most institutions were exerting effort to include non-traditional students, including older, working adults and parents, as well as other culturally and geographically isolated students in their programmes and courses. Moreover, most of these pioneers were working at institutions that had national or international reach. Given that a central tenet of DE is to provide "education for all" (Wedemeyer, 1971), it might be surmised that DE initiatives these pioneers were engaged in would aim to include all learners across the greatest geographic region possible. Due to the sparsity of data on student population size, though, it is not possible to draw definitive statements on this area in the study.

Challenges

Generating one-tenth of all units in this study, the parent code challenges was the third most-discussed topic among the topics that were directly linked to specific research questions. Results related to this parent code answered the eighth research question: "What are some of the challenges that you faced in the field of DE over the years?" All 30 respondents answered this question, generating a total of 25 child codes. Of these child codes, understanding-acceptance of DE was the most dominant theme. Other noteworthy themes were institutional growing pains, funding, technology, gender, faculty, and cultural issues.

Acceptance/Understanding: Acceptance and understanding of DE was the foremost challenge identified; four out of five respondents talked about this concern, resulting in the generation of nearly one-quarter of all challenges units. From the perspective of these respondents, orthodox views held by those who subscribed to traditional education perspectives were most troublesome. This is what some respondents had to say:

> [Respondent 1]: In the very beginning, the biggest challenge was to explain distance education to mainstream practitioners. Our colleagues in mainstream universities found us puzzling. The whole terminology of distance education, the fact that we were not only doing all our work at a distance with students but were also an open institution was a combination they had never encountered before. It was one of our very early challenges as pioneers in the field.
> [Respondent 2]: With specific reference to distance education and the formation of the Open Campus, there were several, but I will cite four of the main ones that we faced in the first few years. One was the attempt to reshape the various outreach entities into a campus with a UWI government structure. There was need for innovation; there was need for difference in order to create a structure that would allow for ease of doing business. We encountered some resistance to this because we were asked at the same time, because we were part of the university, to conform to the traditional ways, but that was not going to serve our purposes. So that was one of the challenges that we had to deal with head on. We had to find creative ways to overcome that resistance and to argue for a system that would really position the Open Campus for success and allow it at the same time to participate fully in the work of the university.
> [Respondent 3]: We went to a huge amount of trouble over an extended period of time to prove ourselves in the rather snooty university environment that then prevailed.
> [Respondent 4]: Some of the other faculty saw this and said, "That's terrible! They're not meeting face-to-face. They won't get a good education." At a faculty meeting, they argued that I should not be able to do this. It should not be allowed. It would destroy education. It would harm the students. They wouldn't learn anything. I actually had a supportive dean who said, "That's not your choice. All faculty has the right to teach courses the way they want to with the permission of the dean, and I have given her permission. End of story. There will be no vote." But basically, some faculty members wanted to string me up as a witch or something. I don't know.

Understanding and acceptance of DE by the traditional educational field are challenges that are not unique to the women in this study. Some scholars perceive DE as merely a branch of traditional education (Keegan, 1990). Others view it as "a poor cousin" who is prompting the commodification of education while destroying the high-quality standards of traditional schooling (Bates, 2005; Larreamendy-Joerns & Leinhardt, 2006; Parker, 2008; Wark, 2018).

Institutional Growing Pains: Two out of five (41.9%) respondents relayed stories about challenging institutional growing pains. One-third (33.3%) felt that developing new systems, departments, and programmes was challenging while 30% indicated that battling institutional-level skepticism was challenging. Debates between and among administrators and faculty were also mentioned by one-fifth of the respondents. Given the trend from the 1980s onward of traditional institutions adding some DE component to their campus offerings, as well as the advent of DE and online learning institutes, it is likely that many of the pioneers involved in this study had front row seats to these events. Here are some of their recollections:

> [Respondent 1]: There were people from multi-disciplines talking about how they were going to bring this about. I may not have made much by the way of contribution, but I certainly heard a lot of the discussions, and believe me, those discussions were heated. At least they could be heated; they weren't always. So it was very interesting.
> [Respondent 2]: Well, very quickly some faculty members at Athabasca took this whole thing on board and developed our Masters of Distance Education, which I think was one of the first graduate degrees ever offered in an online context. The challenges of developing that were considerable, first of all internally, because faculty members were suspicious of this model, and secondly, externally, persuading an eventual student population that they could complete a graduate degree entirely online without ever meeting face-to-face except at convocation.
> [Respondent 3]: Sometimes we have to attend meetings of the Senate and the Council. If you are articulate in these meetings, some statements might not be perceived positively. But I believed strongly that I had to talk about what I felt. I thought that I was not struggling for my own personal gain, but for the benefit of the university.

Funding: Over half the respondents indicated that funding was another key challenge. Some sought funding for their institutions, while others worked to obtain funding for student support and network development. From these pioneers' stories about their struggle against inflexible traditional institutional funding structures and orthodox views emerged a theme that funders believed DE cost less to deliver:

> [Respondent 1]: What I just alluded to is one: The way that ODFL is seen, and if governments measure your success according to formula-like completions, we tend not to stack up well against other organizations. So keeping the organization sustainable and viable has been a challenge. But we've met that challenge. I think that all public sector education is on a formula of reduced funding from government and ministries, and it is hard, very hard for them to thrive. Also, we shift in demographic and economic cycles. It is quite hard to survive on the funding cycles that we get. So, the reputation of ODFL is shifting, but in the early days, that was very hard.
> [Respondent 2]: I think the other is the unfortunate direction that online learning has taken, where many universities in particular, plus these for-profit companies, have seen this as a way of money making. That, to me, is the second greatest challenge. In order to stay true to what I believe are the important motivators for doing online learning, the profit motive can't come into it because it is not cheaper. The fact that universities are putting more and more classes online, thinking this is the answer to their budgetary problems when provinces and states are reducing funding, is very misguided. It ends up giving online

learning a bad reputation for quality when that, as I said, is the other issue that I think is really important. So I find it quite distressing that this has often been the case.

[Respondent 3]: Regrettably, too many policymakers and funding bodies persisted in the belief that DE was a cheap form of education; that's still too often reflected in the resources provided for online learning. . . . DE, done well, is not a cheap form of education, but that was often not well grasped by senior academics under constant pressure to do more with less.

Technology: Two-fifths of the respondents listed technology as a challenge. A number of the pioneers shared anecdotes about their involvement in the establishment of technological infrastructures. Some also recounted their frustrating experiences with, and related perceptions of, early computing and communication technologies. The following quotes reflect such sentiments:

[Respondent 1]: As networks became more sophisticated, trying to get broadband out to rural and remote areas was not without difficulty. Not directly DE but certainly fundamental to its expansion. This is why I ended up working on contracts for the government of Newfoundland and Industry Canada on their broadband rollout. The more sophisticated the networks and uses became, the more difficult it was for a telephone carrier to make a business case and the broader the set of groups that had to buy in to help them make that case. Trying to get broadband Internet to remote areas so that everybody could have education and health programming at their individual desks is a significantly larger undertaking than getting networks out there that are contained to specific agency sites.

[Respondent 2]: A further challenge across the region is that, while we now experience vastly improved, although sometimes patchy, connectivity at our university campuses, there is limited home connectivity and devices only for the elite. This makes it difficult to take advantage of educational technology.

[Respondent 3]: Another challenge that I have been grappling with for well over a decade, maybe 15 years now, is the challenge of analyzing CMC as it becomes increasingly multimodal. The CMDA paradigm that I developed was based on text because that was what there was in the 90s: chat, email, discussion forums, MUDs and MOOs, blogs, text messaging – all primarily text. But CMC has changed a lot. In the early years, there were different varieties of CMC, each requiring different clients or points of access. People would have their email client. If they wanted to go to a public chatroom, they would have to telnet to a special server. And then there were MUDs [multi-user dimensions] and MOOs [MUDs, object oriented]; you had to telnet to a different server if you wanted to access those. And if you wanted to read newsgroups, you had to download a special reader. It wasn't like it is now where you can access many different forms of CMC through a browser very readily. Most people weren't aware of all the different forms that were available. It was much more siloed, if you will. And web pages were not originally considered CMC by CMC researchers because they were more static and less interactive. But the web gradually became dynamic and more interactive, especially with the evolution of weblogs. Blogs were important in that process, as were social network sites.

Gender: Two out of five interviewees felt that gender issues were also a challenge. Female subordination and male dominance themes accounted for nearly two-thirds of the gender units. Most of the remaining third of these units were equally divided between debunking myths and equality issues. While further discussion on this topic is found under the sub-headings General Gender-related

Comments and Gender Themes in this section, a few reflections on the gender-related challenges that respondents shared are offered now:

[Respondent 1]: Not being taken seriously as a woman, especially asking for the gender-inclusive language. I could tell you some episodes that happened to me: for instance, when I had my first-ever presentation at a Cambridge conference. I think this must have been in 1987. You know how you are nervous when you do your first presentation and in a foreign language and so on. I was talking about the situation of women and how difficult it was and so on. When I had finished, this eminent professor from my own university got up, stood in front of me with his back to me, and said something about how this may be somewhere or other true but not at his university, and he didn't know what I was talking about. So some other colleagues, men as well as women, told him that he was demonstrating what I had been talking about, so . . . So that was just one instance of how women who were asking for women's rights in the university were treated by many male colleagues and professors. It was quite a challenge.

[Respondent 2]: Men who don't think that women are as clever as they are, if not sometimes more. I can't think of anything much. I quickly learned that if I needed something, it always paid off to talk to the boss, who has to say yes or no, and tell them how they will be positioned in the activity. I'm always careful about that so they know that they've had a good slice of the pie, even though I did all of the work.

[Respondent 3]: I think also there is definitely – and this probably getting worse, I think – but there is definitely a tendency to not listen to female academics as much as male academics. There is definitely discrimination there. I can say something, but my voice won't be as loud as a male academic working in the field. That can be very frustrating. Although I can see it with my own work, I probably see it more with other female academics who have struggled to have their voices heard. That's a particular challenge for females working in open and distance learning.

Faculty: Faculty issues were identified as a challenge to nearly one-third of the women in this study. While some concerns, such as lack of motivation, research, and publications were mentioned by a handful of these women, eight of the nine women who discussed faculty challenges felt that the lack of faculty skills were (and still are) most disconcerting:

[Respondent 1]: Another challenge is that when I talk with younger scholars or scholars from other disciplines who have been involved in MOOCs or OER, they don't seem to understand the base or root of ODL. They think MOOCs and online education are totally new. As you know, distance education has a long history. During this time, there have been many kinds of research on why people drop out, why people do not accept that type of technology, why learners have a difficult time in keeping their motivation while they are studying in distance education, etc. Those kinds of topics have already been studied. But when I look at recent papers, authors do not seem to understand such knowledge base in ODL. I think they focus mainly on reading about recent online education and ignore what has been researched in older media-based distance education. It was kind of a challenge for me to share some of the traditional, well-established knowledge in our field.

[Respondent 2]: Training teachers in media courses for DE learning environments and changing their pedagogical model from a teacher-centred approach to a learner-centred approach was also a challenge. This comes up often for me because it was a major question.

[Respondent 3]: But I think even though it is slow, we are making progress. Technically, I think that people have a lack of skills in utilizing the materials and resources and everything that can be and should be easily used by people in Indonesia on the technical side.
[Respondent 4]: (Challenges include. . .)

- Working in education systems that are poorly resourced, often with large classes and underqualified educators. . .,
- Working with poorly trained educators who often don't have the necessary pedagogical content knowledge, (and)
- Understanding the achievement levels of our students rather than assuming the expected levels.

Cultural Issues: Cultural challenges were acknowledged by one-third of the study participants. Nearly three-quarters (72.2%) of the units related to this topic focused on the overall social structure in which the pioneers worked. Expressed in their own words, this is what some of these women had to say:

[Respondent 1]: The interest in DE and women studies did not exist at the faculty and in other social organizations. The traditional society did not perceive these issues: the traditional role of women had been naturalized, fixed as the ancestral interaction with men, the view of the everyday communication, the silence and subjacent violence and so on. The socialization in the cultural framework presented a strict psycho-political dissociation and a deep social differentiation between men and women, with women having a minor and prohibited participation in many areas, existing according to stereotypical expectations, first education of the children exclusively in their hands, etc. Also, it was reflected, obviously, in the educational sphere (in formal schooling and informal everyday life), including the teachers training in biased roles, and kept for many centuries until today. The habits, or the mentality, as it is known nowadays, fixes and consolidates the inferiority of women in any social groups and situations.
[Respondent 2]: They talked about the challenges in their countries. They talked about wars and they talked about losing thousands of students in those wars, and they talked about [the] difficulties of training women in an environment where a male teacher could not be communicating with a female student. They talked about religious persecution, these issues that were actually much more significant than my funding one.
[Respondent 3]: Prejudice, I guess, is an issue, especially in my work at the prisons. There are a lot of people who don't think very favourably of prisoners. And it's not that I don't understand that when we incarcerate people, we deprive them of their liberty. That is supposed to be their punishment, not everything else that we inflict on top of that. They should still have access to education, and when we don't provide that, I feel that it is a violation of their human rights. Trying to get people to work with me to get education into prisons has definitely been challenging.
[Respondent 4]: At the time, a huge percentage of black South Africans had received only a rudimentary basic education, and only a small percentage had completed secondary school. Furthermore, black youths and adults of South Africa were being systematically denied the opportunity in the face-to-face system to further their education above certain levels. The apartheid state exercised extremely strong control over education, with all educational institutions segregated according to whether students were African, White, of Indian descent, or so-called Coloured. To this end, in 1959, the South African regime prevented

Africans, Indians, and Coloureds from joining the big urban universities of South Africa unless they had special state permission. If you were African, you were required to attend designated universities in the so-called homelands of the time. If you were Indian or Coloured, you were required to attend the one Indian or Coloured university in the country. Furthermore, universities for Africans were designated for particular ethnic groups. Any organization wanting to provide educational opportunities to black South Africans needed official state permission, which could be withheld easily. . . . In the early days when I was in SACHED, we were considered to be a threat to the South African state, so one of the challenges we faced was that several of our staff members and our projects were "banned" by the South African government. In short, this meant on the one hand that the staff members could not continue to work for us, and on the other that we had to cease the projects.

These were the environments in which our intrepid female pioneers ceaselessly fought to bring education to all.

Accomplishments

All participants responded to the interview question about their accomplishments in the field, making this the fourth-most discussed question in the study. Over half the women generated nearly one-fifth of accomplishment topic data that focused on their involvement in the implementation of new initiatives. Most often these initiatives included the development of new systems, programmes/ courses, or technological infrastructures. Such results would be anticipated as these pioneers were, in their own words, trailblazers at a time when emerging technologies were enabling the field to burgeon across the globe:

[Respondent 1]: There is a vibrant distance education community. To this end, in 1996, I was the main instigator and Founding President of our distance education organization, NADEOSA, in South Africa. I have continued to serve on the executive ever since and am proud that the association has both survived through some tough times and is thriving.
[Respondent 2]: I contributed project management services to three teams that launched trailblazing innovations in DE, ODL (open and distance learning) and Telemedicine in Newfoundland, Labrador, and Ontario, and was supported in making presentations within and outside Canada sharing lessons learned from those projects.
[Respondent 3]: I am very proud of one achievement for my career. I initiated so far the only master's degree and doctoral degree in distance education in China. So, Beijing Normal University is the only university to deliver a master's degree and a PhD degree in distance education. We have a lot of degrees by distance education, but these are the only degrees for distance education.

One out of three respondents mentioned contributions to the literature, DE advocacy, student learning, research, and international endeavours in the field when reflecting on their achievements. One out of three also listed awards that they had received for various contributions. Perhaps what was most interesting, however, was that 11 (36.7% of all) pioneers chose to share team accomplishments, even though the question asked about personal accomplishments. This is what some of the pioneers said:

[Respondent 1]: That is not an easy question – many of my accomplishments were as part of a team – usually as the instructional designer working with subject-matter specialists who were trying to provide access to information to those at a distance, working on anything from a set of learning materials on how to teach nutrition in small groups to a five-university undergraduate credit course on meat evaluation delivered at a distance to a Master's Degree in Engineering Professional Practice, etc. So a lot of my accomplishments I owe to the rest of the team, where I was simply a designer.

[Respondent 2]: When I say my accomplishments, I've done none of this single-handedly by any means. For my team, one of the big accomplishments that we have done is within the graduate programming. (Author note: This respondent then went on to discuss only team accomplishments.)

[Respondent 3]: That's a difficult one to answer, because . . . I need to explain something here. Our cultures in the Pacific are based very firmly on humility. Just like every single island nation in this Pacific Ocean, North and South Pacific and Central Pacific, we share this belief, this practice. That's why it is hard for me to say that these are *my* [emphasis in the original] accomplishments. They're more *our* [emphasis in the original] accomplishments. The instructional design team that I worked with through the University of the South Pacific and now working as the President of the College of the Marshall Islands – there is a whole team that makes things happen here, from building structures to designing to making sure that the resources are maintained and sustained. So, having explained that, I will now talk about the accomplishments that we have made together.

While the third respondent here clarifies that the focus on team, rather than individual, effort is customary in her culture, this may also be a gender-based phenomenon, given the significant number of participants who appeared reluctant to focus on their personal achievements. Some literature on gender-related self-promotion may provide support for this hypothesis. For instance, Exley and Kessler (2019) found that men describe themselves more favourably to potential employers than equally performing women do, even when promotional incentives are removed. This self-promotion gender gap is inherent to individuals' subjective self-evaluation of their own performance; Exley and Kessler note that this gap arises as early as grade six and persists throughout life. A European study in the corporate sector (Guillén et al., 2017) concluded that men gain influence in a company by appearing self-confident, whereas women need to appear self-confident *and* possess a pro-social (team-focused) orientation to garner influence in the company. Lindeman et al. (2019) tested three theoretical explanations for "women's limited self-promotion success: (1) cognitive dissonance, (2) stereotypical threat, and (3) backlash avoidance" (p. 219). The researchers concluded that women seek to avoid backlash; in other words, women fear perceived social consequences if they engage in self-promotion. Such research examples suggest that, in order to be successful in this field, many of these pioneers emulated cultural norms when discussing achievements. Furthermore, these discoveries may also provide some explanation as to why the authors were able to easily amass a plethora of multimedia literature on male pioneers in our field, but turned up nearly empty-handed after an exhaustive search of the literature for information on female pioneers.

Changes over Time

This was the parent code to produce the fifth-greatest number of units related to the changes that occurred in the field from the time that participants entered the field until the time of their interviews. All participants talked about these changes; most focused on the state of the field in the early years, the current state of the field, and what they perceived to be the greatest changes over time. Technology dominated the conversations in each of these areas. The second most-noted change was the movement from an industrial model to a networked system. Experimentation was also a common theme in early and current-year reflections. Some respondents also pointed out that acceptance and understanding of DE is more widespread today. This may be due in part to the increasing reliance on online learning (Marinova, 2020; Paul & Jefferson, 2019; Tejeda-Delgado et al., 2011), as well as to the publication of comprehensive research studies comparing f-2-f and online learning achievements, which indicate no significant difference in student outcomes (Paul & Jefferson, 2019).

Research Interests

The interview question that generated the sixth-most interview question units was about respondents' research interests. Over half the women engaged in research on technology. Two out of five focused on social issues or DE (theory, systems, instructional design, and/or learning environments). Seven women conducted research on support. Five or fewer women explored other issues: quality assurance, policy and governance, student success, or learner autonomy. Four out of five women in the study were involved in research activities. Most of these women either began their careers as researchers or held faculty positions that included research duties. Two-thirds of the pioneers who conducted research reported an evolution in what topics they explored. Explanations for this evolution included changes in roles, personal interests, technologies, and funding structures/availability.

One out of five women did not actively engage in research activities because they held administrative roles throughout their careers. As one administrator explains:

> [Respondent]: I have to take the fifth on this one because as a project manager, I never engaged in research as such. My concerns were more about what we needed to pull together as a document that we could submit to get the funding that we needed. And then making sure that we met all of the objectives and the budget requirements of the funding, because all of them, Memorial University, Telemedicine, the University of Toronto, and the Contact North network – that was all soft money. None of it initially was hard money. If we did get research funding, the research was, to some extent, influenced by what the funding agencies required us to do.

Goals

The interview question that produced the seventh-most units asked respondents about their goals. All participants answered this question. Over half sought to alleviate social issues, such as improving access and learning opportunities or decreasing isolation, as illustrated by the following quotes:

> [Respondent 1]: Can I be honest? I wanted to make the world a better place for learning. I wanted to provide the best education to the rural areas either here in Israel or in the world, in Africa, and even the USA where I was teaching – places that are really rural. I thought that this might be the way to do it. Otherwise, we might not be able to do it.
> [Respondent 2]: One of my initial goals was bridging the digital divide and providing access and looking at access in terms of different types of access: not only the physical access to technology, but also the psychological access, the comfort level, how we bridge the different types of distances in learning environments. It can be social distance; it can be cultural, etc. So providing access is critical; I work in New Mexico. This is a state where a lot of the communities are separated by huge mountain ranges, very rural communities, and they hardly have any access to education. The moment you actually use expensive technologies, even at that time, like television, that really – if they don't have access to it – is difficult for them to participate in the learning process.

Two out of five respondents pursued faculty, student, or technology support or student success goals, while one-quarter of the respondents sought quality assurance goals or worked to promote DE:

> [Respondent 1]: After that, I was interested in quality assurance because one of the reasons for why people's distance education degrees were not fully valued was related to quality assurance. The KNOU was not evaluated and accredited through the same agency as conventional universities; they had a different track. Even though they may have a different track for accreditation, they should have the same kind or level of vigorousness as a four-year college. For this reason, I was actively involved in quality assurance in distance education in collaboration with other ODL scholars from different parts of the world and UNESCO offices in Bangkok and Paris.
>
> [Respondent 2]: I would mention three goals:
>
> 1. To promote distance education as:
>   - an effective and rewarding learning model;
>   - a source of personal growth that gives the learner the feeling of self-confidence and the satisfaction of being able to learn by oneself; [and]
>   - an opportunity for students to become independent learners, which is a competence required to engage in lifelong learning.
>
> 2. To convince all actors of education systems, including decision makers, that the questions to ask are not:
>   - "What are we going to teach?" but "What do they need to learn?"
>   - "How will we teach?" but "How will they learn what they need to learn?"
>
> 3. To convince all actors of education systems, including decision makers, that the finality (purpose) of education:
>   - It is not just about acquiring knowledge and skills related to a discipline or to a field.
>   - It is also about giving all students the opportunity to become independent learners in order to be able to engage in a process of lifelong learning.

As these quotes illustrate, the pioneers' collective goals were seemingly altruistic, emulating the central tenet of DE, "education for all" (Wedemeyer, 1971).

Interesting Memories

Twenty-nine of the women in this study responded to the question about interesting memories that they might like to share with readers. The use of technology was mentioned by two out of three women, generating two-fifths of all interesting memory units. Most commonly cited anecdotes included recollections on the types, limitations, and integration of technologies. Nearly two out of three women recalled positive memories; most highlighted the excitement experienced while working in the field:

> [Respondent 1]: The one thing that I would like readers to know was that it was very exciting: the interaction of a whole lot of ideas on how you do it and why.
>
> [Respondent 2]: There was a tremendous amount of enthusiasm and excitement among those of us who were starting to work in this field. We were early adopters, well educated,

mostly white and middle class, a restricted demographic, mostly men, but there were women as well. I would say there was a lot of enthusiasm, despite the limited technologies that were available.

[Respondent 3]: Should I say the excitement of planning the structure for the campus, long days and nights of collaboration, consuming coffee, and sitting around the table getting frustrated? All of those things bonded us together as colleagues and helped us to work for a common cause. Hopping to islands to determine the state of play there, going to very remote areas, places that I've never been before in the Caribbean, and looking at the places where the university was trying to reach people. Meeting the people themselves and seeing the need. Those are the things that I remember the most. And the collegial friendships that were formed, working for a common cause, working together and sitting with people around a table, just brainstorming and working through things: the collegial camaraderie, the friendship, and the respect that emerged from these times. These are the things that have stayed with me: the respect and admiration for my colleagues, who worked extremely hard and who are all deserving of awards, believe me. And the people, the people we serve, the places where we serve them, and addressing their needs.

Almost half the women recounted memories about their pioneering efforts in the field, most of which related to creating new networks:

[Respondent 1]: During one early international project, we were working with the University of the West Indies network [UWIDEC] to help expand their network and programmes on the island of Jamaica, which was the network hub. CIDA [Canadian International Development Agency] had funded the partnership. Our engineer partner from the Newfoundland Telephone Company, Jamaican Telephone Company, and us were just finished the design and had placed the necessary hardware in the telephone towers in Jamaica when Hurricane Gilbert hit [a Category 5 storm].

[Respondent 2]: I talked a little bit about the GlobalEd project that I did when I initially started as a faculty member here [University of New Mexico (UNM)], where we connected graduate students through a listserv. We connected them through a listserv that I established here at UNM and developed collaborative research experiences across universities. That was one of my wonderful memories.

Over one-third of the women also spoke fondly about collegial experiences:

[Respondent 1]: I think that the international connection of people who are leading and involved with ODFL was one of the things that I found illuminating and quite amazing, actually.

[Respondent 2]: I've just enjoyed talking and learning from great colleagues, being supported by them, thinking and planning with them. I couldn't get a better life.

Early Founders

Everyone participating in the study responded to the question about identifying early female founders/leaders in the field of DE. Even though 26 (86.7%) of the participants mentioned at least one female's name, 12 participants also stated that they knew very few to none in the field. This inability to identify female founders or leaders was explained by participants in three ways: 1) They were among the first in their part of the world to work in the field; 2) They were not an expert in the field, or 3) They had encountered very little literature published by women.

> [Respondent 1]: When I entered into this area at the beginning, I never met very many females, but I met a female leader who was leading the China Radio and TV Open University in China at that time.
> [Respondent 2]: I visited the OU [British Open University] many times between 1985 and 1995. I could see that the OU was a man's world. (This may have changed since. . .)
> [Respondent 3]: I didn't know any at the time. That is a question I have left unanswered because I just didn't know how to answer it. Because I am so old, I'm trying to think about what 80-year-old distance educators were there. I just don't know. I didn't have any early female founders or leaders in mind; they just weren't part of my reality.
> [Respondent 4]: A couple of female colleagues and I were among the first to explore the area/field of e-learning specifically.
> [Respondent 5]: I've never been an expert on distance education per se. My impression when I first came into this was that distance education in 1977 or so was still correspondence. . . . I might have been wrong. There might have been some people doing something more interactive with distance learning, but I wasn't aware of it.

Five respondents talked about DE organizations where they encountered other women in the field. These organizations included the ICDE (International Council for Distance Education), CADE (Canadian Association of Distance Education), and WIN (Women's International Network). During their interviews, some participants explained the impetus for, and evolution of, WIN. Here is what one had to say:

> [Respondent]: (T)he origin of the Women's International Network was the ICDE conference in Vancouver [BC, Canada] in 1982, where the women who attended the conference became increasingly fed up and quite annoyed with the fact that the majority of people working and studying in distance education were women, but on the podiums and in the positions in this international organization, it was all men So, they started the Women's International Network in 1985, creating an acronym – WIN – which is in itself a statement. WIN was "launched" at the next ICDE World Conference in Melbourne [Australia]. It had a big presence of women and had special sessions and a keynote session that women designed and carried out and so on. That was basically the beginning of the network. From then on, women colleagues were represented on the board of ICDE, which also provided money and support to WIN activities and networking.
> So that was quite a powerful thing, supported by a lot of men, too, but basically the initiative of women. For me, it was very important to be part of the WIN network. The first product of the network was this Karlene Faith book, *Toward New Horizons for Women in Distance Education: International Perspectives*. That was the first time that an international cooperation happened with women, I guess, from all continents contributing to this book. It was really very, very important, and it was presented to the distance education world at the ICDE World Conference in 1988 in Oslo. The Oslo conference was an important milestone for WIN, and thanks to the Programme Chair David Sewart, women were more fairly represented in keynotes and sessions.
> In the 1980s and 1990s, WIN was a strong presence at international conferences: namely, ICDE World Conferences, the annual conferences of the Canadian Association of Distance Education (CADE), and the Cambridge Conferences organized bi-annually by the OU UK's Alan Tait and Roger Mills. . . .

WIN is no longer functional. This happened in 1997 at the ICDE conference at Penn State when some woman came forward out of the woodwork and wanted to formalize the organization. But the whole point was that it was an informal network, and it didn't want any statutes and what not. . . . So that was basically the end of WIN at that time. ICDE stopped funding. You do need funding for mailing and all sorts of things to keep up the work. Unless the woman chairing WIN had good enough standing and resources in her institution, it wouldn't work because ICDE wouldn't support it any longer. So that was basically very sad to see this go. But while it was in existence, it was absolutely wonderful.

Others for the Book

Twenty-five participants offered a total of 158 names when asked to suggest the names of other female pioneers in our field. After removing 57 duplicates and 4 partial names, a list of 97 potential candidates for the project remained. This list indicated that were other female founders and leaders whose pioneering stories may not have been recorded or published. During the final few interviews, a lot of the same names were being generated, implying that the snowballing may have been reaching a saturation point. However, the authors were aware that much of English-speaking Europe had yet to be explored. Furthermore, countries where French, Spanish, Chinese, Hindi, Indonesian, Bengali, Japanese, and other languages prevailed had very little representation in the book, due to the authors' reliance on the English language. The work, experiences, and perceptions of female pioneers from across the globe should be made publicly available before their histories become lost to all stakeholders.

Final Comments

Nine out of ten participants replied when asked if they had anything else that they would like to address in their interviews. Four out of five respondents in the study offered advice. The most common pearls of wisdom related to the future of DE, being learner-focused, and remaining current. Nearly half the study participants talked about the barriers that they overcame; the most prevalent barrier discussed was battling perceptions about our field. Two out of five women shared positive memories. These memories were about the joy of DE, what DE offered to the world, and sharing work with others.

Emergent Codes

The original coding framework contained 11 parent codes, each directly related to one or more interview questions (Appendices A and B). During the coding process, three other parent codes (benefits of DE, career history, and general gender-related comments) and two cross-category themes (technology and gender) emerged.

Benefits of DE: Although no research question asked about the benefits of DE, every respondent mentioned this topic during interviews. This resulted in benefits of DE being the parent code with the second largest number of units in the study. The most cited benefit of DE, mentioned by 28 of the 30 participants, was about addressing social justice issues. Three out of five interviewees discussed the benefits that ICT offered for expanding and enriching DE offerings. Half the study participants also mentioned the DE attributes of openness and enabling learners to continue education throughout life. Such conversations by pioneers who have devoted their lives to this field are consistent with the aim of DE to provide "education for all" (Wedemeyer, 1971).

Career History: The second parent code emerging from the interview data was career history. Despite being mentioned by 90% of interviewees, career history only contained four percent of all units, thus ranking in 12th place among all parent codes. Discourse relating to career history was subdivided into early, mid-, and late career themes. Examination of these themes suggested that most participants began in other fields, entering as faculty, researchers, or technologists. By mid-career, some of the pioneers moved into administrative leadership, course design, or advising-consulting positions. Two-thirds of all respondents also mentioned late career activities. Of these, half indicated that they held administrative leadership positions; the remaining women were equally divided between faculty and advisor-consultant positions. Two questions arose from examining this data. First, would a similar career trend be found among male pioneers? Second, was part of the reason so few female pioneers could be identified in the early years because few held leadership positions at that time?

General Gender-related Comments: The last emergent parent code was general gender-related comments. Although nearly two out of three respondents made general comments related to gender, this parent code yielded the fewest parent code units, making it the lowest-ranking parent code in the study. Nearly half of all respondents mentioned male dominance in the field while one out of three respondents noted incidents of female subordination. A third theme, female grit, was also touched upon. As one respondent elaborates:

> [Respondent]: The greatest emotion that I felt during all these years at TÉLUQ was that aroused by the testimony of the women who had completed the studies programme in which they had committed themselves. These were extremely touching testimonials from women who recognized that they have gained valuable knowledge throughout their studies. They wanted to stress that what was most important to them, what they were most proud of, despite the discouragement they felt at the beginning of their studies in distance education, is that they had learned to learn by themselves. They did not regret the efforts made to combine studies, family life, and their professional work. They had courageously undertaken these studies for their personal development and to progress in the labour market. They also told us that they were aware they had become a role model for their children.

Cross-theme Categories: Two dominant themes were identified among most of the 14 parent codes. These cross-category themes were technology and gender.

Technology themes: All respondents identified the role, attributes, types, and challenges of technology during their interviews. This resulted in technology becoming a sub-category under 12 of the 14 parent codes. When aggregated, technology units produced one-fifth of all study units, making technology the most dominate theme to emerge from this study. These results lend support to those who have argued that technology has not only promoted a myriad of definitions for distance learning, but is also a catalyst in the evolution of the field (Bates, 2008; Bingham et al., 1999; Quality Assurance Agency, 2020; State University, n.d.). Such literature would help explain why one-third of technology units were identified in changes over time, and why interesting memories and research interests each held nearly a fifth of the units. Yet even though conversations about technology were primary in these three areas, technology ranked third to social and cultural issues among the benefits and challenges of DE. This implies that definitions of DE would need to include social and cultural elements as well.

Gender themes: Twenty-eight respondents made gender references within the context of 11 (or 78.6%) of all parent codes, making gender themes the code with the seventh-most units among all codes. In other words, gender themes held a moderate-to-average ranking among all themes identified in the study. The parent code containing the most gender theme units (28.1%) was general gender-related comments (discussed under its own heading in this subsection). Two-thirds of the women in the study mentioned gender themes when considering influencers and initiating experiences in their background. This would be expected because two background questions asked respondents to identify women who influenced them and piqued their interest in the field. Two out of five respondents brought up gender issues when discussing the challenges that they faced. Two out of five also discussed gender when asked to identify early female founders; this gender theme was generated from the reasons these respondents could identify few to no female founders. Claims by some respondents that, despite the prevalent numbers of women working and learning in the field, men retained dominion over administrative leadership positions, conference proceedings, and literary works, coupled with the authors' inability to find resources on female pioneers, offer explanation as to why gender theme data was found in the challenges and early founders codes. The cumulative data drawn from the gender theme prompts the hypothesis that the Matilda effect (Rossiter, 1993) may have been, and continues to be, deeply engrained in the field of DE (Schmidt et al., 2021). This hypothesis is explored at greater length in the Key Implications for Stakeholders section of the final chapter.

Conclusion

This study gathered data from interviews with 30 female pioneers in the field of DE. Fourteen main topics, or parent codes, were identified during the data analysis process. Eleven of these parent codes were overtly tied to at least one interview question. Three other parent codes emerged from the data during the coding process. Two more significant cross-category themes also emerged from a number of parent codes. Summaries and related conclusions offered herein are presented in order from the themes containing the greatest number to the least number of data units.

Technology was the most dominant theme to emerge from this study – even though no interview question explicitly asked respondents to discuss technology. Technology themes crossed 12 of the 14 parent categories and secured one out of five units in the study. Technology held a primary position within the conversational contexts of changes over time, interesting memories, and research interests. The centrality of technology in this study lends credence to literary claims that technology preempted a plethora of distance learning definitions, as well as the evolution of our field (Bates, 2008; Bingham et al., 1999; Quality Assurance Agency, 2020; State University, n.d.). Interestingly, though, social and cultural issues outnumbered technology in conversations about the benefits and challenges of DE. This may suggest that any definition of DE would require socio-cultural identifiers as well.

The second most prevalent code in this study was background. This code aggregated data from four interview questions. All other question-related parent codes were devoted to one research question each. Even though this amplifies the ranking of background in relation to the rest of the question-generated parent codes, the authors believed that, given the aim of this volume, it was critical to gather as much data as possible about the backgrounds of these pioneers to help shed light on what their educational and experiential backgrounds were before they entered the field, who and what prompted their entry into the field, and when they joined the field.

Respondents came from six continents: one-third were from North America, one-quarter came from each of Asia and Oceania, and one in ten was from South America. Despite the dominance of English, especially in Northern Europe, the authors were able to find only one European respondent. Due to the authors' reliance on English, most respondents came from countries where English was a dominant language. One out of five participants communicated in English, even though it was not their native tongue.

Three-quarters of the respondents who discussed their educational background did not have education related to distance learning, education, or technology. One in three did not have any experiential background in DE, education, technology, or research when they entered the field. Such findings allude to the pioneering nature of the field at the time these women began their careers.

While two out of three respondents cited personal interest as one reason for joining the field, they did not elaborate much on what these personal interests were. On the other hand, when just over half the women indicated that social justice issues piqued their interest, they generated enough data to produce seven unique social justice sub-categories. Regardless of why they chose to talk more about social justice than personal interest catalysts, these remained the two main reasons for joining the field.

Some respondents found it difficult to identify any women who may have piqued their interest in DE. Others provided the names of men, even though the interview question only asked for women's names. These results helped explain why the authors were able to easily amass a wealth of literature on male pioneers but came up nearly empty-handed after an exhaustive search of resources for female pioneers.

The benefits of DE generated the third-largest number of units among all identified codes, making it the second ranking parent code in the study. (Although technology contained the largest number of codes, it was an emergent cross-category theme, not a parent code.) No interview question asked about the benefits of DE; this topic organically emerged as the interviews unfolded. Primary sub-themes included social justice, ICT, openness, and continuing education. Review of the collective data underscored the deep pride and devotion that these pioneers felt for this field.

Twenty-eight of the 30 women were still actively involved in the field to some extent at the time of their interviews. Two women were engaged in voluntary work. Six acted as national or international consultants. The remaining women were either full-time administrators or educators or had taken on lighter teaching and research roles as emeritus or adjunct professors.

Discussions about the learning environment that these pioneers were currently working in were separated into two distinct areas: institutional description and student demographics. It was concluded that these women worked in very diverse environments. Some institutions had one geographic site while others were spread across eleven or more sites. Institutions had regional, provincial, state, national, or international reach. One institution was strictly f-2-f; the remaining offered a mix of f-2-f, DE, and blended learning. Programmes tended to be offered at pre-university to graduate school levels. Student demographics were also diverse. While a few institutions catered primarily to a traditional demographic of 18- to 24-year-olds, most had expanded their reach to students of all ages and from around the globe. Since most of the pioneers in this study were engaged in DE initiatives, it seems reasonable that they would work for institutions that sought to include a diversity of learners from across the world.

Even though respondents were overtly asked to identify the DE challenges that they faced, but not the benefits of DE, it is interesting to note that the number of units that benefits generated slightly outnumbered the number of challenges units. Challenges ranked fifth among the parent codes and sixth among all identified codes. The most commonly cited challenge was the acceptance and understanding of DE, a sentiment that has been well-documented in DE literature (Bates, 2005; Keegan, 1990; Larreamendy-Joerns & Leinhardt, 2006; Parker, 2008; Wark, 2018). Other significant challenges that respondents noted included institutional growing pains, funding, technology, gender, faculty, and cultural issues.

The next most discussed interview topic was the women's accomplishments. Over half the women focused on their involvement in the implementation of new initiatives, such as the development of new systems, programmes/courses, or technological infrastructures. Given that these women were trailblazers at a time when emerging technologies were helping to expand the field in multiple directions, it is not surprising to learn that such activities were counted among their achievements. One out of three respondents also listed awards that they received, or contributions to the literature, DE advocacy, student learning, research, and international endeavours in the field as part of their achievements. One anomaly emerged. Although the interview question asked respondents to identify personal achievements, over one-third of the women elaborated on team accomplishments. One interviewee explained that it was not acceptable to discuss individual achievements in her culture. However, a review of research literature on gender-related self-promotion offered three other possible explanations. First, women were more reluctant than men to engage in self-promotion (Exley & Kessler, 2019). Second, men who exuded self-confidence gained influence in a company; women were required to display self-confidence *and* pro-social (team-oriented) behaviours to achieve status (Guillén et al., 2017). Lastly, women feared perceived social consequences if they engaged in self-promotion (Lindeman et al., 2019). Thus, it was concluded that, in order to be successful in this field, some pioneers may have emulated perceived cultural norms when discussing achievements. Such research also provided further explanation of why the participants and authors found it difficult to identify female pioneers in this field.

The interview question to generate the sixth greatest number of parent code units related to the changes that participants had observed from the time that they started in the field until the time of their interviews. Many respondents talked about the most significant change that they had perceived as well. Technology was the primary topic in early years, current year, and most significant change conversations. Second to technology was the movement from an industrial model to a network system. The third theme was greater acceptance and understanding of DE today. This may be due in part to the increasing reliance on online learning (Marinova, 2020; Paul & Jefferson, 2019; Tejeda-Delgado et al., 2011), as well as to the publication of comprehensive research studies providing assurance that there are no significant differences in student achievement between f-2-f and online learning environments (Paul & Jefferson, 2019).

The emergent parent code, general gender-related comments, yielded the fewest parent units in the study. Nevertheless, the cross-category theme, gender, which aggregated gender units from all parent codes including general gender-related comments, yielded the seventh greatest number of units among all code groupings. In total, 28 respondents referenced gender topics within the context of 11 out of the 14 parent codes. This gave the cross-category theme, gender, a mid-level ranking among all themes identified in the study. Primary general gender-related comment subthemes included male dominance in the field, female subordination, and female grit. Two-thirds of respondents discussed gender issues when asked to provide background information on women who influenced them and piqued their interest in the field. Two out of five women touched upon gender issues when discussing challenges and early female founders. The early female founders' gender theme was produced from reasons supplied by the women on why they could identify few to no female founders. It was concluded that a number of these pioneers perceived a gender imbalance of power. They believed that, while there were significantly more women learning and working in the field, men dominated administrative leadership positions, conference proceedings, and literary contributions. This would offer further explanation for the absence of resources on female pioneers in our field. A synthesis of the data gathered from this study leads the authors to conclude that the Matilda effect (Rossiter, 1993) may have had, and continues to have, a significant impact on the careers of women in our field (Schmidt et al., 2021). This hypothesis is presented in greater detail in the Key Implications for Stakeholders section of the final chapter.

The parent code containing the seventh greatest number of units was research interests. Four out of five women were involved in research activities. Two-thirds reported an evolution in what topics they pursued due to changing roles, personal interests, technologies, and funding. Over half the women conducted research on technology. Two out of five explored social issues or DE theory, systems, instructional design, and/or learning environments. One-quarter focused on support topics. A small handful of women looked at quality assurance, policy and governance, student success, or learner autonomy. One out of five women did not engage in research because she had been an administrator during her career.

The interview question to generate the next greatest number of units focused on respondent's career goals. It was concluded that over half the women aimed to enhance social conditions, such as improving access and learning opportunities or decreasing isolation. Two out of five respondents followed faculty, student, or technology support or student success goals while one-quarter of the respondents pursued quality assurance or the promotion of DE goals.

The use of technology was the most prevalent theme to emerge in conversations about respondents' interesting memories. Technology topics included recollections about the types, limitations, and integration of technology. Nearly two out of three respondents recounted positive memories; most of these memories highlighted the excitement that they experienced while working in the field. Almost half the women talked about their pioneering efforts; most of these recollections involved the creation of new networks. Over a third also spoke fondly about collegial memories.

Everyone in the study joined the discussion about identification of early female founders/leaders in the field. Even though 12 participants said that they knew very few to no early female founders/leaders, 26 were able to supply at least one name. The inability to identify female founders/leaders was explained by participants in three ways: 1) They were among the first in their part of the world to work in the field; 2) They were not an expert in the field; or 3) They had encountered very little literature published by women. This has led the authors to speculate that there could be a number of pioneers whose stories remain untold.

When asked to suggest names of other female pioneers for the book, 25 participants offered 158 names. Removal of 57 duplicates and 4 partial names left a list of 97 potential candidates for the study. Near the end of the data collection process, duplication of names became more prevalent, implying that the snowballing strategy may have been reaching its saturation point. Nevertheless, the authors knew that some English-speaking areas of Europe were left to be explored. Moreover, there was very little representation among the respondents from countries where other languages prevailed.

The emergent parent code containing the second greatest number of units was career history. Examination of this data indicated that most participants began in other fields and entered DE as faculty, researchers, or technologists. Mid-career found some moving on to administrative leadership, course design, or advising-consulting positions. By the end of their careers, half the women held administrative positions; the remainder were equally divided between faculty and advisor-consultant positions.

The parent code containing the least number of units (outside of general gender-related comments, which is discussed earlier with the emergent cross-category theme gender) was final comments. Four out of five interviewees offered advice when asked to share any final comments. Prevalent recommendations related to the future of DE, being learner-focused, and remaining current. Almost half the women mentioned barriers, the most common being the battle against erroneous perceptions of our field. Two out of five women shared positive memories: the joy of DE, what DE offered the world, and sharing work with others.

Research Limitations

The primary limitation of this research study was the scarcity of resources on female pioneers in the field of DE, which made it difficult to find potential candidates. The authors' reliance on the English language also limited access to potential candidates. Fortunately, due to the authors' background and resources in the field, they were able to identify a sufficient number of pioneers to begin the study. Employment of a snowball strategy with this initial group of pioneers not only provided the remaining number of participants to complete the project, but also left the authors with a list of 47 potential candidates for future consideration. Time and lack of financial resources placed further limitations on the study. However, lack of external funding meant that the authors were free to conduct the study without externally-imposed limitations.

Key implications for stakeholders arising from this study, as well as future research considerations, are considered in the last chapter of this text, Final Thoughts.

References

Adeoye, M. (2009, April 13). Leadership definitions by scholars [Web log post]. *Adeoyemayowaleadership*. http://adeoyemayowaleadership.blogspot.com/

Bates, A. W. (2005). *Technology, e-learning and distance education* (2nd ed.). Routledge. www.routledge.com/Technology-e-learning-and-Distance-Education/Bates/p/book/9780415284370

Bates, A. W. (2008, July 7). What do you mean by...? [Web log post]. *Tony Bates*. www.tonybates.ca/2008/07/07/what-is-distance-education/

Bingham, J., Davis, T., & Moore, C. (1999). Emerging technologies in distance learning. *Horizon: Issues Challenging Education*. http://horizon.unc.edu/projects/issues/papers/Distance_Learning.html

Boyatzis, R. E. (1998). *Transforming qualitative information: Thematic analysis and code development*. Sage Publications.

Campbell, J. L., Quincy, C., Osserman, J., & Pedersen, O. K. (2013). Coding in-depth semi-structured interviews: Problems of unitization and intercoder reliability and agreement. *Sociological Methods & Research*, 42(3), 294–320. https://doi.org/10.1177/0049124113500475

Cohen, L., Manion, L., & Morrison, K. (2011). *Research methods in education* (7th ed.). Routledge.

Demiray, E. (Ed.). (2012). *International women online journal of distance education (intWOJDE)*. www.wojde.org/

Exley, C., & Kessler, J. (2019). The gender gap in self-promotion (No. w26345; p. w26345). *National Bureau of Economic Research*. https://doi.org/10.3386/w26345

Fahy, P. (2001). Addressing some common problems in transcript analysis. *International Review of Research on Open and Distributed Learning (IRRODL)*, 1. www.irrodl.org/index.php/irrodl/article/view/321

Garrison, D. R., Cleveland-Innes, M., Koole, M., & Kappelman, J. (2005). Revisiting methodological issues in transcript analysis: Negotiated coding and reliability. *Internet and Higher Education*, 9, 1–8. www.sciencedirect.com/science/article/abs/pii/S1096751605000771

Gibbs, G. R. (2007). Thematic coding and categorizing. *Analyzing qualitative data*. SAGE Publications.

Guillén, L., Mayo, M., & Karelaia, N. (2017). Appearing self-confident and getting credit for it: Why it may be easier for men than women to gain influence at work. *Human Resource Management*, 57(4), 839–854. https://doi.org/10.1002/hrm.21857

Hodson, R. (1999). *Analyzing documentary accounts*. Sage Publications. https://books.google.ca/books

Hruschka, D. J., Schwartz, D., Cobb St. John, D., Picone-Decaro, E., Jenkins, R. A., & Carey, J. W. (2004). Reliability in coding open-ended data: Lessons learned from HIV behavioral research. *Field Methods*, 16, 307–331. https://pdfs.semanticscholar.org/f62c/0497ffb0096e5200b43b827b9887812f3138.pdf

Keegan, D. (1990). *Foundations of distance education*. Routledge.

Krippendorff, K. (2004). *Content Analysis: An introduction to its methodology* (2nd ed.). Sage Publications.

Kurasaki, K. S. (2000). Intercoder reliability from validating conclusions drawn from open-ended interview data. *Field Methods*, 12, 179–194. http://journals.sagepub.com/doi/abs/10.1177/1525822X0001200301

Larreamendy-Joerns, J., & Leinhardt, G. (2006). Going the distance with online education. *Review of Educational Research*, 76(4), 567–605. http://rer.sagepub.com/content/76/4/567

Legacee. (2018). Definitions of leadership. *Legacee.com*. www.legacee.com/potpourri/leadership-definitions/

Lindeman, M. I. H., Durik, A. M., & Dooley, M. (2019). Women and self-promotion: A test of three theories. *Psychological Reports*, 122(1), 219–230. https://doi.org/10.1177/0033294118755096

Marinova, I. (2020, November 19). 20 fascinating online education statistics to know in 2021 [Web log post]. *Review42*. https://review42.com/resources/online-education-statistics/

Nelson, T. (2003). The persistence of founder influence: Management, ownership, and performance effects at initial public offering. *Strategic Management Journal*, 24(8), 707–724. https://onlinelibrary.wiley.com/doi/full/10.1002/smj.328

Panda, S. (Ed.). (2017–2018). *Journal of Learning for Development (JL4D)*. https://jl4d.org/index.php/ejl4d

Parker, N. (2008). The quality dilemmas of online education revisited. In T. Anderson (Ed.), *The theory and practice of online learning* (2nd ed., pp. 305–341). Athabasca University Press. http://cde.athabascau.ca/online_book/second_edition.htm

Paul, J., & Jefferson, F. (2019). A comparative analysis of student performance in an online vs. face-to-face environmental science course from 2009 to 2016. *Frontiers in Computer Science*, 1. https://doi.org/10.3389/fcomp.2019.00007

Quality Assurance Agency for Higher Education. (2020). *Guidance: Building a taxonomy for digital learning*. www.qaa.ac.uk/docs/qaa/guidance/building-a-taxonomy-for-digital-learning.pdf

Rossiter, M. W. (1993). The Matthew Matilda effect in science. *Social Studies of Science*, *23*(2), 325–342. https://doi.org/10.1177/030631293023002004

Rourke, L., Anderson, T., Garrison, D. R., & Archer, W. (2001). Methodological issues in the content analysis of computer conference transcripts. *International Journal of Artificial Intelligence in Education*, *12*(1), 8–22. www.iaied.org/pub/951/file/951_paper.pdf

Schein, E. H. (1995). The role of the founder in creating organizational culture. *Family Business Review*, *8*(3), 221–238. http://journals.sagepub.com/doi/abs/10.1111/j.1741-6248.1995.00221.x

Schmidt, H., Bainbridge, S.,& Wark, N. (2021). Mitigating the Matilda e ect on Starr Roxanne Hiltz: Asuperlative early online learning researcher. *International Women Online Journal of Distance Education (intWOJDE)*, *20*(2). www.wojde.org/FileUpload/bs295854/File/01_102.pdf

State University. (n.d.). Distance learning in higher education – Related terms and concepts, goals of distance learning, technologies used in distance learning [Web log post]. *Stateuniversity.com*. https://education.stateuniversity.com/pages/1917/Distance-Learning-in-Higher-Education.html

Stemler, S. (2013). Interrater reliability. In N. Salkind & K. Rasmussen (Eds.), *Encyclopedia of measurement and statistics*. Sage Publications. https://sk.sagepub.com/reference/statistics/n224.xml

Tejeda-Delgado, C., Millan, B., & Slate, J. (2011). Distance and face-to-face learning culture and values: A conceptual analysis. *Administrative Issues Journal*, *1*(2). https://files.eric.ed.gov/fulltext/EJ1055022.pdf

Ward, S. (2018, May 25). Leadership definition [Web log post]. *Small Business*. www.thebalancesmb.com/leadership-definition-2948275

Wark, N. (2018). *Shifting Paradigms: A critical pragmatic evaluation of key factors affecting learner-empowered emergent technology integration* [Doctoral dissertation, Athabasca University]. Athabasca University Digital Archive. http://hdl.handle.net/10791/274

Wedemeyer, C. A. (1971). Independent study. In L. C. Deighton (Ed.), *Encyclopedia of education* (1st ed., pp. 548–557). McMillan.

33
FINAL THOUGHTS

Introduction

The main goal of this book was to capture the voices and contributions of female pioneers in online learning. The authors sought to share these women's stories, experiences, and achievements in the pioneers' own words, rather than from others' perspectives.

It is hoped that this living record will become a timeless historical testament of who these women are, what they believe, and what they offer to our field. It is also hoped that, in some small way, this book serves to give these women the recognition that they have so richly earned as pioneers in our field.

The authors' final thoughts on the study are divided into two main sections. The first section, Key Findings, summarizes salient and other interesting discoveries derived primarily from the cumulative interview data results. The second section, Conclusion, begins by pointing out the key implications of this study for policymakers, administrators, educators, historians, researchers, writers, and students who are interested in DE and online learning. The chapter closes with recommendations for further research.

Key Findings

Fourteen main themes, or independent parent codes, were identified in the study. Eleven were overtly tied to the predetermined, open-ended questions that were asked during the interview (Appendices A & B). In order from most to least discussed, these parent codes were: background, learning environment, challenges, accomplishments, changes over time, research interests, goals, interesting memories, early founders, others for the book, and final comments.

Two sets of codes also emerged during the data analysis process. Neither set of codes was generated directly from any interview question but, instead, arose as topics that the pioneers volunteered during their interviews. The first set included two independent parent codes, with the most prevalent one being benefits of distance education (DE) and the lesser-discussed one being career history. The last set to emerge from the data was cross-theme codes. In other words, these latter codes were found as sub-themes within most of the 14 parent codes. These cross-theme codes were technology and gender.

Among the 14 parent and 2 cross-theme codes, the theme that dominated interview discussions was technology. Overall, conversations about technology consumed one-fifth of the pioneers' interview responses, clearly indicating that technology played a dominant role in their careers.

Possessing one-seventh of the data, the parent code, background, appeared to be the second-most dominant theme in the collective interview results. However, this result is somewhat misleading in that this is the only parent code containing data from four interview questions. Only one interview question was connected to each of the remaining ten parent codes that were overtly tied to interview questions. Of these remaining interview question–generated parent codes, learning environment and challenges contained the most data.

The parent code capturing the third-largest portion of interview discussions (10.5% of all data analysis units) focused on the benefits of DE. This was quite a discovery as not one interview question directly or indirectly asked about the benefits of DE. Half of the benefits mentioned dwelled on social justice issues, such as access to education, geographically isolated learners and other marginalized groups, learner support, and gender equality. What was even more illuminating was that the pioneers talked more about the benefits of DE than they did about the challenges that they faced in the field, even though they were intentionally asked to discuss challenges during their interviews. In fact, challenges ranked fifth among all parent codes, producing one-tenth (10.0%) of all collected data.

The fourth most prevalent parent code, learning environment, contained slightly over one-tenth (10.1%) of all interview data. This result would not be surprising, as it was a comprehensive question that asked the interviewees to describe the geographic and institutional setting that they were working in at the time of their interview and to provide details on student demographics within that environment.

Another noteworthy finding was related to discourse on gender. During the coding process, the parent code, general gender-related comments, was identified as a result of some general comments that some respondents made on the topic. The resultant parent code produced the least number of units among all parent codes (1.8% of coded units). Yet, within discussions tied to other parent themes, gender-related sub-themes also emerged. A merger of the parent code, general gender-related comments, with these gender-related sub-codes, resulted in the finding that, as a collective, gender-related discussions emerged as a mid-level theme (producing 6.5% of all units) among all parent themes. This indicated that gender was a moderate issue in these pioneers' career histories.

The possibility of arriving at new insights with the securement of more interview subjects is viable as saturation of data within some themes and sub-themes was just beginning to occur by the end of the collective interview coding process. Nevertheless, if the same selection and recruitment process (described in the Research Methods section of the preceding chapter) was used, the number of potential female candidates who could participate in the English language might be similarly reduced to somewhere between 18 and 25 candidates.

Conclusion

Key Implications for Stakeholders

Perhaps the most profound finding in this study is that pioneering women have not been adequately represented in the literature. Female learners and workers have traditionally outnumbered men in this field. Yet not only have our female pioneers' voices been muzzled, but their ideas and contributions are also in danger of being lost forever. Time is of the essence. While conducting this study, the authors discovered that many female pioneers were too ill to participate or had already passed on. We will never hear their stories in their own words, and it is likely that some of their works will be lost as well. Our individual and collective understanding of our field will be poorer for this.

Final Thoughts

This project may provide partial explanation for why female pioneers are under-represented in the literature. One third of the women in this study elaborated on *team* accomplishments when asked to discuss personal achievements. This may reflect a cultural norm that expects women to emulate pro-social as well as self-confident behaviours in order to succeed in the workplace (Guillén et al., 2017; Lindeman et al., 2019). Some pioneers also pointed out that the field was predominately populated by women students and scholars in the early years, yet men tended to hold most senior administrative positions and lead presentations at conference gatherings. Such claims were supported by the American National Science Foundation (2015a, 2015b), which found that even though women obtained a higher number of PhDs than men in the social sciences from 1994 to 2014, men still held more faculty positions. Controlling for such factors as experience, Bentley and Adamson (2004) learned that this was especially true when it came to senior faculty positions. A thematic synthesis of these results from our study may provide supporting evidence for the Matilda effect in our field (Rossiter, 1993; Schmidt et al., 2021).

The term *Matilda effect* was coined by Rossiter (1993) after a human rights activist and author, Matilda Gage (1826–1898). Among other works, Gage authored a tract, *Woman as Inventor* (1870), and a journal article, *Woman as an Inventor* (1883), which recounted numerous examples of women's work that had been credited to men throughout the ages. In her article, *The Matthew Matilda Effect in Science* (1993; strikethrough of *Matthew* in the original), Rossiter summarizes Gage's observations: "[T]he more [a] woman worked the more the men around her profited and the less credit she got" (pp. 336–337). Despite all her significant contributions, including her efforts to draw attention to this phenomenon, Gage, too, has slipped into obscurity, thus becoming the epitome of the Matilda effect.

Rossiter (1993) points out that "not only have those unrecognized in their own time generally remained so, but others that were well-known in their day have since been obliterated from history, either by laziness or inertia, or by historians with definite axes to grind" (p. 328). Rossiter supports her claim by providing numerous examples of inventions and discoveries by women that have been "suppressed, ignored, or attributed to their male collaborators . . . in virtually every scientific field – physics, chemistry, genetics, biochemistry, medicine, and more" (Schmidt et al., 2021).

Historical and systemic obliteration of women's academic contributions may not only promote a cultural stereotype of males being better scientists, researchers, and academics (Makarova et al., 2019; Miller et al., 2015; Nosek et al., 2009), but also engender a multi-faceted, albeit unconscious, bias (Lincoln et al., 2012). For instance, Storage et al. (2020) report that adults, as well as children, correlate brilliance or ingenuity with men, not women. This finding may be linked to the under-representation of women in some scientific fields, such as science, technology, engineering, and math (STEM: Bentley & Adamson, 2004; National Science Foundation, 2015a, 2015b).

Although the issue of self-citation was not explored when collecting interview or publication data for this volume, this topic arose when investigating possible reasons for the under-representation of female pioneers in the literature. According to Azouly and Lynn (2020), self-citation could be interpreted as a means to artificially promote one's prior work to potentially inflate their long-term professional authority. Some research studies on gender-related self-citation patterns indicated that men were more prone to self-citation. Upon reviewing 1.5 million JSTOR database publications from 1779 to 2011 (a span of 232 years), King et al. (2017) concluded that overall, men were 56% more likely than women to cite themselves. This male tendency to self-cite increased to 70% during the period from 1991 to 2011. Moreover, women were 10% more likely to never cite themselves. Maliniak et al. (2013) not only concurred that women cited themselves less but also found that men cited men more often than women.

Other scholars disagreed with these self-citation results. For example, in considering 1.6 million publications from the database PubMed between the years 2002 and 2005, one study concluded that self-citation was the hallmark of high and consistent career productivity, not gender (Mishra et al., 2018). However, this study only examined trends among first and last authors on works with multiple authors over a very short period of time. Azoulay and Lynn (2020) argued that work by such scholars as King et al. (2017) and Mishra et al. (2018) just considered the quantity of self-cited works between genders. To address this concern, Azoulay and Lynn (2020) conducted a longitudinal study, tracking the careers of 3,667 graduate-level life science students who had earned post-doctoral scholarships from four private American philanthropic foundations between 1970 and 2005. This study collected the same quantitative data as the previous studies on male versus female citation numbers. It also gathered qualitative data meant to determine if men engaged in self-citation for promotional purposes or if practicing self-citation paid off more for men than women (i.e., helped men advance their career with greater ease). By using a comprehensive, longitudinal approach, the researchers concluded that there was "no evidence whatsoever of a gender gap in self-citation practices or returns" (p. 152). Thus, contradictory results found in available literature on self-citation in science and social science disciplines, compounded by an absence of data from male pioneers in our field, leads to an indeterminant conclusion about whether self-citation practices played a role in the level of visibility and academic advancement among the pioneers in this study.

Despite ambivalent findings regarding self-citations and gender, recent research does indicate that the impact value and evaluation of research is gendered (Chubb & Derrick, 2020). Scientific research manuscripts authored by women are less likely to be accepted by academic journals or cited by others (Fox & Paine, 2019; Maliniak et al., 2013). Even comparison of academic letters of recommendation written for men and women of equivalent candidacy standing denote signs of doubt about female candidates (Madera et al., 2019).

Given the pervasiveness of the Matilda effect (Rossiter, 1993) across the STEM and social sciences, it is conceivable that the field of DE is also impacted by this phenomenon, due to the location of our field within the social sciences, and its reliance on computing and emerging technologies (Makarova et al., 2019; Schmidt et al., 2021). This hypothesis could assist in explaining the obscurity of female pioneers and their contributions in our field. It may also provide illumination on some of the pioneers' cumulative challenges, accomplishments, and gender-related comments results, including observations about the domination of men in leadership, administrative, and conference presentations.

One potential example of the Matilda effect involves a pioneer featured in this book, Starr Roxanne Hiltz. While examining Hiltz's pioneering contributions to our field, Schmidt et al. (2021) noted that, over 20 years after Hiltz and Turoff's (1978) national award–winning seminal work, *The Network Nation: Human Communication via Computer*, hit the stands, Garrison et al. (2000) presented many of Hiltz and Turoff's (1978) notions in their seminal work on their Community of Inquiry model, without giving credit to Hiltz and Turoff's work. To illustrate, in 1978, Hiltz and Turoff said:

> [T]he "written equivalent" of the language content tends to be somewhat better organized and more fully thought out than comparable statements recorded from a face-to-face conversation. This is because the participant has a chance to take as long as desired to think about a response or comment, to reorganize and rework it until it presents the idea as fully and succinctly as possible.
>
> (pp. 82–83)

Over 20 years later, Garrison et al. (2000), echoed this finding, stating that:

> Compared to traditional, oral classroom interaction, computer conferencing would appear to offer not only potential deficiencies, but also some advantages. One such advantage is that text-based communication provides time for reflection. For this reason, written

communication may actually be preferable to oral communication when the objective is higher-order cognitive learning.

(p. 90)

What is most curious is that Garrison et al. (2000) not only neglected to cite Hiltz and Turoff in this area but also overlooked Hiltz's extensive work on collaborative online learning (see, for example, Hiltz, 1984, 1994, as well as the Reference section of her chapter in this book). Yet Garrison et al. (2000) did cite Hiltz and Turoff's (1993) revised edition of the *Network Nation*, saying: "In fact, when education based on computer conferencing fails, it is usually because there has not been responsible teaching presence and appropriate leadership and direction exercised (Gunawardena, 1991; Hiltz & Turoff, 1993)" (p. 16). Moreover, the Reference section of this Garrison et al. (2000) publication did not indicate that the 1993 book was a revised edition of Hiltz and Turoff's original 1978 book.

In 2000, Garrison also wrote an article on the shift from structural to transactional issues in DE. According to his abstract, "[i]n order to assess the theoretical challenges facing the field of distance education, the significant theoretical contributions to distance education in the last century [were] briefly reviewed" (p. 1). While the Garrison et al. (2000, discussed earlier) publication indicated that Garrison was aware of Hiltz and Turoff's (1993) work, Garrison's 2000 article made no mention of Hiltz and Turoff's (1993) contributions, let alone their original, groundbreaking findings in 1978. Instead, Garrison (2000) credited himself, declaring, "[t]he next contribution to be discussed here explicitly places sustained real two-way communication at the core of the educational experience, regardless of the separation of teacher and student. This is a framework provided by Garrison (1989)" (p. 9). Although Garrison does admit that some contributions were overlooked because they overlapped with the ones he had already described, they focused on "definitional and historical descriptions," or "their importance and impact [was] less well recognized and understood" (p. 10), he concludes that "it can be stated with some confidence that the selected models [in this publication] accurately reflect the progression of a theoretical development of the field of distance education along an organizational (structural) – transactional (teaching and learning) continuum" (p. 11). Despite this declaration, Garrison does not indicate that an exhaustive search or systematic review of the literature was undertaken for this article. Nor does he state what criteria were used to select, or reject, potential contributions. Intriguingly, his review included ten contributing males but only one contributing female, France Henri (who also has a chapter devoted to her in this book). In summation, the value of this article must be considered as an expression of one expert's opinion, not a product of scholarly research findings.

Two other articles on the Community of Inquiry model, one by Anderson et al. (2001/2019) and the other by Garrison (2007/2019), give a cursory nod to Hiltz and her colleagues' most recent work of that time. Yet founding contributions to the Community of Inquiry model can be traced back to Hiltz and Turoff's (1978) seminal work. Considering the burgeoning popularity of the Community of Inquiry model (Castellanos-Reyes, 2020; Jan et al., 2019; Richardson et al., 2017; Stenbom, 2018), it seems a grave injustice that Hiltz's superlative and original yet historic contributions are downplayed – or downright ignored – by Garrison, Anderson, and their colleagues in the discussed publications.

While, admittedly, the Hiltz example focuses solely on a few articles written by a handful of men, these articles provoke a number of cautionary notes. First, stakeholders need to be able to recognize opinion-based literature by self-declared experts that might, at first blush, appear to represent diligent scholarly research. Second, even if authors imply that their contributions are original or at the forefront of a particular theory, notion, or praxis, this may not be so. Third, an examination of the reviewed literature by Garrison, Anderson, and colleagues indicates that women were notably and consistently under-cited in their articles. The plethora of references furnished by the pioneers in this book that predate these men's publications provides further evidence to support the Matilda hypothesis. Stakeholders should undertake a conscious effort to consider how well publications represent women's and other minorities' views and contributions. Therefore, stakeholders are strongly urged to critically analyze publications, investigate citations, conduct independent research, and draw their own conclusions. The Matilda effect cannot be identified or reversed without stakeholders' due diligence.

In summary, evidence for support of the Matilda effect (Rossiter, 1993) in this study has been derived from three sources. The initial source was the authors' impetus for this book – a lack of resources on female pioneers in our field. This finding has been supported by the second source, data from the pioneers, which indicated a similar absence of such resources. The pioneers' cumulative data results from the early founders, accomplishments, challenges, and general gender-related comments thematic codes have provided further evidence of the Matilda effect. The third source of evidence has been gathered from the literature that was intended to provide stakeholders with explanations for the data results while also positioning this study within the body of known literature. This final source has been drawn from a growing body of STEM and social science literature that underscores the prevalence of the Matilda effect across the globe.

If proven, the Matilda effect (Rossiter, 1993) hypothesis would expose a historic, system-wide gender disparity that has shaped, and perhaps continues to shape, the perceptions of all stakeholders in our field – from policymakers, funders, administrators, and leaders to theorists, researchers, faculty, and students (Schmidt et al., 2021). Such a discovery would have gender equality and leadership implications requiring not only institutional-level restructuring, but also a comprehensive overhaul of the very foundations upon which our field is built.

Another theme emerging from the data was the struggle that not only these women but also all proponents of DE faced in garnering understanding of our field and its contributions to global society. These pioneers' stories remind stakeholders that changing the mindset of people who have little to no experience with a phenomenon can be daunting. It has been the lifelong pioneering efforts of such individuals as these women, coupled with the exponential adoption of emergent technology across the world, exploding market demand for continuous and lifelong learning initiatives, and the current global COVID-19 pandemic, that have played salient roles in the rapid expansion of our field in recent years.

The centrality of technology in the data results holds overwhelming implications for stakeholders. There has been a historical tendency by some scholars to diminish or outright ignore the role of technology in our field. In fact, some definitions of distance learning terms completely sidestep the use of technology, choosing instead to focus on the distance and degree of interactivity between learners (Connick, 1999; State University, n. d.). The domination of technology themes in this study clearly underscores the leading role that technology has played in the existence and expansion of our field. In short, without technology, distance learning would not exist. The pioneers in this study have made this fact abundantly clear.

Another very interesting implication to arise from this project related to the pioneers' desire to talk about the benefits of DE – a topic that was not directly asked about or even implied by the interview questions. Further insight into why all of the pioneers in this study were compelled to point out the benefits of DE may have been gained by discovering that half the benefit of DE discourse content focused on social justice and equity issues. Even though the interview question about challenges prompted nearly as much dialogue as the benefits of DE did, these challenges did not dissuade the women from pursuing their goals in this field. In his 2009 book *Drive: The Surprising Truth About What Motivates Us*, Pink stated that humans were innately driven to achieve autonomy, mastery, and purpose. When people believed that they were working towards something that was for the greater good, they tended to be more hardworking, engaged, and productive. This may suggest that pioneers are driven by an innate force that enables them to overcome adversity when they are committed to a vision of a better future.

One topic that consumed a fair bit of research and discussion between the authors of this book was the definition of terms. It was determined that our field was plagued by a plethora of terms and definitions for *DE*, *online learning*, and *educational technology* that may or may not possess the same meaning (see, for example, Bates, 2008). Rather than becoming sidetracked from the aims of this study by sorting out what scholars' definitions may or may not "be right," the authors accepted whatever terms and definitions that the pioneers offered during their interviews. Knowing how the various uses and definitions of terms have served to complicate and confuse matters in our field, the authors did strive to provide a very clear, concise definition for the term *pioneer*, which was used to select candidates for this study, though. Two recommendations are therefore offered to stakeholders. First, when conducting research or producing a publication in our field, we humbly suggest that stakeholders strive to clarify what terms and definitions are used in their work. Second, stakeholders are cautioned that terms and definitions in our field are not necessarily widely accepted. In other words, what might be *online learning* for one pioneer in this study or a scholar in our field could very well be *e-learning* for another.

While this study was able to provide many insights into common themes and patterns from the synthesis and analysis of the cumulative interview data, saturation was just beginning to be reached in only four of the fourteen main thematic areas, or parent codes, by the end of the coding process. These four were changes over time, challenges, early founders, and others for the book. Upon comparing individual profiles to the average interview profile, it became apparent that no pioneer's profile closely matched the average profile. Not only did most individual profiles have 50% or less in common with the average profile, but the areas of commonality between individual profiles and the average profile also varied greatly. Three prevalent conclusions were drawn from this. First, more interview data was needed in order to reach a greater level of thematic saturation. This meant that, although general patterns and themes were identified in this study, lesser topics required the collection of more data before definitive results could be reported. Second, our field rapidly evolved as emerging technologies enabled the expansion and development of new pedagogies and means of delivery. Finally, the lack of matching between the individual and average interview suggested that what sets pioneers apart is their very nature: what they choose to pursue and how they pursue it is what makes them pioneers.

The origins and expansion of online learning across the globe was precipitated by the development of the Internet and the World Wide Web. The first ARPANET (later known as the "Internet") link was established between University of California, Los Angeles (UCLA) and the Stanford Research Institute in 1969 (SRI; Press, 2015). Tim Berners-Lee proposed the Mesh (later called the "World Wide Web") to the European Council for Nuclear Research (CERN) in 1989 but then moved to the American Massachusetts Institute of Technology (MIT) to found the World Wide Web Consortium (W3C), an organization devoted to open web standards (Berners-Lee, 2021). Once established, the Internet and World Wide Web quickly expanded to other higher-education institutions in North America and then spread across other English-speaking countries before reaching the rest of the world. While it is not known if the voices and academic contributions of most female pioneers of online learning were captured in this study, the number and geographic distribution pattern of these pioneers do reflect the origins and expansion of online learning (see Background in the Results section of Chapter 32). It is possible that a number of English-speaking European pioneers were overlooked. Unfortunately, some European candidates, such as Robin Mason (England) and Ingeborg Bø (Norway), were identified but had passed on before this study began. The use of a snowballing strategy to collect names during interviews conducted in English would have also limited the number of potential candidates to those whom interviewees felt would be able to participate in English. So, although it is believed that many pioneers who could communicate in English,

Final Thoughts

especially those from the New World, have been represented in this volume, stakeholders should be aware that the stories and works of other pioneers, especially in non-English speaking countries, may not be captured yet.

Finally, this study affirms the value of using a snowball strategy for gathering information when other search strategies yield sparse results. Other researchers who are struggling to gather pertinent data may want to consider employing this strategy for their own work.

Future Research

The study concluded with 47 potential female pioneer candidates left to consider. The authors received an overwhelmingly positive response (69.9%) to the invitation to join this study. It is likely that between these remaining 47 candidates, the response rate, engagement of language translation services, and employment of the snowballing strategy with new participants, a second volume could be produced. Aggregation of data from all volumes might lead to new discoveries about common patterns, trends, and traits among female pioneers from across the globe.

Future research might answer some of the questions that arose from this study. Such research questions include:

1. Can the hypothesis of the Matilda effect (Rossiter, 1993), brought forth in this study, be validated by other evidence in our field?
2. Were female pioneers in our field who adopted a more patriarchal role more likely to achieve high status or have their accomplishments better recognized in the academic community?
3. Were female pioneers in our field who emulated self-confidence *and* pro-social attributes more likely to achieve high status and have their accomplishments better recognized in the academic community?
4. Were male pioneers in our field more likely to cite themselves in publications than female pioneers in our field were?
5. Was part of the reason so few female pioneers in our field could be identified in the early years because so few held leadership positions or publications at the time?
6. Would the same study conducted with male/minority pioneers yield similar results?

Who would have guessed that a casual conversation about female citations in academic research in online learning would have seen the authors embark on a three-year journey that spanned the globe and introduced them to so many fascinating women? Our knowledge has expanded exponentially through our engagement with these early female pioneers. We hope that the readers find themselves similarly absorbed as they delve into these women's valuable contributions. More importantly, we hope to see more of these female pioneers cited as we move forward. At this, we smile when we consider that our fundamental motivation for this book was a form of "social justice," a priority with our participants and, perhaps not so surprisingly, with ourselves as well.

References

Anderson, T., Rourke, L., Garrison, R., & Archer, W. (2019). Assessing teaching presence in a computer conferencing context. *Online Learning*, 5(2), Article 2. (Original publication in 2001) https://doi.org/10.24059/olj.v5i2.1875

Azoulay, P., & Lynn, F. (2020). Self-citation, cumulative advantage, and gender inequality in science. *Sociological Science*, 7, 152–186. https://doi.org/10.15195/v7.a7

Bates, A. W. (2008, July 7). What do you mean by…? [Web log post]. *Tony Bates*. www.tonybates.ca/2008/07/07/what-is-distance-education/

Bentley, J. T., Adamson, R. (2004). Gender differences in the careers of academic scientists and engineers: A literature review. *National Science Foundation.* www.nsf.gov/statistics/nsf03322/pdf/nsf03322.pdf

Berners-Lee, T. (2021). The history of the world wide web [Web log post]. *World Wide Web Foundation.* https://webfoundation.org/about/vision/history-of-the-web/

Castellanos-Reyes, D. (2020). 20 years of the Community of Inquiry framework. *TechTrends, 64*(4), 557–560. https://doi.org/10.1007/s11528-020-00491-7

Chubb, J., & Derrick, G. E. (2020). The impact a-gender: Gendered orientations towards research impact and its evaluation. *Palgrave Communications, 6.* https://doi.org/10.1057/s41599-020-0438-z

Connick, G. P. (Ed.). (1999). *The distance learner's guide.* Prentice Hall.

Fox, C. W., & Paine, C. E. T. (2019). Gender differences in peer review outcomes and manuscript impact at six journals of ecology and evolution. *Ecology and Evolution, 9,* 3599–3916. https://doi.org/10.1002/ece3.4993

Gage, M. E. J. (1870). Woman as inventor. *Women's Suffrage Tracts* (No. 1). New York State Women's Suffrage Association. https://iiif.lib.harvard.edu/manifests/view/drs:2575141$32i

Gage, M. E. J. (1883). Woman as an Inventor. *The North American Review, 136*(318), 478–489. www.jstor.org/stable/25118273

Garrison, D. R. (1989). *Understanding distance education: A framework for the future.* Routledge.

Garrison, D. R. (2000). Theoretical challenges for distance education in the 21st century: A shift from structural to transactional issues. *The International Review of Research in Open and Distributed Learning, 1*(1). https://doi.org/10.19173/irrodl.v1i1.2

Garrison, D. R. (2019). Online community of inquiry review: social, cognitive, and teaching presence issues. *Online Learning, 11*(1). http://dx.doi.org/10.24059/olj.v11i1.1737 (Original publication in 2007).

Garrison, D. R., Anderson, T., & Archer, W. (2000). Critical inquiry in a text-based environment: Computer conferencing in higher education. *Internet and Higher Education, 2,* 87–105. https://doi.org/10.1016/S1096-7516(00)00016-6

Guillén, L., Mayo, M., & Karelaia, N. (2017). Appearing self-confident and getting credit for it: Why it may be easier for men than women to gain influence at work. *Human Resource Management, 57*(4), 839–854. https://doi.org/10.1002/hrm.21857

Gunawardena, C. N. (1991). Collaborative learning and group dynamics in computer mediated communication networks. *Research Monograph of the American Center for the Study of Distance Education* (No. 9, pp. 14–24). Pennsylvania State University.

Hiltz, S. R. (1984). *Online communities: A case study of the office of the future.* Ablex.

Hiltz, S. R. (1994). *The virtual classroom: Learning without limits via computer networks.* Ablex.

Hiltz, S. R., & Turoff, M. (1978). *The network nation: Human communication via computer.* Addison-Wesley.

Hiltz, S. R., & Turoff, M. (1993). *The network nation: Human communication via computer.* MIT Press (Original work published in 1978). https://doi.org/10.7551/mitpress/4920.001.0001

Jan, S., Vlachopoulos, P., & Parsell, M. (2019). Social network analysis and online learning in communities in higher education: A systematic literature review. *Online Learning, 23*(1), 249–265. https://doi.org/10.24059/olj.v23i1.1398

King, M. M., Bergstrom, C. T., Correll, S. J., Jacquet, J., & West, J. D. (2017). Men set their own cites high: Gender and self-citation across fields and over time. *Socius, 3,* 2378023117738903. https://doi.org/10.1177/2378023117738903

Lincoln, A. E., Pincus, S., Koster, J. B., & Leboy, P. S. (2012). The Matilda effect in science: Awards and prizes in the US, 1990s and 2000s. *Social Studies of Science, 42*(2), 307–320. https://doi.org/10.1177/0306312711435830

Lindeman, M. I. H., Durik, A. M., & Dooley, M. (2019). Women and self-promotion: A test of three theories. *Psychological Reports, 122*(1), 219–230. https://doi.org/10.1177/0033294118755096

Madera, J. M., Hebl, M. R., Dial, H., Martin, R., & Valian, V. (2019). Raising doubt in letters of recommendation for academia: Gender differences and their impact. *Journal of Business and Psychology, 34,* 287–303. https://doi.org/10.1007/s10869-018-9541-1

Makarova, E., Aeschlimann, B., & Herzog, W. (2019). The gender gap in STEM fields: The impact of the gender stereotype of math and science on secondary students' career aspirations. *Frontiers in Education.* https://doi.org/10.3389/feduc.2019.00060

Maliniak, D., Powers, R., & Walter, B. F. (2013). The gender citation gap in international relations. *International Organization, 67*(4), 889–922. https://doi.org/10.1017/S0020818313000209

Miller, D. I., Eagly, A. H., & Linn, M. C. (2015). Women's representation in science predicts national gender-science stereotypes: Evidence from 66 nations. *Journal of Educational Psychology, 107*(3), 631–644. https://doi.org/10.1037/edu0000005

Mishra, S., Fegley, B. D., Diesner, J., & Torvik, V. I. (2018). Self-citation is the hallmark of productive authors, of any gender. *PLOS One, 13*(9), e0195773. https://doi.org/10.1371/journal.pone.0195773

National Science Foundation. (2015a) *Doctorate recipients from U.S. universities: 2014.* National Science Foundation. www.nsf.gov/statistics/2016/nsf16300/digest/nsf16300.pdf

National Science Foundation. (2015b). *Table 14. Doctorate Recipients, by Sex and Broad Field of Study: Selected Years, 1984–2014.* www.nsf.gov/statistics/2016/nsf16300/data-tables.cfm.

Nosek, B. A., Smyth, F. L., Sriram, N., Lindner, N. M., Devos, T., Ayala, A., Bar-Anan, Y., Bergh, R., Cai, H., Gonsalkorale, K., Kesebir, S., Maliszewski, N., Neto, F., Olli, E., Park, J., Schnabel, K., Shiomura, K., Tulbure, B. T., Wiers, R., Somogyi, M., . . . Greenwald, A. G. (2009). National differences in gender-science stereotype predict national sex differences in science and math achievement. *Proceedings of the National Academy of Sciences of the United States of America, 106*(26), 10593–10597. https://doi.org/10.1073/pnas.0809921106

Press, G. (2015, January 2). A very short history of the Internet and the Web [Web log post]. *Forbes.* www.forbes.com/sites/gilpress/2015/01/02/a-very-short-history-of-the-internet-and-the-web-2/?sh=88a49d07a4e2

Richardson, J. C., Maeda, Y., Lv, J., & Caskurlu, S. (2017). Social presence in relation to students' satisfaction and learning in the online environment: A meta-analysis. *Computers in Human Behavior, 71*, 402–417. https://doi.org/10.1016/j.chb.2017.02.001

Rossiter, M. W. (1993). The Matthew Matilda effect in science. *Social Studies of Science, 23*(2), 325–342. https://doi.org/10.1177/030631293023002004

Schein, E. H. (1995). The role of the founder in creating organizational culture. *Family Business Review, 8*(3), 221–238. http://journals.sagepub.com/doi/abs/10.1111/j.1741-6248.1995.00221.x

Schmidt, H., Bainbridge, S., & Wark, N. (2021). Mitigating the Matilda effect on Starr Roxanne Hiltz: A superlative early online learning researcher. *International Women Online Journal of Distance Education (intWOJDE), 20*(2). www.wojde.org/FileUpload/bs295854/File/01_102.pdf

State University. (n.d.). Distance learning in higher education – Related terms and concepts, goals of distance learning, technologies used in distance learning [Web log post]. *Stateuniversity.com.* https://education.stateuniversity.com/pages/1917/Distance-Learning-in-Higher-Education.html

Stenbom, S. (2018). A systematic review of the Community of Inquiry survey. *Internet and Higher Education, 39*(June), 22–32. https://doi.org/10.1016/j.iheduc.2018.06.001.

Storage, D., Charlesworth, T. E. S., Banii, M. R., & Cimpian, A. (2020). Adults and children implicitly associate brilliance with men more than women. *Journal of Experimental Social Psychology, 90.* https://doi.org/10.1016/j.jesp.2020.104020

Appendix A
INTERVIEW VERSION A

Interview on Your Contributions to the Field of Distance Education

Interview Questions

1. What was your educational and experiential background before you became involved in distance education (DE)?
2. In what year did you begin to look specifically into DE?
3. What were the circumstances in your world that initiated this interest in DE?
4. Which female researchers or female colleagues may have piqued your interest in DE?
5. Who would you identify as the early female leaders/founders in the field of DE?
6. What are some of the goals that you strove to achieve in the field of DE?
7. What are some of your accomplishments in the field of DE that you would like to share?
8. What are some of the challenges that you faced in the field of DE over the years?
9. What was the "state of DE" when you first entered the field as opposed to DE in 2018?
10. What interesting memories would you like to share about the beginning of online DE?
11. What were your specific DE research interests, and have they changed/evolved over the years?
12. Could you please describe the learning environment that you currently work in (e.g., geographic and institutional setting, student demographics)?
13. Is there anything else you would like to address?
14. Can you suggest names of other female pioneers in DE or online learning that you think we should include in the book?

Appendix B
INTERVIEW VERSION B

Interview on Your Contributions to the Field of Distance Education (For English-as-a-Second-Language Participants)

Interview Questions

1. In what year did you begin to look into distance education (DE)?
2. What education and experience did you have before you became involved in DE?
3. What events in your life made you interested in DE?
4. Were there any women who may have helped you become interested in DE?
5. Who would you say are the early female leaders/founders in the DE field?
6. What are some of the goals that you worked to achieve in the DE field?
7. What are some of your accomplishments in the field of DE that you would like to share?
8. What were some of the challenges that you found in the field of DE?
9. What was DE like when you first entered the field as compared to DE in 2018?
10. What interesting memories would you like to share about the beginning of online DE?
11. What were your DE research interests, and have they changed over the years?
12. Could you please describe the learning environment in which you currently work?
13. Is there anything else you would like to address?

REFERENCES

Adeoye, M. (2009, April 13). Leadership definitions by scholars [Web log post]. *Adeoyemayowaleadership*. http://adeoyemayowaleadership.blogspot.com/

Anderson, B., & Simpson, M. (2012). History and heritage in distance education. *Journal of Open, Flexible, and Distance Learning, 16*(2). https://files.eric.ed.gov/fulltext/EJ1080085.pdf

Anderson, T., Rourke, L., Garrison, R., & Archer, W. (2019). Assessing teaching presence in a computer conferencing context. *Online Learning, 5*(2), Article 2. (Original publication in 2001) https://doi.org/10.24059/olj.v5i2.1875

Azoulay, P., & Lynn, F. (2020). Self-citation, cumulative advantage, and gender inequality in science. *Sociological Science, 7*, 152–186. https://doi.org/10.15195/v7.a7

Bates, A. W. (2005). *Technology, e-learning and distance education* (2nd ed.). Routledge. www.routledge.com/Technology-e-learning-and-Distance-Education/Bates/p/book/9780415284370

Bates, A. W. (2008, July 7). What do you mean by. . .? [Web log post]. *Tony Bates*. www.tonybates.ca/2008/07/07/what-is-distance-education/

Bates, A. W. (2016, September 18). Who are the founding fathers of distance education? [Web log post]. *Tony Bates*. www.tonybates.ca/2016/09/17/who-are-the-founding-fathers-of-distance-education/

Bentley, J. T., & Adamson, R. (2004). Gender differences in the careers of academic scientists and engineers: A literature review. *National Science Foundation*. www.nsf.gov/statistics/nsf03322/pdf/nsf03322.pdf

Berners-Lee, T. (2021). The history of the world wide web [Web log post]. *World Wide Web Foundation*. https://webfoundation.org/about/vision/history-of-the-web/

Bingham, J., Davis, T., & Moore, C. (1999). Emerging technologies in distance learning. *Horizon: Issues Challenging Education*. http://horizon.unc.edu/projects/issues/papers/Distance_Learning.html

Boyatzis, R. E. (1998). *Transforming qualitative information: Thematic analysis and code development*. Sage Publications.

Campbell, J. L., Quincy, C., Osserman, J., & Pedersen, O. K. (2013). Coding in-depth semi-structured interviews: Problems of unitization and intercoder reliability and agreement. *Sociological Methods & Research, 42*(3), 294–320. https://doi.org/10.1177/0049124113500475

Castellanos-Reyes, D. (2020). 20 years of the community of inquiry framework. *TechTrends, 64*(4), 557–560. https://doi.org/10.1007/s11528-020-00491-7

Chubb, J., & Derrick, G. E. (2020). The impact a-gender: Gendered orientations towards research impact and its evaluation. *Palgrave Communications, 6*. https://doi.org/10.1057/s41599-020-0438-z

Cohen, L., Manion, L., & Morrison, K. (2011). *Research methods in education* (7th ed.). Routledge.

Connick, G. P. (Ed.). (1999). *The distance learner's guide*. Prentice Hall.

Demiray, E. (Ed.). (2012). *International women online journal of distance education (intWOJDE)*. www.wojde.org/

EDEN Secretariat. (2016, September 16). Learn from three founding fathers of distance education interviewed by Steve Wheeler [YouTube video]. *#EDEN16*. www.youtube.com/watch?v=OEZU89Drkj4

Exley, C., & Kessler, J. (2019). The gender gap in self-promotion (No. w26345; p. w26345). *National Bureau of Economic Research*. https://doi.org/10.3386/w26345

Fahy, P. (2001). Addressing some common problems in transcript analysis. *International Review of Research on Open and Distributed Learning (IRRODL), 1*. www.irrodl.org/index.php/irrodl/article/view/321

References

Foss, K. A. (n.d.). Remote learning isn't new: Radio instruction in the 1937 polio epidemic [Web log post]. *The Conversation.* http://theconversation.com/remote-learning-isnt-new-radio-instruction-in-the-1937-polio-epidemic-143797

Fox, C. W., & Paine, C. E. T. (2019). Gender differences in peer review outcomes and manuscript impact at six journals of ecology and evolution. *Ecology and Evolution, 9,* 3599–3916. https://doi.org/10.1002/ece3.4993

Gage, M. E. J. (1870). Woman as inventor. *Women's Suffrage Tracts* (No. 1). New York State Women's Suffrage Association. https://iiif.lib.harvard.edu/manifests/view/drs:2575141$32i

Gage, M. E. J. (1883). Woman as an inventor. *The North American Review, 136*(318), 478–489. www.jstor.org/stable/25118273

Garrison, D. R. (1989). *Understanding distance education: A framework for the future.* Routledge.

Garrison, D. R. (2000). Theoretical challenges for distance education in the 21st century: A shift from structural to transactional issues. *The International Review of Research in Open and Distributed Learning, 1*(1). https://doi.org/10.19173/irrodl.v1i1.2

Garrison, D. R. (2019). Online community of inquiry review: Social, cognitive, and teaching presence issues. *Online Learning, 11*(1). http://dx.doi.org/10.24059/olj.v11i1.1737 (Original publication in 2007).

Garrison, D. R., Anderson, T., & Archer, W. (2000). Critical inquiry in a text-based environment: Computer conferencing in higher education. *Internet and Higher Education, 2,* 87–105. https://doi.org/10.1016/S1096-7516(00)00016-6

Garrison, D. R., Cleveland-Innes, M., Koole, M., & Kappelman, J. (2005). Revisiting methodological issues in transcript analysis: Negotiated coding and reliability. *Internet and Higher Education, 9,* 1–8. www.sciencedirect.com/science/article/abs/pii/S1096751605000771

Gibbs, G. R. (2007). Thematic coding and categorizing. *Analyzing qualitative data.* SAGE Publications.

Gibson, C. (Ed.). (1998). *Distance learners in higher education: Institutional responses for quality outcomes.* Atwood Publishers.

Guillén, L., Mayo, M., & Karelaia, N. (2017). Appearing self-confident and getting credit for it: Why it may be easier for men than women to gain influence at work. *Human Resource Management, 57*(4), 839–854. https://doi.org/10.1002/hrm.21857

Gunawardena, C. N. (1991). Collaborative learning and group dynamics in computer mediated communication networks. In *Research Monograph of the American Center for the Study of Distance Education* (No. 9, pp. 14–24). Pennsylvania State University.

Hiltz, S. R. (1984). *Online communities: A case study of the office of the future.* Ablex.

Hiltz, S. R. (1994). *The virtual classroom: Learning without limits via computer networks.* Ablex.

Hiltz, S. R., & Turoff, M. (1978). *The network nation: Human communication via computer.* Addison-Wesley.

Hiltz,. S. R., & Turoff, M. (1993). *The network nation: Human communication via computer.* MIT Press (Original work published in 1970). https://doi.org/10.7551/mitpress/4920.001.0001

Hodson, R. (1999). *Analyzing documentary accounts.* Sage Publications. https://books.google.ca/books

Hruschka, D. J., Schwartz, D., Cobb St. John, D., Picone-Decaro, E., Jenkins, R. A., & Carey, J. W. (2004). Reliability in coding open-ended data: Lessons learned from HIV behavioral research. *Field Methods, 16,* 307–331. https://pdfs.semanticscholar.org/f62c/0497ffb0096e5200b43b827b9887812f3138.pdf

Jan, S., Vlachopoulos, P., & Parsell, M. (2019). Social network analysis and online learning in communities in higher education: A systematic literature review. *Online Learning, 23*(1), 249–265. https://doi.org/10.24059/olj.v23i1.1398

Keegan, D. (1990). *Foundations of distance education.* Routledge.

Kentnor, H. (2015). Distance education and the evolution of online learning in the United States. *Curriculum and Teaching Dialogue, 17*(1–2). https://digitalcommons.du.edu/cgi/viewcontent.cgi?article=1026&context=law_facpub

King, M. M., Bergstrom, C. T., Correll, S. J., Jacquet, J., & West, J. D. (2017). Men set their own cites high: Gender and self-citation across fields and over time. *Socius, 3,* 2378023117738903. https://doi.org/10.1177/2378023117738903

Krippendorff, K. (2004). *Content Analysis: An introduction to its methodology* (2nd ed.). Sage Publications.

Kurasaki, K. S. (2000). Intercoder reliability from validating conclusions drawn from open-ended interview data. *Field Methods, 12,* 179–194. http://journals.sagepub.com/doi/abs/10.1177/1525822X0001200301

Larreamendy-Joerns, J., & Leinhardt, G. (2006). Going the distance with online education. *Review of Educational Research, 76*(4), 567–605. http://rer.sagepub.com/content/76/4/567

Legacee. (2018). Definitions of leadership. *Legacee.com.* www.legacee.com/potpourri/leadership-definitions/

Lincoln, A. E., Pincus, S., Koster, J. B., & Leboy, P. S. (2012). The Matilda effect in science: Awards and prizes in the US, 1990s and 2000s. *Social Studies of Science, 42*(2), 307–320. https://doi.org/10.1177/0306312711435830

References

Lindeman, M. I. H., Durik, A. M., & Dooley, M. (2019). Women and self-promotion: A test of three theories. *Psychological Reports*, *122*(1), 219–230. https://doi.org/10.1177/0033294118755096

Madera, J. M., Hebl, M. R., Dial, H, Martin, R., & Valian, V. (2019). Raising doubt in letters of recommendation for academia: Gender differences and their impact. *Journal of Business and Psychology*, *34*, 287–303. https://doi.org/10.1007/s10869-018-9541-1

Makarova, E., Aeschlimann, B., & Herzog, W. (2019). The gender gap in STEM fields: The impact of the gender stereotype of math and science on secondary students' career aspirations. *Frontiers in Education*. https://doi.org/10.3389/feduc.2019.00060

Maliniak, D., Powers, R., & Walter, B. F. (2013). The gender citation gap in international relations. *International Organization*, *67*(4), 889–922. https://doi.org/10.1017/S0020818313000209

Marinova, I. (2020, November 19). 20 fascinating online education statistics to know in 2021 [Web log post]. *Review42*. https://review42.com/resources/online-education-statistics/

McLuhan, M., & McLuhan, H. (1988). *Laws of media: The new science*. University of Toronto Press.

Miller, D. I., Eagly, A. H., & Linn, M. C. (2015). Women's representation in science predicts national gender-science stereotypes: Evidence from 66 nations. *Journal of Educational Psychology*, *107*(3), 631–644. https://doi.org/10.1037/edu0000005

Mishra, S., Fegley, B. D., Diesner, J., & Torvik, V. I. (2018). Self-citation is the hallmark of productive authors, of any gender. *PLOS One*, *13*(9), e0195773. https://doi.org/10.1371/journal.pone.0195773

National Science Foundation. (2015a) *Doctorate recipients from U.S. universities: 2014*. National Science Foundation. www.nsf.gov/statistics/2016/nsf16300/digest/nsf16300.pdf

National Science Foundation. (2015b). *Table 14. Doctorate Recipients, by Sex and Broad Field of Study: Selected Years, 1984–2014*. www.nsf.gov/statistics/2016/nsf16300/data-tables.cfm.

Nelson, T. (2003). The persistence of founder influence: Management, ownership, and performance effects at initial public offering. *Strategic Management Journal*, *24*(8), 707–724. https://onlinelibrary.wiley.com/doi/full/10.1002/smj.328

Nosek, B. A., Smyth, F. L., Sriram, N., Lindner, N. M., Devos, T., Ayala, A., Bar-Anan, Y., Bergh, R., Cai, H., Gonsalkorale, K., Kesebir, S., Maliszewski, N., Neto, F., Olli, E., Park, J., Schnabel, K., Shiomura, K., Tulbure, B. T., Wiers, R., Somogyi, M., . . . Greenwald, A. G. (2009). National differences in gender-science stereotype predict national sex differences in science and math achievement. *Proceedings of the National Academy of Sciences of the United States of America*, *106*(26), 10593–10597. https://doi.org/10.1073/pnas.0809921106

Panda, S. (Ed.). (2017–2018). *Journal of Learning for Development (JL4D)*. https://jl4d.org/index.php/ejl4d

Parker, N. (2008). The quality dilemmas of online education revisited. In T. Anderson (Ed.), *The theory and practice of online learning* (2nd ed., pp. 305–341). Athabasca University Press. http://cde.athabascau.ca/online_book/second_edition.htm

Paul, J., & Jefferson, F. (2019). A comparative analysis of student performance in an online vs. face-to-face environmental science course from 2009 to 2016. *Frontiers in Computer Science*, *1*. https://doi.org/10.3389/fcomp.2019.00007

Pink, D. H. (2009). *Drive: The surprising truth about what motivates us*. Cannongate Books. www.danpink.com/books/drive/

Postman, N. (1992). *Technopoly: The surrender of culture to technology*. Knopf.

Press, G. (2015, January 2). A very short history of the Internet and the Web [Web log post]. *Forbes*. www.forbes.com/sites/gilpress/2015/01/02/a-very-short-history-of-the-internet-and-the-web-2/?sh=88a49d07a4e2

Quality Assurance Agency for Higher Education (2020). *Guidance: Building a taxonomy for digital learning*. www.qaa.ac.uk/docs/qaa/guidance/building-a-taxonomy-for-digital-learning.pdf

Renwick, W., et al. (1992). *Distance education at the University of the West Indies. Report of an appraisal carried out on behalf of the Commonwealth of Learning Organisation for Economic Co-operation and Development (OECD)* (Report No. ISBN-1-895369-14-2). Commonwealth of Learning. https://files.eric.ed.gov/fulltext/ED364768.pdf

Richardson, J. C., Maeda, Y., Lv, J., & Caskurlu, S. (2017). Social presence in relation to students' satisfaction and learning in the online environment: A meta-analysis. *Computers in Human Behavior*, *71*, 402–417. https://doi.org/10.1016/j.chb.2017.02.001

Rossiter, M. W. (1993). The Matthew Matilda effect in science. *Social Studies of Science*, *23*(2), 325–342. https://doi.org/10.1177/030631293023002004

Rourke, L., Anderson, T., Garrison, D. R., & Archer, W. (2001). Methodological issues in the content analysis of computer conference transcripts. *International Journal of Artificial Intelligence in Education*, *12*(1), 8–22. www.iaied.org/pub/951/file/951_paper.pdf

Schein, E. H. (1995). The role of the founder in creating organizational culture. *Family Business Review*, *8*(3), 221–238. http://journals.sagepub.com/doi/abs/10.1111/j.1741-6248.1995.00221.x

References

Schmidt, H., Bainbridge, S., & Wark, N. (2021). Mitigating the Matilda effect on Starr Roxanne Hiltz: A superlative early online learning researcher. *International Women Online Journal of Distance Education (intWOJDE)*, *20*(2). www.wojde.org/FileUpload/bs295854/File/01_102.pdf

State University. (n.d.). Distance learning in higher education – Related terms and concepts, goals of distance learning, technologies used in distance learning [Web log post]. *Stateuniversity.com*. https://education.stateuniversity.com/pages/1917/Distance-Learning-in-Higher-Education.html

Stemler, S. (2013). Interrater reliability. In N. Salkind & K. Rasmussen (Eds.), *Encyclopedia of measurement and statistics*. Sage Publications. https://sk.sagepub.com/reference/statistics/n224.xml

Stenbom, S. (2018). A systematic review of the Community of Inquiry survey. *Internet and Higher Education*, *39*(June), 22–32. https://doi.org/10.1016/j.iheduc.2018.06.001.

Storage, D., Charlesworth, T. E. S., Banii, M. R., & Cimpian, A. (2020). Adults and children implicitly associate brilliance with men more than women. *Journal of Experimental Social Psychology*, *90*. https://doi.org/10.1016/j.jesp.2020.104020

Tejeda-Delgado, C., Millan, B., & Slate, J. (2011). Distance and face-to-face learning culture and values: A conceptual analysis. *Administrative Issues Journal*, *1*(2). https://files.eric.ed.gov/fulltext/EJ1055022.pdf

Ward, S. (2018, May 25). Leadership definition [Web log post]. *Small Business*. www.thebalancesmb.com/leadership-definition-2948275

Wark, N. (2018). *Shifting Paradigms: A critical pragmatic evaluation of key factors affecting learner-empowered emergent technology integration* [Doctoral dissertation, Athabasca University]. Athabasca University Digital Archive. http://hdl.handle.net/10791/274

Wedemeyer, C. A. (1971). Independent study. In L. C. Deighton (Ed.), *Encyclopedia of education* (1st ed., pp. 548–557). McMillan.

Zaitz, A. W. (1960). *The history of educational television – 1932–1958* [PhD Thesis, Wisconsin University]. https://eric.ed.gov/?id=ED016919

INDEX

AAOU *see* Asian Association of Open Universities (AAOU) Meritorious Service Award
Aboriginal peoples *see* marginalized groups
academic boycott *see* Apartheid
academic integrity 32; *see also* quality assurance
acceptance/understanding of distance education 13, 77, 80, 129–130, 181, 215, 246, 257, 287, 299, 301, 338, 365, 424; credibility challenges 12–13, 24, 116, 147, 200–201, 202, 277, 298, 299, 301, 327, 337–338; distance education not commonplace 24, 35, 115, 147–148, 215, 288, 327, 339, 365, 422; government expectations 12–13, 24, 67, 106, 107, 299, 338, 339, 353, 427; orthodoxy 12–13, 24, 32, 58, 76, 104, 116, 146–147, 165, 170, 180, 200–201, 202, 212, 257, 277, 288, 298–299, 301, 338, 352, 366; terminology challenges 5–6, 173, 310–311, 393
accessibility 32, 35, 147, 237, 242, 244–245, 332, 326; *see also* distance learning, benefits of
access to education *see* social justice
accomplishments, team 48–49, 58, 91, 146, 175–176, 245, 256–257, 260–261, 277, 287, 297–298, 300; *see also* awards
ACDE *see* African Council for Distance Education
ACED *see* Association Canadienne de l'Enseignement à Distance
ACOA *see* Atlantic Canada Opportunities Agency
ACODE *see* Australasian Council on Open Distance and eLearning
ACORN-NL *see* Atlantic Consortium of Research Networks – Newfoundland and Labrador
adaptability challenges 75–76, 104, 148, 165, 202, 297, 366, 368, 405
Adelaide College of Advanced Education, Australia 294, 297
advisor-consultant *see* consultant
Africa Top 100 eLearning Award *see* awards

African Council for Distance Education (ACDE) ODL Award *see* awards
African Storybook 105; *see also* Global Digital Library; World Reader
Aguti, Jessica 231
AI *see see* technology, emergence of
AIPU *see* Association Internationale de Pédagogie Universitaire
Alfonso, Grace 15
American Association of University of Women 140
American Journal of Distance Education 91, 146
Anaheim University, United States 308, 310, 312, 316
analytics, learner *see* technology, emergence of
Anderson, Terry 379, 445–446
andragogy *see* pedagogy
animoji *see* technology, emergence of
anti-Apartheid *see* Apartheid
applied linguistics 16, 344–345; *see also* research interests of female pioneers
AQUEDUTO *see* Association for Quality Education & Training Online
AR *see* technology, emergence of
Argentine Association of Distance Education 64
Arizona State University, United States 143
ARPAnet *see* technology, emergence of
artificial intelligence (AI) *see* technology, emergence of
ASCILITE *see* Australasian Society for Computers in Learning in Tertiary Education
Asian Association of Open Universities (AAOU) 9, 13, 216
Asian Association of Open Universities (AAOU) Meritorious Service Award *see* awards
Asian Development Bank 128, 138, 146, 151
ASIS&T *see* Association for Information Science and Technology

ASL *see* asynchronous
Association Canadienne de l'Enseignement à Distance (ACED) 274
Association for Information Science and Technology (ASIS&T) 185; *see also* awards
Association for Information Science and Technology (ASIS&T) Research Award *see* awards
Association for Quality Education & Training Online (AQUEDUTO), United Kingdom 313
Association Internationale de Pédagogie Universitaire (AIPU) 274
Association of American Publishers 194
Association of American Publishers TMS Best Technical Publication Award *see* awards
Association of Community Colleges, Canada 363
Association of Graduates in Educational Sciences 64
asynchronous: communication 186, 200, 203, 329, 388, 404, 414; learning networks (ASL) 148, 194, 200, 202, 203, 404, 414, 420; *see also* systems, network; technologies; technologies, emergence of
Athabasca University (AU), Canada i, xvi, xx, 29, 30, 32–36, 55, 66, 360–368, 373, 374, 376, 383–388, 419
Athabasca University Press 96, 112
Atlantic Canada Opportunities Agency (ACOA) 239, 245
Atlantic Consortium of Research Networks – Newfoundland and Labrador (ACORN-NL) 235; *see also* Hermes Satellite; Telemedicine Project
AU *see* Athabasca University
Auckland University of Technology, New Zealand 171
audiographics *see* technologies, emergence of
audio-video technologies *see* technologies, emergence of
augmented reality (AR) *see* technologies, emergence of
Australasian Council on Open Distance and eLearning (ACODE) 253, 261
Australasian Society for Computers in Learning in Tertiary Education (ASCILITE) 112
Australian National University 294, 297
Australian Virtual Worlds Learning Group 115
avatar *see* technology
awards: Africa Top 100 eLearning Award 23; African Council for Distance Education (ACDE) ODL Award 13; Asian Association of Open Universities (AAOU) Meritorious Service Award 9, 13, 226, 229; Association for Information Science and Technology (ASIS&T) Research Award 171, 185; Association of American Publishers TMS Best Technical Publication Award 194–195; Charles Wedemeyer Award 91–92, 138, 142, 408; Commonwealth of Learning (COL) Fellow Award 100, 106, 333; Google Impact South Africa 105; honorary doctorate (honoris causa) 13, 125, 226, 229, 408; honorary fellowship 100, 106, 195, 333; International Council for Open and Distance Education (ICDE) Prize for Individual Excellence 229; Office of the Order of the British Empire Award 352; Ordre d'excellence en Éducation, Ministry of Education, Quebec, Canada 157, 162; University of Maryland University College (UMUC) Teaching Award 267, 408; University of Namibia Merit Sabbatical Award 23; University of Pretoria Chancellor's Medal 100, 106; University of South Africa (UNISA) Council Award 106; White Rose of Finland 49; World Education Congress Global Distance Learning Awards 352

Bachelor's degree, female pioneer's: Agriculture 8, 11, 283; Anthropology 197, 263, 359, 361, 417; Arts 19, 21, 71, 111, 125, 170, 225, 252, 255, 263, 273, 294, 297, 298, 308, 383, 417; Chemistry 234, 237, 417; Education 19, 21, 63, 66, 125, 127, 211, 335; Electronics 54, 57; English 41, 137, 140, 197, 252, 254, 258, 308, 342, 344–345, 388; French 32, 157, 176; History 157, 273, 294, 308; Library and Records Management 19, 21; Mathematics 99; Nutrition 87; Philosophy 321, 324; Political Science 157; Psychology 321, 324, 383, 388; Science 54, 63, 70, 71, 87, 99, 157, 234, 255, 283; Sociology 263, 270; Veterinary Science 70
Baggaley, Jon 218
Bailey, Kathy 316
Ball, Sarah *see* Robbins, Sarah
Bangladesh Open University (BOU), India 216
Barbera, Elena 151
Bar-Ilan University, Israel 263, 266
barriers *see* challenges
Bates, Tony 3, 5, 12, 38, 66, 142, 394, 447
Baym, Nancy 185
Beaulieu, Claudette 277, 279
Bedford, Tas 82
behavioural paradigm *see* pedagogy
Beijing Normal University (BNU), China 55, 57, 418, 427
Belawati, Tian **6**, *8*, *10*, 8–17, 218
benefits of distance learning *see* distance learning, benefits of
Benke, Meg 15
Berners-Lee, Tim 5, 447; *see also* technology, emergence of
best practices for learning *see* research interests of female pioneers
Beukas-Amiss, Catherine Margaret (Maggy) **6**, *18*, *20*, 18–28, 336
Blaschke, Lisa Marie 37
blended learning xvi, 21–22, 58, 118–119, 129, 141, 217, 230–231, 267, 268, 285, 313, 340, 349, 404, 409, 420, 436
blogs *see* technology
Blue Quills First Nations College, Canada 373
BNU *see* Beijing Normal University

Index

Bø, Ingeborg 12, 15, 447
Bogor Agricultural Institute, Indonesia 8
Botswana College of Distance and Open Learning *see* Botswana Open University
Botswana Open University 230
BOU *see* Bangladesh Open University
boycott, academic *see* Apartheid
brain drain 125, 407; *see also* marginalized groups; research interests of female pioneers
brick-and-mortar institution *see* face-to-face
Brindley, Jane **6**, *29*, *31*, 29–39, 244, 326, 374, 389
British Columbia Open University, Canada *see* Open Learning Institute of British Columbia
British Open University *see* Open University UK
BROG Project 175–176, 180; *see also* gender; Herring, Susan; linguistics; research interests of female pioneers
Buenos Aires University, Argentina 63
bulletin board systems *see* technology, emergence of
Burge, Elizabeth (Liz) **6**, 33, 34, *40*, *42*, 40–53, 96, 143, 228, 244, 277, 280, 325–326, 374, 375, 399; *see also* cat analogy
business model 147, 238, 406, 409; *see also* resource challenges
Butterfield, Shawna 335, 336, 340

CADE *see* Canadian Association for Distance Education
Calder, Judith A. 374
Cambrian College 30, 327
Cameron, Margaret 298
Campbell Gibson, Chere *see* Gibson, Chere Campbell
Canadian Association for Distance Education (CADE)//L'association canadienne de l'éducation à distance 30, 34, 46, 95, 244, 274, 278, 280, 322, 325–330, 363–365, 374, 413, 432
Canadian International Development Agency (CIDA) 12, 91, 243, 246, 247, 351, 360, 362, 431
Canadian National Advanced Research and Education Network (CANARIE) 235
CANARIE *see* Canadian National Advanced Research and Education Network
Candlin, Chris 312
Caribbean Child Development Centre 285, 348, 355
Carlos III University of Madrid, Spain 195
Carrington, Lawrence 345, 348
CASBS *see* Center for Advanced Study in the Behavioral Sciences
Casey-Stahmer, Anna *see* Stahmer, Anna
cat analogy 45–46; *see also* Burge, Elizabeth
CD *see* technology, emergence of
CEDIPROE *see* Centro de Diseño, Producción y Evaluación de Recursos Multimediales para el Aprendizaje
Centennial College, Canada 327
Center for Advanced Study in the Behavioral Sciences (CASBS) 171
Centro de Diseño, Producción y Evaluación de Recursos Multimediales para el Aprendizaje (CEDIPROE) 64
CERN *see* European Council for Nuclear Research
Challenge for Change Program *see* National Film Board of Canada Challenge for Change Program
challenges *see* acceptance/understanding of distance education; adaptability; brain-drain, faculty; gender; institution; instructional delivery; language barriers; marginalized groups; research challenges; resource challenges; student challenges; sustainability; technology
change management 18, 23
Charles Wedemeyer Award *see* awards
chat, online *see* technology
chatrooms, online *see* technology
Chen, Li **6**, *54*, *56*, 54–62, 417, 418
China Radio and TV Open University 57, 58, 419, 432
Chinese Society of Educational Development Strategy 55
Chomsky, Noam 177
Christison, MaryAnn 313, 316, 317
Chulalongkorn University Language Institute, Thailand 308
CIDA *see* Canadian International Development Agency
civil war 140
classroom, flipped *see* technology
CMC *see* technology, emergence of
CMDA *see* Computer-Mediated Discourse Analysis
Cochenour, John 143
Coggins, Chere Campbell *see* Gibson, Chere Campbell
CoI *see* Community of Inquiry model
COL *see* Commonwealth of Learning
Coldeway, Dan 95
collaborative distance learning *see* research interests of female pioneers
Collège Militaire de Saint Jean, Canada 160
College of the Marshall Islands 253–259, 418, 428
Collinge, Joan 244
Collis, Betty 213
Columbia University, United States 194, 197
Commonwealth of Learning (COL) 12, 24, 27, 103, 106, 125, 127, 129, 130, 226, 228, 229, 230–231, 255, 335, 336, 340, 347, 348, 352, 363; *see also* conferences
Commonwealth of Learning (COL) Fellow Award *see* awards
communication, asynchronous *see* asynchronous
communication, computer mediated *see* technology, emergence of
communication, robot-mediated *see* research interests of female pioneers
communication, synchronous *see* synchronous
communication technologies *see* technology, emergence of

459

Index

communities, marginalized *see* marginalized groups
communities of practice *see* research interests of female pioneers
Community of Inquiry (CoI) model 444–445; *see also* gender; Matilda effect
community, online *see* online learning
compact disc (CD) *see* technology, emergence of
comparative education *see* research interests of female pioneers
computer conferencing *see* technology, emergence of
computer conferencing content analysis *see* research interests of female pioneers
computer mediated communication (CMC) *see* technology, emergence of
Computer-Mediated Discourse Analysis (CMDA) 174, 180–182, 424; *see also* Herring, Susan; research interests of female pioneers
computer mediated learning *see* research interests of female pioneers
computer networks 249, 304; *see also* asynchronous learning networks; research interests of female pioneers; systems, network; technology, emergence of
computers *see* technology, emergence of
Concordia University, Canada 157, 159, 161, 274, 362
conferences: Annual Conference on Teaching and Learning at a Distance, United States 91; Canadian Association of Distance Education (CADE) 34, 46, 95, 278, 326, 327, 328, 329, 364, 374, 432; Commonwealth of Learning (COL) 24, 130, 336, 339, 347; eLearning Africa (eLA) 24; International Council for Open and Distance Education (ICDE) 30, 32, 34, 36, 44–45, 95, 96, 143, 216, 274, 329, 355, 364, 374, 376, 379, 432–433; Linguistic Society of America Conference 178; Namibia ODL conference 24; Online Educa Berlin 24; Vice Chancellors' Platform for ODeL 24; Women's Studies Centre of Umeå University, Sweden 45; *see also* distance learning benefits; Women's International Network (WIN)
conferencing, video *see* technology, emergence of
connectivism *see* pedagogy
connectivity *see* technology
Conole, Grainne 151
Conseil Québécois pour la Formation à Distance (CQFD) 274
consultant i, xvi, 12, 23, 30, 64, 144, 146, 186, 266, 274, 304, 308, 327, 347, 404, 415, 420, 434, 436, 438
Contact Nord *see* Contact North
Contact North//Contact Nord, Canada 30, 167, 243, 244, 279. 324, 326, 328, 429
continuing education *see* marginalized groups
conventional institutions *see* face-to-face
Coomaraswamy, Uma 12, 127, 133, 228
Cornell University, United States 171, 186
correspondence, distance education i, 3, 4, 14, 32, 36, 76–77, 88, 107, 124, 129, 141–142, 147–148, 162, 196, 199, 201, 229, 238, 241, 247, 266, 267, 298, 302, 308, 310, 312, 314, 325, 327, 337, 361, 373, 394, 432
course design *see* research interests of female pioneers
CQFD *see* Conseil Québécois pour la Formation à Distance
Crawford, Gail 363, 374, 386, 398
critical thinking *see* research interests of female pioneers
cultural groups *see* marginalized groups
cultural stereotypes *see* gender
culture and distance education 47, 51, 138, 143–146, 148, 149, 151, 213, 214, 215, 217, 230, 258, 335, 338, 343, 367, 408
curriculum 68, 106, 107, 138, 140, 242, 297, 339–340, 350, 371
cyber warfare 202

Daniel, Sir John 161, 335
Danish Ministry of Science and Technology, Denmark 264
D'Antoni, Susan 12, 15
data analysis process: coding 397–399, 415, 420–421, 433, 435, 442, 447; coding framework 397–398, 433; coding themes 398–399; inter-coder reliability 397, *397*; intra-coder reliability 397, *397*; thematic concept 395, 398; unit of analysis 398
Deakin University, Australia 296, 297–304
definition of study terms *see* terms, definition of
demographics, student *see* student demographics
Department of Corrections, New Zealand 79–80
design, instructional *see* instructional design
developing world *see* marginalized groups
development, organizational *see* research interests of female pioneers
Dewan Pendidikan Tinggi 9
Dhanarajan, Gajaraj (Raj) 103
didactic teaching and learning 67–68, 80
digital learning *see* research interests of female pioneers
Dillon, Connie 142–143, 151
disc, compact (CD) *see* technology, emergence of
discourse analysis, online *see* online discourse analysis
discrimination *see* gender
discussion forums, online *see* technology
distance education (DE): definition of terms 5–6, 393–394, 396; industrial model 58, 199, 201, 230, 302, 338, 366, 366, 409, 428–429, 437; history of 5, 14, 25, 32, 58, 77–78, 93, 148, 183, 201–202, 216–217, 230, 258, 278, 288, 295, 303, 304, 315, 328, 339, 346, 354, 367, 377–378, 387–388, 419, 447; *see also* correspondence, distance education; face-to-face; online learning; open distance education learning; open distance learning; open, distant, flexible learning; pedagogy, distance education; research interests of female pioneers; technology; technology, emergence of

Index

distance education and culture *see* research interests of female pioneers
distance education correspondence *see* correspondence, distance education; technology
Distance Education Partnership Program of Sri Lanka 128
distance education pedagogy *see* pedagogy
distance education policy *see* government challenges, policy
distance education, industrial model of *see* distance education
distance education, international development of *see* research interests of female pioneers
distance learning *see* distance education
distance learning, benefits of: asynchronous learning 148, 200, 203, 329, 388; cohorts 74–75, 81, 94, 287, 368, 386; collegiality 30, 33, 34, 36, 44–45, 95–96, 142–143, 146, 175, 212–213, 216–217, 267, 288, 328, 329, 336, 339, 347, 354, 355, 364, 374, 376–377, 379, 412, *414*, 425, 431, 432, 438; community development 145, 245, 247, 324, 414; continuing education 32, 48, 141, 147–148, 199, 238, 241–243, 245, 289, 297, 301, 324–325, 346, 414, 436; economic 66, 230–231, 244–245, 259, 260, 277, 299, 302; flexibility 12, 22–23, 116, 201, 230, 241, 266, 267, 276–277, 278, 279, 335, 337, 339, 340; information communication technologies (ICT) 8, 12, 22–23, 25, 57, 58, 67, 116, 140, 141, 142, 145, 160, 163, 198, 199, 200, 201, 241, 245, 246, 249, 257–258, 263, 266, 267, 276, 278, 300, 310, 327, 336–337, 348, 377; innovation xiv, 107, 130, 160, 162, 163, 235, 242, 248–249, 260, 327, 352, 355, 422, 427; openness 59, 116, 129, 181, 200, 203, 218, 228, 229, 230–231, 276–277, 279, 289, 299, 335, 366–367, 338, 339, 340, 349, 355, 365, 385, 388; socializing 114, 119, 199, 241, 267, 278, 310, 315, 376, 377; superior 15, 22–23, 94, 119, 266–267, 279, 301, 335, 337, 339, 426; *see also* challenges; conferences; marginalized groups; quality assurance; social justice; technology, emergence of
DOC *see* Federal Department of Communications
Doctorate of Philosophy (PhD) degree *see* Doctorate/PhD degree
Doctorate/PhD degree, female pioneer's: Anthropology 359–362, 417; Biology 332; Clinical Psychology 29; Computer-integrated Education/Educational Technology 19, 21, 156, 157, 159, 163, 209, 274; Distance Education xvi, 57, 64, 112, 114, 115, 117–118, 120, 140, 144, 294, 298–299, 301, 303, 311, 312, 427; Education 9, 43, 63–64, 88, 125, 127, 131, 138, 142, 287, 308, 311, 316, 317, 343, 345, 370, 378, 383, 388; English 252, 343, 345; Information Science 185, 202, 203; Linguistics 170, 176, 181; Nutrition 283; Philosophy 225, 228; Political Science 263, 265, 266, 417; Religious Studies 70, 73; Sociology 194, 197, 287, 370, 378
Doctorate, Post-*see* Post-Doctorate degree

domination *see* gender
Donner Canadian Foundation 321, 324; *see also* Fogo Island Project; Hermes Satellite; National Film Board of Canada Challenge for Change Program; TeleMedicine Project
dual mode institution *see* institution

– e-Rita 92; *see also* Educating Rita
Eastern Institute of Technology, New Zealand 333, 335
economies of scale *see* resource challenges
EDEN *see* European Distance Education Network
Educating Rita 92, 300; *see also* – e-Rita
educational background, female pioneers 400, *401*, 417, 435 *see also* Bachelor's degree; Doctorate/PhD degree; Master's degree; Post-Doctorate degree
educational leadership *see* research interests of female pioneers
educational paradigm *see* pedagogy
educational policy *see* government challenges, policy
educational radio broadcasts *see* technology, emergence of
educational technology definition of 447
educational television broadcasts *see* technology, emergence of
education, leadership in language *see* research interests of female pioneers
Education Native American Network (ENAN) 148
education, remote *see* rural education
education, rural *see* rural education
education, sociology of *see* research interests of female pioneers
education system, transformation of 81, 103, 105–106, 109, 163–164, 167, 300, 303, 333, 335, 337, 339, 343, 348, 350–351, 353
eLearning 19, 21–26, 73, 146, 157, 213, 214–215, 248, 249, 266–269, 363, 373–374, 375, 378, 447
ELVW *see* Experiential Learning in Virtual Worlds
email *see* technology, emergence of
emergent technology *see* technology, emergence of
emerging technology *see* technology, emerging
emoji *see* technology, emergence of
ENAN *see* Education Native American Network
Erdos, Renée 298
ethic groups *see* marginalized groups
European Council for Nuclear Research (CERN) 447
European Distance Education Network (EDEN) 23, 264, 267
Evans, Jennie 255, 261
Ewha Womans University, South Korea 212, 213, 214, 218
experiential background, female pioneers 400, *401*, 418, 435
Experiential Learning in Virtual Worlds (ELVW) 112

face-to-face 58, 214, 257, 267, 298, 337, 402; environment 22–23, 54, 58, 104; faculty 64, 147,

461

Index

175, 202, 266, 267, 328, 422, 423; institution 73, 76, 104, 108, 335, 337–338, 340, 346, 349, 423, 426; learner xvi, 14, 15, 21, 77–78, 92–94, 147, 202, 241, 267, 286, 294, 298, 314, 333, 335, 337, 361, 366, 367, 368, 412, 422, 423; meetings 200, 278; programmes/courses 67, 77, 127, 150, 198, 214, 268, 276, 278, 285, 289, 340, 367; *see also* business model; pedagogy
faculty: challenges 13, 18, 23, 107, 115–116, 128, 132–133, 215–216, 257–258, 277–278, 301–302, 425–426; *see also* research challenges; resource challenges
Fage, Judith 33, 34
Fainholc, Beatriz **6**, *63*, *65*, 63–69, 417
Faith, Karlene 34, 44, 45, 374, 376, 432
fake news 175, 184, 202; *see also* post-authentic world
Farley, Helen **6**, *70*, *72*, 70–86, 115, 120, 418
Federal Department of Communications (DOC), Canada 237, 325; *see also* Hermes Satellite
female pioneer selection process *see* research methods
female pioneers, geographic distribution 5, **6**, 237, 325, 399–400, *400*, 447–448; *see also* research interests of female pioneers
feminist ideology 24, 45, 67, 373, 375–376, 378
FernUniversität (FeU), Germany 244, 370, 371, 372, 373, 375–376, 377, 378, 379
Ferrara, Kathleen 179, 182
Ferreira, Francis 229, 340
FeU *see* FernUniversität
fiber optic cable *see* technology
First Nation peoples *see* marginalized groups
flame wars 177–178, 184; *see also* Herring, Susan; linguistics; research interests of female pioneers
flexible learning *see* research interests of female pioneers
flipped classroom *see* technology
Fogo Island Project 321, 324; *see also* Donner Canadian Foundation; Hermes Satellite; National Film Board of Canada Challenge for Change Program; TeleMedicine Project
formal education degree, female pioneer's *see* Bachelor's degree; Doctorate/PhD degree; Master's degree; Post-Doctorate degree
formal learning *see* learning, formal
Forster, Ann 34
founder/trailblazer *see* terms, definition of
freedom of speech 184; *see also* flame wars; gender; Herring, Susan; linguistics; research interests of female pioneers
free speech *see* freedom of speech
Fulbright Scholar 138, 149, 176, 195
funding *see* resource challenges
future learning technologies *see* research interests of female pioneers

Gage, Matilda 443; *see also* Matilda effect
Garrison, Donn Randy (Randy) 312, 398, 444–446

Gaskell, Ann 34
Gaspard-Richards, Denise 290
Gauthier, Cindy 231
gender: cultural stereotypes/traditional roles 443; discrimination 76, 421, 425; gender-related comments *416*; male domination 13–14, 24, 34, 44, 47, 57, 66–67, 70, 76, 114, 120, 146–147, 161, 177–179, 183–184, 198, 325, 373–375, 378, 419, 425, 432; myths 170, 180; self-promotion 427–428, 443, 444; unconscious bias 443; *see also* linguistics; literature; marginalized groups; Matilda effect; research interests of female pioneers; third shift, the
geographic distribution of female pioneers *see* female pioneers, geographic distribution
geographic inclusion *see* social justice
geographic isolation *see* marginalized groups
Gesellschaft für Internationale Zusammenarbeit (GIZ) 22, 23
Gibson, Chere Campbell v, **6**, 33, 34, 48, *87*, *89*, 87–98, 142–143, 151
Gibson, Terry 91
GIZ *see* Gesellschaft für Internationale Zusammenarbeit
Glennie, Jennifer (Jenny) **6**, *34*, *99*, 101, 99–110
Global Digital Library 105; *see also* African Storybooks; World Reader
Global Distance Learning Awards *see* awards
GlobalEd 143, 148, 431; *see also* Gunawardena, Charlotte
Google Impact South Africa *see* awards
Gourley, Brenda 12, 15, 228–229, 231
government challenges: funding 351, 364; policy 12, 58, 67, 103–105, 147, 213, 217, 299, 424; *see also* acceptance/understanding; research interests of female pioneers; research challenges; resource challenges
graphic communication, online *see* research interests of female pioneers
graphic icons *see* technology, emergence of
graphicons *see* technology, emergence of
Gregory, Sue **6**, 74, 83, *111*, *113*, 111–123
Gunawardena, Chandra v, **6**, *124*, *126*, 124–136, 151
Gunawardena, Charlotte Nirmalani (Lani) **6**, *137*, *138*, 137–155, 213, 399
Guri-Rosenblit, Sarah 266, 269

Harasim, Linda 143, 199
Harvey, Claudia 355
Haughey, Margaret 33, 34, 48, 167, 244, 277, 280, 326, 364, 368
Hearns, Meryl 115, 120
Henri, France **6**, *156*, *158*, 156–169, 330, 364, 368, 445
Hermes Satellite 235, 237–238, 243, 324–325, 326; *see also* Federal Department of Communications (DOC); Keough, Erin; Roberts, Judy; Telemedicine Project; technology, emergence of

462

Index

higher education, history of *see* research interests of female pioneers
Hiltz, Starr Roxanne **6**, *194*, *195*, 194–208, 444–445; *see also* Network Nation, The; Turoff, Murray
HIT *see* Holon Institute of Technology
Holmberg, Börje 12
holographics *see* technology
Holon Institute of Technology (HIT), Israel 265, 267
honorary doctorate *see* awards
Hood, Nina 215
House, Max 325
human-computer interaction *see* computer-mediated communication
Hurricane Gilbert 247, 431
Huston, Aletha 141–142

IAM *see* interaction analysis model
ICDE *see* International Council for Open and Distance Education
ICT *see* distance learning, benefits of; technology, emergence of
ICU *see* International Christian University
IGNOU *see* Indira Ghandhi National Open University
immersive learning environments *see* technology
incarcerated learners *see* marginalized groups
Indiana University Bloomington, United States 171, 173, 174–175, 179–180, 185, 209, 211, 215
indigenous peoples *see* marginalized groups
Indira Gandhi National Open University (IGNOU), India 12, 226, 228, 230, 347
Indonesia Open University (*aka* Universitas Terbuka; UT) 9, 11
Industrial Age 4.0 *see* technology, emergence of
Industrial Age 5.0 *see* technology, emergence of
industrial model of distance education *see* distance education
informal learning *see* learning, informal
information communication technologies (ICT) *see* distance learning, benefits of; technology, emergence of
information systems: and aging 194; emergency management 194, 202; evaluation of 194; management 186; *see also* Hiltz, Starr Roxanne; research interests of female pioneers
Institute of the Future 203
institution: competition 32, 67, 147, 174, 256, 257, 287, 338, 348; dual mode 247, 298, 348, 365, 368, 404, 409; growing pains 18, 23, 32, 58, 92, 115, 128, 129, 146–147, 148–149, 200–201, 230, 257–258, 301, 365, 367–368, 386, 388–389, 423; *see also* business model; transformation, institutional
institutional transformation *see* transformation, institutional
institution, conventional *see* face-to-face
institution, face-to-face *see* face-to-face

instructional delivery challenges 13, 107, 199, 277–278, 301–302, 327, 368
instructional design *see* research interests of female pioneers
interaction analysis model (IAM) 145, 149, 150; *see also* Gunawardena, Lani
interactive whiteboards *see* technology
International Adult and Continuing Education Hall of Fame 88
International Christian University (ICU), Japan 210, 211, 212
International Council for Open and Distance Education (ICDE; *aka* International Council for Distance Education) 9, 11, 12, 13, 40, 41, 64, 143, 156, 218, 228, 336, 347, 365, 408, 413; *see also* awards; conferences
International Council for Open and Distance Education (ICDE) Prize for Individual Excellence *see* awards
international development of distance education *see* research interests of female pioneers
International Extension College, United Kingdom 103, 359, 363
International Network for Information Systems for Crisis Response Management (ISCRAM) 202
International Research Foundation for Teacher Language Education, The (TIRF) 313
International Women Online Journal of Distance Education (intWOJDE) 4, 419
Internet *see* technology, emergence of
Internet of Things (IoT) *see* technology, emergence of
Inter-University Center for e-Learning (IUCEL), Israel 264
intWOJDE *see* International Women Online Journal of Distance Education
IOT *see* technology, emergence of
ISCRAM *see* International Network for Information Systems for Crisis Response Management
IUCEL *see* Inter-University Center for e-Learning

Jacka, Lisa 120
Jacquinot, Geneviève 277
Jagannathan, Neela 228, 229
Jayatilleke, Gayathri 144, 151
Jelly, Doris 243, 325
JL4D *see* Journal of Learning for Development
Johannsen, Bob 203
Johns Hopkins 243
Johnson & Johnson *see* Robert Wood Johnson Foundation
Johnston, Sally 143
Journal of Learning for Development (JL4D) 3–4, 419
Judy Roberts & Associates/Associés 324, 327; *see also* Roberts, Judy
Jung, Insung **6**, 12, 15, 144, 145–146, *209*, *210*, 209–224, 417

463

Kafafian, Haig 200
Kanwar, Asha 6, 12, 15, *225, 227*, 225–233, 255, 336, 347
Karunanayaka, Shironica 133, 151
Kaur, Abtar 231
Kaushik, Madhulika 231
Kay, Jo 115
Kelaniya University, Sri Lanka 140
Keller, Suzanne 198, 202
Keough, Erin 6, 33, 234, 236, 234–252, 277, 280, 325, 326
Kettle, Arnold 228
Kiesler, Sara 179, 182, 185
Kirkpatrick, Denise 347
Kirkup, Gill 374–375, 377, 378
Klein, Caroll 363
KNOU *see* Korea National Open University
Korea National Open University (KNOU) 211–212, 213, 216, 218, 430
Koroivulaono, Theresa 6, *252, 253*, 252–262, 418
Kotalawala, Elsie 127
Koul, Badri 230
Kramarae, Cheris 375
Kreitlow, Burton 92
KU *see* University of Kansas
Kurtz, Gila 6, 219, *263, 264*, 263–272

Lakehead University, Canada 327
Lamy, Marie-Noelle 151
Lamy, Thérèse 6, 161, 244, *273, 275*, 273–281, 330, 364, 368
language: barriers 13, 44, 55, 64, 105, 125, 127–128, 132, 145–146, 149, 157, 210, 260, 265, 313, 367, 373, 375, 376, 395, 414, 417, 425, 433, 435, 438, 442; computer 201, 308; *see also* linguistics; research interests of female pioneers
language leadership in education *see* research interests of female pioneers
L'association canadienne de l'éducation à distance *see* Canadian Association for Distance Education
Latchem, Colin 215, 229
La Trobe University *see* Trobe University
La Trobe University, Australia 125, 127, 171
Laurentian University, Canada xvi, 243, 327
Laurillard, Diana 161–162
leader *see* terms, definition of
leadership in language education *see* research interests of female pioneers
learner analytics *see* technology, emergence of
learner attrition *see* student challenges
learner-centredness *see* learner-focused
learner-centric *see* learner-focused
learner competency *see* student competency
learner engagement *see* research interests of female pioneers
learner-focused 105, 160, 276, 277–278, 335, 336, 343, 408, 411, 414, 418, 425–426, 433, 438; *see also* instructional design; personalized learning; research interests of female pioneers

learner motivation 163, 164, 212, 215–216, 217, 314, 337, 386–387, 425 *see also* research interests of female pioneers
learner preferences *see* learner-focused
learners, incarcerated *see* marginalized learners
learners, marginalized *see* marginalized learners
learner support: online 30, 34–36, 37, 38, 90–93, 105, 106, 107, 109, 142, 147, 160, 165, 166, 216, 217, 230, 244, 278; 295, 299, 301–302; 350, 361, 362, 364, 365–367, 386–389, 403, 404–411, 414, 415, 423, 442; *see also* distance learning, benefits of; research interests of female pioneers; student challenges
learning: formal 66, 81–82, 103, 131, 173, 229, 302, 417–418, 419, 426; informal 173, 229, 238; non-formal 103, 173, 213, 215, 229, 238; self-directed 35, 36, 212; transformative 81, 105, 163, 167, 303, 333, 335, 337, 339, 343, 351; *see also* distance learning, benefits of
learning, digital *see* research interests of female pioneers
learning environments, immersive *see* technology
learning environments, online *see* online learning
learning environments, virtual world *see* technology, emergence of
learning management system (LMS) *see* technology
learning, personalized *see* personalized learning
learning resources *see* research interests of female pioneers
learning technologies, future *see* research interests of female pioneers
Lentell, Helen 33, 34, 255, 261, 375
Library Association of Australia 41, 43
life experience students *see* marginalized groups
lifelong learning 34, 48, 58, 162, 165, 166, 214, 218, 231, 326, 333, 354–355, 385, 404, 414, 420, 421, 430, 446; *see also* research interests of female pioneers
LifeLong Learning Associates 296, 303; *see also* Moran, Louise
linguistics xvi, 160, 170, 174, 176–181, 182, 184, 185, 307, 311, 343, 345, 354; *see also* flame wars; research interests of female pioneers
linguistics, applied *see* research interests of female pioneers
Linguistic Society of America 177, 178; *see also* conferences; Herring, Susan; linguistics
listservs *see* technology
literacy, digital 21–22, 311; *see also* African Storybook; research interests of female pioneers
literature: female pioneers, lack of 3–4, 12, 44–45, 70, 76, 347, 419–420, 425, 428, 431–432, 436, 438, 442, 443–446; male pioneers 3, 4, 12, 142, 419–420, 428, 432, 436, 443–446

MacDonald, Jeanette 91–92; *see also* awards; Gibson, Chere Campbell
MacKenzie, Francine 276
Mackintosh, Naomi 374

Index

Macquarie University, Australia 70, 73, 308, 310, 312
Majelis Pendidikan 9
Malaison, Sylvie 277, 279
male domination *see* gender
Manning, Liz 375
Manukau Institute of Technology, New Zealand 115, 120
Manukau Polytech *see* Manukau Institute of Technology
Māori *see* marginalized groups
marginalized groups 66, 67, 132, 141, 277, 279, 339, 373; communities 231, 242-243, 421; continuing education 90, 349; cultural 339, 421; developing world 12, 230-231, 245, 289, 301; ethnic 67, 82, 102, 345; geographically isolated 242-243, 277, 279, 421; life experience students 349; older adults 12, 231, 241, 289, 310, 349, 421; parents 90, 289, 310, 314, 421; poor 66, 277, 279; prisoners 71, 76, 79-83, 421, 426; racial 102, 426-427; refugee 149, 421; special needs 67, 90, 200, 277, 279; working adults 67, 90, 231, 267, 276-277, 289, 310, 314, 421; *see also* brain drain; distance learning, benefits of; gender; research interests of female pioneers; rural education
Mason, Robin 33. 143. 212. 213. 447; *see also* Open University UK
Massachusetts Institute of Technology (MIT), United States 447
Massey University, New Zealand 332-333
massive open online course (MOOC) 9, 23, 55, 68, 133, 149, 150, 164, 166, 209. 210, 214, 215, 217, 218, 231, 268-269, 366, 367, 404-405, 408, 409, 411, 425; *see also* research interests of female pioneers
Master's degree, female pioneer's: Adult Education 88; Anthropology 359, 361; Arts 225, 252; Counselling Psychology 29, 383; Criminology 321, 324; Distance Education xvi, 9; Education 9, 41, 99, 125, 127, 138-139, 140, 294, 342-343, 345; Educational Technology 55, 111, 114, 209, 211; Electronic Information Management 19, 21; English 254; History 157, 159, 273; Linguistics 170, 176, 308; Philosophy 225; Political Science 234, 237, 263, 265, 370, 373; Religious Studies 70; Social Sciences 370, 373; Sociology 63, 66, 194, 197
Matilda effect 435, 437, 443-446; *see also* Gage, Matilda; literature
Mayadas, Frank 202
McGill University, Canada 87, 90, 157, 159
McIsaac, Marina 143, 151
McLaughlin, Katherine 144
McLaughlin, Margaret (Peggy) 180-181, 185
McLuhan and McLuhan 47, 51
McLuhan, Marshall 47
McNamara, Craig 325
Mead Richardson, Alison 340
Meeks Gardner, Julia (Julie) **6**, *282*, *284*, 282-293, 355, 418

Memorial University of Newfoundland, Canada 234, 235, 237-238, 241-243, 245, 247, 248-250, 324, 325, 327, 328, 362, 429
meta-cognition, socially-mediated *see* research interests of female pioneers
midnight hour degree 117, 366; *see also* gender; marginalized groups; third shift, the
Mid Sweden University (Mittuniversitetet), Sweden xx, 41, 303
Mills, Roger 38, 374, 379, 432
MIT *see* Massachusetts Institute of Technology
Mitchell, Betty 244
Mitra, Sushmita 231
Mittuniversitetet *see* Mid Sweden University
mLearning *see* technology, emergence of
mobile devices *see* technology, emergence of
mobile learning *see* technology, emergence of
mobile technologies *see* technology, emergence of
MOOC *see* massive open online course
Moore, Michael 90, 102; *see also* Theory of Transactional Distance
MOOs *see* technology
Moran, Louise **6**, 34, 96, 243, 244, *294*, *296*, 294-306; *see also* LifeLong Learning Associates
Morpeth, Ros 33, 34, 103, 364, 368, 375; *see also* National Extension College, UK
Mosaic *see* technology, emergence of
MUDs *see* technology
MUDs, Object Oriented (MOOs) *see* technology
Mugridge, Ian 299, 303
MulSeMedia *see* technology
multimedia *see* technology
multimodal computer mediated communication *see* technology, emergence of
Multiple Sensorial Media (MulSeMedia) *see* technology
Multi-User Dimensions (MUDs) *see* technology
Murphy, Karen 143
Murray, Denise **6**, 185, *307*, *309*, 307-320
myths, gender *see* gender

NADEOSA *see* National Association of Distance Education
Namibian Open Learning Network Trust (NOLNet) 22
Namibian University of Science and Technology (NUST) 22
NAO, the robot 268; *see also* research interests of female pioneers; technology, emergence of
NASA *see* National Aeronautics and Space Administration
National Aeronautics and Space Administration (NASA), United States 325; *see also* Hermes Satellite
National American Research Centre for Health 138
National Association of Distance Education (NADEOSA), South Africa 104, 106, 109, 427
National Extension College, UK 33, 103, 107, 363-364, 368, 375; *see also* Morpeth, Ros

Index

National Film Board of Canada 159
National Film Board of Canada Challenge for Change Program 321, 324
National Lab for Smart Online Learning, China 55
National Science Foundation (NSF), United States 132, 185–186, 198, 443
National University La Plata, Argentina 63–64
National Women's Aid Foundation, Germany 371
Nelson, Christine 374
Nelson Marlborough Institute of Technology, New Zealand 333, 335
Network Nation, The 194–195, 197–198, 199, 200, 444–446; *see also* Hiltz, Starr Roxanne
networks *see* systems, network
networks, asynchronous learning *see* asynchronous networks, computer *see* computer networks
New Jersey Institute of Technology (NJIT), United States 195, 196, 198, 199, 201–202, 203
New South Wales (NSW) College of External Studies, Australia 298
Ngengebule, Thandi 109
Nielson, Virginia 389
NJIT *see* New Jersey Institute of Technology
NOLNet *see* Namibian Open Learning Network Trust
Nonyongo, Evelyn (Evie) 109
Norquay, Margaret 326
Northeastern Ontario Regional Cancer Centre, Canada 30
NSF *see* National Science Foundation
NSW *see* New South Wales College of External Studies
Nunan, David 312
NUST *see* Namibian University of Science and Technology

Obama, Barak 184
OBE *see* awards
ODeL *see* open and distance education learning
ODFL *see* open, distant, and flexible learning
ODL *see* open and distance learning
OEC *see* Open Education Consortium
OER *see* open educational resources
Office of the Order of the British Empire Award *see* awards
OffLine StudyDesk 71; *see also* Farley, Helen; University of Southern Queensland
OISE *see* Ontario Institute for Studies in Education
Oldenburg University, Germany i, xvi, 30, 36, 37, 38, 215, 329, 379
older students *see* marginalized groups
Olgren, Chris 96
OLI *see* Open Learning Institute of British Columbia
OLIN *see* Open Learning and Innovation Network
online chat *see* technology
online chatrooms *see* technology
online communication, patterns in *see* gender
online community *see* online learning
online discourse analysis i, 171, 174, 177–178, 180–181; *see also* gender; Herring, Susan; linguistics; research interests of female pioneers
online discussion forums *see* technology
online graphic communication *see* research interests of female pioneers
online learner support *see* learner support
Online Learning Consortium, United States 195, 314
online learning pattern of emergence 5, 447
Ontario Institute for Studies in Education (OISE) 41, 43, 46–48, 50, 244, 326; *see also* University of Toronto
open and distance education learning (ODeL) 22, 24, 25, 26, 27; *see also* distance education; online learning; open distance learning; open, distant, flexible learning; research interests of female pioneers
open and distance learning (ODL) 11–14, 21, 34–37, 70, 73–79, 81, 211–219, 226, 229–231, 326–33, 343, 346–355; *see also* awards; conferences; distance education; online learning; open distance education learning; open, distant, flexible learning; research interests of female pioneers
Open and Distance Learning Association of Australia 295, 304
open and distributed learning (ODL) *see* open and distance learning
Open College of Hong Kong, China 299
open, distant, and flexible learning (ODFL) 333, 336–340, 423, 431; *see also* distance education; online learning; open distance education learning; open distance learning; research interests of female pioneers
open educational resources (OER) 9, 12, 78, 100, 104, 105, 109, 129, 130, 133, 151, 209, 210, 214, 215–216, 217–218, 223, 226, 230, 258–259, 404–405, 409, 410, 425; OER Africa 104; *see also* research interests of female pioneers
Open Education Consortium (OEC) 9
open learning 105, 260–261; *see also* distance education
Open Learning Agency, Canada 66, 244, 299; *see also* Open Learning Institute of British Columbia; Thompson Rivers University
Open Learning and Information Network, Canada 237
Open Learning and Innovation Network (OLIN) 240, 242, 246, 248–249
Open Learning Institute (OLI) of British Columbia, Canada 299, 304; *see also* Open Learning Agency; Thompson Rivers University
Open Polytechnic of New Zealand 36, 229, 333, 335–337, 338, 339–340
Open University of Catalonia *see* Open University of Catalunya
Open University of Catalunya (OUC), Spain 68, 151

Index

Open University of Indonesia 11
Open University of Malaysia 218
Open University of Mauritius 229
Open University of Sri Lanka (OUSL) 125, 126, 127–128, 129–130, 131, 132, 144, 226, 229
Open University of the UK *see* Open University UK
Open University UK (OU UK) 90, 92, 96, 102, 143–144, 151, 226, 228–229, 243, 276, 297, 432
Order of the British Empire (OBE) *see* awards
Ordre d'excellence en Éducation, Ministry of Education, Quebec, Canada *see* awards
organizational development *see* research interests of female pioneers
O'Rourke, Jennifer 33, 34, 326
OUC *see* Open University of Catalunya
OUSL *see* Open University of Sri Lanka
OU UK *see* Open University UK

Pacey, Lucille 244, 277, 322, 326
Panjab University, India 225
Paquette-Frenette, Denise 277, 279
paradigm 166, 174, 177, 180, 181–182, 214, 274, 302, 424; *see also* pedagogy
parents *see* marginalized groups
Paul, Ross 364, 376
PBS *see* Public Broadcasting Station
pedagogy 5, 45, 58, 76, 107, 163, 164, 268, 406, 409, 411, 425–426; andragogy 41, 48, 348; connectivism 55, 57; distance education/online learning xvi, 9, 49, 55, 58, 59, 64, 107, 125, 160, 161–162, 164, 166, 199, 214, 231, 266, 274, 277–278, 322, 326, 343, 348, 349, 361, 447; feminist pedagogy 45, 374; *see also* research interests of female pioneers
Penn State University, United States 41, 215, 379, 433
Perry, Debra 213
personalized learning 164; *see also* instructional design; learner-focused; research interests of female pioneers
personal learning environment (PLE) *see* research interests of female pioneers
Peters, Otto 12, 38
PhD degree, female pioneer's *see* Doctorate/PhD degree
pioneer *see* terms, definition of
PLE *see* research interests of female pioneers
policy, educational *see* government challenges
poor people *see* marginalized groups
Porto, Stella 266, 269
postal mail *see* technology
post-authentic world 184; *see also* fake news
Post-Doctorate degree, female pioneer's: Distance Education 142; Virtual Pedagogy 64, 68
Postman, Neil 45, 47–48, 50, 51
Pravda, Gisela 33, 34, 44–45, 228, 375, 379
Preece, Jenny 200
Princess Anne, UK 247

Princeton University, United States 198
print-based *see* technology
prisoners *see* marginalized groups
Public Broadcasting Station (PBS), United States 141, 198, 199

Qayyum, Adnan 215
qualification certification system 58
qualitative study *see* research methods
quality assurance: challenges 58, 77, 104, 147, 212, 257, 301, 302, 314, 337; online learning 4, 88, 104, 105, 125, 130, 210, 213–217, 218, 226, 229–230, 286, 295, 302, 313, 408, 409, 410, 430, 437–438; *see also* distance learning, benefits of; research interests of female pioneers; US accredited institution
Queensland University, Australia 71, 73, 76, 79, 82, 308
Quest Atlantis Project 185–186

race *see* marginalized groups
racial groups *see* marginalized groups
Rafaeli, Sheizaf 181
Redding, Chris 115
refugee groups *see* marginalized groups
remote education *see* rural education
remote learners *see* rural education
research challenges 181–182; faculty 127–128, 132–133, 215, 216, 218, 313–314; funding 202; *see also* government challenges; resource challenges
research contributions *see* gender
researcher/writer *see* terms, definition of
research interests of female pioneers 409–410, *410*; computer-mediated communication (CMC) 173–175, 177–186, 197, 261; distance education, not related to 286; educational theory 55–57, 58, 145, 149, 150, 166, 214, 217; faculty support 58, 93; human-technology interaction 50, 183, 268; institutional development 25, 130, 174, 186, 354–355; instructional design 36–37, 58, 149, 214, 217, 256, 258; learner autonomy 36, 166; learner success 14, 33, 118, 259; learner support 14, 36, 58, 91, 93, 217, 256, 259; learning environments 148–149, 166, 279, 303–304; massive open online courses (MOOCs) 149, 214, 217; open educational resources (OER) 78, 214, 217, 259; pedagogy and technology 14, 36–37, 58, 166, 214, 259, 279; policy and governance 25, 58, 217, 303; quality assurance 25, 130–131; 217, 230, 302, 378; robotics 181, 182, 183, 186, 265, 268; social issues 79, 130, 148–149, 173, 177–179, 180–181, 183–184, 186, 202, 214, 217, 230, 258, 304, 314–315, 367, 378; social media 25, 36–37, 175–176, 180; systems 166, 202, 217; technology, haptic feedback 78–79; technology, low 79; virtual worlds 78, 117–118, 185–186; *see also* distance education, history of; gender; social

467

Index

network analysis; systems, network; technology; technology, emergence of
research methodology 5, 7, 393, 395–398, 418; *see also* research recruitment criteria
research methods: female pioneer selection process 4, 393, **396**, 396–397, 418; qualitative study 3, 6, 7, 391, 395; snowball technique 5, 396, 419, 433, 438, 447, 448; study limitations 438–439, 447–448; thematic analysis process 6, 395; *see also* data analysis process; research interests of female pioneers
research recruitment criteria 4, 5, 394, **396**, 396–397, 442; founding date 5, **396**, 396; guiding terms 5, 394, **396**, 396; snowballing strategy 5, 396, 419, 433, 438, 447, 448; two-stage approach 5, 396; *see also* research methodology; research methods
resource challenges: funding 34, 107, 116, 119, 129–130, 147, 198, 201–203, 246, 256, 259, 287, 299, 310, 314, 327, 337–338, 339, 353, 364–366, 387, 389, 424; human resources 35, 107, 116, 256, 257–258, 277–278, 353, 426; relevant learning resources 107, 259, 337, 347; *see also* government challenges; research challenges
resources, learning *see* research interests of female pioneers
Rezabek, Landra 143
RGU *see* Robert Gordon University
Rilke, Rainer 47
RMIT *see* Royal Melbourne Institute of Technology
Robbins, Sarah 115
Robert Gordon University (RGU), Scotland 19, 21
Roberts, Judy **6**, 33, 34, 46, 48, 96, 167, 243, 277, 279–280, *321*, *323*, 321–331
Roberts, Vivienne 355
Robert Wood Johnson Foundation 93–94
robotics, telepresent *see* research interests of female pioneers
robot-mediated communication *see* research interests of female pioneers
Rodrigues, Reinhild 373
Rogers, Kay 244, 325–326
Rossié, Ute 375, 379
rote learning *see* pedagogy
Royal Melbourne Institute of Technology (RMIT) 74, 83, 114, 120, 336
Royal Military College of Canada 160
rural education 55. 57, 64–67, 115, 132, 144, 146, 150, 235, 237, 238–239, 241–242, 246, 248, 255, 257, 259, 266–267, 310, 312, 314, 321, 324–325, 329, 348, 424, 429; *see also* marginalized groups
Ryan, Yoni 33
Ryerson Institute of Technology, Canada 273–274, 276, 326

Saba, Farhad (Fred) 142–143
SACHED *see* South African Committee for Higher Education
Saide *see* South African Institute for Distance Education
Salmon, Gilly 33, 266
San Diego State University, United States 92, 142–143
San José State University, United States 308
satellite technology *see* technology, emergence of
Schultz, Ulrike 375
Second Life *see* technology, emergence of
Seelig, Caroline **6**, 228–229, 231, *332*, *334*, 332–341, 347
self promotion *see* gender
Seoul National University (SNU), Korea 209, 211
Sewart, David 374. 376. 432
SFU *see* Simon Fraser University
Sharpe, Sydney 386, 398
Simmons-McDonald, Hazel **6**, 286, *342*, *344*, 342–358
Simon Fraser University (SFU), Canada xvi, 8–9, 14, 244
Sir Arthur Lewis Community College, West Indies 342, 345
Sloan Consortium (Sloan-C) *see* Online Learning Consortium
slow-scan TV *see* technology, emergence of
smartphone *see* technology, emergence of
Smith College, United States 370, 372–373, 417
snail mail *see* technology
snowball technique *see* research methods
SNU *see* Seoul National University
social justice xiv, 32, 36, 99, 107, 383, 385, 401–402, 403, 414, 415, 418, 433, 436, 442, 446, 448; access to education 12, 21–22, 58, 67, 129, 132, 140, 141, 150, 160, 198, 199, 201, 228, 229, 237, 241–244, 245, 249, 277, 279, 301, 310, 339, 345, 346, 349–349, 373, 375, 426; human rights 76, 277, 426, 443; *see also* distance learning, benefits of; gender equity; marginalized groups; research interests of female pioneers
socially-mediated meta-cognition *see* research interests of female pioneers
social network analysis 58, 144–145, 149, 150; *see also* systems, network; technology; technology, emergence of; technology, emerging
social presence theory *see* research interests of female pioneers
Social Sciences and Humanities Research Council (SSHRC), Canada 48, 164
social technologies *see* research interests of female pioneers
Society of International Chinese in Educational Technology 55
sociology of education *see* research interests of female pioneers
South African Committee for Higher Education (SACHED), South Africa 100, 102–103, 105–108, 109, 426–427

Index

South African Institute for Distance Education (Saide) 100, 101, 103–106, 108
Southern Cross University, Australia 120
Spronk, Barbara **6**, 33, 34, *359*, *360*, 359–369, 374, 386
Sri Lanka Open University 12, 144
SSHRC *see* Social Sciences and Humanities Research Council
Stahmer, Anna (*aka* Casey-Stahmer, Anna) 243, 325
Stanford University, United States 308, 311, 316–317, 342–343, 345, 447
State University of New York, United States 170
Steele, Caroline 73, 90
stereotypes *see* gender
student attrition *see* student challenges
student-centered *see* learner-focused
student challenges: student attrition 314, 386, 388–389; *see also* learner support; marginalized groups; student competency
student competency 67, 131, 132, 162, 164, 165
student demographics 14–15, 26, 37, 79, 93–94, 118, 131, 149–150, 203, 217–218, 230–231, 268, 289, 316, 329, 339, 367–368, 404, 405, 420–422, 436, 442; *see also* marginalized groups
student engagement *see* research interests of female pioneers
student-focused *see* learner-focused
student, special needs *see* marginalized groups
student success 30, 31, 34–37, 75, 87, 90, 91, 95, 103–106, 109, 160, 161, 216, 300, 328, 337, 386–387, 388, 405, 407, 409, 410; *see also* research interests of female pioneers
student support *see* learner support
study limitations *see* research methods
Sukhothai Thammathirat Open University, Thailand 96
sustainability 34, 100, 256, 260, 276–277, 407, 408; challenges 115–116, 256, 257, 338, 366, 405, 408, 423
Sustainable Development Goals 225, 229; *see also* sustainability; United Nations Educational, Scientific Cultural Organization (UNESCO)
Swan, Karen 199
Swansea University, United Kingdom 332
Swift, Betty 374
synchronous communication 74–75, 145–146, 148, 157, 186, 329, 404, 405, 420; *see also* technologies; technologies, emerging
Syracuse University, United States 264, 267
systematic theory 55, 57; *see also* Chen, Li; connectivism; research interests of female pioneers
systems, bulletin board *see* technology, emergence of
systems, network 67, 127–128, 148, 159, 163–164, 175, 182, 185, 194, 201–203, 230, 235, 237–249, 298, 301, 303, 325–328, 339–340, 363, 374–375, 376, 379, 406–409, 412, 414, 423, 424, 428–429, 431, 437, 438, 444; *see also* social network

analysis; technology; technology, emergence of; technology, emerging

Tai Poutini Polytechnic, New Zealand 333, 335
Tait, Alan 374, 376, 378, 379, 432
Takayama, Leila 181
Tannen, Deborah 177
Taplin, Margaret 229
teaching effectiveness *see* quality assurance
technology: avatar 75, 77, 117–118, 183; blogs 3, 114, 117, 175–176, 180, 181–182, 186, 394, 419, 424; challenges 13, 21–22, 24, 76, 80, 92, 107, 144, 147, 182, 183, 246, 267, 278, 311, 312–313, 315, 327, 338, 424, 426, 429; chat, online 176, 179, 181–183, 199, 203, 307, 311–313, 316, 350, 424; chatrooms, online 182–183, 350, 424; discussion forums, online 74, 130, 161, 181–182, 261, 288, 424; fiber optic cable 108, 183, 256, 259; flipped classroom 23, 58, 268; holographics 119; immersive learning environments 3; interactive whiteboards 118–119; learning management system (LMS) i, 23, 71, 73, 75–77, 81, 117, 118, 242, 257, 261, 333, 335, 336, 340, 343; listservs 92, 93, 143, 148, 175, 177, 312, 431; Object Oriented MUDs (MOOs) 182, 183, 424; multimedia xvi, 5, 64, 79, 108, 230, 249, 257, 310, 311, 312, 314, 380, 428; Multiple Sensorial Media (MulSeMedia) 78–79; Multi-User Dimensions (MUDs) 181–182, 183, 424; postal mail (*aka* snail mail) 4, 25, 196, 361, 394; print-based 3, 4, 14, 23–25, 90, 91, 95, 108, 125, 276, 278, 322, 327, 329, 394; technology sub-themes *416*; telephone 36, 44, 66, 92–93, 147, 163, 239, 245–247, 267, 329, 362, 366, 377, 395, 396, 424, 431; tele-writer 239, 348; webinars 24, 117, 388; wikis 114, 117; *see also* BROG Project; correspondence, distance education; research interests of female pioneers; technology, emergence of
technology, emergence of: Animoji 183–184; ARPAnet 92, 201, 447; artificial intelligence (AI) 27, 116, 119, 265, 268, 316–317; audiographics 146–147; audio-video technologies 148, 159, 240, 278, 329, 394; augmented reality (AR) 119; bulletin board systems 148; compact disc (CD) 310, 312, 394; computer conferencing 43, 50, 156, 161, 163, 165, 185, 408, 444–445; computer mediated communication (CMC) 143, 145, 163, 170, 171–174, 176, 179–181, 197–203, 301, 303, 307, 311; computer networks 163, 185, 201–203, 235, 237–249, 278, 301, 303, 327–329, 339–340, 408, 412, 423, 424, 428–429, 431, 437; computers 97–98, 183, 201, 278, 315, 377; conversational AI 182; DVD 394; educational radio broadcasts 4, 92–93, 216, 217, 288–289, 322, 326, 366, 394; educational television broadcasts 14, 92, 147–148, 366; email 108, 303; emoji 174–175, 182, 183; graphicon

469

183; Industrial Age 4.0 15; Industrial Age 5.0 15; Industrial Revolution 24; information communication technology (ICT) 14, 58, 67, 68, 433; Internet 5, 14, 58, 74, 77, 93, 100–101, 119, 127, 171, 176, 180, 183, 184, 195, 246, 258, 266, 278, 288, 303, 315, 378, 424, 447; Internet of Things (IoT) 268; learner analytics 143, 145, 336; mobile learning (mLearning) 13, 71, 114; mobile technologies 148, 217; Mosaic 367; robot-mediated communication 174, 181, 182; satellite 55, 57, 144, 235, 237–238, 243, 245, 256–257, 259, 266, 322, 324–326, 328; Second Life 71, 75, 77–78, 115, 118; smartphone 108, 288, 315; social robots for learning 268; teleconferencing 163, 229, 241, 347–350, 394; telepresence robots 174, 181, 183, 186; video-conferencing 14, 182–183, 239, 242, 259, 261, 267, 278, 327–328, 350–351, 353, 355, 377; virtual classroom 195, 197, 198, 199, 201, 203; virtual reality (VR) 27, 116, 119, 216; virtual worlds 71, 74, 75, 78, 112–113, 114–120, 185–186, 409; World Wide Web 5, 182, 195, 200, 367, 424, 447; *see also* Berners-Lee, Tim; distance education, history of; distance learning, benefits of; Hermes Satellite; Postman, Neil; research interests of female pioneers; systems, network; technology; technology, emerging

technology, emerging: definition of 5–6; integration of 5, 163, 212, 408, 427, 430–431, 436–437, 438, 447; *see also* systems, network; technology; technology, emergence of

technology infrastructure *see* technology

Tel-Aviv University, Israel 263

teleconference *see* technology

Telemedicine and Educational Technology Resource Agency (TETRA) 235, 239, 240, 242, 248, 249; *see also* TeleMedicine Project

TeleMedicine Project 235, 322, 324–325; *see also* Donner Canadian Foundation; Fogo Island Project; Hermes Satellite; Telemedicine Educational Technology Resource Agency

telephone *see* technology

telepresent robots *see* technology, emergence of

Télé-université (TÉLUQ), Canada 157, 159, 160–165, 166, 167, 275, 276–277, 279, 364, 368, 434; *see also* University of Quebec

television, educational *see* technology, emergence of

television, slow-scan *see* technology, emergence of

tele-writer *see* technology

TÉLUQ *see* Télé-université

terms, definition of: founder/trailblazer xix, 5, 394; leader xix, 394; pioneer xix, 5, 394; researcher/writer xix, 5, 394; *see also* distance education, definition of terms

TETRA *see* Telemedicine and Educational Technology Resource Agency

Texas A&M University 179

thematic analysis process *see* research methods

THEORYNET 92–93

Theory of Transactional Distance 90, 165; *see also* Moore, Michael

third shift, the 375; *see also* gender; marginalized groups; midnight hour degree

Thompson Rivers University, Canada 299, 304; *see also* Open Learning Agency; Open Learning Institute of British Columbia

Thorpe, Mary 33, 34

TIRF *see* International Research Foundation for Teacher Language Education, The

Tobin, Judith 244, 277, 280, 326

Tower, Iva E. 364

traditional higher education institution *see* face-to-face

traditional roles *see* gender

training programs *see* research interests of female pioneers

transformation, institutional 333, 337, 339, 343, 351; *see also* challenges, institutional

transformative learning *see* learning, transformative

Tropical Metabolism Unit *see* Tropical Medicine Research Institute

Tropical Medicine Research Institute, West Indies 283, 285

Tubella, Ema 15

Turkle, Shirley 311

Turoff, Murray 188, 202, 203, 444–445; *see also* Gibson, Chere Campbell

TV *see* technology, emergence of

Tynan, Belinda 15, 74, 83, 114, 120, 336, 340

UBC *see* University of British Columbia

UCWI *see* University College of the West Indies

UMUC *see* University of Maryland University College

UNAM *see* University of Namibia

UNB *see* University of New Brunswick

unconscious bias *see* gender

UNESCO *see* United Nations Educational, Scientific and Cultural Organization

UNISA *see* University of South Africa

United Nations Development Program (UNDP) xvi

United Nations Educational, Scientific and Cultural Organization (UNESCO) xix, 12, 15, 125, 162, 226

United States Distance Learning Association Hall of Fame 88; *see also* awards

Universitas Terbuka (UT; *aka* Indonesia Open University) 9, 11

Universität of Oldenburg (*aka* University of Oldenburg), Germany xvi, 30, 36, 37, 38, 215, 329, 379

Université TÉLUQ *see* Télé-université

University College of London 288; *see also* University College of the West Indies; University of the West Indies

University College of the West Indies (UCWI) 239, 243, 247, 283, 284, 285–290, 342–343, 344–349,

351, 418; *see also* University College of London; University of the West Indies

University of Adelaide, Australia 41, 43, 44, 294, 296, 297, 347

University of Alberta, Canada 33, 244, 359, 361, 364, 383, 417

University of Applied Sciences, Germany 19, 21

University of Auckland, New Zealand 215, 252, 254, 339

University of British Columbia (UBC), Canada 9, 29, 31, 36, 37, 44, 297

University of California, Berkeley (UC Berkeley), United States 170, 175, 176, 264, 267

University of California, Santa Cruz (UC Santa Cruz), United States 171, 181

University of Ceylon *see* University of Sri Lanka

University of Chicago, United States 64

University of Colombo, Sri Lanka 127, 129, 130, 131, 140, 144

University of Constance, Germany 370, 373, 417

University of Eswatini, Swaziland 226, 229

University of Guelph, Canada 361, 363, 368

University of Hawaii, United States 195

University of Helsinki, Finland 41

University of Kansas (KU), United States 137–138, 141

University of London 141

University of Maryland University College (UMUC) 30, 266–267, 329; *see also* awards

University of Maryland University College (UMUC) Teaching Award *see* awards

University of Michigan, United States 266

University of Montreal, Canada 87, 157, 274, 276

University of Namibia (UNAM) 19, 20, 21, 26, 336, 340; *see also* awards

University of Namibia Merit Sabbatical Award *see* awards

University of New Brunswick (UNB), Canada 41, 43, 46–47, 48, 49, 50, 244, 279

University of New England, Australia 74, 83, 111, 113, 115, 118, 302

University of New Mexico (UNM), United States 92, 138, 140, 142, 144–148, 149–150, 429, 431

University of Northern Colorado, United States 143

University of Oklahoma, United States 92, 142–143, 148

University of Oldenburg, Germany *see* Universität of Oldenburg

University of Ottawa, Canada 29, 30, 273

University of Pretoria Chancellor's Medal *see* awards

University of Pretoria, South Africa 19, 21; *see also* awards

University of Prince Edward Island (UPEI), Canada 244

University of Quebec, Canada 157, 244; *see also* Télé-université

University of Queensland, Australia 70, 73, 76, 308

University of Salzburg, Austria 195

University of Sao Paulo, Brazil 63

University of South Africa (UNISA) 102–103, 106, 107, 109; *see also* awards

University of South Africa (UNISA) Council Award *see* awards

University of Southern Queensland (USQ), Australia xvi, 71, 73, 76, 79, 82

University of Sri Lanka 125, 128, 130, 137

University of Sussex, England 225, 228

University of the South Pacific (USP), Fiji 252, 253, 255–261

University of the West Indies (UWI) 283, 284–290, 342–343, 344–345, 347, 349, 351; *see also* University College of London; University College of the West Indies; University of the West Indies Distance Education Centre; University of the West Indies Network; University of the West Indies Open Campus

University of the West Indies (UWI) Open Campus 285, 288, 343–345; *see also* University of the West Indies; University of the West Indies Distance Education Centre

University of the West Indies Distance Education Centre (UWIDEC; *aka* University of the West Indies Network), 247, 285, 347–348; *see also* University of the West Indies; University of the West Indies Open Campus

University of the West Indies Network *see* University of the West Indies Distance Education Centre

University of the Witwatersrand, South Africa 99

University of Toronto, Canada 41, 43, 44, 50, 234, 321, 322, 324, 325–326, 328, 429; *see also* Ontario Institute for Studies in Education (OISE)

University of Twente, Netherlands 215

University of Utah, United States 313, 316, 317

University of Wales, United Kingdom 322

University of Washington, United States 184

University of Windsor, Canada 30

University of Wisconsin-Madison, United States 87–88, 89, 91–93, 142–143

University of Wisconsin-Oshkosh, United States 93–94

University of Wyoming, United States 92, 143

University of Zürich, Germany 181

UNM *see* University of New Mexico

UPEI *see* University of Prince Edward Island

Upsala College, United States 98, 201, 203

US-accredited institution 259; *see also* quality assurance

USP *see* University of the South Pacific

USQ *see* University of Southern Queensland

UT *see* Universitas Terbuka

UTN National Technological University, Argentina 64

UWI *see* University of the West Indies

UWIDEC *see* University of the West Indies Distance Education Centre

Index

Vassar College, United States 194, 197–198
Växjö University, Sweden 171
video conferencing *see* technology, emergence of
video technologies *see* technology, emergence of
virtual classroom *see* technology, emergence of
virtual reality (VR) *see* technology, emergence of
virtual worlds *see* technology, emergence of
von Prümmer, Christine **6**, 33, 34, 228, 244, *370, 371*, 370–382, 417
VR *see* technology, emergence of

Wagner, Ellen 143
Wati Abas, Zuraini 15
Watkins, Barbara 141–142
Wawasan Open University, Malaysia 13, 218, 226, 229
webinars *see* technology
Wedemeyer, Charles 90, 92, 212, 421–422, 430, 433
Wedemeyer, Charles Award *see* awards
Western Interstate Commission for Higher Education (WICHE), United States 143
Whalen, Doreen 250
Whelan, Shannon 389
whiteboards, interactive *see* technology
White Rose of Finland *see* awards
WICHE *see* Western Interstate Commission for Higher Education
Wikipedia 184; *see also* gender
wikis *see* technology
Willems, Julie 74, 83
WIN *see* Women's International Network
Women in Resource Development (WRDC) 235
Women's Aid Movement, Germany 371
Women's International Network (WIN) 30, 41, 45, 156, 228, 274, 363, 374, 377, 379, 403, 413, 432–433
women's studies 67, 155; *see also* gender; research interests of female pioneers
working adults *see* marginalized groups
World Bank 138, 146, 246, 249
World Education Congress Global Distance Learning Awards *see* awards
world, post-authenticity *see* post-authentic world
World Reader 105; *see also* African Storybook; Global Digital Library
worldview *see* paradigm
World Wide Web (WWW) *see* technology, emergence of
WRDC *see* Women in Resource Development
WWW *see* technology, emergence of

York University, Canada 278, 321, 324, 326, 327, 328
Young, Arlene **6**, 33, 363, *383, 384*, 383–390

Zawacki-Richter, Olaf 215, 379
Zawicki, Anna 244
Zuboff, Shoshana 182
Zuckernick, Arlene 325, 330

Printed in the United States
by Baker & Taylor Publisher Services